# Praise for Past Access Developer's Handbooks

"**This book characterizes** all that a computer programming book should be... it explained clearly how to program Access 97 and also how to use it effectively. In particular, I liked the many code examples and have used some of those provided on the CD."

*Robin Edmonds*
*Warwick, England*

"**This is by far the best** Access book on the market. Tons of information on the guts of Access that you don't get from other books... a necessary addition to the professional Access Developer's library. A must have!"

*John Fuex, MCP, MCSD*
*Austin, Texas*

"**If you do not have this book** in you private library, get it! If you are developing MS-Access applications and have Q's, this is the book that will provide you with the A's you want. Save yourself countless hours. What more can I say? GET IT!"

*Michael Borries*
*Copenhagen, Denmark*

"**After programming in Access** since version 1.1, a developer can be hard pressed to find a book with any information worth learning. This is the first book to come along to change this. In the first 100 pages I learned many new programming methods that would have taken the compilation of 4 or more other books. I would recommend this book to ALL Access, VBA, & VB programmers."

*Andrew Ells-O'Brien*
*Malden, Massachusetts*

"**I have used** the Access Developer's Handbook and found it extremely useful... full of samples, tips and tricks."

*Trisha Phoon*
*Kuala Lumpur, Malaysia*

SYBEX®

www.sybex.com

# Access 2000 Developer's Handbook

## Volume 2: Enterprise Edition

# Access 2000 Developer's Handbook™

## Volume 2: Enterprise Edition

Paul Litwin

Ken Getz

Mike Gilbert

SYBEX®

**San Francisco • Paris • Düsseldorf • Soest • London**

Associate Publisher: Harry Helms
Contracts and Licensing Manager: Kristine O'Callaghan
Acquisitions & Developmental Editor: Melanie Spiller
Editor: Dann McDorman
Project Editor: Bronwyn Shone Erickson
Technical Editor: Acey Bunch
Book Designers: Kris Warrenburg, Robin Kibby
Graphic Illustrator: Tony Jonick
Electronic Publishing Specialist: Robin Kibby
Project Team Leader: Lisa Reardon
Proofreaders: Richard Ganis, Patrick J. Peterson
Indexer: Ted Laux
CD Coordinator: Kara Schwartz
CD Technicians: Ginger Warner, Keith McNeil
Cover Designer: Design Site
Cover Illustrator: Jack D. Myers

SYBEX is a registered trademark of SYBEX Inc.

Developer's Handbook is a trademark of SYBEX Inc.

TRADEMARKS: SYBEX has attempted throughout this book to distinguish proprietary trademarks from descriptive terms by following the capitalization style used by the manufacturer.

The author and publisher have made their best efforts to prepare this book, and the content is based upon final release software whenever possible. Portions of the manuscript may be based upon pre-release versions supplied by software manufacturer(s). The author and the publisher make no representation or warranties of any kind with regard to the completeness or accuracy of the contents herein and accept no liability of any kind including but not limited to performance, merchantability, fitness for any particular purpose, or any losses or damages of any kind caused or alleged to be caused directly or indirectly from this book.

Appendix A © 1995–1999 by Gregory Reddick. All rights reserved. Used by permission.

Library of Congress Card Number: 99-67018

ISBN: 0-7821-2372-4

Manufactured in the United States of America

10 9 8 7 6

*To Geoff, the best son a dad could ask for! Thanks for being patient when I said I had to work on the book again and again. - PEL*

*To my parents, Jerry and Chutie Getz. Once just parents, they've become my close friends as the years have gone by. As I was growing up, my mother told me again and again to "act with dignity." I've tried to follow this rule every day of my life. Sometimes I've succeeded better than other times, but I've sincerely tried. Mom and Dad, thanks always for your constant love and support. I owe you more than you can possibly know. - KNG*

*To Ken and Paul, for inviting me along on what turned out to be a great ride. - MTG*

*To the Microsoft Access, VBA, and Jet teams. Thanks for consistently producing a world-class database program. - PEL, KNG, MTG*

# ACKNOWLEDGMENTS

While the names of three individuals appear on the cover of this book, this book would never have been published without the contributions of countless others. First of all, we'd like to thank Melanie Spiller, our acquisitions editor, who's gone to bat for us more times than we care to count. Melanie has been an inspiration, a mentor, and a sensitive, compassionate friend over the past five years.

We'd also like to thank Acey Bunch, our technical editor for the book. Acey came highly recommended by the technical editor of Volume 1, David Shank. And David was certainly right—Acey contributed immeasurably to the quality of this book. Acey identified technical errors and omissions, and challenged us to produce a better book. Of course, any errors that remain are our fault, not Acey's or anyone else's!

Very special thanks also go out to the contributions of Mike Gunderloy, Mary Chipman, and Michael Kaplan. Mike Gunderloy, a friend and business partner, was responsible for writing a number of chapters, including two chapters on client-server development, as well as the setup and deployment chapter. Because of his attention to detail, accuracy, timeliness, and excellence, we never had to worry for a moment about the chapters we asked Mike to help out with. Mary Chipman, another friend and business partner, contributed ideas, insights, text, and code that worked its way into the replication and security chapters. Michael Kaplan, another longtime friend from Trigeminal Software, also contributed a number of ideas, some code, and even a few paragraphs of text to the replication chapter. Michael was also responsible for several utilities that you can find on the CD.

Special thanks go out to Greg Reddick, one of the coauthors of the first two editions of this book. Greg's contributions to those editions are still very much a part of the current edition. In addition, we continue to use his RVBA naming standard, which appears in Appendix A. Thanks, Greg, for all your hard work and friendship!

Thanks to all the current and former members of the Access, VBA, and Jet teams at Microsoft. In particular, the following individuals gave us early access to information, answered technical questions, or reviewed chapters: Neil Charney, Kevin Collins, Clint Covington, Richard Dickinson, Debra Dove, Keith Fink, David Gainer, Alyssa Henry, Michalakis Michael, Kevin Mineweaser, Wesner Moise, Mark Roberts, David Shank, Monte Slichter, Dave Stearns, Doug Stotland, and James Sturms. We'd also like to thank Richard McAniff for providing an all-too-kind foreword.

We appreciate the work of the following people who provided ideas, friendly encouragement, or technical editing support for of one or more editions of the book: Scott Alexander, Dev Ashish, Andy Baron, Doug Behl, Richard Campbell, Tom Howe, Steve Forte, Peter Litwin, Manuel Lopez, Mindy Martin, Rod Paddock, Brian Randell, Erik Ruthruff, Cynthia Sample, Ron Talmage, and Brian Wells.

Thanks also to all the individuals and companies who contributed content to the companion CD.

Of course, without the hard work and support of the staff at Sybex, this book would be nothing more than a dream. We are especially appreciative of the efforts of our astute project editor, Bronwyn Erickson, and our fearless editor, Dann McDorman. Thanks also to the rest of the team at Sybex, including Harry Helms, Lisa Reardon, Rich Ganis, Patrick J. Peterson, and Robin Kibby. And, of course, our thanks to Sybex crew wouldn't be complete if we didn't thank the woman who keeps the checks coming, Kristine O' Callaghan!

Very extra special thanks and love go out to Suzanne White and Peter Mason. Without you guys, we'd never make it! Thanks for putting up with us when we were cranky and not a whole lot of fun.

Finally, we'd like to thank all the other people—including family, business associates, and friends—who we simply don't have room to (or have somehow forgotten to) thank. You know who you are!

# CONTENTS AT A GLANCE

# TABLE OF CONTENTS

# FOREWORD

Challenges. Identifying and conquering new challenges is one of the most exciting aspects of working at Microsoft. In my 12 years at Microsoft, I've been involved in the expansion of desktop productivity applications, as well as the dawn of the Internet as a focal point of businesses and knowledge workers. Contributing to individual empowerment, both on the desktop and now on the Web, has been incredibly satisfying. Yet new challenges arise every day, such as how to support the emergence of new data standards or how to bring together documents, e-mail, and data. How we cope with these challenges as individuals determines our success as an industry. It's that opportunity that makes coming to work an exciting proposition!

The authors of this book have contributed to our industry's success in their own way, empowering developers like you to take the raw material in Microsoft Office and forge valuable solutions for your customers. And they've kept pace with new challenges and demands, this book being the latest evidence. Access 2000 is perhaps the most significant release Microsoft has ever produced, especially in its support for truly enterprise-level development. My team spent several years adding critical, developer-oriented features that make building solutions to leverage corporate data easier and more powerful than ever. In fact, we added so much potential to the product that it took Paul, Ken, and Mike another whole book to explain it completely.

Perhaps the most obvious new aspect of Access' personality is its integration with Microsoft SQL Server through the new ADP file format. Relational databases are the powerhouses of corporate data storage and more and more of you are choosing SQL Server as your database engine of choice. Our latest release, SQL Server 7, represents a leap forward in functionality that parallels that of Access 2000. With better performance, easier management, OLAP support, and true scalability from the desktop (through the Microsoft Data Engine, MSDE) to multi-server database farms, SQL Server 7 provides customers with robust and secure data storage along with tremendous potential for custom solutions.

Integration with Office 2000 was a primary design goal of SQL Server 7 and it shows in Access 2000 ADPs. You can now create custom solutions tied directly to SQL Server data, while at the same time leveraging all the tools and skills you've acquired from years of developing with Access. We took great care to ensure that developing SQL Server-based solutions with Access was a seamless experience. That's why we integrated SQL Server design tools right into the product. Paul, Ken, and Mike spend a great deal of time in this book explaining how to get the most out of these tools, as well as SQL Server in general. If you've been developing SQL Server solutions with prior versions of Access, you'll want to pay careful attention to the nuggets of wisdom contained in these pages.

The second major area of investment my team made was support for Web technologies. If you haven't yet been tasked with building a Web-based solution that integrates Access or SQL Server data, don't worry, you will soon! More and more customers recognize the power of immediate information access that the Web provides, especially within corporations. Everything from corporate policy manuals to purchase orders to the cafeteria menu are now available online to employees. The Access form you design today will be the Web page you design tomorrow.

To help you in this process we introduced a new Access design feature: data access pages. If you've ever tried to create data-bound Web pages before, you'll appreciate how easy it is to do using the Access 2000 data access page designer. With just a few selections from our wizard, or by dragging table fields onto the design surface, you'll have a Web page that displays live data and that's immediately accessible to everyone in your organization. You can even embellish your pages with HTML and scripts using the new integrated Microsoft Script Editor. It's never been easier or faster to get information to your users (not to mention making you look like a hero).

In addition to Access, I oversee the development of Microsoft Excel. In many ways these applications share the same characteristics. Both deal with the storage, presentation, and analysis of data. Over the years we've heard from a great many of you that you'd like to see better integration between the two products. I'm pleased to say that is one of my primary goals as general manager and, as evidence, we've created a new Office 2000 feature: the Office Web Components. These ActiveX controls enable you to embed some of the best parts of Excel (such as the spreadsheet engine, pivot tables, and charting capabilities) within your custom solutions, be they built with Access or Web technologies. Once again, these three authors have wholeheartedly explored these controls, and they share their findings with you in this book.

It's the challenges of our profession that make our jobs interesting. Providing you with the tools to meet those challenges is part of my job. Providing you with the best information for exploiting those tools is a task that Paul, Ken, and Mike took on several years (and thousands of pages) ago and continue to do well today. I hope you share my excitement at the challenges you'll overcome with Access 2000, using what we all have provided and looking forward to the new challenges on the horizon.

Richard McAniff
General Manager, Access and Excel
Microsoft Corporation

# ABOUT THE AUTHORS

**Paul Litwin**

Paul Litwin (MCSD, MCP) is a senior consultant with MCW Technologies specializing in application development employing Microsoft Access, Visual Basic, SQL Server, Visual InterDev, Active Server Pages, HTML, and related Microsoft technologies. In addition to the various editions of *Access Developer's Handbook*, Paul has written books on Internet development and VBA. He has contributed articles to various publications including *Visual Basic Programmer's Journal, Microsoft Internet Developer, Smart Access, Microsoft Office, Visual Basic for Applications Developer*, and *PC World*. Paul regularly travels around the United States training developers for Application Developers Training Company (AppDev) in Access, VB, SQL Server, and Visual InterDev. Along with Ken Getz, Paul has written and recorded Access courseware and training videos for AppDev. He also developed and recorded AppDev's Visual InterDev courseware and videos. Paul has spoken at a variety of U.S. and international conferences, including Microsoft Tech*Ed, Microsoft Office and VBA Solutions, and DevCon 1999. You can reach Paul at `plitwin@developershandbook.com` or visit the MCW Technologies Web site at `http://www.mcwtech.com`.

**Ken Getz**

Ken Getz is a senior consultant with MCW Technologies, focusing on the Microsoft suite of products. He has received Microsoft's MVP award (for providing online technical support) since 1993 and has written several books on developing applications using Microsoft products. Ken is a technical editor for *Access-Office-VB Advisor* (Advisor) and a contributing editor for *Microsoft Office & Visual Basic for Applications Developer* (Informant) magazines. Currently, Ken spends a great deal of time traveling around the country for Application Developer's Training Company, presenting training classes for Access and Visual Basic developers. He also speaks at many conferences and trade shows throughout the world, including Microsoft's Tech*Ed, Advisor Publication's DevCon, and Informant's Microsoft Office and VBA Solutions conference. You can reach Ken at `kgetz@developershandbook.com`.

**Mike Gilbert**

Mike Gilbert works at Microsoft as a program manager designing object models for business productivity and Web collaboration products. Prior to joining Microsoft he was a senior consultant with MCW Technologies, specializing in application development using Microsoft Access, Visual Basic, SQL Server, and Microsoft Office. He writes for several periodicals and is a contributing editor to *Microsoft Office and Visual Basic for Applications Developer* magazine. He is also a regular speaker at conferences such as Microsoft Tech*Ed and the Microsoft Office and VBA Solutions Conference. You can reach Mike at `mgilbert@developershandbook.com`.

# INTRODUCTION

**W**hen it was released in late 1992, Microsoft Access took the database world by storm because of its aggressive $99 price. But when the dust settled after the first million were sold, many users and developers were pleasantly surprised to find a real database hidden beneath that ridiculously cheap price tag. Access 1.0 and the soon-to-follow modest upgrade, version 1.1, were certainly far from perfect, but users found an instantly usable product that broke down the walls of database accessibility. At the same time, almost overnight, a large and healthy developer community (that included the authors of this book) was born and began to develop professional applications that ran businesses of all sizes throughout the world.

Since its introduction, Microsoft has released four major updates: version 2.0, which hit the streets in May of 1994; Access for Windows 95 (aka Access 95 or Access 7.0), which appeared in November of 1995; Access 97 (aka Access 8.0), which appeared in January of 1997, and Access 2000 (aka Access 9.0), released in June of 1999. These updates have made numerous improvements in the areas of usability, programmability, and extendability. In addition, the last two versions made great strides in making Access a primary candidate for client-server and Internet database development.

Access 2000 is a wonderfully powerful development platform, but like any powerful product, it takes considerable time to master. Fortunately for you, the three of us spent many months and countless hours tearing apart Access 2000, exposing its undocumented secrets, and making it do things that few have imagined were possible—all for your benefit.

# Which Volume Should You Buy?

Because the product has gotten larger and larger over the years, and amazingly, book publishing capabilities haven't grown the same way, we've had to split this edition of the *Access 2000 Developer's Handbook* into two volumes. You're holding in your hands Volume 2 of a two-volume set.

*Volume 1: Desktop Edition*, covers issues facing all Access developers, including coverage of database design, SQL, ADO, forms, reports, working with the Windows API, creating class modules, Access events, Automation, optimization, add-ins, and related topics.

*Volume 2: Enterprise Edition* (this book), covers Access from an enterprise-wide point of view. It contains chapters on creating multi-user and client-server applications, working with SQL Server/Microsoft Data Engine (MSDE), and publishing data on the Web using data access pages and active server pages.

The decision of whether to include some chapters in Volume 1 or Volume 2 was somewhat arbitrary, and we hope that this split in the books' chapters makes it possible to include much more information than we could have otherwise.

---

**NOTE**      You'll find the two volumes complementary, so you may wish to buy both books.

---

# Is This Book for You?

This book and its sibling volume are for any Access developer or anyone who would like to become one. It doesn't matter whether you develop Access applications full time, as only one component of your job, or in your spare time during the evenings and weekends. What matters is that you take the product seriously and want your applications to be the very best.

If you only care to get your toes wet with Access and are happy to throw together quick-and-dirty applications that are automated with nothing more than a few macros, you probably don't need this book, nor its sibling volume. However, if you're ready to dive into the thick of Access and get down to the business of developing industrial-strength applications that utilize Access to its fullest, you've picked the right set books.

If you're planning on only picking of one of the volumes, you may be wondering which volume to get. The choice is simple: if you are developing primarily single-user databases or are developing multiple-user databases but need to learn about topics such as database design, SQL, ADO, forms, reports, working with the Windows API, creating class modules, Access events, Automation, and similar topics, then you need Volume 1. If you are primarily concerned with developing enterprise Access applications—that is, Access applications that serve multiple users, use replication or security, work in a client-server environment, or serve up data over the Internet or your corporate intranet—then this is the volume for you.

If you can't make up your mind or need coverage of topics found in both volumes, then pick up both volumes.

# What You Need to Know

For you to benefit most from an advanced book such as this, we've had to dispense with the fundamentals and make several assumptions about you. We assume you already are an Access developer and are familiar with the topics covered in the first volume.

At a minimum, you should be comfortable creating tables and queries, forms, and reports and be up to speed with Visual Basic for Applications (VBA). We also assume you have some experience with ActiveX Data Objects (ADO) and know how to create a class module. If you aren't up to speed, you may wish to put down this book for the moment and get a copy of *Access 2000 Developer's Handbook, Volume 1: Desktop Edition*. You also may need to spend some time with Access and its documentation, the help system, or an introductory text such as *Mastering Access 2000* by Alan Simpson and Celeste Robinson (Sybex, 1999).

# Conventions Used in This Book

It goes without saying that the professional developer must consistently follow some standard. We followed several standard conventions in this book to make it easier for you to follow along.

We have used version 6.0 of the Reddick VBA (RVBA) naming conventions for the naming of Access (and other) objects, which have been accepted by many Access and VBA developers as the naming standard to follow. Greg Reddick, a noted Access and Visual Basic developer and trainer, developed the standard, which bears his name. Even if you don't subscribe to the RVBA standard, however, you'll likely appreciate the fact that it has been consistently used throughout the book. These conventions, which were first published in Smart Access, are included in their entirety in Appendix A. In a few places, you'll find we have used tags that depart from those in Appendix A for a number of reasons, not the least of which was the fact that Greg didn't finalize version 6.0 of the RVBA conventions until we were well into writing this book. Fortunately, when we've departed from the RVBA standard tags, we've still tried to maintain the spirit of the RVBA conventions, although we may not have used the same tags as Greg.

In addition to following the RVBA standard, we have prefaced all public procedures, user-defined types, and enums that you may wish to use in your own code with the "adh" prefix (which stands for Access Developer's Handbook), aliased all public Windows API declarations using an "adh_api" prefix, and prefixed all public constants with "adhc". These conventions should avoid naming conflicts with any existing code in your applications. If, however, you import multiple modules from various chapters' sample databases into a single database, you may find naming conflicts as a result of our using consistent naming throughout the chapters. In that case, you'll need to comment out any conflicting API declarations or user-defined types.

# Chapter Walk-Through

This book consists of sixteen chapters and two appendixes. In every chapter you'll find lots of examples, with all but the most trivial included in sample databases you can find on the CD that accompanies this book.

## Overview of Access

Chapter 1 begins with a brief history of Access and an overview of what's new in Access 2000, with an emphasis on enterprise development. You'll also find a discussion of Microsoft Office Developer in this chapter.

## Multi-User File-Server Development

Chapter 2 focuses on developing multi-user file-server based applications employing the Jet database engine. In this chapter, you'll learn how to split your database into two parts to improve performance and how to manage linked tables. This chapter contrasts page versus row-level locking, and optimistic versus pessimistic locking. You'll also learn how to create a custom write conflict dialog box, a system for timing out users who have locked records for an excessive period of time, a lock retry loop, and a custom AutoNumber routine. We'll also show you how to take advantage of the new user list and connection control features built into Access 2000.

## Client-Server Development

Access 2000 adds a lot of functionality for the client-server developer so we've dug in deep and offer five client-server chapters.

Chapter 3 introduces client-server application development. In this chapter, you'll learn about ODBC and OLEDB, linked tables, pass-through queries, and Access Data Project (ADP) files. Chapter 3 also talks about some of the issues to consider when designing efficient client-server applications.

In Chapter 4 you'll learn how to use ADP files to create SQL Server databases, tables, views, and database diagrams. You'll also learn about the different versions of SQL Server, including SQL Server Enterprise, SQL Server Desktop, and MSDE.

Chapter 5 concentrates on creating stored procedures and triggers for SQL Server and MSDE databases. Here you'll learn how to create stored procedures with both input and output parameters, how to use the built-in SQL Server system procedures, variables, and functions, and how to employ Transact-SQL flow-control statements. You'll also learn how to create SQL Server triggers.

In Chapter 6, you'll learn how to use ActiveX Data Objects (ADO) to work with server data. Here you'll learn how to connect to server databases using the ADO Connection object, how to use the ADO Command object to call stored procedures, and how to use the ADO Recordset object to return server-based recordsets. You'll also learn how to manage concurrency, how to employ ADO events, and how to manage ADO errors.

Chapter 7 discusses how to work with some of the special client-server features of ADP forms and reports. Here you'll learn how to use the UniqueTable and ResyncCommand properties to create updatable forms, even when they're based on multiple server tables. You'll also learn how to use the ServerFilterByForm and ServerFilter properties to create efficient server-based filters. This chapter also discusses using transactions and a reservations table.

## Security and Replication

Chapter 8 takes a look at Access security. Here you'll look in detail at how Jet security works and how to properly secure an Access MDB database. You'll also learn how to secure your code and programmatically manage security using ADOX, DAO, and SQL. Chapter 8 concludes with a discussion of security in ADP files and an introduction to SQL Server security.

Replication is the subject of Chapter 9. This chapter begins by discussing how Jet replication works and when you may wish to consider using it. You will learn how to replicate your database and manage replicas using the Access menus, the Jet Replication Objects (JRO) object model, and Replication Manager. Chapter 9 discusses the newest additions to Jet replication, including column-level conflict tracking, replica visibility, and the new priority-based conflict resolution algorithm. The chapter concludes with a discussion of SQL Server replication and how you can use merge replication to replicate SQL Server data to Jet replicas.

## Web Development

Access 2000 includes a number of features that support the Internet and intranet developer, thus we've devoted five chapters to this important topic.

Chapter 10 shows you how to use Access 2000 data access pages. This exciting new technology makes it incredibly easy to create Web pages that are bound to Jet and SQL Server databases. In this chapter you'll find out how to create data access pages, including numerous tips and tricks on how to produce attractive and functional pages. You'll also learn about some of the shortcomings of data access pages, and how you can work around some of the issues.

In Chapter 11 you'll learn how to add scripting code to your data access pages. Here you'll learn how to use the Microsoft Script Editor and how to hook your scripts into the myriad of objects, events, properties, and methods you'll find in data access pages. The chapter also includes a number of examples that show you how to use VBScript code to add validation code to your pages, create drill-down interfaces, filter records, and add items to a drop-down list.

Chapter 12 focuses on the Office Web components. Here you'll find information on using these power-packed ActiveX controls in your data access pages and your Access forms. You'll learn how to use the spreadsheet calculation engine built into the Office Spreadsheet component, how to employ the analytical capabilities of the Office PivotTable component, and how to take advantage of the graphing abilities of the Office Chart component.

Chapter 13 switches gears somewhat and discusses the browsing capabilities of Access 2000. This chapter begins with a discussion of how to add hyperlinks to your tables, forms, and reports. You'll also learn how to manipulate hyperlinks from VBA code and how to use the Microsoft Web Browser control to add browsing capabilities to any Access form.

In Chapter 14, you'll learn how to publish Access data to the Web without using data access pages. The chapter starts with a discussion of how to use the Access Export dialog box to publish tables, queries, forms, reports, and views as both static HTML and Active Server Pages (ASP). Chapter 14 also shows you how to create ASP pages from scratch without the help of the Export dialog box. Here you'll learn how to create server-side scripts, how to use server-side include files, and how to use the ASP object model to create dynamic, data-driven Web pages that run in any Web browser.

## Source Code Control and Deployment

The last two chapters of the book are concerned with the management and deployment of Access applications.

Developing an Access application with multiple developers presents a number of challenges, because Access doesn't support multiple developers well right out of the box. Chapter 15 shows you how to use Visual SourceSafe, now a part of Microsoft Office Developer (MOD), to manage multiple developer projects. In this chapter you'll learn how to use Visual SourceSafe with Access MDB and ADP files, taking advantage of such features as check out, versioning, differencing, merging, and rollback.

Chapter 16 takes a look at application deployment issues, beginning with a discussion of how the Access runtime program works. You'll learn how to use the Package and Deployment Wizard, a component of MOD that you can use to create installation programs for your Access runtime applications. You'll also learn how to use the Windows Installer program and the Installer SDK to create a unified setup for the runtime program and your application.

## Appendices

This book contains two appendices.

Appendix A provides a description of the RVBA naming conventions used throughout this book. You'll find this useful both when reading this book and if you wish to use the same naming conventions in your own development work.

Appendix B contrasts VBScript to VBA, highlighting the differences between these sibling languages.

# About the CD

The CD that comes with this book is a valuable companion to the book. It includes all the chapter databases discussed in the book, as well as several extra goodies that should make your Access development work more efficient. (For late-breaking information about the CD, including additional files and utilities, see README.TXT in the root directory of the CD.)

## What's on the CD?

On the CD, we've included the chapter databases. We've also included white papers, freeware and shareware utilities, and demo versions of several commercial products on the CD. Most of these files have some restrictions on their use; please read the provided supporting documentation and respect the rights of the vendors who were kind enough to provide these files. For shareware programs, please register these programs with the vendor if you find them useful.

The CD files are described here:

- **Chapter Databases**: (\Chapter) Here's where you'll find the chapter databases containing all the examples from the text. Each chapter database includes all the objects discussed in the book so you can try out the examples yourself. These databases also include lots of reusable code and other objects you can copy and paste into your own applications. We've also included several other supporting files in the Chapter folder. If you want to install all the chapter samples, run the program **Chapter.exe** (a self-extracting ZIP file). See the "Installing the Chapter Samples" section later in this Introduction for more details.

- **SQL Server/MSDE Database**: (\SQLServer) This folder contains three scripts that you use to reconstitute the ADH2KSQL SQL Server database (that also works with MSDE) that is used with many of the examples in the client-server chapters. The ADH2KSQL database contains all of the tables, views, stored procedures, triggers, and other SQL Server objects discussed in the client-server chapters of the book. See the "Installing the ADH2KSQL SQL Server Database" section later in this Introduction for more details on installing the ADH2KSQL database.

- **MCW Unreplicate Add-in**: (\Other\MCW) This free add-in, created by one of the authors of this book, Paul Litwin, will help you convert a replicated Access 2000 design master into an unreplicated database. Use the Access 2000 Add-In Manager to install the add-in file, named UnRreplicate2000.Mda.

- **Trigeminal Software Tools**: (\Other\TSI) This set of free Access utilities from Trigeminal Software Inc. (TSI) includes a utility for converting Access 2000 forms and reports to data access pages, a tool for copying system relationships, a utility for closing one database and opening another, and a tool for removing the replication system fields from a table. And just when you thought one un-replication utility was probably enough, TSI has also included the TSI 2000 Un-Replicator. See **TriGem.Htm** in the \Other\TSI folder for details on installation of each of the utilities.

- **Database Creations Free Software and Demo System**: (\Other\DbCreate) Database Creations has graciously provided some free utilities to ease the Access 2000 development process and demos of their suite of Access offerings. Included on the CD: Yes! I Can Run My Business, EZ Access Developers Suite, and other Database Creations products. To install the Yes! I Can Run My Business demo, go to \Other\Dbcreate\yesdemo2k.exe. To install the EZ Access Developers Suite, go to \Other\Dbcreate\ezdemo2k.exe.

- **Microsoft Replication White Papers**: (\Other\Microsoft) You'll find these white papers from Microsoft provide a good supplement to the replication chapter in the book. They include "Database Replication in Microsoft Jet 4.0" by Debra Dove, a good overview of replication with a focus on the new features in Access 2000 and "Internet Synchronization with Microsoft Jet 4.0" by Michael Wachal, an indispensable reference for setting up Internet-based synchronization.

- **Microsoft Data Access Page White Papers**: (\Other\Microsoft) The data access page white papers fill in a few pieces not covered in the data access page chapters in the book. Even when the content overlaps, it's always nice to have a few extra examples. This set of white papers includes "Connecting Data Access Pages Together" by Brett Tanzer, "Programming Data Access Pages" by Roy Leban, and "Creating Secure Data Access Pages" by Clint Convington.

- **BlueSky Software HTML Help Demo**: (\Other\BlueSky) If you're creating professional applications, you'll need to create help files. BlueSky software provides a popular suite of programs making this arduous task as simple as possible. Check out their limited-time demo by running the **Setup.Exe** program. For more information, visit http://www.blue-sky.com.

- **FMS, Inc Demonstrations**: (\Other\FMS) Although FMS, Inc., the leading vendor of add-ins and tools for Microsoft Access, hadn't completed their Access 2000 tools at the time we went to print, we wanted to make sure you had a way to find them once their tools are finished. We've included, on the CD, demonstration versions of their Access 97 products, with links to the FMS, Inc. Web site. Run the **FMSDemos.exe** program to investigate the various products. Check their site for information on product availability for Access 2000. For more information, visit http://www.fmsinc.com.

- **WinZip 7.0**: (\Other\Winzip) From Nico Mak Computing, Inc. This is a shareware evaluation version of WinZip 7.0 SR-1. WinZip is a Windows 95/NT utility for zipping and unzipping files. It includes its own zipping and unzipping routines, but it also can be configured to call PKZip, LHA, and other archiving programs. Run the provided setup program (**winzip70.exe**) to install WinZip. See the online help for more information on using WinZip and registering the product. For more information, visit http://www.winzip.com.

- **ClickBook 2.2 Demo**: (\Other\Clickbook) From BlueSquirrel Software. ClickBook is a Windows printing utility that makes it easy to print two, four, or more logical pages per single printed page. ClickBook also makes it easy to print double-sided booklets, brochures, and other double-sided printouts. Run the provided setup program (**cbwin.exe**) to install this program. See the online help for more information on using Clickbook. (The Trial Version of Click-Book prints a "Trial Version" header and footer on each page of your printouts. These headers and footers do not appear on any pages printed by the purchased version.) For more information, visit http://www.bluesquirrel.com.

- **Web Whacker 2000 Demo**: (\Other\WebWhacker) Web Whacker, from Blue Squirrel Software, provides a complete facility for browsing Web pages offline. If you need to take the Web with you on the road when a dialup connection isn't convenient, you'll want to try out this demo. Run **ww2k.exe** to install the demo. For more information, visit http://www.bluesquirrel.com.

# Using the Files from the CD

The CD that accompanies this book is organized into several folders (subdirectories) that contain the chapter databases and other files. See the README.TXT file in the root folder of the CD for any late-breaking details on the CD files.

## Installing the Chapter Samples

The sample chapter databases are located in the \Chapter folder. The simplest way to get these files onto your hard drive so that you can use them is to run the CHAPTER.EXE program (a self-extracting ZIP file) in that folder. This program will extract the files and place them where you request.

If you want to work with individual files, you can copy them from the \Chapter folder. To install the files for a particular chapter, copy the files from the chapter folder to a new folder on your hard disk and open the files with Access 2000. See the description of these files in the text of the chapter for more details.

---

**WARNING**    If you copy files manually, you'll need to also clear the read-only attribute for the files. (All files copied directly from a CD to a hard drive come over as read only.) After you've copied the files, you'll need to select one or more files, right-click in Explorer, choose Properties, and then clear the read-only flag manually. If you use the Chapter.exe program that we've provided, you won't need to do this.

---

## Installing the ADH2KSQL SQL Server Database

To install the ADH2KSQL SQL Server/MSDE sample database you need to follow these steps:

1. First install SQL Server 7.0 or MSDE.

2. Copy the script files from the \SQLServer folder of the book CD to a folder on your hard drive.

3. From an MS-DOS Command window (also known as the Command Prompt window), move to the folder you created in Step 2, and enter the following to create the schema for the new database:

    ```
    osql -U sa -P -i adh2ksql1.sql
    ```

**NOTE**
Make sure you type the case of the parameters exactly. That is, the "-U" and "-P" are both uppercase characters and the "-i" is a lowercase character.

As the script is processed, you should see a series of line numbers scroll across the screen. When the script is complete you should see the following:

```
***********************************
Finished loading ADH2KSQL Database Schema.
You can now run ADH2KSQL2.SQL.
***********************************
```

4. From the same Command window, enter the following to run the second of the three scripts. This adds the first half of the data to the database:

```
osql -U sa -P -i adh2ksql2.sql
```

Again, make sure you type the case of the parameters exactly. When the script is complete you should see a similar message to the one displayed after running the first script.

5. From the same Command window, enter the following to run the third of the three scripts. This adds the second half of the data to the database:

```
osql -U sa -P -i adh2ksql3.sql
```

Again, make sure you type the case of the parameters exactly. When the script is complete you should see a similar message to the one displayed after running the first and second scripts.

**WARNING**
If you have changed the password for the SA account (a good idea), then you'll need to enter the password for this account after the "-P" on the command line in Steps 3, 4, and 5.

**TIP**
If you have the full version of SQL Server (as opposed to MSDE), you can execute the three scripts from the SQL Server Query Analyzer instead.

# How to Use This Book

While you may find it easiest to read the chapters in the order in which they appear in the book, it's not essential. One of our goals as we wrote the book was to make it possible for you to pick up and read any individual chapter without having to read through several other chapters first. Thus, the book is *not* a linear progression that starts with Chapter 1 and ends with Chapter 16. Instead, we have logically grouped together similar chapters, but otherwise (with a few exceptions) the chapters do not particularly build upon each other. To make it easy for you to jump from one chapter to another, we have included cross-references throughout the book. We've also noted where chapters build on material you'll find in the *Access 2000 Developer's Handbook, Volume 1: Desktop Edition*.

While we've done a lot of the work for you, you'll get the most benefit from this book by putting the material to real use. Take the examples and generic routines found in the book and expand on them. Add and subtract from them as you incorporate them into your applications. Experiment and enjoy!

# Come Visit Us

We've created a Web site for the book. Here's the address:

```
http://www.developershandbook.com
```

Come by and visit the Web site to find the latest information on *Access 2000 Developer's Handbooks*. You'll find errata, corrections, additional and enhanced examples, and other information about the books. While you're visiting, you may wish to register by filling out a form with information about yourself, so we can let you know about updates.

Be the first person on your block to know about updates to *Access 2000 Developer's Handbooks*: come on by, and sign up now.

# chapter 1

# What's New in Access 2000

- Learning the history of Access changes

- Understanding what's new in Access 2000

- Understanding the new enterprise features in Access 2000

- Learning about the Microsoft Data Engine (MSDE)

If you're reading this book, you've probably already decided that Microsoft Access 2000 (we'll refer to it hereafter as *Access 2000*) is a worthy platform for your development endeavors. Chances are, you're right. Microsoft has created a serious, full-featured, and powerful development environment for creating database applications on single-user and networked personal computers.

In this chapter, we review the history of Access and summarize the new features of Access 2000, especially those features that are relevant to the enterprise.

---

**NOTE**     Access can be used in both stand-alone and enterprise (or shared) environments. In terms of this book, we define enterprise as the use of Access in a shared multi-user environment. The Access enterprise environment might use the Jet engine, the Microsoft Data Engine (MSDE), SQL Server, or perhaps Oracle as its database engine. In addition, the Access enterprise likely encompasses the Internet or an intranet. This book concentrates on the enterprise use of Access. This book's sibling volume, *Access 2000 Developer's Handbook, Volume 1: Desktop Edition*, covers use of Access in a stand-alone or desktop environment.

---

# A Brief History of Access

Access 1 really opened the eyes of many database developers. It was one of the first relational database products available for the Windows 3 platform, and it was certainly the first to fill the needs of many developers, both corporate and independent. Besides its ease of use in getting started, Access 1 made it very easy to create simple applications. It did have some limitations when developers got past a certain point in their applications, including a severe limitation in that databases couldn't be larger than 128MB. Access 1.1 expanded the maximum database size to 1GB, and fixed some other limitations as well. Still, many professional features were lacking. Programmers used to Visual Basic's nearly complete flexibility were stymied by the inability of Access' inability to change control and form properties at runtime, for example. On the other hand, there was no simpler way to get data in and out of forms than Access, so developers worked around Access 1.1's limitations.

Access 2 offered great gains for developers. Although it also provided numerous improvements for end users, the greatest leap from 1.1 came in the improvements for the developer community. For the professional programmer, Access 2 added features in almost every area of the product, including:

- A vastly extended object and event model

- Runtime access to most form and report properties

- Event procedures

- Cascading updates and deletes for referential integrity

- Engine-level enforcement of rules

- New query types—union, data definition, and pass-through queries—and support for subqueries

- Rushmore query optimization

- Data access objects (DAO), a consistent object model for the manipulation of Jet engine data

- OLE automation client support

- Programmable security

- Support for 16-bit OLE custom controls

Access 95 was a major undertaking. Both Access and Jet were ported from 16-bit Windows to 32-bit Windows. The Access Basic language and integrated development environment (IDE) were replaced with Visual Basic for Applications (VBA) and its enhanced IDE. Numerous other improvements were added, including:

- Support for multi-instance forms

- The addition of the KeyPreview property for forms

- Support for multiselect list boxes and improved combo box performance

- New, lightweight image control

- The ability to detect and alter the type of a control with the ControlType property

- The addition of a built-in query-by-form feature, Filter by Form

- Support for form class modules with public functions (methods) and Let, Get, and Set property procedures

- The ability, with the NoData event of reports, to choose not to print a report if there were no records

- The addition of the RepeatSection property, which lets you repeat a group header at the top of continuation pages

- Replacement of counter fields with the more flexible AutoNumber datatype

- The addition of new With...End With and For Each...Next VBA constructs

- The addition of the line continuation character

- Support for named parameters, optional parameters, and parameter arrays

- Support for new Date, Boolean, and Byte data types

- Improvements to the editor and debugger, including Watch variables and color-coded syntax

- Support for replication

- Several concurrency and performance improvements to the Jet 3 Engine

- OLE automation server support

- The addition of start-up properties that let you disable access to the database window and change the application's title bar and icon

Access 97 was a minor release in comparison to Access 95. Still, there were lots of new features and improvements to existing features. These changes included:

- A new Hyperlink data type.

- The Publish to the Web Wizard made it easy to publish static or dynamic data on the Internet or a corporate intranet.

- Lightweight forms load faster because they don't have any code behind them.

- The native tab control made it easy to create a tabbed dialog.

- Menus and toolbars are completely programmable using the CommandBars collection and CommandBar object.

- New RecordSetType, FailOnError, and MaxRecords query properties.

- Support for class modules.

- IntelliSense support makes writing code much easier. When typing VBA code, the editor displays a list of objects, methods, and properties from which to choose. The VBA editor also displays a list of parameters for built-in and user-defined procedures.

- Support for drag-and-drop means you can pick up a snippet of code and move it to a new location with the mouse.

- Several debugging enhancements, including the new Locals pane and Data Tips.

- Support for partial replicas and Internet replication.

- Supports for a new client-server connection mode called ODBCDirect.

- Support for the special MDE format that removes all VBA source code.

# Access 2000—The Best Access Ever

Access 2000 is a major new release. The number of significant changes is staggering. Of those, the most important changes can be grouped into five major areas:

- Data access

- Internet/intranet

- VBA

- Forms and reports

- Other improvements

In the next few sections, we list the most significant changes, grouped by major area.

## Access 2000 Data Access

Data access in Access 2000 has changed in several big ways. Access 2000 comes with a new database engine option, a new data access model, and a new database format. These and other changes are summarized next:

- Although the Jet Engine remains the default database engine, Access also works with the Microsoft Data Engine (MSDE), a limited-connection version of SQL Server 7.

- In addition to being able to create standard Access MDB database files, you can now create Access Data Projects (ADP) files (also known simply as

Access projects). An ADP file is a "dataless" database in which you can store forms, reports, macros, and modules, linking to data that is stored in a SQL Server or MSDE database. This means that you can use the same familiar Access user interface you know and love as a lean and mean frontend to SQL Server data!

- Access projects include additional menu items for integrating with SQL Server's security and replication features.

- Access integrates tightly with the ActiveX Data Objects (ADO), Microsoft's preferred data access model. Existing DAO code works just fine, but you'll want to start writing data access code using ADO, because it provides greater flexibility and capabilities.

- The Jet Engine stores character data in Unicode. This makes changing languages simpler, but also means that strings will now take up twice as much space. Because of this, the maximum size of databases has increased from 1GB to 2GB. In addition, Jet 4 optionally compresses text and memo fields.

- Jet supports row-level locking in addition to the older page-level locking! This means that pessimistic locking is now a much more viable option.

- Jet SQL supports a number of new ANSI-92 SQL extensions. You can take advantage of the new SQL-92 extensions when using ADO and the Jet OLE DB provider.

- Jet provides a user list feature that allows you to determine the machine and username of all users currently logged into a database. You can use Jet's connection control feature to prevent new users from logging into a database; this might be useful, for example, if you wished to take a database offline for backup.

- Replication has been improved on several fronts. Previously, synchronizations could produce both conflicts and errors. With Jet 4, everything's a conflict, which makes resolution simpler. In addition, conflict resolution now occurs at the column level rather than the table level. Thus, if different users change different fields within the same record, the record is no longer flagged as a conflict. Jet 4 defines three levels of replica "visibility," which now allows you to create replica hierarchies within a replica set. You can also create special replicas where records cannot be deleted. In addition, Jet supports bidirectional merge replication with SQL Server.

- Microsoft provides two new object models in the ADO family for working with schemas and replication: ADOX and JRO. You use ADOX to investigate and modify the schema of Access and other ADO providers. JRO, on the other hand, is a Jet-specific object model you can use to compact and repair databases and work with Jet 4's replication features.

Jet multi-user issues are discussed in Chapter 2. Security and ADOX are discussed in Chapter 8. Replication and JRO are discussed in Chapter 9. Because the new client-server features of Access are so important for working in the enterprise, we've devoted five chapters to the discussion of these features. Designing client-server databases is the subject of Chapter 3. Chapters 4 and 5 discuss creating SQL Server and MSDE databases. Chapter 6 looks at ADO in a client-server context, and Chapter 7 discusses client-server implementation issues.

You will find a discussion of non-enterprise features of ADO and ADOX in Chapter 6 of *Access 2000 Developer's Handbook, Volume 1: Desktop Edition*. The new ANSI-92 SQL Jet extensions are discussed in Chapter 5 of *Access 2000 Developer's Handbook, Volume I: Desktop Edition*.

## Access 2000 Internet and Intranet Features

This version of Access replaces the Publish to the Web Wizard with data access pages. A *data access page* is a Web page that you can use to view or edit data from an Access, MSDE, or SQL Server database using Internet Explorer 5 (or greater). Some facts about data access pages:

- Data access pages take advantage of the client-side data-binding capabilities built into IE 5.

- The data in a data access page is embedded in the HTML page using eXtensible Markup Language (XML).

- You can use data access pages from within an MDB database, an ADP project, or IE5.

- Access includes a data access page designer that you can use to design pages.

- You can attach scripting code, written in either VBScript or JavaScript, to your pages. Microsoft has added the Microsoft Script Editor (MSE), a feature-rich script editor based on the Visual InterDev page editor, to Access.

- Data access pages can be created from scratch or can be based on existing Web pages. Access also includes a wizard that makes it easy to create a page in a hurry.

- You can include the Office Web Components within your pages. The Office Web Components are ActiveX controls that componentize features from Microsoft Excel. There are spreadsheet, pivot table, and chart components.

- While you can use data access pages for browsing and editing records, you can also use them for reporting, thanks to built-in grouping features.

In addition to data access pages, Access 2000 has several other Internet/intranet features:

- You can add hyperlinks to standard Access forms and reports.

- You can manipulate hyperlinks from VBA code.

- You can use the Web Browser control on a standard Access form to create a Web browser in a form.

- You can use the File ➤ Export menu command to export Access tables, queries, forms, and reports to several different formats, including HTML and ASP.

Data access pages are discussed in detail in Chapters 10 and 11. The Office Web Components are discussed in Chapter 12. Chapter 13 discusses the Web client features of Access. Publishing Access data to the HTML and ASP formats is the subject of Chapter 14.

## Access 2000 VBA

The Access module editor has been replaced with the VBA 6 editor. If you're a veteran Access developer, you may find the new editing environment a bit disorienting at first, but with time you'll grow to appreciate the benefits of the new VBA editor. In addition, the Access version of the VBA language, VBA 6, which now brings the Access VBA up to par with Visual Basic 6, has several welcome additions.

These changes are summarized here:

- The Access 2000 VBA editor is the same VBA editor that is built into the other Microsoft Office applications, as well as third-party VBA hosts.

- You can password-protect all of the VBA code in global modules and the modules behind forms and reports with a single password. VBA code is no longer protected by user-level (workgroup) security.

- The VBA editor has a programmable object model and supports COM add-ins. You can download, purchase, or build add-ins to help you write, analyze, or format your VBA code.

- VBA has several new functions, including StrRev, MonthName, Split, Join, and Replace, to name a few.

- You can use Debug.Assert to place assertions in your code.

- Access supports the AddressOf operator, and class modules support the new Implements keyword.

New class module features are discussed in Chapter 3 of *Access 2000 Developer's Handbook, Volume 1: Desktop Edition*. Other new language features are scattered about this book and Volume 1. Building add-ins is discussed in Chapter 18 of *Access 2000 Developer's Handbook, Volume 1: Desktop Edition*.

## Access 2000 Forms and Reports

Not a whole lot has changed in Access 2000 forms and reports. The few items that have changed are highlighted here:

- Forms and reports support the grouping and ungrouping of controls.

- Controls that display text allow for a user-specified border around the text, allowing you to move text around within the control.

- You can apply conditional formatting rules to the data in text and combo boxes.

- You can set a form's recordset to point to an arbitrary DAO or ADO recordset. That is, you can now open a recordset and assign it to a form's Recordset property. This means you can finally bind a form to something besides a table, query, or SQL string.

- Because you can assign a recordset to a form, you can wrap transactions around form updates.

New form and report features are discussed in Chapters 7, 8, and 9 of *Access 2000 Developer's Handbook, Volume1: Desktop Edition*.

## Other Access 2000 Improvements

Additional changes have been made to the product that don't fit neatly into any of the above categories, including the following:

- Object name changes have always been troubling to Access users and developers. That is, until now. Access 2000's Name AutoCorrect feature automatically fixes object name changes in dependent forms, reports, and queries. There are certain limitations—for example, Name AutoCorrect doesn't correct VBA code references, nor does it work in ADP files or replicated databases—but it can save you a lot of time when you rename objects.

- In the past, you could download an add-in for Access 97 that printed relationships. The print relationships feature is now built into Access 2000. From the Relationships window, simply select File ➤ Print Relationships to print out your finely crafted database relationships.

- The Access Upsizing Wizard has also been fully integrated into Access. Select Tools ➤ Database Utilities ➤ Upsizing Wizard to start upsizing your Access data to SQL Server.

- The Find and Replace dialog boxes are now nonmodal dialog boxes.

- Access was never big on backward compatibility. Access 2000, however, bucks this trend: select Tools ➤ Database Utilities ➤ Convert Database ➤ To Prior Access Database Versions to save an Access 2000 database to the older Access 97 format.

- Access 2000 lets you compact and repair a database in one step. Plus, there's an option to automatically compact databases when you close them.

Many of these miscellaneous changes are discussed throughout this book and *Access 2000 Developer's Handbook, Volume 1: Desktop Edition.*

# Microsoft Office Developer Features

Many professional Access developers will want to purchase Microsoft Office Developer (MOD). This version of Microsoft Office includes a copy of Microsoft

Office 2000 Premium (the version that comes with everything in Office Professional plus FrontPage, Publisher, and PhotoDraw), plus the following developer tools:

- A runtime distribution license for applications created with Access and either the Jet Engine or MSDE

- The COM Add-In designer, a VBA tool for creating add-ins that work across Office 2000

- A licensed copy of the Visual Source Safe (VSS) 6 source code control utility, not just the hooks into VSS that came with Office 97's ODE

- The Package and Deployment Wizard, Office 2000's successor to the Access Setup Wizard

- A number of ActiveX controls, including the ADO Data control, the Flex-Grid control, and the Data Repeater control

- Several useful add-ins, including the VBA Code Librarian, the VBA String Editor, the VBA Error Handler, and the VBA Code Commenter

- The Windows API Viewer, a utility for viewing and cutting and pasting Windows API Declare statements, constants, and types

- Microsoft Replication Manager, an updated version of Microsoft's replication administration tool

- Printed copies of the *Microsoft Office 2000 Visual Basic Programmer's Guide* and the *Microsoft Office 2000 Object Model Guide*

- An HTML help authoring tool called the HTML Help Workshop

- The Microsoft Agent and the Microsoft Answer Wizard Software Development Kits

---

**NOTE**    If you've already purchased a copy of Microsoft Office, you can get the developer tools that come with MOD by purchasing the Microsoft Office 2000 Developer Tools.

---

Replication Manager is discussed in Chapter 9. Source code control is the subject of Chapter 15. The Package and Deployment Wizard is discussed in Chapter 16. Building COM add-ins is discussed in Chapter 18 of *Access 2000 Developer's Handbook, Volume 1: Desktop Edition*. Programming the Windows API is discussed in Chapter 16 of *Access 2000 Developer's Handbook, Volume 1: Desktop Edition*.

# Summary

Access is the best-selling desktop database program on the market today. It has the right mix of features for developers working in both stand-alone and enterprise environments. The changes Microsoft has made to the product for this release make this version the best Access ever.

# Developing Multi-User Jet Applications

- Understanding page and record locking

- Contrasting optimistic and pessimistic locking

- Handling multi-user errors with the Form Error event

- Implementing a lock retry loop

- Determining who's logged on to a database

- Managing linked tables

**D**eveloping Access applications for multi-user systems requires extra planning and a shift from single-user application thinking, but it's not especially difficult to learn. In this chapter we explore Access' multi-user support and how best to plan and design multi-user database systems using Access 2000.

---

**NOTE**   There are three sample databases for Chapter 2. CH02APP.MDB is the "application" database—it contains all the user interface objects and supporting code, including code that manages links to CH02DAT.MDB. CH02DAT.MDB is the "data" database—it contains only the tables. CH02AUTO.MDB maintains the last AutoNumber value for the custom AutoNumber routine used by the frmMenu form in CH02APP.MDB.

---

# File-Server versus Client-Server

There are three basic ways to share data using Access:

**File-Server**   In this scenario, a copy of the Jet engine runs on each workstation and makes requests of a database file that resides on a centrally-located file server.

**Replication**   In this scenario, replicated copies or replicas of a database are distributed throughout an organization. Data is shared among the replicas by synchronizing the replicas on a regular basis.

**Client-Server**   In this scenario, Access is used as a front end to a SQL-based database management server such as SQL Server, the Microsoft Data Engine (MSDE), or Oracle. All the data is managed by the database server.

In this chapter, we discuss how to share data using shared file-server access with the database managed by the Jet engine. Replication is discussed in more detail in Chapter 9. Client-server access is discussed in several chapters, beginning with Chapter 3.

# Splitting Databases

By default, Access stores all its objects in a single .MDB file. This can adversely affect performance in a multi-user scenario because every time your application needs to use an object (for example, a form), the Jet engine must send the object across the network to the user. In a production setting, where nothing changes but the data, much of this network traffic is unnecessary.

You can eliminate this unnecessary traffic by splitting the database into two: an "application" database and a "data" database. Install the data database (with tables only) on the file server and a copy of the application database (containing all other objects) on each workstation. From each copy of the application database, use the File ➤ Get External Tables ➤ Link Tables command to link to the set of tables in the data database.

The advantages of this approach are:

- Better performance (especially user interface performance).

- You can create temporary tables within the application database stored on each workstation and not worry about naming and locking conflicts for temporary objects.

- Splitting the database makes updating applications easier because the data and application are kept separate. Changes to the application can be made off site and merged back into the application database without disturbing the data.

The major disadvantage of this approach is that Access hard-codes the paths to linked tables. This means that if you move the data database, you have to fix up the table links.

---

**TIP**     Access includes an add-in called the Database Splitter that makes it easy to split a single database into data and application databases.

---

## Managing Linked Tables

Because Access hard-codes linked table paths, their use requires extra maintenance. If you move the data database, you have three options for fixing the broken links:

- Delete and re-establish the link from scratch.

- Use the Access Linked Table Manager to fix up the references and refresh the links (select Tools ➤ Database Utilities ➤ Linked Table Manager).

- Create VBA code to manage links programmatically.

**TIP**

If you use universal naming convention (UNC) names when establishing your links (for example, \\ServerName\ShareName\Data.Mdb), you won't have to bother with fixing up links when you copy or move the application database from one computer to another within your LAN.

The CH02APP.MDB sample database includes a module, basLinkedTables, that contains reusable code for managing linked tables. The entry point to the code is through the adhVerifyLinks function, which is shown in Listing 2.1. (This function is called at database startup from the AutoExec function, which is called from the database's AutoExec macro.)

**NOTE**

If you wish to use adhVeryifyLinks in your application, you'll need to import three modules: basLinkedTables, basFileOpen, and CommonDialog.

## Listing 2.1

```
Function adhVerifyLinks(strDataDatabase As String, _
    strSampleTable As String) As Boolean

    ' Check status of Links and attempt to fix if broken.
    ' If broken, first try the current database directory.
    ' If that fails, present user with file open dialog.
    ' Assumption: all links are to same back-end MDB file.

    On Error GoTo adhVerifyLinksErr

    Dim varReturn As Variant
    Dim strDBDir As String
    Dim strMsg As String
    Dim varFileName As Variant
    Dim intI As Integer
    Dim intNumTables As Integer
    Dim strProcName As String
    Dim strFilter As String
    Dim lngFlags As Long
#If USEDAO Then
    Dim db As DAO.Database
```

```
        Dim tdf As DAO.TableDef
#Else
    Dim cnn As ADODB.Connection
    Dim cat As ADOX.Catalog
    Dim tbl As ADOX.Table
#End If

    strProcName = "adhVerifyLinks"

    ' Verify Links using one sample table.
    varReturn = CheckLink(strSampleTable)

    If varReturn Then
        adhVerifyLinks = True
        GoTo adhVerifyLinksDone
    End If

#If USEDAO Then
    ' Get name of folder where application database
    ' is located.
    strDBDir = adhCurrentDBPath()
#Else
    strDBDir = CurrentProject.Path & "\"
#End If

    If (Dir$(strDBDir & strDataDatabase) <> "") Then
        ' Data database found in current directory.
        varFileName = strDBDir & strDataDatabase
    Else
        ' Let user find data database using common dialog.
        strMsg = "The required file '" & _
        strDataDatabase & _
        "' could not be found." & _
        " You can use the next dialog box" & _
        " to locate the file on your system." & _
        " If you cannot find this file or" & _
        " are unsure what to do choose CANCEL" & _
        " at the next screen and call the" & _
        " database administrator."
        MsgBox strMsg, vbOKOnly + vbCritical, strProcName

        ' Display Open File dialog using
```

```
                            ' adhCommonFileOpenSave from basFileOpen.
                        strFilter = adhAddFilterItem( _
                         strFilter, "Access (*.mdb)", "*.mdb")

                        varFileName = adhCommonFileOpenSave( _
                            OpenFile:=True, _
                            Filter:=strFilter, _
                            Flags:=cdlOFNHideReadOnly + cdlOFNNoChangeDir, _
                            InitDir:=strDBDir, _
                            DialogTitle:="Locate Data database file")

                        If IsNull(varFileName) Then
                            ' User pressed Cancel.
                            strMsg = "You can't use this database " & _
                             "until you locate '" & strDataDatabase & "'."
                            MsgBox strMsg, _
                             vbOKOnly + vbCritical, strProcName
                            adhVerifyLinks = False
                            GoTo adhVerifyLinksDone
                        Else
                            varFileName = adhTrimNull(varFileName)
                        End If
                    End If


                    'Rebuild Links. Check for number of tables first.
            #If USEDAO Then
                    Set db = CurrentDb
                    intNumTables = db.TableDefs.Count
            #Else
                    Set cnn = CurrentProject.Connection
                    Set cat = New ADOX.Catalog
                    cat.ActiveConnection = cnn
                    intNumTables = cat.Tables.Count
            #End If
                    varReturn = SysCmd(acSysCmdInitMeter, _
                     "Relinking tables", intNumTables)

                    ' Loop through all tables. Reattach those
                    ' with nonzero-length Connect strings.
                    intI = 0
            #If USEDAO Then
                    For Each tdf In db.TableDefs
```

```
                     ' If connect is blank, its not an Linked table.
                     If Len(tdf.Connect) > 0 Then
                          intI = intI + 1
                          tdf.Connect = ";DATABASE=" & varFileName

                          ' The RefreshLink might fail if the new
                          ' path isn't OK. So trap errors inline.
                          On Error Resume Next
                          tdf.RefreshLink
                          'If one link bad, return False.
                          If Err.Number <> 0 Then
                               adhVerifyLinks = False
                               GoTo adhVerifyLinksDone
                          End If
                     End If

                     varReturn = SysCmd(acSysCmdUpdateMeter, intI + 1)
               Next tdf
 #Else
          For Each tbl In cat.Tables
                     ' If Type = "LINK, it's a linked table.
                     If tbl.Type = "LINK" Then
                          intI = intI + 1
                          On Error Resume Next
                          ' This next line recreates and refreshes link.
                          ' This might fail if the new path
                          ' isn't OK. So trap errors inline.
                          tbl.Properties("Jet OLEDB:Link Datasource") = _
                           varFileName
                          'If one link bad, return False.
                          If Err.Number <> 0 Then
                               adhVerifyLinks = False
                               GoTo adhVerifyLinksDone
                          End If
                     End If

                     varReturn = SysCmd(acSysCmdUpdateMeter, intI + 1)
               Next tbl
 #End If
          adhVerifyLinks = True
```

```
adhVerifyLinksDone:
    On Error Resume Next
    varReturn = SysCmd(acSysCmdRemoveMeter)
#If USEDAO Then
    Set tdf = Nothing
    Set db = Nothing
#Else
    Set tbl = Nothing
    Set cat = Nothing
    Set cnn = Nothing
#End If
    Exit Function

adhVerifyLinksErr:
    Select Case Err.Number
    Case Else
        Err.Raise Err.Number, Err.Source, _
          Err.Description, Err.HelpFile, Err.HelpContext
    End Select
    Resume adhVerifyLinksDone
End Function
```

---

**TIP**    We've constructed this function so that it will work with either the DAO or ADO object models. By default, the code in this chapter is set to work with ADO. If you wish to use DAO, instead, set the conditional compile constant USEDAO for the module to True.

---

The adhVerifyLinks function takes two parameters: strDataDatabase, the name of the data database containing the linked tables, and strSampleTable, the name of one of the linked tables. adhVerifyLinks starts by checking the validity of this sample linked table. It assumes that if this table's link checks out okay, then all the links are fine. (You can modify the code to check the integrity of all links instead if you'd like.) The function verifies the links by calling the private function Check-Link, which is shown in Listing 2.2.

## ⟳ Listing 2.2

```
Private Function CheckLink(strTable As String) As Boolean

    ' Checks the Link for the named table.
    ' (Actually, CheckLink also returns False if
    '  table doesn't exist.)

    On Error Resume Next

#If USEDAO Then
    Dim varRet As Variant

    ' Check for failure. If can't determine the name of
    ' the first field in the table, link must be bad.
    varRet = CurrentDb.TableDefs(strTable).Fields(0).Name
    If Err.Number <> 0 Then
        CheckLink = False
    Else
        CheckLink = True
    End If
#Else
    Dim cnn As ADODB.Connection
    Dim rst As ADODB.Recordset

    Set cnn = CurrentProject.Connection
    ' Use OpenSchema to fill a recordset with information
    ' about the columns in strTable. If the recordset is
    ' empty then Jet couldn't connect so link must be bad.
    Set rst = cnn.OpenSchema(adSchemaColumns, _
     Array(Empty, Empty, strTable, Empty))
    CheckLink = Not rst.EOF

    rst.Close
    Set rst = Nothing
    Set cnn = Nothing
#End If

End Function
```

When using DAO, CheckLink checks the validity of a link by attempting to retrieve the name of the table's first field. If this operation succeeds, the link is good; if it fails, it's assumed to be bad and the function returns False. Using ADO, the function checks the link by using the special OpenSchema method of the Connection object. You can use OpenSchema to fill a recordset with all sorts of different database schema information. (This is faster than using an ADOX Table object to determine if the link is broken.)

If CheckLink returns False, adhVerifyLinks looks for the data database in the same folder as the application database. If the database is found there, the function relinks all the tables using this database. If the data database isn't in the application folder, the function prompts the user with a common open file dialog.

When the database has been located, adhVerifyLinks attempts to relink the linked tables in the database.. When using DAO, the function determines that a table is linked by checking if the TableDef object's Connect property has a a non-zero length and then relinks the linked tables by modifying the Connect property and using the RefreshLink method, as demonstrated by this code from adhVerifyLinks:

```
tdf.Connect = ";DATABASE=" & varFileName
tdf.RefreshLink
```

Using ADO, adhVerifyLinks determines that a table is linked by checking to see if the Table object's Type property is set to "LINK" and then relinks the linked tables using a Jet provider-specific property of the ADOX Table object, as demonstrated by this section of code from adhVerifyLinks:

```
tbl.Properties("Jet OLEDB:Link Datasource") = _
  varFileName
```

See Chapter 6 of *Access 2000 Developer's Handbook, Volume 1: Desktop Edition* for more information on ADOX provider-specific properties.

## Integrating Linked Tables into Your Applications

When you split an existing single-database application into data and application databases, you may be required to alter some of your VBA code. You can't use table-type recordsets or the Seek method directly on linked tables, but you can use one of these alternative strategies instead:

- Create non-table-type recordsets and use the slower FindFirst (DAO) or Find method (ADO).

- Use the OpenDatabase method of the Workspace object (DAO) or the Open method of the Connection object (ADO) to open the data database directly. You can then create table-type recordsets and use the Seek method just as though the tables were local.

Whichever method you choose, you'll likely have to make changes to your application code. However, it is possible to write code that is able to use the Seek method regardless of whether the table is local or linked, as demonstrated by the code in Listing 2.3 (for DAO) and Listing 2.4 (for ADO)—both from CH02APP.MDB.

### Listing 2.3

```
Sub SeekLocalOrLinkedDAO(ByVal strTable As String, _
ByVal strCompare As String, _
Optional ByVal strIndex As String = "PrimaryKey")

    ' Performs DAO Seek on table using the specified
    ' index and search criteria. Works with both
    ' local and linked Access tables.
    '
    ' In:
    '     strTable: Name of table
    '     strCompare: Comma delimited list of search values
    '     strIndex: Name of index. Default is "PrimaryKey"
    ' Out:
    '     Prints to the debug window list of field values
    '     or 'No match was found'.

    Dim db As DAO.Database
    Dim rst As DAO.Recordset
    Dim fld As DAO.Field
    Dim strConnect As String
    Dim strDB As String
    Dim intDBStart As Integer
    Dim intDBEnd As Integer

    Const adhcDB = "DATABASE="

    Set db = CurrentDb
    ' Grab connection string from tabledef
    strConnect = db.TableDefs(strTable).Connect
```

```
' If connection string is "" then it's a local table.
' Otherwise, need to parse database portion of
' connection string.
strDB = ""
If Len(strConnect) > 0 Then
    intDBStart = InStr(strConnect, adhcDB)
    intDBEnd = InStr(intDBStart + Len(adhcDB), _
     strConnect, ";")
    If intDBEnd = 0 Then intDBEnd = Len(strConnect) + 1
    strDB = Mid(strConnect, intDBStart + Len(adhcDB), _
     intDBEnd - intDBStart)

    ' Open the external database.
    Set db = DBEngine.Workspaces(0).OpenDatabase(strDB)
End If

' Need to open a table-type recordset to use Seek.
Set rst = db.OpenRecordset(strTable, dbOpenTable)
rst.Index = strIndex

rst.Seek "=", strCompare

If Not rst.NoMatch Then
    ' This example is just printing out the
    ' values of each of the fields of the
    ' found record, but you get the idea...
    For Each fld In rst.Fields
        Debug.Print fld.Name & ": " & fld.Value
    Next
Else
    Debug.Print "No match was found."
End If

Set fld = Nothing
rst.Close
Set rst = Nothing
If Len(strDB) > 0 Then
    db.Close
End If
Set db = Nothing
End Sub
```

## ⟲ Listing 2.4

```
Sub SeekLocalOrLinkedADO(ByVal strTable As String, _
ByVal varCompare As Variant, _
Optional ByVal strIndex As String = "PrimaryKey")

    ' Performs ADO Seek on table using the specified
    ' index and search criteria. Works with both
    ' local and linked Access tables.
    '
    ' In:
    '     strTable: Name of table
    '     varCompare: Array of search values
    '     strIndex: Name of index. Default is "PrimaryKey"
    ' Out:
    '     Prints to the debug window list of field values
    '     or 'No match was found'.

    Dim cnn As ADODB.Connection
    Dim cat As ADOX.Catalog
    Dim rst As ADODB.Recordset
    Dim fld As ADODB.Field
    Dim strDB As String

    Set cnn = CurrentProject.Connection
    Set cat = New ADOX.Catalog
    cat.ActiveConnection = cnn

    ' If this is a linked table, strDB will contain
    ' the name of the source database, otherwise it
    ' will contain an empty string.
    strDB = cat.Tables(strTable). _
     Properties("Jet OLEDB:Link Datasource")

    If Len(strDB) > 0 Then
        ' Open a connection to the external database.
        Set cnn = New ADODB.Connection
        cnn.Open "Provider=Microsoft.Jet.OLEDB.4.0;" & _
         "Data Source=" & strDB & ";"
    End If
```

```
Set rst = New ADODB.Recordset
' Need to open a table-type recordset to use Seek.
rst.Open strTable, cnn, adOpenKeyset, _
 adLockOptimistic, adCmdTableDirect
rst.Index = strIndex

rst.Seek varCompare, adSeekFirstEQ

' If no match was found, EOF will be True.
If Not rst.EOF Then
    ' This example is just printing out the
    ' values of each of the fields of the
    ' found record, but you get the idea...
    For Each fld In rst.Fields
        Debug.Print fld.Name & ": " & fld.Value
    Next
Else
    Debug.Print "No match was found."
End If

Set fld = Nothing
rst.Close
Set rst = Nothing
Set cat = Nothing
If Len(strDB) > 0 Then
    cnn.Close
End If
Set cnn = Nothing
End Sub
```

This code works by grabbing the name of the data database from the table schema. The DAO version of the code (SeekLocalOrLinkedDAO found in Listing 2.3) accomplishes this by parsing the name of the database from the DATABASE item of TableDef's Connect property. The ADO version of the code (SeekLocalOr-LinkedADO found in Listing 2.4) is simpler because you don't have to parse the database name from the Jet OLEDB:Link Datasource property of an ADOX Table object (this property contains the name of the database only).

# Multi-User Settings

Several options and settings in Access affect how your applications behave in a multi-user environment, as described in the following sections.

## Database Open Modes

You can affect the way a database is opened in Access in three ways:

- When you start Access, you can include a database name on the command line and either the /Excl or /Ro parameter to open that database in exclusive or read-only mode, respectively.

- Using the File ➢ Open dialog box, you can open a database exclusively, read only, or both.

- You can change the default database open mode by choosing Tools ➢ Options and changing the Default Open Mode setting on the Advanced tab of the Options dialog box. The setting can be set to Exclusive for single-user access or Shared for multi-user access to the database.

**TIP**    You can prevent a user from opening a database in exclusive mode by using the Tools ➢ Security ➢ User and Group Permissions command to uncheck the OpenExclusive permission of the database for that user. See Chapter 8 for more details.

## The Refresh Interval

You can set the default database refresh interval using the Advanced tab of the Options dialog box. Access automatically checks the recordsets of open forms and datasheets to see whether changes have occurred at the frequency you have specified using this setting. The default refresh interval is 60 seconds, which may be too long for some applications. But if you set the refresh interval to a very small value, you may create excessive network traffic. Finding the proper setting for your application may require some experimentation. In general, the smaller the network, the smaller you can set the refresh interval without adverse effect.

You can manually override the default refresh interval in your VBA code. To refresh the current record on a form, use:

```
Me.Refresh
```

To requery the current record on a form, use:

```
Me.Requery
```

There is no Refresh method of DAO or ADO recordsets; however, you can force a refresh of the current record by setting the recordset's Bookmark property to itself like this:

```
rst.Bookmark = rst.Bookmark
```

To requery a DAO or ADO recordset, use:

```
rst.Requery
```

Record refreshes—either automatic refreshes by Access using the refresh interval or manual refreshes using the Refresh method—are faster than requeries. New records added by other users, however, appear only during a requery, and records deleted by other users vanish from your copy only after a requery (unless you are using a dynamic ADO recordset).

---

**TIP**      Even if you set the refresh interval to a long value, Access automatically refreshes the current record whenever a user attempts to edit it. The benefit of a shorter refresh interval lies chiefly in providing quicker visual feedback that someone else has locked or changed a record while you are viewing it.

---

## Locking Granularity

To provide concurrent access to records by multiple users, the Jet engine sets and removes locks. Prior to Access 2000, the Jet engine locked pages of records, rather than individual records. The page size was 2 kilobytes (2048 bytes). This meant that Jet usually locked more than one record at a time. How many? That depended on how many records Jet could fit into a page that was 2 kilobytes (2048 bytes) in size. This could be anywhere from 1 to 30 or more records, depending on the size of the records.

 One of the most exciting new features of Access 2000 is its support for true record locking! You enable record locking for a database by selecting the Open

Databases Using Record-Level Locking checkbox on the Advanced tab of the Options dialog box (see Figure 2.1). Actually, selecting this checkbox enables record/page locking. For most, but not all, data operations this translates to true record locking (see the next section for the exceptions). On the other hand, if you uncheck Open Databases Using Record-Level Locking checkbox, Jet will lock only pages of record. Record-level locking is turned on, by default.

The locking granularity for a database is determined by the first user opening the database. Once the first user opens a database, you can't change the locking granularity until all users have exited the database.

**FIGURE 2.1**
Enabling record locking.

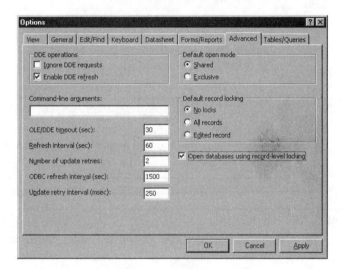

The size of a page in Access 2000/Jet 4.0 has been increased from 2 kilobytes to 4 kilobytes. This was necessary to accommodate support for Unicode.

## Record/Page Locking

When you enable record/page locking for a database, Jet locks individual records for some operations and page locking for other operations.

Jet uses *record-level* locking when reading/writing data records using:

- Access forms

- DAO recordsets

- ADO recordsets, unless overridden by using the "Jet OLE DB: Locking Granularity" property

Jet uses *page-level* locking is used when:

- Updating data using bulk SQL statements

- Updating index pages

- Updating memo data type data

- Using ADO recordsets when the "Jet OLE DB: Locking Granularity" property has been set to 1

**NOTE**   There is one negative side effect of record locking: When you've enabled record/ page locking, Jet is unable to report to you the username and machine name of the user who has a locked a record. (With page locking, Jet is normally able to report this information in error messages.)

**WARNING**   Access 2000 contains a bug that causes Jet to use page locking when you directly open a database from a Windows shortcut or by double-clicking on an .MDB file from Windows Explorer. This happens regardless of whether you have checked the "Open Databases Using Record-Level Locking" checkbox on the Advanced tab of the Options dialog box. To avoid this bug, you need to start Access without loading a database and then open the database once Access has started. There is no way to avoid the bug when using the Access run-time! As we went to press, this bug had not been fixed but it is possible that a future service pack of Access 2000 or the Jet engine may fix the bug.

## Page Locking

When you enable page-level locking for a database, Jet locks pages of records only. This is the same behavior used in earlier versions of the Jet engine.

### Choosing the Right Lock Granularity

Record-level locking provides much better concurrency than page-level locking. This means that more users can be updating records from a given table at the same time when using record-level locking. Record-level locking, however, doesn't necessarily mean better performance. When updating a large number of records, page-level locking may perform better than record-level locking.

> **TIP**　In most situations, you'll find the increased concurrency afforded by record-level locking greatly outweighs any loss in performance over page-level locking.

## Lock Timing

In addition to choosing the locking granularity (record versus page-level locking), you can select the timing of locks, that is, when Jet applies the locks. You can open recordsets in one of three modes (each is discussed in more detail in the following sections):

**No Locks**　This is often called *optimistic locking* and is the default setting. With the No Locks setting, the record (or page of records that contains the currently edited record if employing page locking) is locked only during the instant when the record is saved, not during the editing process.

**Edited Record**　As soon as a user begins to edit a record, the record (or the page containing the currently edited record if employing page locking) is locked until the changes are saved. This is known as *pessimistic locking*.

**All Records**　This setting causes all the records in the entire recordset to be locked. You won't find this option very useful except when doing batch updates or performing administrative maintenance on tables.

You can adjust locking options for database objects that manipulate recordsets. Table 2.1 shows which locking options are available for each database object, as well as the point at which records are actually locked. The default RecordLocks setting for most of these objects is taken from the Default Record Locking option established using the Advanced tab of the Options dialog box, shown back in Figure 2.1.

**TABLE 2.1:** Available RecordLocks Settings for Various Access Objects

| Access Object | No Locks | Edited Record | All Records | Default | When Records Are Locked |
|---|---|---|---|---|---|
| Table datasheets | Yes[1] | Yes[1] | Yes[1] | DRL | Datasheet editing |
| Select query datasheets | Yes | Yes | Yes | DRL | Datasheet editing |
| Crosstab query datasheets | Yes | Yes | Yes | DRL | Query execution |
| Union query datasheets | Yes | Yes | Yes | DRL | Query execution |
| Update and delete queries | No | Yes | Yes | DRL | Query execution |
| Make-table and append queries | No | Yes | Yes | DRL | Query execution[2] |
| Data definition queries | No | No | Yes | All Records[3] | Query execution |
| Forms | Yes | Yes | Yes | DRL | Form and datasheet views |
| Reports | Yes | No | Yes | DRL | Report execution, preview, and printing |
| DAO Recordset | Yes | Yes | Yes | Edited Record[4] | Between Edit and Update methods |
| ADO Recordset | Yes | Yes | Yes | Read Only[5] | Between start of edit and Update method |

Yes = available option
No = option not available for this object
DRL = Default Record Locking option setting for the database
1  There is no RecordLocks property for table datasheets. Datasheets use the Default Record Locking option setting for the database.
2  For make-table and append queries, the target tables are locked.
3  There is no RecordLocks property for data definition queries. Access locks the entire table.
4  Changed using the LockEdits property of a DAO recordset. Edited Record is the default unless you use the dbDenyWrite or dbDenyRead option of theOpenRecordset method, in which case the entire table is locked.
5  Changed using the LockType property of an ADO recordset or the LockType argument of the Recordset.Open method.

## Optimistic Locking

Optimistic locking (record locking = No Locks) allows for concurrent editing of records with fewer locking conflicts. However, because it allows multiple users to be editing the same record at the same time, it carries with it the risk of write conflicts. A *write conflict* occurs when:

1.  A user begins to edit a record.

2.  A second user saves changes to the record.

3.  The first user then attempts to save his/her changes.

A write conflict is bad because it means that the first user is changing a different record than he or she began editing.

### Pessimistic Locking

When you lock records pessimistically (record locking = Edited Record), only one user may edit a record at a time. This is especially problematic when you are using page locking because then only one user may be editing any record on a page at a time.

### Choosing the Right Lock Timing

In general, you don't want two users editing the same record at the same time. This fact would tend to lead you towards using pessimistic locking. However, in versions of Access prior to Access 2000 this meant locking an entire page of records rather than an individual record—often an unacceptable price to pay. Because of this, in prior editions of this book we recommended using optimistic locking except in specialized applications where a write conflict was unacceptable. With Access 2000's support for true record locking, however, we now believe that pessimistic record locking is the preferred choice for most applications. There will be the occasional situation, however, where you may wish to consider optimistic locking. For example, if you have users who tend to lock records for long periods of time, you may prefer to go with optimistic locking. You may also wish to use optimistic locking if you are using page locking because, for example, your application contains links to an Access 97 database.

---

**TIP**     If you are able to use record locking, we recommend using pessimistic locking for most Access 2000 applications that employ the Jet 4 engine.

---

# Locking and Forms

When you use bound forms, Access takes care of the locking of records automatically. In the next few sections we discuss how this works and how to customize Access default locking behaviors.

## Optimistic Locking on Forms

As mentioned earlier in the chapter, the main problem with optimistic locking is the potential for write conflicts. When a write conflict occurs in bound forms, Access displays the Write Conflict dialog box, as shown in Figure 2.2 for the frmCustomerOptimistic1 sample form in the CH02APP.MDB database.

**FIGURE 2.2**

Under optimistic locking, users may encounter the Write Conflict dialog box when attempting to save a record that has been changed by another user.

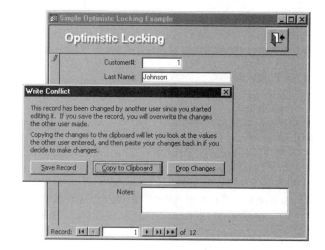

This dialog box offers the user three options:

**Save Record**   If the user selects this option, changes to the record this user has made will overwrite changes made by the other user. In most cases a user should not use this option; it blindly discards the other user's changes.

**Copy to Clipboard**   This option copies this user's changes to the clipboard and refreshes the record with the other user's changes. This option is a good choice for the sophisticated user but requires too much understanding for the naive user. If you used this option back in Access 2.0, you'll be happy to know that the bug that prevented formatted data from being pasted back to the form has been fixed.

**Drop Changes**   If the user selects this option, this user's changes are dropped and the record is refreshed with the other user's changes.

A bug in Access 2000 (it's been there since the days of Access 2—some bugs are slow to be fixed) occurs when you have a one-to-many relationship defined for two tables *without* cascading updates turned on and you choose Save Record in the Write Conflict dialog box for a record on the "one" side of the relationship. You will get a spurious referential integrity violation message even if you have not updated the primary key value (see Figure 2.3). This message occurs because Access blindly copies values for all your fields over the values that have been saved by the other user, without bothering to check whether each field was actually changed. Because the fields include the primary key field, Jet thinks the primary key value has changed and displays the spurious error message.

**FIGURE 2.3**
This spurious error message can occur when you choose Save Record from the Write Conflict dialog box.

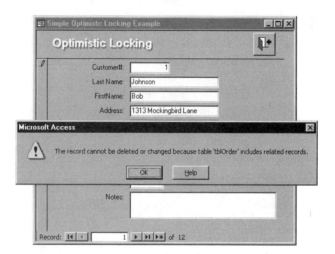

## Optimistic Locking with Custom Error Handling

You can use the Form Error event to intercept write conflict errors and handle them using VBA code by creating an Error event procedure. Access passes to your event procedure the DataErr and Response parameters. The two most common optimistic locking DataErr values are described in Table 2.2

Error 7787 is the standard Write Conflict dialog box error. It occurs when a user attempts to *save changes* to a record that has changed. Error 7878 occurs when a user *begins to edit* a record that has changed since that user began viewing it; this error is more likely to occur with long refresh intervals.

**TABLE 2.2:** Optimistic Locking Errors in Forms

| Error Number | Access Error Message | Comment |
|---|---|---|
| 7787 | Write Conflict: This record has been changed by another user since you started editing it… | A second user saved changes while the first user was editing the record |
| 7878 | The data has been changed… | A second user saved changes while the first user was viewing the record |

**NOTE**    The Error event is triggered anytime a data access error is generated, so any event procedure you create must also be prepared to deal with non-locking data access errors.

You can set the Response parameter to one of two built-in constants:

| Response | When Used |
|---|---|
| acDataErrContinue | To tell Access to continue without displaying the error message; in the case of optimistic errors, this causes a refresh of the record, with the current user's edits discarded |
| acDataErrDisplay | To tell Access to display the normal error message; use this constant for errors you are not handling |

You'll notice that there's no way to tell Jet to overwrite the record with "your" changes. Aside from choosing the built-in error message, your only option is to allow Jet to refresh the user's edits with those the other user has already saved to disk. The built-in Save Record functionality is provided by the Access UI and is, thus, not one of the options available programmatically. However, we have come up with a work-around that produces the same effect—without causing the bug mentioned in the preceding section.

The event procedure attached to the Error event of the frmCustomerOptimistic2 form in the CH02APP.MDB sample database demonstrates this work-around. Listing 2.5 includes this event procedure, as well as supporting code found in the Current event procedure of frmCustomerOptimistic2.

This form uses DAO code to manipulate a "shadow" recordset, but it could easily
be changed to use an ADO recordset instead.

## Listing 2.5

```
Dim mvarCustomerId As Variant

Const adhcErrWriteConflict = 7787
Const adhcErrDataChanged = 7878

Private Sub Form_Error(DataErr As Integer, _
 Response As Integer)
    ' Handle form-level errors

    On Error GoTo Form_ErrorErr

    Dim strMsg As String
    Dim intResp As Integer
    Dim rst As dao.Recordset
    Dim fld As dao.Field
    Dim db As dao.Database

    ' Branch based on value of error
    Select Case DataErr

    Case adhcErrWriteConflict
        ' Write conflict error
        strMsg = "Another user has updated this record " & _
         "since you began editing it." & vbCrLf & vbCrLf & _
         "Do you want to refresh your record with the " & _
         "the other user's changes?" & vbCrLf & vbCrLf & _
         "Choose Yes to refresh your record, " & vbCrLf & _
         "or No to replace the record with your version."
        intResp = MsgBox(strMsg, _
         vbYesNo + vbDefaultButton1 + vbQuestion, _
         "Overwrite Conflict")

        ' Jet only allows other user's changes to
        ' be saved, so we need to trick Jet into using
```

```
' our changes by writing our changes out to
' underlying record, which Access will then
' copy over our changes.
If intResp = vbNo Then

    Set db = CurrentDb

    ' Create recordset of one record that matches
    ' PK value of the record when we began editing
    ' it. This value was stored away by Current
    ' event procedure. This is necessary since we
    ' could've changed the PK value.
    Set rst = db.OpenRecordset("SELECT * FROM " & _
     "tblCustomer WHERE [CustomerId] = " _
     & mvarCustomerId)

    ' Make sure PK value wasn't changed by
    ' other user.
    If rst.RecordCount = 0 Then
        strMsg = "Another user has changed the " & _
         "Customer# for this record. " & _
         "The record will need to be refreshed " & _
         "before continuing."
        MsgBox strMsg, vbOKOnly + vbInformation, _
         "Overwrite Conflict"
    Else
        ' Update values in underlying record
        ' with any changed values from form.
        DoCmd.Hourglass True
        For Each fld In rst.Fields
            rst.Edit
                If (fld <> Me(fld.Name)) Or _
                 (IsNull(fld) <> _
                 IsNull(Me(fld.Name))) _
                 Then
                    fld.Value = _
                     Me(fld.Name).Value
                End If
            rst.Update
        Next fld
    End If
End If
```

```
        ' This will cause record refresh
        Response = acDataErrContinue

    Case adhcErrDataChanged
        ' This error occurs if Access detects that
        ' another user has changed this record when we
        ' attempt to dirty the record. Fairly harmless
        ' since we haven't actually made any changes.
        strMsg = "Another user has updated this record " & _
         "since you began viewing it." & vbCrLf & vbCrLf & _
         "The record will be refreshed with the other " & _
         "user's changes before continuing."
        MsgBox strMsg, vbOKOnly + vbInformation, _
         "Record Refresh"

        ' This will cause record refresh
        Response = acDataErrContinue
    Case Else
        ' Otherwise, let Access display standard
        ' error message
        Response = acDataErrDisplay
        Debug.Print DataErr, Error(DataErr)
    End Select

    DoCmd.Hourglass False

Form_ErrorEnd:
    If Not rst Is Nothing Then
        Set rst = Nothing
    End If
    If Not fld Is Nothing Then
        Set fld = Nothing
    End If
    If Not db Is Nothing Then
        Set db = Nothing
    End If
    Exit Sub

Form_ErrorErr:
    ' It's possible to hit our own error while handling a
    ' data error. For example, someone could pessimistically
```

```
    ' lock the record while we are trying to update it.
    ' Report the error to the user and exit.
    MsgBox "Error " & Err.Number & ": " & Err.Description, _
    vbOKOnly + vbCritical, "Error Handler Error"
End Sub
```

The frmCustomerOptimistic2 form displays a custom write conflict message when error 7787 has been detected (see Figure 2.4). If the user chooses Yes, Response is set to acDataErrContinue and the event procedure exits. If the user chooses No, the event procedure takes the values from the form's current record and writes them out to a newly created recordset based on the conflict record. Then, when the event procedure sets Response to acDataErrContinue and exits, Jet copies "our" values back over the current record, thus providing the equivalent of the Save Record option. However, by copying only the values of fields that differ from the values the other user has saved, the code avoids the referential integrity error message:

```
For Each fld In rst.Fields
    rst.Edit
        If (fld <> Me(fld.Name)) Or _
        (IsNull(fld) <> _
        IsNull(Me(fld.Name))) _
        Then
            fld.Value = _
            Me(fld.Name).Value
        End If
    rst.Update
Next fld
```

This work-around depends on storing the primary key field value for the current record in a module-level global variable, mvarCustomerId, using an event procedure attached to the Current event. This is necessary because you need to be able to open a recordset based on the current record, but you have no guarantee that the user hasn't changed the primary key value. Thus, this technique uses the value of the PK field that was stored away during the Current event. An alternative way to handle this would be to make the PK field read-only or to use the inherently read-only AutoNumber datatype for your PK.

If your form uses a compound primary key field or a query based on multiple tables, you will have to store away the value of multiple fields.

The frmCustomerOptimistic2
form displays a custom
write conflict message.

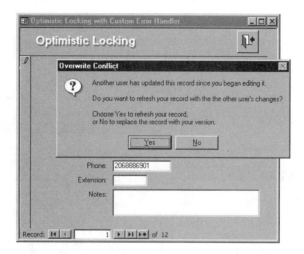

**NOTE**

In many applications, you may not wish to offer your users the ability to save their changes without first viewing the other user's changes. In these cases you may wish to use a much simpler optimistic locking error handler that informs the user that another user has saved changes to the record and then performs a record refresh. An example of this simpler event handler is also included in the sample database attached to the frmCustomerOptimistic3 form (see Figure 2.5).

**FIGURE 2.5**
The frmCustomerOptimistic3
form displays a simpler
custom write conflict
message.

## Pessimistic Locking on Forms

Forms that use pessimistic locking avoid write conflicts because only one user at a time is allowed to edit a record. The presence of the "slashed-O" icon in the record selector notifies other users that a record has been locked, as demonstrated by the frmCustomerPessimistic1 form from the sample database (see Figure 2.6).

**FIGURE 2.6**

Under pessimistic locking, the slashed-O icon in the record selector notifies users that the current record is locked.

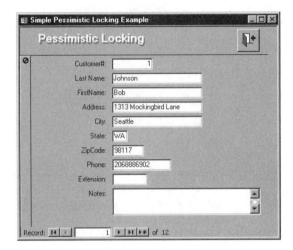

**TIP**

If you have set the RecordSelector property of a form to No, the slashed-O icon does not appear when a record is pessimistically locked. Access beeps at the user, but other than this audible signal, users won't have any clue as to why they can't edit the values in the record. No trappable error is generated, either, because this really isn't an error state. Thus, it's important to leave the RecordSelector property set to Yes when using pessimistic locking unless you create some custom mechanism for notifying users of the lock.

## Pessimistic Locking with a Timeout Option

Access 2000's support for true record locking makes pessimistic (no locks) locking a much more attractive option. Still, even when users can lock only a single record, there is nothing to prevent them from locking that record for an excessive period of time. We've all heard the story of the user who begins to edit a record and then goes out to lunch, or worse, on a two-week vacation!

# The LockTimeout Class

We've created a class module, LockTimeout, that you can use to add timeout functionality to a form. The frmCustomerPessimistic2 form, shown in Figures 2.7 and 2.8, uses the LockTimeout class to undo a user's unsaved changes after ten minutes.

**FIGURE 2.7**

The frmCustomerPessimistic2 form informs users the length of time they have locked a record and how long they have left before their changes will be undone.

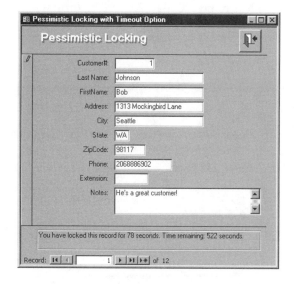

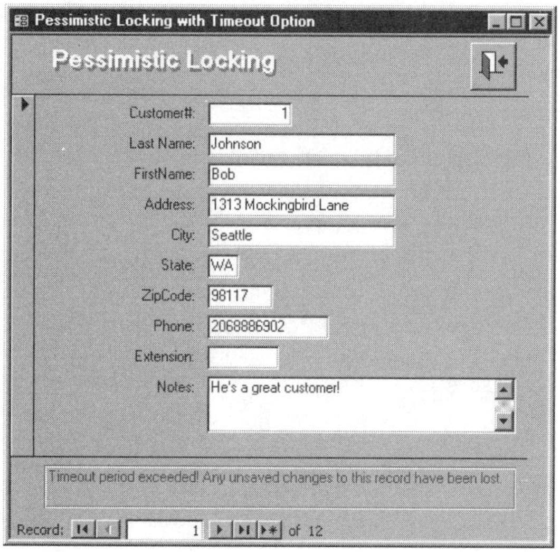

**FIGURE 2.8**

The frmCustomerPessimistic2 form undoes a user's changes if they have locked a record for ten minutes.

The code behind frmCustomerPessimistic2 is shown in Listing 2.6. In the Load event of the form, the code instantiates the mltoCustomer object and calls the BindForm method to bind the form to the LockTimeout class. BindForm takes four arguments:

- A reference to the current form

- A reference to a label on the form that will be used for a status message

- The interval in seconds to update the status message

- The length in seconds before a user is timed out

### Listing 2.6

```
' LockTimeout object variable
Private mltoCustomer As LockTimeout

Private Sub cmdClose_Click()
    DoCmd.Close acForm, Me.Name
End Sub

Private Sub Form_AfterUpdate()
    ' Stop the timer when user saves record
    mltoCustomer.StopTimer
End Sub

Private Sub Form_Dirty(Cancel As Integer)
    ' Start timer when user dirties record
    mltoCustomer.StartTimer
End Sub

Private Sub Form_Load()
    ' Create LockTimeout object
    Set mltoCustomer = New LockTimeout
    ' Bind the LockTimeout object to the current form
    mltoCustomer.BindForm _
      FormRef:=Me, LabelRef:=lblLockStatus, _
      CheckInterval:=1, TimeoutPeriod:=10 * 60
End Sub

Private Sub Form_Timer()
    ' Check for things to do
    mltoCustomer.CheckTimer
End Sub
```

The LockTimeout class module is shown in Listing 2.7. It uses the timeGetTime Windows API function to keep track of time. LockTimeout uses five private variables to keep track of the time a user has locked a record, a reference to the "bound" form, a reference to the label that it should update, the timer interval, and the timeout length.

The BindForm method hooks up the bound form by setting each of the private module-level variables but doesn't actually do anything.

The StartTimer method records the start time using timeGetTime and starts the form's Timer event.

The StopTimer method stops the forms' Timer event and zeros out the mlngLockStart time. It also clears the caption of the status label.

The CheckTimer method does most of the work of the class. First of all, because there is no event that is triggered when the changes on a form are undone, it checks the Dirty property of the form and resets mlngLockStart to 0 if it finds the form is no longer dirty.

If the form is dirty, CheckTimer computes the length of time the user has locked the form and the amount of time that remains before the user will be forcibly timed out. Then it does one of three things: it undoes the user's changes using the form's Undo method if the timeout time has been exceeded, it warns the user of the impending timeout if more than 90% of the time has expired, or merely informs the user of the elapsed lock time if less than 90% of the timeout interval has transpired.

### Listing 2.7

```
' Used to calculate times
Private Declare Function timeGetTime Lib "winmm.dll" () _
  As Long

Private mlngLockStart As Long ' Time user locked record
Private mfrmBound As Form ' Form bound to object
Private mlngTimerInterval As Long ' How often to check
Private mlblStatus As Label ' Label to report to
Private mlngTimeout As Long ' How long is too much

Public Sub BindForm(FormRef As Form, LabelRef As Label, _
  CheckInterval As Long, TimeoutPeriod As Long)
```

```
    ' This procedure used to bind a form
    ' to the LockTimeout object

    mlngLockStart = 0
    Set mfrmBound = FormRef
    Set mlblStatus = LabelRef
    mlngTimerInterval = CheckInterval
    mlngTimeout = TimeoutPeriod
End Sub

Public Sub StartTimer()
    ' Start counting; record locked

    mlngLockStart = timeGetTime()
    mfrmBound.TimerInterval = mlngTimerInterval * 1000
End Sub

Public Sub StopTimer()
    ' Stop counting; record no longer locked

    mlngLockStart = 0
    mfrmBound.TimerInterval = 0
    mlblStatus.Caption = ""
End Sub

Public Sub CheckTimer()
    ' This procedure checks the timer
    ' and acts appropiately based on the
    ' time that has transpired.
    ' Also, it turns the timer off if the
    ' record is no longer dirty as when
    ' the user undoes changes.

    Dim lngLockDuration  As Long ' How long locked
    Dim lngTimetoTimeout As Long ' How much time left

    ' Check if the record is no longer dirty.
    If Not mfrmBound.Dirty Then
        mlngLockStart = 0
    End If

    ' If record is dirty, then do one of three things:
```

```
' 1. Undo changes (which releases lock) if timeout
'    interval exceeded.
' 2. Warn user if 90% of timeout interval has
'    transpired.
' 3. Otherwise (< 90% of timeour interval), just let
'    user know how much time they have left.
If mlngLockStart > 0 Then
    ' Record still dirty, so get to work
    lngLockDuration = _
    (timeGetTime() - mlngLockStart) / 1000
    lngTimetoTimeout = _
    mlngTimeout - lngLockDuration
    If lngLockDuration >= mlngTimeout Then
        ' Time out
        mfrmBound.Undo
        mlngLockStart = 0
        mfrmBound.TimerInterval = 0
        mlblStatus.ForeColor = vbRed
        mlblStatus.Caption = _
         "Timeout period exceeded! " & _
         "Any unsaved changes to this " & _
         "record have been lost."
    ElseIf lngLockDuration >= 0.9 * mlngTimeout _
    Then
        ' Warning message
        mlblStatus.ForeColor = vbRed
        mlblStatus.Caption = _
         "You have locked this record for an " & _
         "excessive period of time. " & _
         "If you do not save your changes within " & _
         lngTimetoTimeout & " seconds " & _
         "you will lose them!"
    Else
        ' Countdown message
        mlblStatus.ForeColor = vbBlack
        mlblStatus.Caption = _
         "You have locked this record for " & _
         lngLockDuration & " seconds. " & _
         "Time remaining: " & _
         lngTimetoTimeout & " seconds."
    End If
    ' This next statement necessary to
```

```
        ' tell form to update the caption.
        mfrmBound.Repaint
    Else
        ' Record no longer dirty so stop counting
        Me.StopTimer
    End If
End Sub
```

## Adding Timeout Functionality to a Form

Follow these steps to hook one of your own forms to the LockTimeout class:

1. Create a bound Access form in an MDB database.

2. Import the LockTimeout class module from the CH02APP.MDB database.

3. Add a label control to the header or footer of the form. Make sure it's big enough to hold the LockTimeout status message. We've found a label that has a width of 4.0 inches and a height of 0.3 inches seems to work well.

4. Add a module-level object variable of type LockTimeout. For example, on the frmEmployee form you might create the following module-level object variable:

    ```
    Private mltoEmployee As LockTimeout
    ```

5. Create event procedures for the form's AfterUpdate, Dirty, and Timer events. In the event procedure attached to the AfterUpdate event, call the StopTimer method of the class; in the Dirty event procedure, call the StartTimer method; and in the Timer event procedure, call the CheckTimer method. For example:

    ```
    Private Sub Form_AfterUpdate()
        mltoEmployee.StopTimer
    End Sub

    Private Sub Form_Dirty(Cancel As Integer)
        mltoEmployee.StartTimer
    End Sub

    Private Sub Form_Timer()
        mltoEmployee.CheckTimer
    End Sub
    ```

6.  Create an event procedure attached to the form's Load event. In this proce-
    dure you need to instantiate the LockTimeout object and call its BindForm
    method, passing BindForm a reference to the form, the label control that will
    hold the status, the interval (in seconds) to update the status, and the length
    of time (in seconds) to wait before timing out the user. For example, the fol-
    lowing code sets the status interval to 1 second and the timeout period to 10
    minutes:

```
Private Sub Form_Load()
    Set mltoCustomer = New LockTimeout
    mltoEmployee.BindForm _
      FormRef:=Me, LabelRef:=lblStatus, _
      CheckInterval:=1, TimeoutPeriod:=10 * 60
End Sub
```

# Locking and Recordsets

These next few sections discuss locking issues with DAO and ADO recordsets.

## DAO Recordsets

The Default Record Locking option is ignored when you use code to open DAO
recordsets using the OpenRecordset method. In this case Access employs pessimistic locking (Edited Record) unless you either a) set the option of the Open-
Recordset method to dbDenyWrite or dbDenyRead, or b) alter the LockEdits
property. You use the dbDenyWrite option to lock all records for updates. You
can go one step further and deny write *and* read access to table-type recordsets
(only) by using the more restrictive dbDenyRead option. (These options apply
only to native Access tables.)

---

**NOTE**    No record locking is performed for snapshot-type recordsets, because they are
read only.

---

You can use the LockEdits property of recordsets to specify the type of locking
to be used. The default of True uses pessimistic (Edited Record) locking. You can
force optimistic (No Locks) record locking by setting this property to False.

For example, the LockingPessDAO subroutine from the basRecordsetLocking module of CH02APP.MDB (see Listing 2.8) opens a recordset against the tblCustomer table using pessimistic locking.

### Listing 2.8

```
Sub LockingPessDAO()
    ' Pessimistic locking

    Dim db As DAO.Database
    Dim rstPessimistic As DAO.Recordset

    Stop

    Set db = CurrentDb()
    Set rstPessimistic = _
     db.OpenRecordset("tblCustomer", dbOpenDynaset)

    ' This next line tells Access to use
    ' pessimistic locking for rstPessimistic.
    rstPessimistic.LockEdits = True

    rstPessimistic.MoveFirst
    ' Record is locked between
    ' Edit and Update methods
    rstPessimistic.Edit
        rstPessimistic!City = "Detroit"
    rstPessimistic.Update

    rstPessimistic.Close
    Set rstPessimistic = Nothing

    Set db = Nothing
End Sub
```

**NOTE** The LockingPessDAO subroutine and other sample locking subroutines in this chapter include a Stop statement. This allows you to experiment with locking. Execute the procedure until it stops. Then open another instance of Access and lock the first record in the tblCustomer table. For example, you might open the frmCustomerPessimistic1 form in the second Access instance and dirty the first record. Come back to the procedure and single-step through the procedure until you run into a run-time locking error. The exact error you get will vary based on how and when you locked the record using another instance of Access.

Similarly, the LockingOptDAO subroutine found in the basRecordsetLocking module (see Listing 2.9) also opens a recordset against the tblCustomer table, this time using optimistic locking.

### Listing 2.9

```
Sub LockingOptDAO()
    ' Optimistic locking

    Dim db As dao.Database
    Dim rstPessimistic As dao.Recordset

    Stop

    Set db = CurrentDb()
    Set rstPessimistic = _
     db.OpenRecordset("tblCustomer", dbOpenDynaset)

    ' This next line tells Access to use
    ' pessimistic locking for rstPessimistic.
    rstPessimistic.LockEdits = True

    rstPessimistic.MoveFirst
    ' Record is locked between
    ' Edit and Update methods
    rstPessimistic.Edit
        rstPessimistic!City = "Detroit"
    rstPessimistic.Update

    rstPessimistic.Close
```

```
              Set rstPessimistic = Nothing
              Set db = Nothing
          End Sub
```

**NOTE**     Like the LockingPessDAO subroutine, the LockingOptDAO subroutine includes a Stop statement. This allows you to experiment with this procedure. Execute the procedure until it stops. Then open another instance of Access and lock the first record in the tblCustomer table, or perhaps create a write conflict by updating the record after you began editing it in the first Access instance. Come back to the procedure and single-step through the procedure until you run into a run-time locking error.

## Multi-User DAO Errors

When using unbound recordsets in a multi-user environment , you need to trap for any multi-user errors that can occur. The most common multi-user errors are summarized in Table 12.3. Error 3197 is equivalent to the write conflict error code 7787 that occurs on bound forms.

 Because the name of the user who has locked a record is unavailable when using record-level locking, Microsoft has added two new errors, 3202 and 3218. These errors are equivalent to errors 3186 and 3260, respectively, but without the user and machine names.

**TABLE 2.3:**   Common VBA Multi-user Error Codes

| Error Code | Error Message |
| --- | --- |
| 3186 | Could not save; currently locked by user *username* on machine *machinename*. |
| 3187 | Could not read; currently locked by user *username* on machine *machinename*. |
| 3188 | Could not update; currently locked by another session on this machine. |
| 3189 | Table *tablename* is exclusively locked by user *username* on machine *machinename*. |
| 3197 | The Microsoft Jet database engine stopped the process because you and another user are attempting to change the same data at the same time. |
| 3202 | Could not save; currently locked by another user. |
| 3218 | Could not update; currently locked. |
| 3260 | Could not update; currently locked by user *username* on machine *machinename* |

## Implementing a DAO Retry Loop

When manipulating recordsets, you'll need to anticipate and handle each of the errors found in Table 12.3. To handle locked records, you will probably want to include an error handler that employs some form of a retry loop that makes several attempts at gaining access to locked records. The basRecordsetLocking module of the CH02APP.MDB database includes an example of a routine that uses such a retry loop. This routine, LockingPessDAO2, along with its module-level constants is shown in Listing 2.10.

### Listing 2.10

```
' Multi-user Error codes
Const adhcLockErrCantSave1 = 3186
Const adhcLockErrCantSave2 = 3202
Const adhcLockErrCantRead = 3187
Const adhcLockErrExclusive = 3189
Const adhcLockErrDatChngd = 3197
Const adhcLockErrCantUpdate1 = 3188
Const adhcLockErrCantUpdate2 = 3260
Const adhcLockErrCantUpdate3 = 3218

' Number of lock retry attempts
Const adhcLockRetries = 5
' Lower bound of range of retry wait
Const adhcLockLBound = 2
' Upper bound of range of retry wait
Const adhcLockUBound = 10

Sub LockingPessDAO2()
    ' Pessimistic locking with error handler

    On Error GoTo ProcErr

    Dim db As DAO.Database
    Dim rstPessimistic As DAO.Recordset
    Dim lngWait As Long
    Dim lngW As Long
    Dim intRetryCount As Integer
    Dim lngReturn As Long
```

```
    Randomize

    Set db = CurrentDb()
    Set rstPessimistic = _
     db.OpenRecordset("tblCustomer", dbOpenDynaset)

    Stop

    ' This next line tells Access to use
    ' pessimistic locking for rstPessimistic.
    rstPessimistic.LockEdits = True

    rstPessimistic.MoveFirst
    ' Record is locked between
    ' Edit and Update methods
    Debug.Print "Attempting to lock record for update."
    rstPessimistic.Edit
        rstPessimistic!City = "Detroit"
    rstPessimistic.Update
    Debug.Print "Record successfully updated!"

ProcEnd:
    On Error Resume Next
    rstPessimistic.Close
    Set rstPessimistic = Nothing
    Set db = Nothing
    Exit Sub

ProcErr:
    Select Case Err.Number
        Case adhcLockErrCantSave1, _
         adhcLockErrCantSave2, _
         adhcLockErrCantRead, _
         adhcLockErrCantUpdate1, _
         adhcLockErrCantUpdate2, _
         adhcLockErrCantUpdate3, _
         adhcLockErrExclusive
            intRetryCount = intRetryCount + 1
            If intRetryCount <= adhcLockRetries Then
                Debug.Print "Lock error, retry #" & _
                    intRetryCount & "."
```

```
            ' Let Jet Engine catch up
            dao.DBEngine.Idle
            ' Space out the retries based on a number
            ' that increases by the number of retries
            ' and a random number
            lngWait = intRetryCount ^ 2 * _
             Int((adhcLockUBound - adhcLockLBound + 1) _
             * Rnd() + adhcLockLBound)
            ' Waste time, but let Windows
            ' multitask during this dead time.
            For lngW = 1 To lngWait
                DoEvents
            Next lngW
            Resume
        Else
            lngReturn = _
             MsgBox("This routine needs to update " & _
             "a record that is locked by another " & _
             "user." & vbCrLf & "Do you wish to " & _
             "try again to update the record?" & _
             vbCrLf & _
             "Press Yes to try again or No to quit.", _
             vbYesNo + vbCritical, _
             "Update Retries Exceeded")
            If lngReturn = vbYes Then
                intRetryCount = 0
                MsgBox _
                 "This routine will retry the " & _
                 "update. " & vbCrLf & _
                 "Note: You will not be " & _
                 "notified again if the update " & _
                 "succeeds.", vbOKOnly + _
                 vbInformation, "Update Retry"
                Debug.Print "Retry count reset to 0."
                Resume
            Else
                MsgBox "Record was not updated!", _
                 vbOKOnly + vbCritical, "Update Abort"
                Debug.Print "Update aborted."
                Resume ProcEnd
            End If
        End If
    End If
```

```
        Case adhcLockErrDatChngd
            ' Record changed while user was editing it
            ' using optimistic locking
            MsgBox "The record you were editing was " & _
                "changed by another user while you were " & _
                "editing it.  Click OK to refresh with " & _
                "the other users changes." & _
                "You can then make your changes and resave.", _
                vbExclamation + vbOKOnly, "Write Conflict"
            rstPessimistic.CancelUpdate
            Resume Next
        Case Else
            MsgBox "Error#" & Err.Number & ": " & _
                Err.Description, vbOKOnly + vbCritical, _
                "Unanticipated Error"
            Resume ProcEnd
    End Select
End Sub
```

---

**NOTE**    The Stop statement in the LockingOptDAO subroutine allows you to experiment with this procedure. Execute the procedure until it breaks. Then open another instance of Access and lock the first record in the tblCustomer table (you can use frmCustomerPessimistic1). Come back to the procedure, open the Debug window and select Run ➢ Continue from the VBA IDE. Notice that the procedure writes information to the Debug window indicating that it is attempting to lock the record. After the first round of unsuccessful lock attempts, indicate that you wish to try again. This time, release the locked record and notice that the retry loop obtained the record lock.

---

The error handler first looks for a variety of errors that might occur when attempting to update a locked record. If one of these errors occurrs, then the code increments the intRetryCount variable. We use this variable to keep track of the number of retries that we have attempted:

```
Select Case Err.Number
    Case adhcLockErrCantSave1, _
        adhcLockErrCantSave2, _
        adhcLockErrCantRead, _
        adhcLockErrCantUpdate1, _
        adhcLockErrCantUpdate2, _
```

```
        adhcLockErrCantUpdate3, _
        adhcLockErrExclusive
            intRetryCount = intRetryCount + 1
```

Next, the code checks if intRetryCount is less than the maximum number of allowable retries (adhcLockRetries). If so, it uses the DAO.DBEngine.Idle method to allow Jet to catch up and perform any pending tasks, such as releasing locks that it didn't have time to release.

```
    If intRetryCount <= adhcLockRetries Then
        Debug.Print "Lock error, retry #" & _
         intRetryCount & "."
        ' Let Jet Engine catch up
        dao.DBEngine.Idle
```

Using DBEngine.Idle may free the lock, but more than likely the code will need to wait a few seconds for the lock to be released by another user or process. Thus, the code also includes some intelligent time-wasting code. It's likely you'll want to include similar code in all your routines that may encounter locking conflicts. A Long Integer, lngWait, is calculated based on a formula that squares the number of retries and multiplies the result by a random number between a lower and upper bound value. Then, a For…Next loop is executed for lngWait iterations to waste time. The inclusion of the DoEvents statement ensures that any other Windows tasks are given processor time during this "dead" time period. By including a random number and squaring the time for each retry, the retry loop attempts to separate out any users who were requesting locks at the same time. After the For…Next loop, the actual retry is accomplished with the Resume statement. Here's the retry loop code:

```
        lngWait = intRetryCount ^ 2 * _
         Int((adhcLockUBound - adhcLockLBound + 1) _
         * Rnd() + adhcLockLBound)
        ' Waste time, but let Windows
        ' multitask during this dead time.
        For lngW = 1 To lngWait
            DoEvents
        Next lngW
        Resume
```

If the maximum number of retries has been exceeded, the error handler code informs the user—in some situations, you may not actually want to inform the user—and gives the user the option to try again or bail out:

```
    Else
        lngReturn = _
```

```
               MsgBox("This routine needs to update " & _
               "a record that is locked by another " & _
               "user." & vbCrLf & "Do you wish to " & _
               "try again to update the record?" & _
               vbCrLf & _
               "Press Yes to try again or No to quit.", _
               vbYesNo + vbCritical, _
               "Update Retries Exceeded")
           If lngReturn = vbYes Then
               intRetryCount = 0
               MsgBox _
                "This routine will retry the " & _
                "update. " & vbCrLf & _
                "Note: You will not be " & _
                "notified again if the update " & _
                "succeeds.", vbOKOnly + _
                 vbInformation, "Update Retry"
               Debug.Print "Retry count reset to 0."
               Resume
           Else
               MsgBox "Record was not updated!", _
                vbOKOnly + vbCritical, "Update Abort"
               Debug.Print "Update aborted."
               Resume ProcEnd
           End If
       End If
```

The error handler also includes a Case statement to handle write conflicts, as shown here. This particular code is not very sophisticated but you get the idea:

```
Case adhcLockErrDatChngd
    ' Record changed while user was editing it
    ' using optimistic locking
    MsgBox "The record you were editing was " & _
     "changed by another user while you were " & _
     "editing it.  Click OK to refresh with " & _
     "the other users changes." & _
     "You can then make your changes and resave.", _
     vbExclamation + vbOKOnly, "Write Conflict"
    rstPessimistic.CancelUpdate
    Resume Next
```

# ADO Recordsets

By default, ADO recordsets are opened in read-only mode. By using either the LockType property of the Recordset object (prior to executing the Open method) or using the LockType argument of the Recordset.Open method, however, you can control the type of record locking used.

You can specify the type and timing of record locking using one of the following constants:

| Constant | value |
| --- | --- |
| adLockReadOnly | 1 |
| adLockPessimistic | 2 |
| adLockOptimistic | 3 |
| adLockBatchOptimistic | 4 |

**WARNING**   ADO recordsets opened against the CurrentProject.Connection do not support pessimistic locking. Although using the Open method of the ADO Recordset object against such a connection appears to allow pessimistic locking, it does not. You can work around this problem by creating a new Connection object rather than using the CurrentProject's connection.

The code shown in Listing 2.11, from the LockingPessADO subroutine of basRecordsetLocking, demonstrates how to open a recordset using pessimistic locking. Notice that we did not use CurrentProject.Connection in this example because that special connection does not support pessimistic locking.

## Listing 2.11

```
Sub LockingPessADO()
    ' Pessimistic locking

    Dim cnn As ADODB.Connection
    Dim rstPessimistic As ADODB.Recordset
    ' In order to use pessimistic locking in Access
    ' you must create a new connection;
    ' CurrentProject.Connection doesn't support
```

```
' pessimistic locking!
' Note that CurrentProject.BaseConnectionString
' returns the connection string used for
' the current connection.
Set cnn = New ADODB.Connection
cnn.Open CurrentProject.BaseConnectionString

Set rstPessimistic = New ADODB.Recordset

' Open a keyset recordset with optimistic locking
rstPessimistic.Open "tblCustomer", cnn, adOpenKeyset, _
 adLockPessimistic, adCmdTable

Stop

rstPessimistic.MoveFirst
    rstPessimistic!City = "Chicago"
' Record locked at the moment the
' update is committed to the database.
rstPessimistic.Update

rstPessimistic.Close
Set rstPessimistic = Nothing
cnn.Close
Set cnn = Nothing
End Sub
```

> **NOTE**
>
> The LockingPessADO subroutine like the other sample locking subroutines in this chapter include a Stop statement. This allows you to experiment with locking. Execute the procedure until it stops. Then open another instance of Access and lock the first record in the tblCustomer table (you can use frmCustomerPessimistic1). Come back to the procedure and single-step through the procedure until you run into a run-time locking error. The exact error you get will vary based on how and when you locked the record using the other instance of Access.

Listing 2.12 shows the equivalent example, LockingOptADO, this time using optimistic locking.

**Listing 2.12**

```
Sub LockingOptADO()
    ' Optimistic locking

    Dim cnn As ADODB.Connection
    Dim rstOptimistic As ADODB.Recordset

    Set cnn = CurrentProject.Connection
    Set rstOptimistic = New ADODB.Recordset

    ' Open a keyset recordset with optimistic locking
    rstOptimistic.Open "tblCustomer", cnn, adOpenKeyset, _
    adLockOptimistic, adCmdTable

    Stop

    rstOptimistic.MoveFirst
        rstOptimistic!City = "Chicago"
    ' Record locked at the moment the
    ' update is committed to the database.
    rstOptimistic.Update

    rstOptimistic.Close
    Set rstOptimistic = Nothing
    cnn.Close
    Set cnn = Nothing
End Sub
```

**NOTE**    Try out LockingOptADO by executing the procedure until it stops at the hard-coded Stop statement. Then open another instance of Access and lock the first record in the tblCustomer table, or perhaps create a write conflict by updating the record after you began editing it in the first Access instance. Come back to the procedure and single-step through the procedure until you run into a run-time locking error.

## Implementing an ADO Retry Loop

As was the case in DAO, when manipulating ADO recordsets, you'll need to anticipate and handle each of the errors found in Table 12.3. This will usually mean using an error handler with a retry loop, just as we did in the DAO example. The CH02APP.MDB database includes an example of an ADO-based routine that uses such a retry loop. This routine, LockingPessADO2 from basRecordsetLocking, is shown in Listing 2.13.

### Listing 2.13

```
' Multi-user Error codes
Const adhcLockErrCantSave1 = 3186
Const adhcLockErrCantSave2 = 3202
Const adhcLockErrCantRead = 3187
Const adhcLockErrExclusive = 3189
Const adhcLockErrDatChngd = 3197
Const adhcLockErrCantUpdate1 = 3188
Const adhcLockErrCantUpdate2 = 3260
Const adhcLockErrCantUpdate3 = 3218

' Number of lock retry attempts
Const adhcLockRetries = 5
' Lower bound of range of retry wait
Const adhcLockLBound = 2
' Upper bound of range of retry wait
Const adhcLockUBound = 10

Sub LockingPessADO2()

    ' Pessimistic locking with error handler

    On Error GoTo ProcErr

    Dim cnn As ADODB.Connection
    Dim rstPessimistic As ADODB.Recordset
    Dim lngWait As Long
    Dim lngW As Long
    Dim intRetryCount As Integer
    Dim lngReturn As Long
```

```
Randomize

' In order to use pessimistic locking in Access
' you must create a new connection;
' CurrentProject.Connection doesn't support
' pessimistic locking!
' Note that CurrentProject.BaseConnectionString
' returns the connection string used for
' the current connection.
Set cnn = New ADODB.Connection
cnn.Open CurrentProject.BaseConnectionString

Set rstPessimistic = New ADODB.Recordset

 ' Open a keyset recordset with optimistic locking
rstPessimistic.Open "tblCustomer", cnn, adOpenKeyset, _
 adLockPessimistic, adCmdTable

Stop

rstPessimistic.MoveFirst
    rstPessimistic!City = "Chicago"
' Record locked at the moment the
' update is committed to the database.
rstPessimistic.Update
Debug.Print "Record successfully updated!"

ProcEnd:
    On Error Resume Next
    rstPessimistic.Close
    Set rstPessimistic = Nothing
    cnn.Close
    Set cnn = Nothing
    Exit Sub

ProcErr:
    ' Need to use the SQLState property
    ' to return the original Jet error code.
    ' Assumption: only 1 error object will
    ' be generated.
    Select Case cnn.Errors(0).SQLState
        Case adhcLockErrCantSave1, _
```

```
adhcLockErrCantSave2, _
adhcLockErrCantRead, _
adhcLockErrCantUpdate1, _
adhcLockErrCantUpdate2, _
adhcLockErrCantUpdate3, _
adhcLockErrExclusive
    intRetryCount = intRetryCount + 1
    If intRetryCount <= adhcLockRetries Then
        Debug.Print "Lock error, retry #" & _
         intRetryCount & "."
        ' Let Windows and the Jet Engine catch up
        DoEvents
        ' Space out the retries based on a number
        ' that increases by the number of retries
        ' and a random number
        lngWait = intRetryCount ^ 2 * _
         Int((adhcLockUBound - adhcLockLBound + 1) _
          * Rnd() + adhcLockLBound)
        ' Waste time, but let Windows
        ' multitask during this dead time.
        For lngW = 1 To lngWait
            DoEvents
        Next lngW
        Resume
    Else
        lngReturn = _
        MsgBox("This routine needs to update " & _
        "a record that is locked by another " & _
        "user." & vbCrLf & "Do you wish to " & _
        "try again to update the record?" & _
        vbCrLf & _
        "Press Yes to try again or No to quit.", _
        vbYesNo + vbCritical, _
        "Update Retries Exceeded")
        If lngReturn = vbYes Then
            intRetryCount = 0
            MsgBox _
             "This routine will retry the " & _
             "update. " & vbCrLf & _
             "Note: You will not be " & _
             "notified again if the update " & _
             "succeeds.", vbOKOnly + _
```

```
                        vbInformation, "Update Retry"
                    Debug.Print "Retry count reset to 0."
                    Resume
                Else
                    MsgBox "Record was not updated!", _
                     vbOKOnly + vbCritical, "Update Abort"
                    Debug.Print "Update aborted."
                    Resume ProcEnd
                End If
            End If
        Case adhcLockErrDatChngd
            ' Record changed while user was editing it
            ' using optimistic locking
            MsgBox "The record you were editing was " & _
             "changed by another user while you were " & _
             "editing it.  Click OK to refresh with " & _
             "the other users changes." & _
             "You can then make your changes and resave.", _
             vbExclamation + vbOKOnly, "Write Conflict"
            rstPessimistic.CancelUpdate
            Resume Next
        Case Else
            MsgBox "Error#" & cnn.Errors(0).SQLState & _
             ": " & cnn.Errors(0).Description, _
             vbOKOnly + vbCritical, "Unanticipated Error"
            Resume ProcEnd
    End Select

End Sub
```

The error handler in Listing 2.13 is very similar to the DAO error handler shown earlier in Listing 2.10. See the explanation of Listing 2.10 for more details on how it works and how to test it.

---

**TIP**    When dealing with Jet errors from your ADO code, you need to check the SQLState property of the Error object to ascertain the correct error number. (As noted in Chapter 6, when working with SQL Server errors, you need to check the Error object's NativeError property instead.)

---

# Transaction Processing

*Transaction processing* is a database term that refers to the process of grouping changes to your data into a batch that is treated as a single atomic unit. Either the entire batch of *transactions* succeeds or they all fail. For example, when moving data from one account to another in a banking application, you wouldn't want to credit the new account without debiting the old account. Thus, you'd wrap this pair of updates in a transaction.

Transaction processing is useful in any application where one action *must* occur in concert with one or more other actions. Transaction processing is commonly required in banking and accounting applications, as well as in many others.

## DAO Transactions

DAO supports transaction processing with the following methods of the *Workspace* object:

- BeginTrans
- CommitTrans
- Rollback

*BeginTrans* allows you to mark the start of a series of operations that should be considered as a single unit. *CommitTrans* takes everything since the most recent BeginTrans and writes it to disk. *Rollback* is the opposite of CommitTrans; it undoes all your changes back to the last CommitTrans. In skeletal form, DAO transaction processing usually looks something like this:

```
On Error GoTo Err_Handler

Dim wrkCurrent As DAO.WorkSpace
Dim fInTrans As Boolean

fInTrans = False
Set wrkCurrent = DAO.DBEngine.Workspaces(0)
    ' ...
wrkCurrent.BeginTrans
    fInTrans = True
    ' (Any series of data changes here)
wrkCurrent.CommitTrans
```

```
        fInTrans = False
  '  ...
Err_Handler:
     if fInTrans Then
         wrkCurrent.Rollback
     End If
     ' (further error processing)
```

Here are some issues you need to be aware of when using DAO transaction processing:

- Not all recordsets support transaction processing. None of the non-native ISAM formats support transactions, but most ODBC data sources do. You can check the *Transactions* property of a Recordset object to see whether it supports transaction processing.

- Transactions affect *all* changes to data in the workspace. Everything you do after a BeginTrans method is committed or rolled back as a single unit. This even applies to changes across multiple databases opened within a single workspace.

- You can nest transactions in Jet databases up to five levels deep. Inner transactions must be committed or rolled back before the surrounding ones. You cannot nest transactions for ODBC tables. To maintain two independent transactions, you can use two separate workspaces.

- If you close a workspace without explicitly committing its transactions, all pending transactions are automatically rolled back.

---

**TIP**    Access 2000 forms allow you to bind an arbitrary recordset to a form. This new feature now makes it possible to use DAO transactions with bound forms. See Chapter 8 in *Access 2000 Developer's Handbook, Volume 1: Desktop Edition* for more details.

---

## ADO Transactions

ADO supports transaction processing with the following methods of the *Connection* object:

- BeginTrans

- CommitTrans

- RollbackTrans

*BeginTrans* allows you to mark the start of a series of operations that should be considered as a single unit. *CommitTrans* takes everything since the most recent BeginTrans and writes it to disk. *RollbackTrans* is the opposite of CommitTrans; it undoes all your changes back to the last CommitTrans. In skeletal form, ADO transaction processing looks very similar to DAO transaction processing:

```
On Error GoTo Err_Handler

Dim cnn As ADO.Connection
Dim fInTrans As Boolean

fInTrans = False
Set cnn = CurrentProject.Connection
' ...
cnn.BeginTrans
    fInTrans = True
    ' (Any series of data changes here)
cnn.CommitTrans
    fInTrans = False
' ...
Err_Handler:
    if fInTrans Then
        cnn.RollbackTrans
    End If
    ' (further error processing)
```

You can see that the only difference is that the transaction processing methods in ADO are methods of the Connection object rather than the Workspace object. In addition, the DAO Rollback method is named RollbackTrans in ADO.

## Transaction Processing in a Multi-User Setting

Transaction processing has extra importance in multi-user applications. When more than one user is modifying the database, you can no longer depend on the results of one change being present when you start another unless you wrap the set of updates in a transaction. Thus, you may wish to use transactions in a multi-user setting.

> **NOTE** When you use transactions, you increase the *integrity* of one user's set of changes at the expense of reduced *concurrency* of the entire shared application, because locks on multiple records are maintained for longer periods of time. Extensive use of transactions will likely cause an increase in the number of locking errors in your application.

When you use transaction processing in a multi-user setting, Jet treats the entire transaction as a single disk write but otherwise respects your specified locking setting. Thus, if you're using pessimistic locking in DAO, Jet locks a record when an Edit method is encountered. When using ADO, Jet locks a record you change the value of the first recordset field. If you're using optimistic locking instead, Jet doesn't lock the record until it encounters an Update method for both DAO and ADO transactions. Within the confines of a transaction, however, Jet accumulates these locks without releasing them until the entire transaction has been either committed or rolled back.

If Jet encounters a locked record within a transaction, the standard set of trappable errors occurs. When this happens, you'll need to either obtain the necessary lock or roll back the transaction.

## Implied Transactions

In addition to *explicit transactions* that you create using the BeginTrans, CommitTrans, and Rollback methods, Jet 4.0 (and its predecessors since Jet 3.0) creates *implicit transactions* to improve the performance of recordset operations. In an exclusively used database, by default, Jet commits implicit transactions every 2 seconds; in a shared environment, Jet commits these transactions every 50 milliseconds. The default setting of 50 milliseconds should ensure no noticeable change in concurrency in a multi-user setting.

The exact effect implicit transactions have on concurrency depends on the values of several Registry settings. These settings are described in Table 12.4. To use non-default settings, you need to edit the Registry keys under the following node:

```
HKEY_LOCAL_MACHINE\SOFTWARE\Microsoft\Jet\4.0\Engines\
Jet 4.
```

There may be some applications for which you wish to sacrifice concurrency for increased performance. In these cases, you may want to increase the value of the SharedAsyncDelay key.

**TABLE 2.4:**   Transaction Registry Settings

| Key | Datatype | Effect | Default |
|---|---|---|---|
| UserCommitSync | String | Determines whether explicit transactions are executed synchronously (unnested transactions are performed one after the other). | Yes |
| ImplicitCommitSync | String | Determines whether Jet creates implicit transactions for recordset updates. A setting of No causes implied transactions to be used | No |
| ExclusiveAsnycDelay | DWORD | Determines the maximum time (in milliseconds) before Jet commits an implicit transaction when the database is opened exclusively. | 2000 |
| SharedAsyncDelay | DWORD | Determines maximum time (in milliseconds) before Jet commits an implicit transaction when the database is opened in shared mode. | 50 |

**TIP**

You can override the Jet Registry settings by using the SetOption method of the DAO DBEngine object or properties of the ADO Connection object. See Chapter 15 in *Access 2000 Developer's Handbook, Volume 1: Desktop Edition* for more information.

# Multi-User Action Queries and Transactions

The Access UI, DAO, and ADO allow you to control the transaction behavior of action queries.

## The UseTransaction Property

Using the property sheet of a saved action query, you can set the UseTransaction property to No to prevent Access from wrapping a single transaction around the query. By default, this setting is Yes, which tells Access to execute all action queries within a single transaction. Setting UseTransaction to No may increase the performance of queries updating a large number of records, but at the expense of not being able to rollback the query if an error occurs.

You can alter the transaction behavior of DAO-saved QueryDefs from DAO as well, but because the UseTransaction property isn't a built-in Jet property, you must first add the property to the QueryDef object's properties collection using code similar to this:

```
' Don't wrap the query in a transaction
Set prp = qdf.CreateProperty("UseTransaction", _
 dbBoolean, False)
qdf.Properties.Append prp
```

Likewise, you tell ADO not to use a transaction when executing an action query by setting the Jet OLEDB:Bulk Transactions property of an ADO Command object to 1 (meaning *don't* use transactions; a value of 2 tells Jet to use a transaction):

```
' Don't wrap the query in a transaction
cmd.Properties("JET OLEDB:Bulk Transactions") = 1
```

**TIP**  You can also set a global property that affects all bulk operations for a connection. To do this, you need to set the Jet OLEDB:Global Bulk Transactions property of the ADO Connection object.

## The FailOnError Property

Update and Delete queries have a property that's related to the UseTransaction property called FailOnError. Normally, the Access UI will allow an action query to partially execute after warning users that some record updates may fail. If you set the FailOnError property to Yes, however, Access will never allow an Update or Delete query to partially succeed.

Using DAO, you can modify the FailOnError property of the recordset or you can set the Options argument of the QueryDef.Execute method to dbFailOnError as shown here:

```
' Fail if any records cannot be updated
qdf.Execute dbFailOnError
```

Listing 12.14 shows an example of using the dbFailOnError option of a DAO QueryDef object.

**Listing 12.14**

```
Function DeleteTempOrdersDAO()

    ' An example of the use of the dbFailOnError option
    ' and the RecordsAffected property of action queries.

    On Error GoTo ProcErr

    Dim db As DAO.Database
    Dim wrk As DAO.Workspace
    Dim qdf As DAO.QueryDef
    Dim lngRecsEstimated As Long
    Dim lngRecsAffected As Long
    Dim intResp As Integer
    Dim strWhere As String
    Dim fInTrans As Boolean

    DeleteTempOrdersDAO = False
    fInTrans = False

    Set db = CurrentDb
    Set wrk = DAO.DBEngine.Workspaces(0)

    ' Where clause for query
    strWhere = "[OrderId] BETWEEN 1 AND 100"

    ' Count number of recs to be deleted

    lngRecsEstimated = _
     DCount("*", "tblTempOrders", strWhere)
    Set qdf = db.CreateQueryDef("", _
     "DELETE * FROM tblTempOrders WHERE " & strWhere)

    ' Fail on error?
    intResp = MsgBox("About to delete " & _
     lngRecsEstimated & " records." & vbCrLf & _
     "Fail if any record can't be deleted?", _
     vbYesNo + vbInformation + vbDefaultButton1, _
     "Action Query Example")
```

```
wrk.BeginTrans
    fInTrans = True
    If intResp = vbYes Then
        qdf.Execute dbFailOnError
    Else
        qdf.Execute
    End If
    ' Now calculate the records that were
    ' actually deleted
    lngRecsAffected = qdf.RecordsAffected
    If lngRecsAffected < lngRecsEstimated Then
        intResp = MsgBox("Only " & lngRecsAffected & _
            " out of " & lngRecsEstimated & _
            " records will be deleted." & vbCrLf & _
            "OK to continue?", _
            vbOKCancel + vbInformation, _
            "Action Query Example")
        ' Rollback transaction upon user request
        If intResp = vbCancel Then
            MsgBox "Transaction rolled back!", _
                vbOKOnly + vbCritical, _
                "Action Query Example"
            wrk.Rollback
            GoTo ProcDone
        End If
    End If
    wrk.CommitTrans
    fInTrans = False

    DeleteTempOrdersDAO = True

ProcDone:
    qdf.Close
    Set qdf = Nothing
    wrk.Close
    Set wrk = Nothing
    Exit Function

ProcErr:
    If fInTrans Then
        wrk.Rollback
        MsgBox "Error occurred. Rolled back.", _
```

```
            vbOKOnly + vbCritical, "Action Query Example"
    Else
        MsgBox "Error#" & Err.Number & ": " & _
        Err.Description, _
        vbOKOnly + vbCritical, "Action Query Example"
    End If
    Resume ProcDone

End Function
```

Using ADO, you can get the equivalent effect by setting the Jet OLEDB:Partial Bulk Ops property of the ADO Command object to 2 (meaning no partial completion allowed; a value of 1 allows partial completion):

```
' Fail if any records cannot be updated
cmd.Properties("JET OLEDB:Partial Bulk Ops") = 2
```

---

**TIP**    You can also set a global property that affects all bulk operations for a connection. To do this, you need to set the Jet OLEDB:Global Partial Bulk Ops property of the ADO Connection object.

---

Listing 12.15 shows an example of using the Jet OLEDB:Partial Bulk Ops property of an ADO Command object.

**Listing 12.15**

```
Function DeleteTempOrdersADO()

    ' An example of the use of the "Jet OLEDB:Partial Bulk Ops"
    ' property of the ADO Command object.
    '

    On Error GoTo ProcErr

    Dim cnn As ADODB.Connection
    Dim cmd As ADODB.Command
    Dim lngRecsEstimated As Long
    Dim lngRecsAffected As Long
    Dim intResp As Integer
    Dim strWhere As String
```

```
Dim fInTrans As Boolean

DeleteTempOrdersADO = False
fInTrans = False

Set cnn = CurrentProject.Connection

' Where clause for query
strWhere = "[OrderId] BETWEEN 1 AND 100"

' Count number of recs to be deleted

lngRecsEstimated = _
 DCount("*", "tblTempOrders", strWhere)
Set cmd = New ADODB.Command
cmd.ActiveConnection = cnn
cmd.CommandText = _
 "DELETE * FROM tblTempOrders WHERE " & strWhere
cmd.CommandType = adCmdText

' Fail on error?
intResp = MsgBox("About to delete " & _
 lngRecsEstimated & " records." & vbCrLf & _
 "Fail if any record can't be deleted?", _
 vbYesNo + vbInformation + vbDefaultButton1, _
 "Action Query Example")

cnn.BeginTrans
    fInTrans = True
    If intResp = vbYes Then
        cmd.Properties("JET OLEDB:Partial Bulk Ops") = 2
    Else
        cmd.Properties("JET OLEDB:Partial Bulk Ops") = 1
    End If
    cmd.Execute lngRecsAffected
    If lngRecsAffected < lngRecsEstimated Then
        intResp = MsgBox("Only " & lngRecsAffected & _
        " out of " & lngRecsEstimated & _
        " records will be deleted." & vbCrLf & _
        "OK to continue?", _
        vbOKCancel + vbInformation, _
        "Action Query Example")
```

```
                        ' Rollback transaction upon user request
                        If intResp = vbCancel Then
                            MsgBox "Transaction rolled back!", _
                             vbOKOnly + vbCritical, _
                             "Action Query Example"
                            cnn.RollbackTrans
                            GoTo ProcDone
                        End If
                    End If
              cnn.CommitTrans
              fInTrans = False

              DeleteTempOrdersADO = True

        ProcDone:
                    Set cmd = Nothing
                    cnn.Close
              Set cnn = Nothing
              Exit Function

        ProcErr:
              If fInTrans Then
                  cnn.RollbackTrans
                  MsgBox "Error occurred. Rolled back.", _
                   vbOKOnly + vbCritical, "Action Query Example"
              Else
                  MsgBox "Error#" & cnn.Errors(0).SQLState & ": " & _
                   cnn.Errors(0).Description, _
                   vbOKOnly + vbCritical, "Action Query Example"
              End If
              Resume ProcDone

        End Function
```

# Using a Custom AutoNumber Routine

The Jet engine offers a great deal of flexibility in choosing AutoNumber fields (called
Counter fields prior to Access 95). You can choose an AutoNumber field with Long
Integer values that are made up of sequentially incremented or randomly chosen

numbers, or you can use a 16-byte globally unique identifier (GUID) instead. (See Chapter 9 for more on GUIDs.) At times, however, you may prefer to use a custom routine for assigning some type of incremented value for one of the following reasons:

- You need to use an alphanumeric string.

- You need to use an increment greater than 1. (Although the Access UI, DAO, and ADOX don't support the specification of increments greater than 1, you can create such an AutoNumber using a SQL DDL query that employs the CREATE TABLE statement. See Chapter 5 in *Access 2000 Developer's Handbook, Volume 1: Desktop Edition* for more details.)

- You wish to recover values for discarded records.

- You need to create values that are computed using other fields in the record.

- You have the data stored in a non-native table that has no support for AutoNumber fields.

- You replicate the database and don't want to use randomly-generated AutoNumber values.

---

**TIP**    It's important that you not place too much faith in surrogate primary keys, such as those that can be generated using AutoNumber (built-in or custom) fields. While these fields can certainly guarantee uniqueness of the record, you still have to ensure, through the use of additional indexes or event procedures, that a user can't create five customer records for the same customer.

---

## Custom AutoNumber Setup

You can implement your own custom AutoNumber fields for an Access database by maintaining a separate table to hold the next AutoNumber value. You must lock this table when you retrieve a new AutoNumber value and trap for errors that may occur when multiple users attempt to retrieve a new value at the same time.

We have created a custom AutoNumber routine for the MenuId field of tblMenu in the CH02APP.MDB sample database. The routine—written using DAO—is called from the frmMenu form; the table that holds the AutoNumber value is kept in the CH02AUTO.MDB database.

---

**NOTE**        This routine could also have been implemented using ADO.

---

## Implementing a Custom AutoNumber

We have split the activity of obtaining a new AutoNumber value into two parts. A low-level routine handles the AutoNumber increment or returns –1 if an AutoNumber value cannot be retrieved. A high-level routine handles the assignment of this AutoNumber to a new record and determines what to do about any errors. Both routines are contained in the module basAutoNumber in the CH02APP.MDB database.

The adhGetNextAutoNumber function is the low-level routine that interfaces directly with the AutoNumber database. It takes a single parameter—the name of the table that requires the new AutoNumber value. The next AutoNumber value is stored in a table (in the adhcAutoNumDb database) with _ID appended to the base table name. For example, the AutoNumber for tblMenu is stored in tblMenu_ID. This table has a simple structure: it consists of a single Long Integer field named NextAutoNumber. The adhGetNextAutoNumber function is shown in Listing 12.16.

**Listing 12.16**

```
' Database storing autonumber values
Const adhcAutoNumDb = "Ch02Auto.Mdb"

' Number of lock retry attempts
Const adhcLockRetries = 5
' Lower bound of range of retry wait
Const adhcLockLBound = 2
' Upper bound of range of retry wait
Const adhcLockUBound = 10

'Error constants
Const adhcErrRI = 3000
Const adhcLockErrCantUpdate2 = 3260
Const adhcLockErrTableInUse = 3262

Function adhGetNextAutoNumber(ByVal strTableName _
  As String) As Long
```

```
' Returns the next custom autonumber value for a
' particular table. Autonumbers are stored in the
' database adhcAutoNumDb in tables with _ID appended
' for which they supply autonumbers.
' Returns -1 if a valid autonumber value cannot be
' retrieved due to locking problems.

On Error GoTo adhGetNextAutoNumber_Err

Dim wrk As DAO.Workspace
Dim db As DAO.Database
Dim rstAutoNum As DAO.Recordset
Dim lngNextAutoNum As Long
Dim lngW As Long
Dim lngX As Long
Dim intRetryCount As Integer

Randomize
DoCmd.Hourglass True
intRetryCount = 0

' Open a recordset on the appropriate table in the
' autonumbers database denying all reads to others
' while it is open
Set wrk = DAO.DBEngine.Workspaces(0)
Set db = wrk.OpenDatabase(adhCurrentDBPath() & _
 adhcAutoNumDb, False)
Set rstAutoNum = db.OpenRecordset(strTableName _
 & "_ID", dbOpenTable, dbDenyRead)

' Increment and return the autonumber value
rstAutoNum.MoveFirst
rstAutoNum.Edit
    lngNextAutoNum = rstAutoNum![NextAutoNumber]
    rstAutoNum![NextAutoNumber] = lngNextAutoNum + 1
rstAutoNum.Update

adhGetNextAutoNumber = lngNextAutoNum

adhGetNextAutoNumber_Exit:
    DoCmd.Hourglass False
```

```
        On Error Resume Next
        rstAutoNum.Close
        Set rstAutoNum = Nothing
        db.Close
        Set db = Nothing
        wrk.Close
        Set wrk = Nothing
        Exit Function

adhGetNextAutoNumber_Err:
    Select Case Err.Number
    Case adhcErrRI, _
      adhcLockErrCantUpdate2, _
      adhcLockErrTableInUse
        ' Table locked by another user
        intRetryCount = intRetryCount + 1
        ' Tried too many times, give up
        If intRetryCount > adhcLockRetries Then
            adhGetNextAutoNumber = -1
            Resume adhGetNextAutoNumber_Exit
        Else
            ' Let Windows and the Jet Engine catch up
            DAO.DBEngine.Idle
            ' Space out the retries based on a number
            ' that increases by the number of retries
            ' and a random number
            lngW = intRetryCount ^ 2 * _
             Int((adhcLockUBound - adhcLockLBound + 1) _
             * Rnd() + adhcLockLBound)
            ' Waste time, but let Windows
            ' multitask during this dead time.
            For lngW = 1 To lngW
                DoEvents
            Next lngW
            Resume
        End If
    Case Else
        ' Unexpected error
        MsgBox "Error " & Err.Number & ": " _
         & Err.Description, _
         vbOKOnly + vbCritical, "adhGetNextAutoNumber"
        adhGetNextAutoNumber = -1
```

```
        Resume adhGetNextAutoNumber_Exit
    End Select

End Function
```

When there is no contention for AutoNumber values, adhGetNextAutoNumber does its work by simply retrieving and incrementing the NextAutoNumber field. In a multi-user situation, however, it is possible for one user to request an AutoNumber value while another user already has the table locked. adhGetNextAutoNumber handles these types of errors using a retry loop similar to the one discussed earlier in the chapter in the section entitled "Implementing a DAO Retry Loop."

The function adhAssignID, also located in basAutoNumbers (shown in Listing 2.17), handles the high-level AutoNumber assignment. It is called from the Before-Insert event of the form and is passed three parameters: a reference to the Form object, the name of the underlying table that holds the custom AutoNumber field, and the name of the custom AutoNumber field. adhAssignID deletes any record that cannot be assigned an AutoNumber. Depending on your particular circumstances, you may need a more sophisticated high-level control routine. For example, you might want to save records that couldn't be assigned a value to a temporary local table rather than discard them entirely.

### Listing 12.17

```
Function adhAssignID(frm As Form, ByVal _
strTableName As String, _
ByVal strAutoNumField As String) As Variant

    ' Called from BeforeInsert event of a form to assign
    ' a new custom autonumber value for a field.
    ' Removes any record that cannot be saved.

    On Error GoTo adhAssignID_Err

    Dim lngNewID As Long

    lngNewID = adhGetNextAutoNumber(strTableName)
    If lngNewID <> -1 Then
        frm(strAutoNumField) = lngNewID
    Else
        MsgBox "Can't Add Record; autonumber " & _
```

```
                    "Not Available", vbOKOnly + vbCritical, _
                    "Error Saving Record"
                    frm.Undo
            End If

    adhAssignID_Exit:
        Exit Function

    adhAssignID_Err:
        frm.Undo
        MsgBox "Error " & Err.Number & ": " & Err.Description, _
         vbOKOnly + vbCritical, "adhAssignID"
        Resume adhAssignID_Exit


    End Function
```

You may wish to modify adhGetNextAutoNumber to return an AutoNumber in some custom format that uses an increment other than 1 or that uses an alphanumeric string.

# User Lists and Connection Control

 The Jet 4.0 engine supports two new multi-user features that allow you to manage users more effectively: the user list and connection control.

## User List

You can create a special provider-specific recordset in ADO (using the OpenSchema method of the Connection object) that supplies information about the current users in the database. This requires you to pass a special magic number GUID to the OpenSchema method. The number, a GUID equal to {947bb102-5d43-11d1-bdbf-00c04fb92675}, has no real meaning except that it's the only one that you can use to get the user list information back from Jet. (You can use OpenSchema to fill a recordset with all sorts of different database schema information. We used the OpenSchema method earlier in the chapter in the "Managing Linked Tables" section.)

The code from Listing 2.18—which you'll find behind the frmViewUsers form of CH02APP.MDB—demonstrates the use of the list user feature.

### Listing 12.18

```
' The user list schema information requires this magic
' number. Why isn't a constant predefined for this?
' Who knows.
Const adhcUsers = "{947bb102-5d43-11d1-bdbf-00c04fb92675}"

Sub BuildUserList()

    ' Builds a list of users in the database
    ' using the OpenSchema method on the
    ' Connection object.

    Dim cnn As ADODB.Connection
    Dim rst As ADODB.Recordset
    Dim fld As ADODB.Field
    Dim intUser As Integer
    Dim strUser As String
    Dim varVal As Variant

    ' Headings
    strUser = "Computer;UserName;Connected?;Suspect?"

    Set cnn = CurrentProject.Connection

    Set rst = cnn.OpenSchema( _
     Schema:=adSchemaProviderSpecific, _
     SchemaId:=adhcUsers)

    With rst
        Do Until .EOF
            intUser = intUser + 1
            For Each fld In .Fields
                varVal = fld.Value
                ' Some of the returned values are
                ' null-terminated strings so you need
                ' to lop off the null characters
                If InStr(varVal, vbNullChar) > 0 Then
                    varVal = Left(varVal, _
                     InStr(varVal, vbNullChar) - 1)
                End If
```

```
                    strUser = strUser & ";" & varVal
            Next
            .MoveNext
        Loop
    End With
    txtUsers = intUser
    lboUsers.RowSource = strUser

    ' Cleanup
    rst.Close
    Set rst = Nothing
    Set fld = Nothing
    Set cnn = Nothing
End Sub
```

When passed the correct SchemaId value, the OpenSchema method fills the ADO recordset with the user list data. Some of the values returned by Open-Schema, however, are null-terminated strings. Thus, the code in the BuildUserList subroutine lops off everything after the null character before building a string, which it then stuffs into a listbox control on the frmViewUsers form (by setting the value of the listbox control's RowSource property). An example of the resulting listbox with three current users is shown in Figure 2.9.

**FIGURE 2.9**

frmViewUsers uses the OpenSchema method to display a list of current database users.

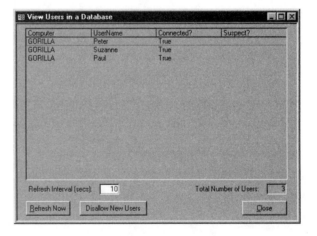

# Connection Control

Jet 4.0 provides a feature called *connection control* (also known as *passive shutdown*) that allows you to prevent users from connecting to a database. This may be useful if you wish to limit the number of simultaneous users of a database or you wish to perform some administrative task, such as backup. Note that this feature is passive—there's no way to forcibly boot users out of a database.

You control connections using the Jet OLEDB:Connection Control property of the ADO Connection object. To disallow any new users of the database, set this property to 1. To revert back to allowing new users, set the property to 2.

Listing 2.19 illustrates the passive shutdown feature with an example from frm-ViewUsers.

### Listing 12.19

```
Const adhcAllowUsers = "Allow New Users"
Const adhcDisallowUsers = "Disallow New Users"

Private Sub cmdShutdown_Click()
    If cmdShutdown.Caption = adhcDisallowUsers Then
        ' Initiate connection control and fixup
        ' button caption
        CurrentProject.Connection. _
         Properties("Jet OLEDB:Connection Control") = 1
        cmdShutdown.Caption = adhcAllowUsers
    Else
        ' Undo connection control and fixup
        ' button caption
        CurrentProject.Connection. _
         Properties("Jet OLEDB:Connection Control") = 2
        cmdShutdown.Caption = adhcDisallowUsers
    End If
End Sub
```

Figure 2.10 shows the error message users will encounter when trying to connect to a database that has been passively shutdown.

**FIGURE 2.10**

If you've initiated connection control, users will encounter this error message when attempting to open the database.

# Other Considerations

The next few sections discuss several other issues that you may wish to consider when developing multi-user applications.

## Security

Although security is not specific to a multi-user scenarios, it certainly becomes more necessary in a multi-user environment. As the number of workstations running your application increases, the more likely it is you'll want to prevent unauthorized users from gaining access to either the data *or* the application.

If you're using page locking, security also allows Access to accurately inform users as to who has locked a record. Unfortunately, as currently implemented, record-level locking does not allow reporting of the name of the user who has locked a record.

**NOTE**    See Chapter 8 for more details on security.

## The Wire

When moving from single-user to multi-user applications, you need to start thinking about potential data bottlenecks. Remember that every time your application requests data, it is sent over the network (also know as *the wire*) to the workstation. Thus, you'll want to minimize sending large amounts of data over the wire, for the sake of both the user requesting the data and the network traffic.

One area that demands special attention is how *much* of a recordset you offer your users in a form. Although Access makes it easy to bind a form to an entire table or query, letting users navigate to their hearts' content, you'll quickly find this doesn't work well with even moderately large tables (more than 30,000–50,000 rows) on a network. You're better off presenting each user with a single record at a time and programmatically changing the record source of the form rather than using one of the Find methods to move to a specific record.

## Test, Test, Test!

You need to test your applications more thoroughly if they will be used on a network. The rule to remember here is, if something *can* go wrong, it will. This means you must set aside a significant amount of time for testing and debugging your multi-user applications.

One advantage of developing in the Windows environment is that you can develop, test, and debug multi-user applications on a single machine by starting two instances of Access and switching back and forth between the instances. While this should allow you to test for and fix many potential problems, you'll still need to test the application on the target network under a typical load of users to find all potential problems. In other words, there's no substitute for the real thing.

# Summary

The important point to remember when writing multi-user Jet applications is to anticipate problems. Multi-user applications need to handle—that is, recover from—the errors that occur when locks are placed on records. In general, there is no set of perfect answers that applies to all multi-user Jet applications. You'll have to develop the appropriate solution for your particular database and consider each of the following:

- Adjust your multi-user settings to achieve optimum performance for your particular application.

- Split your database into separate data and application databases for increased performance.

- Use VBA code to manage the linked tables in a split database architecture.

- Use record-level locking unless you have a good reason for using page-level locking.

- Balance ease of use, data integrity, and ease of programming in developing your locking strategy.

- Be aware of the errors that can occur when multiple users share data.

- Use custom error-handling code when using bound forms with optimistic locking.

- Consider using a timeout feature when using bound forms with pessimistic locking.

- Use transactions to ensure the integrity of your data when multiple operations must occur in concert.

- Use the user list and connection control features of Jet to manage user connections.

- Minimize data going across the network wire.

- Be sure to adequately test your applications.

# chapter 3

# Designing Client-Server Applications

- Understanding client-server architecture

- Using Access as a client development tool

- Managing connections to your server

- Controlling the flow of data

The term *client-server* has come to represent many types of computer processing systems. In its most basic sense, a client-server application is one that divides the execution of tasks between two or more separate processes (running programs). A *server* is any process that offers services to other processes (the *clients*). These processes are typically located on different computers connected by some sort of network, but they need not be. Of interest to Access developers are *client-server database applications.* These are applications that shift the burden of data storage and manipulation to a dedicated application, usually running on a powerful server on the network. (Often these are referred to simply as *client-server applications.*) The role of Access in these applications is to provide the interface, or *front end*, to the server data.

In this chapter we outline the basic principles behind client-server application design, with an emphasis on Access as the client-side component. The chapter provides an overview of client-server features in Access 2000, including the new ADP file format, as well as database connectivity options such as ADO and ODBC. Numerous other chapters will explain the practical implementation details.

# Comparing Client-Server and File-Server Systems

When you first look at using Access in a client-server system, you may think it's an easy task. After all, if you bought this book, you've probably developed in Access for a while. Migrating to client-server should just mean loading your data tables onto the server and changing the links, right?

Wrong. Client-server systems are a completely different architecture from that used by the Microsoft Jet database engine. Migrating from one to the other often requires many changes in the design, implementation, and support of your application. Before you convert your application, you should understand the differences and the impact they will have on your application. Above all, if you're writing your first client-server application, be sure to leave plenty of time for testing in a non-production environment.

## The Goals of Client-Server Application Design

The goals of client-server application design are pretty straightforward:

- Better application performance
- Greater scalability with large numbers of users
- Tighter security and reliability

You achieve these goals through careful design of your client-server application. It's not enough to simply transfer your Access database to SQL Server, for example, and fix up the table links. (Although this is exactly what the Access Upsizing Wizard does.) You need to evaluate how the server database is used by any client applications that access it.

## ODBC versus OLE DB

Since we last published a book on Access development, a lot has changed on the data access front. The biggest shift has been the widespread adoption of OLE DB as the favored way of programmatically interacting with data. When we wrote the Access 97 edition of this book, OLE DB (and its high-level programming model, ADO) was just starting to appear on the scene. OLE DB is now supported by a large number of vendors of both relational and non-relational databases as a native data access method.

You can still develop client-server applications using the older Open Database Connectivity (ODBC) technology. In fact, some features of Access are only available by using ODBC. Before beginning a discussion of client-server development with Access, we'll explain the differences between these two technologies.

### The First Generation: ODBC

ODBC was conceived as a way to deal with one of the biggest problems of early database servers: proprietary data access. When database software vendors first began delivering their solutions, the only way to develop front-end applications was to use proprietary function libraries that were linked into your program executable. This meant that switching database server technologies was very difficult because every application would need to be rewritten.

Along with several other relational database vendors, Microsoft developed ODBC as an API-based standard for data access that used dynamically loaded drivers to provide access to different systems. This meant that developers of front-end applications could write to a single API set and ODBC would translate the calls to appropriate server commands using the specified database driver. Although ODBC took some time to catch on, it eventually emerged as one of the first real breakthroughs in accessing relational data on a variety of platforms.

ODBC has two major pitfalls, however. First, it was designed specifically to deal with relational data. While this provided access to huge amounts of data, especially transactional data, there are even bigger amounts of data stored in non-relational formats. E-mail messages, documents, and Web pages are all examples of data that does not reside in a relational database. Second, ODBC was API-based. That meant that anyone that wanted to program an ODBC-based application had to call dozens of complex functions just to perform simple tasks. Vendors like Microsoft did provide shortcuts (like ODBC support in DAO) that helped somewhat, but at its core ODBC was a very complicated technology.

## The Next Generation: OLE DB

OLE DB is the successor to ODBC and attempts to remedy its shortcomings. First off, as the name implies, OLE DB is not API-based but rather COM-based. Developing is easier because you can rely on a variety of COM core services. Furthermore, since OLE DB is COM-based, any COM component can act as a data provider. It's even possible to add OLE DB support to existing COM components, thus extending their usefulness.

OLE DB was created to deal with both relational and non-relational data. This makes it easy for software vendors to supply OLE DB *providers* (the functional equivalent of *drivers* in ODBC) for their data stores, increasing the opportunity for developers to access data and integrate it into their solutions.

Still, OLE DB is quite a complex technology that includes new features like disconnected recordsets and batch updates. To simplify the task of programming OLE DB common data access scenarios, Microsoft released ActiveX Data Objects (ADO) as an integral component of OLE DB. ADO offers a simplified object model that in many ways resembles DAO, an object model familiar to all serious Access developers. If you are an experienced DAO programmer with existing applications, you will find moving your skills (and, to some extent, your applications) to ADO relatively painless.

Since this book covers the enterprise features of Access 2000, we concentrate on Access support for OLE DB and ADO, especially in conjunction with SQL Server, Microsoft's enterprise database technology. You should still read the sections on ODBC in this chapter, however, since it is still a viable technology and does provide additional capabilities over those provided by OLE DB in Access 2000.

**NOTE**    This book is not meant to provide an introduction to ADO. Instead, it focuses on the application of ADO to client-server scenarios. If you want more complete coverage of ADO, you should refer to the companion book, *Access 2000 Developer's Handbook, Volume 1: Desktop Edition.*

## Summary of Data Access Methods

Figure 3.1 shows different methods of retrieving data from a server using Access 2000:

- File-server using Jet databases
- Linked ODBC tables
- SQL pass-through (SPT) queries
- Client-server using ADP files
- Programmatic access using DAO or ADO
- ODBCDirect, formerly called Remote Data Objects (RDO)

A *file-server* application is what you get when you simply move your database to a network server's hard drive. (File-server is covered extensively in Chapter 2.) In this case, no active components at all are running on the server. (The black vertical line in Figure 3.1 indicates the boundary between client and server components.) The Jet database engine that runs on the client workstation does all data processing. This is inherently inefficient due to the amount of data that must move across the network to satisfy queries. For example, suppose you need to retrieve all the customers in Alaska. In this case, assuming the State field of the Customers table was indexed, the Jet engine would read the entire index for this field from the server. It would then retrieve the records it required.

**FIGURE 3.1**
Differing methods of
accessing server data

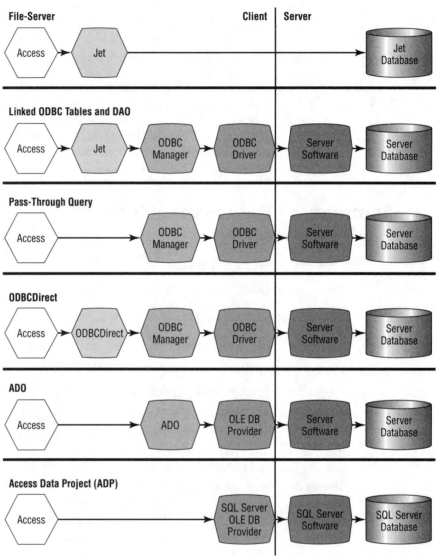

Linking to server tables using *Open Database Connectivity (ODBC)* takes a more
complex route to retrieve server data. In this case, the Jet engine translates the
original SQL for your query into a universal SQL dialect. This SQL statement,

together with information identifying which server contains the data, is passed to the ODBC manager. The ODBC manager locates the appropriate database server driver and hands it the SQL statement. The ODBC driver then translates the universal SQL to a SQL dialect understood by the particular database server and hands it to that server to process. Ideally, in this scenario the only network traffic is the SQL statement going out and the final result set coming back. The advantage of using linked tables is that you can still take advantage of Access features such as bound forms.

*SQL pass-through* adds another wrinkle to this means of communication. Although the "plumbing" components are still present, none of them will perform any translation on a SQL pass-through query. Instead, you must write the exact SQL statement that the server will execute within Access itself. SQL pass-through is mainly useful when you need to use some advanced feature of your database server that ODBC SQL is incapable of understanding. It can also speed processing of regular queries because Jet and ODBC do not intercede to translate your SQL.

**NOTE**    ODBC linked tables and pass-through queries are only available in Jet (MDB) databases.

Access 2000 adds a powerful new capability in the form of *Access Data Project (ADP)* files. This new file format replaces the Jet database in storaging application objects (forms, reports, macros, modules) and uses a direct OLE DB connection to SQL Server for data storage. ADP files provide capabilities similar to linked ODBC tables in previous versions of Access, but are a much cleaner implementation of true client-server architecture since there is no client-side database engine.

Connecting to data sources programmatically using ADO (or DAO) is one more way you can manipulate server data. This approach is similar to manipulating local Jet databases, but you specify either an OLE DB or ODBC data source. You can then create recordsets and execute queries against the server database.

Finally, *ODBCDirect* provides another alternative to the standard ODBC connection. With ODBCDirect, instead of sending your query to Jet to be translated, you send it directly to the database server using an extension to the Jet DAO object model. ODBCDirect is integrated into the Jet DAO, so using it is a simple extension of using straight DAO. Rather than manipulating Jet data, however, ODBC-Direct provides a very thin wrapper around native ODBC function calls. It can produce additional execution speed because, like SQL pass-through, it sends queries directly to the server.

---

**NOTE**   ODBCDirect support is provided in Jet 4.0, but it is effectively obsolete now that you can use ADO.

---

## Key Differences from File-Server Applications

When you use Access in file-server mode, each instance of Jet manages its own cache of physical pages from the file, updates the pages on each client's machine, and sends the updated physical pages back over the network. Each copy of Jet performs the index updating, system table maintenance, and other database management functions required to process your application's work.

In marked contrast, when you use Access as a front-end application and the database resides on a database server, the database server provides all the data-management functions for the application. Only the database server updates the physical file and sees the physical pages in the database. Each user's copy of Access sends requests to the database server and gets data, or pointers to the data, back from the server. It's this single point of control that makes client-server computing more robust than file-server computing, and that makes it a better choice for mission-critical applications.

Table 3.1 shows some of the key processing differences between an Access-only multi-user application and a client-server application using Access and a database server.

**TABLE 3.1:**   Key Differences between File-Server and Client-Server Applications

| Process | Native Access (File-Server) Processing | Client-Server Access Processing |
| --- | --- | --- |
| Updating data | Each user's machine retrieves the physical pages over the network, updates them, and writes them back to the shared drive. Because of this, a failure on any client machine has a good chance of corrupting the database and requiring shutdown and repair. | The server database engine manages all updates of the physical database. Because of this, management problems with the network and individual machine failures are greatly reduced. |

**TABLE 3.1:**    Key Differences between File-Server and Client-Server Applications *(continued)*

| Process | Native Access (File-Server) Processing | Client-Server Access Processing |
|---|---|---|
| Security | The Access security model covers all portions of a multi-user Access application. | For Jet/ODBC solutions, the Access security model is applied to the Access portions of the application (forms, reports, modules, and macros). The security system of the database server controls accessing and updating the actual data. For ADP solutions. you cannot set security on application components, only the data. |
| Validation rules | Validation rules are part of native Access and the data engine. | Validation rules and triggers must be defined at the server. They will not display the Access-defined error message when triggered. Your application will need to handle notifying the user appropriately. |
| Support for special data types | Supports Counter, OLE, and Memo data types. | Server dependent. |
| Referential integrity | Defined within Access. | Referential integrity must be defined directly at the server if the server supports it. |
| Updateable queries/views | Access allows updates of almost any type of join. Access also allows update of both sides of a one-to-many join. | Most servers prohibit updates to joined queries. Using ODBC will sometimes work around this by sending multiple updates. Using pass-through limits you to updates the server allows. |

**WARNING**    Be careful if you're migrating a secure Access application to a client-server platform! ADP files do not have the concept of a workgroup database that allows for object-level (forms, reports, macros, and modules) security. You must handle security of ADP files using file system mechanisms like Windows NT Access Control Lists (ACLs), or by setting a password on the ADP file itself. If you must maintain object-level security, you'll need to stick with a Jet database for application components.

By now you are probably wondering whether client-server is such a good idea after all. This is a good frame of mind from which to approach the native-Access versus client-server decision, because moving to a client-server implementation requires learning a new approach to application programming. It also requires giving up many of your familiar tools and losing some of the strong integration you find in Access. (Although ADP files help with integration to some extent.) There are, nonetheless, several compelling reasons why you might choose to use a database server as a back end to Access applications:

- Reliability and data protection

- Transaction and data integrity

- Performance considerations

- Improved system management

- Unique server capabilities

Each of these considerations is discussed in the following sections.

> **NOTE**    Each of the preceding reasons assumes you have a choice as to where to store the data. However, often you will consider using Access in a client-server environment simply because the data already resides on a database server and you wish to use Access to gain access to the data while continuing to keep the data on the server to support existing applications.

## Reliability and Data Protection

Access runs a copy of the database engine on every client machine and has no synchronized transaction log or distributed transaction commit system. A failure of any single client machine or network component, therefore, has the potential to corrupt the entire database. Usually the database can be fixed, but repairing an Access database requires all users to log off the database. Repair of a large database can take several hours, and no user can use the database during the repair. On the other hand, because all updating and data management on a server occurs at the *server*, failures on the network or client machines rarely affect the database. Also, most database servers have fast and robust recovery facilities. Database servers also typically run on operating systems such as Windows NT, UNIX, or MVS, which have their own fault-recovery systems, making the database almost incorruptible. For example, you can literally pull the plug on a Windows NT server running Microsoft SQL Server with no data loss. Don't try that with your Access database!

# Transaction Processing and Data Integrity

The transaction support built into Jet has access to the data only for its own current session. It cannot resolve problems left from a previous failed session or from another copy of Jet that failed somewhere else on the network. This transaction support also does not have full protection for the database if a failure occurs while Jet is committing a transaction. In addition, the current implementation of Jet can leave locks orphaned in the shared locking (LDB) file, requiring a shutdown and purge of the shared locking file before anyone can access or repair the data. As a result, failures that occur while a copy of Access is committing a transaction can result in data loss, data lockout, or database corruption. The windows are small, but they may be sufficient to cause you to seriously consider client-server if you are implementing systems that, for example, process fund transactions. In this case money will not be properly transferred or accounted for if the transaction partially commits. In contrast, most database servers are capable of maintaining a full audit trail, enabling the database administrator to reconstruct the state of the database at any time. Popular servers, such as Microsoft SQL Server, also offer hot backup facilities, letting you save a second copy of critical data in real time without suspending database operations.

# Performance Considerations

Performance is another important reason to consider client-server, but one that is often misrepresented. Unlike the reliability issues, there are many approaches to providing good performance from a native Access multi-user system. However, there are cases in which a server is the only way to achieve appropriate performance. Generally speaking, if you often need to find small amounts of data in a sea of records, client-server will provide a speed boost. On the other hand, if you're frequently analyzing records from the bulk of your database or running multiple reports with only slight variations between them, a client-server environment might prove slower than the equivalent file-server system.

---

**TIP**    Relational databases have traditionally been biased towards *transactional* applications—those that write to single records. *Analytical* applications—those that summarized large numbers of records—have not been well suited to relational databases. That is changing with the advent of On Line Analytical Processing (OLAP) services in products like Microsoft SQL Server 7.0. For more information on SQL Server OLAP services, see `http://www.microsoft.com/sql/70/gen/olap.htm`.

---

It's important to remember that client-server is not a performance panacea. Simply moving your database tables to a server database will, in all likelihood, result in drastically *lower* performance. You must rethink your application in terms of client-server. We'll discuss this in more detail later in the chapter.

## System Management

One often-overlooked area in client-server is overall system management and administration. Windows and the Access Workgroup Administrator program offer only very limited management services compared to a Windows NT or a UNIX server machine. Adding a robust, modern server database to the package further increases the management tools. Microsoft SQL Server, for example, is capable of monitoring its own operation and sending e-mail or even pager messages to the database administrator in case of trouble.

## Unique Server Capabilities

Sometimes you will need to use a server for your database simply because it offers some capabilities that Access doesn't. Here is a list of the most important features built into SQL Server that might make it the right choice for your applications:

- Data replication triggered by a specific transaction load.

- Central management of distributed servers.

- Scalability to high-performance machines. (SQL Server will make use of multiple processors; Access will not.)

- Support for very large databases (up to terabytes of data).

- Querying via electronic mail.

- Deadlock and livelock resolution, ensuring that two users cannot lock each other out of needed data.

- Dynamic backup, even while the database is in use.

- Automatic recovery—backups plus log files can be used to regenerate a database lost to hardware failure.

- Device mirroring—your data can be written to multiple drives at one time, for instantaneous backups.

- Integrated security resulting in a single logon for both the network and the database.

When you think about the amount of code you would have to write to get most of these capabilities in Access itself, you can see that a database server can save considerable development time and expense.

# Understanding OLE DB

As we mentioned earlier, OLE DB has become the preeminent data access technology for server data. (At least it was when we wrote this book. Who knows what methods will dominate in the next few years.) The bulk of the remaining chapters deal with creating applications using OLE DB and ADO, so it makes sense at this point to give you some background on OLE DB architecture and how it works. This section will be relatively brief, covering only enough to provide a base level of understanding to support the examples in other chapters.

## OLE DB Components

OLE DB identifies four key components of a solution: data provider, data consumer, data service provider, and business component.

- A *data provider* is any relational or non-relational data store that offers data for consumption. A software component that exposes a well-defined set of COM interfaces is required to access the data.

- A *data consumer* is any application that calls OLE DB methods to connect to and query a data provider. Access is the data consumer in an ADP-based application.

- A *data service provider* is any component that provides services such as query processing or cursor management. OLE DB was designed to be modular, in the sense that third parties could provide key pieces of the data access architecture.

- A *business component* is a COM-based application that implements business rules and that may, itself, act as a data consumer. Business components can also implement OLE DB interfaces so that client applications can interact with them as if they were communicating directly with the database.

# Using OLE DB Providers with ADO

Chapter 4 covers creating and using OLE DB data providers with Access ADP files. This section deals with the basics of using OLE DB data providers with ADO through VBA. Later chapters will have more examples.

Since ADO was modeled to be similar to DAO, you should have no trouble working with data once you've established a connection to the server and run a query. ADO and DAO diverge on how this is done.

DAO uses the concept of a *workspace* to denote a session between an application and the Jet database engine. Workspaces are useful for scoping transactions and they also enforce user-level security. Once an application obtains a pointer to a workspace, it can then open a database *connection* and process queries. Jet provides a default workspace, Workspaces(0), using security credentials stored in the Windows Registry to simplify the programmer's job.

ADO combines the concepts of workspaces and connections. ADO applications request a data source connection using whatever security credentials the data source requires. This connection supplies the scoping necessary for transactions.

---

**NOTE**     If you want finer control over connections and transaction scoping, you can call OLE DB interfaces directly from C++.

---

## Establishing an ADO Connection

Establishing a persistent connection in ADO is a relatively straightforward process. You begin by creating a new ADO Connection object. You can either explicitly create an ADO connection object or use the Application.CurrentProject.Connection object provided by Access in an ADP file. This is similar to the CurrentDB object in Jet databases.

Once you've created the Connection object, you must supply the provider to use as well as other pertinent connection information. The easiest way to do this is by using the ConnectionString property. ConnectionString accepts a tagged string containing details on provider, database, security credentials, and other information. OLE DB and ODBC share many of the same tags for connection strings. (For more information on connection strings and ODBC see "Establishing ODBC Connections" later in this chapter.) Listing 3.1 shows a test procedure that opens a connection to a server and lists properties of the Connection object.

---

**NOTE**     If you use the Application.CurrentProject.Connection object instead of creating a new object, you don't need to set the connection properties. Instead you'll inherit the settings used by the ADP file itself.

---

⟩ **Listing 3.1**

```
Sub TestConnection()
    Dim cnn As ADODB.Connection
    Dim l As Long

    ' Create a new Connection object
    Set cnn = New ADODB.Connection

    With cnn

        ' Set the connection string and open the
        ' connection
        .ConnectionString = _
        "Provider=SQLOLEDB;SERVER=myserver;UID=sa"
        .Open

        ' List out all the connection properties
        For l = 0 To .Properties.Count - 1
            With .Properties.Item(l)
                Debug.Print .Name, .Value
            End With
        Next

        ' Drop the connection
        .Close
    End With

    ' Destroy the Connection object
    Set cnn = Nothing
End Sub
```

## Specifying Providers

As you can see from Listing 3.1, the connection string specifies which OLEDB provider to use, the database to connect to, and the logon ID to use. Each OLE DB provider installed on your machine expects a particular provider string. Table 3.2 lists the provider strings associated with some of the more popular OLE DB providers. Many of these providers ship as part of Microsoft products like Office 2000 and Visual Studio 6.

# Using ODBC Data Sources with OLE DB

You'll notice that Table 3.2 lists ODBC Data Sources as an OLE DB provider. Because ODBC has a head start on OLE DB as a data access standard, there are more ODBC drivers in existence (especially for obscure database systems) than there are equivalent OLE DB providers. The ODBC provider for OLE DB lets you use existing ODBC drivers with OLE DB data consumers and, more importantly, ADO.

Using the ODBC provider is simple: just pass an ODBC connect string as the ConnectString property of an ADO Connection object. OLE DB will automatically append "PROVIDER=MSDASQL;" to the connect string, as MSDASQL is the default provider for OLE DB. (You can, of course, explicitly add this to the connect string yourself if you like.) This works with both ODBC connections, for which there is a Data Source Name (DSN) in the Windows Registry, as well as for "DSN-less" connections.

**TABLE 3.2:**  OLE DB Provider Strings

| Provider | String |
|---|---|
| ODBC Data Sources | MSDASQL |
| SQL Server | SQLOLEDB |
| Jet 4.0 | Microsoft.Jet.OLEDB.4.0 |
| Jet 3.5 | Microsoft.Jet.OLEDB.3.5 |
| Oracle | MSDAORA |
| Microsoft Active Directory | ADSDSOObject |
| Microsoft Internet Publishing Service | MSDAIPP.DSO |
| Microsoft Indexing Service | MSIDXS |

You can also specify the OLE DB provider separately from the connection information using the Connection object's Provider property, as in this example:

```
cnn.Provider = "SQLOLEDB"
cnn.ConnectionString = "SERVER=myserver;UID=sa"
cnn.Open
```

## Per Query Connections

Creating and opening a Connection object is useful when you have a number of queries you need to process in the context of your application. That's because you can pass a Connection object to a Recordset object's Open method, providing ADO with all the information it needs to process your query:

```
Dim rst As ADODB.Recordset
Set rst = New ADODB.Recordset
cnn.Properties("Current Catalog") = "Northwind"
rst.Open "SELECT * FROM Customers", cnn
```

If you simply want to process a single query and have no need to maintain a connection to the database, you can pass a connect string as the second argument to the Open method:

```
Dim rst As ADODB.Recordset
Set rst = New ADODB.Recordset
rst.Open "SELECT * FROM Customers", _
  "Provider=SQLOLEDB;SERVER=myserver;UID=sa;DATABASE=Northwind"
```

There is a small amount of overhead associated with establishing a connection, so if you plan on executing many queries you should create and maintain an ADO Connection object instead.

---

**NOTE**     The examples shown above illustrate two ways of specifying which SQL Server database to use. The first example sets a property of the Connection object, Current Catalog, to the name of the server database. In the second example the database is specified as part of the connection string.

---

# Understanding ODBC

A good portion of this chapter deals with the Open Database Connectivity (ODBC) data access standard. You might be asking yourself why we're covering this in such detail, since Access 2000 now supports OLE DB in ADP files (and ADO in MDB files). The reason is that ADP files can only be used with Microsoft SQL Server 6.5 and 7.0 database servers (including the Microsoft Data Engine—MSDE). As of this writing, Oracle still held the biggest share of the database server market and there are dozens of other server types that you may wish to connect to. To do this, you can either write ADO code (in MDB or ADP files) or use linked tables in an old-style Jet database. The latter requires an ODBC connection and so it makes sense to understand how ODBC works. This chapter is really the only place in the book where we discuss ODBC.

ODBC is a common language definition and a set of protocols that allow a client to interactively determine a server's capabilities and adapt the processing to work within the functions the server supports. To use ODBC to connect Access to a back-end database, you need three things:

- A network that allows communications between the client machine and the machine that holds the back-end database

- The ODBC driver manager that comes with Access

- An ODBC driver that can work with your back-end database

Many sources exist for ODBC-compliant drivers. Many database and hardware vendors now provide them, and there are several third-party sources for drivers. For lists of drivers and vendors consult the Microsoft Universal Data Access Web site at `http://www.microsoft.com/data/`.

ODBC processing consists of three major activities:

- Establishing connections

- Parsing queries

- Managing record sources

The key to getting reliable performance lies in understanding all three of these areas, especially how your specific ODBC driver and back-end server handle each.

# Establishing ODBC Connections

ODBC processing revolves around *connections*. When a client needs access to data on a server, the ODBC software at the client end (in the case of Access, Jet and the underlying ODBC drivers) performs a number of steps to establish a connection:

1. Finds the system and path information for the appropriate connection

2. Connects over the appropriate network(s) to the database server

3. Checks for a stored login for the database

4. Prompts the user (if required) for login and password information

5. Gathers information about the capabilities of the server

6. Gathers information about the capabilities of the ODBC driver

7. Gathers information about the table(s) that are being connected

To make a connection, an application must pass an ODBC connect string to the ODBC manager. An ODBC connect string is an encoded string that consists of the data source name and other required information. A sample connect string is shown here:

```
DSN=PerfTest;APP=MicrosoftAccess;UID=sa;PWD=;DATABASE=ADHTestDB;
```

You can see that each piece of information is designated by a tag and separated from the next by a semicolon. Table 3.3 lists a few of the most common tags used in ODBC connect strings.

---

**NOTE**       An ODBC data source name is used to identify factors such as driver and server names. For more information on creating a data source, see the "Configuring ODBC" section later in this chapter.

---

**TABLE 3.3:**   Common ODBC Connect String Tags

| Tag | Description |
| --- | --- |
| DSN | Data source name |
| UID | User ID |
| PWD | User password |

**TABLE 3.3:** Common ODBC Connect String Tags *(continued)*

| Tag | Description |
| --- | --- |
| DATABASE | Database name (if the DSN does not specify a specific database, you can include it here) |
| APP | Application name (used by servers to identify the user of a connection) |
| DRIVER | ODBC driver name given as its file name (e.g., SQLSRV32.DLL for SQL Server) |
| SERVER | Server name |

One unique feature of ODBC is that every piece of connection information is optional. If the ODBC manager or database driver doesn't find what it needs in the connect string, it prompts the user for the missing information. When you link to an ODBC data source, Access stores the connect string in the linked table's Connect property. If you want to work with server data programmatically, you'll need to become comfortable constructing connect strings yourself.

**TIP** You do not always need to create a persisted ODBC data source in order to use ODBC. If you don't want to create a data source that gets saved to the user's workstation, you must include the DRIVER tag (and SERVER if it's a server database) in the connect string.

You generally want to make connections only once for each session. Once a connection has been established, you can execute multiple queries using it. This is what happens when you use linked tables, because Access caches connection information for linked tables locally. This in turn allows Jet to connect to the table when you reference it without all the overhead of a dynamic connection.

When converting your Access application to a client-server application, you should examine all uses of the OpenDatabase function or method. When used against an ODBC data source, the OpenDatabase method triggers the steps listed above. If you need to open a database programmatically, consider opening a single connection and storing a pointer to it in a global Database variable.

**NOTE**      Starting with ODBC version 2.5, some drivers include a "fast connect" option. When you invoke this option (during the driver setup), the driver defers as much of the connection processing as possible until you actually request records from the data source. Using this option can speed the initial load of your application, at the cost of making the first access to each table slower.

# Query Parsing

Jet handles a query for an ODBC connection in one of three ways. You can use any of the following:

- A regular Jet-optimized Access query
- A SQL pass-through (SPT) query
- A query passed using ADO or ODBCDirect

If you use an SPT, or an ADO or ODBCDirect query, Jet does no parsing of the query and passes the SQL string directly to the database server for processing. It is your responsibility to ensure that the string is a valid SQL statement. On the other hand, you can also use a regular Access query, whereupon Jet interprets and optimizes the query locally, determining the best execution path. During the optimization step, Jet partitions the query execution into a Jet-executed component and a server-executed component. It is at this point that Jet may make inappropriate choices concerning the best SQL to send to the server.

SQL pass-through and ADO and ODBCDirect querying generally work best for activities during which the server can do a large amount of processing, or for which Access is incapable of expressing the query in native SQL. You might consider using one of these technologies in lieu of Jet queries in the following situations:

- To perform data definition language (DDL) operations or other administrative actions on the server. Often, there is no Jet equivalent for these queries.
- To execute SQL when the SQL syntax is not supported by Access.
- To execute very short SQL actions, such as single-row retrievals or updates.
- To process SQL statements that join tables from two different databases on the same server.

- To process SQL updates when you need to check on the number of rows updated.

- To process large action queries within transactions.

# Managing Record Sources

When you convert an application from using Jet data to using ODBC data, you may find that complex forms open slowly compared to other forms. This is because there is more overhead associated with creating a connection to an ODBC data source than to a Jet table. Each record source on a form (the form itself, plus any subforms or list or combo boxes) may require its own connection. When you built your forms in Access and bound them to Jet data, you probably didn't worry about how many different sources of data the form used, because the data all came from local Jet tables. When you use ODBC, you need to limit the number of different record sources on a form to ensure reasonable performance and usability.

As mentioned earlier in this chapter, ODBC uses connections to talk to the server. Depending on the server, a single physical connection may be opened or a separate physical connection may exist for each active recordset. If a recordset is updatable, Jet will maintain two connections (except when there are fewer than 100 records, in which case only one connection is used). Whether they are physical links or logical links over a shared path, all connections use memory and processing resources. In addition, some servers impose a licensing limit on the number of open connections. Thus, to work efficiently under ODBC, you need to be careful about the number of active recordsets your application uses. Each row source on your form (whether for the form itself or a combo or list box) is a separate connection. Each bound subform will have one or more connections. A connection remains open in each of these situations:

- Until all associated data has been returned from the server

- While any transactions are outstanding

Jet may cache a connection to avoid the cost of reestablishing the connection the next time it requires the data. You can control this caching process by way of ODBC parameters in the Registry. (See the "Configuring ODBC for Your System" section later in this chapter.)

# Configuring ODBC

Regardless of the approach you take to client-server development with Access, you'll need to know something about using ODBC. In this section, we briefly discuss the ODBC Administrator applet you can use to configure ODBC data sources.

## ODBC Data Sources

ODBC data sources define the distinct servers and databases you want to connect to. You use the ODBC Administrator applet to manage data sources. Conceptually, a data source consists of three items:

- A name unique to the workstation on which the data source is defined

- The ODBC driver used

- Any other driver-specific information

ODBC supports *user* and *system* data source names (DSNs). User DSN information is linked to a particular workstation user, while system DSNs are available to all users of a workstation. DSN information is stored in the Registry in the Software\ODBC\ODBC.INI subkey of either the HKEY_CURRENT_USER hive (for user DSNs) or the HKEY_LOCAL_MACHINE hive (for system DSNs).

ODBC versions 3 and later also support *file data sources*. File data sources store configuration information in a file rather than in the Registry. This makes it very easy, for example, to define a data source on one computer and transfer the definition to another. You just need to copy the definition file (which ODBC creates with a .DSN file extension) to the other computer. ODBC stores configuration files in the \Program Files\Common Files\Odbc\Data Sources directory.

---

**NOTE**    You can change the directory ODBC looks in to find file data sources. Modify the DefaultDSNDir entry of the HKEY_LOCAL_MACHINE\Software\ ODBC\ODBC.INI\ODBC File DSN Registry key.

---

Once you've established a data source, the only thing an ODBC-compliant application such as Access needs to know in order to connect to it is the data source name. ODBC then allows the driver to prompt the user for any additional information.

# Running ODBC Administrator

Although you can configure data sources by editing Registry settings, it is usually easier to use the ODBC Administrator applet. This software is normally installed as part of any application that supports ODBC and appears as a Control Panel icon labeled "32-bit ODBC." (You can also run the executable file, ODBCAD32 .EXE, installed in the Windows, Windows\System, or Windows\System32 directory, separately.) Figure 3.2 shows the Administrator's user interface. Using the tabs, you can view user, system, and file data sources, as well as information on ODBC drivers and system files.

---

**NOTE**    Windows 2000 does not display the ODBC Administrator icon in its Control Panel. Instead it appears in the Start ➢ Programs ➢ Administrative Tools menu group. Furthermore, Windows 2000 Professional does not display this menu group by default. You must right-click the Taskbar, select Properties from the pop-up menu, click the Advanced tab on the Properties dialog box, and select the checkbox next to Display Administrative Tools in the Start menu Settings list.

---

**FIGURE 3.2**
ODBC Administrator applet
showing system data
source names

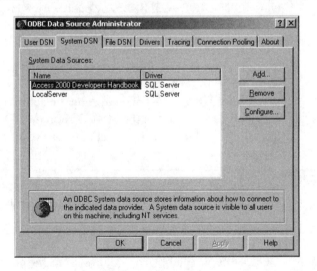

## Setting Up a Data Source

To create a new user data source, click the Add button on the initial ODBC Administrator dialog box. (To add a new system data source, click the Add button on the System DSN tab.) You are prompted to select a driver from a list of those installed on your workstation (see Figure 3.3). As an example, we'll show you how to set up the Microsoft SQL Server data source used by our sample database. You start by selecting the SQL Server driver from the list and clicking the Finish button.

**FIGURE 3.3**
Choosing an ODBC driver
for a new data source

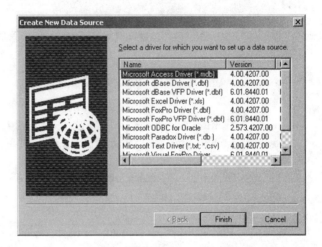

**NOTE**   You should note that the list of ODBC drivers is built from Registry entries in the HKEY_LOCAL_MACHINE\Software\ODBC\ODBCINST.INI Registry key and should correspond to those installed on your workstation. If you do not see a particular driver listed, you should rerun that driver's setup program.

After selecting a driver, you see a dialog box like the one shown in Figure 3.4. Don't be alarmed, however, if the one you see differs greatly, because the ODBC driver itself generates the dialog box. It will therefore differ between drivers and driver versions, given the varying pieces of information each needs.

**FIGURE 3.4**
Configuring the sample SQL
Server data source

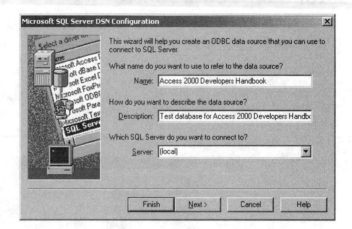

At a minimum, however, you'll need to supply a name for the data source. The name must be unique with respect to other DSNs defined on the same workstation. If you want to set up the data source for this chapter, fill out the remaining fields as shown in the dialog box in Figure 3.4. (Substitute the name of your SQL Server in the Server field.)

# Getting at Server Data

You can retrieve data in each of the four ways we've been describing—the native Jet query, SQL pass-through, ADO, and ODBCDirect—using VBA code. Let's look at the syntax for each of these alternatives in turn, using the query shown in Figure 3.5. You can find this query, qrySales, in the CH03.MDB sample database. This query uses three of the tables from the sample Pizza database, named ADH2KSQL in SQL Server, built from the SQL script files included on the companion CD-ROM.

We've provided you with a test form, frmTestbed, shown in Figure 3.6, with which to test the various data access methods.

To use the form first select one of the sample queries from the combo box. This populates the four text boxes with SQL statements corresponding to each query formatted for either Jet SQL or standard ANSI SQL. Next, select the ODBC data source you created in the last section that points to the same Pizza database and fill in a user ID and password (if necessary). Now you can execute each query using the command buttons to see how each method performs. You should execute each several times (and optionally vary the number of iterations) to reduce the effects of network traffic, disk caching, etc.

**FIGURE 3.5**

The test query used for our data access examples

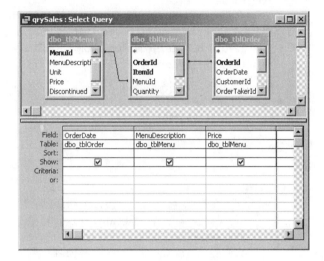

**FIGURE 3.6**

Use frmTestbed to test the performance characteristics of each data access method.

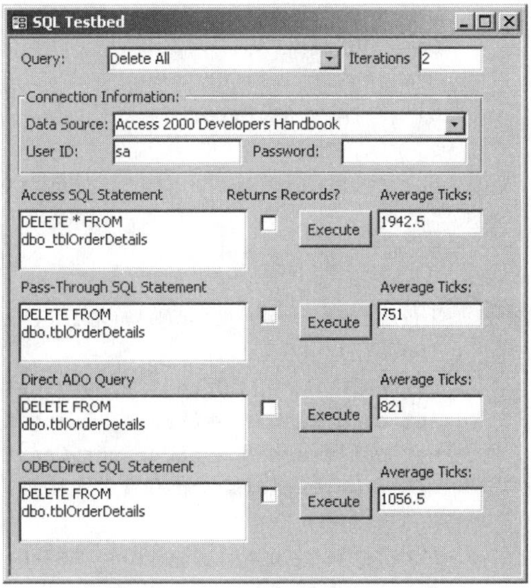

## Using a Native Jet Query

Finding the proper SQL for a native Jet query is simple: just construct the query on the QBE grid and switch to SQL view. Here's the Jet SQL for the sample query:

```
SELECT dbo_tblOrder.OrderDate, dbo_tblMenu.MenuDescription,
dbo_tblMenu.Price
FROM (dbo_tblMenu INNER JOIN dbo_tblOrderDetails
ON dbo_tblMenu.MenuId = dbo_tblOrderDetails.MenuId)
INNER JOIN dbo_tblOrder ON dbo_tblOrderDetails.OrderId =
dbo_tblOrder.OrderId;
```

For the native Jet query, we create a QueryDef object using the linked tables directly and then base a recordset on this QueryDef. Listing 3.2 shows the relevant portion of the code.

### ⟳ Listing 3.2

```
Private Sub cmdExecuteAttached_Click()
    Dim wsCurrent As DAO.Workspace
    Dim dbCurrent As DAO.Database
    Dim qdfAttached As DAO.QueryDef
    Dim rstAttached As DAO.Recordset
    Dim lngIterations As Long
    Dim cIterations As Long
    Dim lngStart As Long
    Dim lngTotal As Long
    Dim errAny As Error

    On Error GoTo cmdExecuteLinkedErr

    DoCmd.Hourglass True

    lngIterations = CLng(Me.txtIterations)
    lngTotal = 0
    Set wsCurrent = DBEngine.Workspaces(0)
    Set dbCurrent = wsCurrent.Databases(0)
    Set qdfAttached = dbCurrent.CreateQueryDef _
      ("", Me.txtAttachedSQL)

    ' Tell Jet to wait as long as the query takes
    qdfAttached.ODBCTimeout = 0
```

```
For cIterations = 1 To lngIterations
    lngStart = GetTickCount()

    ' If query returns records create Recordset,
    ' otherwise execute it
    If Me.chkJetRec Then
        Set rstAttached = qdfAttached.OpenRecordset()
        rstAttached.MoveLast
        rstAttached.Close
    Else
        wsCurrent.BeginTrans
        qdfAttached.Execute
        wsCurrent.Rollback
    End If
    lngTotal = lngTotal + GetTickCount() - lngStart
Next cIterations
Me.txtAttachedTicks = lngTotal / lngIterations

cmdExecuteLinkedExit:
    DoCmd.Hourglass False
    Exit Sub
cmdExecuteLinkedErr:
    If Err.Number = DBEngine.Errors(0).Number And _
    DBEngine.Errors.Count > 1 Then
        For Each errAny In DBEngine.Errors
            MsgBox "Error " & errAny.Number & " raised by " _
            & errAny.Source & ": " & errAny.Description, _
            vbCritical, "cmdExecuteAttached()"
        Next errAny
    Else
        MsgBox "Error " & Err.Number & " raised by " _
        & Err.Source & ": " & Err.Description, _
        vbCritical, "cmdExecuteAttached()"
    End If
    Resume cmdExecuteLinkedExit
End Sub
```

The only major complication here is setting the query timeout. By default, Jet will wait only 60 seconds for a query to execute before deciding that the server is down and aborting all processing on that query. You can use the query's ODBC-Timeout property (available through code, as shown here, or on any query's property sheet) to increase this time. If you set the timeout to 0, Jet will wait until either the server returns data or you give up and press Ctrl+Break to abort the query.

You should also note the error handling in this function. Because we're dealing with multiple components (Access, Jet, ODBC, and SQL Server), it's possible for a single operation to produce more than one error. If multiple errors occur in any Jet operation, Jet will populate the Errors collection of the DBEngine object with Error objects—one for each component to report an error. Jet will also put the last error into the Err object, which belongs to Access. However, if an error occurs in some non-data component (for example, VBA), Jet will not be notified, and consequently the Errors collection won't match the actual error. In this case you must retrieve the information from the Err object.

When it senses an error, the code checks to see whether there are multiple errors in the Errors collection and, if so, checks to see whether the first member of this collection matches the one stored in Err. If so, it dumps every member of the collection using a For...Each loop. If not, it simply dumps the error information from the Err object.

## Using a SQL Pass-Through Query

To execute the same query using SQL pass-through, you must rewrite it in SQL that the server can understand directly—which means you need to know the dialect of SQL used on your server. To translate this query to Microsoft SQL Server, you need to change the underlines in the table names back to dots, as shown here:

```
SELECT dbo.tblOrder.OrderDate, dbo.tblMenu.MenuDescription,
dbo.tblMenu.Price
FROM (dbo.tblMenu INNER JOIN dbo.tblOrderDetails
ON dbo.tblMenu.MenuId = dbo.tblOrderDetails.MenuId)
INNER JOIN dbo.tblOrder ON dbo.tblOrderDetails.OrderId =
dbo.tblOrder.OrderId
```

---

**TIP**    If you're unsure of the proper SQL but have a sniffer tool such as SQL Profiler, which comes with Microsoft SQL Server (and is explained in detail in the "Looking In on Jet and ODBC" section later in this chapter), you can execute your query using the regular QBE grid and then inspect the trace of the conversation with the server to see how ODBC chose to translate it for you.

---

Executing a pass-through query in code also requires creating a QueryDef object. You create pass-through queries using the same technique as for normal queries, except that you set the QueryDef's Connect property to a valid ODBC connect string. In this case, we're setting it to the return value of a function called GetConnect. GetConnect constructs a connect string from values entered on the form. Listing 3.3 shows how to construct and execute a pass-through query using code.

### Listing 3.3

```
Private Sub cmdExecutePassthrough_Click()
    Dim wsCurrent As DAO.Workspace
    Dim dbCurrent As DAO.Database
    Dim qdfPassthrough As DAO.QueryDef
    Dim rstPassthrough As DAO.Recordset
    Dim lngIterations As Long
    Dim cIterations As Long
    Dim lngStart As Long
    Dim lngTotal As Long
    Dim errAny As DAO.Error

    On Error GoTo cmdExecutePassthroughErr

    DoCmd.Hourglass True

    lngIterations = CLng(Me.txtIterations)
    lngTotal = 0
    Set wsCurrent = DBEngine.Workspaces(0)
    Set dbCurrent = wsCurrent.Databases(0)

    ' Create pass-through query
    Set qdfPassthrough = dbCurrent.CreateQueryDef("")
    qdfPassthrough.Connect = "ODBC;" & GetConnect()
    qdfPassthrough.SQL = Me.txtPassthroughSQL

    ' Tell Access to wait as long as the query takes
    qdfPassthrough.ODBCTimeout = 0
    For cIterations = 1 To lngIterations
        lngStart = GetTickCount()

        ' If query returns records create Recordset,
        ' otherwise execute it
        If Me.chkPassRec Then
            Set rstPassthrough = qdfPassthrough.OpenRecordset()
```

```
                    rstPassthrough.MoveLast
                    rstPassthrough.Close
                Else
                    qdfPassthrough.ReturnsRecords = False
                    wsCurrent.BeginTrans
                    qdfPassthrough.Execute
                    wsCurrent.Rollback
                End If
                lngTotal = lngTotal + GetTickCount() - lngStart
            Next cIterations
            Me.txtPassthroughTicks = lngTotal / lngIterations

cmdExecutePassthroughExit:
    DoCmd.Hourglass False
    Exit Sub
cmdExecutePassthroughErr:
    If Err.Number = DBEngine.Errors(0).Number And _
      DBEngine.Errors.Count > 1 Then
        For Each errAny In DBEngine.Errors
            MsgBox "Error " & errAny.Number & " raised by " _
                & errAny.Source & ": " & errAny.Description, _
                vbCritical, "cmdExecutePassthrough()"
        Next errAny
    Else
        MsgBox "Error " & Err.Number & " raised by " _
            & Err.Source & ": " & Err.Description, _
            vbCritical, "cmdExecutePassthrough()"
    End If
    Resume cmdExecutePassthroughExit
End Sub
```

To create a pass-through query, you need to take the following steps in order. (Setting properties in the wrong order will result in a runtime error.)

1. Create the QueryDef.

2. Set the QueryDef's Connect property. If you're unsure of the syntax for the Connect property, check the Description property of a linked table from the same database.

3. Assign the proper server SQL to the query's SQL property.

4. Set the ReturnsRecords property to True if the query returns records. (You would set this to False for queries that don't return records, such as DDL queries.)

---

**WARNING**  If you want your pass-through query to execute with no user intervention, make sure you include every piece of information the server requires in your connect string. Otherwise the user may have to supply it by means of a driver-generated dialog box. For example, if you omit the UID or PWD component when connecting to a SQL Server database, the ODBC driver will display a dialog each time the query is run.

---

Once you have created the proper QueryDef, a pass-through query behaves much like a native query in Jet—with one significant difference. Because Jet can't know how the server is retrieving records, a pass-through query is always read only. (If you need to update records in a pass-through query, you can write an update query and execute it by means of pass-through, as well.)

## Using Direct ADO to Execute Queries

Even in a Jet database with linked ODBC tables, you still may choose to execute queries directly using ADO to gain more control over the SQL sent to the server. Listing 3.4 shows code that executes a query against a database using the OLE DB provider for ODBC data sources.

---

**NOTE**  We used the ODBC OLE DB provider rather than a specific server driver to enable the query to work with any ODBC data source. If you write your own ADO queries, you'll want to choose the OLE DB provider for your specific server.

---

**Listing 3.4**

```
Private Sub cmdExecuteADO_Click()
    Dim strServer As String
    Dim conADO As ADODB.Connection
    Dim rstADO As ADODB.Recordset
    Dim lngIterations As Long
    Dim cIterations As Long
```

```
Dim lngStart As Long
Dim lngTotal As Long
Dim errAny As ADODB.Error

On Error GoTo HandleError

DoCmd.Hourglass True

lngIterations = CLng(Me.txtIterations)
lngTotal = 0

' Establish a connection using the ODBC OLEDB provider
Set conADO = New ADODB.Connection
With conADO
    .ConnectionString = "Provider=MSDASQL;" & _
     GetConnect()
    .Open
End With

For cIterations = 1 To lngIterations
    lngStart = GetTickCount()

    ' If query returns records create Recordset,
    ' otherwise execute it
    If Me.chkADORec Then
        Set rstADO = New ADODB.Recordset

        rstADO.Open CStr(Me.txtADOSQL), conADO, adOpenStatic
        rstADO.MoveLast
        rstADO.Close
        Set rstADO = Nothing
    Else
        conADO.BeginTrans
        conADO.Execute Me.txtADOSQL
        conADO.RollbackTrans
    End If
    lngTotal = lngTotal + GetTickCount() - lngStart
Next cIterations
Me.txtADOTicks = lngTotal / lngIterations

ExitHere:
    conADO.Close
```

```
            Set conADO = Nothing
            DoCmd.Hourglass False
            Exit Sub
    HandleError:
        If conADO.Errors.Count > 0 Then
            If Err.Number = conADO.Errors(0).Number And _
              conADO.Errors.Count > 1 Then
                For Each errAny In conADO.Errors
                    MsgBox "Error " & errAny.Number & " raised by " _
                      & errAny.Source & ": " & errAny.Description, _
                      vbCritical, "cmdExecuteADO()"
                Next errAny
            Else
                MsgBox "Error " & Err.Number & " raised by " _
                  & Err.Source & ": " & Err.Description, _
                  vbCritical, "cmdExecuteADO()"
            End If
        Else
            MsgBox "Error " & Err.Number & " raised by " _
              & Err.Source & ": " & Err.Description, _
              vbCritical, "cmdExecuteADO()"
        End If
        Resume ExitHere
    End Sub
```

---

**WARNING**   Take a look at the explicit data type conversion (CStr) in the Recordset's Open method. When passing a query from an Access form control make sure you convert it to a String, otherwise ADO will raise a runtime error.

---

You'll notice that this code is very similar to DAO, with one difference being that ADO objects are *creatable*. That is, you must instantiate them using the VBA New keyword.

The procedure first establishes a connection with the ODBC data source by setting the ADO Connection object's ConnectionString property. Note the inclusion of the Provider=MSDASQL; clause. This specifies that OLE DB should use the ODBC provider. (Although as we mentioned earlier, this is the default driver and thus the string could have been omitted.)

After establishing the connection the procedure can then create a recordset based on the supplied SQL or execute an SQL statement. Error handling is done in a manner similar to DAO, using the Errors collection on the ADO Connection object instead of DBEngine.

## Using ODBCDirect

Because ODBCDirect queries also send their SQL directly to the server, they use the same SQL syntax as pass-through queries. The code needed to execute an ODBCDirect query, however, is quite different from SQL pass-through (though very similar to DAO). Listing 3.5 shows the code necessary to execute an ODBC-Direct query.

### Listing 3.5

```
Private Sub cmdExecuteRDO_Click()
    Dim lngIterations As Long
    Dim cIterations As Long
    Dim lngStart As Long
    Dim lngTotal As Long
    Dim wsDirect As DAO.Workspace
    Dim dbDirect As DAO.Database
    Dim cnDirect As DAO.Connection
    Dim rsDirect As DAO.Recordset
    Dim errAny As DAO.Error

    On Error GoTo cmdExecuteRDOErr

    DoCmd.Hourglass True

    lngIterations = CLng(Me.txtIterations)
    lngTotal = 0

    ' Create an ODBCDirect workspace
    Set wsDirect = DBEngine.CreateWorkspace _
     ("ODBCDirect", CurrentUser(), "", dbUseODBC)

    ' Open the database using an ODBC connect string
    Set cnDirect = wsDirect.OpenConnection _
     ("ODBCDirectConnection", _
     dbDriverComplete, False, "ODBC;" & GetConnect())
```

```vb
    For cIterations = 1 To lngIterations
        lngStart = GetTickCount()

        ' If query returns records create Recordset,
        ' otherwise execute it
        If Me.chkODBCRec Then
            ' Open the recordset using server-specific SQL
            Set rsDirect = cnDirect.OpenRecordset( _
            Me.txtRDOSQL, dbOpenDynaset)
            rsDirect.MoveLast
            rsDirect.Close
            Set rsDirect = Nothing
        Else
            wsDirect.BeginTrans
            cnDirect.Execute Me.txtRDOSQL
            wsDirect.Rollback
        End If
        lngTotal = lngTotal + GetTickCount() - lngStart
    Next cIterations
    Me.txtRDOTicks = lngTotal / lngIterations

    cnDirect.Close
    wsDirect.Close

cmdExecuteRDOExit:
    DoCmd.Hourglass False
    Exit Sub
cmdExecuteRDOErr:
    If Err.Number = DBEngine.Errors(0).Number And _
     DBEngine.Errors.Count > 1 Then
        For Each errAny In DBEngine.Errors
            MsgBox "Error " & errAny.Number & " raised by " _
            & errAny.Source & ": " & errAny.Description, _
            vbCritical, "cmdExecuteRDO()"
        Next errAny
    Else
        MsgBox "Error " & Err.Number & " raised by " _
        & Err.Source & ": " & Err.Description, _
        vbCritical, "cmdExecuteRDO()"
    End If
    Resume cmdExecuteRDOExit
End Sub
```

As you can see, ODBCDirect works much like DAO. The key is to create a new Workspace object using the dbUseODBC constant. This tells Jet that you want to use ODBCDirect for any database operations carried out in that workspace. Once that's done you need to establish an ODBCDirect connection using the Workspace's OpenConnection method. Everything else should look familiar. Just remember to use server-specific SQL, not Jet SQL, when running queries.

# Evaluating Query Alternatives

Choosing a query strategy blindly is unlikely to get you the best possible query performance. In any sizable application, you'll need to test the various approaches for your important queries; that is, those that retrieve or modify large data sets and that are likely to take a long time to complete. We've provided a simple test bed application in the sample database. It includes a form that lets you execute a query using each of the methods we've mentioned, as well as code to use the Windows API call GetTickCount to do precise timings.

On frmTestbed, you can type a SQL statement to be executed by any of the four methods of querying we've discussed. You can also choose the number of iterations of testing you wish to run. Always test a query multiple times when you're evaluating its performance because data may end up cached on both the server and the client during a working session. You want your test to be extensive enough to get an average time, without the initial load of getting tables into memory.

> **NOTE**     While frmTestbed is set up to test queries against the sample database, you can test any query either by adding it to the SampleQueries table or by simply typing in the text boxes on the form.

# Configuring ODBC for Your System

In the Windows Registry, Access provides a wide range of configuration options for controlling ODBC. All the settings in Table 3.4 are made in the \HKEY_ LOCAL_MACHINE\SOFTWARE\Microsoft\Jet\4.0\Engines\ODBC Registry key. Table 3.4 contains descriptions of each configuration option and points out some potential settings for various conditions.

**TABLE 3.4:**    Registry Settings for Jet ODBC Behavior

| Key Name | Value | Use |
| --- | --- | --- |
| TraceSQLMode | 0 | Turns off tracing of Jet-to-server SQL statements (default). |
| | 1 | Traces all SQL statements sent from Jet to the ODBC interface. The output will be in a file named SQLOUT.TXT. |
| TraceODBCAPI | 0 | Disables tracing the ODBC API-level interface (default). |
| | 1 | Traces ODBC API calls into file ODBCAPI.TXT. You would use this only for debugging an ODBC driver or resolving a problem when working with a vendor. Normally, for working on your application's performance or debugging your SQL, use a SQL trace instead. |
| DisableAsync | 0 | Allows Access to continue processing while the server processes an ODBC request (default). |
| | 1 | Forces Access to wait for each ODBC request to complete before proceeding. You should set this only for debugging purposes or when dealing with a server that has problems with asynchronous queries, because it can have severe performance problems. |
| LoginTimeout | $s$ | Aborts a login attempt if the server has not responded in $s$ seconds (default: 20). |
| QueryTimeout | $s$ | Provides a default value for query-processing timeouts in seconds. Individual queries can override this with the ODBCTimeout property of the QueryDef. If you set this to 0, queries will not time out; instead, they will wait forever for data (default: 60). |
| ConnectionTimeout | $s$ | Sets the length of time, in seconds, during which Jet will maintain an inactive connection before releasing it. If your server is not licensed on a per-connection basis, setting this higher may improve response time. If you frequently run out of connections, lower this value (default: 600). |
| AsyncRetryInterval | $m$ | Sets the length of time, in milliseconds, that Jet waits each time it checks on the progress of an async query (default: 500). |
| AttachCaseSensitive | 0 | Does not use case when matching table names (default). If you use this setting, the first matching table that ODBC finds is attached. |
| | 1 | Performs a case-sensitive search when opening tables. |
| SnapshotOnly | 0 | Allows processing that uses updatable recordsets (default). |
| | 1 | Forces the use of read-only Snapshot recordsets. |

**TABLE 3.4:**   Registry Settings for Jet ODBC Behavior *(continued)*

| Key Name | Value | Use |
|---|---|---|
| AttachableObjects | *string* | Includes the server's system objects in the selection list for attaching tables. *string* is a list of all the system objects to include in the selection list (default: TABLE, VIEW, SYSTEM TABLE, ALIAS, and SYNONYM). |
| JetTryAuth | 1 | Try Jet Userid & Password before prompting the user for a different ID and password (default). You can use this setting if you keep IDs and passwords in sync between Access and the server. |
| | 0 | Prompts the user for a different ID and password. Use this setting if your Access IDs are not kept in sync with the server. |
| PreparedInsert | 0 | Generates data-specific inserts that reflect only the supplied columns (default). You should normally use this setting. |
| | 1 | Uses a predefined INSERT that uses all columns in the table. Using prepared INSERT statements can cause nulls to overwrite server defaults and can cause triggers to execute on columns that weren't inserted explicitly. |
| PreparedUpdate | 0 | Generates data-specific updates that reflect only the supplied columns (default). You should normally use this setting. |
| | 1 | Uses a predefined UPDATE that updates all columns. Using prepared UPDATE statements can cause triggers to execute on unchanged columns. |
| FastRequery | 0 | Uses a new SELECT statement each time a parameterized query is executed (default). |
| | 1 | Uses a prepared SELECT statement on the server when executing a parameterized query. |

# Configuring Your Server for Access

You can provide additional information for Access to use in managing your server connections in an optional table, MSysConf. You must add this table to each *server* database. It provides Access-specific information to assist in managing connections. Each time you connect to the database using Jet, Jet looks for this table and, if it exists, reads in the configuration information. The table should be defined as described in Table 3.5. Table 3.6 describes each of the settings for the MSysConf table.

**TABLE 3.5:** Structure of the MSysConf Table

| Column Name | Data Type | Allows Nulls? |
| --- | --- | --- |
| Config | 2-byte integer | No |
| chValue | VARCHAR(255) | Yes |
| nValue | 4-byte integer | Yes |
| Comments | VARCHAR(255) | Yes |

**TABLE 3.6:** Settings in Your MSysConf Table

| Config | nValue | Use |
| --- | --- | --- |
| 101 | 0 | Does not store user IDs and passwords for attached tables. This value prompts the user for ID and password information each time the tables are attached. |
| | 1 | Stores the user ID and password information with the connect string information for attached tables (default). |
| 102 | *d* | Sets the data retrieval delay time. Jet will delay *d* seconds between each retrieval of a block of rows from the server (default: 10; range: not documented [appears to be 1–32767]). |
| 103 | *n* | Sets the *n* number of rows to fetch from the server at each interval. You use these two settings (102 and 103) to control the rate at which data is brought from a server to Access during idle time (default: 100; range: not documented [appears to be 1–32767]). |

**WARNING** If you include an MSysConf table on the server, it must have the proper format and data, or you won't be able to connect to that server at all.

# Editing ODBC Data

You may on occasion link a server table only to discover that Access is treating it as a read-only data source. The Jet engine requires a unique index for every non-Access table it will allow you to edit. When you link a table from an ODBC data source, Access chooses the clustered unique index as the primary key. If there is no clustered unique index, Access chooses the (alphabetically) first unique index as the primary key of the table. This has a couple of implications:

- A table with no unique index will always be read only.

- If you have an index on the server that you wish to use as the primary key, you must a) make sure it is named something like AAA_PrimaryKey so that it will alphabetize before any other unique indexes; or b) make it a clustered unique index.

Should you have a table with no indexes, you can fix the problem in two ways. First, you can use whatever tools your server provides to create an index and then detach and re-link the table. (Doing this forces Access to query the server again for the new structure of the table.) If someone other than yourself is maintaining your server database, this method may be the best way to go, because changing the table on the server will make it read-write for all users.

You can also correct the problem in Access by creating a pseudo-index. Access 2000 automatically offers to do this for you when you link a table without a unique index on the server. You'll see the dialog box shown in Figure 3.7, and you can choose any combination of fields that you know is unique on the server.

**FIGURE 3.7**

Selecting unique fields for a server view

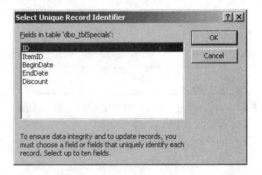

Alternately, you can use a DDL (Data Definition Language) query in Access to create the pseudo-index. This has the general form

```
CREATE UNIQUE INDEX index ON table (field [ASC|DESC][,
  field [ASC|DESC], ...])
```

Using either the automatic method or the CREATE INDEX method causes Access to maintain a local index on the linked table, enabling it to update the data in the table.

---

**NOTE**    While you can view indexes created using DDL in the Access Index Properties dialog box, you cannot use the dialog box to create, delete, or change indexes on attached ODBC tables. You must use a DDL query.

---

**WARNING**    A local index created in this manner is for your convenience only and may not reflect which fields in the server table actually determine uniqueness. Create these indexes with care! If you create a local index on fields that aren't unique, you could experience strange behavior when updating server tables.

---

Although any table with a unique index can be updated, you can make another optimization to speed updates on some servers. If your server supports a Timestamp data type (a date/time field the server updates whenever any value in the record is changed), tables with a Timestamp field can be updated much more efficiently. Whenever Jet updates a row using ODBC, it has to ensure that another user did not change the record while you were editing it. Normally it will check by retrieving all non-memo and non-OLE fields from the table and comparing them to the locally cached values, to make sure there were no changes to any field. If the table has a timestamp, it can just check to make sure the timestamp hasn't changed since you started editing the record.

# Understanding Your Server

Part of the promise of ODBC is that you can develop applications that are server independent. It turns out, though, that while ODBC certainly makes it easier to move from server to server, it is still important to write your application with the target server in mind. Both the server and the connecting software will affect the processing of your SQL. The SQL language used in Access differs from ANSI-standard SQL and has several features not supported by most servers. It also lacks features present in some servers.

ANSI SQL standards define data types differently from Access. You need to understand how ODBC maps data types, both from the server to Access and from Access tables to the server.

Some important areas to check for different servers are security, AutoNumber fields or their equivalent, joins, support for the use of multiple indexes within a single query, declarative referential integrity (DRI), and transaction processing support. The level of transaction support is a function of both the server and the ODBC driver. You need to match the features of your server with the features of Access that your application uses. If your application functionality depends on features your server does not support, you should look at a different server, rework your application, or consider not migrating the application. You will often end up splitting your application's logic between parts that can be performed on the server and parts that must be performed locally in the front end.

Consider the following server characteristics when picking a server and developing your Access applications:

- Does the server support SQL-92 join syntax?
- What join syntax is supported?
  - Inner joins only
  - Outer joins
  - Nested inner and outer joins (note that this would require SPT or ODBCDirect queries)
- Does the server support subqueries?
- Does the server support auto-incrementing or identity fields (counters)?
- Does the server support referential integrity?
- Does the server allow updates on any joined queries? If so, which updates and deletes are supported?
- Does the server support stored procedures or triggers?
- Does the server support cascading updates or deletes?
- Which built-in functions does the server support?
- Which date/time functions does the server support?

# Designing an Efficient Client-Server Application

When implementing client-server systems, you need to address several design areas that you typically do not need to deal with in a stand-alone Access application. The next few sections cover each of these design areas in detail.

## Establishing Rules for Transactions

You must clearly define and document all your data activity that is to be grouped together so that the transaction protection and recovery features of your server can work correctly.

Jet applies the following rules regarding transactions when processing against an ODBC data source:

- Forms must use optimistic locking.

- Recordsets must use optimistic locking.

- Only the outermost transaction is used if nested transactions are encountered.

- Only a single workspace is used for an ODBC connection. Multiple workspaces are consolidated.

- Action queries are processed in a single transaction.

- Recordsets created inside a VBA transaction are processed under that transaction.

Jet precludes the use of pessimistic locking because it has no way of knowing whether a particular record is locked. (This feature is not available through ODBC.) Therefore, bound forms are of limited usefulness in an update-intensive application where optimistic locking can lead to problems (records locked on save or data changing during edits). The same problems exist with records created using VBA, but with these you have much more control over how to handle the error.

You may, however, be able to successfully use bound forms directly against server tables or views in the following circumstances:

- When the form is based on a single table

- When the system is coded to handle update contention that will occur from optimistic locking

- When the data being updated does not need to be kept private while a set of changes is completed

- When the amount of data shown on the form at any one time is strictly limited

Forms that will usually meet these criteria include:

- Enquiry-only forms (based on read-only recordsets)

- Master table maintenance forms

- Browse forms that accept a key value from the user and then change their record source to fetch only the record with that key

Processing that generally does *not* work well using bound forms in the client-server setup includes:

- Updates or inserts of master/detail combinations, such as orders

- Updates in which multiple rows of a table must be changed at once

**NOTE** Chapter 7 describes another approach to record contention and locking: reservation tables. See "Using a Reservations Table" in that chapter for more information.

## Using Local Tables

At times you will want to keep a local copy of some of your server database tables within the Access client application. When splitting the workload between Access and the server, always remember that Access is a complete database system. You can take advantage of this by caching data locally on each client machine as it is first used or even at login time, refreshing your local tables during your AutoExec macro or Startup Form Form_Open procedure. This way you can reduce both network traffic and the load on your server, allowing you to support many more concurrent users on the same server and network. This procedure is especially easy to implement if you are converting an existing application, because you already have the native Access processing coded.

Review all your data requirements and identify the data that matches the following conditions:

- Data is static or relatively static.

- Users do not need to see each other's changes immediately.

- Data is always used together as a set, with each set needing to be used together exclusively.

Also, review your processing requirements to look for the following situations:

- Data entry systems in which several detail records are entered to build a complete transaction. This may be an order, an invoice, a parts list, or one of several other cases matching the traditional header-detail data pairing.

- Reports showing several aspects of the same data.

- Reports that do a great deal of data consolidation.

When you have processing needs matching the above types, you can benefit by downloading the data onto the client machine for processing or, when going the other way, by capturing the user's activity locally and uploading data to the server only when the user's session or activity is complete.

If your application uses a number of lookup tables, set up your system to load them at startup time. You can then design your forms and reports to use the local data in pick lists, in combo boxes, or when displaying descriptive lookup text instead of codes.

If your users typically work on a particular set of data for an extended period and other users should not work on this same data concurrently, you have a prime candidate for downloading the data and processing it locally—for example, a problem management system or an order processing system.

You'll have to choose carefully when to use the client copy of a table and when to use the server copy. A table of U.S. states used as the row source for a combo box, for example, should be the local copy because opening the combo will cause it to be requeried multiple times. On the other hand, when you're writing a query that joins that table with other server tables, you'll want to use the server copy, to avoid the heavy network traffic of doing a join between two different data sources.

# Creating Efficient Queries

At the heart of any database application are queries. They are the way you interact with data. Creating efficient client-server queries requires that you follow two guidelines:

- Construct queries that can be executed entirely on the server.

- Move as little data as possible across the network.

Remember, your major benefits from a client-server application come when you move less data over the network cable than you would in a file-server application. These guidelines are discussed in the next two sections.

## Execute on the Server

A database server's strength is its ability to process queries very quickly and efficiently. To take advantage of this, you must make sure that any queries you generate (including bound forms and update operations) are executed entirely by the server. When would this not be the case? If you're using pass-through queries, ADO queries against a server, or ODBCDirect, you needn't worry about this because your queries are sent directly to the server with no intervention from Jet. If you're using linked tables, however, you can get into trouble.

Problems arise as Jet parses your query. Based on its knowledge of ODBC and the server you're using, Jet breaks down your query into the portions the server can execute directly and those it can't. It then executes one query for each server component, brings back the resulting data, and then processes the final result locally. This leads to longer execution time and increased network traffic.

Ideally, when Jet finishes parsing your query, it is left with a single SQL statement that it can then send to the server. Often, however, it will not be able to resolve your query to ODBC-compliant SQL. Specifically, Jet will need to perform local processing if you've used any of these features:

- Access or user-defined functions that take field values as inputs

- Access SQL that ODBC doesn't support (TRANSFORM/PIVOT is one example)

- Multiple-level GROUP BYs

- GROUP BYs, including DISTINCT

- Joins over GROUP BYs

- Joins over DISTINCT clauses

- Certain combinations of outer and inner joins

- Queries stacked on unions

- Subqueries that include data from more than one source

- Joins between multiple data sources (ODBC or ISAM)

- Other complex queries

If you've used any of the features listed above, you should rewrite those portions of the application to use simpler Jet queries, pass-through or ADO queries, or ODBCDirect.

For most developers, however, the final item in the list is of most concern. Often it is difficult to predetermine whether a particular query will result in local processing. To troubleshoot these situations, you need a way to see what SQL Jet is actually generating. (See the "Looking In on Jet and ODBC" section later in this chapter for more information.)

## Move Only What You Need

Network traffic is costly in terms of execution time, so you must reduce it as much as possible. If you've satisfied the first guideline above, you've met this one halfway. You've reduced the amount of data going *to* the server to a single SQL statement. The other half is to reduce the amount of data coming *back*.

It is important to avoid recordsets based on all fields and all rows of a table. If you really need this level of data, consider importing or downloading the data from the server instead of linking to it. You can always refresh the data from the server by dropping your local table and re-importing. For forms, always define a query for the record source, and always include a WHERE clause that is as restrictive as possible—one row is best, but may not be enough to meet your needs. Avoid the use of the all-fields identifier (*) in your queries. Create form-specific queries that contain only the fields required for that form.

One way to limit the data returned when you're writing queries to serve as the record source for a form is to start with a blank record source. Force the user to make some type of selection that can be used in a WHERE clause to limit the rows returned. You can then include this in a SQL statement and dynamically change the RecordSource property at runtime. You can accomplish this by using an event procedure similar to this one:

```
Private Sub cboMenuDescription_AfterUpdate()
    ' Reset form's recordource based on local query
    Me.RecordSource = "SELECT * FROM dbo_tblMenu WHERE " & _
      "MenuId = " & Me.cboMenuDescription
End Sub
```

In the sample database, frmMenuSingleItem demonstrates this same technique with the tblMenu table from the sample SQL Server database for this chapter. It also demonstrates another technique mentioned earlier: downloading lookup information to a local table. Menu items are downloaded to a local table, and this information is used to populate a combo box on the form. After the user makes a selection, the remaining fields are retrieved. A Refresh button on the form lets the user download new values from the server table in the event new menu items are added.

| NOTE | Before using the sample Access database on your workstation, you will need to run the Linked Table Manager to re-establish the links to SQL Server on your computer. You can find the utility by selecting Tools ➤ Database Utilities ➤ Linked Table Manager. |
|------|---|

Another consideration concerns retrieving memo or OLE fields from the server. Because these tend to involve a substantial amount of data, they will vastly increase your network traffic. For example, if you have a table containing employee data, including employee pictures, you might start by bringing back only the text data and including a command button to retrieve a picture only if the user wants to see one.

For reports, consider defining the base data for the report as a local table and running an append query to load it from the server. Doing so avoids many of the pitfalls you will find when trying to interpret all the data access requirements of a report. It will also allow you to base multiple reports on the same set of data and yet query the server only once.

# Building Your Forms

Building forms for client-server applications requires some special consideration. You must pay special attention to how your searching and navigation processes work. You must also be closely aware of your data sources.

## Choosing Bound and Unbound Fields

After you have identified all the data requirements and data sources for your forms, you need to create the forms and link all the fields to their data sources. Whenever possible, link bound fields to a field from the record source of the form, instead of creating a separate row source for each control. In a client-server environment, each row source will result in a separate connection to the server.

If you do use controls bound to separate data sources (including subforms, list boxes, or combo boxes) try to limit the rows they display by specifying criteria in the record sources used to populate them. If you don't know the criteria values until after the form is opened (perhaps because the values come from other fields on the form), hide the controls until the criteria are set. Then use an explicit action, such as button click, to display them. Firing off the query for a subform with null criteria can create a major, unnecessary workload for your network. This is especially important for subforms because they tend to be more complex than list boxes or combo boxes.

## Choosing an Appropriate Design for Your Forms

Often an Access form allows a user to navigate to a specific record and then perform detailed work on the record. Several approaches to form design provide good performance for these situations. The goal of each approach is to present the user with a small subset of the fields to select the records they need and a separate recordset for the detail. The form should be set up to fill the detail recordset only *after* the user selects the criteria.

## Using an Unbound Main Form and a Subform for Detail

One of the simplest approaches you can use for forms mainly used to search or edit data is to create your edit form as though it will be used directly, and then embed it as a subform on an unbound form. You can set the record source of the subform based on a query that references fields on the unbound main form rather than use the master and child-linking fields. On the main form, create the controls users will use to establish the criteria for their final recordset. You should set the default value on each of the criteria fields to a value that will cause the subform to return no rows when the form is first opened. If you use a combo box, list box, or other pick-list mechanism to allow the user to find records, use a hidden field to hold the criteria and fill it in the AfterUpdate event procedure of the pick-list type control. Provide a command button, toolbar button, or menu selection for users to indicate that they are finished setting criteria. If the pick lists are based on fairly static data, such as order types, lists of valid codes, or processing status codes, this data should be downloaded to the client at startup. For more volatile data, you should accept the overhead of retrieving it from the server each time the form is opened to ensure that users receive the most current data.

## Using a Dynamic Record Source

You can provide more flexibility by using a modified version of the form/sub-form model presented in the preceding section. Create the SQL for the detail form dynamically, based on the values filled in on the unbound main form. This eliminates the need for hidden fields for criteria and helps ensure that the most efficient SQL can be used for each alternative set of criteria. You must use dynamic SQL (instead of a fixed query with parameters) if you are using LIKE in your criteria and appending wildcard characters to the user's selections. If you use fixed criteria, you will end up with a full table scan because the optimizer cannot predict how to use the indexes. You should also use dynamic SQL instead of a fixed query if your table has multiple indexes but your server can use only a single index for each table in a query. By building the SQL based on the fields the user selects, you have the best chance of using the most restrictive index each time.

## Using Unbound Controls in the Header or Footer

On a single form, you can use a variation on the approach just described. Place the unbound controls that are used for criteria entry in the header or footer, and at runtime either filter the form using the ApplyFilter action or reset the form's record source using the form's RecordSource property. This approach has the advantage of using only a single bound form, but it offers fewer user interface design alternatives because the header and footer must always appear at a specific location.

## Using FindFirst

One approach to record navigation and searching that works much better in client-server than in native Access is the FindFirst method. In Access this method always results in a scan, but with servers, Jet will often use a new query, and the server can process an efficient search. You can take advantage of this by placing your search criteria in the header or footer area of a form and using FindFirst to move the detail section to the desired data.

# Building Reports

Reports often cause problems for client-server work in Access. Access has a powerful reporting module that offers many data-analysis tools. Most of these tools assume that the data with which they are working is local and that retrieving the data multiple times will not cause unacceptable overhead.

You may find that the easiest solution is to split your report processing into two parts. First, set up a query that extracts all the required data from your server. While building this query, do not worry about obtaining totals, grouping, or other reporting requirements. After you have isolated the data for the report, build the query or queries used by the report based on the server query. When you need to run multiple reports from a single data source, you should download the data into local Access tables and base the reports on these temporary tables.

Exceptions to this general approach are:

- Generating a summary report from a very large database

- Generating a report using statistics (such as median) that are supported by your server directly but are not supported in Access

## Effects of Grouping and Sorting

Access cannot send multiple-field GROUP BYs directly to servers. If you do not download the data into an Access table with indexes that support the GROUP BYs, the recordset is sorted on the client machine. The grouping and sorting in the report design will override the grouping and sorting in a query, so do not use grouping and sorting in the query when you are grouping and sorting data within the report.

### Selecting Data Sources for Fields

Because reports represent a read-only snapshot of a database, you will find more cases in which downloaded data can be used than for forms. Applying all formatting on the report fields instead of the query fields also helps with query optimization.

### Creating Header and Footer Fields and Expressions

You should try to base the summary fields in your headers and footers on fields from the Detail sections of your reports, instead of on expressions against the tables.

### Graphs

When including graphs in a report, you must pay close attention to the data source and the location of the OLE server. You usually use a separate record source for each chart on a report. Make sure the record source is restricted to exactly what should be graphed. Do not use the query to add formatting or titles or to provide anything other than the raw data for the graph. Provide all legends, titles, and formatting by means of Automation. Allowing the server to do what it does best—provide data from its tables—should keep your reports working smoothly.

# Common Client-Server Migration Problems

It's likely you will encounter problems when moving existing file-server applications to a client-server environment. While much of this chapter has provided useful information for this process, the following sections offer additional troubleshooting assistance.

### Nonupdatable Queries

One of the first problems you may run into is that some queries (or views) that are updatable in Access will be read only on your server. In these cases, Jet processes the join operation locally and manages the retrievals and updates to the server's tables on the client side. This is not as efficient as handling the updates solely on the server, and it may also introduce increased contention problems, depending on how Access and your server define the transactions for these updates. You may want to consider redesigning your system to avoid doing updates on joined data. Typically, as long as your network is well designed, the server will be fast enough to allow the split in updating that Jet produces. The major problem comes with the increased network load that sometimes occurs with this type of system.

## Converting Validation Rules

Validation rules are another area that requires special consideration during migration. If your server supports triggers and stored procedures, you should be able to convert most Access rules to server-based triggers. If you do this, you will need to add in your own error handling to replace the validation text and error trapping you had in your native Access application. You will also need to test your specific server to determine the error processing related to stored procedures and triggers. Take extra care when converting table-level validation rules and validation rules that use Access functions. Most servers will not have the same set of predefined functions as Access, so you may need to have stored procedures written to replace them. In some cases, you may need to do the validation locally in VBA before the data is sent to the server.

## User-Defined Functions

Any queries that make use of user-defined functions or built-in Access functions also require special attention. Since the server will not support them, Jet returns them to your application to perform locally. This may not be too much of a problem if the functions are only on the final output, because they will be applied only as the data is sent from the server to the client. You will experience severe performance problems, however, if they are part of query criteria, ORDER BY, GROUP BY, or aggregate expressions. If you have any of these cases, consider converting the functions to stored procedures on the server. You could also split your query to allow the server processing that doesn't involve the Access function to occur in one server query, returning a recordset that is then processed locally.

## Counter, OLE, and Memo Fields

The presence of counter fields in your database requires the use of a stored procedure or special field datatype on many servers to provide a similar function. Most servers now support equivalents of OLE and memo fields, but if you use either of these, make sure you understand exactly *how* the server supports them.

## Combo and List Boxes

Combo and list boxes that reference large numbers of server rows will be a problem. You'll get much better performance if you either cache the data locally or use appropriate criteria to restrict the list to a small number of entries.

# Looking in on Jet and ODBC

To some extent, the interaction between Jet and ODBC is a black box. When you run queries against linked ODBC tables, you really have no control over how Jet retrieves or updates the data. This makes it difficult to troubleshoot problems involving Jet and ODBC and to make informed decisions regarding when to use features such as SQL pass-through or ODBCDirect. Fortunately, there may be a solution. Some database server vendors supply software that allows you to examine the actual SQL statements being sent to the server. While we can't cover every database server, in this section we'll look at using the SQL Profiler tool that ships with Microsoft SQL Server 7.

---

**NOTE**    SQL Server 6.5 shipped with an analogous tool called SQL Trace. While the user interface differs from SQL Profiler, the concepts are similar and you should be able use the techniques we describe in this section. Prior to SQL Server 6.5, SQL tracing was possible through the use of a third-party program called SQLEye. This program may still be available through Microsoft's TechNet program. To locate the utility go to the TechNet Web site at `http://www.microsoft.com/technet` and search for SQLEye.

---

## Running SQL Profiler

SQL Profiler is one of the utilities you can install as part of the SQL Server package; it appears as an icon in your program group or Start menu. When you start SQL Profiler for the first time, you are prompted to define a *trace.* (You can also create new traces whenever you want by selecting File ≻ New ≻ Trace from the menus.) Traces tell SQL Profiler what to monitor—for example, which servers, processes, and activities. Figure 3.8 shows the Trace Properties dialog box. You can also access this dialog box at any time by selecting File ≻ New ≻ Trace.

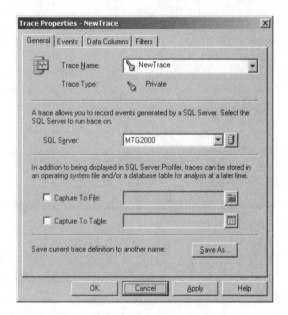

**FIGURE 3.8**
Defining a SQL Profiler trace to monitor statements sent to the server

You must give the trace a name that is unique among all other defined traces. You can optionally select individual logins, applications, or hosts to monitor. For example, you could define a trace to include only those statements sent from the application "Microsoft Access."

For the purposes of this chapter we'll ignore the advanced options found on the dialog box's Events, Data Columns, and Filters tabs. Consult the SQL Server 7 documentation for information on these options. If you'd like to test SQL Profiler with the sample database, and you're not monitoring a busy production server, simply enter a trace name and click the OK button.

Once you've defined at least one trace, you can begin monitoring activity. SQL Profiler will update its display with any active connections. You can define and use additional traces as you deem necessary.

## Monitoring Jet and ODBC Interaction

As you execute queries (or anything involving the server you're monitoring, for that matter), SQL Profiler displays the actual statements being sent to the server. If you're using linked ODBC tables, these statements will be the translated SQL coming from the SQL Server ODBC driver. In the case of pass-through queries or ODBCDirect, these will be statements you've defined yourself.

When you begin using SQL Profiler, you will find it enlightening just to watch the statements generated by Jet and the ODBC driver as you perform tasks such as linking to tables, running queries, and modifying data. Figure 3.9 shows the statements generated by opening the frmMenu form in the sample database immediately after opening the database itself.

**FIGURE 3.9**

Tracing commands sent to SQL Server using SQL Profiler

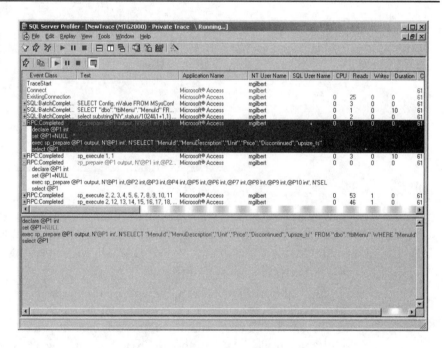

Each of the statements is described briefly here:

1.  Access logs on to SQL Server.

2.  Jet attempts to query the MsysConf table (if it exists).

3.  Jet queries the tblMenu table for the primary key values.

4.  Jet queries the sysDatabases table to determine whether the database is read only.

5.  The ODBC driver creates a stored procedure to retrieve additional records from the table.

6.  Jet calls this stored procedure to cache records for display.

7.  The ODBC driver creates a stored procedure to perform update overwrite validation.

8.  Jet calls this stored procedure twice to place values on the form.

What you don't see in Figure 3.9 is the data being returned to Access. You'll have to infer this from the SQL statements. For example, the statement requesting the primary key values might not make much of an impact with a 20-row table, but what if the table had a million records!

## Troubleshooting Poor Performance

Using tools like SQL Profiler, you can troubleshoot parts of your application that perform poorly after moving to client-server. For instance, suppose you use a delete query to remove rows from a table on the server. After migrating the data to SQL Server, you find that this query all of a sudden takes a very long time to execute. By using SQL Profiler you'd notice that when you run a delete query against a linked ODBC table, Jet issues a DELETE statement for *each row in the table!* It does this to ensure that you delete only records that haven't changed since you created the result set. Armed with this knowledge, you could then replace the standard query with a SQL pass-through query that issued a single DELETE statement. As you become more familiar with how Jet and ODBC interact, you'll be able to spot instances where converting to SQL pass-through or ODBCDirect make sense.

# Summary

In this chapter we have covered the basics of implementing a client-server system using Access. We introduced the major areas to consider when planning a client-server system or planning a migration to client-server. More specifically, we covered these issues:

- Understanding the mechanics of ODBC processing
- Choosing a query strategy for client-server applications
- Configuring Access for ODBC
- Mapping your transactions in client-server systems
- Taking advantage of Access' strengths in creating client-server applications
- Choosing the best form and control design for efficient processing
- Building efficient reports
- Identifying problem areas when migrating an application to client-server

# Creating SQL Server Databases

- SQL Server and MSDE

- Connecting to SQL Server databases

- Creating SQL Server databases

- Upsizing Access databases

- Creating tables and indexes

- Creating views

- Creating database diagrams

- Managing SQL Server databases from Access

**N**ow that you understand the basics of client-server databases, it's time to investigate the way that Access implements these basics. The vehicle for client-server databases in Access 2000 is, for the most part, the *Access project*, or *ADP file*. Chapter 3 discussed general client-server design principles that can be applied to any server database, but the remainder of the book will focus on using ADP files to connect an Access 2000 client to a Microsoft SQL Server database. Access projects use what looks like the familiar Access user interface atop the Microsoft SQL Server database engine, combining ease of use with powerful storage capabilities and true client-server computing.

However, you shouldn't be fooled by the superficial resemblance of Access projects to traditional Access databases. Access projects include a new set of designers for SQL Server objects and change some of the existing designers. In this and the following chapters, you'll learn how to use these new designers productively. But let's start at the start: how do you create an Access project that uses SQL Server data of your choice?

# SQL Server Versions

Access projects, as you already know, allow you to use the Access user interface to view and manipulate data that's stored by the Microsoft SQL Server database engine. Access projects also support creating and modifying SQL Server objects like tables, views, and stored procedures, right from within the Access 2000 user interface. It turns out that there are multiple products that use this database engine. In fact, there are (in the current version, SQL Server 7.0) four distinct versions of SQL Server:

- SQL Server Enterprise Edition
- SQL Server Standard Edition
- SQL Server Desktop Edition
- Microsoft Database Engine (MSDE)

In order to choose the best storage engine for your Access project data, you should understand the major differences between these four versions of SQL Server.

**NOTE** Access projects can also use SQL Server 6.5 for data storage. The SQL Server needs to be updated with Service Pack 5. There's no Desktop or MSDE version of SQL Server 6.5. For the most part, projects based on SQL Server 6.5 behave exactly the same as those based on SQL Server 7.0. We'll use SQL Server 7.0 databases for all of our examples, because that's the version that supplies the MSDE that ships with Office.

## SQL Server Enterprise Edition

SQL Server Enterprise Edition is the most powerful version of Microsoft SQL Server currently available. SQL Server Enterprise Edition can only be installed on Windows NT Server Enterprise Edition. It delivers a number of high-end features not present in other versions of SQL Server:

- Failover clustering

- Partitioned OLAP Services

- Support for up to 32 processors

- Support for up to 64 gigabytes of RAM

## SQL Server Standard Edition

This is the "regular" version of SQL Server. It can only be installed on Windows NT Server (*not* Windows NT Workstation or Windows 9x). It supports up to four processors.

If you read something about SQL Server 7.0 without mention of a particular edition, then the writer is probably referring to the Standard Edition. SQL Server ships with Microsoft OLAP Server (for storing and querying multidimensional data) and Microsoft English Query (for natural language query resolution).

## SQL Server Desktop Edition

SQL Server Desktop Edition is intended to be a single-user version of SQL Server. It includes all of the tools that are present in the regular edition (but not optional components such as Microsoft OLAP Server or Microsoft English Query), and can be installed on Windows 95, Windows 98, or Windows NT Workstation (as well as Windows NT Server). You're legally entitled to install SQL Server Desktop Edition on any computer that has a proper SQL Server client access license. This makes SQL Server Desktop ideal for supporting mobile applications that use merge replication and conflict resolution to remain synchronized with a master SQL Server database.

SQL Server Desktop can utilize up to two processors. This edition is optimized for five or fewer users. If you expect more than five simultaneous users of the database, Microsoft recommends upgrading to either the Standard or the Enterprise Edition.

If you install SQL Server Desktop on Windows 95 or Windows 98, some features are disabled (because they don't work on non-Windows NT operating systems). These features include:

- Named pipes connectivity

- Integrated security

- Asynchronous I/O

- Transaction-based publishing

- Clustering

- Full text search

- Multiprocessor support

---

**NOTE**    To install any version of SQL Server on Windows 95, you must first install DCOM for Windows 95. You can install this manually by running the DCOM95.EXE program located in the x86\OTHER subdirectory on the SQL Server 7.0 CD-ROM.

---

## MSDE

While Microsoft has been careful not to refer to the Microsoft Data Engine (MSDE) as a version of SQL Server (for legal reasons) MSDE is essentially SQL Server Desktop without some of the management tools (see the "SQL Server Tools" sidebar later in this chapter for more information). MSDE is compiled from the same source tree as full SQL Server and is described by Microsoft as "a SQL Server-compatible database engine." It's designed to provide a zero-maintenance version of SQL Server that runs on Windows NT, Windows 95, or Windows 98. It has the same limitations as SQL Server Desktop as well as some additional limitations:

- Maximum database size of 2 gigabytes in a single database file (other versions of SQL Server support databases up to one million terabytes), although you can have multiple database files on a single computer

- Supports two processors

- Can only be a replication subscriber, not a publisher

- Cannot participate in transactions distributed across multiple servers.

MSDE is shipped with all versions of Microsoft Office 2000 as well as the stand-alone Access 2000 product, although it's not integrated into the setup program. To install MSDE, run the SETUPSQL.EXE program found in the \SQL\X86\Setup folder on the installation CD-ROM.

**WARNING**    Although the MSDE setup program does not force a reboot when it's done, you must reboot your computer to enable full MSDE and Access project functionality, unless you install it on Windows NT.

Because MSDE is a version of SQL Server, it can be updated by applying the SQL Server service packs. As of this writing, Microsoft recommends that SQL Server 7.0 Service Pack 1 be applied to all MSDE installations.

**TIP**    You can download SQL Server service packs from the SQL Server Support Web site at `http://support.microsoft.com/support/sql/content/spack.asp`.

# SQL Server Tools

The full versions of SQL Server include a number of tools that are not shipped with MSDE. These tools are:

**Books Online**    Provides complete documentation for SQL Server.

**Enterprise Manager**    A Microsoft Management Console snap-in that allows you to manage all objects within SQL Server databases throughout your enterprise.

**MSDTC Administrative Console**    Controls the Microsoft Distributed Transaction Coordinator.

**Performance Monitor**    Adds additional PerfMon counters so that SQL Server can be monitored on Windows NT.

**Profiler**    Allows the collection of traffic data to and from your SQL Server for later analysis.

**Query Analyzer**    Provides a graphical interface for submitting Transact-SQL queries and viewing their results.

In addition, the full version of SQL Server includes several optional components that are not available with MSDE

**English Query**    Supports natural language queries.

**OLAP Services**    Provides data warehousing services.

If your organization uses SQL Server Standard Edition and your computer is licensed to connect to that server, it's perfectly legal for you to install the utilities from SQL Server Desktop Edition on your computer, even if you use MSDE for your local SQL Server database engine. If this option is available to you, we recommend that you make use of it in order to obtain your own copies of the very useful Enterprise Manager, Profiler, and Query Analyzer applications. Using those applications is beyond the scope of this book, but they're well covered in other books such as *SQL Server 7 In Record Time*, by Mike Gunderloy and Mary Chipman (Sybex, 1999).

# Creating Access Projects

In order to use an Access project, you need to hook up the Access user interface to a SQL Server data source. There are three ways you can do this:

- You can create a new Access project and connect it to an existing SQL Server database.

- You can use the Microsoft SQL Server Database Wizard to create a new Access project based on a brand new SQL Server database.

- You can use the Upsizing Wizard to create a new Access project from an existing Access database, converting the data from Jet to SQL Server in the process.

In this section we'll briefly cover each of these alternatives.

## Connecting to an Existing SQL Server Database

To connect to an existing SQL Server database, choose File ➢ New from the Access menus and then select Project (Existing Database) from the General tab in the New dialog box. This will open the File New Database dialog box, where you assign a filename to the new Access project. This is just like creating a new Jet database, although the default file extension is .ADP and the file created is *not* a Jet database.

Next, Access will open the Data Link Properties dialog box, shown in Figure 4.1.

**FIGURE 4.1**
The Data Link Properties
dialog box

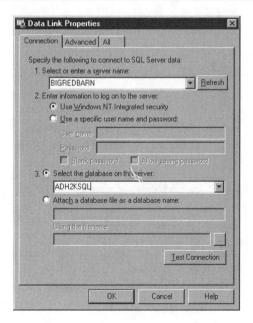

If you've seen the Data Link Properties dialog box in other contexts (for example, when working with the Visual Basic Data Environment), you'll notice that the Providers tab is missing from this instance of the dialog box. That's because Access projects require the Microsoft Data Shape OLE DB Provider, using the Microsoft SQL Server OLE DB Provider as the Data Provider. There's no point to even trying to connect to any other data source. They simply won't work.

You must supply three pieces of information to connect an Access project to an existing SQL Server database. First, you need to supply the name of the server. This is normally the network name of the computer on which SQL Server is running. The special name "(local)" can be used to refer to an instance of SQL Server or MSDE running on the same computer as Access 2000 itself. Second, you need to supply security information. This can take the form of a SQL Server username and password, or you can choose to use Windows NT integrated security, in which case your logon identity is used to access SQL Server.

**TIP**    If you're in doubt as to what security information to supply, consult your database administrator. If you installed MSDE in its default mode, use integrated security.

Finally, you need to supply the name of a SQL Server database or database file that the Access project will use to store data. This database will supply all of the data-bearing objects (tables, views, database diagrams, and stored procedures) for your new Access project. If you've supplied appropriate security credentials, you can browse the databases on the server using the drop-down list.

**TIP**    Click the Test Connection button to ensure that your connection is configured properly before attempting to browse databases or committing your changes.

**TIP**    At any time, you can inspect the Data Link Properties dialog box by choosing File ➢ Connection from the Access menus.

Provided that the information you supplied is correct, Access will connect to the server, query the system catalog for object information, and display a list of SQL Server objects in the familiar database window.

**NOTE**    The Advanced and All tabs of the dialog box let you specify individual OLE DB options. Covering each of the options is beyond the scope of this book. A good source of information on the other options provided by OLE DB is the Microsoft Developer Network Library site on the Web (`http://msdn.microsoft.com/library/`).

## The Microsoft SQL Server Database Wizard

The second way to create an Access project is to create a new SQL Server database at the same time that you create the Access project. To do this, you use the Microsoft SQL Server Database Wizard. To start, choose File ➤ New from the Access menus and then select Project (New Database) from the General tab in the New dialog box. This will open the File New Database dialog box, where you assign a filename to the new Access project (just as with existing SQL Server databases).

Next, the Microsoft SQL Server Database Wizard launches. This wizard, shown in Figure 4.2, has only two screens.

**NOTE**    If you did not install the client-server tools when you installed Access, you may be prompted to insert your CD by the Windows Installer.

**FIGURE 4.2**
The Microsoft SQL Server Database Wizard

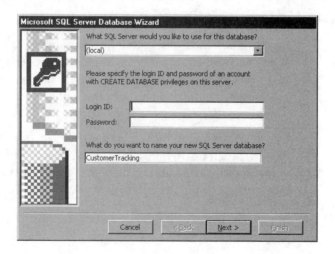

On the first screen of the Microsoft SQL Server Database Wizard, you specify the SQL Server where you want to create the database, supply a login ID and password, and assign a name to the database. On the second screen, you need only click the Finish button. The wizard doesn't need any other information to create the database.

**TIP**
Although it's not explicitly stated on the wizard interface, supplying a SQL Server username and password is optional if you're running Windows NT. If you leave these settings blank, the wizard will create your new database using Windows NT integrated security.

The new database is created with a default size of 2 megabytes, with a 2-megabyte transaction log. Both the database and the transaction log files are saved in the same folder as the master database for the server, and both are set to automatically grow by 10% whenever they become full and will grow repeatedly as long as you have enough disk space.

**NOTE**
If you're not happy with the default settings applied by the wizard, consider using SQL Server Enterprise Manager to create the new database first, then create a new Access project based on the new, existing database.

## The Upsizing Wizard

Finally, if you have an existing Access database that you'd like to migrate to an Access project, you can use the Microsoft Access Upsizing Wizard to create both the project and the underlying SQL Server database. While it's far from perfect, the Upsizing Wizard will do most of the routine work involved in moving data from your Access database to an Access project.

As you'll see in this section, though, the Upsizing Wizard is not a magical tool. It does the best it can to translate an Access database (using the Jet engine) into an Access project (using the SQL Server engine). Then it gives you a report on what it's done and leaves the scene. It's up to you to test, and probably fix, your application.

## Using the Upsizing Wizard

Although the Upsizing Wizard has been available since Access 2.0, it's always been an add-in that you could download from the Internet and install after you installed the project. Access 2000 is the first version where the Upsizing Wizard is built into the main product. Because it wasn't previously part of the product, you may never have seen the Upsizing Wizard in action. First, we'll walk through the typical steps of converting an Access database to an Access project using the Upsizing Wizard. Then, we'll look at what might go wrong in the process.

To use the Upsizing Wizard, open your existing Access database and then choose Tools ➤ Database Utilities ➤ Upsizing Wizard from the Access menus. This will open the first screen of the Upsizing Wizard (Figure 4.3). Your first choice is whether to create a new database or use an existing SQL Server database to hold your data. In almost all cases, you should choose to create a new database. This will help ensure that the Upsizing Wizard doesn't accidentally harm existing data.

**FIGURE 4.3**

Choosing database options from the Upsizing Wizard

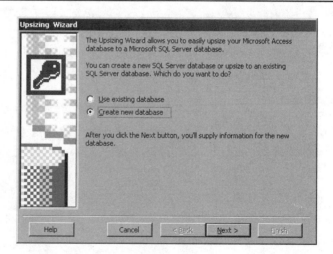

The second screen of the Upsizing Wizard (Figure 4.4) allows you to choose a server, name the new SQL Server database, and provide login information. As with the SQL Server Database Wizard, if you want to use integrated security, you don't need to supply a login ID or password. If you're using the default local installation of MSDE for your SQL Server, integrated security is automatically enabled.

FIGURE 4.4
Selecting server and
database names

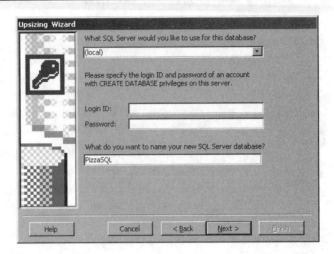

The third screen of the Upsizing Wizard (Figure 4.5) allows you to select the tables to be moved from the existing Access database to the new SQL Server database. Generally, you should select all of the tables in your Access database to avoid any potential problems with upsizing other objects (such as queries or forms that depend on a particular table).

FIGURE 4.5
Choosing which tables
to upsize

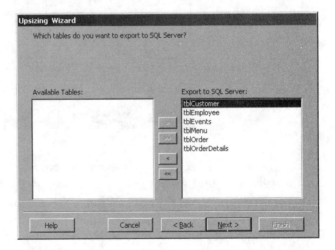

**TIP**  The list of available tables respects the settings for hidden and system objects that you've made for the Database container within Access. So if you don't see the tables you want to upsize, be sure to select Show Hidden Objects from the Access Options dialog box before running the wizard.

The fourth screen of the Upsizing Wizard (Figure 4.6) allows you to choose which table attributes to upsize. The table attributes you can upsize are:

**Indexes**    Creates SQL Server indexes to match the existing Access indexes. Because Access creates hidden indexes when you relate two tables, it may appear that there are more indexes in the SQL Server database than there were in the Access database.

**Validation Rules**    Attempts to translate existing validation rules to constraints on the SQL Server table.

**Defaults**    Attempts to translate existing defaults to constraints on the SQL Server table.

**Table Relationships**    Creates relationships in the SQL Server database to match the existing relationships in the Access database. If you choose Use DRI, the SQL Server relationships are implemented with PRIMARY KEY and FOREIGN KEY constraints. If you choose Use Triggers, the SQL Server relationships are implemented with Transact-SQL code in triggers. Generally, you should choose to use triggers, since DRI is not compatible with cascading updates or deletes.

In addition, there are two other options that indicate which data options you want to include:

**Add Timestamp Fields to Tables**    If the Upsizing Wizard can't find a unique key for a table, it will add a timestamp field to the table to make it possible to update the table after it's upsized. The wizard will normally make the correct decision if you leave this option set to "Yes, let wizard decide."

**Only Create the Table Structure...**    This option can be useful if you just want a quick test of problems in upsizing your database. Generally, you want to leave this box unchecked.

**FIGURE 4.6**
Selecting options for tables
created in SQL Server

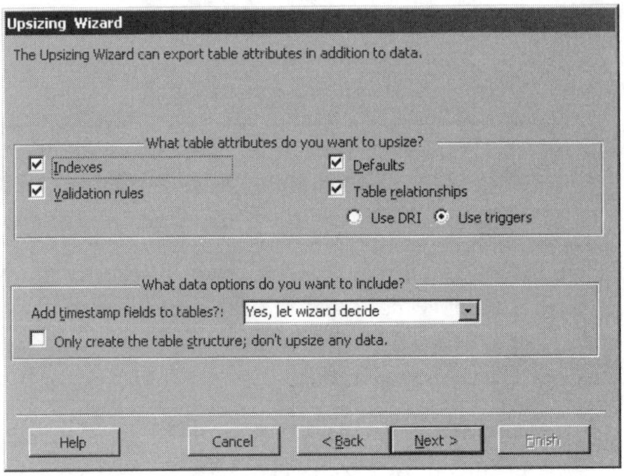

The fifth screen of the Upsizing Wizard (Figure 4.7) allows you to choose which application changes the wizard should make:

**No Application Changes**    This option creates a SQL Server database to match your Access database, but does not create an Access project.

**Link SQL Server Tables to Existing Application**    This option creates a SQL Server database and links the tables to the existing Access database.

**Create a New Access Client/Server Application**    This option creates a SQL Server database and then uses it to build a new Access project. Existing Access objects are moved to the new Access project. If you're using the Upsizing Wizard to transfer an Access database to an Access project, this is the option you should choose.

**ADP File Name**    This is the name to be used for the new Access project.

**Save Password and User ID**    If you check this box, the login ID and password you chose on the second screen of the wizard will be saved in the Access project's connection string. This makes it easier to open the new Access project, but does not protect the data from prying eyes.

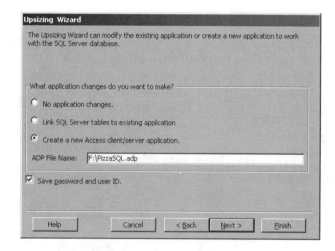

After making these selections, you can click Finish to begin the upsizing process. Assuming you're using the Upsizing Wizard to create an Access project from an Access database, the Upsizing Wizard will:

- Create a new SQL Server database.

- Transfer tables, the attributes you selected, and the data the tables contain to the new SQL Server database.

- Create a new Access project using the new SQL Server database.

- Create views and stored procedures in the SQL Server database that have the same names as the queries in the Access database, and translate the Jet SQL to Transact SQL. In some cases, one query in the Access database may give rise to both a view and a stored procedure in the SQL Server database.

- Copy the forms and reports from the Access database to the Access project. In some cases, the RecordSource, ControlSource, and RowSource properties of forms, reports, and controls may be modified to translate Jet SQL into Transact SQL.

- Create new data access pages that function the same as the existing data access pages, but that use data from the SQL Server database instead of the Jet database.

- Copy all macros and modules from the Access database to the Access project without making any changes to these objects.

When the Upsizing Wizard finishes its work, it will display an Upsizing Wizard report like the one shown in Figure 4.8. This report will tell you exactly what it did and, more importantly, what objects it was unable to upsize. When you close the report, your new Access project will be opened in place of the existing database.

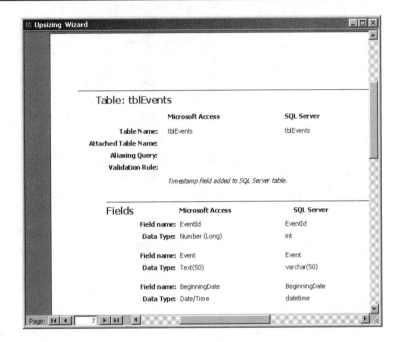

**FIGURE 4.8**
The Upsizing Wizard report shows what the wizard did to create the SQL Server database.

**TIP**  The report automatically saves itself as a snapshot in the same directory as the original database, so you can reopen it later.

Sounds easy, right? Well, as you'll see in the next section, there are many things that can go wrong with upsizing a database.

## Upsizing Wizard Problems and Solutions

There are a number of things that you need to be aware of in order to upsize successfully. In this section, we'll review the most important of these traps for the unwary.

You need to be aware of Access security before you attempt to upsize a database. In particular:

- You must have Read Design permissions on all objects that you want to upsize, and you must have Read Data permissions on tables if you want to move their data.

- You must know the VBA password and be prepared to supply it if your VBA project is password protected.

- You can't convert an MDE database to an Access project with the Upsizing Wizard. The Upsizing Wizard requires the original VBA in your Access database to do its job of checking for recordsource changes. You need to start with an MDB, not with the converted MDE database.

Some features of your Access database simply won't be transferred to your new Access project. These include:

- Input masks.

- Some validation rules and default values. The Upsizing Wizard attempts to translate such properties from Jet to SQL Server syntax, but if it fails, the property won't be upsized. You should inspect the design of every single table you upsize to make sure validation rules and default values were upsized.

- The Allow Zero Length property (you can create a CHECK constraint in your new SQL Server database to mimic the functionality of this property).

- Hyperlink fields will be upsized to text, but will no longer function as hyperlinks.

You'll also find that the Upsizing Wizard's ability to upsize queries is spotty in this version, to say the least. This is the first version of Access where the Upsizing Wizard has attempted this difficult task, and it's definitely version 1.0 technology. You should inspect the upsizing report carefully to determine which queries were upsized and which queries failed to upsize. Fortunately, the upsizing report includes the SQL text that the Upsizing Wizard generated, even for failed queries, and you can often modify this text to create a proper stored procedure or view in your SQL Server database.

Some specific query issues to consider:

- Crosstab queries won't be upsized.

- Action queries that take parameters won't be upsized.

- Action queries based on other queries won't be upsized.

- SQL pass-through and SQL DDL queries won't be upsized.

- If a query fails to upsize, all queries based on that query, directly or indirectly, will also fail to upsize.

Because forms, reports, combo boxes, and list boxes can all be based on queries, you'll find that they have the same upsizing problems that queries have.

---

**TIP**    You will have more success upsizing objects if you make sure that all fields referenced in RecordSource and RowSource properties are fully qualified, that is, that they are referred to with the full [TableName].[FieldName] syntax.

---

Finally, you need to inspect all of your upsized modules carefully. Remember, in an Access project the Jet engine, and hence DAO, is not loaded. Any code you've upsized that relies on Data Access Objects won't work in the new Access project. You'll need to manually convert all of your DAO code to use ADO instead or add DAO as an explicit reference, though we don't recommend the latter.

So, with all these problems, is it worth running the Upsizing Wizard? Generally, we think it is, because it does handle data upsizing very well, and will at least make a start on other objects. But there's no substitute for thorough testing of any upsized application.

## The Import and Export Utility

If you've installed MSDE on your system, you have another alternative for moving data from an Access database to a SQL Server database. This is the SQL Server

Data Transformation Services Wizard, which you can launch from Programs ➤ MSDE ➤ Import and Export Data. Data Transformation Services (DTS) is SQL Server's native interface for translating tables from one database to another.

To use DTS to move data from an existing Access database to a new Access project, follow these steps:

1. Create a new Access project using the Microsoft SQL Server Database Wizard (as discussed earlier in this chapter). This will put in place the Access project front-end and a blank SQL Server database to use as the back end.

2. Launch the DTS wizard.

3. On the Choose a Data Source screen, select your existing Access database, as shown in Figure 4.9. You don't need to supply a username or password unless the database is secured.

**FIGURE 4.9**
Selecting the data source for imported data

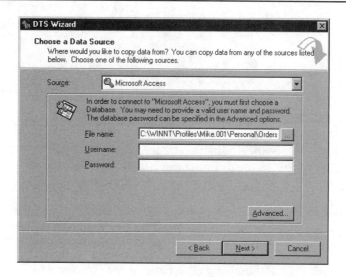

4. On the Choose a Destination screen, select the OLE DB Provider for SQL Server, provide login information for your SQL Server, and choose a destination database. Figure 4.10 shows how this screen might look if you're targeting a database on MSDE. Note the use of the special "(local)" server name and Windows NT authentication.

Generally, you'll choose to copy tables from the source to the destination. However, the DTS Wizard also allows you the option of copying the results of a query. This is useful if your Access database contains some fields that you don't want to transfer to your Access project.

**FIGURE 4.10**

Selecting the data destination for imported data

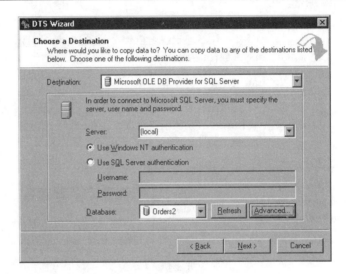

5. On the next screen, you can choose the tables to transfer, specify names for the destination tables, and optionally choose to create a transform for each table. A transform allows you to alter field properties, specify target data types, or even write a VBScript program to alter the data as it's copied.

6. Next, you can choose whether to run or save the DTS package. If you're using this tool to set up a new Access project on your local machine, you should generally choose to run the package immediately.

7. When you click Finish, the DTS Wizard will transfer the selected tables, keeping you notified as to its progress. Figure 4.11 shows the progress dialog box from the DTS Wizard. As you can see, it keeps track of the number of records moved in each table.

When you're done with the wizard, close and re-open your Access project to see the new tables that have been created for you.

While the DTS Wizard is a useful tool for transferring data, it won't do as much work for you as the Upsizing Wizard. In particular, it won't transfer indexes or relationships between tables. You can use the Access project table designer and database diagram designer to re-create indexes and relationships in your new Access project.

**FIGURE 4.11**
DTS Wizard progress
dialog box

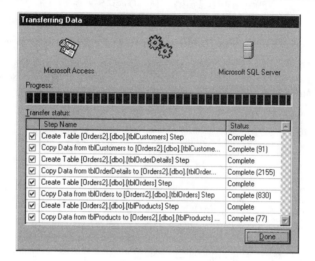

# Creating Tables and Indexes

No matter how you create your Access project, you'll find that it contains a slightly different list of objects than you might be used to from Jet databases. The Database container in an Access project includes nine types of objects. Tables, views, database diagrams, and stored procedures are stored in the SQL Server database. Forms, reports, pages, macros and modules are stored in the Access project.

In the remaining sections of this chapter, we'll introduce you to tables, views and database diagrams. Chapter 5 covers the use of stored procedures. Forms and reports are discussed in Chapter 7. Data pages are the subject of Chapters 10 and 11, while modules are discussed in Chapter 6 and elsewhere.

But for any of these objects to be useful, you need data, and data is always stored in tables. So, let's begin at the beginning, with the table designer.

# Using the Table Designer

The first time you open a table in design view in an Access project, you might get a bit of a shock from how it looks, as shown in Figure 4.12. On the other hand, your shock might be one of recognition. Access projects use the Visual Data Tools designers. These same designers are shared by the Visual Basic DataView and by Visual Studio Data Projects, so if you've worked with data in those environments, the Access project table designer will be familiar.

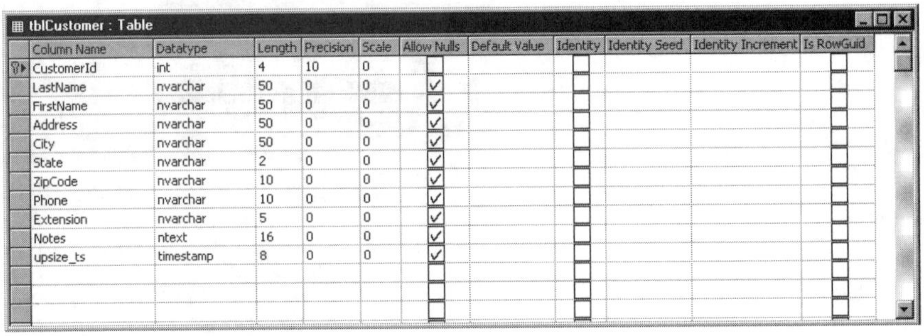

**FIGURE 4.12**
Designing a table in an Access project

| Column Name | Datatype | Length | Precision | Scale | Allow Nulls | Default Value | Identity | Identity Seed | Identity Increment | Is RowGuid |
|---|---|---|---|---|---|---|---|---|---|---|
| CustomerId | int | 4 | 10 | 0 | | | | | | |
| LastName | nvarchar | 50 | 0 | 0 | ✓ | | | | | |
| FirstName | nvarchar | 50 | 0 | 0 | ✓ | | | | | |
| Address | nvarchar | 50 | 0 | 0 | ✓ | | | | | |
| City | nvarchar | 50 | 0 | 0 | ✓ | | | | | |
| State | nvarchar | 2 | 0 | 0 | ✓ | | | | | |
| ZipCode | nvarchar | 10 | 0 | 0 | ✓ | | | | | |
| Phone | nvarchar | 10 | 0 | 0 | ✓ | | | | | |
| Extension | nvarchar | 5 | 0 | 0 | ✓ | | | | | |
| Notes | ntext | 16 | 0 | 0 | ✓ | | | | | |
| upsize_ts | timestamp | 8 | 0 | 0 | ✓ | | | | | |

**NOTE**   While other environments use the Visual Data Tools designers for any sort of data, in Access projects their use is limited to SQL Server objects.

Rather than the two-pane design of the Access database table designer, this designer uses a single pane to show fields (usually called *columns* in a SQL Server database) and their properties. The properties that you can edit in the table designer are:

**Column Name**   Name of the column.

**Datatype**   SQL Server data type to use. (See the next section for an explanation of SQL Server data types.)

**Length**   Number of bytes of storage used for this column.

**Precision**   For numeric columns only, the maximum number of digits that can be stored.

**Scale**   For numeric columns only, the maximum number of digits to the right of the decimal point that can be stored.

**Allow Nulls**    If checked, you can save a row with a null in this column.

**Default Value**    Default value for this field.

**Identity**    If checked, values for this field are automatically generated.

**Identity Seed**    Value assigned to the identity column in the first row of the table.

**Identity Increment**    Difference between successive values of the identity column.

**IsRowGuid**    Identifies a column with the GUID data type that uniquely identifies a row (for replication programming)

Just as with the Access database table designer, you can design entirely new tables with this interface, or alter existing tables. If you've worked with server databases in the past, you'll be pleasantly surprised at the ease with which you can alter existing tables. For example, to change the length of an nvarchar field in a SQL Server database, just highlight the existing length and type the new value. This may not seem like much to a seasoned Access developer, but it used to be extremely difficult to make changes to existing SQL Server table designs.

By right-clicking in the table designer and choosing Properties, you can also alter table-level properties. The operations you can perform from the property sheet include:

- Adding and removing CHECK constraints

- Editing the table's relationships

- Creating and deleting indexes

CHECK constraints fulfill the same purpose that validation rules do in Access. That is, they provide expressions that are checked when new data is entered in a table or when existing data is edited. If all CHECK constraints return True when you attempt to enter or edit data, you're allowed to make the changes. If any of them return False, the changes are rejected.

CHECK constraints follow the same general syntax that validation rules do, although they are required to use SQL Server expressions rather than Jet expressions. For example, this would be a valid CHECK constraint:

```
(Price > 0)
```

As Figure 4.13 shows, you can choose several options when you create a CHECK constraint. You can choose whether or not to check existing data in the table (if any) when you create the constraint. You can also choose whether this constraint should apply during routine insert and update operations, during replication operations, or both.

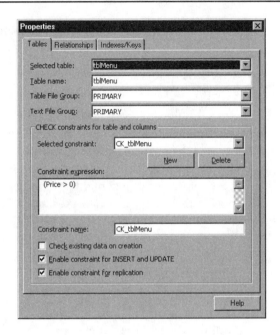

If you like, you can create and edit relationships from the Relationships tab of the table's property sheet. However, you'll probably find it easier to do this within the database diagram designer, discussed later in this chapter.

The third tab in the table property sheet allows you to create indexes and keys for the table. Figure 4.14 shows this tab. Creating indexes in SQL Server table is broadly similar to index creation in a Jet table, but there are some additional options:

**Selected Index** This combo box allows you to choose the index you'd like to work with from all of the indexes on the table.

**New**    Creates a new index.

**Delete**    Deletes the selected index.

**Column Name**    Allows you to choose the column, or combination of columns, to be indexed. SQL Server indexes can contain up to 16 columns, though the total combined size of all the columns in an index cannot exceed 900 bytes.

**Index Name**    Allows you to edit the name of the index

**Index File Group**    Allows you to select a file group where this index will be stored. This is an advanced option allowing you to enhance performance in some cases by keeping an index on a different physical device than the table it refers to. For MSDE operations, you should leave this set to the default PRIMARY.

**Create UNIQUE**    Choose this checkbox to create a unique constraint or a unique index. The options you can select here are:

**Constraint**    Creates a unique constraint, which prevents entering duplicate data.

**Index**    Creates a unique index, which speeds searching and sorting.

**Ignore Duplicate Key**    If you select this option, SQL Server allows inserting duplicate data but does not index the duplicate rows.

**Fill Factor**    Specifies the percent of each index page that can be filled with data. You should probably not alter this option.

**Pad Index**    Tells SQL Server to leave space open between rows in an index page.

**Create as CLUSTERED**    A clustered index is stored in the same physical order as the table and is the fastest index for search operations. A table can have only one clustered index.

**Don't Automatically Recompute Statistics**    Tells SQL Server not to dynamically maintain index statistics. You should leave this box unchecked.

**FIGURE 4.14**
An index in the table
designer

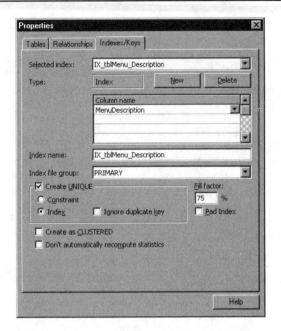

## Understanding SQL Server Data Types

SQL Server data types are similar—but not identical—to Access data types. When you're designing a SQL Server table, you can choose from among these types:

- Binary data (binary, varbinary)

- Large data (text, ntext, image)

- Character data (char, varchar, nchar, nvarchar)

- Date and time data (datetime, smalldatetime)

- Exact numeric data (decimal, numeric)

- Approximate numeric data (float, real)

- Integer numeric data (int, smallint, tinyint)

- Monetary data (money, smallmoney)

- Miscellaneous data (bit, timestamp, uniqueidentifier)

Let's examine each of these data types in turn.

## Binary

Binary data up to 8,000 bytes in length can be stored in either a binary or varbinary field. The difference between the two is in what the length property of the field specifies. For a binary field, the length specifies the *exact* number of bytes that should always be stored. For a varbinary field, the length specifies the *maximum* number of bytes that can be stored. Thus, binary columns are more suited for data that seldom varies in size, while varbinary columns are more suited for data that is of variable length.

However, if the variation is slight, you might be better off using a binary column than a varbinary column. That's because SQL Server can retrieve data more efficiently from a fixed-length column that a variable-length column.

## Large Data

The text, ntext, and image data types can be used to store very large amounts of data. In this respect, they're similar to the Jet memo and OLE Object data types. Like those data types, the data these columns hold is not stored in the actual table rows. Rather, they're stored in data pages, and the table just holds a pointer to the actual data. This is transparent to the user but means that a text or image column only takes up 4 bytes within a table row.

---

**WARNING**   You can't use text or image columns in ORDER BY, COMPUTE, or GROUP BY clauses, in an index, or as a local variable in a stored procedure.

---

A text column can hold from 0 to $2^{31} - 1$ characters of non-Unicode data. An ntext column can hold from 0 to $2^{30} - 1$ characters of Unicode data. An image column can hold from 0 to $2^{31} - 1$ characters of binary data. Note than an ntext column can only hold half as many characters as a text column, because each Unicode character requires 2 bytes of storage.

## Character Data

SQL Server supports four distinct character data types, depending on whether the column should be fixed-width or variable-width, and whether it should accept ANSI or Unicode data:

- char columns accept fixed-width, ANSI data

- varchar columns accept variable-width, ANSI data

- nchar columns accept fixed-width, Unicode data

- nvarchar columns accept variable-width, Unicode data

Of these, nvarchar is the closest to the Access text data type. The char and varchar columns can hold up to 8,000 ANSI characters, while the nchar and nvarchar columns can hold up to 4,000 Unicode characters.

## Date and Time Data

SQL Server supports two different date and time data types: datetime and smalldatetime. Datetime columns take up a total of 8 bytes and have higher precision than smalldatetime columns, which take up 4 bytes each.

A datetime column can accept any date from January 1, 1753 though December 31, 9999, with an accuracy of one three-hundredth of a second. A smalldatetime column can accept any date from January 1, 1900 through June 6, 2079, with an accuracy of one minute.

## Exact Numeric Data

SQL Server appears to support two exact numeric data types: decimal and numeric. However, this is an illusion; both words are really synonyms for the same data type. When creating a decimal column, you must specify both a precision and a scale for the column.

The precision specifies the total number of digits to save, while the scale specifies the number of digits to save to the right of the decimal point. The maximum precision is 38. The scale must be equal to or less than the precision. Within the limits that you define, numbers are stored exactly and are not subject to rounding errors.

Depending on the precision you choose, a decimal column will occupy between 5 and 17 bytes in your table:

- A precision of 1 through 9 occupies 5 bytes.

- A precision of 10 through 19 occupies 9 bytes.

- A precision of 20 through 28 occupies 13 bytes.

- A precision of 29 through 38 occupies 17 bytes.

## Approximate Numeric Data

SQL Server supplies two data types to hold large numeric values that may be rounded: float and real. When you specify a float column, you must specify a precision between 1 and 53. This is the number of bits that SQL Server will use to store the number. With maximum precision, a float column can store numbers to $\pm10^{308}$.

A real column is the same as a float(24) column, storing numbers to $\pm10^{38}$.

Floating-point columns with precision through 24 store seven significant digits and take up 4 bytes. Floating-point columns with precision 25 through 53 store 15 significant digits and take up 8 bytes.

---

**TIP**  Floating-point numbers are useful for representing large values where accuracy is not required. Since the values stored are approximations, you should avoid using floating-point numbers (and use decimal and numeric types instead) if you want to eliminate potential rounding errors.

---

## Integer Data

SQL Server provides three data types for integer data: int, smallint, and tinyint.

- int takes 4 bytes of storage and has a range of whole numbers from $-2\times10^{31}$ through $2\times10^{31}$. This is the equivalent of the Jet long data type.

- smallint takes 2 bytes of storage and has a range of whole numbers from $-32,768$ through $32,767$. This is the equivalent of the Jet integer data type.

- tinyint takes 1 byte of storage and has a range of whole numbers from 0 through 255. This is the equivalent of the Jet byte data type.

---

**TIP**  If this is your first experience with SQL Server, be sure to note that a SQL Server int is the equivalent of a Jet long, not a Jet integer!

---

## Monetary Data

SQL Server provides two data types that hold non-rounded data with both integer and fractional parts, similar to Jet currency fields. These are the money and smallmoney data types.

A money column stores values from $-2^{63}$ to $2^{63}-1$, with up to four digits to the right of the decimal point. It requires 8 bytes of storage. A smallmoney column stores values from –214,748 to 214,748, with up to four digits to the right of the decimal point. It requires 4 bytes of storage. The closest equivalent to the Jet currency data type is the SQL Server money data type.

## Miscellaneous Data

SQL Server supports three specialized data types: bit, timestamp, and uniqueidentifier.

A bit column holds a single bit, set to either 1 or 0. SQL Server will collect multiple bit fields into bytes for more efficient storage.

---

**WARNING**    Although a bit column holds the same amount of information as the Jet Yes/No data type, the range of information differs between the two. Bit columns hold 1 or 0, while Yes/No columns hold –1 or 0.

---

A timestamp column is an auto-incrementing data type that is updated every time the row containing a timestamp column is inserted or updated. The timestamp has nothing to do with the datetime data type or the actual time on your computer clock, but is a monotonically increasing counter whose values are always guaranteed to be unique within a database. A table can only have one timestamp column.

A uniqueidentifier column holds a 16-byte hexadecimal GUID, similar to a Jet Replication ID.

# Understanding Table Limitations

As with any database engine, the SQL Server engine imposes particular limitations on data it stores. Table 4.1 lists the limitations that apply to tables and related objects

**TABLE 4.1:** SQL Server 7.0 Limits

| Feature | Limit |
| --- | --- |
| Column name length | 128 |
| Bytes per character column | 8,000 |
| Bytes per text or image column | 2GB |
| Bytes per index | 900 |
| Bytes per foreign key | 900 |
| Bytes per primary key | 900 |
| Columns per index or key | 16 |
| Foreign keys per table | 253 |
| Bytes per row | 8,060 |
| Columns per table | 1,024 |
| Clustered indexes per table | 1 |
| Nonclustered indexes per table | 249 |
| UNIQUE constraints per table | 250 |
| Tables per database | 2,147,483,647 |
| Bytes per GROUP BY or ORDER BY | 8,060 |
| Columns per SELECT statement | 4,096 |
| Tables per SELECT statement | 256 |
| Columns per INSERT statement | 1,024 |
| Columns per View | 1,024 |

# Creating Views

*Views* in an Access project are nearly the same as queries in an Access database. The primary difference is that views cannot contain an ORDER BY clause.

**TIP** One way to work around the lack of ORDER BY in a view is to create the view without the ORDER BY and then create a stored procedure that draws all of its records from the view and adds the ORDER BY clause. You'll learn about stored procedures in Chapter 5.

## Designing a View

As with tables, you'll find a new designer for views in an Access project (see Figure 4.15). In this section, you'll learn how to work with this new designer that, once again, is part of the Visual Database Tools.

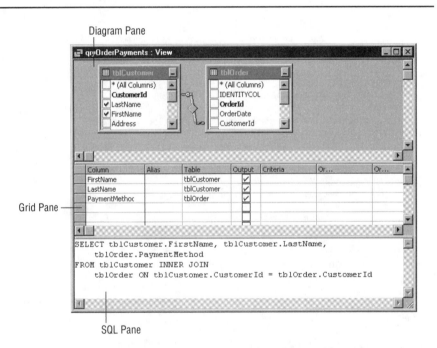

**FIGURE 4.15**
View open in the view designer

The view designer shows you three different views of your query. From top to bottom, these are:

- The Diagram Pane provides a graphical representation of the tables and fields used as the sources of data for your query. Lines show how the tables are joined, and checkmarks show the fields included in the result set of the query.

- The Grid Pane provides a way to further control the fields that are included in the query. You can specify sorting, grouping and searching conditions, the results of action queries, or the names of aliases here.

- The SQL Pane shows you the SQL statement that represents this query in the database. You can verify the syntax of this statement or edit it by hand.

---

**NOTE**    If you've worked with the view designer in other products, you'll have seen a Results Pane integrated into the same window with the design information. The Access designers chose to omit this pane. To see and edit the results of a view in an Access project, you must change to the datasheet for the view.

---

The view designer keeps the information in all three panes synchronized. For example, if you check a new field in the Diagram Pane, it will appear in the Grid and SQL Panes automatically.

## The Diagram Pane

When you open a new view from the Database container, you'll find that you can work with it using only minor variations of the techniques that work in an Access database.

To add a new table to the view, drag the table from the Show Table dialog box (shown in Figure 4.16), which presents a TreeView of all the tables and views in your database, or drag it directly from the Database container. To remove a table, right-click on the table and choose Remove from the pop-up menu, or click the table's title bar and then press Delete.

To add or remove a column from the query's output, check or uncheck the checkbox to the left of the field, as shown in Figure 4.15. In addition to individual columns, you can check the box for "* (All Columns)" to include all of the columns from this table in the result set. Some tables include an additional choice named IDENTITYCOL. This column will include the column with its Identity property set to True from this table in the query's output.

**FIGURE 4.16**
Show Table dialog box

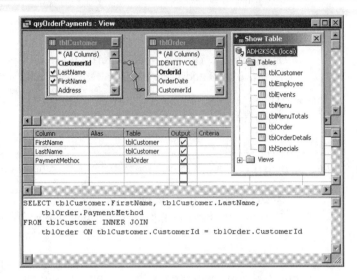

To see the data type of a column, just hover the cursor over that column name in the Diagram Pane, and the information will appear in a data tip.

If your view includes multiple tables, you'll almost certainly want to specify a join between the tables. If the database includes referential integrity information (PRIMARY KEY and FOREIGN KEY constraints), the view designer will automatically include these joins when you drop related tables. Otherwise, you can create joins by dragging a column from the many-side table and dropping it on the corresponding one-side column. The view designer also makes it easy to create non-equijoins and outer joins. To create a join other than an equijoin, first create the equijoin and then right-click on the join line and choose Properties. This will open the Properties dialog box shown in Figure 4.17.

To create a non-equijoin, select a different join criterion from the combo box. To create an outer join, select one of the two checkboxes in the Include Rows section of the dialog box. In either case, the view designer will alter the appearance of the graphic on the join line so you can determine the type of join without looking at the join properties.

FIGURE 4.17
Editing join properties

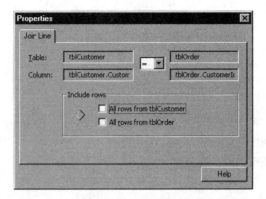

If there's a criterion set on a field, you can remove it by right-clicking on the field and choosing Remove Filter from the pop-up menu. This isn't all that useful, since there's no way to put the criterion back in this pane. Usually, you'll want to make filtering changes in the Grid Pane instead.

Finally, by right-clicking within the Diagram Pane and choosing Properties, you can select options for the query as a whole. The most common of these is the TOP option, which allows you to limit the size of the result set returned by the query. However, there are other choices available here as well:

**Top**　Limits query results to a certain number or certain percent of records.

**Output All Columns**　Puts all columns from all tables in the result set of the view, just as if you'd chosen the * column for each table.

**DISTINCT Values**　Equivalent to distinct values in an Access database, removing duplicate rows from the result set.

**Encrypt View**　Encrypts the view when you save it.

**GROUP BY WITH CUBE**　Creates a multidimensional summary from the GROUP BY fields in the query.

**GROUP BY WITH ROLLUP**　Creates summary values for the GROUP BY fields in the query.

**GROUP BY ALL**　Includes duplicate rows in an aggregate query.

**WARNING**     If you encrypt a view, you can no longer open it with the view designer. You can still retrieve results from the view by opening it, but to change it you must write a stored procedure that uses the ALTER VIEW statement.

## The Grid Pane

The Grid Pane allows you to fine-tune the result set of the view. This includes creating aliases for columns, setting criteria used to filter the query, and selecting grouping options.

To add a new column to the result set, select the column and table names from the combo boxes in a blank row of the Grid pane. The drop-down arrows for these boxes are hidden until you click in the grid, but they're always there.

To create an alias for a column, just type the new name into the Alias column of the grid on that column's row. An Alias specifies the name used to refer to that column within the view's results set.

To create a calculated column, type an arbitrary name into the Alias column and type the expression itself into the Column column. For example, you might enter "Total" in the Alias column and "Price * Quantity" in the Column column.

To set a criterion used to filter the result set (part of a SQL WHERE clause), type the appropriate restriction in the Criteria column of the row with the column you want to restrict. You can set multiple criteria by using more of the grid. To connect two criteria on the same field with an OR, type the criteria into successive columns on the same row. To connect them with an AND, create a second row for the same field and enter the criteria on successive rows.

To transform your view into a grouping view, right-click in the Grid Pane and select Group By. This will add a Group By column to the grid. You can then select an appropriate aggregate expression for each row in the grid by clicking in this column and choosing from the drop-down list.

## The SQL Pane

The SQL Pane is primarily there as a reference for new users and a tool for advanced SQL authors. You can use it as a tool to learn SQL by constructing a view with the Diagram and Grid Panes and watching to see what the view designer does with it.

Alternately, if you already know SQL, you can make changes in this pane and they'll be propagated back to the other panes.

If you make a change in the SQL Pane, it's not reflected in the other panes until you move out of the SQL Pane. This allows you to edit and revise without worrying about extraneous error messages.

Although not all SQL statements are supported by the view designer, there are some statements that are supported in the SQL Pane but not in the Diagram and Grid Panes. For example, the basic union query

```
SELECT CompanyName
FROM Customers
UNION
SELECT CompanyName
FROM Suppliers
```

can be successfully designed and executed by the view designer, but only by starting in the SQL Pane. When you move out of that pane, the query designer warns you that the query cannot be displayed graphically. If you choose to continue, the Diagram and Grid Panes will be grayed out, but you can still work with the query's data.

## View Datasheets

At first glance, the datasheet created by opening a view might seem straightforward: just a place where the results of executing your view are displayed. But, just as with Access database queries, this pane is more than just a static display. Within certain broad limits (discussed below) you can edit the data shown in this pane as well.

To edit data in the datasheet, just navigate to the cell containing the value you wish to change, using the arrow keys, scroll bars, and mouse. Highlight the value and type in the new data. To enter a null, simply delete the existing value. To enter an empty string, type two double quotes with no space between them. When you leave the row that you're editing, Access will attempt to save the data back to the database.

Of course, Access might not succeed for a variety of reasons. Here are some of the limits on what you can edit in views:

- You can only edit text and other long columns that contain less than 900 characters of data.

- You cannot edit binary large object (BLOB) data.

- You must have the appropriate permissions to change data in the database.

- The result set must contain the primary key of the output, or enough other information to uniquely identify the source rows for the data being edited.

- You cannot edit data if the view contains a table that isn't joined to the other tables in the view.

- You cannot edit data if the view displays multiple tables in a many-to-many relationship.

- You cannot edit aggregate views.

- You cannot edit views that use the DISTINCT keyword.

- You cannot edit columns based on expressions.

- You cannot edit timestamp columns.

## The SQL Server SELECT Statement

As you've seen, SQL Server views are basically a wrapper for SELECT statements. You may think you already know all about SELECT statements from your experience with Access queries. Unfortunately, if you've never worked with a server database, you may be in for a bit of a shock. Despite the fact that SQL is a standardized language, the fact is that every product implements this standard with its own set of quirks and extensions. Access has one set of deviations from the standard, while SQL Server has another. In this section, we'll explore the syntax of the SQL Server SELECT statement, so you can get a sense of how it differs from the Access version.

> **NOTE**  This section documents the full SELECT statement, which is used in both views and stored procedures. Some of this syntax does not apply to views. Views cannot use the ORDER BY, COMPUTER, COMPUTE BY, or INTO clauses in the SELECT statement.

Here's the formal syntax of the SQL Server SELECT statement:

```
SELECT statement ::=
<query_expression>
```

```
            [ ORDER BY { order_by_expression | column_position
            [ ASC | DESC ] }
            [,...n]
        ]
            [ COMPUTE
            { { AVG | COUNT | MAX | MIN | SUM } (expression) }
            [,...n]
            [ BY expression [,...n] ]
            ]
        [FOR BROWSE]
        [ OPTION (<query_hint> [,...n]) ]

    <query expression> ::=
        { <query specification> | (<query expression>) }
        [UNION [ALL] <query specification | (<query expression>)
[...n] ]

    <query specification> ::=
        SELECT [ ALL | DISTINCT ]
        [ {TOP integer | TOP integer PERCENT} [ WITH TIES] ]
        <select_list>
        [ INTO new_table ]
        [ FROM {<table_source>} [,...n] ]
        [ WHERE <search_condition> ]
        [ GROUP BY [ALL] group_by_expression [,...n]
        [ WITH { CUBE | ROLLUP } ]
            ]
        [ HAVING <search_condition> ]

    <select_list> ::=
    { *
        | { table_name | view_name | table_alias }.*
        | { column_name | expression | IDENTITYCOL | ROWGUIDCOL }
        [ [AS] column_alias ]
        | column_alias = expression
        } [,...n]

    <table_source> ::=
        table_name [ [AS] table_alias ] [ WITH ( <table_hint>
[,...n]) ]
        | view_name [ [AS] table_alias ]
        | rowset_function [ [AS] table_alias ]
```

```
        | derived_table [AS] table_alias [ (column_alias [,...n] ) ]
        | <joined_table>

    <table_hint> ::=
        { INDEX(index_val [,...n])
        | FASTFIRSTROW
        | HOLDLOCK
        | NOLOCK
        | PAGLOCK
        | READCOMMITTED
        | READPAST
        | READUNCOMMITTED
        | REPEATABLEREAD
        | ROWLOCK
        | SERIALIZABLE
        | TABLOCK
        | TABLOCKX
        | UPDLOCK
        }
                                                    <joined_table> ::=
        <table_source> <join_type> <table_source> ON
<search_condition>
        | <table_source> CROSS JOIN <table_source>
        | <joined_table>

    <join_type> ::=
        [ INNER | { { LEFT | RIGHT | FULL } [OUTER] } ]
        [ <join_hint> ]
        JOIN

    <search_condition> ::=
        { [ NOT ] <predicate> | ( <search_condition> ) }
        [ {AND | OR} [NOT] {<predicate> | ( <search_condition> )
        } ]
        } [,...n]

    <predicate> ::=
        {
        expression { = | <> | != | > | >= | !> | < | <= | !< }
expression
        | string_expression [NOT] LIKE string_expression
        [ESCAPE 'escape_character']
```

```
     | expression [NOT] BETWEEN expression AND expression
     | expression IS [NOT] NULL
     | CONTAINS
     ( {column | * }, '<contains_search_condition>' )
     | FREETEXT ( {column | * }, 'freetext_string' )
     | expression [NOT] IN (subquery | expression [,...n])
     | expression { = | <> | != | > | >= | !> | < | <= | !< }
     {ALL | SOME | ANY} (subquery)
     | EXISTS (subquery)
     }

<query_hint> ::=
     { { HASH | ORDER } GROUP
     | { CONCAT | HASH | MERGE } UNION
     | { LOOP | MERGE | HASH } JOIN
     | FAST number_rows
     | FORCE ORDER
     | MAXDOP number
     | ROBUST PLAN
     | KEEP PLAN
     }
```

If you've never seen a SQL Statement defined in a formal grammar before, you might find this a bit overwhelming. Here are some hints on reading the formal definition:

- Keywords in all upper case must be typed exactly as shown.

- Keywords in angle brackets are expanded later in the syntax diagram. For example, the first clause in a SELECT statement is a query expression, and later in the syntax diagram you're told what a query expression consists of.

- Keywords in italics should be replaced by the name of an actual database objects.

- Choices are separated by pipe ( | ) characters.

- Keywords in square brackets are optional.

- Keywords in curly brackets must be included. If there's a series of keywords separated by pipe characters in curly brackets, at least one of these keywords must be included.

- The special [,...n] sequence indicates that the previous clause may be repeated more than once if you desire.

Let's look at the parts of the SQL statement in more detail.

## The SELECT clause

You can specify SELECT ALL or SELECT DISTINCT. SELECT ALL (the default, if you don't specify ALL or DISTINCT) includes all returned rows in the result set. SELECT DISTINCT removes duplicate rows.

---

**TIP**  SQL Server has no equivalent of the Access SELECT DISTINCTROW.

---

In addition to TOP *n* and TOP *n* PERCENT, SQL Server also supports TOP *n* [PERCENT] WITH TIES. This causes the result set to contain at least as many rows as you've specified, and additional rows that fall into the same place in the ordering as the last row. You can only use WITH TIES if there's an ORDER BY clause, so it's for stored procedures rather than views.

SQL Server requires that all of the column names in a SELECT statement be unique. This is more restrictive than Jet's rule. For example, this is a legal Jet query:

```
SELECT *
FROM tblCustomer INNER JOIN tblOrder
ON tblCustomer.CustomerID = tblOrder.CustomerID
```

The same statement cannot even be saved for a SQL Server view. The problem is that both tables contain a CustomerID field, and you can't have two CustomerID fields without qualification in the view. You need to modify the SQL to work on SQL Server:

```
SELECT tblCustomer.*, tblOrder.CustomerID as OrdCustomerID
FROM tblCustomer INNER JOIN tblOrder
ON tblCustomer.CustomerID = tblOrder.CustomerID
```

Obviously, if you wanted to include all of the fields from the tblOrder table in this view, you'd need to list them all individually.

There are two special names available for columns. You can use IDENTITYCOL to refer to the column in the table that has its IDENTITY property set, or

ROWGUIDCOL to refer to the column in the table that has its ROWGUIDCOL property set.

## The INTO clause

The INTO clause creates a make table statement, just as it does in Access queries. This clause can only be used in stored procedures. Another limitation is that by default, SQL Server databases do not allow this sort of statement to be executed. You must make sure the Select Into/Bulkcopy option is turned on in the database before trying to execute a SELECT…INTO. You can do this by creating a stored procedure to call the sp_dboption system stored procedure.

## The FROM clause

The FROM clause specifies the sources for the SELECT statement. A source can be a table or a view, but not a stored procedure.

The FROM clause is the first place that you can specify a hint as part of your SQL statement. A hint is an instruction to the SQL Server query optimizer, telling it what operations it should perform to return the results of the SELECT statement. SQL Server's query optimizer is very good all by itself. We included the hints in our syntax diagram for the sake of completeness, but our recommendation is simple: don't use hints. Hints are provided for advanced SQL Server database administrators, and the rest of us should trust the optimizer to do the right thing.

SQL Server supports full outer joins in the FROM clause. That is, you can join two tables so that all rows from both tables are included, with matching rows matched and unmatching rows generating nulls in the other table. The only way to do this in Access is to use a UNION query that puts together a LEFT JOIN and a RIGHT JOIN query.

A CROSS JOIN is the same as no join at all. That is, these two FROM clauses are equivalent:

```
FROM Customers, Employees
FROM Customers CROSS JOIN Employees
```

## The WHERE Clause

The WHERE clause accepts SQL syntax in its search conditions that the Jet engine doesn't understand:

- FREETEXT performs a natural language search on the specified column using full text searching. This search is less "precise" than the exact match required by LIKE.

- CONTAINS can perform a weighted search or a search for words near other words.

- ALL, SOME, and ANY return True, depending on whether all, some or any rows in the subquery match the specified condition.

- EXISTS returns True if a subquery returns any rows.

**NOTE**   Older versions of SQL Server used the WHERE clause to perform joins between tables. This syntax is obsolete.

## The GROUP BY Clause

SQL Server GROUP BY clauses support two extensions that can create summary rows: CUBE and ROLLUP. The simplest way to understand these two extensions is by considering the result sets that they generate.

First, let's look at ROLLUP. Figure 4.18 shows a portion of the result set from this view:

```
SELECT tblCustomer.LastName, tblOrder.OrderID,
COUNT(tblOrderDetails.ItemID) AS ItemCount
FROM tblOrderDetails INNER JOIN
tblOrder ON
tblOrderDetails.OrderID = tblOrder.OrderID INNER JOIN
tblCustomer ON
tblOrder.CustomerID = tblCustomer.CustomerID
GROUP BY tblCustomer.LastName, tblOrder.OrderID
WITH ROLLUP
```

The WITH ROLLUP result set contains a row for the grand total of the aggregation across all rows (this is the last row in the figure, with nulls for LastName and OrderID) and a row with the total for each grouping other than the last one (for example, the row showing that Stevens had 41 items in all).

**FIGURE 4.18**
Result set WITH ROLLUP

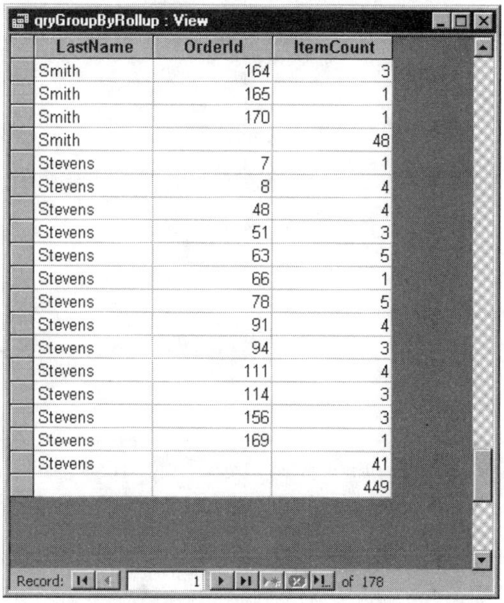
qryGroupByRollup : View

| LastName | OrderId | ItemCount |
|---|---|---|
| Smith | 164 | 3 |
| Smith | 165 | 1 |
| Smith | 170 | 1 |
| Smith | | 48 |
| Stevens | 7 | 1 |
| Stevens | 8 | 4 |
| Stevens | 48 | 4 |
| Stevens | 51 | 3 |
| Stevens | 63 | 5 |
| Stevens | 66 | 1 |
| Stevens | 78 | 5 |
| Stevens | 91 | 4 |
| Stevens | 94 | 3 |
| Stevens | 111 | 4 |
| Stevens | 114 | 3 |
| Stevens | 156 | 3 |
| Stevens | 169 | 1 |
| Stevens | | 41 |
| | | 449 |

Record: 1 of 178

By contrast, WITH CUBE provides even more summary information. Figure 4.19 shows a portion of the result set from this view:

```
SELECT tblCustomer.LastName, tblOrder.OrderID,
COUNT(tblOrderDetails.ItemID) AS ItemCount
FROM tblOrderDetails INNER JOIN
tblOrder ON
tblOrderDetails.OrderID = tblOrder.OrderID INNER JOIN
tblCustomer ON
tblOrder.CustomerID = tblCustomer.CustomerID
GROUP BY tblCustomer.LastName, tblOrder.OrderID
WITH CUBE
```

As you can see, the WITH CUBE result set contains even more rows than the WITH ROLLUP result set. The WITH CUBE result set contains rows for every aggregate of every column, considered with or without all of the other columns.

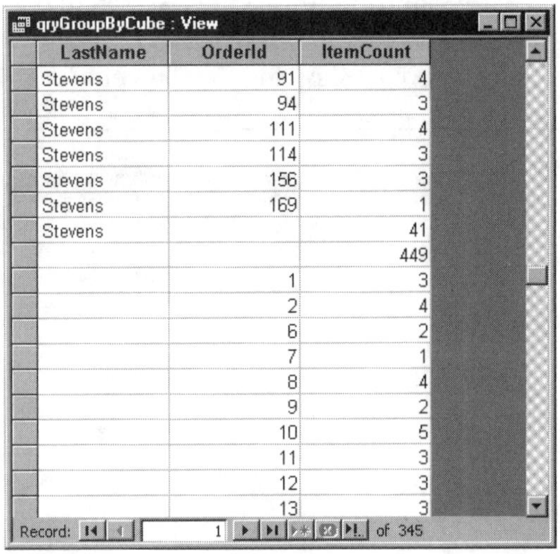

**FIGURE 4.19**
Result set WITH CUBE

| LastName | OrderId | ItemCount |
|----------|---------|-----------|
| Stevens | 91 | 4 |
| Stevens | 94 | 3 |
| Stevens | 111 | 4 |
| Stevens | 114 | 3 |
| Stevens | 156 | 3 |
| Stevens | 169 | 1 |
| Stevens |  | 41 |
|  |  | 449 |
|  | 1 | 3 |
|  | 2 | 4 |
|  | 6 | 2 |
|  | 7 | 1 |
|  | 8 | 4 |
|  | 9 | 2 |
|  | 10 | 5 |
|  | 11 | 3 |
|  | 12 | 3 |
|  | 13 | 3 |

qryGroupByCube : View

Record: ◄◄ ◄ 1 ► ►► ►* of 345

**TIP**    If you find that you frequently need the result sets generated by the WITH ROLLUP or WITH CUBE operators, you should investigate Microsoft OLAP Server, which ships with the Standard and Enterprise Editions of SQL Server 7.0. Microsoft OLAP Server is designed to precalculate and store this sort of aggregate information so that you can retrieve rolled up result sets much more quickly than they can ordinarily be generated by SQL Server.

# Creating Database Diagrams

Database diagrams bear a superficial resemblance to the Relationships window in an Access database, but they are much more flexible. To create a database diagram in an Access project, select the Database Diagrams tab of the Database container and click the New button. For example, right-click on the Database Diagrams folder and choose New Diagram. This will give you a blank window. Now you can populate this window with tables. The easiest way to start this process is by simply dragging a table from the Database container into your new database diagram. Alternately, you can right-click the database diagram, select Show Table, and drag tables in from the Show Table dialog box. By default, new tables will be displayed as a list of column names. This is the view used for the tblCustomer and tblOrder tables in Figure 4.20. But there are four other views available, which you can select by right clicking on the table in the database diagram:

**Column Properties**   Displays all of the properties of the columns in the table. The tblMenu table in Figure 4.20 uses this view.

**Keys**   Shows only column names for primary and foreign keys. The tblOrder table in Figure 4.20 uses this view.

**Name Only**   Shrinks the table display to a title bar only. The tblOrderDetails table in Figure 4.20 uses this view.

**Custom**   Shows a selection of the properties for the column in the table (you can change the properties shown by choosing Modify Custom View from the Diagram menu). The tblEmployee table in Figure 4.20 is displayed using this view.

**FIGURE 4.20**
A database diagram

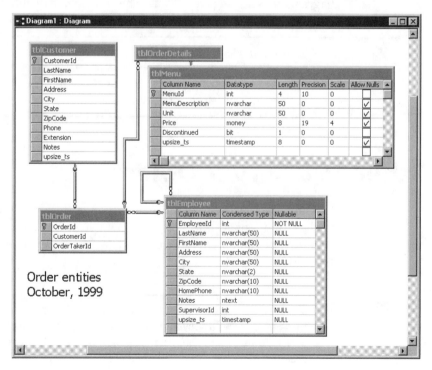

No matter which view you choose, the database diagram will show the relationships between the tables in the view. These are the "pipes" between the tables. The key symbols identify primary keys, while the infinity symbols identify foreign keys. In a self-join the pipe will make a loop, as shown for the tblEmployee table in Figure 4.20.

Context menus within the database diagram let you control its appearance. You can add text annotations to the diagram, show or hide the names of the relationships, set up the page for printing, automatically arrange the tables and control the zoom of the display. You can also right-click on any table or relationship to view its properties.

The database diagram is not simply a display, but also a workspace for designing databases. You can create new relationships by dragging and dropping a foreign key field to a primary key field. You can delete relationships with the shortcut menu for the relationship. You can even create new tables by right-clicking in the diagram and selecting New Table. This will open a blank table designer.

**TIP**  Microsoft product managers are fond of showing how you can literally design your entire database schema right from the Database Diagram window. In fact, this is a very handy addition to the product—the ability to design tables and relationships simultaneously and interactively.

# Other SQL Server Objects

Although the Database container shows you most objects in your SQL Server database, it does not show you all of them. In particular, you may need to know about rules, defaults, and user-defined data types. We'll discuss those objects in this section.

**TIP**  If you have any version of SQL Server other than MSDE, the SQL Server Enterprise Manager provides a convenient interface for managing all of the objects in a SQL Server database, including those that are not directly accessible from an Access project.

# Rules

You may run across SQL Server databases that contain rules. You can think of a SQL Server rule as similar to an Access database validation rule, but, unlike a validation rule, a rule exists as an independent object. In SQL Server, you can create a rule by executing a CREATE RULE statement, for example:

```
CREATE RULE price_rule
AS
@price > 0
```

Once a rule has been created, you can apply it to as many columns of data in as many tables as you like. The rule has to be bound to each column where it will be used by executing the sp_bindrule stored procedure:

```
sp_bindrule 'price_rule', 'tblOrders.Price'
```

Once you've bound a rule, it serves to check data entry to the specified column.

In SQL Server 7.0, rules are provided strictly for backwards compatibility. You can still create and bind rules, but you can perform any function that a rule would perform with a CHECK constraint instead. Since you can create CHECK constraints with the table designer, we recommend that you simply not use rules.

**TIP**  To execute an arbitrary SQL statement such as CREATE RULE or sp_bindrule from an Access project, create a new stored procedure and type in the SQL that you wish to execute. Then save and execute the stored procedure. (If you are executing a stored procedure like sp_bindrule, you must precede it with the EXEC or EXECUTE keywords.) You may wish to keep a scratch stored procedure in databases under development that you can reuse for such arbitrary SQL statements.

# Defaults

SQL Server defaults are similar to SQL Server rules in that they are independent objects. As you might guess, these are default values that can be attached to multiple columns. To create a default, you'd use the CREATE DEFAULT statement:

```
CREATE DEFAULT salary AS 20000
```

Once you've created a default, you can use sp_bindefault to attach it to a particular column:

```
sp_bindefault 'salary', 'tblEmployee.Salary'
```

Like rules, defaults are considered obsolete in SQL Server 7.0. You can simply use the Default column in the table designer to create DEFAULT constraints on your tables instead.

## User-Defined Data Types

Finally, SQL Server allows you to create your own user-defined data types. These data types are based on the built-in types and are created with the sp_addtype stored procedure. For example, if five-character alphanumeric fields identify all of the customers in your database, you could create a special data type that will hold that much data:

```
sp_addtype customerid, 'char(5)', 'NOT NULL'
```

Although Access provides no direct interface for creating user-defined data types, once they're created in a database (possibly by executing a temporary stored procedure as detailed above) you can use them in table design. Figure 4.21 shows the table designer listing several user-defined data types (id, tid, and empid) and their underlying equivalents.

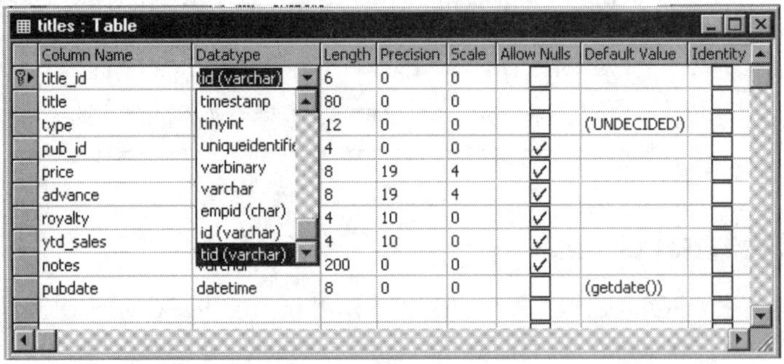

**FIGURE 4.21**

Choosing a user-defined data type

| Column Name | Datatype | Length | Precision | Scale | Allow Nulls | Default Value | Identity |
|---|---|---|---|---|---|---|---|
| title_id | id (varchar) | 6 | 0 | 0 | | | |
| title | timestamp | 80 | 0 | 0 | | | |
| type | tinyint | 12 | 0 | 0 | | ('UNDECIDED') | |
| pub_id | uniqueidentifi | 4 | 0 | 0 | ✓ | | |
| price | varbinary | 8 | 19 | 4 | ✓ | | |
| advance | varchar | 8 | 19 | 4 | ✓ | | |
| royalty | empid (char) | 4 | 10 | 0 | ✓ | | |
| ytd_sales | id (varchar) | 4 | 10 | 0 | ✓ | | |
| notes | tid (varchar) | 200 | 0 | 0 | ✓ | | |
| pubdate | datetime | 8 | 0 | 0 | | (getdate()) | |

# Managing SQL Server Databases from Access

You can perform some simple SQL Server database management tasks from within an Access project. The Access developers provided this capability so that MSDE databases can be managed, even though SQL Enterprise Manager isn't shipped with that version. However, you can use these tools to manage any SQL Server database, as long as the database engine is running on the same computer as Access.

Here's a summary of the management operations you can perform:

- Tools ➤ Database Utilities ➤ Backup will make a backup copy of the SQL Server data in an Access project.

- Tools ➤ Database Utilities ➤ Restore will restore the data from a previously saved backup.

- Tools ➤ Database Utilities ➤ Drop SQL Database will destroy the SQL Server database and all of the objects and data that it contains.

- Tools ➤ Security ➤ Database Security allows you to manage database users, roles, and logins. This security information is stored in the SQL Server database and pertains only to objects stored in that database.

- Tools ➤ Replication provides an interface to the SQL Server replication engine, which works on a publish-and-subscribe metaphor.

Overall, Access provides just the minimum necessary administrative interface to a SQL Server database. For serious use, you'll want to install the utilities from SQL Server Desktop, Standard, or Enterprise Editions instead. You can also create your own utilities using either SQL Distributed Management Objects (SQL-DMO) or Transact-SQL (T-SQL) commands. Information on using SQL-DMO and T-SQL can be found in the SQL Server documentation or on the MSDN Web site (`http:/ /msdn.microsoft.com/library`).

---

**TIP**    For more information on SQL Server administration, see *SQL Server 7 In Record Time*, by Mike Gunderloy and Mary Chipman (Sybex, 1999).

---

# Summary

This chapter introduced you to creating Access projects and manipulating the objects that are stored in the SQL Server database behind the project. Although the overall Access interface looks similar whether you're working with a database or a project, the details differ in many respects. Even if you're an experienced Access developer, you'll want to study the new tools carefully to find their differences from what you're used to.

This chapter has covered these major topics:

- Editions of SQL Server
- Creating new SQL Server databases
- Connecting to existing SQL Server databases
- Using the Access Upsizing Wizard
- Using the Import and Export utility
- Creating tables and indexes
- SQL Server data types
- Table capacities and limitations
- Creating views
- The SQL Server SELECT statement
- Database diagrams
- Rules, defaults, and user-defined data types
- Managing SQL Server databases from Access

# Creating Stored Procedures and Triggers

- Understanding stored procedures

- Creating stored procedures with parameters, variables, and return values

- Using T-SQL flow-of-control statements and built-in variables, functions, and procedures

- Creating triggers

- Using stored procedures to cascade primary key updates and deletions

*S*tored procedures are sets of SQL statements and control-of-flow statements that are compiled and stored in a database on the server. *Triggers* are special versions of stored procedures that you attach to server database events. Stored procedures and triggers are supported by many relational database management systems (RDBMS), including SQL Server, the Microsoft Data Engine (MSDE), and Oracle. In this chapter, we discuss how to create, manage, and use stored procedures and triggers in Access project files (ADP). Thus, we'll limit the discussion to SQL Server and MSDE stored procedures and triggers.

# The Stored Procedure Advantage

Whenever you have the choice of executing SQL that is stored on the client (either as an ad hoc SQL statement or an Access query in an MDB file), or executing the same code stored on the server in a stored procedure, you're better off using the stored procedure. There are many reasons for this:

- Because they are precompiled and stored on the server, stored procedures execute faster than SQL that's stored on the client and must be sent to the server, interpreted, and compiled before it can be executed.

- The judicious use of stored procedures allows you centralize business rules and other application logic. This reduces redundancy and eases maintenance issues.

- Stored procedures can include complex flow-control and transaction processing statements that simplify the programming you need to do on the client.

- By removing user permissions to tables and providing a stored procedure interface to these same objects, you can simplify security and reduce the chances that users make catastrophic changes to the database.

Stored procedures are an important part of any client/server application.

# Creating Stored Procedures

Select Insert ➤ Stored Procedure to create a stored procedure in Access. The procGetCustomer1 stored procedure is about as simple a stored procedure as you can create. It returns all of the records from tblCustomer:

```
Create Procedure procGetCustomer1
As
        SELECT * FROM tblCustomer
```

Figure 5.1 shows procGetCustomer1 in the Access stored procedure designer.

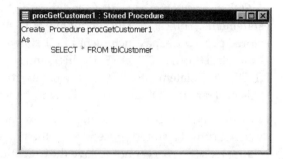

**FIGURE 5.1**
The procGetCustomer1
stored procedure returns all
of the records from
tblCustomer.

---

**TIP**    If you open an existing stored procedure in the stored procedure designer, the designer changes the Create Procedure statement to Alter Procedure. You use the Alter Procedure statement to update an existing stored procedure.

---

## Stored Procedure Syntax

You create a SQL Server stored procedure using the CREATE PROCEDURE statement, whose syntax is shown here:

```
CREATE PROC[EDURE] procedure_name
[@param1 datatype [= default] [OUTPUT] ]
[, @param2 datatype [=default] [OUTPUT] ]
[, …]
[WITH {RECOMPILE | ENCRYPTION |
RECOMPILE, ENCRYPTION]}
[FOR REPLICATION]
AS
SQL statements
```

Parameter *datatypes* may be any of the following (see SQL Server Books Online for a description of each datatype):

| | | | |
|---|---|---|---|
| int | smallint | tinyint | bit |
| decimal | numeric | float | real |
| money | smallmoney | datetime | smalldatetime |
| cursor | timestamp | uniqueidentifier | char |
| varchar | text | nchar | nvarchar |
| ntext | binary | varbinary | image |

Parameters are discussed in more detail in a later section of this chapter entitled "Understanding Parameters and Variables."

*SQL statements* may consist of one or more SQL statements or flow-of-control T-SQL statements. You can use just about any SQL statement in a stored procedure; a stored procedure may include SELECT statements, action query statements (for example, DELETE, UPDATE, INSERT, and so forth) and Data Definition Language (DDL) SQL statements. T-SQL flow-of-control statements are discussed in the "Using Transact-SQL Control-Of-Flow Statements" section later in this chapter.

Normally, SQL Server determines an execution plan for the stored procedure when it runs the stored procedure for the first time. The WITH RECOMPILE clause tells SQL Server not to save the execution plan with the stored procedure and to re-evaluate the execution plan every time it runs the stored procedure.

The WITH ENCRYPTION clause stores the source code of the stored procedure in encrypted form. This prevents users from seeing the source code using the sp_helptext system stored procedure.

You use the FOR REPLICATION clause to tell SQL Server to mark the stored procedure as a replication filter procedure that will be executed by the replication engine.

---

**NOTE**    This is a slightly simplified version of the CREATE PROCEDURE statement. See the SQL Server Books Online for a more complete definition.

---

Here's an example of a stored procedure, procMenuPricesIncrease, that uses an UDPATE statement to increase the prices of menu items by 10 percent:

```
Create Procedure procMenuPricesIncrease
As
    UPDATE tblMenu
    SET Price = Price*1.1
```

The following stored procedure, procCreateTestTable1, creates a two-column table named tblTest:

```
Create Procedure procCreateTestTable1
As
    CREATE TABLE tblTest
    (Id INT CONSTRAINT PrimaryKey PRIMARY KEY,
    Description VARCHAR(20))
```

# Understanding Parameters and Variables

Just like VBA procedures, SQL Server stored procedures can have parameters, variables, and a return value.

## Parameters

Although a stored procedure without parameters may be useful, a stored procedure *with* parameters is considerably more flexible. You can create both input and output parameters.

All stored procedure parameter names begin with "@" and are local to the procedure. By default, all parameters are for input. If you want to create an output parameter, follow the parameter's data type with the keyword "OUTPUT."

### Input Parameters

You use input parameters to send information to a stored procedure. For example, you might use input parameters to filter the records returned by a SELECT statement.

In the following stored procedure, procGetCustomer2, we have defined a single integer input parameter that is used to filter the SELECT statement:

```
Create Procedure procGetCustomer2
    @custid INT
As
    SELECT * FROM tblCustomer
    WHERE CustomerId = @custid
```

---

**TIP**    When you execute a stored procedure from the Access database container, Access prompts you for each parameter just like Access' own parameter queries.

---

### Output Parameters

Sometimes you'd like a stored procedure to return information back to the calling procedure. This is where an output parameter comes in handy. For example, you might use an output parameter to send the value of an automatically assigned identity column back to the calling program.

In the following stored procedure, procInsertOrder, we've defined six input parameters and one output parameter:

```
Create Procedure procInsertOrder
    @orderdate datetime,
    @customerid int,
    @ordertakerid int,
    @deliverydate datetime,
    @paymentmethod nvarchar(50),
    @notes ntext,
    @orderid int OUTPUT
As
    set nocount on
    INSERT INTO tblOrder
    (OrderDate, CustomerId,
    OrderTakerId, DeliveryDate,
    PaymentMethod, Notes)
    VALUES
    (@orderdate, @customerid,
    @ordertakerid, @deliverydate,
    @paymentmethod, @notes)

    -- Pass back the new OrderId value
    -- to the calling program as an output parameter
    SELECT @orderid = @@IDENTITY
```

You can use a special form of the SELECT statement to set an output parameter or variable to a value:

```
SELECT @param = value
```

Alternately, you can use the SET statement whose syntax is identical to this special form of the SELECT statement:

```
SET @param = value
```

In procInsertOrder, we have set @orderid to the special T-SQL @@IDENTITY variable. This variable returns the value of the last assigned identity value.

---

**NOTE**     The Access UI is unable to directly process stored procedure output parameters. You can use the procInsertOrderTest stored procedure (discussed in the next section) to test the procInsertOrder stored procedure.

---

## Declaring and Using Variables

In addition to parameters, you can create local variables. You define a variable using the DECLARE statement, as shown here:

```
DECLARE @variable datatype [, …]
```

Just as with output parameters, you use a special form of the SELECT statement (or the equivalent SET statement) to set the value of a local variable:

```
-- The next two statements are equivalent
SELECT @variable = value
SET @variable = value
```

For example, you could use the following stored procedure, procInsertOrderTest, to test procInsertOrder:

```
Create Procedure procInsertOrderTest
As
    DECLARE @intOrderId INT

    EXECUTE procInsertOrder
    '1/1/2000', 1, 1, '1/1/2000',
    'Cash', 'Test order', @intOrderId OUTPUT

    -- return a recordset containing the newly
    -- assigned Orderid value
    SELECT @intOrderId AS NewOrderId
```

In this example, procInsertOrderTest executes procInsertOrder using the T-SQL EXECUTE statement. procInsertOrderTest then uses a SELECT statement to return a single record to the calling program containing the value of the newly inserted identity column. Notice that this SELECT statement looks similar to, but is different from, the one used in the procInsertOrder stored procedure. In procInsertOrder we used a special T-SQL version of the SELECT statement to set a parameter to a value without returning any records. In procInsertOrderTest, however, we use the AS keyword to create a single-row recordset containing a computed column whose value is set equal to @intOrderId.

---

**NOTE**    The EXECUTE statement is discussed in the next section.

---

Figure 5.2 shows the result of executing the procInsertOrderTest stored procedure.

**FIGURE 5.2**
When executed
from Access, the
procInsertOrde Test
stored procedure returns
the value of the new
OrderId identity column.

## Return Values

In addition to output parameters, you can return information to the calling program using the stored procedure's return value. You use the RETURN statement to return a value:

```
RETURN [integer_value]
```

When a stored procedure processes a RETURN statement, the stored procedure unconditionally terminates and sends back the optional return value to the calling program. The return value must be an integer.

SQL Server's built-in system stored procedures return zero if they succeed or a non-zero value if they fail. You don't have to follow this convention, but it's not a bad idea to be consistent with the built-in stored procedures.

The following stored procedure, procCustomerExist, returns 0 if a customer with a matching CustomerId is found or 1 if the customer's record is not found:

```
Create Procedure procCustomerExist
   @custid INT
As
   IF (SELECT Count(*) FROM tblCustomer
      WHERE CustomerId = @custid) >= 1
      -- Success
      RETURN 0
   ELSE
      -- Failure
      RETURN 1
```

**NOTE**
When you execute a stored procedure from the Access database container, you have no way of accessing the stored procedure's return value. You can test procCustomerExist, however, by running procCustomerExistTest.

**TIP**
It's usually best to reserve the return value for indicating if the stored procedure succeeded or failed. If you need to pass back additional information to the calling program—for example, the value of an identity column or the total sales for a region—you should instead use either an output parameter or a recordset.

# Executing Stored Procedures

How you execute a stored procedure depends on from where you are executing it.

## Executing a Stored Procedure from the Access Database Container

To execute a stored procedure from the database container of an ADP file, double-click on the stored procedure. If the stored procedure has one or more input parameters, Access prompts you for the parameters before it executes the stored procedure.

If the stored procedure returns records, Access displays the datasheet containing the records returned by the stored procedure, as shown in Figure 5.3.

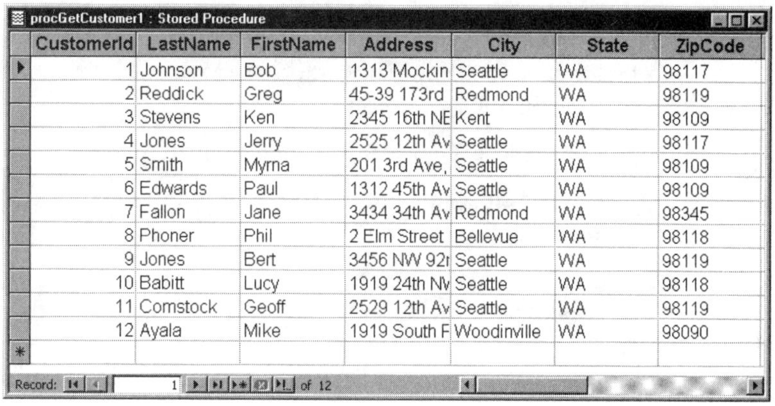

**FIGURE 5.3**
The datasheet returned by procGetCustomer1

| CustomerId | LastName | FirstName | Address | City | State | ZipCode |
|---|---|---|---|---|---|---|
| 1 | Johnson | Bob | 1313 Mockin | Seattle | WA | 98117 |
| 2 | Reddick | Greg | 45-39 173rd | Redmond | WA | 98119 |
| 3 | Stevens | Ken | 2345 16th NE | Kent | WA | 98109 |
| 4 | Jones | Jerry | 2525 12th Av | Seattle | WA | 98117 |
| 5 | Smith | Myrna | 201 3rd Ave, | Seattle | WA | 98109 |
| 6 | Edwards | Paul | 1312 45th Av | Seattle | WA | 98109 |
| 7 | Fallon | Jane | 3434 34th Av | Redmond | WA | 98345 |
| 8 | Phoner | Phil | 2 Elm Street | Bellevue | WA | 98118 |
| 9 | Jones | Bert | 3456 NW 92r | Seattle | WA | 98119 |
| 10 | Babitt | Lucy | 1919 24th Nv | Seattle | WA | 98118 |
| 11 | Comstock | Geoff | 2529 12th Av | Seattle | WA | 98119 |
| 12 | Ayala | Mike | 1919 South F | Woodinville | WA | 98090 |

If the stored procedure doesn't return any records, Access displays a dialog box informing you that it executed your stored procedure, as shown in Figure 5.4.

**FIGURE 5.4**

Access displays this dialog box when you execute a stored procedure that doesn't return any records from the database container.

## Executing a Stored Procedure from Another Stored Procedure

You can call one stored procedure from another using the EXECUTE statement, which you can abbreviate to EXEC. Here's the syntax:

```
EXEC[UTE] [@return_variable = ] procedure_name
[{value | variable OUTPUT |
@param = value | @param = variable OUTPUT}] [, …]]
```

where *procedure_name* is the name of the stored procedure you wish to execute, *@return_variable* is a local variable that will contain the return value of the stored procedure, *@param* is the name of a stored procedure parameter, *value* is a value you wish to pass to the stored procedure, and *variable* is a local variable that will contain the value of an output parameter.

For example, to execute the procGetCustomer1 stored procedure, which has no parameters, you might use this EXECUTE statement:

```
EXECUTE procGetCustomer1
```

If a stored procedure has parameters, you can pass the parameters either by position or by name. This example executes a stored procedure with two input parameters, by position:

```
EXEC procGetCustomer3 "Greg", "Reddick"
```

This example executes the same stored procedure, this time passing parameters to the procedure by name:

```
EXEC procGetCustomer3
@LastName = "Reddick", @FirstName = "Greg"
```

When you pass parameters by name you don't need to be concerned about the order of the parameters. Passing parameters by name is a bit more cumbersome but makes your code more readable.

If you need to execute a stored procedure with an output parameter, you need to pass it a variable into which it can place the output value. In addition, you need to include the keyword OUTPUT. For example, here's the EXECUTE statement from the procInsertOrderTest stored procedure that was shown earlier in the chapter. This stored procedure calls procInsertOrder, a stored procedure with six input parameters and one output parameter:

```
EXECUTE procInsertOrder
'1/1/2000', 1, 1, '1/1/2000',
'Cash', 'Test order', @intOrderId OUTPUT
```

The following code, from procInserOrderTestN, also calls procInsertOrder, but passes parameters to it by name:

```
EXECUTE procInsertOrder
    @orderdate = '1/1/2000',
    @customerid = 1,
    @ordertakerid = 1,
    @deliverydate = '1/1/2000',
    @paymentmethod = 'Cash',
    @notes = 'Test order',
    @orderid = @intOrderId OUTPUT
```

The following stored procedure, procCustomerExistTest, calls a stored procedure with a return value, procCustomerExist:

```
Create Procedure procCustomerExistTest
    @custid INT
As
    DECLARE @intReturn INT
    -- execute a stored procedure with a return
    -- value and a single input parameter
    EXECUTE @intReturn = procCustomerExist @custid
    IF (@intReturn = 0)
        SELECT 'Sucess' AS Status
    ELSE
        SELECT 'Failure' AS Status
```

**NOTE**    The IF...ELSE statement is discussed later in this chapter.

# Executing a Stored Procedure from a Pass-Through Query

You can use SQL pass-through (SPT) queries in Access MDB databases to send uninterpreted SQL statements to a server database. You create a SQL pass-through query by creating a new blank query and then choosing Query ➤ SQL Specific ➤ Pass-Through. (You can't create SPT queries in ADP files.)

To call a stored procedure from an SPT query, you use the EXECUTE statement. SPT queries provide no mechanism for dealing with output parameters or the return value of a stored procedure.

Figure 5.5 shows the query designer with an SPT query loaded in design view.

**FIGURE 5.5**
The qryGetCustomerPst pass-through query calls the procGetCustomer3 stored procedure.

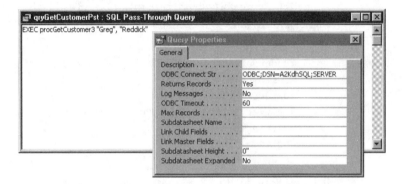

---

**TIP**　　You can use the ReturnsRecords property of a pass-through query to let Access know whether the SPT query returns records.

---

# Executing a Stored Procedure from ADO

You can use ADO (ActiveX Data Objects) to directly execute stored procedures using the ADO Command object. If the stored procedure has parameters, you can use the Command object's Parameters collection to pass parameters to and from the stored procedure. Here's an example of how you might execute the procInsertOrder stored procedure using ADO, from the basStoredProcedures module of CH05.ADP:

```
Sub TestProcInsertOrder()
    Dim cnn As ADODB.Connection
    Dim cmd As ADODB.Command
    Dim prm As ADODB.Parameter

    Set cnn = CurrentProject.Connection
    Set cmd = New ADODB.Command

    cmd.ActiveConnection = cnn
    cmd.CommandText = "procInsertOrder"
    cmd.CommandType = adCmdStoredProc

    Set prm = cmd.CreateParameter("OrderDate", _
      adDBDate, adParamInput, , #1/1/2000#)
    cmd.Parameters.Append prm

    Set prm = cmd.CreateParameter("CustomerId", _
      adInteger, adParamInput, , 1)
    cmd.Parameters.Append prm

    Set prm = cmd.CreateParameter("OrderTakerId", _
      adInteger, adParamInput, , 1)
    cmd.Parameters.Append prm

    Set prm = cmd.CreateParameter("DeliveryDate", _
      adDBDate, adParamInput, , #1/1/2000#)
    cmd.Parameters.Append prm

    Set prm = cmd.CreateParameter("PaymentMethod", _
      adVarWChar, adParamInput, 50, "Cash")
    cmd.Parameters.Append prm

    Set prm = cmd.CreateParameter("Notes", _
      adVarWChar, adParamInput, 1024, "Test Record")
    cmd.Parameters.Append prm

    Set prm = cmd.CreateParameter("OrderId", _
      adInteger, adParamOutput)
    cmd.Parameters.Append prm
```

```
        cmd.Execute

        Debug.Print "New OrderId: " & cmd.Parameters("OrderId")

        Set prm = Nothing
        Set cmd = Nothing
        Set cnn = Nothing
    End Sub
```

The ADO Command object and its Parameters collection are discussed in more detail in Chapter 6.

## Executing a Stored Procedure from DAO

You can use DAO (Data Access Objects) to execute SQL pass-through queries that reference stored procedures. For example, the following subroutine, RunSPTQuery from the basDAOSPT module of CH05SPT.MDB, executes the qryGetCustomerPst pass-through query, which in turn executes the procGetCustomer stored procedure:

```
Sub RunSPTQuery()
    Dim db As DAO.Database
    Dim qdf As DAO.QueryDef
    Dim rst As DAO.Recordset

    Set db = CurrentDb
    Set qdf = db.QueryDefs("qryGetCustomerPst")
    Set rst = qdf.OpenRecordset()

    Do While Not rst.EOF
        Debug.Print rst.Fields("CustomerId")
        Debug.Print rst.Fields("LastName")
        Debug.Print rst.Fields("FirstName")
        rst.MoveNext
    Loop

    rst.Close
    Set rst = Nothing
    Set qdf = Nothing

End Sub
```

---

**NOTE**    You can find additional information about SPT queries in Chapter 5 of *Access 2000 Developer's Handbook, Volume 1: Desktop Edition.*

---

# Using Transact-SQL Control-of-Flow Statements

Transact-SQL (T-SQL) has a number of statements that, while not part of the SQL language, you can use to control the flow of stored procedures. These statements are summarized in Table 5.1

**T A B L E   5 . 1 :**   T-SQL Control-of-Flow Statements

| Statement | Description |
| --- | --- |
| BEGIN…END | Creates a block of T-SQL statements. Required for some T-SQL statements such as WHILE. |
| BREAK | Breaks out of a WHILE loop. |
| *comment* | Designates a comment. Comments may be single-line (-- ) or multi-line (/* … */). |
| CONTINUE | Restarts a WHILE loop. |
| DECLARE | Creates a local variable.* |
| EXECUTE | Executes a stored procedure.* |
| GOTO | Unconditionally jumps to a label. |
| IF…ELSE | Branches based on the value of an expression. |
| PRINT | Prints a string to the Query Analyzer, ISQL, or OSQL window. Access and most clients ignore the printed text. |
| SET NOCOUNT ON/OFF | When set to ON, SQL Server doesn't return rowcounts to the client. When set to OFF, SQL Server returns rowcounts. |
| RETURN | Execution is unconditionally terminated and an optional return value is returned to the client.* |
| WAITFOR | Pauses execution for a specified time interval. |
| WHILE | Repeatedly executes a block of statements while a condition is true. |

* Discussed in an earlier section of the chapter.

Each of the control-of-flow T-SQL statements (except for those that have already been discussed in earlier sections of the chapter) is discussed in greater detail in the following sections.

## BEGIN...END Statements

You use the BEGIN and END statements to create a block of T-SQL statements. Here's the basic syntax:

```
BEGIN
one_or_more_statements
END
```

Certain T-SQL statements require you to use the BEGIN and END statements if you need to execute more than one statement within a clause.

For example, in the following IF...ELSE statement from procCustomerExist, no BEGIN/END statements are needed because each clause of the IF...ELSE statement only includes a single statement (a comment statement is not counted as a statement):

```
IF (SELECT Count(*) FROM tblCustomer
    WHERE CustomerId = @custid) >= 1
    -- Success
    RETURN 0
ELSE
    -- Failure
    RETURN 1
```

If, however, you wished to add a second statement to each of the IF...ELSE clauses, for example, a PRINT statement, you would then need to use BEGIN/END statements as shown here (from procCustomerExist2):

```
IF (SELECT Count(*) FROM tblCustomer
    WHERE CustomerId = @custid) >= 1
    BEGIN
    -- Success
    PRINT 'Success'
    RETURN 0
    END
ELSE
    BEGIN
    -- Failure
    PRINT 'Failure'
    RETURN 1
    END
```

## Comments

You can create two types of comments in T-SQL: single-line and multi-line comments. The basic syntax is shown here:

```
-- single-line comment
/* this comment spans
more than one line */
```

You create a single-line comment using "--" as shown in this example:

```
-- Failure
RETURN 1
```

The T-SQL single-line comment works much like a VBA comment.

A multi-line comment, as its name implies, can span multiple lines. You designate the beginning of a multi-line comment with "/*" and the end with "*/". Here's an example:

```
/* return a recordset containing the newly-
assigned OrderId value */
SELECT @intOrderId AS NewOrderId
```

## GOTO Statement

The T-SQL GOTO statement is very much like its VBA counterpart: GOTO unconditionally redirects execution flow to the statement following the label. Here's the basic syntax:

```
GOTO label
...
label:
```

The label may appear before or after the GOTO statement. Like the VBA GoTo statement, the T-SQL GOTO statement should only be used as a last resort because it tends to make your code less readable.

## IF...ELSE Statement

You use the IF...ELSE statement to branch in your code based on the value of a condition. The basic syntax is:

```
IF expression
{statement | statement block}
ELSE
{statement | statement block}
```

The expression can be either a simple Boolean expression or a SELECT statement that results in a True/False value. SELECT statements must be enclosed in parentheses. Each clause of the IF…ELSE statement may consist of a single statement or a block of statements between BEGIN and END statements.

The procCustomerExistTest stored procedure, shown earlier, contained an IF…ELSE statement:

```
IF (@intReturn = 0)
    SELECT 'Sucess' AS Status
ELSE
    SELECT 'Failure' AS Status
```

The following IF…ELSE statement from procCustomerExist2 (which was also shown earlier) uses a SELECT statement for the condition and BEGIN…END blocks:

```
IF (SELECT Count(*) FROM tblCustomer
    WHERE CustomerId = @custid) >= 1
    BEGIN
    -- Success
    PRINT 'Success'
    RETURN 0
    END
ELSE
    BEGIN
    -- Failure
    PRINT 'Failure'
    RETURN 1
    END
```

## PRINT Statement

The PRINT statement is similar to the VBA Debug.Print method. It prints a line of text to the SQL Server Query Analyzer, ISQL, and QSQL windows but is ignored by most clients, including Access. The basic syntax is:

```
PRINT string_expression
```

For example, the following PRINT statement from procCustomerExist2 prints "Failure" to the SQL Server Query Analyzer window:

```
PRINT 'Failure'
```

The following stored procedure, procCustomerOrderCount, uses the PRINT statement to print a count of the number of orders placed by a particular customer:

```
Create Procedure procCustomerOrderCount
    @custid INT
As
    Declare @ordercount INT
    SELECT @ordercount = Count(*) FROM tblOrder
    WHERE CustomerId = @custid
    PRINT 'Customer #' + CAST(@custid AS varchar(5)) +
    ' has made ' + CAST(@ordercount AS varchar(5)) +
    ' orders.'
```

Figure 5.6 shows the results of running procCustomerOrderCount in the SQL Server Query Analyzer.

**FIGURE 5.6**
The procCustomerOrder-
Count stored procedure
uses a PRINT statement to
display a count of the
number of orders a
particular customer
has made.

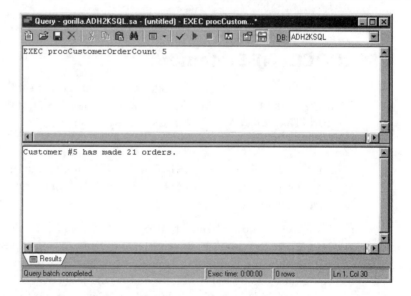

**NOTE**    The procCustomerOrderCount stored procedure won't return anything when executed from Access. You'll need to run it within the SQL Server Query Analyzer, ISQL, or OSQL programs to see the resulting PRINT statement.

A few points about PRINT and string expressions:

- You use a single quote (') to delimit strings.

- You use a plus (+) to concatenate strings.

- T-SQL doesn't automatically convert datatypes as does VBA. Thus, you must use a function such as CAST to explicitly convert a non-string expression to a string before concatenating the expression to a string.

---

**WARNING**   If you include a PRINT statement before a SQL statement that returns a recordset, the PRINT statement returns a zero rowcount that fools the client program into thinking that no recordset is coming. The net result is that no recordset is returned to the client. If you encounter this problem, either move the PRINT statement after the SQL statement or use the SET NOCOUNT ON statement (see next section for more details).

---

## SET NOCOUNT Statement

You use the SET NOCOUNT statement to turn on or off the rowcount messages that are sent to the client after every executable T-SQL statement in a stored procedure. The syntax of SET NOCOUNT is shown here:

```
SET NOCOUNT {ON | OFF}
```

If you do not include a SET NOCOUNT statement in your stored procedure, SQL Server sends rowcount messages to the client (which is the equivalent to SET NOCOUNT OFF).

Whether or not you need to use SET NOCOUNT ON depends on the stored procedure and the client. For example, if you're running stored procedures from the Access database container, Access will normally determine whether records are being returned by the stored procedure using the rowcount of the first executable statement. This may be a problem if the first executable statement doesn't return any records, as in procInsertOrder2a:

```
Create Procedure procInsertOrder2a
    @orderdate datetime,
    @customerid int,
    @ordertakerid int,
    @deliverydate datetime,
    @paymentmethod nvarchar(50),
```

```
    @notes ntext,
    @orderid int OUTPUT
As

    INSERT INTO tblOrder
    (OrderDate, CustomerId,
    OrderTakerId, DeliveryDate,
    PaymentMethod, Notes)
    VALUES
    (@orderdate, @customerid,
    @ordertakerid, @deliverydate,
    @paymentmethod, @notes)

    SELECT @@IDENTITY AS "NewCustomerId"
```

If you execute this stored procedure from the Access database container and enter the necessary parameters, Access reports that the stored procedure executed but did not return any records, as shown in Figure 5.7.

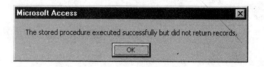

The procInsertOrder2b stored procedure is identical to procInsertOrder2a, with the addition of a SET NOCOUNT ON statement:

```
Create Procedure procInsertOrder2b
    @orderdate datetime,
    @customerid int,
    @ordertakerid int,
    @deliverydate datetime,
    @paymentmethod nvarchar(50),
    @notes ntext,
    @orderid int OUTPUT
As
    set nocount on
    INSERT INTO tblOrder
    (OrderDate, CustomerId,
    OrderTakerId, DeliveryDate,
    PaymentMethod, Notes)
```

```
VALUES
(@orderdate, @customerid,
@ordertakerid, @deliverydate,
@paymentmethod, @notes)

SELECT @@IDENTITY AS "NewCustomerId"
```

When you execute procInsertOrder2b from the Access database container and enter the necessary parameters, Access waits until it encounters the first SQL statement that returns records before it decides whether or not to create a datasheet. In this case, the SET NOCOUNT ON statement forces Access to create a recordset, as shown in Figure 5.8.

**FIGURE 5.8**
By adding the SET NOCOUNT ON statement to the beginning of the procInsertOrder2b stored procedure, Access returns a datasheet with the value of the CustomerId column.

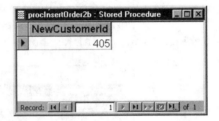

**TIP**

The ADO Command's Execute method returns the number of records affected by the execution of a stored procedure. For some stored procedures, this count may be wrong because of the reporting of intermediate results. In these cases, you may want to add SET NOCOUNT ON statement. When you use SET NOCOUNT ON with ADO, the Execute method returns -1 to indicate that the stored procedure executed successfully but a rowcount was unavailable. See Chapter 6 for more on ADO Command objects.

## WAITFOR Statement

You use the WAITFOR statement to insert a time delay into your stored procedure code. The syntax is as follows:

```
WAITFOR {DELAY 'delay' | TIME 'time'}
```

You can specify the WAITFOR delay time as either a relative or absolute time. Use *delay* to specify a relative time in hours:minutes:seconds format; use *time* to specify an absolute time in hours:minutes:seconds format. Both *delay* and *time* values must be 24 hours or less and delimited using single quotes.

For example, the following WAITFOR statement stops execution for 5 seconds:

```
WAITFOR DELAY '0:0:5'
```

The following WAITFOR statement stops execution until 5:00 PM:

```
WAITFOR TIME '17:00:00'
```

# WHILE, BREAK, and CONTINUE Statements

You use the WHILE statement to repeatedly execute a block of statements while a condition is true. The WHILE statement is similar to the VBA DO...WHILE loop. The syntax is as follows:

```
WHILE condition
    {statement | statement block}
```

A WHILE loop may consist of a single statement or a block of statements between BEGIN and END statements. The *statement* or *statement block* is executed repeatedly until the *condition* evaluates to false.

Within a statement block, you may use the BREAK or CONTINUE statements. You use the BREAK statement to terminate the WHILE loop and continue execution at the statement following the END statement. You use the CONTINUE statement to restart the WHILE loop.

The procIncreaseAvgPrice stored procedure increases the prices of menu items by $0.01 until the average price of menu items is $5.00 or greater. This feat is accomplished using a WHILE loop:

```
Create Procedure procIncreaseAvgPrice
As
    set nocount on
    DECLARE @oldavg MONEY, @newavg MONEY
    -- Calculate and store away old average price
    SELECT @oldavg = (SELECT Avg(Price) FROM tblMenu)

    WHILE (SELECT Avg(Price) FROM tblMenu) < 5
        BEGIN
        UPDATE tblMenu
        SET Price = Price + 0.01
        END
```

```
-- Calculate new average price
SELECT @newavg = (SELECT Avg(Price) FROM tblMenu)
-- Output old and new average prices
SELECT @oldavg AS OldAvgPrice, @newavg AS NewAvgPrice
```

# Using Built-in Variables, Functions, and Procedures

Like Access and VBA, SQL Server provides a number of built-in variables and functions that you can take advantage of in your stored procedures. You can also take advantage of SQL Server's system stored procedures. In this section, we present some of the more commonly used built-in variables, functions, and system stored procedures. For a more complete reference of these items, see SQL Server Books Online.

## System Variables

You can use system variables to retrieve various pieces of system data. System variables all begin with "@@". Some of the more commonly used system variables are summarized in Table 5.2

**T A B L E   5 . 2 :**   Commonly Used T-SQL System Variables

| Variable | Description |
| --- | --- |
| @@ERROR | Returns the error number of the last executed T-SQL statement, or 0 if the statement executed successfully. |
| @@IDENTITY | Returns the last-assigned identity column value for the current connection. |
| @@ROWCOUNT | Returns the number of rows affected by the last SQL statement. |
| @@SERVERNAME | Returns the name of the SQL Server machine. |
| @@SPID | Returns the server process ID for the current connection. |
| @@VERSION | Returns the date and version number of the SQL Server installation. |

The procInsertOrder stored procedure (shown earlier) used @@IDENTITY to determine the value of the new OrderId column for the inserted row. Here's the source for procInsertOrder:

```
Create Procedure procInsertOrder
    @orderdate datetime,
    @customerid int,
    @ordertakerid int,
    @deliverydate datetime,
    @paymentmethod nvarchar(50),
    @notes ntext,
    @orderid int OUTPUT
As
    set nocount on
    INSERT INTO tblOrder
    (OrderDate, CustomerId,
    OrderTakerId, DeliveryDate,
    PaymentMethod, Notes)
    VALUES
    (@orderdate, @customerid,
    @ordertakerid, @deliverydate,
    @paymentmethod, @notes)
    -- Pass back the new OrderId value
    -- to the calling program as an output parameter
    SELECT @orderid = @@IDENTITY
```

**NOTE**    The complete listing of system variables can be found in the SQL Server Books Online help system.

## Built-in Functions

SQL Server provides a variety of built-in functions you can use in your stored procedures. There are several types of built-in functions: date/time, mathematical, string, and system. Some of the more commonly used built-in functions are summarized in Table 5.3

The following example, from procOrderRenewal, demonstrates the use of DATEADD to add five years to a date:

```
Create Procedure procOrderRenewal
```

**T A B L E  5 . 3 :**   Commonly Used Built-in T-SQL Functions

| Type | Function | Description |
|------|----------|-------------|
| Date/Time | DATEADD | Returns a date based on adding an interval to a date. |
| Date/Time | DATEDIFF | Returns the number of days, months, years, etc. between two dates. |
| Date/Time | DATEPART | Returns a portion of a datetime value. |
| Date/Time | GETDATE | Returns the system date and time. |
| Math | RAND | Returns a random number between 0 and 1. |
| Math | ROUND | Returns a number rounded to a specified level of precision. |
| Math | SQRT | Returns the square root of a number. |
| String | CHARINDEX | Returns the starting position of a substring within a string. |
| String | LTRIM | Returns a string with leading blanks removed. |
| String | SOUNDEX | Returns the Soundex sound-alike code for a string. |
| String | STUFF | Inserts one string into another. |
| String | SUBSTRING | Returns a portion of a string. |
| System | CAST | Converts one datatype to another. (CONVERT provides similar functionality.) |
| System | DB_NAME | Returns the name of the database. |
| System | ISDATE | Returns true if the expression is a valid date. |
| System | IS_MEMBER | Returns true if the user is a member of the named group or role. |
| System | ISNULL | Replaces Null with a specified replacement value. |
| System | ISNUMERIC | Returns true if the expression is a valid number. |
| System | SUSER_NAME | Returns the login name. |

```
As
    SELECT OrderDate,
    DateAdd(year, 5, OrderDate) AS RenewalDate
    FROM tblOrder
```

The procCustomerOrderCount stored procedure, which was shown earlier in the chapter, uses the CAST function to convert numeric values into string values which it then prints using the PRINT statement (you'll need to run this stored procedure from SQL Server Query Analyzer, ISQL, or OSQL to see the printed result):

```
Create Procedure procCustomerOrderCount
    @custid INT
As
    Declare @ordercount INT
    SELECT @ordercount = Count(*) FROM tblOrder
    WHERE CustomerId = @custid
    PRINT 'Customer #' + CAST(@custid AS varchar(5)) +
    ' has made ' + CAST(@ordercount AS varchar(5)) +
    ' orders.'
```

> **NOTE**  The complete listing of built-in functions, their arguments, and usage can be found in the SQL Server Books Online help system.

## System Stored Procedures

SQL Server contains a number of system stored procedures—or just system procedures—that you can use to query SQL Server's system tables and configure SQL Server. All of the system procedures begin with either "sp_" for *system procedure* or "xp_" for *extended procedure*. System procedures are like regular user-stored procedures that are written in T-SQL—except they are stored in SQL Server's master database and perform their work on the current database. Extended procedures are similar to system procedures but they call external DLL or EXE libraries to perform their work.

Some of the more commonly used system procedures are summarized in Table 5.4.

**TABLE 5.4:** Commonly Used System Stored Procedures

| System/Extended | Procedure | Description |
| --- | --- | --- |
| System | sp_columns | Returns information about columns in a table. |
| System | sp_configure | Views or changes various SQL Server configuration options. |
| System | sp_dboption | Views or changes database options. |
| System | sp_help | Returns information about database objects. |

**TABLE 5.4:** Commonly Used System Stored Procedures *(continued)*

| System/Extended | Procedure | Description |
|---|---|---|
| System | sp_helpdb | Returns information about databases. |
| System | sp_helpsql | Provides syntax help for T-SQL statements. |
| System | sp_helptext | Returns the T-SQL source code for stored procedures, views, and other objects. |
| System | sp_lock | Returns information about locks that are currently placed on the server. |
| System | sp_recompile | Recompiles a stored procedure or all of the stored procedures associated with a table or view. |
| System | sp_server_info | Returns a wealth of information about the server. |
| System | sp_statistics | Returns information about indexes for a table. |
| System | sp_who | Returns information on active SQL Server users. |
| Extended | xp_commandshell | Executes a Windows command. |
| Extended | xp_sendmail | Sends an e-mail message using SQLMail. |

For example, you might use sp_columns to retrieve information on the columns in the tblMenu table:

```
EXECUTE sp_columns 'tblMenu'
```

Figure 5.9 shows the resulting recordset returned by running sp_columns on tblMenu.

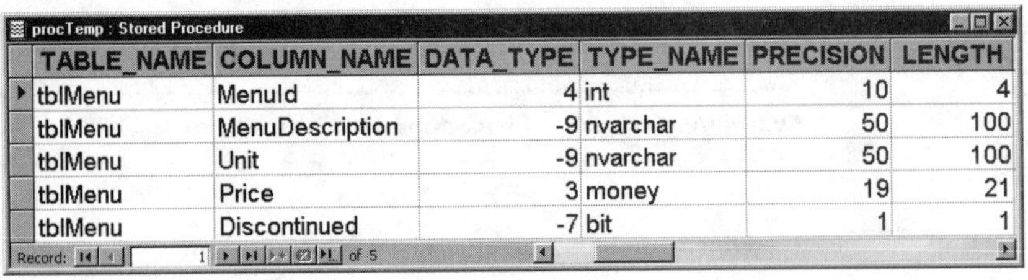

procTemp : Stored Procedure

| TABLE_NAME | COLUMN_NAME | DATA_TYPE | TYPE_NAME | PRECISION | LENGTH |
|---|---|---|---|---|---|
| tblMenu | MenuId | 4 | int | 10 | 4 |
| tblMenu | MenuDescription | -9 | nvarchar | 50 | 100 |
| tblMenu | Unit | -9 | nvarchar | 50 | 100 |
| tblMenu | Price | 3 | money | 19 | 21 |
| tblMenu | Discontinued | -7 | bit | 1 | 1 |

Record: 1 of 5

**FIGURE 5.9**
The information returned by sp_columns for tblMenu

You might use sp_help to get information about the procInsertOrder stored procedure:

```
EXECUTE sp_help 'procInsertOrder'
```

The recordset returned by sp_help is shown in Figure 5.10.

**FIGURE 5.10**

The information returned by sp_help for procInsertOrder

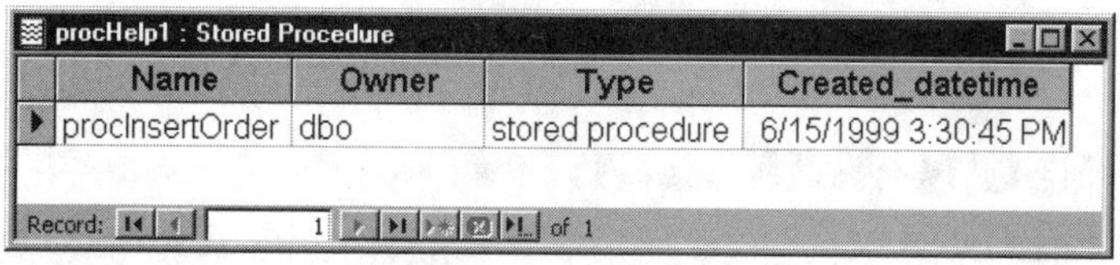

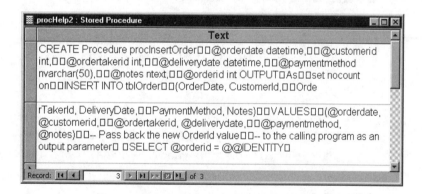

While sp_help returns information *about* a stored procedure, sp_helptext returns the *source* of the stored procedure. For example:

```
EXECUTE sp_helptext 'procInsertOrder'
```

The recordset returned by sp_helptext is shown in Figure 5.11. The returned text includes embedded line feed/carriage return characters.

**FIGURE 5.11**

sp_helptext returns the source of the procInsertOrder stored procedure.

# Grouping Operations with Transactions

*Transactions* are useful whenever you wish to treat a series of operations as a single atomic unit. Either all of the operations succeed or none of the operations succeed. For example, if you were moving cash from a customer's checking account to a customer's savings account, this would normally consist of two operations: copy record from checking account to savings account, and delete record from checking account. You wouldn't want the first operation to succeed and the second to fail; thus you would execute these two operations within a transaction.

T-SQL has three statements for managing transactions in your stored procedures: BEGIN TRANSACTION, COMMIT TRANSACTION, and ROLLBACK TRANSACTION.

## BEGIN TRANSACTION

To begin a transaction you use BEGIN TRANSACTION. Its syntax is shown here:

```
BEGIN TRAN[SACTION] [transaction_name |
  @tran_name_variable]
```

BEGIN TRANSACTION can be abbreviated to BEGIN TRAN. You can use *transaction_name* or *@tran_name_variable* to optionally assign a name to the transaction.

## COMMIT TRANSACTION

To commit a transaction—that is, to tell SQL Server that it's okay to go ahead and complete the transaction because all of the operations have succeeded—you use the COMMIT TRANSACTION statement. Its syntax is as follows:

```
COMMIT [TRAN[SACTION]] transaction_name |
  @tran_name_variable]
```

COMMIT TRANSACTION can be abbreviated to COMMIT TRAN or simply COMMIT. You can use *transaction_name* or *@tran_name_variable* to refer to the name you assigned to the transaction back in the BEGIN TRANSACTION statement.

## ROLLBACK TRANSACTION

To abort a transaction, you use the ROLLBACK TRANSACTION statement. Its syntax is shown here:

```
ROLLBACK [TRAN[SACTION]] transaction_name |
  @tran_name_variable]
```

ROLLBACK TRANSACTION can be abbreviated to ROLLBACK TRAN or simply ROLLBACK. You can use *transaction_name* or *@tran_name_variable* to refer to the name you assigned to the transaction back in the BEGIN TRANSACTION statement.

## Determining When a Transaction Has Succeeded

Any stored procedures that use transactions must use some mechanism to determine if the transaction should be committed. This is where the T-SQL @@ERROR and @@ROWCOUNT system variables come in handy.

For example, the procMoveCustomertoEmployee stored procedure moves a customer record to the employee table. It uses both @@ERROR and @@ROW-COUNT to determine if the transaction should be committed:

```
Create Procedure procMoveCustomertoEmployee
    @CustomerId INT,
    @EmployeeId INT,
    @SupervisorId INT
As
    set nocount on
    -- intError keeps track of current @@ERROR
    -- value which may be 0 to indicate no error.
    -- intSaveError keeps track of last non-zero
    -- @@ERROR value.
    -- intRowCount keeps track of rowcount.
    DECLARE @intError INT, @intSaveError INT
    DECLARE @intRowCount INT
    SELECT @intSaveError = 0

    BEGIN TRAN
    -- Copy row from tblCustomer to tblEmployee.
    INSERT INTO tblEmployee
    (EmployeeId, LastName, FirstName,
    Address, City, State, ZipCode,
    HomePhone, Notes, SupervisorId)
    SELECT @EmployeeId AS EmployeeId,
    LastName, FirstName,
    Address, City, State, ZipCode,
    Phone, Notes, @SupervisorId AS SupervisorId
    FROM tblCustomer
    WHERE CustomerId = @CustomerId
    -- Save away error code and rowcount.
    SELECT @intError = @@ERROR, @intRowCount = @@ROWCOUNT
```

```
IF @intError <> 0
   BEGIN
   SELECT @intSaveError = @intError
   PRINT 'Error: ' + CAST(@intError AS VARCHAR(5)) +
   ' occurred.'
   END
ELSE
   BEGIN
   -- If no row is found in tblCustomer, no error will
   -- be generated. However, we can check @@ROWCOUNT
   -- to test for this condition. In this case, we
   -- create a dummy errror condition.
   IF @intRowCount = 0
      BEGIN
      SELECT @intSaveError = 5000
      END
   END

-- Now delete the tblCustomer record.
DELETE FROM tblCustomer
WHERE CustomerId = @CustomerId
SELECT @intError = @@ERROR
PRINT @intError
IF @intError <> 0
   BEGIN
   SELECT @intSaveError = @intError
   PRINT 'Error: ' +
   CAST(@intError AS VARCHAR(5)) + ' occurred.'
   END

IF @intSaveError = 0
   BEGIN
   -- All is well, so commit transaction and
   -- report success.
   COMMIT TRAN
   SELECT 'Customer record moved to employee table.'
   AS Status
   END
ELSE
   BEGIN
   -- Something went wrong, so rollback
   -- the transaction and report the problem.
```

```
ROLLBACK TRAN
IF @intSaveError = 5000
    SELECT 'Transaction aborted. ' +
    'No row in tblCustomer to move.'
    AS Status
ELSE
    SELECT 'Transaction aborted. ' +
    'Last error code: ' +
    CAST(@intSaveError AS VARCHAR(5)) AS Status
END
```

# Creating Triggers

A *trigger* is a stored procedure that is automatically executed when a row is inserted, updated, or deleted. You can think of a trigger as an event procedure for a table.

To create a trigger in Access, select a server table in the database container, right-click on the table and select Triggers from the popup menu. At the Triggers for Table dialog box (see Figure 5.12), click New to create a new trigger for the table. If the table already has triggers defined, you can select an existing trigger and click the Edit or Delete buttons.

**FIGURE 5.12**
The Triggers for Table dialog box lets you create a new trigger or edit or delete an existing trigger.

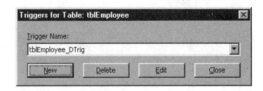

For example, the tblMenu table has a trigger that updates summary values in tblMenuTotals every time a record is updated, inserted, or deleted.

```
Create Trigger trgtblMenuUpdateTotalsUID
On dbo.tblMenu
For  Insert, Update, Delete
As
    SET NOCOUNT on
    DECLARE @curAvgPrice MONEY,
    @curMinPrice MONEY,
```

```
@curMaxPrice MONEY

SELECT @curAvgPrice = Avg(Price),
@curMinPrice = Min(Price),
@curMaxPrice = Max(Price)
FROM tblMenu

UPDATE tblMenuTotals
SET AvgPrice = @curAvgPrice,
MinPrice = @curMinPrice,
MaxPrice = @curMaxPrice
WHERE Id = 1
```

# Trigger Syntax

You create triggers using the CREATE TRIGGER statement whose syntax is shown here:

```
CREATE TRIGGER trigger_name
ON table_name
FOR {Insert | Update | Delete | Insert, Update | Insert, Delete |
Update, Delete | Insert, Update, Delete}
[WITH ENCRYPTION]
AS
SQL statements
```

Triggers must be uniquely named across the database, but each trigger may only apply to a single table. You may create as many triggers for a table that you like as long as each has a unique name.

You specify when the trigger is called using the FOR clause. You can specify Insert, Update, Delete, or some combination of these actions. The body of the trigger comes after the AS keyword. This is where you specify the statements that are to execute when the trigger is called.

---

**TIP**    If you edit an existing trigger in the trigger designer, the designer changes the CREATE TRIGGER statement to ALTER TRIGGER. You use the ALTER TRIGGER statement to update an existing trigger.

---

## Inserted and Deleted Tables

Triggers are similar to the Access BeforeUpdate event procedures in that they are called just prior to the updating of the data. The trigger code runs before the data is actually committed, but the trigger code sees the changes in the trigger table (the table to which the trigger is attached) as if they have already occurred. The trigger runs within a transaction so no other user sees these changes until the trigger has successfully completed.

SQL Server populates two special tables named *inserted* and *deleted* with copies of the affected rows. By looking at the rows in these tables, your trigger code can determine which rows were updated, inserted, or deleted. This is exactly the information you will need to know while your trigger code is running.

During the course of a trigger, SQL Server performs the following operations on the trigger, inserted, and deleted tables:

- For an Insert trigger, SQL Server adds the new rows to the *trigger* table and also adds a copy of the new rows to the *inserted* table.

- For a Delete trigger, SQL Server removes the deleted rows from the *trigger* table and copies them to the *deleted* table.

- For an Update trigger, SQL Server deletes the old rows (the rows that are being replaced with the updated rows) from the *trigger* table and copies them to the *deleted* table. At the same time, SQL Server adds the updated rows to the *trigger* table and copies the updated rows to the *inserted* table.

The following Update/Insert trigger, trgtblMenuPriceUI, is used to enforce a simple rule (Price must be > 0). Notice how it uses the inserted table to determine the value of Price in the new/updated row:

```
Create Trigger trgtblMenuPriceUI
On dbo.tblMenu
For Insert, Update
As
    set nocount on
    If (SELECT Count(*) FROM inserted WHERE Price <= 0) > 0
        BEGIN
        RAISERROR 50001 'Price must be greater than 0.'
        ROLLBACK TRANSACTION
        END
```

---

**WARNING** If a trigger is triggered from a bulk action query statement, the inserted and deleted tables are populated with all the rows affected by the bulk operation. Keep this in mind when constructing your triggers.

---

## Transactions and the RAISERROR Statement

Triggers automatically run within an implied transaction. You don't include a BEGIN TRANSACTION statement at the beginning of the trigger—it's implied. In fact, you don't even include a COMMIT TRANSACTION statement at the end of the trigger—it too is implied. The only part of the transaction that's not implied is the ROLLBACK TRANSACTION statement, which you include if you wish to abort the insert, update, or delete action.

For example, the trgtblMenuPriceUI trigger introduced in the last section contains this code:

```
If (SELECT Count(*) FROM inserted WHERE Price <= 0) > 0
    BEGIN
    RAISERROR 50001 'Price must be greater than 0.'
    ROLLBACK TRANSACTION
    END
```

This trigger uses the ROLLBACK TRANSACTION statement to abort the transaction if Price is determined to be zero or less. It also uses the RAISERROR statement to generate a SQL Server error. This error is sent back to the client just as if SQL Server had generated it.

There are two forms of RAISERROR: the first form is shown here:

```
RAISERROR error_number error_message
```

You set *error_number* to an integer number and *error_message* to a string that you wish to be displayed by the client when the RAISERROR statement is executed. To make sure you don't conflict with SQL Server's built-in errors, you should set the error number to a value greater than 50,000.

For example, the RAISERROR statement from the trgtblMenuPriceUI trigger used this first form of RAISERROR:

```
RAISERROR 50001 'Price must be greater than 0.'
```

The second form of RAISERROR is more complex:

```
RAISERROR ({error_number | error_message}, severity, state)
```

In this form of RAISERROR, you only get to set an *error_number or* an ad hoc *error_message*. If choose to set the message, SQL Server arbitrarily sets the error number to a value of 50,000. If you choose to set the error number, this number must point to a user-defined error that you have previously created using the sp_addmessage system stored procedure.

You set *severity* to a value from 0 to 18. Values less than 11 are considered warnings, not errors. (If you're a member of the sysadmin role, you can use values above 18, however, these values should only be used with caution.)

You set *state* to an arbitrary integer value from 1 through 127 that represents information about the invocation state of the error. A value of 1 works just fine.

For example, the RAISERROR statement from the trgtblMenuPriceUI trigger could have been rewritten as:

```
RAISERROR ('Price must be greater than 0.', 16, 1)
```

**NOTE**    The second form of RAISERROR has additional arguments that let you create ad hoc messages with replaceable strings. See SQL Server Books Online for more details.

## Checking if a Column Has Been Updated

You can use a special form of the IF statement within a trigger to determine if a particular column was updated by the action that triggered the trigger:

```
IF UPDATE(column_name) [{AND|OR} UPDATE(column_name)
[,...n]
```

For example, we could rewrite the trgtblMenuPriceUI trigger as follows:

```
Create Trigger trgtblMenuPriceUI
On dbo.tblMenu
For Insert, Update
As
    set nocount on
    If UPDATE(Price)
        IF(SELECT Count(*) FROM inserted WHERE Price <= 0)
        > 0
            BEGIN
            RAISERROR 50001 'Price must be greater than 0.'
            ROLLBACK TRANSACTION
            END
```

Using the IF UPDATE() statement is especially useful when your trigger updates data in other tables. In these cases, you can use IF UPDATE() to be more selective and execute the updates only when necessary.

# Using Stored Procedures to Implement Cascading

While you can use SQL Server's declarative referential integrity (DRI) to create primary key/foreign key relationships between tables, DRI doesn't currently support the cascading of record deletions or primary key updates to foreign key tables. However, you can use stored procedures in concert with DRI to implement this commonly needed functionality. (See Chapter 4 for more on DRI.)

## Why Not Use Triggers?

You can easily create triggers to implement the cascading of primary key updates and deletions that work for single record updates and deletions. Problems arise, however, when these triggers are called from a bulk operation that updates or deletes multiple records. While it's not impossible to create triggers that work for multiple record operations, in order to create them you'll have to use inefficient server cursors inside the triggers. Since triggers get called for many record operations, it's not a good idea to place inefficient code in them. Thus, the bottom line is to avoid using triggers to implement cascading of primary key updates and deletions.

Follow these steps to implement cascading using a combination of DRI and stored procedures:

1. Create the relationship using DRI. This would normally disallow updates to the primary key and deletes of rows in the primary key table when related rows were present in the foreign key table.

2. Create a stored procedure that performs the cascading operation and then call this stored procedure anytime you wished to delete or update records with cascading.

For example, say you wished to implement a one-to-many relationship between tblEmployee and tblOrder with cascading of updates and deletes implemented via stored procedures. To implement this scenario, you would first have to implement DRI using a database diagram (see Chapter 4). You would also create two stored procedures.

Cascading the deletion is fairly straightforward. First delete the dependent foreign key records, and then delete the primary key records. Here's the code to do this for the tblEmployee/tblOrder relationship:

```
Create Procedure procCascadeEmployeeIdDelete
    @empid INT
As
    set nocount on
    /* Only need to perform the cascade if there
       are dependent records */
    IF (SELECT COUNT(*) FROM tblOrder
    WHERE OrderTakerId = @empid) > 0
    BEGIN
    /* Delete foreign key records first. */
    DELETE tblOrder
    WHERE OrderTakerId = @empid
    IF @@ERROR <> 0
        ROLLBACK TRANSACTION
    ELSE
        BEGIN
        /* Now delete the primary key records. */
        DELETE tblEmployee
        WHERE EmployeeId = @empid
        IF @@ERROR <> 0
            ROLLBACK TRANSACTION
        END
    END
```

Once you've created procCascadeEmployeeIdDelete, you can now delete an employee record and his or her orders by calling the stored procedure. For example:

```
EXECUTE procCascadeEmployeeIdDelete @empid=10
```

Cascading the update is a little more involved. You first have to copy the existing record to a new record with the new primary key value. Then you can update the foreign key of the dependent records. Finally, you must delete the old primary key record. Here's the code to do this for the tblEmployee/tblOrder relationship:

```
Create Procedure procCascadeEmployeeIdUpdate
    @oldid INT,
    @newid INT
As
    set nocount on
    /* Only need to perform the cascade if there
       are dependent records */
    IF (SELECT COUNT(*) FROM tblOrder
    WHERE OrderTakerId = @oldid) > 0
    BEGIN
    /* Create the new tblEmployee record by copying
       the old record with the new EmployeeId. */
    INSERT INTO tblEmployee
    (EmployeeId, LastName, FirstName,
    Address, City, State, ZipCode,
    HomePhone, Notes, SupervisorId)
    SELECT @newid AS EmployeeId,
    LastName, FirstName,
    Address, City, State, ZipCode,
    HomePhone, Notes, SupervisorId
    FROM tblEmployee
    WHERE EmployeeId = @oldid

    /* Now cascade the change. */
    UPDATE tblOrder
    SET OrderTakerId = @newid
    WHERE OrderTakerId = @oldid
    IF @@ERROR <> 0
        ROLLBACK TRANSACTION
    ELSE
        BEGIN
        /* And remove the old employee record. */
        DELETE tblEmployee
        WHERE EmployeeId = @oldid
        IF @@ERROR <> 0
            ROLLBACK TRANSACTION
        END
    END
```

Once you've created the stored procedure, you can now delete an employee record and his or her orders by calling the stored procedure. For example:

```
EXECUTE procCascadeEmployeeIdUpdate @oldid=7, @newid=23
```

**NOTE**    If multiple relationships are affected by the operation, you will have to cascade the update or delete to all involved tables. For example, you might want to extend the procCascadeEmployeeIdDelete and procCascadeEmployeeIdUpdate stored procedures so they cascade the delete/update operation to the tblOrderDetails table.

# Summary

In this chapter, we discussed how to create stored procedures and triggers. This included the following topics:

- The basic syntax of a SQL Server stored procedure
- How to use parameters and variables in your stored procedures
- How to execute stored procedures
- Using Transact-SQL control-of-flow statements within stored procedures
- Using built-in variables, functions, and system stored procedures
- Wrapping stored procedure operations within transactions and trapping for errors
- Creating SQL Server triggers
- How to use the special inserted and deleted tables
- How to rollback trigger transactions and generate error messages
- Cascading primary key updates and deletes using stored procedures

# Using ActiveX Data Objects with Server Data

- Creating connections to server databases

- Executing parameterized stored procedures using Command objects

- Executing ad hoc SQL and prepared statements using Command objects

- Managing concurrent access to server data

- Sinking to ADO events

- Dealing with ADO errors

In Chapter 6 of the *Access 2000 Developer's Handbook, Volume 1,* we examined how to use ActiveX Data Objects (ADO) to work with Access MDB data. In this chapter, we'll take a look at how you use ADO to work with server data instead. While the examples in this chapter will focus on the use of ADO with SQL Server/MSDE data, much of the discussion also applies to the use of Access with other server databases such as Oracle and DB2.

# ADO Object Model

The objects and collections of the ADO 2.1 object model are summarized in Figure 6.1. Just as when working with Jet data, when you work with server data, you'll primarily focus on three ADO objects: Connection, Command, and Recordset. You use a Connection object to establish a connection to an OLE DB data provider, a Command object to execute a query or stored procedure, and a Recordset object to retrieve a set of records.

**FIGURE 6.1**
The ADO Object Model

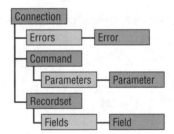

# Creating Connections

ADO provides two ways to establish a connection to an OLE DB data source: implicit and explicit connections. ADO creates an implicit connection for you when you create a Recordset or Command object and provide the Recordset or Command object a connection string without first creating an explicit ADO Connection object. In most cases, however, it's more efficient to create an explicit Connection object that you can then reuse with multiple Recordset and Command objects. Using an explicit Connection object also affords you greater control over the type of connection that ADO creates.

---

**NOTE**   If you're using an Access project file (ADP) with MSDE or SQL Server, you can use the project's existing connection. See the "Using CurrentProject.Connection" section later in this chapter for more details.

---

# Creating a Connection to a Server Database

You use the Connection object's Open method to establish a connection to a server database. The first order of business is in selecting the correct OLE DB provider.

## Selecting a Provider

When connecting to SQL Server or MSDE using the Microsoft SQL Server 6.5/7.0 OLE DB data provider, you set the Provider keyword of the connection string or the Provider property of the Connection object to *"SQLOLEDB."* To connect to Oracle using the Microsoft Oracle OLE DB provider, you set the Provider keyword of the connection string or the Provider property to *"MSDAORA."*

There are, of course, many other server databases besides SQL Server and Oracle. See the server database's documentation for more details. If your server doesn't have a native OLE DB provider available, you may also be able to use the ODBC data provider (*MSDASQL*) along with the server's ODBC driver.

---

**TIP**   While you can connect to any server database (including SQL Server and Oracle) via the ODBC data provider (MSDASQL), this adds an extra layer to the connection. In general, it's best to use a native OLE DB provider if one is available.

---

## Creating the Connection

ADO provides considerable flexibility in how you specify the type of connection to open. You can specify everything about the connection using the ConnectionString argument of the Open method. (Alternately, you can use the ConnectionString property of the Connection object.) You can also specify characteristics of the connection using various Connection object properties. Finally, you can use a combination of these methods. The exact connection string keywords or Connection properties you use depends on the provider you are using. Some of the more common connection string keywords and Connection properties for SQL Server are summarized in Table 6.1

**TABLE 6.1:** Common SQL Server/MSDE Connection String Keywords and Connection Object Properties

| Item | Connection String Keyword | Connection Object Property |
|------|---------------------------|----------------------------|
| Database | Initial Catalog (or Database) | Initial Catalog |
| Server | Data Source (or Server) | Data Source |
| User ID | User ID (or UID) | User ID |
| Password | Password (or Pwd) | Password |
| Integrated Security | Trusted_Connection = yes | Integrated Security = SSPI |
| Force Password Prompt | N/A | Prompt = adPromptAlways |
| Don't save password with connection string | N/A | Persist Security Info = False |
| Use client-side cursors | N/A | CursorLocation = adUseClient |

For example, to open a connection to a SQL Server database named "ADH2KSQL" on a server named "gorilla" with a user ID of "Suzanne" and a password of "mud", you might use the following code (from the Connect1 subroutine of the basConnection module of the CH06A.MDB sample database):

```
Sub Connect1()
    Dim cnn As ADODB.Connection
    Set cnn = New ADODB.Connection

    cnn.Open "Provider=SQLOLEDB;Data Source=Gorilla;" & _
      "Database=ADH2KSQL;User Id=Suzanne;Password=mud"

    cnn.Close
    Set cnn = Nothing
End Sub
```

The Connect2 subroutine uses the ConnectionString property to open the same SQL Server database:

```
Sub Connect2()
    Dim cnn As ADODB.Connection
    Set cnn = New ADODB.Connection

    cnn.ConnectionString = _
     "Provider=SQLOLEDB;Data Source=Gorilla;" & _
     "Database=ADH2KSQL;User Id=Suzanne;Password=mud"
    cnn.Open

    cnn.Close
    Set cnn = Nothing
End Sub
```

In the Connect3 subroutine, we have used properties of the Connection object instead:

```
Sub Connect3()
    Dim cnn As ADODB.Connection
    Set cnn = New ADODB.Connection

    With cnn
        .Provider = "SQLOLEDB"
        .Properties("Data Source") = "Gorilla"
        .Properties("Initial Catalog") = "ADH2KSQL"
        .Properties("User Id") = "Suzanne"
        .Properties("Password") = "mud"
        .Open
    End With

    cnn.Close
    Set cnn = Nothing
End Sub
```

## Using Integrated Security

If you wish to use SQL Server or MSDE with integrated security (also known as Windows NT/2000 authentication), then you can use either the Integrated Security Connection property or the Trusted_Connection connection string keyword. When you're using integrated security, your Windows NT or Windows 2000 authentication is used to log you onto SQL Server, obviating the need to log in a second time to SQL Server.

**NOTE** Before you can use integrated security, you must add Windows NT/2000 user accounts to SQL Server. See Chapter 8 for more details.

The code in Connect4 demonstrates how to create a connection to a SQL Server database using the Integrated Security Connection property:

```
Sub Connect4()
    Dim cnn As ADODB.Connection

    Set cnn = New ADODB.Connection

    With cnn
        .Provider = "SQLOLEDB"
        .Properties("Data Source") = "Gorilla"
        .Properties("Initial Catalog") = "ADH2KSQL"
        .Properties("Integrated Security") = "SSPI"
        .Open
    End With

    cnn.Close
    Set cnn = Nothing
End Sub
```

Similarly, Connect5 demonstrates how to create a connection to a SQL Server database using the Trusted_Connection connection string keyword:

```
Sub Connect5()
    Dim cnn As ADODB.Connection

    Set cnn = New ADODB.Connection

    cnn.Open "Provider=SQLOLEDB;Data Source=Gorilla;" & _
      "Database=ADH2KSQL;Trusted_Connection=yes;"

    cnn.Close
    Set cnn = Nothing
End Sub
```

**TIP**     Integrated security is only available for Windows NT and Windows 2000 users.

## Password Persistence

By default, ADO embeds your password in the connection string. Thus, if you read the value of the ConnectionString property, you'll be able to view a user's password. To demonstrate this, add the following statement to any of the Connect subroutines:

```
Debug.Print cnn.ConnectionString
```

When you do this, Access prints something similar to the following to the Debug window:

```
Provider=SQLOLEDB.1;Password=mud;User ID=Suzanne;
Initial Catalog=ADH2KSQL;Data Source=Gorilla;
Locale Identifier=1033;Connect Timeout=15;
Use Procedure for Prepare=1;Auto Translate=True;
Packet Size=4096;Workstation ID=GORILLA
```

This is of course a potential security hole, but one you can easily plug up by setting the Persist Security Info property to False. For example, in Connect6, we've set the Persist Security Info property to False:

```
Sub Connect6()
    Dim cnn As ADODB.Connection

    Set cnn = New ADODB.Connection

    With cnn
        .Provider = "SQLOLEDB"
        .Properties("Data Source") = "Gorilla"
        .Properties("Initial Catalog") = "ADH2KSQL"
        .Properties("User Id") = "Suzanne"
        .Properties("Password") = "mud"
        .Properties("Persist Security Info") = False
        .Open
    End With

    Debug.Print cnn.ConnectionString

    cnn.Close
    Set cnn = Nothing
End Sub
```

This time, the Connection object's ConnectionString property doesn't include the password:

```
Provider=SQLOLEDB.1;Persist Security Info=False;
User ID=Suzanne;Initial Catalog=ADH2KSQL;
Data Source=Gorilla;Locale Identifier=1033;
Connect Timeout=15;Use Procedure for Prepare=1;
Auto Translate=True;Packet Size=4096;Workstation ID=GORILLA
```

---

**TIP**    When working with secured servers without integrated security, you should always set the Persist Security Info property of the Connection object to False. If you're using integrated security, this isn't an issue. See Chapter 8 for more information on SQL Server/MSDE security.

---

## Prompting Users

You can use the Prompt property to control if and when the data provider prompts the user for user ID, password, and other connection information. You can set the Prompt property to any of the values from Table 6.2; adPromptNever is the default setting.

**T A B L E   6 . 2 :**   Prompt Connection Property Values

| Prompt Constant | Description |
| --- | --- |
| adPromptAlways | Always prompt for connection information, even if complete information was provided. |
| adPromptComplete | Prompt only if additional information was needed. |
| adPromptComplete Required | Prompt for more information if necessary, but don't accept optional information. |
| adPromptNever | Never prompt for information; fail if not enough information was provided (default). |

The Connect7 subroutine from basConnection demonstrates how to connect to a SQL Server database using a prompt dialog box:

```
Sub Connect7()
    Dim cnn As ADODB.Connection

    Set cnn = New ADODB.Connection
```

```
With cnn
    .Provider = "SQLOLEDB"
    .Properties("Data Source") = "Gorilla"
    .Properties("Initial Catalog") = "ADH2KSQL"
    .Properties("Prompt") = adPromptAlways
    .Properties("Persist Security Info") = False
    .Open
End With

cnn.Close
Set cnn = Nothing
End Sub
```

The SQL Server Login dialog box produced by Connect7 is shown in Figure 6.2.

**FIGURE 6.2**
The SQL Server Login dialog box

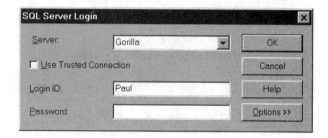

## Cursor Location

You can use the CursorLocation property of a Connection object to specify where ADO should build recordset cursors. By default, ADO uses server-side cursors for most data providers (adUseServer), including SQL Server. However, certain ADO features, such as use of the use of the Recordset property of ADP forms, require the use of client-side cursors. The following code creates a connection that uses client-side cursors:

```
Dim cnnClient as Connection
Set cnnClient = New ADODB.Connection
cnnClient.CursorLocation = adUseClient
```

**TIP**   In general, it's more efficient to use server-side cursors. Only use a client-side cursor when you need to.

## Using CurrentProject.Connection

If you're using an Access project, Access maintains a connection to SQL Server or MSDE automatically. When using ADO, you can use the existing connection to SQL Server by using the Connection property of the CurrentProject object:

```
Dim cnn As ADODB.Connection
Set cnn = CurrentProject.Connection
```

For example, the UseCurrentProjectCnn subroutine from basADPConnection of the CH06B.ADP project makes use of the connection of the CurrentProject object to create a simple recordset:

```
Sub UseCurrentProjectCnn()
    Dim cnn As ADODB.Connection
    Dim rst As ADODB.Recordset

    Set cnn = CurrentProject.Connection
    Set rst = New ADODB.Recordset

    rst.Open "SELECT LastName FROM tblCustomer", cnn
    Do While Not rst.EOF
        Debug.Print rst!LastName
        rst.MoveNext
    Loop
    rst.Close
    Set rst = Nothing
    Set cnn = Nothing
End Sub
```

If you display the ConnectionString property of the project's connection, you may be surprised to find that the ADP files use the Microsoft Data Shaping Service for OLE DB (MSDataShape) instead of directly using the SQL Server OLE DB data provider (SQLOLEDB). By using the Microsoft Data Shaping Service, which in turn calls the SQL Server OLE DB data provider, Access is able to create hierarchical or shaped recordsets out of SQL Server data. Of course, you can directly use the Microsoft Data Shaping Service if you'd like—see *Visual Basic Developer's Guide to ADO* (Sybex, 1999) by Mike Gunderloy for more information on ADO data shaping.

# Using Command Objects

You use an ADO Command object to execute a query. When used with a server database, the source of the query may be the name of a table or view, a SQL statement, or a stored procedure.

You can use Command objects to execute queries that both return records and those that do not. In this section, we'll limit the discussion to queries that don't return records—that is, *action queries*. We discuss the use of Command objects with record-returning queries in the later section entitled "Creating Server Recordsets."

## Command Object Properties and Methods

The Command object has a number of methods and properties. These are summarized in Table 6.3.

**TABLE 6.3:**   The Methods and Properties of the Command Object

| Type | Property/Method | Description |
| --- | --- | --- |
| Property | ActiveConnection | Sets the Connection object or connection string used by the Command |
| Property | CommandText | SQL string or name of stored procedure, table, or view to be used as the source of the query |
| Property | CommandType | Describes the type of CommandText used; may be adCmdText (SQL query), adCmdTable (query against table), adCmdTableDirect (directly opened table), adCmdStoredProc (stored procedure or action query), adCmdUnknown (unknown; default), or adCmdFile (persisted recordset) |

**TABLE 6.3:** The Methods and Properties of the Command Object *(continued)*

| Type | Property/Method | Description |
| --- | --- | --- |
| Property | CommandTimeout | Number of seconds to wait before abandoning the execution of a query; defaults to 30 |
| Property | Prepared | If True, indicates that the CommandText should be run as a prepared statement |
| Property | State | Returns information about the state of the Command object—open (adStateOpen) or closed (adStateClosed) |
| Method | Cancel | Terminates the execution of an asynchronous Command query |
| Method | CreateParameter | Creates a parameter for a parameterized action query or stored procedure |
| Method | Execute | Executes the Command object's query |

You use the Execute method of a Command object to run a query. At a bare minimum, you must set the ActiveConnection and CommandText properties before using the Execute method, as shown in the following example (CmdSQL1 from basADPCommand in CH06B.ADP):

```
Sub CmdSQL1()
    Dim cmd As ADODB.Command
    Dim strSQL As String

    Set cmd = New ADODB.Command
    ' Set Notes field to current date & time
    strSQL = "UPDATE tblCustomer SET Notes = '" & _
      CStr(Now()) & "'"

    Set cmd.ActiveConnection = CurrentProject.Connection
    cmd.CommandText = strSQL
    cmd.Execute

    Set cmd = Nothing
End Sub
```

While CmdSQL1 works, you'll want to also set the CommandType property of the Command Object. If you don't use the CommandType property, ADO has to guess as to what type of CommandText you are sending it, wasting valuable time. You should always use the CommandType property as shown in CmdSQL2:

```
Sub CmdSQL2()
    Dim cmd As ADODB.Command
    Dim strSQL As String

    Set cmd = New ADODB.Command
    ' Set Notes field to current date & time
    strSQL = "UPDATE tblCustomer SET Notes = '" & _
    CStr(Now()) & "'"

    Set cmd.ActiveConnection = CurrentProject.Connection
    cmd.CommandText = strSQL
    cmd.CommandType = adCmdText
    cmd.Execute

    Set cmd = Nothing
End Sub
```

## The Execute Method

The Command object's Execute method has the following syntax when used with non-row returning queries:

```
cmd.Execute [recordsaffected,] [parameters,] [options]
```

where:

- *cmd* is a Command object variable.

- *recordsaffected* is an optional long variable into which ADO returns the number of records affected by the action query or stored procedure.

- *parameters* is an optional array of input parameters.

- *options* is an optional long integer indicating the type of command contained in the CommandText property; it may be adCmdText (SQL query), adCmdTable (query against table), adCmdTableDirect (directly opened table), adCmdStoredProc (stored procedure or action query), adCmdUnknown (unknown; the default), or adCmdFile (persisted recordset); it can be combined with adExecuteNoRecords (the query doesn't return records), adAsyncExecute (execute query asynchronously), or adAsyncFetch (fetch the remaining asynchronous rows).

**NOTE**  You can also use the Execute method of a Connection object to execute an action query. When you use a Connection object's Execute method, however, you are more limited in what you can do. For example, you can't pass parameters to a stored procedure when using a Connection object's Execute method.

## The Options Argument

You'll notice you can set the *options* argument to a similar set of constants as the CommandType property. However, the last three constants (adExecuteNoRecords, adAsyncExecute, and adAsyncFetch ) are not supported by the CommandType property.

By default, ADO sets up a recordset in which to place the results of a Command object, even when the query doesn't return records. This is an unnecessary waste of resources that you can easily prevent by including the adCmdExecuteNoRecords constant in the Options argument, as illustrated by CmdSQLNoRecs:

```
Sub CmdSQLNoRecs()
    Dim cmd As ADODB.Command
    Dim strSQL As String

    Set cmd = New ADODB.Command
    ' Set Notes field to current date & time
    strSQL = "UPDATE tblCustomer SET Notes = '" & _
     CStr(Now()) & "'"

    Set cmd.ActiveConnection = CurrentProject.Connection
    cmd.CommandText = strSQL
    cmd.CommandType = adCmdText
    cmd.Execute Options:=adExecuteNoRecords

    Set cmd = Nothing
End Sub
```

## The RecordsAffected Argument

You can use the Execute method's *RecordsAffected* argument to check whether your bulk SQL operation worked and, if so, how many records were affected by the operation. CmdSQLRecsAffected illustrates how you can use this argument:

```
Sub CmdSQLRecsAffected()
    Dim cmd As ADODB.Command
```

```
        Dim strSQL As String
        Dim lngRecs As Long

        Set cmd = New ADODB.Command
        ' Set Notes field to current date & time
        strSQL = "UPDATE tblCustomer SET Notes = '" & _
         CStr(Now()) & "'"

        Set cmd.ActiveConnection = CurrentProject.Connection
        cmd.CommandText = strSQL
        cmd.CommandType = adCmdText
        cmd.Execute RecordsAffected:=lngRecs, _
         Options:=adExecuteNoRecords
        Debug.Print lngRecs & " records were updated."

        Set cmd = Nothing
    End Sub
```

---

**NOTE**    Under certain conditions, RecordsAffected can report a spurious number. This might happen, for example, if the query or stored procedure causes a trigger to be executed or a stored procedure includes multiple SQL statements.

---

**TIP**    If you use the SET NOCOUNT ON statement within a SQL Server stored procedure, RecordsAffected will be set to −1 if the procedure succeeded and 0 if it did not.

---

## Executing Stored Procedures

In Chapter 5, we discussed the many advantages of stored procedures. The judicious use of stored procedures helps to make your applications faster, easier to maintain, and more secure.

The RunMenuPricesSP subroutine (from basADPCommand in CH06B.ADP) illustrates how to execute a simple stored procedure:

```
Sub RunMenuPriceSP()
    Dim cmd As ADODB.Command
    Dim strSQL As String
    Dim lngRecs As Long
```

```
Set cmd = New ADODB.Command

Set cmd.ActiveConnection = CurrentProject.Connection
cmd.CommandText = "procMenuPricesIncrease"
cmd.CommandType = adCmdStoredProc
cmd.Execute RecordsAffected:=lngRecs, _
 Options:=adExecuteNoRecords

Debug.Print "Price was increased by 10% for " & _
 lngRecs & " records."

Set cmd = Nothing
End Sub
```

The procMenuPricesIncrease stored procedure increases the prices of all tblMenu records by 10%. Its source is shown here:

```
CREATE Procedure procMenuPricesIncrease
As
    UPDATE tblMenu
    SET Price = Price*1.1
```

---

**TIP**     See Chapter 5 for more information on creating stored procedures.

---

# Passing Parameters to and from Stored Procedures

While you may occasionally create a stored procedure like procMenuPrices-Increase that doesn't have any parameters, this type of stored procedure will be rare. Most stored procedures have parameters. Fortunately, the ADO Command object is well equipped to handle stored procedures with parameters.

There are several different methods for passing parameters to and retrieving parameters from a stored procedure. We'll take a look at each.

## Using the Parameters Argument

You can pass input parameters to a stored procedure using the Parameters argument of a Command object's Execute method. This argument accepts either a single value or an array of values.

For example, the procDeleteCustomer stored procedure deletes a single customer record from tblCustomer. It accepts a single input parameter, @custid, the CustomerId of the record you wish to delete:

```
Create Procedure procDeleteCustomer
    @custid integer
As
    DELETE
    FROM tblCustomer
    WHERE CustomerId = @custid
```

If a stored procedure has only one input parameter, you can simply pass the value of the parameter in the Parameters argument as demonstrated by the Del-CustSPArray subroutine (from the basCommand module of the CH06A.MDB database):

```
Private Const adhcADH2KSQLCnn = "Provider=SQLOLEDB;" & _
  "Data Source=Gorilla;Database=ADH2KSQL;" & _
  "User Id=sa;Password=;"

Sub DelCustSPArray(lngCustId As Long)
    ' Execute a stored procedure
    ' by passing parameters in
    ' Parameters argument of Execute method.
    Dim cnn As ADODB.Connection
    Dim cmd As ADODB.Command
    Dim lngRecs As Long

    Set cnn = New ADODB.Connection
    Set cmd = New ADODB.Command

    cnn.Open adhcADH2KSQLCnn

    Set cmd.ActiveConnection = cnn
    cmd.CommandText = "procDeleteCustomer"
    cmd.CommandType = adCmdStoredProc

    ' Pass parameter to the stored proc.
    ' This method cannot be used with
    ' output parameters or the return value.
    cmd.Execute RecordsAffected:=lngRecs, _
     Parameters:=lngCustId, _
     Options:=adExecuteNoRecords
```

```
If lngRecs <> 0 Then
    Debug.Print "Deleted customer record #" & _
     lngCustId
Else
    Debug.Print "Couldn't delete customer record #" & _
     lngCustId
End If

Set cmd = Nothing
cnn.Close
Set cnn = NothingEnd Sub
```

---

**NOTE**  Since many of the examples in this chapter need to connect to the same database, ADH2KSQL, using an ADO connection string, we've defined a constant, adhcADH2KSQLCnn, that defines that connection string in one place. Then, if we ever change the connection string, we need to change it in only one place. (Actually, we've defined this constant once for each module of CH06A.MDB— we've been slightly redundant to make each module independent of the others in the chapter.)

---

If you need to pass multiple input parameters to a stored procedure, you can use the VBA Array function to create an array from a list of parameter values. For example, the following code from the MoveCustSPArray subroutine uses the Array function to pass three parameters to the procMoveCustomertoEmployee stored procedure.

```
cmd.CommandText = "procMoveCustomertoEmployee"
cmd.CommandType = adCmdStoredProc
cmd.Execute RecordsAffected:=lngRecs, _
 Parameters:=Array(21, 11, 1), _
 Options:=adExecuteNoRecords
```

The biggest drawback with using the Parameters argument of the Execute method to pass parameters to a stored procedure is that it can handle only *input* parameters. If you need to retrieve the return value or an output parameter from a stored procedure, then you need to use the Refresh or Append method instead.

## Using the Refresh Method

By default, a Command object knows nothing about a stored procedure's set of parameters. Using the Refresh method of a Command object's Parameters collection, however, you can ask the Command object to query the server to learn about the stored procedure's parameters.

The Refresh method takes no arguments. Its syntax is as follows:

*command*`.Parameters.Refresh`

Once you've used the Refresh method, you can then reference the stored procedure's parameters by name. The DelCustSPRefresh subroutine demonstrates the use of the Refresh method to execute the procDeleteCustomer stored procedure:

```
Sub DelCustSPRefresh(lngCustId As Long)
    ' Execute a stored procedure
    ' using Refresh method of Command
    ' object's Parameters collection.

    ' Note: this method doesn't work
    ' with CurrentProject.ActiveConnection

    Dim cnn As ADODB.Connection
    Dim cmd As ADODB.Command
    Dim lngRecs As Long

    Set cnn = New ADODB.Connection
    Set cmd = New ADODB.Command

    cnn.Open adhcADH2KSQLCnn

    Set cmd.ActiveConnection = cnn
    cmd.CommandText = "procDeleteCustomer"
    cmd.CommandType = adCmdStoredProc

    ' Refresh parameters collection so we
    ' can use parameters.
    cmd.Parameters.Refresh
    ' Set the value of the parameter using
    ' the name of the parameter as defined
    ' in the stored procedure.
    cmd.Parameters("@custid") = lngCustId
```

```
    cmd.Execute RecordsAffected:=lngRecs, _
     Options:=adExecuteNoRecords

    If lngRecs <> 0 Then
        Debug.Print "Deleted customer record #" & _
         lngCustId
    Else
        Debug.Print "Couldn't delete customer record #" & _
         lngCustId
    End If

    Set cmd = Nothing
    cnn.Close
    Set cnn = Nothing
End Sub
```

When you execute the Refresh method, ADO fills the Command object's Parameters collection with the name, datatype, type (input, output, input and output, or return value) and size of each of the stored procedure's parameters.

---

**TIP**   You can use the Refresh method *without* explicitly including it in your code. If you reference a stored procedure parameter by name (or by position using its ordinal value) without first executing the Refresh method, ADO calls the Refresh method implicitly.

---

The main disadvantage of using the Refresh method is that its use requires an extra roundtrip to the server. When the Refresh method is executed—either explicitly or implicitly—ADO must query the server for its Parameters collection, an extra step that you can avoid by using the Append method instead (which is discussed next).

---

**WARNING**   The Refresh method doesn't work using an ADP's CurrentProject.Connection connection. If you want to use Refresh in an ADP, you'll need to connect to the SQL Server database using a new connection.

---

## Using the Append Method

As you just learned, you can use the Refresh method to tell a Command object to download information about a stored procedure's Parameters collection from the server. You can avoid the extra roundtrip to the server at runtime, however, by appending the parameters to the Command object at design time.

Appending a parameter to a Command object's Parameters collection at design time requires two basic steps:

1.  Create the parameter using the CreateParameter method of the Command object's Parameters collection, supplying information about each parameter, including its datatype, size, type, and value.

2.  Use the Append method to append the new Parameter object to the Command object's Parameters collection.

For example, the DeleteCustSPAppend subroutine demonstrates the use of the Append method to execute the procDeleteCustomer stored procedure:

```
Sub DelCustSPAppend(lngCustId As Long)
    ' Execute a stored procedure
    ' by appending the parameters to Command
    ' object's Parameters collection.
    Dim cnn As ADODB.Connection
    Dim cmd As ADODB.Command
    Dim prm As ADODB.Parameter
    Dim lngRecs As Long

    Set cnn = New ADODB.Connection
    Set cmd = New ADODB.Command

    cnn.Open adhcADH2KSQLCnn

    Set cmd.ActiveConnection = cnn
    cmd.CommandText = "procDeleteCustomer"
    cmd.CommandType = adCmdStoredProc

    ' Create the parameter and append it to
    ' the Command object's Parameters collection.
    ' Each parameter must match by posistion and
    ' datatype. The name doesn't have to match
    ' the name used in the stored procedure.
    Set prm = cmd.CreateParameter("custid", adInteger, _
```

```
        adParamInput, , lngCustId)
    cmd.Parameters.Append prm

    cmd.Execute RecordsAffected:=lngRecs, _
     Options:=adExecuteNoRecords

    If lngRecs <> 0 Then
        Debug.Print "Deleted customer record #" & _
         lngCustId
    Else
        Debug.Print "Couldn't delete customer record #" & _
         lngCustId
    End If

    Set prm = Nothing
    Set cmd = Nothing
    cnn.Close
    Set cnn = Nothing
End Sub
```

When using this technique, you must append the Parameter objects in the exact same order in which they are defined in the stored procedure, being careful to match the datatype, size, and parameter type (adParamInput, adParamOutput, adParamInputOutput, or adParamReturnValue) of each parameter. While this requires a little extra work at design time, you avoid the extra roundtrip to the server that the Refresh method requires each time ADO runs the stored procedure.

## Retrieving Output Parameters

Up till now, the examples in this chapter have only used input parameters. You can also use Command objects to execute stored procedures with output values. To retrieve an output parameter you must use either the Refresh or Append method to define the output parameters. The Execute method's Parameters argument doesn't support output parameters.

For example, the procInsertOrder stored procedure takes six input parameters and one output parameter. The stored procedure uses the output parameter, @orderid, to return the value of the identity column of the newly added record back to the calling program. The procInsertOrder stored procedure follows. For more information on creating stored procedures with output parameters, see Chapter 5.

```
Create Procedure procInsertOrder
    @orderdate datetime,
    @customerid int,
    @ordertakerid int,
    @deliverydate datetime,
    @paymentmethod nvarchar(50),
    @notes ntext,
    @orderid int OUTPUT
As
    set nocount on
    INSERT INTO tblOrder
    (OrderDate, CustomerId,
    OrderTakerId, DeliveryDate,
    PaymentMethod, Notes)
    VALUES
    (@orderdate, @customerid,
    @ordertakerid, @deliverydate,
    @paymentmethod, @notes)
    -- Pass back the new OrderId value
    -- to the calling program as an output parameter
    SELECT @orderid = @@IDENTITY
```

To use the Refresh method with an output parameter, you simply retrieve the value of the output parameter—by either name or position—after you've used the Execute method to run the stored procedure. The AddOrderSPRefresh subroutine (from basCommand of the CH06A.MDB database) uses the Refresh method to execute the procInsertOrder stored procedure and retrieve the value of the @orderid output parameter:

```
Sub AddOrderSPRefresh()
    ' Execute a stored procedure
    ' with an Output parameter
    ' using Refresh method of Command
    ' object's Parameters collection.

    ' Note: this method doesn't work
    ' with CurrentProject.ActiveConnection

    Dim cnn As ADODB.Connection
    Dim cmd As ADODB.Command
```

```
Dim lngRecs As Long

Set cnn = New ADODB.Connection
Set cmd = New ADODB.Command

cnn.Open adhcADH2KSQLCnn

Set cmd.ActiveConnection = cnn
cmd.CommandText = "procInsertOrder"
cmd.CommandType = adCmdStoredProc

cmd.Parameters.Refresh
cmd.Parameters("@orderdate") = "1/1/2000"
cmd.Parameters("@customerid") = 1
cmd.Parameters("@ordertakerid") = 1
cmd.Parameters("@deliverydate") = "1/1/2000"
cmd.Parameters("@paymentmethod") = "Cash"
cmd.Parameters("@notes") = "ADO Test Record"

cmd.Execute RecordsAffected:=lngRecs, _
 Options:=adExecuteNoRecords

If lngRecs <> 0 Then
    Debug.Print "Added new order with OrderId of " & _
      cmd.Parameters("@orderid") & "."
Else
    Debug.Print "Couldn't add new order."
End If

Set cmd = Nothing
cnn.Close
Set cnn = NothingEnd Sub
```

You can also use the Append method to execute a stored procedure containing an output parameter. To use the Append method to retrieve an output parameter requires three basic steps:

1. Create a Parameter object for the output parameter using the CreateParameter and Append methods. (If the parameter is used only for output purposes, then use the adParamOutput constant for its parameter type. If the parameter is used for both input and output, then use the adParamInputOutput.)

2. Execute the stored procedure.

3. Retrieve the value of the output parameter using the name you assigned to the parameter in Step 1.

The AddOrderSPAppend subroutine uses the Append method to execute the procInsertOrder stored procedure and retrieve the value of the @orderid output parameter:

```
Sub AddOrderSPAppend()
    ' Execute a stored procedure
    ' with an output parameter
    ' by appending the parameters to Command
    ' object's Parameters collection.
    Dim cnn As ADODB.Connection
    Dim cmd As ADODB.Command
    Dim prm As ADODB.Parameter
    Dim lngRecs As Long

    Set cnn = New ADODB.Connection
    Set cmd = New ADODB.Command

    cnn.Open adhcADH2KSQLCnn

    Set cmd.ActiveConnection = cnn
    cmd.CommandText = "procInsertOrder"
    cmd.CommandType = adCmdStoredProc

    Set prm = cmd.CreateParameter("OrderDate", _
      adDBDate, adParamInput, , #1/1/2000#)
    cmd.Parameters.Append prm

    Set prm = cmd.CreateParameter("CustomerId", _
      adInteger, adParamInput, , 1)
    cmd.Parameters.Append prm

    Set prm = cmd.CreateParameter("OrderTakerId", _
      adInteger, adParamInput, , 1)
    cmd.Parameters.Append prm

    Set prm = cmd.CreateParameter("DeliveryDate", _
      adDBDate, adParamInput, , #1/1/2000#)
    cmd.Parameters.Append prm
```

```
Set prm = cmd.CreateParameter("PaymentMethod", _
 adVarWChar, adParamInput, 50, "Cash")
cmd.Parameters.Append prm

Set prm = cmd.CreateParameter("Notes", _
 adVarWChar, adParamInput, 1024, "Test Record")
cmd.Parameters.Append prm

Set prm = cmd.CreateParameter("OrderId", _
 adInteger, adParamOutput)
cmd.Parameters.Append prm

cmd.Execute RecordsAffected:=lngRecs, _
 Options:=adExecuteNoRecords

If lngRecs <> 0 Then
    Debug.Print "Added new order with OrderId of " & _
      cmd.Parameters("OrderId") & "."
Else
    Debug.Print "Couldn't add new order."
End If

Set prm = Nothing
Set cmd = Nothing
cnn.Close
Set cnn = NothingEnd Sub
```

## Retrieving a Stored Procedure's Return Value

A SQL Server stored procedure's return value is really just a special type of output parameter with the name "return_value" and the parameter type adParamReturn-Value.

The procCustomerExist stored procedure takes one input parameter, @custid, which is the CustomerId of the tblCustomer record to check. It returns 0 if the customer record exists and 1 if it doesn't exist. Its source is shown here:

```
Create Procedure procCustomerExist
    @custid INT
As
    IF (SELECT Count(*) FROM tblCustomer
        WHERE CustomerId = @custid) >= 1
```

```
      -- Success
      RETURN 0
ELSE
      -- Failure
      RETURN 1
```

The CustWithReturnSPRefresh subroutine illustrates how to retrieve the return value from the procCustomerExist stored procedure:

```
Sub CustWithReturnSPRefresh(lngCustId As Long)
    ' Execute a stored procedure
    ' with a return value
    ' by refreshing the parameters to Command
    ' object's Parameters collection.
    Dim cnn As ADODB.Connection
    Dim cmd As ADODB.Command

    Set cnn = New ADODB.Connection
    Set cmd = New ADODB.Command

    cnn.Open adhcADH2KSQLCnn

    Set cmd.ActiveConnection = cnn
    cmd.CommandText = "procCustomerExist"
    cmd.CommandType = adCmdStoredProc

    cmd.Parameters.Refresh
    cmd.Parameters("@custid") = lngCustId

    cmd.Execute

    ' Return value is sent back via
    ' the "return_value" parameter.
    If cmd.Parameters("return_value") = 0 Then
        Debug.Print "Customer #" & _
          lngCustId & " exists."
    Else
        Debug.Print "Customer #" & _
          lngCustId & " does not exist."
    End If

    Set cmd = Nothing
    cnn.Close
    Set cnn = NothingEnd Sub
```

The only trick when using the Refresh method is to realize that the name of the return value parameter is "return_value."

You can also use the Append method to retrieve a stored procedure's return value. The trick in this case is to realize that the return value is always the first parameter in the Command object's Parameters collection. The Append method is demonstrated by the CustWithReturnSPAppend subroutine:

```
Sub CustWithReturnSPAppend(lngCustId As Long)
    ' Execute a stored procedure
    ' with a return value
    ' by appending the parameters to Command
    ' object's Parameters collection.
    Dim cnn As ADODB.Connection
    Dim cmd As ADODB.Command
    Dim prm As ADODB.Parameter

    Set cnn = New ADODB.Connection
    Set cmd = New ADODB.Command

    cnn.Open adhcADH2KSQLCnn

    Set cmd.ActiveConnection = cnn
    cmd.CommandText = "procCustomerExist"
    cmd.CommandType = adCmdStoredProc

    ' Return value parameter must always
    ' be the first appended parameter.
    Set prm = cmd.CreateParameter("Return", _
      adInteger, adParamReturnValue)
    cmd.Parameters.Append prm

    Set prm = cmd.CreateParameter("CustomerId", _
      adInteger, adParamInput, , lngCustId)
    cmd.Parameters.Append prm

    cmd.Execute

    If cmd.Parameters("Return") = 0 Then
        Debug.Print "Customer #" & _
          lngCustId & " exists."
    Else
```

```
        Debug.Print "Customer #" & _
          lngCustId & " does not exist."
      End If

      Set prm = Nothing
      Set cmd = Nothing
      cnn.Close
      Set cnn = NothingEnd Sub
```

### Which Method Should You Use?

We've presented three different techniques—using the Parameters argument, Refresh method, and Append method—for executing stored procedures with parameters using the ADO Command object. Which technique you use depends on the stored procedure and your needs. The following points may help you make your decision on which method works best for you:

- If you must use an ADP file's CurrentProject.Connection to connect to the database, then you can't use the Refresh technique. However, you can circumvent this problem by creating a new Connection object to connect to the server database and using this new connection for your Command objects.

- If the stored procedure has only input parameters, then you'll likely find the Parameters argument technique the easiest to use. However, both the Refresh and Append techniques also work.

- If the stored procedure has output parameters or a return value that you wish to retrieve, then you need to use either the Append or Refresh method.

- If you need to work with output parameters or a return value, and if runtime performance is most important, then you should use the Append method.

- If you need to work with output parameters or a return value, and if design time simplicity and runtime flexibility is most important, then you should use the Refresh method.

## Using Prepared Statements

Some ADO providers, including SQL Server, support the use of *prepared statements*. A prepared statement is a SQL statement that has been compiled and optimized. If you set a Command object's Prepared property to True, the query string associated with the Command object is parsed, compiled, and optimized the first time it is executed. For subsequent executions of the same Command object, the prepared statement runs faster than the equivalent unprepared Command object. The first time you execute a prepared statement, however, execution is actually slower because of the time it takes to prepare the statement.

Prepared statements make the most sense when used with parameterized ad hoc SQL statements. To create a prepared statement, follow these steps:

1. When entering the parameterized SQL statement, use a question mark (?) to indicate a parameter.

2. Set the Command object's Prepared property to True.

3. For each parameter, use the CreateParameter and Append methods to add the parameter to the Parameters collection of the Command object. Don't set the values of the parameters yet.

4. Before you execute the Command object, set the parameter values using the parameter names you assigned in Step 3.

For example, the PrepareStatement subroutine (found in the basPrepared module of the CH06A.MDB database) prepares an Update SQL statement for execution. Because the Command object will be executed multiple times, we have made the Command and Connection objects module-level variables. Here's the source of PrepareStatement, along with the module-level variable declarations:

```
Private Const adhcADH2KSQLCnn = "Provider=SQLOLEDB;" & _
  "Data Source=Gorilla;Database=ADH2KSQL;" & _
  User Id=sa;Password=;"

Private mcnn As ADODB.Connection
Private mcmd As ADODB.Command

Sub PrepareStatement()
    Dim strSQL As String
    Dim prm As ADODB.Parameter

    Set mcnn = New ADODB.Connection
    mcnn.Open adhcADH2KSQLCnn

    Set mcmd = New ADODB.Command

    ' Create Update statement with two parameters.
    ' Use ? as a placeholder for parameters.
```

```
    strSQL = "UPDATE tblMenu SET Price = ? " & _
     "WHERE MenuId = ?"

    Set mcmd.ActiveConnection = mcnn
    mcmd.CommandType = adCmdText
    mcmd.CommandText = strSQL
    mcmd.Prepared = True

    ' Append the two parameters to the
    ' Command object's Parameters collection.
    Set prm = mcmd.CreateParameter("NewPrice", _
     adCurrency, adParamInput)
    mcmd.Parameters.Append prm

    Set prm = mcmd.CreateParameter("MenuId", _
     adInteger, adParamInput)
    mcmd.Parameters.Append prm

    Debug.Print "Statement prepared."

    Set prm = Nothing

End Sub
```

Once you've run PrepareStatement, you can use the ExecuteStatement subroutine from basPrepared to execute the prepared statement multiple times. The source for ExecuteStatement is quite simple:

```
Sub ExecuteStatement(lngMenuId As Long, _
  curNewPrice As Currency)
    Dim lngRecs As Long

    ' Set the value of prepared statement
    ' parameters.
    mcmd.Parameters("NewPrice") = curNewPrice
    mcmd.Parameters("MenuId") = lngMenuId

    mcmd.Execute RecordsAffected:=lngRecs, _
     Options:=adExecuteNoRecords

    If lngRecs <> 0 Then
        Debug.Print "Price updated."
    Else
```

```
            Debug.Print "Unable to update price."
        End If
    End Sub
```

Because of the extra overhead in preparing prepared statements, you should only use them when you will be executing a SQL statement a number of times using the same Connection and Command objects. Prepared statements are implemented in SQL Server using temporary stored procedures that are deleted when the Connection or Command object is dropped.

If you need to execute the same parameterized SQL statement many times but can't use the same Connection and Command object, consider creating a stored procedure instead.

---

**WARNING**    Don't set the Command object's Prepared property to True when executing stored procedures. This will do nothing but slow down the execution of the stored procedure.

---

# Creating Server Recordsets

You create recordsets in ADO to retrieve the records returned by a query. ADO recordsets were discussed in great detail in Chapter 6 of the *Access 2000 Developer's Handbook, Volume 1: Desktop Edition*. In this section, we'll detail some of the server-specific features of ADO recordsets.

## Creating Recordsets Based on Stored Procedures

How you create a recordset based on a stored procedure depends on whether the stored procedure has parameters and whether you need to create a recordset that's updatable or uses a non-forward-only cursor.

### Using the Recordset's Open Method without Parameters

If the stored procedure has no parameters, creating a recordset based on it differs little from creating a recordset from a SQL statement or a table. The only difference is that you need to set the options argument of the Recordset object's Open method to adCmdStoredProc.

The GetCustomersSP subroutine (from the basRecordset module of CH06A .MDB) demonstrates how to create a recordset from the procGetCustomer1 SQL Server stored procedure:

```
Sub GetCustomersSP()
    ' Execute a stored procedure
    ' without parameters
    ' that returns records.

    Dim cnn As ADODB.Connection
    Dim rst As ADODB.Recordset

    Set cnn = New ADODB.Connection
    Set rst = New ADODB.Recordset

    cnn.Open adhcADH2KSQLCnn

    rst.Open "procGetCustomer1", cnn, _
     adOpenKeyset, adLockReadOnly, adCmdStoredProc

    Do While Not rst.EOF
        Debug.Print rst!FirstName & " " & rst!LastName
        rst.MoveNext
    Loop

    rst.Close
    Set rst = Nothing
    cnn.Close
    Set cnn = Nothing
End Sub
```

## Using the Command Object's Execute Method with Parameters

In the earlier section "Using Command Objects," we discussed how to use Command objects to execute parameterized stored procedures and prepared statements that don't return any rows. You can also use Command objects along with recordsets to execute parameterized stored procedures and prepared statements that return rows.

To create a recordset based on a Command object, you use the following syntax of the Execute method

```
Set rst = cmd.Execute(recordsaffected, parameters, options)
```

where:

- *rst* is a Recordset object variable.

- *cmd* is a Command object variable.

- *recordsaffected* is an optional long variable into which ADO returns the number of records affected by the action query or stored procedure.

- *parameters* is an optional array of input parameters.

- *options* is an optional long indicating the type of command contained in the CommandText property (see the earlier section "The Execute Method" for more details).

You can use any of three techniques for passing parameters to a stored procedure (the Parameters argument, the Refresh method, or the Append method) that were described in the "Passing Parameters to and from Stored Procedures" section earlier in this chapter.

The GetEmployeeSPAppend subroutine (from the basRecordset module of CH06A.MDB) demonstrates how to pass parameters to a stored procedure that returns records using the Append method of the Command object's Parameters collection:

```
Sub GetEmployeeSPAppend(lngEmpId As Long)
    ' Execute a stored procedure
    ' that returns records
    ' by appending the parameters to Command
    ' object's Parameters collection.
    Dim cnn As ADODB.Connection
    Dim cmd As ADODB.Command
    Dim prm As ADODB.Parameter
    Dim rst As ADODB.Recordset

    Set cnn = New ADODB.Connection
    Set cmd = New ADODB.Command

    cnn.Open adhcADH2KSQLCnn

    Set cmd.ActiveConnection = cnn
```

```
        cmd.CommandText = "procGetEmployee"
        cmd.CommandType = adCmdStoredProc

        ' Create the parameter and append it to
        ' the Command object's Parameters collection.
        Set prm = cmd.CreateParameter("employeeid", _
         adInteger, adParamInput, , lngEmpId)
        cmd.Parameters.Append prm

        ' Execute Command and place results
        ' in Recordset object.
        Set rst = cmd.Execute()

        If Not rst.EOF Then
            Debug.Print rst!FirstName & " " & rst!LastName
        Else
            Debug.Print "No such employee."
        End If

        rst.Close
        Set prm = Nothing
        Set rst = Nothing
        Set cmd = Nothing
        cnn.Close
        Set cnn = Nothing
    End Sub
```

**NOTE**    The basRecordset module of CH06A.MDB also contains an example that uses the Parameters argument of the Execute method (GetEmployeeSPArray) and another example that uses the Refresh method of the Command object's Parameters collection (GetEmployeeSPRefresh).

## Using the Recordset's Open Method with Parameters

When you use the Command object's Execute method to create a recordset from a parameterized stored procedure, you always end up with a forward-only, read-only recordset. It isn't obvious, but you can also use the Open method of the Recordset object to create a recordset from a parameterized stored procedure. The advantage of this technique is that you can control the type of recordset created.

To create a recordset based on a parameterized stored procedure using the Open method requires that you follow these two steps:

1. Create a Command object and populate the Parameters collection of the Command object using either the Refresh or Append methods.

2. Use the Recordset object's Open method to fill the recordset, setting the Source argument to the Command object variable with no ActiveConnection argument.

For example, the GetEmployeesSPKeysetAppend subroutine creates a optimistic keyset recordset based on the procGetEmployee parameterized stored procedure:

```
Sub GetEmployeeSPKeysetAppend(lngEmpId As Long)
    ' Use the Recordset.Open method and the
    ' Append method of a Command obejct to run
    ' a parameterized stored procedure that
    ' returns records, producing a keyset
    ' recordset with optimistic locking.

    Dim cnn As ADODB.Connection
    Dim cmd As ADODB.Command
    Dim prm As ADODB.Parameter
    Dim rst As ADODB.Recordset

    Set cnn = New ADODB.Connection
    Set cmd = New ADODB.Command
    Set rst = New ADODB.Recordset

    cnn.Open adhcADH2KSQLCnn

    Set cmd.ActiveConnection = cnn
    cmd.CommandText = "procGetEmployee"
    cmd.CommandType = adCmdStoredProc

    ' Create the parameter and append it to
    ' the Command object's Parameters collection.
    Set prm = cmd.CreateParameter("employeeid", _
      adInteger, adParamInput, , lngEmpId)
    cmd.Parameters.Append prm
```

```
' Fill the Recordset using the Command object
' with the appended parameter.
rst.Open cmd, , adOpenKeyset, _
 adLockOptimistic, adCmdStoredProc

If Not rst.EOF Then
    Debug.Print rst!FirstName & " " & rst!LastName
Else
    Debug.Print "No such employee."
End If

rst.Close
Set prm = Nothing
Set rst = Nothing
Set cmd = Nothing
cnn.Close
Set cnn = Nothing
End Sub
```

The advantage of this technique is that you can create any type of recordset you'd like. You aren't limited to a forward-only, read-only recordset like when using the Execute method.

## Recordset Property Interactions

With two cursor locations, four cursor types, and four lock types, there are theoretically 32 variations of recordsets. ADO is designed to be very forgiving on this count. You can request any combination of location, cursor type, and lock type, and ADO will open a recordset without error. However, it may not open precisely what you've requested. For combinations that aren't supported, ADO will change one or more options to get a recordset type that it's able to deliver.

How ADO changes the options you request depends on the data provider and the cursor library. In *Access 2000 Developer's Handbook, Volume 1: Desktop Edition*, we outlined the mappings between what you ask for and what you get for the Jet OLEDB provider. Things are a bit different for SQL Server. Table 6.4 shows the mappings for SQL Server server-side recordsets for connections using the SQLOLEDB provider and for ADP connections using the MSDataShape service. Table 6.5 shows the same mappings for client-side recordsets.

**TABLE 6.4:** Server-Side Recordset Properties

| Requested | Delivered for SQLOLEDB Connection | Delivered For ADP CurrentProject. Connection (MSDataShape Service) |
| --- | --- | --- |
| Forward-only, read-only | Forward-only, read-only | Static, read-only |
| Forward-only, pessimistic | Forward-only, pessimistic | Static, batch optimistic |
| Forward-only, optimistic | Forward-only, optimistic | Static, optimistic |
| Forward-only, batch optimistic | Forward-only, batch optimistic | Static, batch optimistic |
| Keyset, read-only | Keyset, read-only | Static, read-only |
| Keyset, pessimistic | Keyset, pessimistic | Static, batch optimistic |
| Keyset, optimistic | Keyset, optimistic | Static, optimistic |
| Keyset, batch optimistic | Keyset, batch optimistic | Static, batch optimistic |
| Dynamic, read-only | Dynamic, read-only | Static, read-only |
| Dynamic, pessimistic | Dynamic, pessimistic | Static, batch optimistic |
| Dynamic, optimistic | Dynamic, optimistic | Static, optimistic |
| Dynamic, batch optimistic | Dynamic, batch optimistic | Static, batch optimistic |
| Static, read-only | Static, read-only | Static, read-only |
| Static, pessimistic | Keyset, pessimistic | Static, batch optimistic |
| Static, optimistic | Keyset, optimistic | Static, optimistic |
| Static, batch optimistic | Keyset, batch optimistic | Static, batch optimistic |

**TABLE 6.5:** Client-Side Recordset Properties

| Requested | Delivered for SQLOLEDB Connection | Delivered For ADP CurrentProject. Connection (MSDataShape Service) |
| --- | --- | --- |
| Forward-only, read-only | Static, read-only | Static, read-only |
| Forward-only, pessimistic | Static, batch optimistic | Static, batch optimistic |
| Forward-only, optimistic | Static, optimistic | Static, optimistic |

**TABLE 6.5:**   Client-Side Recordset Properties *(continued)*

| Requested | Delivered for SQLOLEDB Connection | Delivered For ADP CurrentProject. Connection (MSDataShape Service) |
| --- | --- | --- |
| Forward-only, batch optimistic | Static, batch optimistic | Static, batch optimistic |
| Keyset, read-only | Static, read-only | Static, read-only |
| Keyset, pessimistic | Static, batch optimistic | Static, batch optimistic |
| Keyset, optimistic | Static, optimistic | Static, optimistic |
| Keyset, batch optimistic | Static, batch optimistic | Static, batch optimistic |
| Dynamic, read-only | Static, read-only | Static, read-only |
| Dynamic, pessimistic | Static, batch optimistic | Static, batch optimistic |
| Dynamic, optimistic | Static, optimistic | Static, optimistic |
| Dynamic, batch optimistic | Static, batch optimistic | Static, batch optimistic |
| Static, read-only | Static, read-only | Static, read-only |
| Static, pessimistic | Static, batch optimistic | Static, batch optimistic |
| Static, optimistic | Static, optimistic | Static, optimistic |
| Static, batch optimistic | Static, batch optimistic | Static, batch optimistic |

If you study these tables, several interesting patterns emerge:

- Only static recordset cursors are supported by the ADP CurrentProject .Connection connection's server-side cursor library. In addition, any request for pessimistic locking is changed to batch-optimistic locking. These facts must be a side effect of ADPs using the MSDataShape service.

- No matter which type of connection is used (SQLOLEDB or MSDataShape), only static recordset cursors are supported by the client-side cursor library. Pessimistic locking requests of the client-side library are changed to batch-optimistic locking.

- The SQLOLEDB data provider server-side cursor library satisfies most requests for recordsets with the exact type of recordset requested. The one exception is for static recordsets. When requesting an updatable static cursor, SQLOLEDB substitutes the equivalent keyset cursor.

**NOTE**   If you attempt to create a dynamic server-side cursor based on a SQL Server SELECT statement containing an ORDER BY clause, the SQL Server provider gives you a keyset cursor, even though CursorType returns acOpenDynamic. The reason: it's not possible to maintain an ordered recordset with other users adding and deleting rows.

## Pessimistic Locking

Pessimistic locking when using SQL Server recordsets doesn't work like pessimistic locking when using Jet recordsets. Instead of using record locks, SQL Server uses something called *scroll locks*. When you employ pessimistic locking using the Jet Engine, Jet locks an individual record (or page of records) when you begin to edit that record. When using SQL Server, however, the entire recordset is locked when the recordset is created!

Because of the way SQL Server locks records, you have two basic options for locking with SQL Server recordsets:

• Create very small recordsets.

• Use optimistic locking.

The next section discusses how to manage concurrency when using optimistic locking.

# Managing Concurrency

Because of the way the SQLOLEDB provider works, it is quite likely that you will have to use optimistic locking in your SQL Server applications.

The biggest issue when using optimistic locking is how to manage concurrent users accessing the same records so that you avoid a write conflict. A *write conflict* (also known as a *write-after-write error*) occurs when:

1. A user begins to edit a record.

2. A second user saves changes to the record.

3. The first user then attempts to save his/her changes.

It should be obvious that a write conflict is bad because it means that the first user is changing a different record than he or she began editing.

# Using Bound Forms

If you're using bound ADP-based forms, you can let Access deal with concurrency. Just as with Jet databases, Access will display its built-in (and somewhat confusing) Write Conflict dialog box when a write conflict occurs, as shown in Figure 6.3.

**FIGURE 6.3**
The default Access Write
Conflict dialog box.

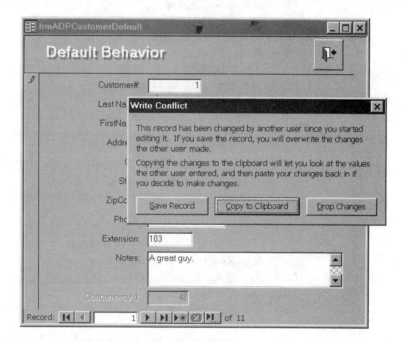

Fortunately, as with Jet databases, you can create an event handler attached to the Error event of the form to customize how Access behaves when a write conflict occurs. The code in Listing 6.1 (from the frmADPCustomerCustom form in the CH06B.ADP sample database) substitutes a much simpler (and safer) dialog box for the built-in one. The custom Write Conflict dialog box displayed by frmADPCustomerCustom is shown in Figure 6.4.

## Listing 6.1

```
Const adhcErrWriteConflict = 7787
Const adhcErrDataChanged = 7878

Private Sub Form_Error(DataErr As Integer, _
```

```
Response As Integer)

    ' Handle form-level errors

    On Error GoTo Form_ErrorErr

    Dim strMsg As String

    ' Branch based on value of error
    Select Case DataErr

    Case adhcErrWriteConflict
        ' Write conflict error
        strMsg = "Another user has updated this " & _
         "record since you began editing it. " & _
         vbCrLf & vbCrLf & _
         "The record will be refreshed with the other " & _
         "user's changes before continuing."
        MsgBox strMsg, vbOKOnly + vbInformation, _
         "Record Refresh"

        ' This will cause record refresh
        Response = acDataErrContinue

    Case adhcErrDataChanged
        ' This error occurs if Access detects that
        ' another user has changed this record when we
        ' attempt to dirty the record. Fairly harmless
        ' since we haven't actually made any changes.
        strMsg = "Another user has updated this " & _
         "record since you began viewing it. " & _
         vbCrLf & vbCrLf & _
         "The record will be refreshed with the other " & _
         "user's changes before continuing."
        MsgBox strMsg, vbOKOnly + vbInformation, _
         "Record Refresh"

        ' This will cause record refresh
        Response = acDataErrContinue
    Case Else
        ' Otherwise, let Access display
        ' standard error message
        Response = acDataErrDisplay
    End Select
```

```
    DoCmd.Hourglass False

Form_ErrorEnd:
    Exit Sub

Form_ErrorErr:
    ' It's possible to hit or own error while handling a
    ' data error. For example, someone could pessimstically
    ' lock the record while we are trying to update it.
    ' Report the error to the user and exit.
    MsgBox "Error " & Err.Number & ": " & _
    Err.Description, _
        vbOKOnly + vbCritical, "Error Handler Error"
End Sub
```

**NOTE**    See Chapter 2 for an explanation of the Error event and how this code works.

**FIGURE 6.4**
A custom Access write
conflict dialog box.

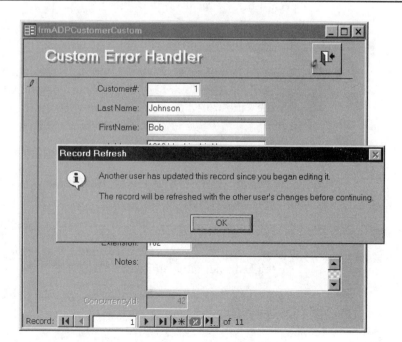

## Using Unbound Forms

If you're using unbound forms (either within an ADP or MDB file), you have to do a little more work to manage concurrent access to SQL Server records. There are two basic approaches:

- Use a read/write Recordset object to both read and update the records.

- Use a read-only Recordset object to read the records and a stored procedure-based Command object to update the records.

While you might be inclined to use the first approach, it's always best to avoid keeping a recordset—especially an updatable recordset—open for long periods of time. The second (minimalist) approach can be generalized more easily and is more scalable.

We've created a sample form that employs the minimalist approach to managing unbound form concurrency. This approach revolves around the following features:

- A SQL Server Integer column that can be used to track concurrency. This column is named ConcurrencyId, but in reality could be named anything you'd like. This approach depends on this column being incremented by one every time the record is updated.

- A stored procedure that retrieves a single record from the table, including the ConcurrencyId.

- A second stored procedure that updates a single record in the underlying table only if the primary key and ConcurrencyId match. If the ConcurrencyId matches, the stored procedure increments it by one. Otherwise, it returns an error.

### A Concurrency Example

We've created an example that demonstrates this approach. The example consists of the following elements:

- An unbound form, frmADOConcurrency, in the CH06A.MDB database.

- A stored procedure, procGetCustomer2, that retrieves a single record from the tblCustomer table of the ADH2KSQL SQL Server database.

- A stored procedure, procInsertCustomer2, that adds a new record to the tblCustomer table.

- A stored procedure, procDeleteCustomer, that deletes a record from the tblCustomer table.

- A stored procedure, procUpdateCustomer1, that updates a record in the tblCustomer table. This stored procedure contains the bulk of the concurrency checking logic.

- Code attached to frmADOConcurrency that manages record retrieval, display, and updating using the four stored procedures.

The frmADOConcurrency form is shown in Figure 6.5.

**FIGURE 6.5**
The frmADOConcurrency form has encountered a write conflict.

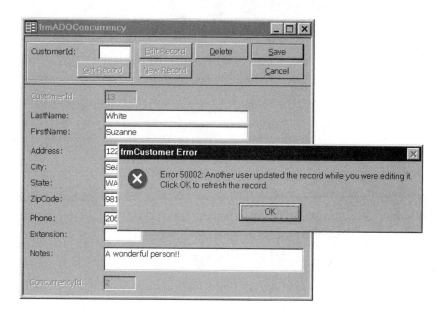

## The Stored Procedures

The procGetCustomer2 stored procedure retrieves a single record from the Ch06A.MDB database. Its source is displayed here:

```
Create Procedure procGetCustomer2
   @custid INT
As
   SELECT * FROM tblCustomer
   WHERE CustomerId = @custid
```

The procInsertCustomer2 is responsible for inserting a new tblCustomer record. Since you don't need to worry about concurrency during an insert operation, there's nothing special about this stored procedure:

```
Create Procedure procInsertCustomer2
    @CustomerId INT,
    @LastName VARCHAR(50),
    @FirstName VARCHAR(50),
    @Address VARCHAR(50) = Null,
    @City VARCHAR(50) = Null,
    @State VARCHAR(2) = Null,
    @ZipCode VARCHAR(10) = Null,
    @Phone VARCHAR(10) = Null,
    @Extension VARCHAR(5) = Null,
    @Notes VARCHAR(100) = Null
As
    INSERT INTO tblCustomer
    (CustomerId, LastName, FirstName,
    Address, City, State, ZipCode,
    Phone, Extension, Notes)
    VALUES
    (@CustomerId, @LastName, @FirstName,
    @Address, @City, @State, @ZipCode,
    @Phone, @Extension, @Notes)
```

The procDeleteCustomer stored procedure is also pretty basic. Again, no concurrency concerns are necessary here:

```
Create Procedure procDeleteCustomer
    @custid integer
As
    DELETE
    FROM tblCustomer
    WHERE CustomerId = @custid
```

---

**NOTE**    We've decided in this example not to be concerned about deleting a record that was updated by another user. This may be an oversimplification. You could add concurrency-checking code to the procDeleteCustomer stored procedure that ensures that you don't delete a customer record that has changed since you began editing the record.

---

In contrast to the other stored procedures, procUpdateCustomer1 is a bit more complicated. The stored procedure begins with the following code:

```
Create Procedure procUpdateCustomer1
/* This stored procedure updates a single record
   in the tblCustomer table. It uses a ConcurrencyId
   to manage concurrent access to the record. */
   @CustomerId INT,
   @ConcurrencyId INT,
   @LastName VARCHAR(50),
   @FirstName VARCHAR(50),
   @Address VARCHAR(50),
   @City VARCHAR(50),
   @State VARCHAR(2),
   @ZipCode VARCHAR(10),
   @Phone VARCHAR(10),
   @Extension VARCHAR(5),
   @Notes VARCHAR(100)
As
   set nocount on
   DECLARE @intCurrentCId INT
```

The procUpdateCustomer1 stored procedure uses the @intCurrentCId variable to hold the current value of the ConcurrencyId field. This value is retrieved by the next piece of code:

```
/* Check current state of record. */
SELECT @intCurrentCId = ConcurrencyId
FROM tblCustomer WHERE CustomerId = @CustomerId
```

If no record is found, the stored procedure raises an error. A different error is raised if the record is found but the ConcurrencyId field is different that the expected value:

```
/* No record at all, so it must have been deleted. */
IF @@ROWCOUNT = 0
   BEGIN
   RAISERROR 50001
   'Another user deleted the record while you were editing it.'
   RETURN 1
   END

/* The record is there but its ConcurrencyId is
   different. This indicates that a write conflict has
```

```
occurred. */
IF @intCurrentCId != @ConcurrencyId
  BEGIN
  RAISERROR 50002
  'Another user updated the record while you were editing it.'
  RETURN 1
  END
```

If the stored procedure has gotten past the concurrency check, then it's time to update the record with the following code:

```
/* All is well, so go ahead and update the record,
   incrementing the ConcurrencyId during the update. */
UPDATE tblCustomer
SET LastName = @LastName,
FirstName = @FirstName,
Address = @Address,
City = @City,
State = @State,
ZipCode = @ZipCode,
Phone = @Phone,
Extension = @Extension,
Notes = @Notes,
ConcurrencyId = ConcurrencyId + 1
WHERE CustomerId =  @CustomerId
AND ConcurrencyId = @ConcurrencyId

IF @@ERROR = 0
  BEGIN
    RETURN 0
  END
```

The UPDATE statement increments the ConcurrencyId field as the record is saved.

---

**NOTE**     This scheme will not work if you allow users to update the underlying table without incrementing the ConcurrencyId field. Fortunately, using security you can prevent users from updating the table directly. See Chapter 8 for more on SQL Server security.

---

The ADH2KSQL database also contains a stored procedure named procUpdateCustomer2 that is identical to procUpdateCustomer1, except that it allows you to update only the fields that have changed.

### The frmADOConcurrency Form

The code behind fmADOConcurrency glues the solution together. All the code behind frmADOConcurrency can be found in the CH06A.MDB sample database. We've included only the most interesting code here.

When a user clicks the Get Record button, the following code is called:

```
Private Sub cmdGet_Click()
    ' Retrieve a record from tblCustomer
    ' using the procGetCustomer2
    ' stored procedure.
    Dim cnn As ADODB.Connection
    Dim cmd As ADODB.Command
    Dim prm As ADODB.Parameter
    Dim rst As ADODB.Recordset
    Dim ctl As Control

    If Not IsNull(Me.txtCustId) Then
        Set cnn = New ADODB.Connection
        Set cmd = New ADODB.Command

        cnn.Open adhcADH2KSQLCnn

        Set cmd.ActiveConnection = cnn
        cmd.CommandText = "procGetCustomer2"
        cmd.CommandType = adCmdStoredProc

        ' Create the parameter and append it to
        ' the Command object's Parameters collection.
        Set prm = cmd.CreateParameter("custid", _
         adInteger, adParamInput, , Me.txtCustId)
        cmd.Parameters.Append prm

        ' Execute Command and place results
        ' in Recordset object.
        Set rst = cmd.Execute()
```

```
        If Not rst.EOF Then
            For Each ctl In Form.Controls
                If ctl.ControlType = acTextBox And _
                ctl.Name <> "txtCustId" Then
                    ctl.Value = rst(ctl.Name)
                End If
            Next ctl
            mfInsert = False
            Me.txtCustId = Null
            Call HandleControls(True, False)
        Else
            MsgBox "No such record.", _
             vbInformation + vbOKOnly, conForm
            Call HandleControls(False, False)
        End If
    End If

    rst.Close
    Set rst = Nothing
    Set cmd = Nothing
    Set prm = Nothing
    cnn.Close
    Set cnn = Nothing
End Sub
```

The cmdGet_Click event procedure uses a Command object to execute a parameterized stored procedure, procGetCustomer2, to retrieve a single record into a recordset. A For…Each loop is then used to fill the textbox controls with the fields from the recordset bearing the same name. The cmdGet_Click event procedure calls a helper subroutine, HandleControls, to manage the enabling and disabling of various form controls.

The cmdSave_Click event procedure calls the SaveCustomer subroutine to save an edited record. This subroutine uses a Command object to execute the procUpdateCustomer1 stored procedure and deal with any errors that are raised by the stored procedure.

Here's the first half of the SaveCustomer subroutine. This code is responsible for creating the Command object, appending parameters to it, executing it, and retrieving the return value from the procUpdateCustomer1 stored procedure:

```
Sub SaveCustomer()
    ' Saves edits to tblCustomer
```

```
' by executing the procUpdateCustomer1
' stored procedure.
' Includes error handler to deal with
' concurrency errors raised by the
' stored procedure.
Dim cnn As ADODB.Connection
Dim cmd As ADODB.Command
Dim prm As ADODB.Parameter
Dim lngReturn As Long
Dim strError As String
Dim lngError As Long
Dim intResp As Integer

On Error GoTo ErrorHandler

Set cnn = New ADODB.Connection
Set cmd = New ADODB.Command

cnn.Open adhcADH2KSQLCnn

Set cmd.ActiveConnection = cnn

cmd.CommandText = "procUpdateCustomer1"
cmd.CommandType = adCmdStoredProc

' Append parameters to the Command
' object's Parameters collection.
Set prm = cmd.CreateParameter("Return", _
 adInteger, adParamReturnValue)
cmd.Parameters.Append prm
Set prm = cmd.CreateParameter("CustomerId", _
 adInteger, adParamInput, , Me.CustomerId)
cmd.Parameters.Append prm
Set prm = cmd.CreateParameter("ConcurrenyId", _
 adInteger, adParamInput, , Me.ConcurrencyId)
cmd.Parameters.Append prm
Set prm = cmd.CreateParameter("LastName", _
 adVarChar, adParamInput, 50, Me.LastName)
cmd.Parameters.Append prm
Set prm = cmd.CreateParameter("FirstName", _
 adVarChar, adParamInput, 50, Me.FirstName)
cmd.Parameters.Append prm
```

```
Set prm = cmd.CreateParameter("Address", _
 adVarChar, adParamInput, 50, Me.Address)
cmd.Parameters.Append prm
Set prm = cmd.CreateParameter("City", _
 adVarChar, adParamInput, 50, Me.City)
cmd.Parameters.Append prm
Set prm = cmd.CreateParameter("State", _
 adVarChar, adParamInput, 2, Me.State)
cmd.Parameters.Append prm
Set prm = cmd.CreateParameter("ZipCode", _
 adVarChar, adParamInput, 10, Me.ZipCode)
cmd.Parameters.Append prm
Set prm = cmd.CreateParameter("Phone", _
 adVarChar, adParamInput, 10, Me.Phone)
cmd.Parameters.Append prm
Set prm = cmd.CreateParameter("Extension", _
 adVarChar, adParamInput, 5, Me.Extension)
cmd.Parameters.Append prm
Set prm = cmd.CreateParameter("Notes", _
 adVarChar, adParamInput, 100, Me.Notes)
cmd.Parameters.Append prm

cmd.Execute Options:=adExecuteNoRecords

lngReturn = cmd.Parameters("Return")

' Check return value to see if
' the stored proc worked.
If lngReturn = 0 Then
    MsgBox "Record saved.", _
     vbInformation + vbOKOnly, Me.Name
Else
    MsgBox "Unable to save changes.", _
     vbCritical + vbOKOnly, Me.Name
End If

' No longer editing, so clear the
' textbox controls and call
' HandleControls to fixup other controls.
Call ClearControls
Call HandleControls(False, False)
```

The second half of SaveCustomer contains the error-handling code. The error handler deals with the deleted and updated record errors that are raised by proc-UpdateCustomer1:

```
ExitHere:
    Set cmd = Nothing
    Set prm = Nothing
    cnn.close
    Set cnn = Nothing
    Exit Sub
ErrorHandler:
    ' Grab Access/VBA Error
    lngError = Err.Number
    strError = Err.Description
    ' If ADO Error available grab
    ' the first one in the collection.
    If cnn.Errors.Count > 0 Then
        lngError = cnn.Errors(0).NativeError
        strError = cnn.Errors(0).Description
    End If
    Select Case lngError
        Case 50002 ' Record updated
            MsgBox "Error " & lngError & ": " & _
             strError & vbCrLf & _
             "Click OK to refresh the record.", _
             vbCritical + vbOKOnly, _
             "frmCustomer Error"
            Me.txtCustId = Me.CustomerId
            Call cmdGet_Click
            Call cmdEdit_Click
        Case 50001 'Record deleted
            intResp = MsgBox("Error " & lngError & ": " & _
             strError & vbCrLf & _
             "Click OK to add the record " & _
             "back to the database or Cancel " & _
             "to abort save.", _
             vbCritical + vbOKCancel, _
             "frmCustomer Error")
            If intResp = vbOK Then
                Call InsertCustomer
            Else
                Call ClearControls
```

```
                        Call HandleControls(False, False)
                    End If
              Case Else
                  MsgBox "Error " & lngError & ": " & _
                      strError, vbCritical + vbOKOnly, _
                      "frmCustomer Error"
          End Select
          Resume ExitHere
    End Sub
```

If the error handler determines that a write conflict error has occurred (error # 50002), it informs the user of the write conflict and then calls the cmdGet_Click and cmdEdit_Click subroutines to refresh the record with the updated values.

Similarly, if the error handler determines that the edited record was deleted (error #50001), it informs the user of the situation and offers to add the deleted record back to the database. This feat is accomplished by calling the Insert-Customer subroutine, the same subroutine used to save a new record to the database. InsertCustomer saves the new record by executing the procInsertCustomer2 stored procedure:

```
Sub InsertCustomer()
    ' Saves new record to tblCustomer
    ' by executing the procInsertCustomer2
    ' stored procedure.
    Dim cnn As ADODB.Connection
    Dim cmd As ADODB.Command
    Dim prm As ADODB.Parameter
    Dim lngRecs As Long
    Dim strError As String
    Dim lngError As Long

    On Error GoTo ErrorHandler

    Set cnn = New ADODB.Connection
    Set cmd = New ADODB.Command

    cnn.Open adhcADH2KSQLCnn

    Set cmd.ActiveConnection = cnn

    cmd.CommandText = "procInsertCustomer2"
    cmd.CommandType = adCmdStoredProc
```

```
' Check that CustomerId, LastName, and
' FirstName are completed.
If IsNull(Me.CustomerId) Or _
 Me.CustomerID = vbNullString Then
    MsgBox "CustomerId is a required field", _
     vbCritical + vbOKOnly, Me.Name
    Me.CustomerId.SetFocus
    GoTo ExitHere
ElseIf IsNull(Me.LastName) Or _
 Me.LastName = vbNullString Then
    MsgBox "LastName is a required field", _
     vbCritical + vbOKOnly, Me.Name
    Me.LastName.SetFocus
    GoTo ExitHere
ElseIf IsNull(Me.FirstName) Or _
 Me.FirstName = vbNullString Then
    MsgBox "FirstName is a required field", _
     vbCritical + vbOKOnly, Me.Name
    Me.FirstName.SetFocus
    GoTo ExitHere
End If

' Append parameters to the Command
' object's Parameters collection.
Set prm = cmd.CreateParameter("CustomerId", _
 adInteger, adParamInput, , Me.CustomerId)
cmd.Parameters.Append prm
Set prm = cmd.CreateParameter("LastName", _
 adVarChar, adParamInput, 50, Me.LastName)
cmd.Parameters.Append prm
Set prm = cmd.CreateParameter("FirstName", _
 adVarChar, adParamInput, 50, Me.FirstName)
cmd.Parameters.Append prm
Set prm = cmd.CreateParameter("Address", _
 adVarChar, adParamInput, 50, Me.Address)
cmd.Parameters.Append prm
Set prm = cmd.CreateParameter("City", _
 adVarChar, adParamInput, 50, Me.City)
cmd.Parameters.Append prm
Set prm = cmd.CreateParameter("State", _
 adVarChar, adParamInput, 2, Me.State)
cmd.Parameters.Append prm
```

```
    Set prm = cmd.CreateParameter("ZipCode", _
     adVarChar, adParamInput, 10, Me.ZipCode)
    cmd.Parameters.Append prm
    Set prm = cmd.CreateParameter("Phone", _
     adVarChar, adParamInput, 10, Me.Phone)
    cmd.Parameters.Append prm
    Set prm = cmd.CreateParameter("Extension", _
     adVarChar, adParamInput, 5, Me.Extension)
    cmd.Parameters.Append prm
    Set prm = cmd.CreateParameter("Notes", _
     adVarChar, adParamInput, 100, Me.Notes)
    cmd.Parameters.Append prm

    cmd.Execute RecordsAffected:=lngRecs, _
     Options:=adExecuteNoRecords

    ' Check if stored proc worked.
    If lngRecs <> 0 Then
        MsgBox "Record saved.", _
         vbInformation + vbOKOnly, Me.Name
    Else
        MsgBox "Unable to save record.", _
         vbCritical + vbOKOnly, Me.Name
    End If

    ' No longer inserting, so disable
    ' the CustomerId control, reset
    ' insert flag, clear the textbox
    ' controls, and call HandleControls
    ' to fixup other controls.
    Me.CustomerId.Enabled = False
    mfInsert = False
    Call ClearControls
    Call HandleControls(False, False)

ExitHere:
    Set cmd = Nothing
    Set prm = Nothing
    cnn.Close
    Set cnn = Nothing
    Exit Sub
ErrorHandler:
```

```
        ' Grab Access/VBA Error
        lngError = Err.Number
        strError = Err.Description
        ' If ADO Error available grab
        ' the first one in the collection.
        If cnn.Errors.Count > 0 Then
            lngError = cnn.Errors(0).NativeError
            strError = cnn.Errors(0).Description
        End If
        MsgBox "Error " & lngError & ": " & _
         strError, vbCritical + vbOKOnly, _
         "frmCustomer Error"
        Resume ExitHere
    End Sub
```

InsertCustomer includes additional logic to require that users complete the CustomerId, LastName, and FirstName fields.

---

**NOTE**       See Chapter 7 for more on multi-user sharing issues and locking. Chapter 7 also
includes an example that uses application logic to get the equivalent of pessimistic
locking with SQL Server databases.

---

# Handling ADO Events

ADO exposes a number of events that you can hook into using a WithEvents variable. Two ADO objects expose events: Connection and Recordset objects. The
events are summarized in Table 6.6.

**TABLE 6.6:**  ADO Events

| Object | Event | Description |
| --- | --- | --- |
| Connection | WillConnect | Called just before a connection is opened |
| Connection | ConnectComplete | Called when the connection is opened |
| Connection | Disconnect | Called when the connection is closed |
| Connection | WillExecute | Called just before a command on this connection is executed |

**TABLE 6.6:** ADO Events (continued)

| Object | Event | Description |
|---|---|---|
| Connection | ExecuteComplete | Called when the command is done executing |
| Connection | BeginTransComplete | Called when a BeginTrans method is complete |
| Connection | CommitTransComplete | Called when a CommitTrans method is complete |
| Connection | RollbackTransComplete | Called when a RollbackTrans method is complete |
| Connection | InfoMessage | Called whenever a completed connection event needs to return additional information from the provider |
| Recordset | FetchProgress | Called periodically during a lengthy asynchronous operation to report how many rows have been retrieved into the recordset |
| Recordset | FetchComplete | Called after all the rows have been retrieved into the recordset |
| Recordset | WillChangeField | Called just before the value of one or more fields has changed, using the Value property or the values argument of the Update method |
| Recordset | FieldChangeComplete | Called after the value of one or more fields has changed, using the Value property or the values argument of the Update method |
| Recordset | WillMove | Called just prior to a recordset move operation |
| Recordset | MoveComplete | Called after the recordset move operation has completed |
| Recordset | EndOfRecordset | Called when the end of the recordset has been reached |
| Recordset | WillChangeRecord | Called just before a record is changed using an Update, UpdateBatch, AddNew, Delete, Cancel, or CancelBatch method |
| Recordset | RecordChange Complete | Called after a record is changed using an Update, UpdateBatch, AddNew, Delete, Cancel, or CancelBatch method |
| Recordset | WillChange Recordset | Called just before a recordset is altered using a Requery, Resync, Close, Open, or Filter method |
| Recordset | RecordsetChange Complete | Called after a recordset is altered using a Requery, Resync, Close, Open, or Filter method |

Many of the events pass parameters to the event procedures.

## Sinking to ADO Event

To sink to an ADO event, you must create a class module, either a stand-alone class module or a form's class module. Then, follow these steps:

1. Add a WithEvents variable to the module. While you can add this variable anywhere, you typically will want to add it to the declarations section of the module. For example, the following code creates a WithEvents variable for the ADO Recordset object:

```
Private WithEvents rstSink as ADODB.Recordset
```

2. When you add the WithEvents variable to the class module, the VBA editor adds the event sink variable to the editor's object drop-down list. Select the event sink variable from the object drop-down, and the event to which you wish to respond from the procedures drop-down list, to create one or more event procedures for the event sink. Write code in the event procedure to react to the event.

3. Somewhere in your code—for example, in the form's Load event procedure—instantiate the event sink variable. For example:

```
Set rstSink = New ADODB.Recordset
```

4. Somewhere else in your code—for example, in the form's Unload event procedure—destroy the event sink by setting it to Nothing. For example:

```
Set rstSink = Nothing
```

---

**NOTE**    See Chapter 3 of *Access 2000 Developer's Handbook, Volume 1: Desktop Edition* for more details on event sinking.

---

## An Example

The CH06A.MDB database includes a form, frmADOEvents, that contains an event sink variable, mcnn, that responds to events of the ADO Connection object. The frmADOEvents form is shown in Figure 6.6.

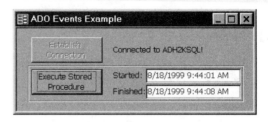

**FIGURE 6.6**

The frmADOEvents form

Here's the declarations section of the formADOEvents module:

```
Private Const adhcADH2KSQLCnn = "Provider=SQLOLEDB;" & _
    "Data Source=Gorilla;Database=ADH2KSQL;User Id=sa;Password=;"

' Create an event sink variable for
' the Connection object
Private WithEvents mcnn As ADODB.Connection
Private mcmd As ADODB.Command
Private mrst As ADODB.Recordset
```

Here's the code attached to the cmdConnect command button to establish the connection:

```
Private Sub cmdConnect_Click()
    ' Establish the connection
    Set mcnn = New ADODB.Connection
    mcnn.Open adhcADH2KSQLCnn
End Sub
```

As the connection is established, it calls the WillConnect and ConnectComplete event procedures:

```
Private Sub mcnn_WillConnect( _
  ConnectionString As String, _
  UserID As String, Password As String, _
  Options As Long, _
  adStatus As ADODB.EventStatusEnum, _
  ByVal pConnection As ADODB.Connection)
    Me.lblConnect.Caption = "Connecting..."
End Sub

Private Sub mcnn_ConnectComplete( _
  ByVal pError As  ADODB.Error, _
```

```
        adStatus As ADODB.EventStatusEnum, _
      ByVal pConnection As ADODB.Connection)
          ' Display the connected message and
          ' enable the execute controls. Also
          ' disable the cmdConnect command button.
          Me.lblConnect.Caption = "Connected to ADH2KSQL!"
          Me.cmdExecute.Enabled = True
          Me.txtStart.Enabled = True
          Me.txtFinish.Enabled = True
          Me.cmdExecute.SetFocus
          Me.cmdConnect.Enabled = False
    End Sub
```

In addition to displaying a "connected" message on the form, the code attached to the ConnectComplete event enables several controls on the form.

When the user clicks the cmdExecute button, the code executes the procWait stored Procedure using a Command object. The procWait stored procedure simulates a long-running query using the WaitFor statement. Here's procWait's source:

```
Create Procedure procWait
As
    DECLARE @start DATETIME
    SELECT @start = GETDATE()
    WAITFOR DELAY '0:0:5'
    SELECT @start AS Started, GETDATE() As Finished
```

When finished executing, procWait returns the start and finish time in a recordset.

Here's the code attached to the cmdExecute's click event that creates the Command object and executes it asynchronously:

```
Private Sub cmdExecute_Click()
    ' Setup the command
    Set mcmd = New ADODB.Command
    Set mcmd.ActiveConnection = mcnn
    mcmd.CommandText = "procWait"
    mcmd.CommandType = adCmdStoredProc

    ' Execute the command asynchronously
    Set mrst = mcmd.Execute(Options:=adAsyncExecute)
End Sub
```

**TIP**

It's important that you use the adAsyncExecute constant to execute the Command asynchronously. If you don't, Access will pause to wait for the Command object to complete execution, defeating the purpose of using an event sink.

As the Command is executed, the WillExecute and ExecuteComplete events are called:

```
Private Sub mcnn_WillExecute( _
 Source As String, _
 CursorType As ADODB.CursorTypeEnum, _
 LockType As ADODB.LockTypeEnum, _
 Options As Long, _
 adStatus As ADODB.EventStatusEnum, _
 ByVal pCommand As ADODB.Command, _
 ByVal pRecordset As ADODB.Recordset, _
 ByVal pConnection As ADODB.Connection)
    Me.txtStart = "Running..."
    Me.txtFinish = "Running..."
End Sub

Private Sub mcnn_ExecuteComplete( _
 ByVal RecordsAffected As Long, _
 ByVal pError As ADODB.Error, _
 adStatus As ADODB.EventStatusEnum, _
 ByVal pCommand As ADODB.Command, _
 ByVal pRecordset As ADODB.Recordset, _
 ByVal pConnection As ADODB.Connection)
    ' Update the text boxes with the
    ' start and finish times returned
    ' by the procWait stored procedure.
    Me.txtStart = mrst("Started")
    Me.txtFinish = mrst("Finished")
End Sub
```

Once the ExecuteComplete event is triggered, we can be sure the recordset was created.

Finally, the following clean-up code executes as the form unloads:

```
Private Sub Form_Unload(Cancel As Integer)
    Set mcmd = Nothing
    mrst.Close
```

```
        Set mrst = Nothing
        mcnn.Close
        Set mcnn = Nothing
    End Sub
```

---

**NOTE**          Many of the events pass parameters to your event procedures. You can use these
                  parameters to determine, for example, the number of records affected by a
                  command or whether the operation succeeded and, if not, what errors occurred.

---

# Dealing with Errors

You have two choices in dealing with errors when you encounter an error in executing an ADO operation. You can use either the VBA Err object or the ADO
Errors collection.

The VBA Err object holds the number, description, and other information about
the last executed VBA statement. When working with ADO, however, the VBA
Err object has two shortcomings. First, the number it reports is essentially useless.
Second, VBA can only capture one ADO error, the topmost object in the ADO
Errors collection.

---

**NOTE**          See Chapter 14 of the *Access 2000 Developer's Handbook, Volume 1: Desktop
                  Edition* for more information on using VBA Err object.

---

By using the ADO Errors collection, you are able to retrieve a considerable
amount of information on the errors generated by the last ADO operation.

## Using the Errors Collection

When an error is encountered in an ADO operation, ADO fills the Errors collection with one or more Error objects. The Errors collection is descendent of the
Connection object. If you have opened multiple connections, then each Connection object has its own Errors collection.

You can check the number of errors in the Errors collection using the Errors collection's Count property. For the vast majority of ADO errors, the Errors collection will have only one Error object. Each Error object has a number of properties that are summarized in Table 6.7.

**TABLE 6.7:** Properties of the ADO Error Object

| Error Object Property | Description |
|---|---|
| Description | The error message |
| NativeError | The error number reported by the data provider; for the SQL Server provider, this property (not the Number) contains the number you'll want to use |
| Number | The error number as processed by ADO; for the SQL Server provider, this number is not useful |
| Source | The provider or ADO object that generated the error |
| SQLState | A five-character code returned by the data provider; for the SQL Server provider, this number is not useful |

**TIP**

If wish to branch in your code based on the number of the ADO error, you should use the NativeError property.

The MakeAnADOError subroutine in the basErrors module of CH06A.MDB demonstrates the use of the ADO Errors collection:

```
Sub MakeAnADOError()
    ' This subroutine demonstrates how
    ' to use the ADO Errors collection.
    Dim cnn As ADODB.Connection
    Dim cmd As ADODB.Command
    Dim prm As ADODB.Parameter
    Dim rst As ADODB.Recordset
    Dim errADO As ADODB.Error
    Dim lngError As Long
    Dim strError As String

    On Error GoTo ErrorHandler

    Set cnn = New ADODB.Connection
```

```
    Set cmd = New ADODB.Command

    cnn.Open adhcADH2KSQLCnn

    Set cmd.ActiveConnection = cnn
    cmd.CommandText = "procGetEmployee"
    cmd.CommandType = adCmdStoredProc

    Set prm = cmd.CreateParameter("employeeid", _
     adInteger, adParamInput, , 5)
    cmd.Parameters.Append prm

    ' This code should trigger an error because
    ' the procGetEmployee stored procedure only
    ' has one parameter.
    Set prm = cmd.CreateParameter("extrparam", _
     adInteger, adParamInput, , 5)
    cmd.Parameters.Append prm

    ' Execute Command and place results
    ' in Recordset object.
    Set rst = cmd.Execute()

    If Not rst.EOF Then
        Debug.Print rst!FirstName & " " & rst!LastName
    Else
        Debug.Print "No such employee."
    End If

ExitHere:
    Set rst = Nothing
    Set prm = Nothing
    Set cmd = Nothing
    cnn.Close
    Set cnn = Nothing
    Exit Sub
ErrorHandler:
    ' Iterate through the ADO Errors collection
    ' if it contains any errors.
    If cnn.Errors.Count > 0 Then
        For Each errADO In cnn.Errors
            Debug.Print "ADO Error Information:"
```

```
                 Debug.Print ">NativeError: " & _
                   errADO.NativeError
                 Debug.Print ">Description: " & _
                   errADO.Description
                 Debug.Print ">Number: " & errADO.Number
                 Debug.Print ">Source: " & errADO.Source
                 Debug.Print ">SQLState: " & errADO.SQLState
             Next errADO
         End If
         Set errADO = Nothing
         Resume ExitHere
     End Sub
```

The error handler of MakeAnADOError displays information on each Error object in the ADO Errors collection.

Because errors can occur in both ADO and non-ADO areas of your code, it's a good idea to check both places for errors and only use the Errors collection if it has a count greater than 0. This is demonstrated in the error handler from the Save-Customer subroutine of frmADOConcurrency shown earlier in the chapter:

```
ErrorHandler:
    ' Grab Access/VBA Error
    lngError = Err.Number
    strError = Err.Description
    ' If ADO Error available grab
    ' the first one in the collection.
    If cnn.Errors.Count > 0 Then
        lngError = cnn.Errors(0).NativeError
        strError = cnn.Errors(0).Description
    End If
```

Because the Errors collection will usually only contain a single Error object, you can often get away with code that looks only at the first item of the Errors collection, as shown in this example.

# Summary

In this chapter, we explored the use of ADO with server databases. We covered the following topics:

- An overview of the ADO object model

- How to use the Connection object to establish a connection to a server database

- How to connect to secured SQL Server and MSDE databases

- How to prompt users for login information

- How the ADP CurrentProject.Connection differs from a regular SQL Server connection

- How to use the Command object and its properties and methods

- The various ways to execute a parameterized stored procedure using the Command object

- How to create prepared statements

- How to return a recordset from a parameterized stored procedure

- The various interactions between data provider, cursor type, lock type, and cursor location when using SQL Server data

- How to manage concurrency when using optimistic locking

- How to sink to ADO events

- How to use the ADO Errors collection

While all of the examples in this chapter used SQL Server data, many of the concepts are the same regardless of the particular server database you use.

# Developing ADP Applications

- Using forms in Access projects

- Using reports in Access projects

- Multi-user, sharing, and replication issues

**N**ow that you've seen how to store and manipulate data stored in Access projects, you're ready to consider the problem of actual ADP applications. As you know, the data is only part of the story. If you want to create an application that end users can work with safely and successfully, you need to create a user interface that goes beyond the built-in datasheets for tables, views, and stored procedures.

The good news is that you can use the same tools for this purpose in Access projects that you're already familiar with from Access databases: forms, reports, and data access pages. Your previous experience with Access will help you get quickly up to speed with Access project applications. But you need to be somewhat cautious, because there are a few differences between databases and projects in the design and behavior of Access user interface objects.

You'll learn about data access pages in Chapters 10 and 11. In this chapter, you'll see the details of using forms and reports in Access projects.

---

**NOTE**    We've provided a sample file, CH07.ADP, which illustrates the techniques discussed in this chapter. Before using the project, however, be sure the connection properties match those for your computer. Select File ➤ Connection and make sure the entries in the Data Link Properties dialog box are correct.

---

# Using Forms in Access Projects

Forms in Access projects are very much like forms in Access databases. The design surface looks and feels the same, and the individual controls are identical between the two varieties of Access. However, there are some subtle changes. Access projects add a few new properties to forms and dispense with some properties that aren't useful in projects. Also, you'll find that you have some increased flexibility in data management, thanks to the combination of ADO and SQL Server used to hold data in these forms.

In this section, we'll cover the property differences you'll find when you create a form in an Access project. We'll also show you how you can use ADO transactions to manage data on bound forms in Access projects.

# Changes to the Form User Interface

You'll notice one major change to the user interface of forms in an Access project: the navigation buttons are more extensive than they are in an Access database.

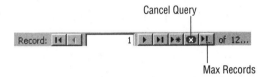

The additional buttons on the navigation bar are designed to help when there are many records on the server, perhaps too many to be easily retrieved to a form. If a form is taking too long to retrieve data, you can hit the Cancel Query button to cancel the retrieval of the remaining records. The form's recordset will contain only the records that were retrieved before the query was cancelled. For example, if you cancel after retrieving 450 of 5,000 records, hitting the Last Record navigation button will take you to record 450, not to record 5,000. To see all the records, you'd need to refresh or requery the form.

Click the Max Records button to bring up the sliding scale shown below. By default, forms will retrieve no more than 10,000 records when you open them. You can change this default for all future forms by choosing Tools ➢ Options ➢ Advanced and setting a value for Default Max Records in the Client-Server Settings section. Alternately, you can change it for an individual form interactively with the slider or programatically with the MaxRecords property of the form. When a form has fetched the maximum records you allow it with this setting, it behaves as if you had hit the Cancel Query button. The only way to get more records into the form is to change the Max Records setting.

**NOTE**    If you change the Max Records setting for a form, it requeries the form's recordset. This has several side effects, including moving the form back to the first record.

When you set MaxRecords for a form, Access issues a SET ROWCOUNT statement to the server before it issues the query for the form's recordsource. For example, if you have a form based directly on tblCustomer and set the MaxRecords value to 100, Access issues two SQL statements to return records to the form:

```
SET ROWCOUNT 100
SELECT * FROM "tblCustomer"
```

# New and Changed Form Properties

Forms in Access projects have seven properties that aren't present for forms in Access databases (each of which is discussed in the following sections):

- InputParameters
- MaxRecButton
- MaxRecords
- ResyncCommand
- ServerFilter
- ServerFilterByForm
- UniqueTable

In addition, the RecordsetType property has different values for a form in an Access project than for a form in an Access database.

## InputParameters

The InputParameters property helps you construct forms that retrieve a subset of records from a table. These forms can use either a SQL statement or a stored procedure as their record source. The InputParameters property of the form holds the same information that would be stored via the Parameters window of a query in an Access database.

For example, consider frmInputParametersSQL. Figure 7.1 shows the Data tab from the property sheet for this form.

FIGURE 7.1
Using the InputParameters
property

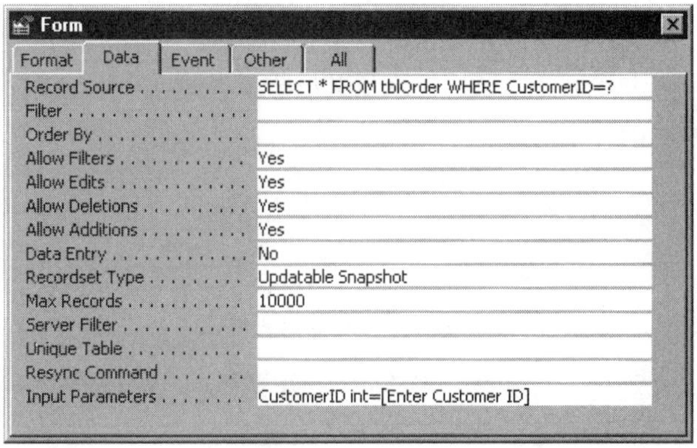

To use InputParameters with a SQL statement, you must construct a Recordsource in the form of a SQL SELECT statement with a WHERE clause. Instead of supplying values in the WHERE clause, though, you use the "?" character as a placeholder. In Figure 7.1, for example, the SQL statement is set up to filter on the CustomerID column, but does not contain an actual value to use for this column. You can test this for yourself by looking at the frmInputParametersSQL form in CH07.ADP.

Supplying the filter is the job of the InputParameters property. This property lists the name of the parameter (in this case, of the column), the SQL Server data type, and where Access should retrieve the value for this property. This can be a prompt, as shown here, or the name of a control on an open form. You can also use commas to separate multiple parameters. So, for example, you might have a form based on this pair of properties:

- Recordsource: `SELECT * FROM tblOrder WHERE CustomerID=? AND OrderDate>?`

- InputParameters: `CustomerID int=[Enter Customer ID], OrderDate datetime=[Form]![FirstDate]`

These properties would result in the user being prompted for the Customer ID to use, and the Order Date being filled in automatically from the value of the First-Date control.

When using InputParameters with a SQL statement, the SQL statement is stored on the form, not in the back-end database. You can also use InputParameters to work with forms based on stored procedures with parameters that are persisted to the server. In this case, you must use the actual stored procedure parameter names in the InputParameters property and precede each one with an @ symbol. For example, you might base a form on the procGetCustomer2 stored procedure, which has this definition:

```
CREATE PROCEDURE procGetCustomer2
@custid INT
AS
SELECT * FROM tblCustomer
WHERE CustomerID = @custid
```

In this case, the form properties could be set this way:

- RecordSource: `procGetCustomer2`

- InputParameters: `@custid int=[Enter Customer ID]`

CH07.ADP contains a form, frmInputParametersSP, that illustrates this technique.

---

**NOTE**    If you base a form on a stored procedure with parameters and leave the InputParameters property empty, the user will still get prompted for each parameter, but the prompting dialog box will just use the name of the parameter as the prompt.

---

---

**WARNING**    Basing forms on stored procedures is not perfectly integrated into Access 2000. The New Form dialog box, for example, won't let you select the name of a stored procedure as the recordsource of a form. Worse, the wizards are completely incapable of creating forms, reports, or pages based on stored procedures. To use a stored procedure as a recordsource, you must create a blank object and then select the name of the stored procedure as the recordsource in the property sheet. To get around these problems, you can often base a form on a view rather than on a stored procedure.

---

## MaxRecords

The MaxRecords property is the analog of the visual setting for maximum records discussed above. Unlike the visual property, though, changes to MaxRecords made in code do not take effect immediately. If you want a change to MaxRecords made in code to take effect, you should call the form's Requery method.

## MaxRecButton

The MaxRecButton property is a Boolean property that controls whether or not the Max Records button is displayed on the form. The MaxRecords property continues to function as discussed above, but if you remove the button, the user has no way to change the value of this property (and no visual indication that the form might not be showing all of the records in the table). You should be very cautious about setting this property to No.

## UniqueTable and ResyncCommand

Although Access projects try to preserve the same updatability semantics as Access databases, they're not always successful. We'll discuss this later on in the chapter, but there are some cases where Access can almost (but not quite!) figure out how to update data from joined tables. For example, if you have a form based on a stored procedure that joins tables, you need to help Access out a bit by telling it how to retrieve updated data after it's been saved.

For example, suppose you have a form based on procCustomerOrders, which is defined like this:

```
CREATE PROCEDURE procCustomerOrders
AS
SELECT tblCustomer.LastName, tblCustomer.FirstName,
tblOrder.*
FROM tblCustomer INNER JOIN tblOrder
ON tblCustomer.CustomerID = tblOrder.CustomerID
ORDER BY tblOrder.OrderID
```

Figure 7.2 shows a simple form (see frmCustomerOrdersSP in CH07.ADP) based on this stored procedure. The CustomerID field, of course, comes from the tblOrder table.

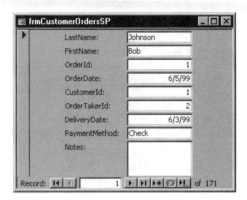

In an Access database, this form would perform row fixup and allow you to change any field, updating other fields as necessary. In an Access project, by default, you won't get this behavior. Indeed, if you construct such a form and attempt to make any updates, you'll get the message, "Form is read-only because the Unique Table property is not set," in the status bar.

In order to be able to edit the data at all, you need to set the UniqueTable property. Perhaps a better name for this property would be the MostManyTable property. The table to choose is the one that supplies different values for every row in the recordset—that is, the one that is on the many side of any possible join. In the case of a form based on procCustomerOrders, for example, you should set this property to tblOrder.

Once you've done this, you'll discover that the data from the unique table can be edited on the form, but you'll have another problem. Access still won't retrieve all of the fields it should after you've edited data. For example, suppose you change the CustomerID field on the form and save the record. You know that this should change the values of the LastName and FirstName fields, but the Access project doesn't know that. It will continue to display the original values for these fields until you requery the data.

In order to have Access fix up fields on the one side of the one-to-many join for this example, you must supply a value for the form's ResyncCommand property. This property holds a SQL statement that is used to retrieve new values for a record after a change to that record is saved, with "?" parameter placeholders in place of every field in the UniqueTable's key. For example, an appropriate ResyncCommand for the form we've been working with in this section is

```
SELECT tblCustomer.LastName, tblCustomer.FirstName,
tblOrder.*
FROM tblCustomer INNER JOIN tblOrder
ON tblCustomer.CustomerID = tblOrder.CustomerID
WHERE tblOrder.OrderID = ?
```

If the Unique Table has multiple fields in its key, there must be multiple question marks in the ResyncCommand, and these must be in the same order as the key fields in the table.

Whether you need to supply UniqueTable and ResyncCommand properties depends on the form's recordsource. If the form is based on a view with a join, you must supply the UniqueTable property (or else the form is read only). If the form is based on a parameterized SQL statement or a stored procedure with a join or expression, you must also supply the ResyncCommand property (or else Access won't automatically show the correct data after an update).

**TIP**     Forms in Access projects never allow updating fields from any table other than the Unique Table.

## ServerFilterByForm and ServerFilter

While the regular Access Filter by Form interface is very useful for finding data, it doesn't do anything to limit the amount of data retrieved from the server. That's because Filter by Form is strictly a client-side technology. If you do a Filter by Form, even in an Access project, it follows these steps:

1. When you open the form, Access retrieves all the records in the recordset.

2. When you place the form in Filter by Form view, Access uses the retrieved records to construct the choices in the filtering combo boxes.

3. When you apply the filter, Access uses the fields you've selected for filtering to show a subset of the already-retrieved data.

In order to make filtering useful for limiting the amount of data retrieved in an Access project, Access adds the ServerFilterByForm property to Access forms in a project. (See the frmCustomerServerFilter form for an example.) If you set this property to Yes, Access follows these steps:

1. When you open the form, Access does not retrieve any data. Instead, the form is opened in Filter by Form view.

2. Because there's no data yet, Access only presents "Is Null" and "Is Not Null" in the filtering combo boxes. You can supply any literal value you like, though, because these boxes are not limited to the list.

3. When you apply the filter by clicking the Apply Server Filter button on the toolbar, Access constructs a WHERE clause based on your filter choices and uses that as part of the SQL statement that populates the form.

The WHERE clause that Access creates is available as the form's ServerFilter property. For a demonstration of this feature check out the frmCustomerServerFilter form in CH07.ADP.

---

**WARNING** When you set the ServerFilterByForm property to Yes, regular (client-side) filtering on this form is no longer available.

---

**TIP** ServerFilterByForm can't be set to Yes if the recordsource of the form is a stored procedure. In that case, you should consider using input parameters for filtering instead.

---

# RecordsetType

The RecordsetType property in an Access project has two possible settings. If you set the property to Snapshot, none of the fields displayed on the form can be edited. If you set the property to Updatable Snapshot (the default) controls from the most-many table can be edited (provided you set the UniqueTable property if necessary, as described above).

# What's Missing

Forms in an Access project have all of the properties that forms in an Access database do except for one: the RecordLocks property. You'll recall that in an Access database, this property lets you choose between optimistic and pessimistic locking. In an Access project you have no choice; the recordset created for a form always employs optimistic locking.

There are also a few shortcut keys that don't work in Access projects. These are

- Ctrl+Alt+Spacebar, which inserts the default value for a field in an Access database.

- F9, to refresh the contents of a lookup field (this key still works to refresh an entire form).

# Data Updatability

As you might expect, the rules for updating data displayed on a form in an Access project are different from those in an Access database. After all, the data engine is different, and this is really only the first version of the Access project technology. So you won't be surprised to find that the rules for updating are somewhat more restrictive in Access projects.

Here are the general rules for updating data on forms in Access projects:

- To be updatable at all, a table must have either a primary key constraint, a unique constraint on some field, or a unique index on some field.

- Fields on forms based on a single table are updatable as long as the table meets the primary key, unique index, or unique constraint requirement.

- Fields on forms based on a view that is in turn based on a single updateable table are themselves updatable. This is true even if the unique field is not included in the view.

- Fields on forms based on a one-to-many join represented as a SQL statement are updateable if they're in the most-many table.

- Fields on forms based on a one-to-many join from a view or stored procedure are updateable if they're in the most-many table and this table has been specified as the Unique Table for the form.

- Fields based on a self-join are never updateable.

- Fields based on a many-to-many join are never updateable.

- Fields based on expressions are not updateable.

- Fields based on a SQL statement containing a GROUP BY or COMPUTE clause are not updateable.

---

**TIP**    If you need to update fields on both the one side and the many side of a join, consider creating a form based on the one-side table with a subform based on the many-side table. Because Access will create separate recordsets for the form and the subform, both sides of the join can be updated in this situation.

---

# Using Transactions with Bound Forms

In a few areas, Access projects provide substantially more functionality for forms than Access databases provide. One of these areas is in transactional processing for bound forms. For years, Access developers have been asking for a way to group multiple changes made via a form into a transaction and then either commit the entire group or roll back the entire group as a unit. The only way to do this has been to utilize temporary tables or unbound forms and write a great deal of code. In Access projects, a combination of the newly exposed Form.Recordset property and ADO code allows you to manage transactions easily on bound forms.

The easiest way to create a bound form that supports transactions is to first use the normal Access design tools to create a bound form with no reference to transactions. You might choose to work directly in Form Design view or to use the Form Wizard. In either case, when you're done designing the form, you need to switch to the Visual Basic Editor and add the code necessary to support transactions. Listing 7.1 shows the code for a form (frmTransactions) based on tblCustomers.

### Listing 7.1

```
Option Compare Database
Option Explicit

Private mfDirty As Boolean
Private mfPendingChanges As Boolean
Private mcnnMain As New ADODB.Connection
Private mrstCustomers As New ADODB.Recordset

Private Sub Form_AfterDelConfirm(Status As Integer)
    If Not mfPendingChanges Then
        mfPendingChanges = (Status = acDeleteOK)
    End If
End Sub

Private Sub Form_AfterUpdate()
    mfPendingChanges = True
End Sub

Private Sub Form_Delete(Cancel As Integer)
    If Not mfDirty Then
        mcnnMain.BeginTrans
        mfDirty = True
    End If
End Sub

Private Sub Form_Dirty(Cancel As Integer)
    If Not mfDirty Then
        mcnnMain.BeginTrans
        mfDirty = True
    End If
End Sub

Private Sub Form_Open(Cancel As Integer)
    mcnnMain.ConnectionString = CurrentProject.Connection
    mcnnMain.Open
    mrstCustomers.Open "SELECT * FROM tblCustomer", _
     mcnnMain, adOpenKeyset, adLockOptimistic
    Set Me.Recordset = mrstCustomers
End Sub
```

```
Private Sub Form_Unload(Cancel As Integer)
    Dim intRet As Integer
    If mfPendingChanges Then
        intRet = MsgBox("Commit all changes?", vbYesNoCancel)
        If intRet = vbYes Then
            mcnnMain.CommitTrans
        ElseIf intRet = vbNo Then
            mcnnMain.RollbackTrans
        Else
            Cancel = True
        End If
    Else
        If mfDirty Then
            mcnnMain.RollbackTrans
        End If
    End If
    Set mrstCustomers = Nothing
    Set mcnnMain = Nothing
End Sub
```

This code creates two ADO variables to support transactional processing. The mcnnMain variable is an ADO connection that's used as the context for transactions. The mrstCustomers variable is an ADO recordset that contains exactly the same records as the form would display if you left it bound to the original record-source. By opening this recordset from the separate connection, though, you enable it to participate in that connection's transaction processing. The form's Open event enables the code to open this recordset before records are actually displayed, and to assign it to the form's Recordset property once it's open.

---

**TIP**

If your form is based on a join between multiple tables, you need to remember to set the UniqueTable property in code after you set the Recordset property to make this technique work.

---

When the user changes a record, either the Delete or the Dirty event will occur. In either of these events, if you haven't already started a transaction, you call the BeginTrans method. When the user commits a change, either the AfterUpdate or AfterDelConfirm event will fire. In these events, the code makes note that there are pending changes.

When the user closes the form, the Unload event fires. Based on user response to a message box, the code either commits or rolls back the pending transactions at this point.

---

**WARNING**  This technique won't work in Access databases. If you set the Recordset property of a form to an ADO recordset based on Jet data instead of SQL Server data, the form will become read only.

---

**TIP**  If you expect users to hold the form open for long periods of time, you might consider placing a textbox with a count of open transactions and separate Commit and Rollback buttons on the form as well.

---

# Optimizing Forms

There are no secret special tricks for optimizing forms in Access projects. The basic optimization is the same as for any client-server database application: fetch only the data you need and only when you need it. Here's a small checklist of things to consider:

- Use the MaxRecords property to limit the number of records returned.
- If the user is likely to want only a subset of the form's records, open the form in Server Filter by Form mode.
- If the form will be used mainly for entering new data, set the DataEntry property to Yes.
- Display only the fields that the user is likely to need. In particular, don't display text or image fields in bound controls unless it's absolutely necessary to do so.
- Set the HasModule property of the form to No if you don't need any code behind the form.
- Base forms and subforms on queries rather than tables, so that you can include only the necessary records.

# Using Reports in Access Projects

There are very few differences between reports in an Access database and reports in an Access project. You'll find a few new properties, but otherwise, using reports should be quite familiar to you.

## New Report Properties

Reports in an Access project add two useful properties (each of these is discussed in the following sections):

- InputParameters
- ServerFilter

The RecordLocks property, however, has been dropped from reports in an Access project. There's no way to lock the records in a report in an Access project while the report is being previewed.

> **NOTE**   If you use code to iterate through the Properties collection of a report in an Access project, you'll also find some properties that have no business being there: MaxRecButton, ResyncCommand, ServerFilterByForm, and UniqueTable. But since you can't retrieve or set a value for these properties, see them on the property sheet, in the locals window, or in the Object Browser, they might as well not be there.

### InputParameters

The InputParameters property on a report allows you to prompt the user for filtering information at runtime. Syntactically, it works exactly the same as the InputParameters property on a form.

To use InputParameters with a report whose recordsource is a SQL statement, you include "?" markers in the SQL statement for each runtime parameter. For example, this would be a valid combination of properties for a report with runtime prompting:

- Recordsource: `SELECT * FROM tblCustomers WHERE CustomerID = ?`
- InputParameters: `CustomerID int=[Enter Customer ID]`

Of course, you can also use the InputParameters property to prompt the user for parameters for a stored procedure. In this case, just as with forms, you must use the @name syntax to identify the parameters in the stored procedure. Using the same stored procedure that was used for the form example above, you could have this combination of properties on a report:

- RecordSource: `procGetCustomer2`

- InputParameters: `@custid int=[Enter Customer ID]`

When your report is based on a stored procedure with parameters, you can also use the parameters as the control source for a control. To do this, you use the full parameter name, including the @ sign. For example, in the case of procGetCustomer2, this would be a valid control source:

`=[@custid]`

## ServerFilter

Alternately, you can use the ServerFilter property to programatically supply a filter for a report. In this case, the filter is used by Access directly in the SQL database to limit the number of records returned. This property has the same format as the ServerFilter constructed in Server Filter by Form mode on a form. Of course, a report has no Server Filter by Form mode. However, you can take advantage of this correspondence of properties to use the form interface to let users choose the records to show on a report.

To see this technique in action, open the frmCustomerReport form in CH07.ADP. This form, shown in Figure 7.3, is based on the tblCustomers table and saved with its ServerFilterByForm property set to True, so that it automatically opens in server filter by form mode.

The form's MaxRecords property is set to 1 so that it won't waste time retrieving a lot of records from the server when the user chooses a set of records to display. The only way to get the ServerFilter property is to actually apply the filter, so the form has to retrieve something. Fortunately the filter doesn't contain the MaxRecords setting, so this won't be inherited by the report.

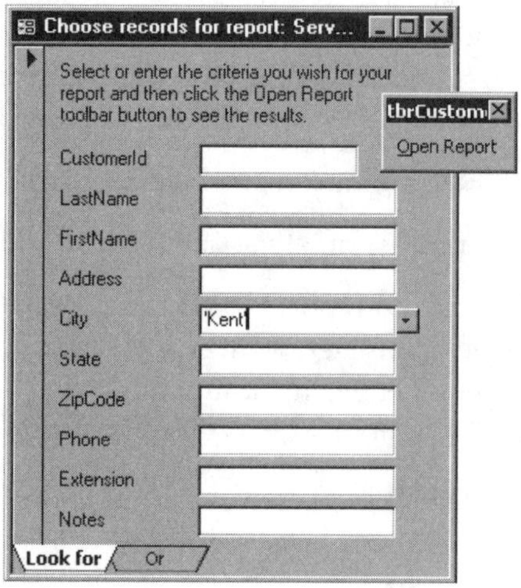

**FIGURE 7.3**

Choosing records to display on a report

You might think that you can set MaxRecords to zero to prevent retrieving records entirely, but Access interprets this as "retrieve all records from the table." Avoid setting this property to zero when using large data sets.

The form automatically displays a custom toolbar with a single button. This button is just a copy of the built-in Apply Server Filter button from the form's toolbar. This allows you to supply a custom caption, rather than trying to explain to users why they need to choose "Apply Server Filter" in order to open a report.

**TIP** The Customize Toolbar dialog box doesn't contain a copy of the Apply Server Filter button. You can make a copy on your own custom toolbar by using Ctrl+drag to copy it from the existing toolbar with your mouse.

When the user clicks the Open Report toolbar button, their selected filter is applied. This triggers the form's ApplyFilter event, which contains this bit of code:

```
Private Sub Form_ApplyFilter(Cancel As Integer, _
  ApplyType As Integer)
    DoCmd.OpenReport "rptCustomerFilter", acViewPreview
    DoCmd.Close acForm, Me.Name
End Sub
```

In turn, the report uses its own Open event to copy the ServerFilter property from the form:

```
Private Sub Report_Open(Cancel As Integer)
    On Error Resume Next
    Me.ServerFilter = Forms!frmCustomerReport.ServerFilter
End Sub
```

The end result is that the report opens showing exactly the records that the user chose from the form. The On Error Resume Next in the Report_Open procedure allows the report to open showing all records if it's called directly rather than from the filtering form.

# Record Locking

From working with Access databases, you're familiar with the distinction between optimistic and pessimistic locking used with the Jet engine:

- With optimistic locking, records are locked only for the duration of the update.

- With pessimistic locking, records are locked when the edit begins and unlocked when the update is complete.

Bound forms in Access projects natively support optimistic locking via ADO to SQL Server. Optimistic locking makes sure that users aren't locked out of records or groups of records while other records are editing. However, optimistic locking does not prevent multiple users from editing the same record at the same time. Whoever saves their changes last wins (that is, their changes are the ones that are ultimately saved in the database).

What if you require the pessimistic locking functionality you're used to from Access databases, where users can't start editing records that other users are working with? Let's look at two possibilities for implementing this form of locking in Access projects: unbound forms and reservation tables.

## Using Unbound Forms

Your first impulse for implementing pessimistic locking will probably be the same one that we had: take advantage of the form's Recordset property. If Access insists on using optimistic locking, what's to prevent you from opening your own record-set with pessimistic locking and assigning it to the form's Recordset property?

Well, nothing, except that it won't work. ADO won't allow you to open a recordset with pessimistic locking using the client cursor engine, so you have to use a server-side cursor. And if you assign a recordset using a server-side cursor to the Recordset property of a form, Access immediately makes the form read-only, despite anything else you might do.

The next obvious alternative is to use an unbound form with a pessimistic recordset. In outline, this strategy looks something like this:

1. Open a recordset with pessimistic locking when you open the form.

2. Leave all the form's fields unbound and write code to move the values from the current row of the recordset to controls on the form.

3. Create your own navigation buttons and use them to call the Move methods of the recordset.

4. When the user changes the value in a control, write the change back to the recordset, starting an edit.

5. When the user commits a record, update the recordset.

6. Write additional code to handle record insertions and deletions.

It's an obvious idea, and it is indeed possible to write code to do all of these things. But if you do go down this road, you'll discover a big problem when you try to test your solution using two sessions of your application. The problem is that SQL Server implements pessimistic locking differently than the Jet engine does.

When you use ADO to open a server-side updatable recordset on SQL Server, ADO creates a SQL Server Cursor object to handle the records and tells it to use what are called *scroll locks*. With scroll locks, the records are locked, not when they're edited, but when they're read into the recordset! The locks don't prevent other users from reading those records, but they do prevent other users from obtaining the necessary locks to open their own pessimistic recordset. The net result is that using unbound forms with a recordset with pessimistic locks works fine…as long as your application has a maximum of one simultaneous user.

There appears to be no way with the current versions of Access and SQL Server to use true pessimistic locking on the database engine level with data in Access projects. The closest you can get is to write your own application logic to reserve records on edit and release them on update. We'll demonstrate this technique in the next section.

## Using a Reservations Table

If you can't use the engine to give you automatic pessimistic locking, the only alternative is to use application logic to achieve the same result. Fortunately, with stored procedures the application logic can reside on the server, where it's easily available to client applications.

The technique demonstrated here uses a separate table to reserve records to be edited. By keeping the table on the server and using an appropriate primary key, it's possible to make sure that no two client applications can reserve the same record. Figure 7.4 shows the design of the reservation table.

**FIGURE 7.4**
The reservation table

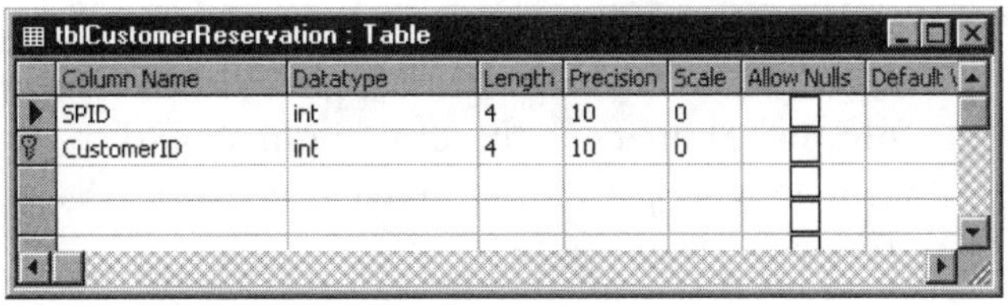

tblCustomerReservation : Table

| Column Name | Datatype | Length | Precision | Scale | Allow Nulls | Default V |
|---|---|---|---|---|---|---|
| SPID | int | 4 | 10 | 0 | ☐ | |
| CustomerID | int | 4 | 10 | 0 | ☐ | |

SPID stands for SQL Server Process ID. The server assigns a unique SPID every application that connects to SQL Server. This SPID can be retrieved from the @@SPID system variable and remains constant as long as the application remains connected. It provides a handy way to uniquely identify a particular instance of an Access project.

The database also contains a stored procedure that writes rows to the reservation table, procReserveCustomer:

```
CREATE PROCEDURE procReserveCustomer
   (
      @custid int,
      @ok int OUTPUT
   )
AS
   SET NOCOUNT ON
   DECLARE @error_save int, @rowcount_save int
```

```
INSERT INTO tblCustomerReservation (SPID, CustomerID)
 VALUES (@@SPID, @custid)
SELECT @error_save=@@ERROR, @rowcount_save=@@ROWCOUNT
IF @error_save <> 0
   SELECT @ok = 0
ELSE
BEGIN
   IF @rowcount_save = 1
      SELECT @ok = -1
   ELSE
      SELECT @ok = 0
END
RETURN
```

This stored procedure inserts a row into the reservations table, using a customer ID supplied as an input parameter and the SPID of the current process. It then checks both the @@ERROR and @@ROWCOUNT system variables to determine what happened. Only if the @@ERROR variable is 0 (no errors occurred) and the @@ROWCOUNT variable is 1 (a single row was inserted) does it return –1 in the output parameter. A bit of thought should convince you that, no matter the sequence of operations, no two clients could possibly reserve the same customer ID using this procedure.

The stored procedure is called by the Dirty event of the frmCustomerReservation form. This event is fired, of course, whenever the user changes any field displayed on the form. Listing 7.2 shows the code behind the Dirty event.

### Listing 7.2

```
Private Sub Form_Dirty(Cancel As Integer)
    Dim intRet As Integer
    Dim cmdReserve As New ADODB.Command
    Dim prm As ADODB.Parameter
    On Error GoTo HandleErr
    With cmdReserve
        .ActiveConnection = CurrentProject.Connection
        .CommandType = adCmdStoredProc
        .CommandText = "procReserveCustomer"
        Set prm = .CreateParameter( _
          "@custid", adInteger, adParamInput)
        prm.Value = txtCustomerId.OldValue
        mfOriginalCustID = txtCustomerId.OldValue
```

```
                .Parameters.Append prm
                Set prm = .CreateParameter( _
                 "@ok", adInteger, adParamOutput)
                .Parameters.Append prm
                .Execute options:=adExecuteNoRecords
                If .Parameters("@ok") <> -1 Then
                    Err.Raise 1
                End If
        End With
    ExitHere:
        Set cmdReserve = Nothing
        Set prm = Nothing
        Exit Sub
    HandleErr:
        MsgBox "This record is being edited by another " & _
         "user. Please try again later"
        Cancel = True
        Resume ExitHere

    End Sub
```

If the stored procedure returns 0, or if any error bubbles up from the server operation, this event procedure ends up in its error handler. That error handler cancels the Dirty event, which has the effect of throwing away any change the user made, and tells the user what's going on.

---

**NOTE**    The error handling in this sample is extremely simplistic in that it assumes all errors are due to another user editing the record. In a real application you'd want to use more robust error handling.

---

When the user saves their changes, it's time to remove the reservation. This is done by another stored procedure:

```
CREATE PROCEDURE procUnreserveCustomer
    (
        @custid int
    )
AS
    SET NOCOUNT ON
    DELETE tblCustomerReservation
    WHERE SPID=@@SPID AND CustomerID=@custid
    RETURN
```

As you've probably guessed, this stored procedure is called from the form's AfterUpdate event, so it gets called whenever the user saves a record. Listing 7.3 shows this procedure.

### Listing 7.3

```
Private Sub Form_AfterUpdate()
    Dim cmdUnreserve As New ADODB.Command
    Dim prm As ADODB.Parameter
    On Error GoTo HandleErr
    ' No reservation to remove if this is an insertion
    If mfInserting Then
        GoTo ExitHere
    End If
    ' Unreserve this record
    With cmdUnreserve
        .ActiveConnection = CurrentProject.Connection
        .CommandType = adCmdStoredProc
        .CommandText = "procUnreserveCustomer"
        Set prm = .CreateParameter( _
          "@custid", adInteger, adParamInput)
        prm.Value = mfOriginalCustID
        .Parameters.Append prm
        .Execute options:=adExecuteNoRecords
    End With
ExitHere:
    Set cmdUnreserve = Nothing
    Set prm = Nothing
    Exit Sub
HandleErr:
    MsgBox "Unexpected error saving record"
    Resume ExitHere

End Sub
```

The mfInserting variable is set to True in the form's BeforeInsert event, since there's no point in trying to reserve a record that hasn't been inserted into the table yet. The logic for handling deletions is similar to that for handling updates: it doesn't allow a deletion if someone else has the record reserved.

**WARNING**    This technique is by no means foolproof. In particular, note that any application could simply write to the tblCustomer table directly and so defeat the purpose of the reservations table. You could, however, use SQL Server security to prevent this by revoking UPDATE permissions on the table, rewriting the stored procedure that removes reservations to also save the data, and granting permissions on that procedure. See Chapter 8 for more information on SQL Server security.

# Summary

This chapter has reviewed form and report issues in Access projects. For the most part, you'll find that all of your form and report knowledge from Access databases carries over intact. There are just a few new properties to learn about, and some record locking considerations that are unique to SQL Server, and then you'll be up to speed.

This chapter has covered these major topics:

- Form user interface differences
- Form property differences
- Updatability
- Using transactions with bound forms
- Optimizing forms
- Report property differences
- Simulating pessimistic locking

# Securing Your Application

- Understanding Jet security

- Securing your databases properly

- Programming security using ADOX, DAO, and SQL

- Setting up SQL Server/MDSE security

**A**ccess security can be confusing and cumbersome to use. More than one developer has supposedly "secured" his or her database only to find out later that unauthorized users could easily get in. In this chapter we cover Jet security in detail, outlining how and why it works the way it does, and how to avoid common "gotchas." We also show you how to manipulate security programmatically using DAO, ADOX, and SQL. Finally, we discuss how to secure MSDE and SQL Server databases.

> **NOTE**     Security in Access is a function of the Jet (or MSDE/SQL Server) database engine, not the Access User Interface (UI). While the Access UI provides one means of managing security, Jet and MSDE/SQL Server maintain security no matter what client application you are using.

# Jet Security Basics

Jet 4.0 offers two overlapping security models:

- Workgroup-based security
- Database password security

## Workgroup-Based Security

Since Access 1.0, the Jet engine has offered a sophisticated *workgroup-based* security model (it's also referred to as a *user-level* security model) rather than the more common database-based model most other desktop database management systems use. Under the simpler file-oriented model, security revolves around a database and is self-contained within the confines of that database. Each database has its own security system that is independent of others. In contrast, in Jet's workgroup-based security model, every database used by members of a workgroup shares the same security system.

## Database Passwords

With the introduction of Jet 3.0 (Access 95), Microsoft added a much simpler alternative to workgroup security: database passwords. This system allows you to set a single password for a database that all users must know to open the database. While much simpler to implement and use, this system is very easily compromised because all users use the same password. In addition, it doesn't let you track individual users' activity in a shared database. On the other hand, you can use both workgroup-based security and database passwords at the same time.

You set a database password by selecting Tools ➤ Security ➤ Set Database Password. Once this option is set, whenever you open the database you will be met with the Password Required dialog box, as shown in Figure 8.1.

| TIP | You must have the database open exclusively to set the database password. |
| --- | --- |

**FIGURE 8.1**
Entering a password for a database

To open a database that's been password-protected programmatically using DAO, you must use the connect parameter of the OpenDatabase method. For example, the following code opens the sample_dpwd.mdb database with a password of "password" using DAO:

```
Dim wrk As DAO.Workspace
Dim dbTest As DAO.Database

Set wrk = DBEngine.Workspaces(0)
Set dbTest = wrk. _
  OpenDatabase(adhCurrentDBPath() & "sample_dpwd.mdb", _
  False, False, ";PWD=password")
```

A couple of notes about using the OpenDatabase method are in order. First, the connect parameter of the OpenDatabase method is case sensitive. In addition, you must set the exclusive and read-only parameters (the second and third parameters) if you use the connect parameter.

To open a database that's been password-protected programmatically using ADO, you must use the "Jet OLEDB:Database Password" property of the Connection object. Here's the equivalent code using ADO:

```
Dim cnnTest As ADODB.Connection

Set cnnTest = New ADODB.Connection
cnnTest.Open "Provider=Microsoft.Jet.OLEDB.4.0;" & _
  "Data Source=" & CurrentProject.Path & _
  "\sample_dpwd.mdb;" & _
  "Jet OLEDB:Database Password=password;"
```

---

**TIP**

If you're using workgroup-based security, you may wish to prevent a user from creating or removing a database password. To do so, remove the user's Administer permission for the database object. You'll also need to remove this user from any groups that have this permission set. (See the "Assigning Permissions" section later in this chapter.)

---

---

**WARNING**

You can't replicate a database for which you have set a database password; you must first remove the password. Nor can you set a database password for a replicated database.

---

# Jet Workgroup-Based Security

Jet's workgroup-based security is based on *users and their permissions,* not passwords. Most desktop databases employ password-based security if they implement any security features at all. (Jet offers a limited password-based system, too—see the previous section.) In these systems, users enter a password that identifies them to the system as valid users. Every user who shares a given security level shares that same password, so the system is incapable of identifying individual users. In contrast, Jet's security model requires each user to have both a username and a password. The password merely verifies that users are who they claim to be. Once verified, the password leaves the picture. With Jet, users manage their own individual passwords, which they can change at will without affecting other users. Passwords can be more secure since they're not shared by lots of users.

In a password-based system, each object has passwords associated with it that define its security. For example, the Orders table in Paradox might have a read-only password and a read/write password, so a user named Joe who knew both passwords would have read/write access to the table. With Jet, however, an object doesn't have any associated passwords or permissions. Instead, a user (or a group of users) has an associated set of permissions on a per-object basis. Thus, in Access/Jet, the user Joe or the Managers group of which he is a member might have Read-Data and UpdateData permissions for the Orders table.

## Two Parts to Security

Jet security is made up of two parts:

- *User and group accounts and their passwords* are stored in the workgroup file. This file, usually kept centrally on a file server in a multi-user environment, is, by default, named SYSTEM.MDW.

- *Object permissions* are stored in each database.

For example, the security system for a small business, with three employees and four Access databases, might look like that shown in Figure 8.2. The workgroup for this company is defined by the company's workgroup file, BIZSYS.MDW, which contains the three user accounts (Joe, Mary, and Sally) and their passwords and the two group accounts (Managers and Programmers). Object permissions are stored in each of the four databases.

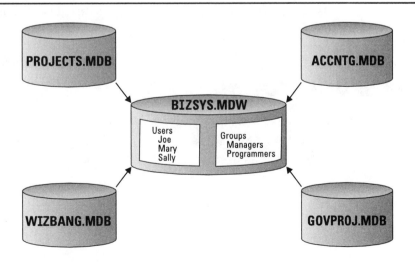

**FIGURE 8.2**
A security system for a small business

Each of the databases for this company—PROJECTS.MDB, ACCNTG.MDB, WIZBANG.MDB, and GOVPROJ.MDB—would be tied to the BIZSYS.MDW workgroup file. Jet stores the access rights to each of the database objects in the individual databases. For example, the Managers group might have Administer rights on the tblCustomers table in ACCNTNG.MDB, while the Programmers group might have only ReadData and UpdateData rights for this table. The rights for this table and for all the other objects in ACCNTNG.MDB would be stored in this database, along with pointers to the account information stored in BIZSYS.MDW.

**NOTE**   This example assumes you wish to use the same workgroup file with all databases. If you prefer, you can use a different workgroup file for each database by using the /wrkgrp startup command-line option.

## Enabling Jet Security

Security in Jet is always on; it can't be turned off. The security system, however, remains invisible until you're ready to use it. This is possible because of the presence of several default user and group accounts.

Every workgroup file starts out with two predefined group accounts (Admins and Users) and one predefined user account (Admin).

When a user starts an Access session, Jet attempts to log in as Admin with a blank password. Only if this logon attempt fails does Jet prompt the user for a username and password using the Logon dialog box. Thus, as long as you keep the Admin password blank (a zero-length string), security remains invisible.

# Jet Workgroups

Security in Jet revolves around *workgroups*. At the interface level, a workgroup is defined as a group of users who work together. At the Jet level, a workgroup is defined as all users sharing the same workgroup file.

The workgroup file is a special encrypted database, by default named SYSTEM .MDW, that Access and Jet use to store a number of pieces of information having to do with users, including:

- User account names, their personal identifiers (PIDs), and passwords

- Group account names and their PIDs

- Information regarding which users belong to which groups

In a multi-user environment, you can choose to place the workgroup file either on the file server or on each workstation. Usually, you'll want to place it on the file server, which makes maintaining user and group accounts much easier. On the other hand, if your security settings are fairly static, you could reduce network traffic by placing a copy of the workgroup file on each workstation.

## Creating a New Workgroup

Microsoft includes a utility program called the *Workgroup Administrator (WRKGADM .EXE)*, which you can use to create a new workgroup (workgroup file) or to change to the default workgroup. If you run this utility and choose to create a new workgroup, you are met with the Workgroup Owner Information dialog box, as shown in Figure 8.3.

---

**NOTE**    The Access 2000 install program copies the Workgroup Administrator utility to the localized Office folder (for example, in the U.S. version of Office, this would be located in the Program Files\Microsoft Office\Office\1033 folder), but doesn't add this program to the Start menu.

---

**FIGURE 8.3**
The information entered into the Workgroup Owner Information dialog box is used to uniquely identify a workgroup.

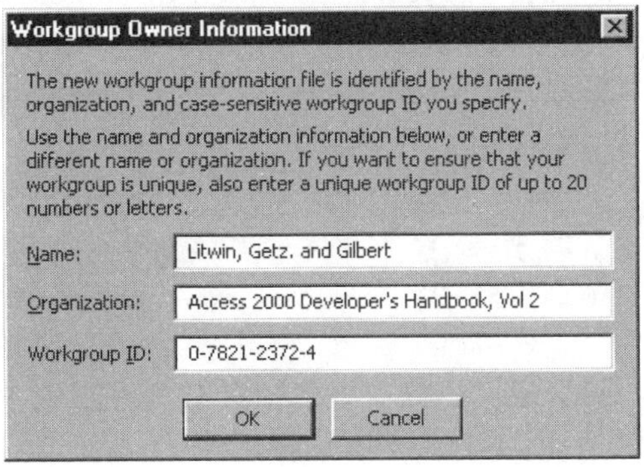

Workgroup Owner Information

The new workgroup information file is identified by the name, organization, and case-sensitive workgroup ID you specify.

Use the name and organization information below, or enter a different name or organization. If you want to ensure that your workgroup is unique, also enter a unique workgroup ID of up to 20 numbers or letters.

Name: Litwin, Getz. and Gilbert

Organization: Access 2000 Developer's Handbook, Vol 2

Workgroup ID: 0-7821-2372-4

OK    Cancel

**TIP**

Because the workgroup file is such a vital part of security, we recommend regularly backing up this file and storing a copy of it safely off-site. You should also store a copy of the Name, Organization, and Workgroup ID fields in hard-copy form in a secure off-site location.

You enter three fields into the Workgroup Owner Information dialog box: Name, Organization, and Workgroup ID. The last field, Workgroup ID, is the most critical one. You can enter from 0 to 20 numbers or *case-sensitive* letters into this field. Take extra care to keep this entry secret but backed up somewhere off site. If you leave this field blank, you'll be warned, but you won't be prevented from proceeding. Once you commit your entries to these fields by clicking the OK button, you will have one more chance to change your mind, and then you won't be able to view or change them again. Thus, it's important to write them down.

**WARNING**

Until you change it, Access normally attaches to the default SYSTEM.MDW workgroup file that is copied to your hard drive by the Access 2000 installation program. This default workgroup file is identical on every Access 2000 installation and thus is neither secure nor securable. When you need to secure a database, the first thing you should do is create a brand-new secured workgroup file. In Access 2000, the Security Wizard now creates a new secured workgroup file—see the "Properly Securing a Database with the Access 2000 Security Wizard" section later in this chapter for more details.

Based on your entries in the Workgroup Owner Information dialog box, Jet generates an encrypted binary ID called the Workgroup SID. Jet uses the Workgroup SID to uniquely identify the Admins group account in the workgroup. The significance of this built-in account is discussed in the "Special Status: Built-In Accounts" section later in this chapter.

## Joining a Workgroup

You can use the Workgroup Administrator program to change the default workgroup. This allows you to participate in multiple workgroups, although only one workgroup can be active at a time.

The Workgroup Administrator program writes the name of the workgroup file to the following Registry key:

```
HKEY_LOCAL_MACHINE\SOFTWARE\Microsoft\Office\9.0\
Access\Jet4.0\Engines\SystemDB
```

You can open a database using a workgroup that differs from the default workgroup by using the /wrkgrp startup command-line option. For example, to open an Access database named C:\DB\MYDB.MDB with a workgroup file named C:\WRK\MYWRK.MDW, you might create a shortcut that looked like the following:

```
"C:\Program Files\Microsoft Office\Office\MSACCESS.EXE"
C:\Db\Mydb.mdb /wrkgrp "C:\Wrk\Mywrk.mdw"
```

# Jet User and Group Accounts

Jet uses user and group accounts to dole out security permissions. Both types of accounts share the same name space, so you need to ensure that all names are unique for a workgroup. Thus, you can't have a user and a group with the same name.

---

**TIP**      Microsoft uses the convention whereby usernames are singular and group names are plural (for example, the Admin user and the Admins group). We've adopted (and recommend that you adopt) this account-naming scheme.

---

In Access, select Tools ➢ Security ➢ User and Group Accounts to create and manage user and group accounts (see Figure 8.4).

Only members of the Admins group can add, delete, and change the membership for user and group accounts, but any user can view accounts and change his or her account password.

## PIDs, SIDs, and Passwords

When you create a new user or group account in Jet, you must enter a non-blank, 4–20 character, case-sensitive *personal identifier* (*PID*). Jet combines the name of the account with the PID to create a *security identifier* (*SID*) for each user or group account. Once you've entered a PID, you can *never* view or change it.

---

**TIP**  We recommend that only a single database administrator create accounts and PIDs and that this individual keep a written off-site record. This will be useful if someone deletes an account that you need to re-create at a later date. This same person should keep a written off-site record of the user and organization names and the workgroup ID entered into the Workgroup Owner Information dialog box, as well as a recent backup of the workgroup file.

---

After you create a new user account, you can add an optional 1–14 character, case-sensitive password using the Change Logon Password tab of the User and Group Accounts dialog box. (Unlike PIDs, passwords are optional.) Jet uses passwords only at logon time to verify the identity of the user.

Only users can change their own passwords, but members of the Admins group can clear another user's password. You *can't* view an existing password either through the UI or programmatically.

Both passwords and PIDs are stored in the workgroup file in an encrypted format.

Jet uses the internally generated account SIDs to uniquely identify user and group accounts across workgroups. Except for some of the special built-in accounts that are discussed in the "Special Status: Built-In Accounts" section later in this chapter, Jet treats accounts in different workgroups with the same name but different PIDs (and thus different SIDs) as distinct.

## Groups Are More Than Collections of Users

A group account is more than simply a collection of users. In many situations you can use a group account in place of a user account. Table 8.1 contrasts the two types of accounts.

**TABLE 8.1:**   User and Group Account Attributes

| Attribute | User Accounts | Group Accounts |
| --- | --- | --- |
| Has associated permissions for objects | Yes | Yes |
| Has a personal ID (PID) | Yes | Yes |
| May own objects | Yes | Yes |
| May log on | Yes | No |
| Has password | Yes | No |
| May own a database | Yes | No |

Although you cannot log on as a group, you can do almost anything else with a group account, including owning objects. A group account may not own a database.

## Special Status: Built-In Accounts

As mentioned earlier in this chapter, the Jet security system includes several built-in accounts that make it possible for security to remain invisible until it's needed. These built-in accounts include the Admin *user* and the Admins and Users *groups*.

It's important that you understand how these "special status" accounts work; otherwise your database won't be secure. Table 8.2 describes the three built-in accounts.

**T A B L E   8 . 2 :**   Admin (User) and Admins and Users (Groups)

| Account Type | Account | Same SID for All Workgroups? | Comments |
|---|---|---|---|
| User | Admin | Yes | Default user account |
| Group | Admins | No | Members have special privileges |
| Group | Users | Yes | All user accounts are members of Users |

None of the special accounts can ever be deleted from a workgroup. Each built-in account is described in more detail in the next few sections.

## Admin User

All new workgroups initially contain the Admin user account with a blank password. As mentioned previously, Jet attempts to log you on as the Admin user with a blank password. Only if this logon attempt fails does Jet prompt you for a username and password.

You cannot delete the Admin user, but you can remove it from the Admins group as long as Admins has at least one other member. This is one of the steps for making a database secure that are discussed in the "Properly Securing a Database with the Access 2000 Security Wizard" section later in this chapter.

> **NOTE**    The Admin user has the same SID across all workgroups. Thus, the Admin user is not a secure account.

The Admin user is somewhat misnamed; even though it is initially a member of the Admins group, it has no special administrative powers of its own. It might have been more accurate for Microsoft to have named the Admin user account User or DefaultUser.

As long as the Admin user is not the current user when you create objects, it will not have any explicit permissions on newly created objects.

## Admins Group

The Admins group is uniquely identified across workgroups. (This differs from all other built-in accounts, which are not unique from one workgroup to another.) In fact, the Admins group draws its SID from the workgroup SID created by the Workgroup Administrator program. Access requires that there always be at least one member of the Admins group. This requirement makes it impossible to have a workgroup with no administrator.

> **NOTE**    If you really want to, you can write code to remove the last member of the Admins group. If you do so, however, you will have no way to administer the database. In other words, don't do it!

Members of the Admins group have special, irrevocable administrative rights. Their membership in Admins, however, *is* revocable by another Admins member. Any members of the Admins group can grant themselves permissions to all database objects in the databases in their workgroup. (Access, but not the Jet engine, enforces this. It is possible, using code, to revoke Administer permission from the Admins group for an object. The object's owner will retain Administer permissions for the object.) In addition, members of Admins always have the ability to manage user and group accounts in their workgroup.

By default, when you create a new object, the Admins group gets full permissions to the new object.

## Users Group

The Users group is the default group for all Access users. All built-in user accounts—as well as new user accounts created using the Access UI—will be members of the Users group. Access won't allow you to remove users from the Users group. (This is an Access limitation, but it's not one that Jet enforces. Using code, you can remove user accounts from the Users group, but these users will no longer be able to log on to Access.)

Along with the Admin user account, it is the presence of the Users group account that allows Jet to keep security invisible until needed. This is possible because the Users group account has the same SID across all workgroups. Thus, if you wish to secure a workgroup, you must remove all object permissions from the Users group and refrain from using it to assign permissions. On the other hand, the easiest way to make a secure Jet database unsecured is to assign full object permissions for each of its objects to the Users group.

By default, the Users group gets full permissions on newly created objects.

# Assigning Jet Permissions

Using the Access UI, you assign permissions to database objects with the Tools ➢ Security ➢ User and Group Permissions command (see Figure 8.5). Although you can change only one *type* of object at a time, you can select multiple objects (in contiguous or discontiguous groups) on the Permissions tab.

**FIGURE 8.5**
The Programmers group account is assigned Open/ Run, ReadDesign, and ModifyDesign permissions for the frmCustomer and frmEmployee forms.

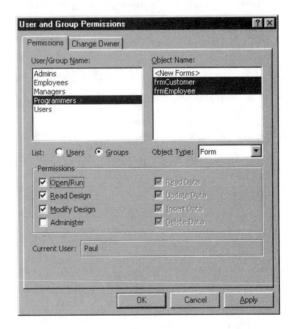

# Which Objects Have Which Permissions?

Each database container object in Jet has a set of associated permissions you can set. The set of permissions varies by object. For example, tables and queries don't have the Open/Run permission, but they have several permissions that control how data may be read or updated. On the other hand, forms, reports, and macros have no data permissions but do have the Open/Run permission. Table 8.3 lists each object and its permission set.

**NOTE**

New for Access 2000: You can no longer use the Jet security model to secure code. You secure Access global and class modules and the modules attached to forms and reports via the VBA Editor's Project Properties dialog box. See the later section "Security for Modules" for more details.

**TABLE 8.3:**   Permission Sets for Each Type of Object

| Object | Open/ Run | Read- Design | Modify- Design | Administer | Read- Data | Update- Data | Insert- Data | Delete- Data | Open Exclusive |
|---|---|---|---|---|---|---|---|---|---|
| Table |  | ✓ | ✓ | ✓ | ✓ | ✓ | ✓ | ✓ |  |
| Query |  | ✓ | ✓ | ✓ | ✓ | ✓ | ✓ | ✓ |  |
| Form | ✓ | ✓ | ✓ | ✓ |  |  |  |  |  |
| Report | ✓ | ✓ | ✓ | ✓ |  |  |  |  |  |
| Macro | ✓ | ✓ | ✓ | ✓ |  |  |  |  |  |
| Database | ✓ |  |  | ✓ |  |  |  |  | ✓ |

With the release of Access 95, Microsoft added a new permission for the database object: Administer. Although its name implies otherwise, this permission does *not* control the ability to administer permissions for the database. The database's Administer permission, however, does control access to:

- Converting the database into a replicated design master (this doesn't include creating additional replicas; a user needs only the Open/Run permission to create additional replicas)

- Creating and removing the database password (the user must also have the OpenExclusive permission)

- Saving changes to the database startup properties (this affects only Access applications)

Permissions are not completely independent of each other; some permissions imply other permissions. For example, you can't have UpdateData permissions for a table if you don't also have ReadDesign and ReadData permissions. Thus, UpdateData permission also implies these other permissions. Table 8.4 shows the interdependencies of permissions for table and query objects.

**TABLE 8.4:** Relationship between Permissions for Table and Query Objects*

| Permission | Read-Design | Modify-Design | Administer | Read-Data | Update-Data | InsertData | Delete-Data |
|---|---|---|---|---|---|---|---|
| ReadDesign | N/A | | | | | | |
| ModifyDesign | ✓ | N/A | | ✓ | ✓ | | ✓ |
| Administer | ✓ | ✓ | N/A | ✓ | ✓ | ✓ | ✓ |
| ReadData | ✓ | | | N/A | | | |
| UpdateData | ✓ | | | ✓ | N/A | | |
| InsertData | ✓ | | | ✓ | | N/A | |
| DeleteData | ✓ | | | ✓ | | | N/A |

*If you have the permission in the first column, you also have the checked permissions to the right.

# Permissions for New Objects

In addition to setting permissions on existing objects, you can set permissions on new objects. You do this by choosing <New *objectname*> in the User and Group Permissions dialog box (see Figure 8.5). This setting does *not* control the ability to create new objects; it controls only the permissions the account will receive for new objects. Although you can remove all permissions for new objects, this will *not* prevent users from creating new objects. In addition, since they will become the owner of any objects *they* create, they can always grant themselves Administer rights to these objects.

You can prevent users from creating new Access objects by removing Open-Exclusive permissions on the database. However, there doesn't seem to be any way to prevent users from creating new tables and queries in this version of Access.

# Explicit versus Implicit Permissions

Users in the Jet security model receive both implicit and explicit permissions. *Explicit permissions* are those permissions you explicitly assign to a user and are directly associated with the user account. *Implicit permissions* are those permissions a user account receives by virtue of their membership in groups.

A user's set of permissions for an object will be based on the union of the user's explicit permissions and implicit permissions. A user's security level is always the *least restrictive* of the user's explicit permissions and the permissions of any and all groups to which the user belongs.

For example, say that user Anna has no permissions for the tblCustomer table. Anna also belongs to two groups: Employees and Programmers. The Employees group has Administer permissions (which implies all the other permissions for an object) for tblCustomer, and the Programmers group has only ReadDesign permissions for tblCustomer. Anna will have Administer permissions for tblCustomer because this is the least restrictive (or highest) permission for tblCustomer.

---

**WARNING**     Don't make the mistake of removing a user's explicit permissions without bothering to check his or her implicit permissions.

---

Members of the Admins group (and those users having the Administer permission for a particular object) can directly view and set explicit permissions, but they can't directly view or set implicit permissions. Instead, you view implicit permissions by noting the group membership of a user and then looking at the permissions for each of these groups. To change implicit permissions, you must either modify the permissions for each of the groups to which a user belongs, or add or remove the user from groups.

**TIP**    Jet 3.0 added a new property, AllPermissions, for the quick querying of a user's complete permission set using DAO. There's no equivalent to AllPermissions, however, when using ADOX or SQL to manage permissions.

# Security for Modules

**NEW!**    As mentioned previously, modules no longer fall under the Jet security model. The only way to secure your code is using the VBA project password. Select Tools ➤ *name_of_project* Properties from the VBA Editor. On the Protection tab of the Project Properties dialog box, select Lock Project for Viewing and enter (and confirm) a password to password protect the VBA code in the project, as shown in Figure 8.6.

**FIGURE 8.6**

Password protecting the
VBA project for the
CH08A.MDB database

Once you password protect the VBA project for a database, you'll be prompted for a password any time you attempt to view or modify code in the database. This applies to global modules, as well as class, form, and report modules. You'll only be prompted once for the VBA project password per database session.

**NOTE**    Another way to secure your code is to not include it in your shipping database! You can do this by creating an MDE file (Tools ➤ Database Utilities ➤ Make MDE File). MDE files are discussed in more detail in Chapter 18 of the *Access Developer's Handbook, Volume 1*.

## Security for Data Access Pages

A data access page is made up of two components:

- The shortcut to the page that's stored in the Access database

- The actual HTML file stored outside of the database

The best way to secure the page is to publish it to a secured Windows NT Web server. Then you can use the Web server's security system to secure the page. Things get a bit more complicated if you wish to have data access pages work with data in a secured Access database. For more information on the issues involved, see the *Creating Secure Data Access Pages* white paper which you'll find on the CD that accompanies this book.

# Who Can Change Permissions?

The following users can change object permissions:

- Members of the Admins group (for the workgroup in which the database was created) can always change permissions on any users. These rights can never be taken away using the Access UI (but they can be taken away using code).

- An object's owner—either the user who created the object or the user or group to which ownership of the object was transferred—can always modify the permissions for the object. This includes the ability of owners to give themselves Administer permissions for the object, even if someone else previously revoked these privileges. These rights can never be taken away.

- Any user with explicit or implicit Administer permissions to the object can administer permissions for that object. Another user with Administer rights can take away these rights.

- The database owner—the user who created the database—can always open a database and create new objects in it, even if the owner's rights to all the database's objects have been revoked. (The Access UI will allow members of the Admins group to *think* they have revoked the Open/Run permission from the database owner, but the owner will retain that right.) The only way to remove these rights is to import all of a database's objects into a new database and delete the original database. This will effectively change the ownership of the database.

**WARNING**    Access won't allow you—even if you are a member of the Admins group—to view or set permissions of the database itself if the database was created using a different workgroup (MDW) file than the current workgroup file. The only known workaround is to create a new database using the new workgroup file and import all of the objects from the old database into it.

# What Happens to Permissions for Deleted Accounts?

When you delete a user or group account from a workgroup for an account that still has associated permissions, those permissions remain in the database. This can be a security concern; if someone can re-create the account and its PID, that person has a *backdoor pass* into your secured database. Thus, it's important that you remove all permissions (and transfer any objects the to-be-deleted account owns to a new owner) before deleting an account.

If someone re-creates an account with the same name but a *different* PID, Jet treats that account as a completely different account. It will not inherit any of the old account's permissions, because its SID is different from the SID of the old account.

**TIP**    The CurrentUser function returns only the name of a user and therefore cannot be counted on to distinguish between users with the same name but different SIDs (either in the same workgroup at different points in time or across workgroups). This might be an issue when you are using the value of CurrentUser to branch in your code or log activity to a file.

When you use the Change Owner tab of the User and Group Permissions dialog box to list the owner of an object whose account has been deleted, Access lists the owner as "<Unknown>".

# Jet Object Ownership

In addition to the permissions that are granted to accounts, you need to be aware of ownership, because database owners and object owners have special privileges.

## Who Owns a Database?

The user who creates a database is the database's owner. This user maintains special irrevocable rights to the database. As mentioned previously, this user will always be able to open the database. Only user accounts, not group accounts, can own databases.

Database ownership cannot be changed, but you can always create a new database using a different user account and import all the database's objects into another database. (This is how the Microsoft Security Wizard works.) If you then delete the original database and rename the new database to the name of the original, you have effectively transferred its ownership. The account used to transfer ownership must have ReadDesign and ReadData (where applicable) permissions to each of the database's objects.

You can use the Change Owner tab of the Tools ➤ Security ➤ User and Group Permissions command to view, but not change, the database owner.

## Who Owns a Database's Objects?

Each database container object also has an owner. Initially, this is the user who created the object and may or may not be the same user account as the database owner. You can use the Change Owner tab of the Tools ➤ Security ➤ User and Group Permissions command to view and change object owners (see Figure 8.7).

The new owner for an object may be a group account. This is especially useful when you are managing OwnerAccess queries, which are discussed in the next section.

**FIGURE 8.7**
Anna is about to change
the ownership for five
tables from the Admin user
to the Managers group.

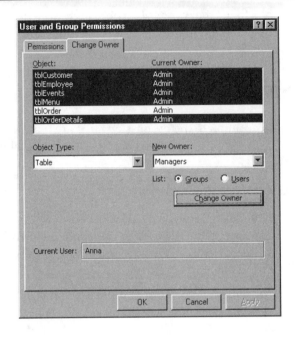

## OwnerAccess Queries

Queries created in Access QBE have a property, RunPermissions, that governs whether Jet uses the query user's (the person running the query) permissions or the query owner's permissions when checking the security permissions for each of the source tables in a query. In Access SQL, setting this property to "Owner's" translates to the "WITH OWNERACCESS OPTION" clause.

This property allows you to present data to users who lack access rights to the underlying tables. Using this feature, you can effectively apply column-level and row-level security to a table.

For example, using an OwnerAccess query, you could let members of the Programmers group view and update all the columns in the tblEmployee table except for the Salary field. To do this, you would perform the following steps:

1. Remove all permissions to tblEmployee for the Programmers group.

2. Using an account that has ReadData and UpdateData permissions to tblEmployee, create a query, qryEmployee, that includes all the columns from tblEmployee except Salary.

3. Set the RunPermissions property of qryEmployee to "Owner's" (or include the "WITH OWNERACCESS OPTION" clause in the SQL statement for the query).

One problem with OwnerAccess queries is that Jet allows only the query's owner to save changes to the query. Even other users with Administer rights to the query are prevented from saving changes to the query. This can present a problem if you are sharing the management of these queries among multiple users. In this case, you may wish to transfer ownership of the query to a group account, but you'll have to temporarily change the RunPermissions property of the query back to "User's" before you can change the query's owner.

# Jet Database Encryption

As good as Jet security is, a very knowledgeable hacker equipped with a low-level disk editor might be able to directly open the MDB file and break into your database. The only way to guard against such a hacker is to encrypt the database. Hacking your way into a database is far from a trivial task, but there are those who love such a challenge.

Encrypting a database does not secure it, it merely protects the database when you are not using Access or Jet to access the database.

Only the database owner or members of the Admins group can encrypt or decrypt a database. Jet uses an RSA- (Rivest, Shamir, and Adleman—the names of the inventors of the algorithm) based encryption algorithm with a key based on your workgroup ID to encrypt the database. Using Access, you can encrypt or decrypt a database using the Tools ➤ Security ➤ Encrypt/Decrypt Database command.

Encryption has two negative side effects. First, it reduces database performance (according to Microsoft estimates) by approximately 10 to 15 percent. Second, it makes the database uncompressible by programs such as PKZip, LHA, Stacker, and DriveSpace. You won't be prevented from compressing the database, but the compression step won't significantly reduce the size.

> **NOTE** The Access 2000 Security Wizard does not encrypt the database.

# Programming Jet Security

In contrast to prior versions of Access, Access 2000 provides *three* different mechanisms for programmatically manipulating Jet security:

- Data Access Objects (DAO)
- ActiveX Data Objects Extensions for DDL and Security (ADOX)
- Jet SQL

In the sections that follow, you'll learn how to program Jet security. We'll cover how to manipulate Jet user and group accounts and set object permissions using DAO, ADOX, and SQL.

## The ADH2K.MDW Sample Workgroup File

We've included a sample workgroup file on the CD, ADH2K.MDW, that you can use with the various programming examples in this chapter. You don't really need to use this workgroup because the sample database hasn't been secured, but it may prove helpful when you try out the examples.

In addition to the Admin user, the sample workgroup contains the following user accounts:

- Geoff
- Paul
- Peter
- Suzanne

All of the user accounts have blank passwords.

The sample workgroup also contains the following group accounts (in addition to the built-in Admins and Users groups):

- Employees

- Managers

- Programmers

# DAO Security Overview

Programming security with DAO revolves around two parts of the DAO object model:

- You use the Users and Groups collections to manipulate user and group accounts.

- You use the Containers and Documents collections to set permissions on Jet and Access objects.

The DAO object model is shown in Figure 8.8. As you can see, the Users and Groups collections are descendents of the Workspace object, which is consistent with the fact that they are physically stored in the workgroup (MDW) file. In contrast, the Containers and Documents collections are descendents of the Database object, which is also consistent with the location of the Jet and Access objects—in the MDB file.

**FIGURE 8.8**
The DAO object model

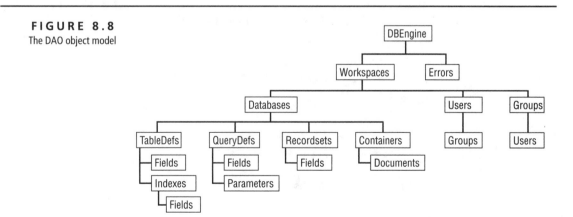

## Managing Accounts with DAO

The Users collection is a descendant of the Workspace object that contains all users in the workgroup. The code in Listing 8.1, from basSecurityExamplesDAO, enumerates the user accounts in the workgroup to the Debug window.

⟳ **Listing 8.1**

```
Sub ListUsersDAO()
    ' List all users in workgroup
    ' to debug window using DAO.
    Dim wrk As DAO.Workspace
    Dim usr As DAO.User

    Set wrk = DBEngine.Workspaces(0)

    Debug.Print "The Users collection has " & _
     wrk.Users.Count & " members:"
    For Each usr In wrk.Users
        Debug.Print usr.Name
    Next usr

    Set usr = Nothing
    wrk.Close
    Set wrk = Nothing
End Sub
```

Like the Users collection, the Groups collection is a direct descendant of the Workspace object. You might use the code shown in Listing 8.2 (also from basSecurityExamplesDAO) to enumerate the names of all the groups in the Groups collection of the default workspace.

⟳ **Listing 8.2**

```
Sub ListGroupsDAO()
    ' List all groups in workgroup
    ' to debug window using DAO.

    Dim wrk As DAO.Workspace
```

```
        Dim grp As DAO.Group

        Set wrk = DBEngine.Workspaces(0)

        Debug.Print "The Groups collection has " & _
         wrk.Groups.Count & " members:"
        For Each grp In wrk.Groups
            Debug.Print grp.Name
        Next grp

        Set grp = Nothing
        wrk.Close
        Set wrk = Nothing
    End Sub
```

In addition to the Workspace object's Users collection, each Group object contains its own Users collection. This collection represents all users that are members of the group. Likewise, each User object contains its own Groups collection that represents all groups to which the user belongs. These collections make it very easy to write code that determines the users who belong to a particular group or the groups to which a particular user belongs.

For example, if you wished to list user accounts that were members of the Managers group, you could use code similar to that shown in Listing 8.3.

## Listing 8.3

```
Sub ListManagersDAO()
    ' List all members of Managers group
    ' to debug window using DAO.
    Dim wrk As DAO.Workspace
    Dim grpManagers As DAO.Group
    Dim usr As DAO.User

    Set wrk = DBEngine.Workspaces(0)
    Set grpManagers = wrk.Groups!Managers

    For Each usr In grpManagers.Users
        Debug.Print usr.Name
    Next usr
```

```
              Set usr = Nothing
              Set grpManagers = Nothing
              wrk.Close
              Set wrk = Nothing
          End Sub
```

## Creating Accounts using DAO

To create a new user account, you use the CreateUser method of a Workspace object. For example, the CreateNewUserDAO subroutine, found in basSecurity-ExamplesDAO, and shown in Listing 8.4, creates a new user named Anna with a PID of "1234whatR" and a password of "foo".

### Listing 8.4

```
Sub CreateNewUserDAO()
    ' Create new user account using DAO.

    ' Creates following new account:
    '    User     = Anna,
    '    PID      = 123whatR
    '    Password = foo

    Dim wrk As DAO.Workspace
    Dim usrNew As DAO.User
    Dim grpUsers As DAO.Group

    Set wrk = DBEngine.Workspaces(0)
    Set usrNew = wrk.CreateUser("Anna", "123whatR", "foo")
    wrk.Users.Append usrNew

    Set grpUsers = usrNew.CreateGroup("Users")
    usrNew.Groups.Append grpUsers

    Set usrNew = Nothing
    Set grpUsers = Nothing
    wrk.Close
    Set wrk = Nothing
End Sub
```

Any time you create a new account programmatically, you should add the account to the built-in Users group. If you don't, the user will not be able to log in to the workgroup.

To create a new group account, you use the CreateGroup method of a workspace object. For example, the CreateNewGroupDAO subroutine in Listing 8.5 creates a new group named Drones with a PID of "crazy8s".

### Listing 8.5

```
Sub CreateNewGroupDAO()
    ' Create new group account using DAO.

    ' Creates following new account:
    '   Group     = Drones,
    '   PID       = crazy8s

    Dim wrk As DAO.Workspace
    Dim grpNew As DAO.Group

    Set wrk = DBEngine.Workspaces(0)
    Set grpNew = wrk.CreateGroup("Drones", "crazy8s")
    wrk.Groups.Append grpNew

    Set grpNew = Nothing
    wrk.Close
    Set wrk = Nothing
End Sub
```

Both the Groups and Users collections of the Workspace object have a Delete method for deleting accounts. The example shown in Listing 8.6 illustrates deleting a user account.

### Listing 8.6

```
Sub DeleteUserDAO()
    ' Delete Anna user account using DAO.

    Dim wrk As DAO.Workspace
```

```
        Set wrk = DBEngine.Workspaces(0)
        wrk.Users.Delete "Anna"

        wrk.Close
        Set wrk = Nothing]
    End Sub
```

The code to delete a group account is virtually identical, as you can see in Listing 8.7.

## Listing 8.7

```
Sub DeleteGroupDAO()
    ' Delete Drones group account using DAO.
    Dim wrk As DAO.Workspace

    Set wrk = DBEngine.Workspaces(0)
    wrk.Groups.Delete "Drones"

    wrk.Close
    Set wrk = Nothing
End Sub
```

## Adding and Removing Users from Groups in DAO

Because of the symmetry in the DAO Users and Groups collections, you can use either the CreateGroup method of the User object or the CreateUser method of the Group object to add a user to a group. The code shown in Listing 8.8, and found in basSecurityExamplesDAO, uses the User.CreateGroup method.

## Listing 8.8

```
Sub AddUserToGroupDAO()
    ' Adds Anna to Drones group using DAO.
    Dim wrk As DAO.Workspace
    Dim usr As DAO.User
    Dim grp As DAO.Group
```

```
            Set wrk = DBEngine.Workspaces(0)

            Set usr = wrk.Users("Anna")
            Set grp = usr.CreateGroup("Drones")
            usr.Groups.Append grp

            Set usr = Nothing
            Set grp = Nothing
            wrk.Close
            Set wrk = Nothing
        End Sub
```

You can use the Delete method of the Users collection of a Group object to remove a user from a group. This is illustrated by RemoveUserFromGroupDAO, which is shown in Listing 8.9.

### Listing 8.9

```
    Sub RemoveUserFromGroupDAO()
        ' Removes Anna from Drones group using DAO.

        Dim wrk As DAO.Workspace

        Set wrk = DBEngine.Workspaces(0)

        wrk.Groups("Drones").Users.Delete "Anna"

        wrk.Close
        Set wrk = Nothing
    End Sub
```

## Determining if a User is a Member of a Group using DAO

You can easily determine if a user is a member of a particular group by simply checking if the Group object's Users collection contains the user. (Again, because of the symmetry in the Users and Groups collections, you could also check if the User object's Groups collection contains the group.) The IsUserMemberDAO function shown in Listing 8.10 checks if a user is a member of a particular group.

**Listing 8.10**

```
Function IsUserMemberDAO(strGroup As String, _
Optional varUser As Variant) As Boolean
    ' Determines if user is a member of a group
    ' using DAO.
    Dim wrk As DAO.Workspace

    ' Turn off error reporting
    On Error Resume Next

    Set wrk = DBEngine.Workspaces(0)

    If IsMissing(varUser) Then
        varUser = CurrentUser()
    End If

    IsUserMemberDAO = _
     (wrk.Groups(strGroup).Users(varUser).Name = varUser)

    wrk.Close
    Set wrk = Nothing
End Function
```

The IsUserMemberDAO function uses the currently logged-in user, determined with the CurrentUser() function, if no user account name is specified.

## Managing User Passwords in DAO

You can use the NewPassword method of the User object to change a user's password. You must supply both old and new passwords; however, if you're a member of Admins and are changing another user's password, the old password argument is ignored. This allows Admins members to change the passwords of other users. The subroutine ChangeUserPasswordDAO from basSecurityExamplesDAO, shown in Listing 8.11, illustrates how to change a user's password using DAO.

### Listing 8.11

```
Sub ChangeUserPasswordDAO(strUser As String, _
  strOld As String, strNew As String)
    ' Changes a user's password.
    Dim wrk As DAO.Workspace
    Dim usr As DAO.User

    Set wrk = DBEngine.Workspaces(0)
    Set usr = wrk.Users(strUser)

    ' For Admins members, the old password
    ' value is ignored.
    usr.NewPassword strOld, strNew

    Set usr = Nothing
    wrk.Close
    Set wrk = Nothing
End Sub
```

A user account with blank passwords is the Achilles heel of a supposedly secure workgroup. Using the Access UI, there's no way for a database administrator to quickly determine which users have left their passwords blank. Using DAO, however, you can accomplish this easily. You can use the adhListUsersWithBlankPwd function, which can be found in the basGenericDAOSecurityUtilities module, to determine which users have blank passwords. This function is shown in Listing 8.12.

### Listing 8.12

```
Function adhListUsersWithBlankPwd() As Boolean

    ' Prints all users with blank passwords to a text file.

    On Error GoTo adhListUsersWithBlankPwdErr

    Dim wrkDefault As DAO.Workspace
    Dim wrkNew As DAO.Workspace
    Dim usr As DAO.User
```

```
Dim strUser As String
Dim fNonBlankPwd As Boolean
Dim fAnyBlankPwds As Boolean
Dim strAccessDir As String
Dim strMsg As String

Const adhcBlankPwdFile = "BlankPwd.Txt"

Const adhcProcName = "adhListUsersWithBlankPwd"

' Output will be placed in same
' folder as MSACCESS.EXE
strAccessDir = SysCmd(acSysCmdAccessDir) + _
 adhcBlankPwddFile

' Intialize flag to track if any blank Pwds occur
fAnyBlankPwds = False

' Open output file and create header
Open strAccessDir For Append As #1
Print #1, String$(70, "=")
Print #1, "Users with Blank Passwords      " & _
 "Produced: " & Format(Now, "mm/dd/yy hh:nn") & _
 "  By: " & CurrentUser()
Print #1, String$(70, "=")

Set wrkDefault = DBEngine.Workspaces(0)

' Iterate through all users in workgroup
For Each usr In wrkDefault.Users
    strUser = usr.Name

    ' Skip if special engine-level users
    If strUser <> "Creator" And strUser <> "Engine" Then
        ' Initialize flag that tracks blank Pwd
        fNonBlankPwd = False

        ' Attempt to log on to new workspace
        ' with blank Pwd
        Set wrkNew = DBEngine. _
         CreateWorkspace("NewWorkspace", strUser, "")
```

```
                    ' If an error occurred on last statement, then
                    ' error handler will set flag to True.
                    ' Otherwise, able to log on, so Pwd must've
                    ' been blank.
                    If Not fNonBlankPwd Then
                        Print #1, strUser
                        fAnyBlankPwds = True
                    End If
                End If

        Next usr

        If fAnyBlankPwds Then
            strMsg = "Accounts with blank passwords " & _
                "were found!" & vbCrLf & vbCrLf & _
                "The names have been logged to " & _
                strAccessDir
        Else
            strMsg = "No accounts with blank passwords " & _
                "were found. " & vbCrLf & vbCrLf & _
                "This fact has been logged to " & _
                strAccessDir
            Print #1, "<NONE>"
        End If
        MsgBox strMsg, vbInformation + vbOKOnly, _
         "Procedure " & adhcProcName

        'Return True if any passwords are blank
        adhListUsersWithBlankPwd = fAnyBlankPwds

adhListUsersWithBlankPwdDone:
    If Not wrkNew Is Nothing Then wrkNew.Close
    Print #1, String$(70, "=")
    Print #1, ""
    Print #1, ""
    Close #1
    On Error GoTo 0
    Exit Function

adhListUsersWithBlankPwdErr:
    Select Case Err
    Case adhcErrBadAccntOrPwd
```

```
                    'Could not log on user account with blank Pwd
                    fNonBlankPwd = True
                    Resume Next
              Case Else
                    strMsg = "Error " & Err.Number & ": " & Err.Description
              End Select
                    MsgBox strMsg, vbCritical + vbOKOnly, _
                    "Procedure " & adhcProcName
              Resume adhListUsersWithBlankPwdDone

       End Function
```

The adhUsersWithBlankPwd function works by iterating through the Users collection in the default workspace and attempting to log on to each account using a blank password. If it is able to log on to an account, it prints the username to a file.

## Programming Permissions using DAO

You check and set permissions of Jet and Access objects in DAO by manipulating the Permissions property of Document objects. You can also manipulate the Permissions property of a Container object to affect new objects. Microsoft defines a number of Jet and Access security constants that you can use when checking and setting permissions. These constants are summarized in Table 8.5.

**TABLE 8.5:**  DAO Security Constants for Access and Jet objects

| Constant | Meaning |
| --- | --- |
| dbSecNoAccess | No access to the object |
| dbSecFullAccess | Full access to the object |
| dbSecDelete | Can delete the object |
| dbSecReadSec | Can read the object's security-related information |
| dbSecWriteSec | Can alter access permissions |
| dbSecWriteOwner | Can change the Owner property setting |
| dbSecCreate | Can create new documents; valid only with a Container object |
| dbSecReadDef | Can read the table definition, including column and index information |

**TABLE 8.5:** DAO Security Constants for Access and Jet objects *(continued)*

| Constant | Meaning |
| --- | --- |
| dbSecWriteDef | Can modify or delete the table definition, including column and index information |
| dbSecRetrieveData | Can retrieve data from the Document object |
| dbSecInsertData | Can add records |
| dbSecReplaceData | Can modify records |
| dbSecDeleteData | Can delete records |
| dbSecDBAdmin | Gives user permission to make a database replicable, change the database password, and set startup properties |
| dbSecDBCreate | Can create new databases; valid only on the Databases container object in the workgroup file (SYSTEM.MDW) |
| dbSecDBExclusive | Can open the database exclusively |
| dbSecDBOpen | Can open the database |
| acSecMacExecute | Can run the macro |
| acSecMacReadDef | Can read the definition of the macro |
| acSecMacWriteDef | Can modify the definition of the macro |
| acSecFrmRptExecute | Can open the form or report |
| acSecFrmRptReadDef | Can read the definition of the form or report and its module |
| acSecFrmRptWriteDef | Can modify the definition of the form or report and its module |

## Reading Permissions with DAO

You can read the permissions of an object in DAO simply by checking the value of the Permissions or AllPermissions property of the object. The Permissions property returns explicit permissions only, whereas AllPermissions returns the union of explicit and implicit permissions. They both return a long integer value corresponding to the user's permissions for the object. For example, you could query the permissions of the tblOrder table and store the value into the variable lngPermissions with the following assignment statement (assuming you had previously set the db object variable to point to the database):

```
lngPermissions = _
  db.Containers!Tables.Documents!tblOrder.Permissions
```

Often, you'll want to check whether a user has some minimum permissions to an object. You can do this using bitwise arithmetic (also referred to as *bit twiddling*). This works because Jet stores each individual permission as a different bit of the 4-byte long integer value. You check a permission value for a specific set of bits—some permissions are actually the result of setting several bits—by using the And operator to mask off the bits in which you are interested and comparing the result of the operation to these same bits.

For example, say you wished to determine if the current user had the ability to insert rows into the tblEmployee table. You could use the following code to check to see if the user had this right:

```
doc = db.Containers!Tables.Documents!tblEmployee
fOK = ((doc.Permissions And dbSecInsertData) = _
  dbSecInsertData)
```

In this example, fOK will be set to True if the document object has that permission—as defined by dbSecInsertData—set to True, and False if the document object does not.

## Checking Permissions with Constants That Have One Bit Set

There's another way to check a permission value against a constant that works *only* if one bit is set on in the constant:

```
fOk = (doc.Permissions And dbSecInsertData) <> 0
```

This method, however, will fail with constants that have more than one bit set. Thus, because many of the security constants have multiple bits set, you shouldn't use this method.

You aren't limited to checking a single permission—by adding several permission constants together with the bitwise Or operator, you can check if a user or group has some minimal set of rights. For example, you could use the following code to check if a user has read, insert, update, and delete record rights for tblEmployee:

```
doc = db.Containers!Tables.Documents!tblEmployee
fOK = ((doc.Permissions And (dbSecRetrieveData Or _
  dbSecInsertData Or dbSecReplaceData _
```

```
   Or dbSecDeleteData)) = _
(dbSecRetrieveData Or dbSecInsertData Or dbSecReplaceData _
   Or dbSecDeleteData))
```

The CanCurrentUserReadCustomersDAO function from basSecurityExamples-DAO demonstrates how to determine whether the current user has read permission for the tblCustomer table. This function is shown in Listing 8.13.

### Listing 8.13

```
Function CanCurrentUserReadCustomerDAO() As Boolean
      ' Illustrates correct DAO syntax to check
      ' a permission of a table for the current user.

      ' Checks explicit permissions for:
      '    User = --Current User--
      '    Object = tblCustomer
      '    Permission = dbSecRetrieveData

      Dim db As DAO.Database
      Dim doc As DAO.Document

      Set db = CurrentDb()
      Set doc = db.Containers!Tables.Documents!tblCustomer

      CanCurrentUserReadCustomerDAO = _
       ((doc.Permissions And dbSecRetrieveData) _
       = dbSecRetrieveData)

      Set doc = Nothing
      Set db = Nothing
   End Function
```

If the current user has ReadData permission to tblCustomer, CanCurrentUser-ReadCustomersDAO returns True; otherwise it returns False. The trick in this example is to use the bitwise And operator to mask off the complete permissions with only the permission you are interested in—in this case, dbSecRetrieveData (ReadData permission).

The CanCurrentUserReadCustomersDAO function checks the permissions of the currently logged-in user. If you set the UserName property of the Document object prior to checking the value of the Permissions property, you can check the permissions of any user or group in the workgroup. The use of the UserName property is shown in Listing 8.14.

## Listing 8.14

```
Function CanUserReadCustomersDAO(strUser As String) _
As Boolean
    ' Illustrates correct DAO syntax to check
    ' a permission of a table for a particular user.

    ' Checks explicit permissions for:
    '    Object = tblCustomer
    '    Permission = dbSecRetrieveData

    Dim db As DAO.Database
    Dim doc As DAO.Document

    Set db = CurrentDb()
    Set doc = db.Containers!Tables.Documents!tblCustomer

    doc.UserName = strUser

    CanUserReadCustomersDAO = _
     ((doc.Permissions And dbSecRetrieveData) _
     = dbSecRetrieveData)

    Set doc = Nothing
    Set db = Nothing
End Function
```

**NOTE**  Contrary to what its name might suggest, the UserName property of Document and Container objects can be set to the name of either a user or a group account.

CanUserReadCustomersDAO and CanCurrentUserReadCustomersDAO check only for explicit permissions. You can also use a Document object's AllPermissions property to check the union of both explicit (direct user-assigned) and implicit (permissions obtained by membership in a group) permissions using the following syntax:

```
fOK = _
((doc.AllPermissions And dbSecConstant) = dbSecConstant)
```

The AllPermissions property is unique to DAO. ADOX doesn't have an equivalent property. The CanUserReadCustomersDAO2 function shown in Listing 8.15 illustrates the use of AllPermssions.

### Listing 8.15

```
Function CanUserReadCustomersDAO2(strUser As String) _
As Boolean
    ' Illustrates correct DAO syntax to check
    ' both direct and indirect permissions for
    ' a table using the AllPermissions property.

    ' Checks all permissions for:
    '    Object = tblCustomer
    '    Permission = dbSecRetrieveData

    Dim doc As DAO.Document

    Set db = CurrentDb()
    Set doc = db.Containers!Tables.Documents!tblCustomer

    doc.UserName = strUser

    CanUserReadCustomersDAO2 = _
     ((doc.AllPermissions And dbSecRetrieveData) _
     = dbSecRetrieveData)

    Set doc = Nothing
    Set db = Nothing
End Function
```

**NOTE**    The AllPermissions property is read only. You can't use it to set the permissions of a Document object.

## Writing Permissions Using DAO

Writing permissions using DAO is similar to reading them. You have two choices when writing the permissions of an object:

- You can replace the existing permissions with a brand-new set of permissions.

- You can add to or subtract from the existing set of permissions.

To *replace* a set of permissions, you simply set the permissions to the new value. For example, you could change the permission set for tblOrder to give the user only ModifyDesign permission rights using the following code:

```
Set doc = db.Containers!Tables.Documents!tblOrder
doc.Permissions = dbSecWriteDef
```

You can set multiple rights in one step by using the bitwise Or operator. For example, the following code assigns both ReadDesign and ReadData rights to the user:

```
Set doc = db.Containers!Tables.Documents!tblOrder
doc.Permissions = dbSecReadDef Or dbSecRetrieveData
```

To *add* a particular permission to the existing permission set, you use the bitwise Or operator with the value of the existing permissions. For example, you could use the following code to add ModifyDesign permission to the existing set of permissions for tblOrder:

```
Set doc = db.Containers!Tables.Documents!tblOrder
doc.Permissions = doc.Permissions Or dbSecWriteDef
```

Using this method of assigning permissions is often preferable because it guards against inadvertently removing other permissions the user may have. For example, if the user also had ReadData permission to tblOrder, that permission would be preserved using this technique.

To *subtract* a particular permission from a user while preserving all other permissions, you use the bitwise And Not operators. For example, to take away the same permission from a user, replace the second line in the preceding example with the following:

```
doc.Permissions = doc.Permissions And Not dbSecWriteDef
```

The SetUserReadCustomersDAO subroutine (from basSecurityExamplesDAO), shown in Listing 8.16, illustrates how to add a permission to or subtract a permission from the existing permission set of the tblCustomer table.

### Listing 8.16

```
Sub SetUserReadCustomersDAO(strUser As String, _
fRead As Boolean)
    ' Illustrates correct DAO
    ' syntax to set a specfic permission.

    ' Sets permission for:
    '    Object = tblCustomer
    '    Permission = dbSecRetrieveData

    Dim db As DAO.Database
    Dim doc As DAO.Document

    Set db = CurrentDb()
    Set doc = db.Containers!Tables.Documents!tblCustomer

    doc.UserName = strUser

    If fRead Then
        doc.Permissions = _
          doc.Permissions Or dbSecRetrieveData
    Else
        doc.Permissions = _
          doc.Permissions And Not dbSecRetrieveData
    End If

    Set doc = Nothing
    Set db = Nothing
End Sub
```

For example, the following call to SetUserReadCustomersDAO adds the Read-Data permission for tblCustomer to Anna's permission set for the table:

```
Call SetUserReadCustomersDAO "Anna", True
```

On the other hand, this call to SetUserReadCustomersDAO subtracts the Read-Data permission for tblCustomer from Geoff's permission set for the table:

```
Call SetUserReadCustomersDAO "Geoff", False
```

You aren't limited to viewing and setting permissions of tables. You can also view and set the permissions of Access objects using DAO. For example, the Set-UserExecFormDAO subroutine, shown in Listing 8.17, adds and subtracts the Execute right for the frmCustomer form.

### Listing 8.17

```
Sub SetUserExecFormDAO(strUser As String, fExec As Boolean)
    ' Illustrates correct DAO syntax to set
    ' execute (Open) permission for a form.

    ' Sets permission for:
    '    Object = frmCustomer
    '    Permission = acSecFrmRptExecute

    Dim db As DAO.Database
    Dim doc As DAO.Document

    Set db = CurrentDb()
    Set doc = db.Containers!Forms.Documents!frmCustomer

    doc.UserName = strUser

    If fExec Then
        doc.Permissions = _
          doc.Permissions Or acSecFrmRptExecute
    Else
        doc.Permissions = _
          doc.Permissions And Not acSecFrmRptExecute
    End If

    Set doc = Nothing
    Set db = Nothing
End Sub
```

## Setting Permissions for New Objects using DAO

To set the permissions for any new objects, you set the Permissions property of the parent Container object. In addition, you must set the Inherit property of the Container object to True prior to setting the value of the Permissions property. The SetUserReadNewTablesDAO subroutine in Listing 8.18 illustrates how to set permissions for new tables.

**Listing 8.18**

```
Sub SetUserReadNewTablesDAO(strUser As String, _
fRead As Boolean)
    ' Illustrates correct DAO
    ' syntax to set the read permission
    ' for the tables container.

    ' Sets permission for:
    '   Container = Tables
    '   Permission = dbSecRetrieveData

    Dim db As DAO.Database
    Dim cnt As DAO.Container

    Set db = CurrentDb()
    Set cnt = db.Containers!Tables
    cnt.Inherit = True

    cnt.UserName = strUser

    If fRead Then
        cnt.Permissions = _
         cnt.Permissions Or dbSecRetrieveData
    Else
        cnt.Permissions = _
         cnt.Permissions And Not dbSecRetrieveData
    End If

    Set cnt = Nothing
    Set db = Nothing
End Sub
```

## Manipulating Database Permissions using DAO

In order to view or set permissions for the database itself, you set permissions of
the MSysDB document of the Database container. By subtracting the dbSecDB-
Open permission of the MSysDB document, you can prevent a user from opening
a database. This is demonstrated by the SetUserDatabaseOpenDAO subroutine of
basSecurityExamplesDAO, which is shown in Listing 8.19.

## Listing 8.19

```
Sub SetUserDatabaseOpenDAO(strUser As String, _
fOpen As Boolean)
    ' Illustrates correct DAO syntax to set
    ' the Open permission for a database.

    ' Sets permission for:
    '    Object = Database
    '    Permission = dbSecDBOpen

    Dim db As DAO.Database
    Dim doc As DAO.Document

    Set db = CurrentDb()
    Set doc = db.Containers!Databases.Documents!MSysDB

    doc.UserName = strUser

    If fOpen Then
        doc.Permissions = _
         doc.Permissions Or dbSecDBOpen
    Else
        doc.Permissions = _
         doc.Permissions And Not dbSecDBOpen
    End If

    Set doc = Nothing
    Set db = Nothing
End Sub
```

Any user that attempts to open a database without the dbSecDBOpen right to the database will be met with a dialog box similar to the one shown in Figure 8.9.

**FIGURE 8.9**
A user who lacks the Database Open right (dbSecDBOpen) to a database will be met with this dialog box when they attempt to open the database.

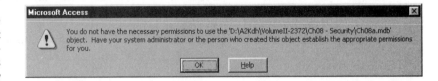

**TIP**

A user will still be able to open a database if the Users group or any other groups to which the user belongs have the dbSecDBOpen right.

## Disabling the Creation of New Databases using DAO

Jet exposes a permission, dbSecDBCreate, that is not exposed by the Access UI. If you remove this right from the Databases container of the workgroup file (typically, SYSTEM.MDW) using DAO, you will prevent users from creating new databases. The function adhSetDbCreate in basGenericDAOSecurityUtilities does just this. You pass it the name of the user or group account, and a Boolean parameter that you set to False to disable database creation or True to enable the creation of databases.

**NOTE**

If you use this function to disable the dbSecDBCreate permission of a user, you'll want to make sure the user doesn't have implicit dbSecDBCreate permission. That is, you'll want to also remove this permission from the Users group and any other groups to which the user belongs.

The adhSetDbCreate function is shown in Listing 8.20.

### Listing 8.20

```
Function adhSetDbCreate(ByVal strAccount As String, _
ByVal fEnable As Boolean) As Boolean

    ' Enables or disables the ability
    ' to create new databases.

    On Error GoTo adhSetDbCreateErr

    Dim strSystemDB As String
    Dim dbSys As Database
    Dim cnt As Container
    Dim strMsg As String

    Const adhcProcName = "adhSetDbCreate"
```

```
        adhSetDbCreate = False

        strSystemDB = SysCmd(acSysCmdGetWorkgroupFile)

        Set dbSys = _
         DBEngine.Workspaces(0).OpenDatabase(strSystemDB)
        Set cnt = dbSys.Containers!Databases
        cnt.UserName = strAccount

        'Turn on or off the permission to create new databases
        If fEnable Then
            cnt.Permissions = cnt.Permissions Or dbSecDBCreate
        Else
            cnt.Permissions = cnt.Permissions _
             And Not dbSecDBCreate
        End If

        adhSetDbCreate = True

adhSetDbCreateDone:
    If Not dbSys Is Nothing Then dbSys.Close
    On Error GoTo 0
    Exit Function

adhSetDbCreateErr:
    Select Case Err
    Case adhcErrNoPermission
        adhSetDbCreate = False
        Resume adhSetDbCreateDone
    Case adhcErrNameNotInCollection
        strMsg = "The account '" & strAccount & _
         "' doesn't exist."
    Case Else
        strMsg = "Error " & Err.Number & ": " & Err.Description
    End Select
        MsgBox strMsg, vbCritical + vbOKOnly, _
         "Procedure " & adhcProcName
    Resume adhSetDbCreateDone

End Function
```

To determine the path to the workgroup file, adhSetDbCreate uses the Access SysCmd function, passing it the acSysCmdGetWorkgroupFile constant.

## Changing Object Ownership using DAO

You can change the owner of a Jet or Access object by setting the Owner property of the object to the name of a user or group account in the workgroup. The Change-OwnerOfTableDAO subroutine from basSecurityExamplesDAO demonstrates how to use the Owner property to change the owner of the tblCustomer table to the Drones group. ChangeOwnerOfTableDAO is shown in Listing 8.21.

### Listing 8.21

```
Sub ChangeOwnerOfTableDAO()
    ' Illustrates correct DAO
    ' syntax to change a table's owner.

    ' Sets permission for:
    '    Object = tblCustomer
    '    New Owner = Drones

    Dim db As DAO.Database
    Dim doc As DAO.Document

    Set db = CurrentDb()
    Set doc = db.Containers!Tables.Documents!tblCustomer

    doc.Owner = "Drones"

    Set doc = Nothing
    Set db = Nothing
End Sub
```

Similarly, the ChangeOwnerOfFormDAO subroutine shown in Listing 8.22 demonstrates that you can also change the owner of an Access object—in this example the frmCustomer form.

⟲ **Listing 8.22**

```
Sub ChangeOwnerOfFormDAO()
    ' Illustrates correct DAO
    ' syntax to change a form's owner.

    ' Sets permission for:
    '    Object = frmCustomer
    '    New Owner = Drones

    Dim db As DAO.Database
    Dim doc As DAO.Document

    Set db = CurrentDb()
    Set doc = db.Containers!Forms.Documents!frmCustomer

    doc.Owner = "Drones"

    Set doc = Nothing
    Set db = Nothing
End Sub
```

# Reusable DAO Security Functions

In prior editions of the *Access Developer's Handbook,* we included a number of generic, reusable security functions that you could incorporate into your applications to manipulate Jet security. While we have decided to present simpler functions in this edition that make it easier to contrast the differences between DAO, ADOX, and SQL, we have still included the more generic functions in the basGenericDAOSecurityUtilities module of the CH08.MDB database. The following table summarizes the security functions contained in basGenericDAOSecurityUtilities:

**adhAddGroupMember**   Adds a user to a group.

**adhCheckPermission**   Checks the particular bit or set of bits of a permission value for a document or container.

**adhCreateGroup**   Creates a new group account.

**adhCreateUser**   Creates a new user account.

**adhDeleteAccount**   Deletes a user or group account from the workgroup.

**adhGetAccount**   Checks for the existence of an account and returns the type (user or group) if found.

**adhGetObjectOwner**   Gets the account name of an object's owner.

**adhIsGroupMember**   Verifies whether a user is a member of a group.

**adhGetPermission**   Gets the entire permission value for a document or container.

**adhListUsersWithBlankPwd**   Prints all users with blank passwords to a text file.

**adhRemoveGroupMember**   Removes a user from a group.

**adhSetDbCreate**   Enables or disables an account from being able to create databases.

**adhSetDbPwd**   Sets the database password.

**adhSetOwner**   Changes the owner of a document or container.

**adhSetPermission**   Adds or subtracts a particular bit or set of bits, or replaces a permission value for a document or container.

**adhSetPermissionAdd**   Adds a particular permission bit or set of bits for a document or container. Wrapper function that calls adhSetPermission.

**adhSetPermissionDocCreate**   Enables or disables the ability of an account to create documents of a particular type. Wrapper function that calls adhSetPermission.

**adhSetPermissionReplace**   Replaces a permission value for a document or container. Wrapper function that calls adhSetPermission.

**adhSetPermissionSubtract**   Subtracts a particular permission bit or set of bits for a document or container. Wrapper function that calls adhSetPermission.

**adhSetPwd**   Sets the password for a user account.

# ADOX Security Overview

The ADOX object model is pictured in Figure 8.10. To manipulate user and group accounts, you use the Users and Groups collections. These two collections are descendants of the Catalog object that represents the schema catalog of a data source. Unlike the DAO object model there is no equivalent of the Containers and Documents collection in ADOX. Instead, you programmatically manipulate permissions in ADXO using methods of the User and Group objects.

**FIGURE 8.10**
The ADOX object model contains Users and Groups collections that are descendants of the Catalog object.

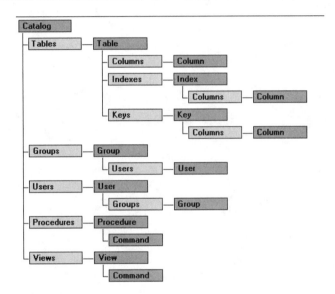

## Managing Accounts with ADOX

The ADOX Catalog object contains the Users collection. The ADOX Users collection in ADOX is similar to the Workgroup object's Users collection in DAO. It contains a collection of User objects, which represent each user in the workgroup. The ListUsersADOX subroutine shown in Listing 8.23 illustrates how to iterate through the members of the Users collection. This subroutine can be found in basSecurity-ExamplesADOX module of CH08.MDB.

**Listing 8.23**

```
Sub ListUsersADOX()
    ' List all users in workgroup
    ' to debug window using ADOX.
    Dim cat As ADOX.Catalog
    Dim usr As ADOX.User

    Set cat = New ADOX.Catalog
    cat.ActiveConnection = CurrentProject.Connection

    Debug.Print "The Users collection has " & _
    cat.Users.Count & " members:"
    For Each usr In cat.Users
        Debug.Print usr.Name
    Next usr

    Set usr = Nothing
    Set cat = Nothing
End Sub
```

ListUsersADOX begins by creating a new instance of the ADOX Catalog object and points it to the current database by setting the Catalog's ActiveConnection property to the CurrentProject's Connection property. The code then displays a count of the number of users using the Count property of the Users collection. Finally, ListUsersADOX iterates through each of the User objects in the Catalog's Users collection and prints the value of each User object's Name property to the debug window.

The Catalog object has a Group's collection that is analogous to the Users collection. The ListGroupsADOX subroutine in Listing 8.24 iterates through each of the Groups collection's Group objects and prints the name of the group to the Debug window.

**Listing 8.24**

```
Sub ListGroupsADOX()
    ' List all groups in workgroup
    ' to debug window using ADOX.
    Dim cat As ADOX.Catalog
```

```
Dim grp As ADOX.Group

Set cat = New ADOX.Catalog
cat.ActiveConnection = CurrentProject.Connection

Debug.Print "The Groups collection has " & _
cat.Groups.Count & " members:"
For Each grp In cat.Groups
   Debug.Print grp.Name
Next grp

Set grp = Nothing
Set cat = Nothing
End Sub
```

Each User object in ADOX contains its own Groups collection that represents each of the groups to which the user belongs. Similarly, each Group object contains its own Users collection that represents each of the users that are members of the group. This redundancy in the ADOX hierarchy is analogous to the Users and Groups collections in DAO.

The ListManagersADOX subroutine from basSecurityExamplesADOX, shown in Listing 8.25, uses the Managers group's Users collection to list all of the members of the Managers group.

### Listing 8.25

```
Sub ListManagersADOX()
   ' List all members of Managers group
   ' to debug window using ADOX.
   Dim cat As ADOX.Catalog
   Dim grpManagers As ADOX.Group
   Dim usr As ADOX.User

   Set cat = New ADOX.Catalog
   cat.ActiveConnection = CurrentProject.Connection

   Set grpManagers = cat.Groups!Managers

   For Each usr In grpManagers.Users
      Debug.Print usr.Name
```

```
    Next usr

        Set usr = Nothing
        Set grpManagers = Nothing
        Set cat = Nothing
    End Sub
```

## Creating Accounts Using ADOX

To create a new user account in ADOX, you simply use the Append method of the Catalog.Users group, passing it the name of the user and the user's password. ADOX automatically assigns a random personal identifier (PID) to the new account. Because you never have access to this PID, you won't be able to re-create the same account if for some reason the account is inadvertently deleted or the workgroup is destroyed.

The CreateNewUserADOX subroutine, shown in Listing 8.26, creates a new user account named "Anna" with a password of "foo".

### Listing 8.26

```
Sub CreateNewUserADOX()
    ' Create new user account using ADOX.

    ' Creates following new account:
    '   User     = Anna,
    '   PID      = --ADO assigns this automatically--
    '   Password = foo

    Dim cat As ADOX.Catalog

    Set cat = New ADOX.Catalog
    cat.ActiveConnection = CurrentProject.Connection

    cat.Users.Append "Anna", "foo"
    cat.Users("Anna").Groups.Append "Users"

    Set cat = Nothing
End Sub
```

Just as was the case when using DAO, you must add any newly created accounts to the built-in Users group or the user will be unable to log in to the workgroup.

> **TIP**
>
> The inability to specify the PID of a new account is a serious shortcoming of ADOX that hopefully will be remedied in the future. In the mean time, you can work around this problem by creating new accounts using a SQL DDL query (see the "Managing Accounts with SQL" section later in this chapter).

Creating a new group account is even simpler: use the Append method of the Catalog.Groups object, passing it the name of the new group. An example that illustrates this is shown in Listing 8.27.

### Listing 8.27

```
Sub CreateNewGroupADOX()
    ' Create new group account using ADOX.

    ' Creates following new account:
    '   Group    = Drones,
    '   PID      = --ADO assigns this automatically--

    Dim cat As ADOX.Catalog

    Set cat = New ADOX.Catalog
    cat.ActiveConnection = CurrentProject.Connection

    cat.Groups.Append "Drones"

    Set cat = Nothing
End Sub
```

As was the case with creating a new user, you can't specify a PID when creating a new group account using ADOX.

You can use the Delete method of the Users or Groups collections to delete a user or group account, respectively. Listing 8.28 shows an example of deleting a user account. Listing 8.29 shows how to delete a group account.

### Listing 8.28

```
Sub DeleteUserADOX()
    ' Delete Anna user account using ADOX.
    Dim cat As ADOX.Catalog

    Set cat = New ADOX.Catalog
    cat.ActiveConnection = CurrentProject.Connection

    cat.Users.Delete "Anna"

    Set cat = Nothing
End Sub
```

### Listing 8.29

```
Sub DeleteGroupADOX()
    ' Delete Drones group account using ADOX.
    Dim cat As ADOX.Catalog

    Set cat = New ADOX.Catalog
    cat.ActiveConnection = CurrentProject.Connection

    cat.Groups.Delete "Drones"

    Set cat = Nothing
End Sub
```

## Adding and Removing Users from Groups in ADOX

As was the case in DAO, you have two ways to add a user to a group in ADOX: either use the Append method of the User object's Groups collection or use the Append method of the Group object's Users collection. The AddUserToGroup-ADOX subroutine shown in Listing 8.30 uses the former technique.

**Listing 8.30**

```
Sub AddUserToGroupADOX()
    ' Adds Anna to Drones group using ADOX.
    Dim cat As ADOX.Catalog
    Dim usr As ADOX.User

    Set cat = New ADOX.Catalog
    cat.ActiveConnection = CurrentProject.Connection

    Set usr = cat.Users("Anna")
    usr.Groups.Append "Drones"

    Set usr = Nothing
    Set cat = Nothing
End Sub
```

Removing a user from a group is analogous to adding the user to the group:
only the method changes. You can use either the Delete method of the User object's
Groups collection or the Delete method of the Group object's Users collection. The
RemoveUserFromGroupADOX subroutine shown in Listing 8.31 uses the former
technique.

**Listing 8.31**

```
Sub RemoveUserFromGroupADOX()
    ' Removes Anna from Drones group using ADOX.
    Dim cat As ADOX.Catalog
    Dim usr As ADOX.User

    Set cat = New ADOX.Catalog
    cat.ActiveConnection = CurrentProject.Connection

    Set usr = cat.Users("Anna")
    usr.Groups.Delete "Drones"

    Set usr = Nothing
    Set cat = Nothing
End Sub
```

## Determining If a User Is a Member of a Group Using ADOX

Again, because of the symmetry in the Users and Groups collections, you have two ways to determine if a user is a member of a group using ADOX: you can either check if the Groups collection of the User object contains the group or if the Users collection of the Group object contains the user.

The IsUserMemberADOX function from basSecurityExamplesADOX, shown in Listing 8.32, determines if a user is a member of a group by checking the Users collection of the Group object.

### Listing 8.32

```
Function IsUserMemberADOX(strGroup As String, _
Optional varUser As Variant) As Boolean
    ' Determines if user is a member of a group
    ' using ADOX.
    Dim cat As ADOX.Catalog

    ' Turn off error reporting
    On Error Resume Next

    Set cat = New ADOX.Catalog
    cat.ActiveConnection = CurrentProject.Connection

    If IsMissing(varUser) Then
        varUser = CurrentUser()
    End If

    IsUserMemberADOX = _
      (cat.Groups(strGroup).Users(varUser).Name = varUser)

    Set cat = Nothing
End Function
```

To make it more useful, we added code to the IsUserMemberADOX function that sets the username to the value returned by the CurrentUser function if the varUser is not provided. The built-in CurrentUser function returns the name of the currently logged-in user.

## Managing User Passwords in ADOX

You can use the ChangePassword method of the User object to change a user's password. The ChangePassword method is very similar to DAO's NewPassword method. You must supply both old and new passwords, but the old password value is ignored if you are changing another user's password and you're a member of the Admins group. This allows Admins members to change the passwords of other users. The ChangeUserPasswordADOX from basSecurityExamplesADOX, shown in Listing 8.33, demonstrates the use of the ChangePassword method.

### Listing 8.33

```
Sub ChangeUserPasswordADOX(strUser As String, _
  strOld As String, strNew As String)
    ' Changes Anna's password.

    Dim cat As ADOX.Catalog
    Dim usr As ADOX.User

    Set cat = New ADOX.Catalog
    cat.ActiveConnection = CurrentProject.Connection

    Set usr = cat.Users("Anna")

    ' For Admins members, the old password
    ' value is ignored.
    usr.ChangePassword strOld, strNew

    Set usr = Nothing
    Set cat = Nothing
End Sub
```

# Programming Permissions Using ADOX

You manipulate object permissions in ADOX by using methods of User and Group objects. As in DAO, you use constants to specify which rights you wish to view or set in ADOX. The ADOX rights constants are summarized in Table 8.6.

**TABLE 8.6:** ADOX Rights Constants

| Constant | Description |
|---|---|
| adRightNone | No access to the object |
| adRightFull | Full access to the object; when used with Databases container, user can make a database replicable, change the database password, and set startup properties |
| adRightDrop | Can delete the object |
| adRightReadPermissions | Can read the object's security-related information |
| adRightWritePermissions | Can alter access permissions |
| adRightWriteOwner | Can change the Owner property setting |
| adRightCreate | Can create new documents; when used with Databases container of system database, can create new databases |
| adRightReadDesign | Can read the table definition, including column and index information |
| adRightWriteDesign | Can modify or delete the table definition, including column and index information |
| adRightRead | Can read records; when used with Databases container, can open database |
| adRightInsert | Can add records |
| adRightUpdate | Can modify records |
| adRightDelete | Can delete records |
| adRightExclusive | When used with Databases container, can open the database exclusively |
| adRightExecute | Can execute the object |
| adRightWithGrant | Can grant other users the right to administer permissions for the object |

## Reading Permissions with ADOX

You can read the existing set of permissions a user or group has for an object using the GetPermissions method of the user or group object. GetPermissions returns a long integer corresponding to the existing set of permissions for the object. For example, you might use the following statement to retrieve the Users group's permission set for the tblCustomer table and place the value in lngPerm:

```
lngPerm = _
  cat.Groups("Users").GetPermissions("tblCustomer", _
  adPermObjTable)
```

You pass the GetPermissions method the name of the object and a constant specifying its type. As is the case when using the Permissions property in DAO, GetPermissions returns a long integer containing the entire set of permissions for the object, with each bit of the 4-byte long integer value indicating a different permission (or right). Often, you'll want to check if the user has some minimum rights to an object, which you can do using bitwise arithmetic. You check a permission value for a specific set of bits—some permissions are actually the result of setting several bits—by using the bitwise And operator to mask off the bits in which you are interested and comparing the result of the operations to these same bits. Using the ADOX rights constants from Table 8.6 makes this easier.

---

**NOTE**      The adPermObjTable objecttype constant of GetPermissions works with both tables and queries.

---

For example, say that you wished to determine if the Drones group had the ability to insert rows into the tblEmployee table. You could use the following code to check to see if Drones had this right:

```
lngPerm = _
  cat.Groups("Drones").GetPermissions("tblEmployee", _
  adPermObjTable)
fOK = ((lngPerm And adRightInsert) = adRightInsert)
```

In this case, fOK will be set to True if the Drones group has insert rights to tblEmployee. Otherwise, fOK will be set to False.

---

**WARNING**   Because some rights may be the result of setting more than one bit, you *can't* use the following simplified syntax to check for a particular right: fOK = ((lng-Permissions And adRightInsert) <> 0). Yes, it might work some of the time, but if you ever check a right that is made up of multiple bits, the above will report a spurious result.

---

You aren't limited to checking a single right—by adding several rights together with the bitwise Or operator, you can check if a user or group has some minimal set of rights. For example, you could use the following code to check if Suzanne has read, insert, update, and delete record rights for tblMenu:

```
lngPerm = _
cat.Users("Suzanne").GetPermissions("tblMenu", _
adPermObjTable)
fOK = ((lngPerm And (adRightRead Or adRightInsert Or _
adRightUpdate Or adRightDelete)) = _
(adRightRead Or adRightInsert Or adRightUpdate Or _
adRightDelete))
```

The CanUserReadCustomersADOX function from basSecurityExamplesADOX is shown in Listing 8.34. This function returns True if the user has the right to read records from tblCustomer, or False otherwise.

### Listing 8.34

```
Function CanUserReadCustomersADOX(strUser As String) _
As Boolean
    ' Illustrates correct ADOX syntax to check
    ' a permission of a table for a user.

    ' Checks explicit permissions only for:
    '    Object = tblCustomer
    '    Permission = adRightRead

    Dim cat As ADOX.Catalog

    Set cat = New ADOX.Catalog
    cat.ActiveConnection = CurrentProject.Connection

    CanUserReadCustomersADOX = _
      ((cat.Users(strUser).GetPermissions("tblCustomer", _
      adPermObjTable) And adRightRead) = adRightRead)

    Set cat = Nothing
End Function
```

This example used the GetPermissions method of the User object. Group objects also have a GetPermissions method that has the identical syntax.

To check the permissions for the currently logged-in user, you use the built-in CurrentUser function to return the name of the current user. The following code from CanCurrentUserReadCustomersADOX of basSecurityExamplesADOX does just this:

```
CanCurrentUserReadCustomersADOX = _
((cat.Users(CurrentUser()).GetPermissions("tblCustomer", _
adPermObjTable) And adRightRead) = adRightRead)
```

The CanUserReadCustomersADOX and CanCurrentUserReadCustomersADOX functions report only the user's explicit permissions. A user may also have implicit permissions to an object by virtue of his or her membership in groups. In DAO, you can check both implicit and explicit permissions by looking at a user's AllPermissions property. ADOX has no equivalent property or method; however, you can get the same effect by checking a user's explicit permissions and the permissions of every group to which he or she belongs.

For example, the CanUserReadCustomersADOX2 function demonstrates how to check both a user's explicit and implicit permissions for a particular right—in this case, the right to read records from tblCustomer. CanUserReadCustomersADOX2 can be found in basSecurityExamplesADOX and is shown in Listing 8.35.

### Listing 8.35

```
Function CanUserReadCustomersADOX2(strUser As String) _
As Boolean
    ' Illustrates correct ADOX syntax to check both
    ' direct and indirect permissions for a table.
    ' This is more complex than DAO because ADOX lacks
    ' anything like DAO's AllPermissions property.

    ' Checks all permissions for:
    '    Object = tblCustomer
    '    Permission = dbSecRetrieveData

    Dim cat As ADOX.Catalog
    Dim usr As ADOX.User
    Dim grp As ADOX.Group
    Dim fPerm As Boolean
    ' Assume false
```

```
        fPerm = False

        Set cat = New ADOX.Catalog
        cat.ActiveConnection = CurrentProject.Connection

        Set usr = cat.Users(strUser)
        ' Check explicit permission for user.
        fPerm = ((usr.GetPermissions( _
         "tblCustomer", adPermObjTable) _
         And adRightRead) = adRightRead)

        ' If not part of explicit permission set,
        ' then check implicit permissions.
        If Not fPerm Then
            For Each grp In usr.Groups
                fPerm = ((grp.GetPermissions( _
                 "tblCustomer", adPermObjTable) _
                 And adRightRead) = adRightRead)
                If fPerm Then Exit For
            Next
        End If
        CanUserReadCustomersADOX2 = fPerm

        Set usr = Nothing
        Set grp = Nothing
        Set cat = Nothing
    End Function
```

CanUserReadCustomersADOX2 starts by checking the explicit permissions for tblCustomer using the GetPermissions method of the User object. If the explicit permission set for tblCustomer does not include the right to read records, CanUserReadCustomersADOX2 proceeds to check the permission of each of the groups to which the user belongs using the Groups collection of the User object. The code exits the For loop using a Exit For statement as soon as the adRightRead permission is found for one of the groups.

## Writing Permissions using ADOX

To update permissions in ADOX, you use the SetPermissions method of the User or Group object. Using the action argument of the SetPermissions method, you can choose from several different ways to update permissions. The different action argument values are summarized in Table 8.7.

**TABLE 8.7:** Action Argument Constants for the ADOX SetPermissions Method

| Action argument | Description |
| --- | --- |
| adAccessGrant | Adds the specified right or rights to the existing permission set |
| adAccessSet | Replaces the permission set with the specified right or rights |
| adAccessDeny | Removes the specified right or rights from the existing permission set |
| adAccessRevoke | Removes all rights to the object |

For example, the following statement adds the ability to delete records to Geoff's existing permission set for tblMenu:

```
cat.Users("Geoff").SetPermissions "tblMenu", _
    adPermObjTable, adAccessGrant, adRightDelete
```

The following statement removes the ability to delete records from Geoff's existing permission set for tblMenu:

```
cat.Users("Geoff").SetPermissions "tblMenu", _
    adPermObjTable, adAccessDeny, adRightDelete
```

This next version of the statement completely replaces Geoff's permission set so he now has the ability to delete records and no other rights to tblMenu:

```
cat.Users("Geoff").SetPermissions "tblMenu", _
    adPermObjTable, adAccessSet, adRightDelete
```

The SetUserReadCustomersADOX in basSecurityExamplesADOX illustrates how to add or subtract a permission from the existing permission set for tblCustomer using the SetPermissions method. SetUserReadCustomersADOX is shown in Listing 8.36.

### Listing 8.36

```
Sub SetUserReadCustomersADOX(strUser As String, _
    fRead As Boolean)
    ' Illustrates correct ADOX syntax
    ' to add or remove a specfic permission.

    ' Sets permission for:
    '   Object = tblCustomer
```

```
'    Permission = adRightRead

Dim cat As ADOX.Catalog

Set cat = New ADOX.Catalog
cat.ActiveConnection = CurrentProject.Connection

If fRead Then
    cat.Users(strUser).SetPermissions "tblCustomer", _
    adPermObjTable, adAccessGrant, adRightRead
Else
    cat.Users(strUser).SetPermissions "tblCustomer", _
    adPermObjTable, adAccessDeny, adRightRead
End If

Set cat = Nothing
End Sub
```

If you pass a value of True to SetUserReadCustomersADOX for its second argument, it sets the action argument of SetPermissions to adAccessGrant. This adds the adRightRead right to the existing permission set for tblCustomer. For example:

```
Call SetUserReadCustomersADOX "Peter", True
```

On the other hand, if you pass a value of False to SetUserReadCustomersADOX for its second argument, it sets the action argument of SetPermissions to adAccessDeny. This subtracts the adRightRead right from the existing permission set for tblCustomer:

```
Call SetUserReadCustomersADOX "Peter", False
```

By setting the second argument (the objectype argument) of the SetPermissions method to adPermObjTable, you indicate that you wish to set the permissions for a table or query. The SetPermissions method also includes a provision for setting the rights of provider-specific objects. When working with the Jet provider, forms, reports, and macros are considered provider-specific objects. To set the rights of provider-specific objects, you set the ObjectType argument to adPermObjProviderSpecific and then supply the sixth argument, ObjectTypeID, with a GUID that identifies the provider-specific object. You can also use a provider-specific ObjectTypeID with the GetPermissions method. The ObjectTypeID GUID values for Access objects are summarized in Table 8.8

**TABLE 8.8:** ObjectTypeID Argument GUIDs for the Access Objects and the basSecurityExamplesADOX Constants

| Access Object | basSecurityExamplesADOX Constant | ObjectTypeID Argument |
|---|---|---|
| Forms | JET_SECURITY_FORMS | {c49c842e-9dcb-11d1-9f0a-00c04fc2c2e0} |
| Reports | JET_SECURITY_REPORTS | {c49c8430-9dcb-11d1-9f0a-00c04fc2c2e0} |
| Macros | JET_SECURITY_MACROS | {c49c842f-9dcb-11d1-9f0a-00c04fc2c2e0} |

We've defined three constants that correspond to the Access object GUIDs in the Declarations section of basSecurityExamplesADOX. The SetUserExecFormADOX subroutine, also found in basSecurityExamplesADOX and shown in Listing 8.37, shows how to go about using these constants (that is, if they worked). Unfortunately, a bug in the ADOX 2.1 OLEDB provider maps the permissions for the Access objects incorrectly. At the time this book went to press (version ADOX 2.1), the problem had not been fixed. Microsoft, however, has stated that it will make a fix available at sometime in the future.

**Listing 8.37**

```
Public Const JET_SECURITY_FORMS = _
  "{c49c842e-9dcb-11d1-9f0a-00c04fc2c2e0}"


Sub SetUserExecFormADOX(strUser As String, fExec As Boolean)
    ' Illustrates correct ADOX syntax to set
    ' execute (Open) permission for a form.
    Dim cat As ADOX.Catalog

    Set cat = New ADOX.Catalog
    cat.ActiveConnection = CurrentProject.Connection

    ' ***************************************************
    ' Note: this should work, but doesn't in ADOX 2.1
    ' It may be fixed in a later ADOX release.
    ' ***************************************************
    If fExec Then
        cat.Users(strUser).SetPermissions "frmCustomer", _
        adPermObjProviderSpecific, adAccessGrant, _
```

```
            adRightExecute, , JET_SECURITY_FORMS
    Else
            cat.Users(strUser).SetPermissions "frmCustomer", _
            adPermObjProviderSpecific, adAccessDeny, _
            adRightExecute, , JET_SECURITY_FORMS
    End If

    Set cat = Nothing
End Sub
```

**WARNING**   At the time this book went to press, the provider-specific constants for Access objects did not work properly because of a bug in the JET OLEDB provider. Check http://www.microsoft.com/data for details on updates to MDAC (Microsoft Data Access Components), ADOX, or the JET OLEDB provider that fix this bug.

## Setting Permissions for New Objects Using ADOX

You can set permissions for new objects using ADOX by passing the SetPermission method an empty string for the name argument and the type of the container for the ObjectType argument. When you do this, you also need to set the fourth SetPermission argument (inherit) to adInheritObjects. For example:

```
cat.Users("Anna").SetPermissions "", adPermObjTable, _
  adAccessGrant, adRightRead, adInheritObjects
```

The SetUserReadNewTablesADOX subroutine in Listing 8.38 demonstrates how to set permissions for the tables container.

### Listing 8.38

```
Sub SetUserReadNewTablesADOX(strUser As String,_
    fRead As Boolean)
    ' Illustrates correct ADOX syntax to set
    ' the read permission for the tables container.

    ' Sets permission for:
    '   Container = Tables
    '   Permission = adRightRead
```

```
        Dim cat As ADOX.Catalog

        Set cat = New ADOX.Catalog
        cat.ActiveConnection = CurrentProject.Connection

        ' Use "" for name argument and adInhertiObjects
        ' for the inherit argument to set permissions
        ' for a container which will then affect new objects.
        If fRead Then
            cat.Users(strUser).SetPermissions "", _
            adPermObjTable, adAccessGrant, adRightRead, _
            adInheritObjects
        Else
            cat.Users(strUser).SetPermissions "", _
            adPermObjTable, adAccessDeny, adRightRead, _
            adInheritObjects
        End If

        Set cat = Nothing
    End Sub
```

## Manipulating Database Permissions Using ADOX

By using an ObjectType value of adPermObjDatabase with the GetPermissions and SetPermissions methods, you can view and set properties of the database itself. For example, the SetUserDatabaseOpenADOX subroutine shown in Listing 8.39 illustrates how you can use the adPermObjDatabase objectype constant to add or remove the database Open right for a user.

### Listing 8.39

```
    Sub SetUserDatabaseOpenADOX(strUser As String, _
      fOpen As Boolean)
        ' Illustrates correct ADOX syntax to set
        ' the Open permission for a database.

        ' Sets permission for:
        '   Object = Database
        '   Permission = adRightOpen
```

```
        Dim cat As ADOX.Catalog

        Set cat = New ADOX.Catalog
        cat.ActiveConnection = CurrentProject.Connection

        If fOpen Then
            cat.Users(strUser).SetPermissions "", _
            adPermObjDatabase, adAccessGrant, adRightRead
        Else
            cat.Users(strUser).SetPermissions "", _
            adPermObjDatabase, adAccessDeny, adRightRead
        End If

        Set cat = Nothing
    End Sub
```

## Changing Object Ownership Using ADOX

The ADOX Catalog object has a method, SetObjectOwner, which you can use to change the owner of an object. Its syntax is similar to the SetPermissions method. For example, to change the owner of the qryMenu query to the Programmers group, you might use the following code:

```
    cat.SetObjectOwner "qryMenu", adPermObjTable, "Programmers"
```

The ChangeOwnerOfTableADOX subroutine from basSecurityExamplesADOX demonstrates the use of the SetObjectOwner method with a table. ChangeOwnerOfTableADOX is shown in Listing 8.40.

### Listing 8.40

```
    Sub ChangeOwnerOfTableADOX()
        ' Illustrates correct ADOX
        ' syntax to change a table's owner.

        ' Sets permission for:
        '   Object = tblCustomer
        '   New Owner = Drones

        Dim cat As ADOX.Catalog
```

```
      Set cat = New ADOX.Catalog
      cat.ActiveConnection = CurrentProject.Connection

      cat.SetObjectOwner "tblCustomer", _
       adPermObjTable, "Drones"

      Set cat = Nothing
    End Sub
```

The ChangeOwnerOfFormADOX subroutine shown in Listing 8.41 demonstrates how to change the owner of a form.

> **Listing 8.41**

```
    Public Const JET_SECURITY_FORMS = _
     "{c49c842e-9dcb-11d1-9f0a-00c04fc2c2e0}"

Sub ChangeOwnerOfFormADOX()
    ' Illustrates correct ADOX
    ' syntax to change a form's owner.

    ' Sets permission for:
    '    Object = frmCustomer
    '    New Owner = Drones

    Dim cat As ADOX.Catalog

    Set cat = New ADOX.Catalog
    cat.ActiveConnection = CurrentProject.Connection

    cat.SetObjectOwner "frmCustomer", _
     adPermObjProviderSpecific, "Drones", JET_SECURITY_FORMS

    Set cat = Nothing
End Sub
```

---

**NOTE**     The bug that prevents you from setting the permissions of Access objects using ADOX 2.1 *doesn't* prevent you from changing the ownership of Access objects.

---

# Managing Jet Security with SQL

Versions of Access prior to Access 2000 did not allow you to manage Jet security using SQL. However, Microsoft made a number of improvements to the SQL language that ships with Access 2000 and Jet 4.0 that are collectively known as the Jet 4.0 ANSI SQL-92 extensions. These extensions are discussed in great detail in Chapter 5 of the *Access Developer's Handbook, Volume 1: Desktop Edition*. In this section, we'll concentrate on how to employ the new Jet SQL for manipulating security.

The SQL statements for security are summarized in Table 8.9.

**TABLE 8.9:**   The Jet 4 ANSI-92 SQL Extensions for Security

| SQL Statement | Description |
| --- | --- |
| ADD USER | Adds a user to a group |
| ALTER DATABASE | Changes the database password |
| ALTER USER | Changes a user's password |
| CREATE GROUP | Adds a new group account to the workgroup |
| CREATE USER | Adds a new user account to the workgroup |
| DROP GROUP | Deletes a group account |
| DROP USER | Deletes a user account or removes a user from a group |
| GRANT | Grants privileges to a user or group |
| REVOKE | Revokes privileges from a user or group |

In general, the SQL support for security is not as strong as the support found in either DAO or ADOX. One place where SQL falls short is in its inability to let you view the names of either existing users or groups or the existing permission sets of objects. On the other hand, many developers—especially those proficient in SQL—will undoubtedly find manipulating Jet security with SQL to be considerably easier than either of the alternatives.

In order to use the Jet 4.0 ANSI-92 SQL extensions, you must be using ADO and the Jet 4.0 (or later) OLE DB provider. The extensions are not supported by DAO or the Access query designer.

## Managing Accounts with SQL

You use the CREATE USER statement to create a new user account using SQL. You pass CREATE USER the name of the new user, a password, and a personal identifier or PID, separating each item with a space. For example, to create a new user named Phil with a password of "openME" and a PID of "99hello88", you would use the following CREATE USER statement:

```
CREATE USER Phil openME 99hello88
```

The CreateNewUserSQL subroutine from basSecurityExamplesSQL illustrates how to use the CREATE USER statement to add the user Anna with a password of "foo" and a Personal Identifier (PID) of "123whatR". CreateNewUserSQL is shown in Listing 8.42.

**Listing 8.42**

```
Sub CreateNewUserSQL()
    ' Create new user account using SQL.

    ' Creates following new account:
    '   User     = Anna
    '   PID      = 123whatR
    '   Password = foo

    Dim cnn As ADODB.Connection

    Set cnn = CurrentProject.Connection
    cnn.Execute "CREATE USER Anna foo 123whatR"
    cnn.Execute "ADD USER Anna TO Users"

    Set cnn = Nothing
End Sub
```

Just as when creating new users using DAO or ADOX, the CREATE USER statement doesn't automatically add the new user to the built-in Users group, which the user must belong to if he or she will open any databases in the workgroup. Thus, CreateNewUserSQL also executes an ADD USER statement to add the new user to the Users group.

---

**TIP**

Like the DAO CreateUser method, the SQL CREATE USER statement has a distinct advantage over the ADOX User collection's Append method: it allows you to specify a PID when creating a new user account. (This is also true for the CREATE GROUP statement.)

---

You use the CREATE GROUP statement to create a new group account. The CreateNewGroupSQL subroutine shown in Listing 8.43 creates a new group named Drones with a PID of "crazy8s".

### Listing 8.43

```
Sub CreateNewGroupSQL()
    ' Create new group account using SQL.

    ' Creates following new account:
    '    Group      = Drones
    '    PID        = crazy8s

    Dim cnn As ADODB.Connection

    Set cnn = CurrentProject.Connection
    cnn.Execute "CREATE GROUP Drones crazy8s"

    Set cnn = Nothing
End Sub
```

You use the ADD USER statement to add a user to a group. An example that adds Anna to the Drones group is shown in Listing 8.44.

**Listing 8.44**

```
Sub AddUserToGroupSQL()
    ' Adds Anna to Drones group using SQL.
    Dim cnn As ADODB.Connection

    Set cnn = CurrentProject.Connection
    cnn.Execute "ADD USER Anna TO Drones"

    Set cnn = Nothing
End Sub
```

The DROP USER statement does double duty. First, you can use it to delete a user account using the following syntax:

```
DROP USER Paul
```

You can also use DROP USER to remove a remove a user from a group. For example, to remove Paul from the Admins group, you would use the following DROP USER statement:

```
DROP USER Paul FROM Admins
```

The DeleteUserSQL subroutine shown in Listing 8.45 illustrates how to use DROP USER to delete a user account. The RemoveUserFromGroupSQL subroutine shown in Listing 8.46 illustrates how to use DROP USER to remove a user from a group.

**Listing 8.45**

```
Sub DeleteUserSQL()
    ' Delete Anna user account using SQL.
    Dim cnn As ADODB.Connection

    Set cnn = CurrentProject.Connection
    cnn.Execute "DROP USER Anna"

    Set cnn = Nothing
End Sub
```

## Listing 8.46

```
Sub RemoveUserFromGroupSQL()
    ' Removes Anna from Drones group using SQL.
    Dim cnn As ADODB.Connection

    Set cnn = CurrentProject.Connection
    cnn.Execute "DROP USER Anna FROM Drones"

    Set cnn = Nothing
End Sub
```

To delete a group account, you use the DROP GROUP statement, as illustrated by DeleteGroupSQL in Listing 8.47.

## Listing 8.47

```
Sub DeleteGroupSQL()
    ' Delete Drones group account using SQL.
    Dim cnn As ADODB.Connection

    Set cnn = CurrentProject.Connection
    cnn.Execute "DROP GROUP Drones"

    cnn.Close
End Sub
```

You use the ALTER USER statement in SQL to change a user's password. For example, to change Peter's password from blue to red, you would use the following statement:

```
ALTER USER Peter PASSWORD red blue
```

You specify the new password first separated from the existing password with a space.

The ChangeUserPasswordSQL subroutine from basSecurityExamplesSQL, shown in Listing 8.48, demonstrates how to change a user password.

**Listing 8.48**

```
Sub ChangeUserPasswordSQL()
    ' Changes Anna's password
    ' from "foo" to "bar" using SQL.
    Dim cnn As ADODB.Connection

    Set cnn = CurrentProject.Connection
    cnn.Execute "ALTER USER Anna PASSWORD bar foo"

    Set cnn = Nothing
End Sub
```

## Programming Permissions using SQL

You use the GRANT statement to grant a right to a user or group account. The syntax of the GRANT statement is shown here:

```
GRANT {privilege1 [, privilege2 [, ...] } ON
{TABLE table | OBJECT object | CONTAINER container}
TO account1 [, account2 [, ...] ]
```

You use the analogous REVOKE statement to revoke a right from a user or group account. Its syntax is shown here:

```
REVOKE {privilege1 [, privilege2 [, ...] } ON
{TABLE table | OBJECT object | CONTAINER container}
FROM account1 [, account2 [, ...] ]
```

*Privilege* can be any of the following privileges listed in Table 8.10.

*Table* is the name of any table or query; *object* can be the name of any non-table object; *container* is the name of any object container. Valid object container names include:

- Tables
- Forms
- Reports
- Scripts

**TABLE 8.10:**   Privileges That Can Be Used With the GRANT and REVOKE Statements

| Privilege | Description |
| --- | --- |
| SELECT | User or group can read rows |
| DELETE | User or group can delete rows |
| INSERT | User or group can insert rows |
| UPDATE | User or group can update rows |
| DROP | User or group can delete the object |
| SELECTSECURITY | User or group can view security settings of the object |
| UPDATESECURITY | User or group can update security settings of the object |
| DBPASSWORD | User or group can change the database password |
| UPDATEIDENTITY | User or group can update identity columns |
| CREATE | User or group can create new objects |
| SELECTSCHEMA | User or group can read the schema of the object |
| UPDATESCHEMA | User or group can update the schema of the object |
| UPDATEOWNER | User or group can update owner of the object |

**WARNING**   At the time of this writing, the ability to alter permissions on non-Jet objects did not work. Most likely, this is related to the problem with setting Access object permissions in ADOX and may be fixed in an update of MDAC, ADOX, or the Jet OLE DB provider.

The SetUserReadCustomersSQL subroutine from basSecurityExamplesSQL, shown in Listing 8.49, demonstrates the use of the GRANT and REVOKE statements with the tblCustomer table.

### Listing 8.49

```
Sub SetUserReadCustomersSQL(strUser As String, _
    fRead As Boolean)
        ' Illustrates correct SQL syntax
        ' to set a specfic permission.

        ' Sets permission for:
```

```
'   Object = tblCustomer,
'   Permission = SELECT

Dim strSQL As String

If fRead Then
    strSQL = "GRANT SELECT ON TABLE tblCustomer " & _
    "TO " & strUser
Else
    strSQL = "REVOKE SELECT ON TABLE tblCustomer " & _
    "FROM " & strUser
End If

CurrentProject.Connection.Execute strSQL
End Sub
```

The SetUserReadNewTablesSQL subroutine, shown in Listing 8.50, uses the GRANT and REVOKE statements with the CONTAINER keyword to affect the permissions assigned to new tables.

### Listing 8.50

```
Sub SetUserReadNewTablesSQL(strUser As String, _
fRead As Boolean)
    ' Illustrates correct SQL syntax to set
    ' read permission for the tables container.

    ' Sets permission for:
    '   Container = Tables
    '   Permission = SELECT

    Dim strSQL As String

    If fRead Then
        strSQL = "GRANT SELECT ON CONTAINER Tables " & _
        "TO " & strUser
    Else
        strSQL = "REVOKE SELECT ON CONTAINER Tables " & _
        "FROM " & strUser
    End If

    CurrentProject.Connection.Execute strSQL
End Sub
```

# Choosing DAO, ADOX, or SQL

The advantages and disadvantages of the three different ways to program security are contrasted in Table 8.11.

**TABLE 8.11:** Comparison of Using DAO, ADOX, or SQL to Manage Jet Security

| Feature | DAO | ADOX | SQL |
| --- | --- | --- | --- |
| Creating User and Group accounts | Complete support | Doesn't let you specify a PID | Complete support |
| Querying account membership/existence | Complete support | Complete support | No support |
| Other account maintenance (adding users to groups, removing users and groups) | Complete support | Complete support | Complete support |
| Granting/revoking permissions to tables and queries | Complete support | Complete support | Complete support |
| Granting/revoking permissions to Access objects (forms, reports, data access pages, and macros) | Complete support | Doesn't work correctly in ADOX 2.1* | Doesn't work correctly in ADOX 2.1* |
| Querying permissions | Complete support | Works with tables and queries* | No support |
| Managing object ownerships | Complete support | Complete support | No support |
| Backwards compatibility | Yes | No | No |
| Future support | DAO's days are numbered | Definitely | Most likely |
| Simplicity | Not always so simple | Simpler than DAO | Simpler than DAO and ADOX |
| Compatibility with SQL Server and other databases | No | Works with SQL Server; may work with other databases in future | Yes |

*The current version of ADOX (version 2.1) at the time of this writing contains a bug in the mapping of provider-specific object permissions to the Jet 4.0 OLEDB provider. This bug precludes the use of ADOX and SQL to set permissions on Access objects (forms, reports, and macros). This bug will likely be fixed in a service pack of ADOX, Access, or MDAC (Microsoft Data Access Components). Check http://www.microsoft.com/data for details of updates.

So which model should you use? At the time of this writing, DAO has the most complete support for programming security; however, ADOX is simpler to use and DAO's lifespan is limited. Once the Access objects permissions problem is fixed, ADOX will be able to do 95% of what DAO can do. One remaining issue is that ADOX doesn't let you specify the personal identifier (PID) for newly created accounts. However, you can get around this shortcoming by creating your new accounts using the SQL CREATE USER and CREATE GROUP statements.

# Securing a Jet Database with the Access 2000 Security Wizard

Securing a database properly takes great care. It's very easy to make a mistake and leave yourself open to possible security intrusions. Fortunately, Microsoft has created a wizard that ships with Access to help secure databases properly.

The Security Wizard for Access 2000 has been totally reworked. The new wizard now accomplishes many of the steps you had to perform manually in prior versions of Access.

The Access 2000 Security Wizard has seven steps:

1. Choose to create a new workgroup file or to work with an existing workgroup file, as shown in Figure 8.11. If you opt to create a new workgroup, the wizard prompts you for the name of the workgroup, the workgroup ID, and an optional name and company name.

2. Choose the objects to secure. In most cases, you'll want to select all objects.

3. Next, the wizard presents a list of security groups, as shown in Figure 8.12. This list includes any existing groups you created, plus the following wizard-created groups: Backup Operators, Full Data Users, Full Permissions, New Data Users, Project Designers, Read-Only Users, and Update Data Users. You can select or unselect each listed group. Any unselected groups will not be included in the workgroup file.

**FIGURE 8.11**

In the first step of the Security Wizard, you get to choose the workgroup file.

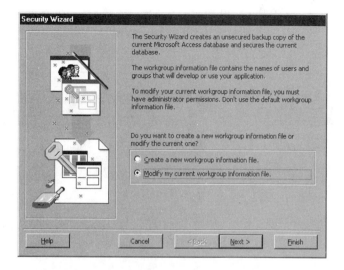

**FIGURE 8.12**

In the third step of the Security Wizard, you get to choose which groups to include in the workgroup file.

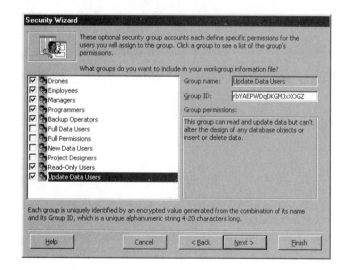

4. Next, you are given the option to assign some limited set of permissions to the built-in and unsecured Users group, as shown in Figure 8.13. This might be useful if, for example, you wanted all users to be able to read records from certain tables.

**FIGURE 8.13**

In the fourth step of the Security Wizard, you are given the option to assign permissions to the Users group.

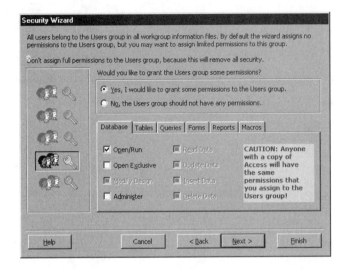

5. Next, the wizard displays the list of users in the workgroup. You can add or delete users from this list. The wizard doesn't list the built-in Admin user.

6. Next, the wizard lets you add and remove users from the groups you selected back in Step 3. The wizard requires that you add at least one of the users to the Admins group.

7. Finally, you are asked to name the backup unsecured version of the database.

When you click the Finish button, the wizard creates the new workgroup (if needed) and secures the database. Amongst other things, the wizard removes the Admin user from the Admins group and adds an undisclosed password to the Admin account to force database logins.

**NOTE**   In contrast to prior versions of the Security Wizard, the Access 2000 Security Wizard does not encrypt the database.

When it's done, the wizard presents you with a report summarizing its work, as shown in Figure 8.14. You should print this report because it lists all of the information you will need if you ever need to re-create the workgroup. This report details sensitive information, including the workgroup ID and personal identifier codes, so you should store it away in a secure location.

---

**TIP**    You can rerun the Security Wizard at any time to add additional users and groups or to secure additional objects.

---

If you want to selectively secure elements of a database but not have users log in, then you should run the wizard, giving some limited set of permissions to the Users group in Step 4 of the wizard. Users who do not log in to the database will get any permissions you assign to the built-in Users group. Then ship the database without the workgroup file you used to secure it.

---

**NOTE**    The Security Wizard doesn't secure code. You'll have to add a VBA project password if you wish to secure your modules.

---

**FIGURE 8.14**
The Security Wizard report

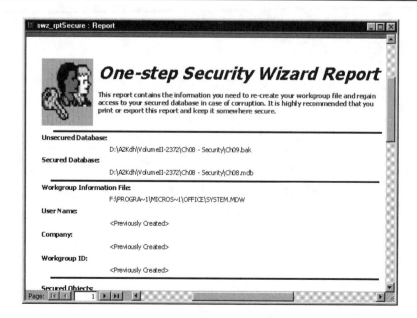

# Unsecuring a Secured Jet Database

You can reverse the process of securing a database by following these steps:

1. Log on as a member of the Admins group.

2. Grant full permissions, including Administer permission, to the built-in Users group for all objects in the database.

3. Put the Admin user back in the Admins group.

4. Clear the password for the Admin user.

5. Exit Access.

6. Restart Access and log on as Admin.

7. Create a new blank database and import all the secured database's objects using the File ➢ Get External Data ➢ Import command.

The trick to this technique is to give an unsecured group (Users) full permissions on all the objects and to then transfer ownership of the database and all its objects to an unsecured user (Admin).

# Migrating Secured Jet Databases to Access 2000

If you're migrating a secured database from a prior version of Access to Access 2000, you have several options, which are contrasted in Table 8.12.

**TABLE 8.12:**   Strategies for Migrating Older Secured Databases to Access

| Strategy | Advantages | Disadvantages |
| --- | --- | --- |
| Convert your secured database while joined to your existing Access workgroup file; after conversion, continue to use the old Access workgroup file | Easy | Performance will likely be worse because Jet will need to work with two different database versions. In addition, if you're migrating from Access 2, you won't be able to take advantage of new security features, such as the ability of non-Admins members to view their group membership |

**TABLE 8.12:**   Strategies for Migrating Older Secured Databases to Access *(continued)*

| Strategy | Advantages | Disadvantages |
| --- | --- | --- |
| Convert your secured database; create a new Access 2000 workgroup file with the same WID; create the same accounts with the same SIDs as the old Access workgroup | Takes full advantage of new security features | Requires you to have a written record of all accounts and PIDs |
| Document existing security system (account names, group membership, object permissions); unsecure database by assigning all permissions of all objects to the Users group; convert the unsecured database; rebuild security system from the ground up using different PIDs | Takes full advantage of new security features; can be used when you don't have a written record of the workgroup WID or account SIDs | Requires the most work |

In general, it's best to use the second or third strategy from Table 8.12, especially if you're upgrading from Access 2. Even when upgrading from a later version of Access, however, you'll likely realize better performance by using an Access 2000 version of the workgroup file.

**NOTE**    Regardless of which version you are migrating from, you no longer will be able to secure VBA modules using Jet workgroup security. You'll need to password-protect your VBA project (see the "Security for Modules" section earlier in this chapter for more details).

# Jet Security and Linked Tables

When you secure linked tables in an application database of a classic split database architecture (see Chapter 2), you are securing only the links, not the data in the tables. To properly secure the data, you must secure the tables in the *data database*. Don't bother securing the links stored in the application database; this security will be overlaid on top of the security of the data tables and doesn't really add anything because users will always be able to directly open the tables in the data database.

To link to (or refresh links to) tables in the data database, users must have Open/Run permission to the data database and Modify Design permission to the linked tables in the application database.

# Access Project (ADP) Security

If you're working with an Access project file (ADP) rather than a Jet database (MDB), you no longer are working with Jet security. To secure the objects in an Access project, you must use one or more of the following:

- To secure tables, stored procedures, and other SQL Server/MSDE objects, you must use SQL Server's security system.

- To secure modules you can use a VBA project password. See the "Security for Modules" section earlier in this chapter for more details.

- To secure forms, reports, and modules, you can remove the source code for the project by converting it to an ADE file (the ADP version of an MDE file). You can do this by selecting Tools ➤ Database Utilities ➤ Make ADE File. (Make sure you keep the original ADP file for making schema changes.)

- To secure data access pages, you can publish the pages to a secured Web server. See the "Security for Data Access Pages" sidebar earlier in this chapter for more details.

In this section, we'll introduce you to SQL Server's security system and discuss how to secure the database objects in an ADP file.

---

**NOTE**    In many larger enterprises, you may be prevented from directly manipulating security settings of a SQL Server database. In these cases, you will need to work with your company's database administrator (DBA) to manipulate the SQL Server database security. Even in these cases, however, you'll likely find this section's discussion of SQL Server's security system helpful.

---

# SQL Server Security Overview

SQL Server security is a bit more complex than Jet security. Before you can begin to understand SQL Server security, you must first understand the following terms:

**Logins**   Before a user can log on to a SQL Server server, he or she must have a login ID. SQL Server supports the integration with the Windows NT and Windows 2000 security systems so that you can add Windows NT/2000 login accounts to a server. You can also create SQL Server logins; this is necessary if Windows 95/98 users will be logging into the server.

**Users**   While the login ID allows a user onto the server, it won't allow the user to do anything with a database until that login ID also becomes a database user. To complicate things, a login ID can point to a database user of a different name.

**Groups**   You can set permissions on two different kinds of user groupings: groups and roles. The term *groups* applies only to Windows NT/2000 groups. If you wish to apply permissions to groups of SQL Server users that are not Windows NT/2000 groups, then you need to use *roles*.

**Roles**   For the most part, roles work pretty much like Jet security groups, despite the different name. SQL Server predefines a number of fixed roles (for example, public, sysadmin, and db_owner). In addition, you can create user-defined roles. Roles can contain users, groups, and even other roles.

**Application Roles**   In addition to standard roles, SQL Server lets you create special application roles. Application roles are useful when you wish your applications to log in and assume their own permission settings independent of the user.

**Permissions**   You can assign permissions to objects for users, groups, and roles (including application roles).

---

**TIP**   Just like when dealing with Jet security, it's best to assign permissions for objects to roles rather than individual users.

---

## Managing SQL Security from an ADP File

From an ADP file, you manage SQL Server security using the SQL Server Security dialog box. To display this dialog box, shown in Figure 8.15, select Tools ➤ Security ➤ Database Security.

From this single dialog box, you can manage SQL Server logins, users, groups, roles, and set permissions on server objects.

---

**NOTE**   If you are using SQL Server, you may prefer to use SQL Server Enterprise Manager to manage security settings. Enterprise Manager gives you added power and flexibility. You can also use Transact-SQL and system stored procedures to manage SQL Server security.

---

## Authentication Systems

SQL Server can use one of two basic authentication systems:

**NT Authentication**   Users don't have to log in to SQL Server because their Windows NT/2000 login ID is passed along to SQL Server.

**SQL Server Authentication**   Users log in to SQL Server separately. You need to use this authentication system if Windows 95/98 users or non-Windows or Internet users will be logging into the database.

If SQL Server or MSDE is running on a Windows NT or Windows 2000 operating system, you can use either authentication system or both. If SQL Server or MSDE is running on a Windows 95 or Windows 98 desktop operating system, your only option is to use SQL Server authentication.

# Managing SQL Server Logins, Users, and Roles

Before you can assign permissions to SQL Server objects, you need to create SQL Server logins, users, and roles. In most cases, you'll want to create roles first and then logins and users. Before we discuss how to create these accounts, we need to talk about SQL Server's default account: SA.

## The SA Login ID

Every SQL Server installation starts with a single login, SA (which stands for server administrator), with a blank password. In many ways, the SA account is similar to the Admin account in Jet. This account is a member of the System Administrators server role, which means that the SA account has full access to all databases on the server. The first step to securing any SQL Server installation is to add a password to this very important account. You should avoid using this account thereafter. The SA login maps to the DBO (for database owner) user in each SQL Server database.

## Creating Roles

Think of roles as equivalent to Jet groups. To create a new user-defined role from the SQL Server Security dialog box, select the Database Roles tab and click the Add button as shown in Figure 8.16. Access displays the Database Roles Properties dialog box as shown Figure 8.17.

At the Database Roles Properties – New Role dialog box, enter the name for the new role in the Name textbox, select the Standard Role radio button, and click the OK button to create the new role. If you wish to add members at this time, you can click the Add button prior to clicking the OK button. You'll see the Add Role Members dialog box as shown in Figure 8.18.

FIGURE 8.16
The Databases Roles tab of
the SQL Server Security
dialog box

FIGURE 8.17
The Database Roles
Properties – New Role
dialog box

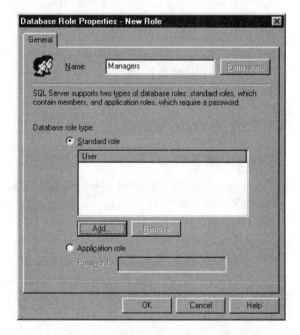

**NOTE**   You can't associate permissions for objects with roles until you first create the role. Once created, you can return to the Database Roles Properties dialog box and click the Permissions button to set permissions. This is discussed in more detail in the "Securing SQL Server Objects" section later in this chapter.

**FIGURE 8.18**
The Add Role Members
dialog box

## Creating Logins

Before you can create a user account for a database, you must first create a login ID. Recall that a login ID gets you into the server, whereas the user account gets you into a particular database.

To create a new login ID and user account, select the Server Logins tab of the SQL Server Security dialog box (shown earlier in Figure 8.15) and click Add. Access displays the SQL Server Login Properties – New Login dialog box as shown in Figure 8.19.

What you do next at the SQL Server Login Properties – New Login dialog box depends on whether you are creating a login from an existing Windows NT authenticated user account or creating a new SQL Server authentication login from scratch.

**FIGURE 8.19**
The General tab of the SQL
Server Login Properties –
New Login dialog box

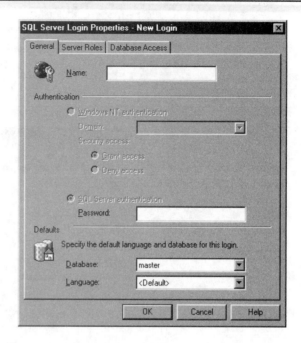

If you're creating a login from an existing Windows NT authenticated user account, select the Windows NT/2000 domain, from the Domain drop-down control, and then enter the name of the user in the Name textbox in the format *domain\user*. (You can also enter the name of a Windows NT/2000 group to add the group to SQL Server.)

If you're creating a new SQL Server authentication login from scratch, enter the name of the user in the Name text box and the password for the user in the SQL Server authentication password text box.

Regardless of which type of login ID you are creating, you can also specify a default database and language for the login.

At this point, you can either click the OK button to create the login or first add the login to one or more databases and roles.

## Giving Login IDs Administrative Capabilities

If the new login ID will need to perform administrative duties, select the Server Roles tab to add the user to one or more fixed server roles. The Server Roles tab is shown in Figure 8.20.

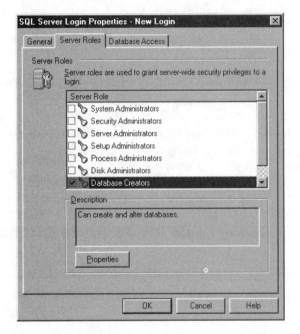

Adding a login to one of these roles is similar to adding a Jet user to the Admins group. What's different, however, is that SQL Server has broken up the administrator job into a number of smaller pieces. You can select from one or more of the following fixed server roles:

**System Administrators (sysadmin)**   Members of this role can perform any SQL Server activity. In other words, this is the president, CEO, and chairman of the board of SQL Server security. This is the SQL Server equivalent of the Admins group.

**Security Administrators (sercurityadmin)**   Members of this role can manage logins and permissions.

**Server Administrators (serveradmin)**    Members of this role can configure the server.

**Setup Administrators (setupadmin)**    Members of this role can manage linked servers, replication, and startup procedures.

**Process Administrators (processadmin)**    Members of this role can manage and shut down processes.

**Disk Administrators (diskadmin)**    Members of this role can manage disk files.

**Database Creators (dbcreator)**    Members of this role can create and manage the schema of databases.

---

| **TIP** | Be careful about adding users to the fixed server roles. Only add a user to one of the fixed server roles if that user will need to perform an administrative task such as creating databases or managing security. |
|---|---|

---

## Giving Login IDs Access to Databases

Select the Database Access tab of the SQL Server Login Properties – New Login dialog box to make the login ID a user in one or more databases and a member or one or more database roles. The Database Access tab is shown in Figure 8.21.

---

**FIGURE 8.21**

The Database Access tab
of the SQL Server Login
Properties – New Login
dialog box

To give the login access to a database, select the checkbox next to the database name in the upper portion of the dialog box. SQL Server responds by adding the login ID name to the User column for the selected database. If you want to, you can change the username to an alias that's different from the login ID. This allows you to log in to the server using one name, but appear to the database under another name. (In fact, this is what happens with the SA login which appears in each database under the name "DBO".) To avoid confusion, it's best to keep the login and usernames the same.

Once you've added a login to a database, you can add the user to one or more roles for the database. Select the name of the database in the upper portion of the dialog box and then select one or more roles in the lower portion of the dialog box. You can add the user to both fixed database roles and user-defined roles.

The fixed database roles are summarized here:

**public**   All users are members of this role which is very similar conceptually to the Jet Users group.

**db_owner**   Members of this role can do anything with the database.

**db_accessadmin**   Members of this role can manage logins for the database.

**db_securityadmin**   Members of this role can manage permissions and roles for the database.

**db_ddladmin**   Members of this role can create and update the schema of database objects.

**db_backupopertor**   Members of this role can back up the database.

**db_datareader**   Members of this role can read data from any table in the database.

**db_datawriter**   Members of this role can modify data in any table in the database.

**db_denydatareader**   Members of this role are prevented from reading data from any table in the database.

**db_denydatawriter**   Members of this role are prevented from updating data in any table in the database.

While the fixed database roles can be useful, more than likely you'll also want to add users to your own user-defined roles.

# Securing SQL Server Objects

You can view and set permissions for objects for both users and roles using the SQL Server Security dialog box. But before we show you how, we must first discuss how permissions work in SQL Server.

## Explicit and Implicit SQL Server Permissions

For the most part, SQL Server permissions are inherited just like Jet's permissions. That is, users inherit the permissions from any roles to which they belong just like Jet users inherit permissions from any groups to which they belong. There is one important difference, however. In SQL Server, you can remove permissions from a user or role in two different ways:

- If you *revoke* a permission from a user or role, the user or role may still acquire the permission implicitly by any roles to which the user or role belongs. This is how Jet security works.

- If you *deny* a permission to a user or role, the user or role cannot acquire the permission, regardless of whether the user or role belongs to any roles that have that permission. That is, when you deny a permission it can not be acquired implicitly. The only way a user can reacquire a denied permission is to have that permission explicitly granted back to the user.

## Viewing and Setting SQL Server Permissions

To view or set permissions for a role or user, select the appropriate tab—Database Users or Database Roles—of the SQL Server Security dialog box, select the account for which you wish to set permissions, and click the Edit button. Access displays the Database Users or Database Roles Properties dialog box, as shown in Figures 8.22 and 8.23.

From the Database Users or Roles Properties dialog box, click the Permissions button to display the Permissions tab of the Database Users/Roles Properties dialog box, shown in Figure 8.24.

**FIGURE 8.22**
The Database Users
Properties dialog box for
the user Geoff

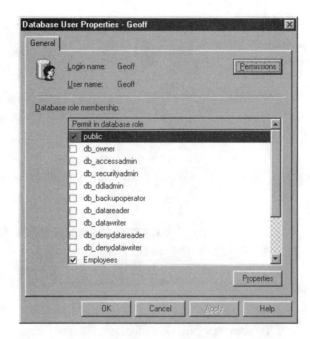

**FIGURE 8.23**
The Database Roles Proper-
ties dialog box for the
Employees role

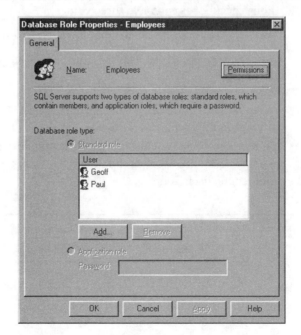

**FIGURE 8.24**
You can use this dialog box
to update the permissions
of SQL Server objects and
statements.

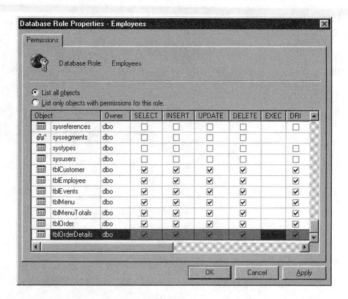

To alter a permission displayed on the Permissions tab, click the permission checkbox next to the object for which you wish to set permissions. The permissions checkboxes can have three values:

- A checkmark indicates that the permission is *granted* to the user or role.

- Nothing in the checkbox indicates that the permission is *revoked* from the user or role.

- A red X indicates that the permission is *denied* to the user or role.

You can toggle between the three different states by repeatedly clicking on a permission checkbox. Click the Apply button to commit your changes. In Figure 8.25 we have granted, revoked, and denied various permission for the tblCustomer table to the user Geoff.

**TIP**   The ability to deny permissions that cannot be acquired implicitly is a valuable feature of SQL Server's security system.

**FIGURE 8.25**
Geoff has been granted
Select and Insert permissions to tblCustomer, the
Update permission has
been revoked, and the
Delete permission has been
denied.

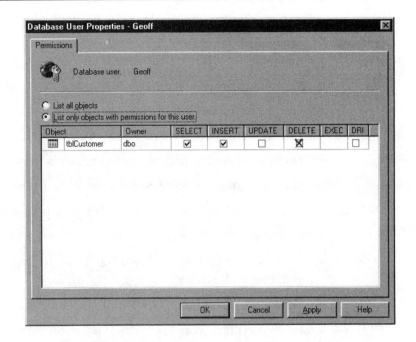

**NOTE**    See *SQL Server 7 In Record Time* by Mike Gunderloy and Mary Chipman (Sybex, 1999) for a more complete discussion of SQL Server security.

# Summary

In this chapter we have covered security in detail. You should now have a good understanding of the Jet and SQL Server security models and how best to take advantage of them.

You have learned:

- The basic structure of the Jet security model

- How to set database passwords

- How to use the more powerful workgroup-based Jet security model

- That Jet workgroup-based security is made up of two components: user and group accounts stored in the workgroup file and object permissions stored in each database

- How to enable Jet security

- How to use the Access security menus to manage Jet security

- How to create a secure Jet workgroup file

- How to manage Jet user and group accounts

- How the Jet built-in user and group accounts work

- How to manage Jet object permissions for users

- The difference between explicit and implicit permissions

- How object and database ownership works in Jet security

- What Jet OwnerAccess queries are and how to use them to get column-level and row-level security

- How to set a VBA project password to secure code

- How encryption works and what it has to do with security

- How to program security using DAO, ADOX, and SQL

- How to properly secure and unsecure Jet databases

- How to migrate secured Jet databases to Access 2000

- How to secure Access Data Project (ADP) files

- How SQL Server and MSDE security works

- How to use the ADP security menus to manage SQL Server/MDSE security

- How to create SQL Server login IDs, roles, and user accounts

- How to grant, revoke, and deny permissions to SQL Server users and roles

- How to view and set permissions for SQL Server objects

# Mastering Replication

■ Understanding how replication works

■ Using Replication Manager

■ Creating a custom conflict-resolution function

■ Synchronizing data over the Internet

■ Creating partial replicas

■ Configuring SQL Server merge replication with Jet subscribers

If you wanted to keep two or more copies of a database synchronized using Access 2, you faced many hurdles. In fact, this functionality required so much coding that few developers attempted it. Microsoft changed all that with the addition of replication support to Access 95. With each subsequent release of Access and the Jet engine, replication has gotten better and better. In this chapter we discuss Jet replication in detail, including how replication works and when to use it. In addition, we discuss how to replicate and synchronize databases and manage replication conflicts—both through the built-in user interfaces and programmatically. Finally, we also discuss how SQL Server replication works and how to synchronize between SQL Server and Jet databases.

---

**NOTE**    There are two sample databases for this chapter: CH09.MDB and CH09DAO.MDB. Neither is replicated. CH09.MDB contains all of the examples discussed in the chapter, including the examples that use JRO to programmatically manipulate replication. CH09DAO.MDB contains many equivalent examples coded using the older DAO object model. These versions of the examples are not discussed in the chapter, but are included here for those readers who wish to use DAO.

---

# Jet Replication: What Is It and How Does It Work?

Access or Jet *replication* allows you to make special copies of a regular MDB database that are enabled in such a way that you can easily transfer changes made in one copy to each of the other copies. There are three basic parts to replication:

1. Replication

2. Synchronization

3. Conflict resolution

## Replication

When you convert a normal Access MDB database into a replication-enabled database, Jet makes a number of changes to the schema of the database that enables the database to clone or replicate itself. These schema changes, which are discussed in more detail later in the chapter, include the addition of system tables, the modification of existing tables, and the creation of new properties of the database and many of its objects.

When you convert a nonreplicated database into a replicated database, you end up with the *design master* of a new *replica set*. A replica set of one, however, is not very useful since you wouldn't have anyone to swap changes with, so you normally create a second member of the replica set by replicating the design master. You can create additional members of a replica set by replicating any of its existing replicas.

The design master is a special member of a replica set. You can make schema changes only in the design master. You can make changes to data in any replica of a replica set. The decentralized replication model Jet uses is termed a *multi-master* replication model.

---

**NOTE**    In contrast to Jet's multi-master replication model, SQL Server uses a publish-and-subscribe replication model.

---

 Previous versions of Access and Jet supported two classes of replicas: ordinary (or full) replicas, and partial replicas. *Partial replicas* differ from ordinary replicas in that they contain a filtered subset of the database and can only synchronize with an ordinary replica. Jet 4.0 adds support for *replica visibility*, which allows you more flexible control over which replicas can synchronize with other replicas. In addition, Jet 4.0 lets you create special *prevent deletes* replicas that disallow record deletions.

## Synchronization

When you make updates to a replica that's a member of a replica set, Jet tracks the updates using the extra tables and fields it added to the database when you first replicated it. Jet does not, however, send changes to the other members of the replica set without your intervention. In fact, unlike networked databases in a multi-user file-server or client-server environment, replicas are not connected except when you temporarily connect them—two at a time—during a *synchronization exchange*.

When you synchronize two replicas, Jet sends updates from one replica to another. What makes replication so useful is that Jet sends only the *updates*. This makes synchronization much more efficient than importing and exporting records between two nonreplicated databases. Normally, synchronization occurs in both directions, but you can elect to synchronize in only one direction if you wish. It's up to you to control when synchronization occurs and between which replicas.

## Conflict Resolution

A conflict is triggered any time a change to a row made in one replica conflicts with a change to a row made in another replica. Jet notifies you of conflicts after a synchronization exchange.

Prior to Access 2000, the Jet engine used a row-level tracking system for conflicts. Thus, a modification to the same row in two replicas caused a *conflict*. Access 2000 and Jet 4.0 now support column-level tracking of changes in addition to the older row-level tracking. This means that if one user changed the description of a menu item in one replica and another user changed the price of the same menu item in another replica, a conflict would not be triggered under column-level conflict tracking. Jet 4.0 allows you to determine for each table whether you wish to use column- or row-level conflict tracking.

---

**NOTE**    Column-level tracking is the default for new replicated databases. Row-level tracking is the default for replicas converted from earlier versions of Access.

---

Prior to Access 2000, Jet used an algorithm to determine which record's changes were preserved that was based on which replica modified the record the greatest number of times. Access 2000 and Jet 4.0 now resolve conflicts based on a priority-based algorithm. Each replica is assigned a priority and the highest priority replica wins in the event of a conflict.

Also new for Access 2000 and Jet 4.0: Microsoft has dispensed with replication errors. In prior versions of Access, Jet would mark certain types of synchronization problems as data or design errors. Errors often blocked synchronization and required developer intervention to fix. Jet 4.0 unifies the treatment of the older conflicts and errors so that everything is now simply a conflict. These changes make resolution much simpler.

Access 2000 includes the Replication Conflict Viewer, which you can use to alter this automated decision and swap the winning and losing records. In addition, you can write a custom conflict resolution function to use instead of the Replication Conflict Viewer.

# When to Use Replication

When you stop and think about it, replication is nothing more than a different way to share a database. Replication offers a major advantage over the more traditional file-server and client-server approaches: replicas don't have to be physically connected except during synchronization. Replication does have several drawbacks, however. For example, replication:

- Adds overhead to a database

- Can't guarantee that a record is updated by only one user at a time

- Increases the likelihood that a record will be in different states for different users at the same time

- Changes AutoNumber fields so they assign numbers randomly

You shouldn't use replication for situations in which the more classic file-sharing approaches are better suited. In many cases, it will be fairly obvious which file-sharing strategy is best suited for your particular application, but there are some situations where no one solution is obvious. The next few sections explore some of these situations.

**WARNING**   Replication may significantly slow down larger Access applications. It also may require you to make a number of application changes to compensate for some of replication's side effects. Any move of an existing database application to replication requires careful planning and testing. Don't replicate your production database without testing!

## Local Area Networks

When designing a system for a local area network (LAN), you may have difficulty deciding whether to:

- Share a single copy of a nonreplicated database (or at least a single copy of a "data" database in a classic split Access database system—see Chapter 2 for more details) across a workgroup

  *or*

- Distribute replicated copies of the database to each user and regularly synchronize changes between the replicated copies

In most cases, the more traditional file-server approach makes more sense because of the need for the immediate dissemination of updates to all users. In a replicated system, there is a greater time lag between the dissemination of updates. This lag period may vary from an hour to several hours or days, depending on the number of users, the volume of updates, the frequency of conflicts, the synchronization topology, and the synchronization schedule.

On the other hand, using replication in this scenario might make sense if:

- Data is updated infrequently

- Updates do not usually affect other users

- The network is already overloaded

- The network is often down

In these cases, it might make sense to use a replicated database instead of the traditional file-server approach.

---

**TIP**  Another alternative, especially when you have an overloaded network and can't afford to move to a client-server system, might be to create a hybrid system that uses replication *and* file-server sharing. Create multiple workgroups, each tied to a workgroup server machine. Users within a workgroup would use a split database system with the data database residing on the workgroup's file server. The data database would be replicated across workgroup servers, which would be synchronized on a regular schedule. This hybrid system would distribute the load over multiple servers. *Update latency*—the time it takes for an update to be propagated to all replicas in the replica set—would be small within a workgroup but would be greater between machines in different workgroups.

---

# Wide Area Networks

Wide area networks (WANs) are usually larger than LANs (have more nodes) and are spread out across greater distances. Perhaps most important, the speed of the connection between two nodes (computers) on a WAN is slower than on a LAN. These factors usually rule out the use of a file-server sharing model on a WAN in favor of a client-server system. On the other hand, you may wish to consider using replication instead of a classic client-server system when using a WAN. Recall that synchronization exchanges transfer only the changed records, not whole tables, which makes replication well suited for WANs.

Replication may make sense on a WAN if:

- Data is updated infrequently
- Updates do not usually affect other users
- The network is already overloaded
- The network is often down
- The move to a client-server system is considered too expensive

On the other hand, replication is probably not a good candidate if:

- There are a great number of updates, especially if multiple users will be updating the same records (creating a potentially large number of conflicts)
- There is a need for the immediate dissemination of updates to all users
- Data consistency is critical

In these situations, you'd be better off using a more classic client-server, transaction-oriented approach or the replication services of SQL Server or another server database.

# Loosely Connected Networks

Mobile users on laptops that connect to a network infrequently or that connect over slow modem lines do not fit well into the classic file-server or client-server system, especially when two-way transfer of updates is needed. This type of system is often ideally suited for Jet replication.

*Partial replication* is especially attractive for loosely connected networks because you can partition tables so that each replica receives only a small subset of the rows present in the master database. See the "Partial Replication" section later in the chapter for more details.

## Other Replication Uses

Replication may also be useful in the following situations:

- Warm backups
- Distribution of application updates

Even if you decide not to use replication to share data in a file-server environment, you may wish to consider using it for maintaining warm backups. By replicating a database and regularly (perhaps every 15 minutes or hourly) synchronizing it with another replica, you'll be ready in the event of a disaster that corrupts or destroys your main database. And if the backup replica is located on a different machine—perhaps even in another building—you're insulating yourself even further if the server itself goes down.

You may also wish to consider using replication to distribute application updates. This could significantly reduce the maintenance burden associated with updating an application that has been distributed to tens or hundreds of workstations. In this situation, you'd synchronize with each workstation to distribute your update.

In both these scenarios, you'd have to weigh the potential benefits of using replication against the extra overhead replication adds to a database. (See the "Changes Made to a Database When It Is Replicated" section later in this chapter for more on replication overhead.)

# The Many Faces of Replication

You can replicate and synchronize Jet databases through a variety of means, as shown in Table 9.1. Each method has its own set of advantages and disadvantages, as described in more detail in the next few sections. Your situation will usually dictate which method to choose. For example, if you're developing an application that will be run by sophisticated power users, you may wish to employ the Access menus. On the other hand, if you're developing an application for naive users, you'll want to use JRO or Replication Manager, or some combination of the two.

**TABLE 9.1:** Various Mechanisms for Managing Jet Replication

| Method | Advantages | Disadvantages | Comments |
|---|---|---|---|
| Windows Briefcase | Simple drag-and-drop action; can be performed by users. | Requires user intervention; cannot be controlled programmatically; requires Windows Briefcase; can only create full replicas. | Not as simple as it seems; can be confusing for some users; very limited capabilities. |
| Access menus | Simple; can be performed by users; includes basic conflict-management facility; supports partial replicas, replica visibility, and prevent deletes replicas. | Requires user intervention and an understanding of basic replication terminology. | Requires retail copy of Access on each desktop. |
| JRO | Can be automated; insulates user from process; doesn't require Access; can create and populate partial replicas; supports replica visibility, replica priorities, and indirect synchronization. | Requires programming; no built-in conflict-management mechanism; can't create prevent deletes replicas. | Probably the best solution for most developers. |
| DAO | Can be automated; insulates user from process; doesn't require Access; can create and populate partial replicas. | Requires programming; no built-in conflict management mechanism; doesn't support replica visibility, replica priorities, prevent deletes replicas, or indirect synchronization. | JRO is a better choice. |
| Replication Manager | Can be automated; doesn't require Access. | Not all aspects of replication can be handled with Replication Manager. Not included with Visual Basic or Visual C++; doesn't support replica visibility, replica priorities, or prevent deletes replicas. | Only a partial solution; you will need to supplement with JRO or the Access menus. |

# Briefcase Replication

The Windows Briefcase is an operating system utility that makes it easy for users to manage files on multiple PCs. Typically, you drag files to and from the Briefcase on your laptop. The Briefcase makes it easy to keep multiple copies of the same files synchronized. Normally, the Briefcase works at the file level, performing simple file date/time comparisons to ensure that the most recent copy of a file is never overwritten.

If you choose the replication option when you install Access, it registers a special Jet replication reconciler to be used instead of Briefcase's normal reconciler when an MDB file is dragged to and from the Briefcase. With the Jet replication reconciler installed and registered, the first time you drag an MDB file to the Briefcase, the MDB file is converted into a replication design master, and on your laptop, a replica of the database is made. Thereafter, when you choose the Update option within the Briefcase, the two replicas of the database are synchronized using the Jet replication reconciler.

To use the Windows Briefcase-based replication facilities, you must have:

- The Windows Briefcase installed

- Access on the laptop with the replication option installed

There's no way to automate Briefcase replication or integrate it into an existing application, so its use for the professional developer is limited. In addition, Briefcase replication doesn't support many of the newer replication features, such as partial replicas and replica visibility.

---

**WARNING**    Once the special Jet replication reconciler has been registered, the Briefcase will attempt to replicate or synchronize all MDB files, even if the MDB file is an nonreplicated database. There's no way to direct the Briefcase to perform file date/time comparisons only for certain MDB files.

---

## Access Menu-Based Replication

The Access user interface includes a set of menus found under Tools ➤ Replication that expose most of the Jet replication functionality to the Access user. The Access replication menus are summarized in Table 9.2

**TABLE 9.2:**    Access Replication Menus

| Menu | Description |
| --- | --- |
| Synchronize Now | Specifies another replica with which to synchronize; can also be used to transfer design master status to another replica. |
| Create Replica | For nonreplicated databases, creates a design master and a second replica; for replicated databases, creates an additional replica. |

**TABLE 9.2:**   Access Replication Menus *(continued)*

| Menu | Description |
|------|-------------|
| Partial Replica Wizard | Starts the Partial Replica Wizard that guides you through the process of creating and populating a partial replica; for Access 97, you had to download this wizard; Access 2000 integrates into to the product. |
| Resolve Conflicts | If there are synchronization conflict records in the currently open replica, this command opens the Microsoft Replication Conflict Viewer, which you can use to resolve conflict records. (This command is automatically executed when you open a replica that contains synchronization conflicts.) |
| Recover Design Master | If the currently open replica is not the design master, you can use this command to make this replica the design master for the replica set. You should use this command only if the design master has been damaged or destroyed. |

# Programming Replication Using Data Access Objects (DAO)

In prior versions of Access, you programmatically manipulated Jet replication using DAO. Access 2000 and Jet 4.0 have introduced Jet and Replication Objects (JRO), an ADO-compatible object model for programming replication. While it's still supported, Microsoft has not updated DAO replication support in Jet 4.0. Thus, DAO doesn't support any of the new features of Jet 4.0, such as replica priority, replica visibility, or indirect synchronization.

## Undocumented DAO MakeReplica Constants

Actually, DAO *does* support replica visibility, read-only replicas, and prevent deletes replicas through some undocumented constants you can use with the MakeReplica method:

```
Const dbRepMakePartial = &H1
Const dbRepMakeReadOnly = &H2
Const dbRepMakePreventDeletes = &H4
Const dbRepMakeGlobal = &H1000
Const dbRepMakeLocal = &H2000
Const dbRepMakeAnonymous = &H4000
```

The first two of these six constants are defined in the DAO type library, so you can use them without defining them. You'll need to define the last four before using them. Because they are undocumented, you should use these DAO constants with caution.

If you have older replication applications using DAO, and you don't want to take advantage of the new replication features, you can still use DAO. If you're creating new replication applications or want to take advantage of the new features of Jet 4.0, however, you should migrate to JRO.

---

With a few minor exceptions, you can use the Jet and Replication Objects (JRO) object model to do anything that DAO can do and more. Thus, we haven't included DAO code examples in this chapter. You will find on the CD that accompanies this book, however, a sample database, CH09DAO.MDB, that contains equivalent examples to many of the JRO examples.

---

## Programming Replication Using Jet and Replication Objects (JRO)

Briefcase replication and replication through the Access menus may be useful, but if you're a developer, you're probably most concerned about how to programmatically manipulate replication from Jet and Replication Objects (JRO) and VBA. The good news is that it's all—okay not 100% but 99% of it—there. Everything you can do from the Windows Briefcase or the Access menus is programmable through JRO—from Access, Visual Basic, and Visual C++.

The JRO object model is shown in Figure 9.1. The methods and properties of the JRO objects are summarized in Table 9.3.

---

**FIGURE 9.1**
The JRO object model has only a few objects.

**TABLE 9.3:**   The Methods and Properties of the JRO Objects

| Object/ Collection | Property or Method? | Item | Description |
|---|---|---|---|
| Jet Engine | Method | Compact Database | Compacts the database |
| | | RefreshCache | Forces pending writes and refreshes memory with database data |
| Replica | Property | ActiveConnection | ADO Connection object to which replica belongs; read/write |
| | | ConflictFunction | Name of conflict resolution function to call; read/write |
| | | ConflictTables | Returns a recordset containing a list of tables and their associated conflict tables; read only |
| | | DesignMasterID | Returns the unique identifier of the design master replica; can also be used to make the current replica the design master; read/write |
| | | Priority | Relative priority of replica for conflict resolution; read/write |
| | | ReplicaID | Unique identifier for replica; read only |
| | | ReplicaType | Returns a constant that indicates the type of replica (jrRepTypeDesignMaster, jrRepTypeFull, jrRepTypeNotReplicable, jrRepTypePartial); read only |
| | | RetentionPeriod | Number of days to keep replication histories (may range from 5 to 32,000); read/write for design master; read only for other replicas; defaults to 60 for replicas created by DAO, JRO, or Replication Manager; defaults to 1000 for replicas created by Access |
| | | Visibility | Visibility of replica (jrRepVisibilityAnon, jrRepVisibilityGlobal, jrRepVisibilityLocal); read only |
| | Method | CreateReplica | Creates a new replica |
| | | GetObjectReplica bility | In a replicated database, returns True if an object is replicated; in a nonreplicated database, returns True if object will be replicated |

**TABLE 9.3:**   The Methods and Properties of the JRO Objects *(continued)*

| Object/ Collection | Property or Method? | Item | Description |
|---|---|---|---|
| | | MakeReplicable | Converts a nonreplicated database into a replicated design master |
| | | PopulatePartial | Populates a partial replica with rows |
| | | SetObject-Replicability | Makes an object replicable or local; does not apply to Access objects (forms, reports, data access pages, macros, and modules) |
| | | Synchronize | Initiates a synchronization exchange with another replica |
| Filters | Property | Count | Returns the number of Filter objects; read only |
| | | Item | Returns a Filter object |
| | Method | Append | Adds a new Filter object to the Filters collection |
| | | Delete | Removes a Filter object from the Filters collection |
| | | Refresh | Refreshes the Filters collection |
| Filter | Property | FilterCriteria | Specifies the criteria that must be met for the record to be replicated to a partial replica; read/write before filter is set; read only after it has been set |
| | | FilterType | Type of filter (jrFltrTypeTable, jrFltrTypeRelationships); read/write before filter is set; read only after it has been set |
| | | TableName | Name of table to which filter applies; read/write before filter is set; read only after it has been set |

# Replication Manager

If you've purchased a copy of the Microsoft Office Developer, you have an additional mechanism for managing replication and synchronization: Replication Manager and its companion program, Synchronizer. Replication Manager is shown in Figure 9.2.

**FIGURE 9.2**
Replication Manager is managing two replicas on a local area network. The replica set also contains a third unmanaged replica.

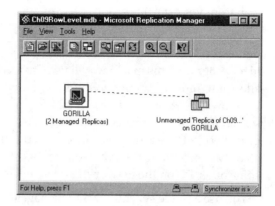

Using Replication Manager, you can:

- Replicate a database
- Create additional replicas for a replica set
- Synchronize replicas
- Create a regular synchronization schedule for a replica set
- Review the synchronization history of a replica
- Manage various replica properties
- Set up a synchronization scheme for remote sites
- Set up Internet/intranet synchronization

Replication Manager makes it easy to plan your replication topology and manage the synchronization schedules for a replica set. This allows you to set up a regular synchronization schedule without programming. It also comes in handy if you need to review the synchronization history for a replica set.

## Synchronizers

You use Replication Manager to create replicas, design replication topologies, and set up synchronization schedules, but it is the accompanying Synchronizer program that actually carries out the scheduled synchronization exchanges, moving data between replicas at the times you have designated using Replication Manager. When you install Replication Manager, it defaults to loading Synchronizer when you start Windows. If you don't plan on using Replication Manager and

Synchronizer to perform synchronization, you'll want to remove the Synchronizer icon from your startup group.

When you use Replication Manager and Synchronizer to manage synchronization of replicas on your LAN, you need to decide which PC will host the Synchronizer program. This machine will need to load Synchronizer upon bootup and allow it to remain running in the background. If your LAN server runs under Windows 95/98 or Windows NT/2000, you can run Synchronizer directly on the server. If your server runs under NetWare, Windows for Workgroups, or some other network operating system, or you'd rather not increase the load on an already overburdened server, you can elect to run the Synchronizer program from some other PC on the network.

You use a single synchronizer to manage the synchronization of all replicas on a LAN. On a WAN, or in a distributed system of workgroups occasionally connected by modem, you need to use multiple synchronizers, one for each workgroup. Each synchronizer manages the synchronization schedule of the local workgroup's replicas and cooperatively manages (along with the other sites' synchronizers) the synchronization between workgroups. See the "Replication Topologies" section later in this chapter for more information on replicating over a WAN.

## The Replication Manager Map

The Replication Manager user interface can be a bit confusing. For locally managed replicas, Replication Manager draws a single machine icon (labeled with the machine name) on the screen (the map) to represent a replica set. The total number of local replicas managed by the local synchronizer appears below the icon.

If replicas in the selected replica set are managed by multiple synchronizers, Replication Manager draws an icon for each synchronizer site (see Figure 9.3).

**FIGURE 9.3**

This replica set is managed by two synchronizers: one on the local PC (GORILLA) and another on the remote PC (COHO).

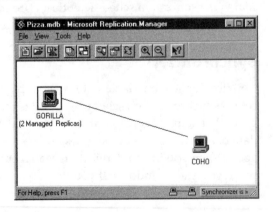

# Replication Topologies

When replicating a database, you must decide on a synchronization topology and schedule for the replica set. The *topology* defines which replicas exchange updates with which other replicas and the direction of these exchanges. The *schedule* defines when the exchanges occur and who initiates the exchanges. The topology and schedule you choose for your replica set affect the update latency.

## LAN Topologies

Various topologies that might be used on a LAN are depicted in Figure 9.4 and contrasted in Table 9.4.

**FIGURE 9.4**
Common replication topologies for a local area network

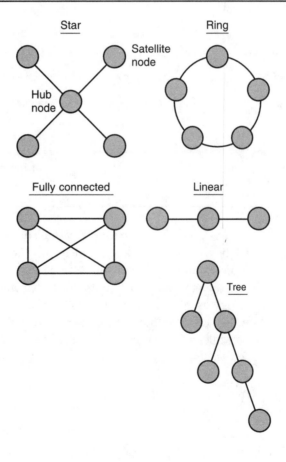

**TABLE 9.4:** Contrasting Various Replication Topologies

| Topology | Latency | Load Distribution | Network Traffic | Reliability | Comments |
|---|---|---|---|---|---|
| Star | Moderate | Uneven | Low | Good as long as hub doesn't fail; bad if hub fails | Appropriate for many situations. Two rounds of synchronization exchanges may be necessary to fully propagate updates. |
| Ring | Moderate | Even | Low | Good if direction can be reversed in the event of a node failure | Appropriate for many situations, especially when you need to evenly distribute the load. |
| Fully connected | Low | Even | High | Good | Best latency but the most network traffic. Appropriate for applications with a small number of nodes where latency must be kept to a minimum. |
| Linear | High | Even | Low | Bad; if any node fails, synchronization is disrupted | Simple to implement but worst update latency. May be appropriate for single-master model (data updates made only to the design master). |
| Tree | Variable | Uneven | Low | Depends on where the failure occurs | May be most efficient for applications where data updates occur only in selected nodes. |

Which synchronization topology you choose will depend on the importance of latency, network load, and synchronization reliability. If a very short latency is of utmost importance, network traffic is not a concern, and you don't have many nodes, then you may wish to use the fully connected topology. Otherwise, the star topology usually works best, with the ring topology another good choice. Replication Manager uses the star topology for locally managed replicas. The replica in the middle of a star topology is called the *hub replica*, and the other replicas are called *satellite replicas*.

## WAN Topologies

All the topologies shown in Figure 9.4 are also possible on a wide area network (WAN) or a loosely connected network. More likely, however, you'll use a topology that interconnects several stars or rings, as depicted in Figure 9.5.

**FIGURE 9.5**
Common replication topologies for a wide area network

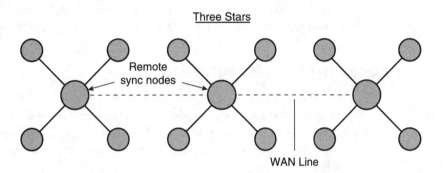

Three Stars

Remote sync nodes

WAN Line

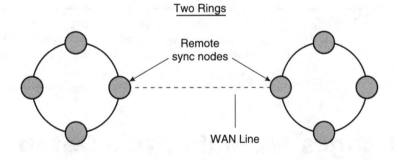

Two Rings

Remote sync nodes

WAN Line

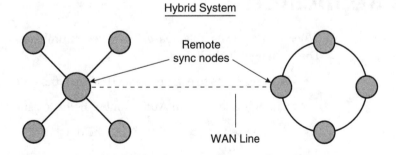

Hybrid System

Remote sync nodes

WAN Line

In a WAN or loosely connected network, each replica that exchanges updates with remote replicas is called a *remote sync node*. (This is our terminology, not Microsoft's.) If you're using Replication Manager, the synchronizers will most likely be located on these machines. WANs and loosely connected networks actually have two sets of topologies: the topology that connects the remote sync nodes (this topology shows up in the Replication Manager map) and the topology used at each workgroup site. In a topology that consisted of several interconnected stars, the hubs of each star would also be remote sync nodes.

## Locating the Design Master

You should place the design master for a replica set on a non-hub computer when using the star topology. In addition, the design master should not be a remote sync node. This allows you to insulate the design master from the rest of the replicas and to better control when design changes are rolled out to the other members of the replica set.

---

**TIP**    When you will be making design changes over an extended time period, you should remove the design master from the normal synchronization schedule so that inconsistent design changes are not propagated to other members of the replica set.

---

# Changes Jet Makes to a Database When It Is Replicated

When you replicate a database, Jet makes a number of changes to the database. These changes include:

- Adding fields to each replicated table in the database

- Changing sequential AutoNumber fields to random AutoNumber fields

- Adding several system tables to the database

These changes, which can significantly increase the size of your database, are explored in the next few sections.

# New Tables

Several new system tables are added to the database when it is replicated. These tables track the names and locations of replicas and replicated tables in the replica set, log synchronization exchanges, track deleted records, and log synchronization conflicts and errors. The replication system tables are summarized in Table 9.5

**TABLE 9.5:**   System Tables Added to a Replicated Database

| Table | Present When | Purpose | Replicated?* |
|---|---|---|---|
| MSysConflicts | Always | Stores information about conflicts. | Yes |
| MSysContents | Replica is a partial replica | Stores information about which records should be included in the partial replica. | No |
| MSysExchangeLog | Always | Logs information on each synchronization exchange with this replica. | No |
| MSysFilters | Replica is a partial replica | Stores information about partial replica filters. | No |
| MSysGenHistory | Always | Logs the history of every generation of updates in the replica set (of which this replica is aware). Used to avoid sending unchanged records during synchronization exchanges. | No |
| MSysOthersHistory | Always | Logs the generations received from other replicas in the replica set. | No |
| MSysRepInfo | Always | Stores information about the replica set, including the GUID of the design master; contains a single record. | Yes |
| MSysReplicas | Always | Stores the GUID of each replica in the replica set. | Yes |
| MSysSchChange | Always | Stores all schema changes made to the design master. Jet deletes records in this table periodically to minimize the size of this table. | No |

*Even though many of these tables are not replicated, the records in many of them are kept up-to-date across all replicas of a replica set.

**TABLE 9.5:** System Tables Added to a Replicated Database *(continued)*

| Table | Present When | Purpose | Replicated?* |
|---|---|---|---|
| MSysSchedule | Always | Schedule information used by Replication Manager and the Synchronizer. Used only with these utilities. | Yes |
| MSysSideTables | When conflicts are present | Stores the name of the conflict table and GUID of the user table to which it applies. Contains one record for each table with outstanding conflicts. | Yes |
| MSysTableGuids | Always | Stores the name of all replicated tables in the database and their GUIDs. | No |
| MSysTombstone | Always | Stores the table and row GUIDs for all deleted rows in the replica. | No |
| MSysTranspAddress | Always | Stores settings used by the Synchronizer. | Yes |
| MSysTranspCoords | Replication Manager–managed replicas | Stores the *x* and *y* coordinates of the topology map used in Replication Manager. | No |

*Even though many of these tables are not replicated, the records in many of them are kept up-to-date across all replicas of a replica set.

All the replication system tables are read only. Most of the fields in these tables are readable, although some of the fields are not because the data is stored in binary form as OLE objects. An example of one of the system tables, MSysReplicas, is shown in Datasheet view in Figure 9.6.

**FIGURE 9.6**

The MSysReplicas system table contains information on all replicas in the replica set.

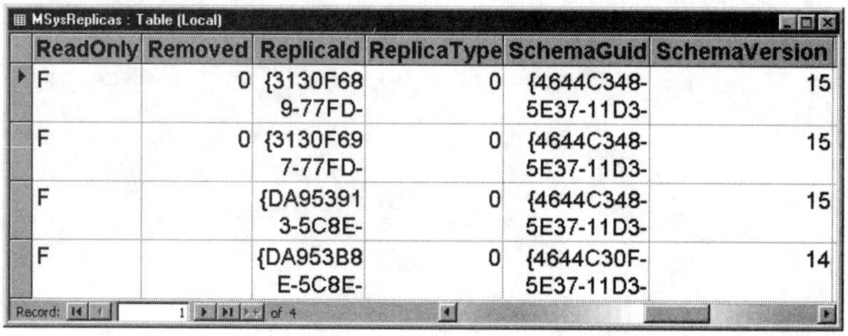

| ReadOnly | Removed | ReplicaId | ReplicaType | SchemaGuid | SchemaVersion |
|---|---|---|---|---|---|
| F | 0 | {3130F689-77FD- | 0 | {4644C348-5E37-11D3- | 15 |
| F | 0 | {3130F697-77FD- | 0 | {4644C348-5E37-11D3- | 15 |
| F | | {DA953913-5C8E- | 0 | {4644C348-5E37-11D3- | 15 |
| F | | {DA953B8E-5C8E- | 0 | {4644C30F-5E37-11D3- | 14 |

Record: 1 of 4

In addition to the hidden system tables outlined in Table 9.5, Jet creates local (nonreplicated) conflict tables whenever there are outstanding conflicts in a database table as a result of a synchronization exchange. Jet constructs the name of the conflict table by appending "_Conflict" to the end of the table that contains conflicts. For example, a conflict table for tblCustomer would be named tblCustomer _Conflict. The schema of the conflict table is the same as that of the original database table with which it is associated, except that the conflict table doesn't contain indexes (other than an index on the s_GUID field) or most field properties.

When a conflict occurs during synchronization because a row has been updated in both replicas, Jet creates a row in the conflict table (if this is the first conflict for a table, Jet first creates the conflict table) and stores the losing row in it. The algorithm used to determine the losing row is discussed in the "Managing Conflicts" section later in this chapter.

# Table Changes

Jet makes two types of changes to each replicated table when a database is replicated or a local table is made replicable:

- It adds new replication fields.
- It changes existing AutoNumber fields.

## Additional Replication Fields

Jet adds several fields to each replicated table. The additional replication fields are summarized in Table 9.6. All the replication fields are read only.

**TABLE 9.6:**   Replication Fields Added to Each Table

| Field | Datatype | Purpose | Comments |
|---|---|---|---|
| s_Generation | Long Integer | Tracks changes (generations) to a row. | Always present in replicated tables. If the s_Generation field value is 0, it represents an added row or a changed row that needs to be sent to other replicas during the next synchronization exchange. If it is a non-zero value, it represents the generation of the replica during which this change was made. |
| s_GUID | AutoNumber— Replication ID | Added to tables to uniquely identify the row across replicas, even if the primary key values change. | This field will not be added to the table if the table contains an existing AutoNumber field with a field size of Replication ID. |

**TABLE 9.6:** Replication Fields Added to Each Table *(continued)*

| Field | Datatype | Purpose | Comments |
|---|---|---|---|
| s_Lineage | OLE Object | Tracks the history of changes to the record. | Used to determine which replicas have already received changes and who wins a conflict. |
| s_ColLineage | OLE Object | Added to tables where column-level conflict tracking is enabled. | Used to determine who wins a conflict when column-level conflict tracking is enabled. |
| Gen_Field | Long Integer | One Gen field is added for each large object (memo or OLE object) user field in the table. This field tracks changes (generations) to the large object field independent of the other fields in the row. | Its name takes the format Gen_*Field,* where *Field* is the name of the large object field. If this name is not unique, the rightmost characters are changed until a unique name is produced. |

## AutoNumber Fields

Jet adds the fields from Table 9.6 to each database table, but it also alters the behavior of existing AutoNumber fields. If a table contains a Long Integer AutoNumber field with a NewValues property setting of Increment, Jet changes the property to Random. This significantly reduces the chance that two replicas assign the same AutoNumber value because each AutoNumber field will be based on a randomly selected number between –2 billion and +2 billion.

**NOTE**  This change to the behavior of AutoNumber fields may adversely affect existing applications that depend on these fields being assigned sequentially. In these situations, you may need to create a custom AutoNumber routine that ensures each replica's numbers are unique by selecting values from different pools of numbers. We presented a custom AutoNumber routine in Chapter 2, which you can modify for use with replicas.

## Globally Unique Identifiers (GUIDs)

A globally unique identifier (GUID) is a 16-byte string made up of several parts that, when concatenated, have an infinitesimal chance of ever generating duplicate values. And the *global* in GUID means that each GUID will be unique throughout the world, regardless of where or when it was generated. The datasheet for a replicated table with a GUID row identifier field (s_GUID) is shown in Figure 9.7.

**FIGURE 9.7**
The normally hidden replication fields can be seen in the tblCustomer table.

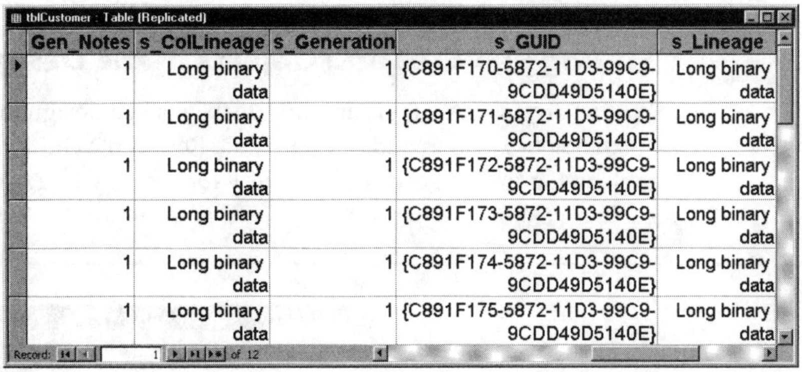
tblCustomer : Table (Replicated)

| Gen_Notes | s_ColLineage | s_Generation | s_GUID | s_Lineage |
|---|---|---|---|---|
| 1 | Long binary data | 1 | {C891F170-5872-11D3-99C9-9CDD49D5140E} | Long binary data |
| 1 | Long binary data | 1 | {C891F171-5872-11D3-99C9-9CDD49D5140E} | Long binary data |
| 1 | Long binary data | 1 | {C891F172-5872-11D3-99C9-9CDD49D5140E} | Long binary data |
| 1 | Long binary data | 1 | {C891F173-5872-11D3-99C9-9CDD49D5140E} | Long binary data |
| 1 | Long binary data | 1 | {C891F174-5872-11D3-99C9-9CDD49D5140E} | Long binary data |
| 1 | Long binary data | 1 | {C891F175-5872-11D3-99C9-9CDD49D5140E} | Long binary data |

Record: 1 of 12

GUIDs are used in several places in a replicated database to uniquely identify many parts of a replicated system, including:

- Rows in a replicated table
- Each table in a replicated database
- Each replica in a replica set
- Each synchronization exchange
- Each database generation
- Each schema change
- Each synchronizer

## Other Changes

When you replicate a database, Access makes several changes to the look and behavior of the database that are a result of the underlying changes Jet makes to the database schema.

One of the first changes you will notice is to the title bar of the database window. Nonreplicated databases have title bars of the form *database_name*: *Database*. After replication, the title bar changes to *database_name*: Design Master, *database_name*: Replica, or *database_name*: Partial Replica.

## Editing and Creating Objects in the Design Master

When you save new table and query objects in a design master replica, the Save As dialog box will include a new Make Replicable checkbox, as shown for a new table in Figure 9.8. Any table or query for which you don't check the Make Replicable checkbox will become a local—that is, nonreplicated—object.

**FIGURE 9.8**
Saving a table in a replicated database

To make a local object replicable in a design master, open the object's property dialog box by using the View ➤ Properties menu command (or the equivalent right-click shortcut menu command) and select the Replicated checkbox. Similarly, to make a replicated object a local object, deselected the Replicated checkbox in this dialog box.

## Editing and Creating Objects in Replicas

All saved tables and queries in non–design master replicas will automatically be local. You can't change this. The only way you can make a local object replicable in a non–design master replica is to import that object into the design master, delete it from the replica, and then make it replicable in the design master by using the View ➤ Properties command.

For the purposes of replication, Jet 4.0 now treats non-Jet objects—that is, forms, reports, macros, modules, and data access pages—as a single replicable object. It's all or nothing; you either replicate all non-Jet objects or you don't replicate any non-Jet objects. What's more, you must decide whether the Access application objects are replicated *before* you replicate the database. See "Pre-Replication Decisions" later in this chapter for more details.

Once you've replicated a database for which you've chosen to replicate the Access application objects, you can only edit or create new non-Jet objects from the design master. You won't be able to edit or create local non-Jet objects in non-design master replicas. As previously mentioned, however, you can create local tables and queries in non-design master replicas.

# Replicating a Database

The first step in employing Jet's replication services is to convert an existing non-replicated database into a replicated design master. You can do this using the Access menus, the Window Briefcase, Replication Manager, JOR, or DAO.

## Pre-Replication Decisions

Prior to replicating a database, you need to make a few decisions.

### Do You Want to Replicate Tables and Queries?

By default, Access replicates all tables and queries in the database. But if you are using JRO or Replication Manager, you can selectively choose whether to exclude some tables or queries from being replicated. You can choose to replicate a table or query either before or after the database is replicated. See the "Replicating a Database Using JRO" and "Replicating a Database Using Replication Manager" sections later in this chapter for more details.

### Do You Want to Use Row-Level or Column-Level Conflict Tracking?

Before a table is replicated, you can choose whether to resolve conflicts at the row level or column level. By default, Jet uses column-level tracking for newly replicated tables. To use row-level tracking instead, right-click the table in the database container and select Properties from the pop-up menu. From the Properties dialog box, select the Row Level Tracking checkbox to enable row-level tracking, as shown in Figure 9.9.

**FIGURE 9.9**

Enabling row-level conflict tracking for the tblProduct table.

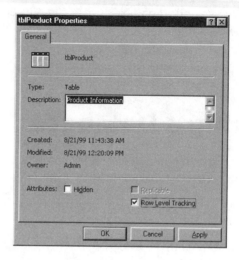

## Do You Want to Replicate Access Application Objects?

In Access 2000 and Jet 4.0, you can elect to either replicate all Access application objects or replicate none of them. Unlike earlier versions of the Jet engine, version 4.0 saves the entire set of Access objects—forms, reports, macros, modules, and data access pages—as a single binary object. Therefore, you no longer can selectively replicate some Access objects. You must choose to replicate or not replicate the Access objects prior to replicating the database. After you replicate the database, you cannot change your mind.

By default, Jet replicates Access application objects. To choose not to replicate the Access objects, select File ➤ Database Properties. At the database's Properties dialog box, click the Custom tab and select ReplicateProject under Properties. Change the value from Yes to No and click Modify to save your changes, as shown in Figure 9.10. After you replicate the database, all of the Access application objects will be local to the design master replica.

---

**TIP**    Unless you're replicating a tables-only database, you'll more than likely want to also replicate the Access application objects.

---

**FIGURE 9.10**
Changing the Replicate-Project property of a database affects whether the Access application objects are replicated.

> **TIP**
>
> If you upgrade a database from an earlier version of Access to Access 2000, it will not contain the ReplicateProject property. If this is an issue, you'll need to create a new Access 2000 database and import all of the older database's objects into it.

## Replica Visibility

Jet 4.0 supports three levels of replica *visibility*:

- Global
- Local
- Anonymous

Replica visibility affects whether other replicas can see the replica and synchronize with it.

A *global* replica is a replica that can be seen by and synchronized with all other global replicas. Prior to Jet 4.0, all replicas—with the exception of partial replicas—were global replicas; that is, all other replicas could see them. In most cases, you'll want to create global replicas because they are the most flexible type of replica. Global replicas appear in the MSysReplicas table. Global replicas can create any other type of replica, including global, local, and anonymous replicas. The default visibility for a replica created from a global replica is global.

A *local* replica is a replica that can only synchronize with its parent replica (the replica that created it). You can use a local replica to enforce a star topology or another type of replica hierarchy. Only the parent replica of a local replica sees the local replica. The parent of a local replica proxies updates and conflicts for the local replica. A local replica has a fixed priority of 0. Local replicas appear in the MSys-Replicas table.

An *anonymous* replica is similar to a local replica in that it can only synchronize with its parent replica. It also has a fixed priority of 0 and its updates and conflicts are proxied by its parent replica. The one difference between an anonymous replica and a local replica is that information about an anonymous replica is only stored in the MSysReplicas table temporarily. Jet removes information about anonymous replicas from MSysReplicas after a period of inactivity. Anonymous replicas make sense when you have a lot of replicas that only occasionally participate in synchronization exchanges. Once it has been removed from MSysReplicas, an anonymous replica will need to initiate a synchronization exchange with its parent replica in order to synchronize again.

By default, all of the replication tools create global replicas. You can create local and anonymous replicas using either Access or JRO.

## Partial Replicas

A *partial replica* is a replica that contains only a *subset* of data from one or more replicated tables. For example, if you were distributing your sales database to salespeople with laptops that contain limited hard disk space, it would be nice to be able to give each salesperson data pertaining only to that salesperson's sales territory.

You can create partial replicas using JRO, DAO, or the Partial Replica Wizard, which is built into Access 2000. See the "Partial Replication" section later in this chapter for more information on creating partial replicas using JRO.

## Prevent Deletes Replicas

When you create a replica using the Access menus, you have the option to disallow the deletion of records in the new replica. This may be useful in situations where you want to distribute a full replica, but not allow users of the replica to delete existing records.

You can only create a prevent deletes replica using the Access menus.

**NOTE**    The inability of JRO to create a prevent deletes replica is one of the few places where JRO can't do something that another replication tool can.

## Replicating a Database Using the Access Menus

You use Tools ➤ Replication ➤ Create Replica to convert an existing nonreplicated database into a replicated design master. After executing this command, you are met with a warning dialog box explaining that Access will close the database and then convert it into a replicated design master.

If you choose to proceed, you will see a second dialog box asking whether you want Access to create a backup of your database before converting it. If you haven't already backed up the database, do so now, because there's no simple way to "un-replicate" a database. Access names the backup database name with the same root name and the extension .BAK. You won't have a chance to change this now, but you can always rename the backup later using Windows Explorer. After you dismiss this dialog box, Access converts the database to the design master of the new replica set. After the database has been converted, Access displays a File Save As dialog box, which asks for a name for the second replica of the replica set.

You can create additional replicas from any existing replica using the same command (Tools ➤ Replication ➤ Create Replica) you used to convert a database to a replicated design master. Access responds with the Location of New Replica dialog box, as shown in Figure 9.11. Notice that this dialog box includes controls you can use to set the visibility and priority of the new replica. In addition, you can use the Prevent Deletes checkbox to create a prevent deletes replica.

**FIGURE 9.11**

The Location of New Replica dialog lets you control the visibility and priority of the new replica.

# Replicating a Database Using Replication Manager

You use Replication Manager's Tools ➢ Convert Database to Design Master command to convert a nonreplicated database into a replicated design master. Executing this command launches the Convert Database to Design Master Wizard. Like the Access menus, Replication Manager gives you the option of creating a backup with the .BAK extension when it replicates the database.

## Selectively Replicating Objects

On the fourth screen of the Convert Database to Design Master Wizard, shown in Figure 9.12, you get the chance to replicate all database objects or some subset of objects. Select Make Some Objects Available to the Entire Replica Set and click the Choose Objects button to selectively replicate objects. The wizard displays the Select Replicated Objects dialog box.

**FIGURE 9.12**
The fourth screen of the Convert Database to Design Master Wizard

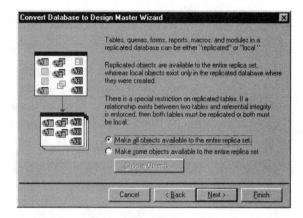

The Select Replicated Objects dialog box has three tabs. Using the tabs, you can selectively replicate tables, queries, and the Access project. On the Project Items tab, shown in Figure 9.13, you decide whether the Access objects—forms, reports, macros, modules, and data access pages—are replicated. Your choices are limited to replicating all of the Access objects or none of them.

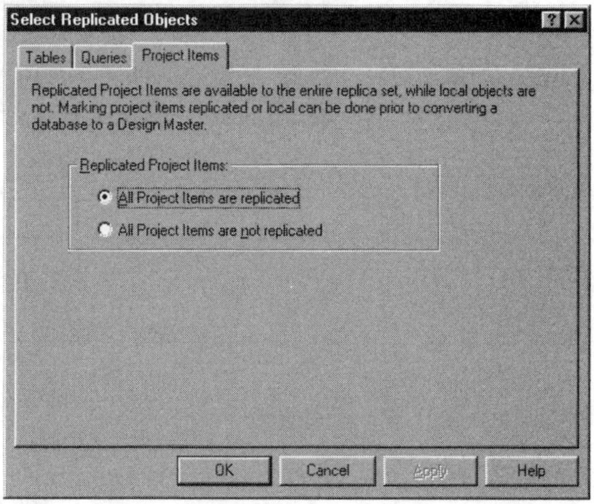

**FIGURE 9.13**
The Project Items tab of the Select Replicated Objects dialog box

## Single Master Replica Sets

When converting a database to a design master, Replication Manager gives you the option of creating a replica set based on the *single master model* (see Figure 9.14). In this model, schema *and* data changes can be made only at the design master. If you choose the single master model (the second radio button option shown in Figure 9.14), all replicas other than the design master will be read only (even if you specify otherwise when creating replicas using JRO or DAO). When you choose this option, Jet sets the SingleMaster field in the MSysRepInfo table to "T." You can get the equivalent effect in JRO or DAO by always creating read-only replicas.

The default setting of the Convert Database to Design Master Wizard is to allow data changes in all replicas.

**FIGURE 9.14**
Using Replication Manager, you can create replica sets that allow data changes only in the design master.

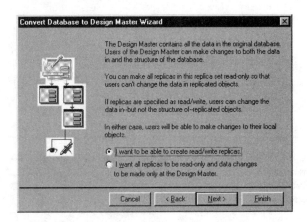

| WARNING | Take care before creating a single master replica set. There's no way to reverse this operation. |

## Managed Replicas

When converting a database to a design master or creating additional replicas with the File ➤ New Replica command, Replication Manager asks if you wish to have the replica managed by this synchronizer (see Figure 9.15). When a synchronizer manages a replica, it is able to schedule synchronizations that originate from the replica.

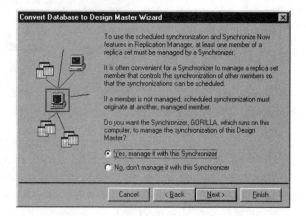

If you create an unmanaged replica, you will be unable to schedule synchronizations using the replica. To synchronize the replica you will have to either originate a synchronizer-based synchronization using another managed replica (or a different synchronizer that *is* managing this replica) or synchronize using Access, JRO, or DAO.

## Replica Retention Period

The replica retention period controls how long Jet maintains schema changes and deleted records for replicas that have not been synchronized. This Integer value must be between 5 and 32,000 days and can be set only for the design master. You can alter the retention period value, which defaults to 1,000 days for replica sets created by the Access UI or the Windows Briefcase, and 60 days for replica sets created using Replication Manager, JRO, or DAO, via the replica Properties sheet in Replication Manager (see Figure 9.16). You can also use the RetentionPeriod property of the JRO Replica object to alter the replica set's retention period.

**FIGURE 9.16**
You can adjust the replica
retention period for a
replica set using the
replica Properties sheet in
Replication Manager.

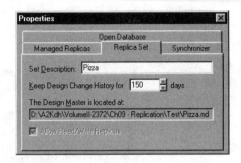

When you use Access or Replication Manager to open a replica that is within five days of expiring, you are reminded of the impending replica expiration with a warning message. If the retention period expires for a replica, Replication Manager and Access will refuse to synchronize changes between this replica and other replicas in the replica set.

## Replicating a Database using JRO

You use the MakeReplicable method of the JRO Replica object to convert a non-replicated database into a replicated design master. Replication requires an exclusive connection to the database, so no other users can have the to-be-replicated database open. The syntax of the MakeReplicable method is:

```
replica.MakeReplicable [connectionstring] [, columntracking]
```

where:

- *replica* is a Replica object variable.

- *connectionstring* is a connection string or an object variable pointing to an open ADO connection; if you use this argument, it overrides the ActiveConnection property of the Replica object.

- *columntracking* is True to use column-level conflict tracking or False to use row-level conflict tracking; the default is True.

For example, you could use the following syntax to create a new design master named C:\PIZZA.MDB with column-level tracking:

```
rpl.MakeReplicable "c:\pizza.mdb", True
```

The adhCreateNewReplicaSet subroutine (from the basReplicationJRO module of CH09.MDB) demonstrates the use of the MakeReplicable method:

```
Public Sub adhCreateReplicatSet(strDB As String, _
  Optional fColTrack As Boolean = True)
    ' Creates a new replica set using JRO.

  Dim rplNew As JRO.Replica

  Set rplNew = New JRO.Replica

  rplNew.MakeReplicable ConnectionString:=strDB, _
    ColumnTracking:=fColTrack

  Set rplNew = Nothing
End Sub
```

## Creating Additional Replicas Using JRO

To create a replica from an existing replica, you use the CreateReplica method of the Replica object. The syntax of the CreateReplica method is:

```
replica.CreateReplica replicaname, description _
  [, replicatype] [, visibility] [, priority] _
  [, updatability]
```

where:

- *replica* is a Replica object variable pointing to an existing replica.

- *replicaname* is the name of the new replica.

- *description* is a string describing the replica; while this argument is required, you can set it to an empty string.

- *replicatype* is an optional constant specifying the type of replica to create; it may be either jrRepTypeFull (default) or jrRepTypePartial.

- *visibility* is an optional constant specifying the visibility of the replica; it may be jrRepVisibilityAnon, jrRepVisiblityGlobal (default), or jrRepVisibilityLocal.

- *priority* is an optional number ranging between –1 and 100; only users with the database administrator privilege can set priority to a value greater than

90% of the parent replica's priority; must be 0 for local and anonymous replicas; –1 is the default, which indicates a value that is 90% of the parent replica's priority for global replicas or a value of 0 for local and anonymous replicas.

- *updatability* is an optional constant specifying whether data updates can be made in the new replica; it may be either jrRepUpdFull (default) or jrRepUpdReadOnly.

---

**NOTE**    The creation of partial replicas is discussed in the "Partial Replication" section later in this chapter.

---

For example, you could use the following syntax to create a full, global replica named FULLGLOBALREPLICA.MDB with default priority of 90% of its parent:

```
rpl.CreateReplica "fullglobalreplica.mdb", _
    "A full, global replica", jrRepTypeFull, _
    jrRepVisiblityGlobal, -1, jrRepUpdFull
```

You could you use the following code to create a local replica named LOCALREPLICA.MDB:

```
rpl.CreateReplica "localreplica.mdb", _
    "A full, local replica", jrRepTypeFull, _
    jrRepVisiblityLocal
```

You might use the following code to create a read-only full, global replica named READONLY50.MDB with a priority of 50:

```
rpl.CreateReplica "readonly50.mdb", _
    "A full, read-only replica with a priority of 50", _
    jrRepTypeFull, jrRepVisiblityGlobal, 50, jrRepUpdReadOnly
```

The adhCreateNewReplica subroutine (from the basReplicationJRO module of CH09.MDB) demonstrates the use of the CreateReplica method:

```
Public Sub adhCreateNewReplica(strDB As String, _
    strDesc As String, _
    Optional lngType As ReplicaTypeEnum = jrRepTypeFull, _
    Optional lngVis As VisibilityEnum = _
    jrRepVisibilityGlobal, _
    Optional lngPriority As Long = -1, _
    Optional lngUpdate As UpdatabilityEnum = jrRepUpdFull)
```

```
' Creates a new replica from the current replica

Dim rpl As JRO.Replica

Set rpl = New JRO.Replica

' Set the ActiveConnection to the current database
Set rpl.ActiveConnection = CurrentProject.Connection
' Create the replica

rpl.CreateReplica _
  ReplicaName:=strDB, _
  Description:=strDesc, _
  ReplicaType:=lngType, _
  Visibility:=lngVis, _
  Priority:=lngPriority, _
  Updatability:=lngUpdate

Set rpl = Nothing
End Sub
```

The Replica object's ActiveConnection property is identical in purpose and syntax to the ADO Command object's ActiveConnection property. You use the Replica object's ActiveConnection property to connect to a Jet replica. You can set it to an existing ADO Connection object—including the CurrentProject's Connection—or to a connection string.

## Selectively Replicating Database Objects Using JRO

You can use JRO to selectively choose whether to exclude some tables or queries from being replicated. To set the replicability status of a table or query you use the SetObjectReplicability method of the Replica object. Its syntax is shown here:

```
replica.SetObjectReplicability objectname, objecttype, _
  replicability
```

where:

- *replica* is a Replica object variable.
- *objectname* is the name of the object.

- *objecttype* is the type of object; use "Tables" for tables or queries; *objecttype* can also be set to the name of one of the Access containers, but any attempts to change the replicability of these objects are ignored.

- *replicability* is True to replicate the object or False to not replicate it.

You can use the SetObjectReplicability method either before or after the database is replicated. For example, to replicate the tblCustomer table, you could use the following:

```
rpl.SetObjectReplicability  "tblCustomer",  "Tables",  True
```

To stop replicating the qryEmployee query, you could use the following:

```
rpl.SetObjectReplicability  "qryEmployee",  "Tables",  False
```

> **NOTE**　In order to create a relationship between two tables, both tables either must be replicated or not replicated. That is, you can't establish a relationship between a replicated and a nonreplicated table. Furthermore, if two tables are involved in a relationship, you must first delete the relationship before changing the replicability status of either of the tables.

As mentioned in the "Pre-Replication Decisions" section earlier in this chapter, Jet 4.0 doesn't let you selectively replicate Access objects. Instead, these objects are treated as a single binary object—the Access project—whose replicability is governed by a user-defined property of the database, ReplicateProject. You can only change the ReplicateProject property prior to converting the database into a replicated design master. Furthermore, JRO doesn't provide any way to change this property.

> **NOTE**　See the "Pre-Replication Decisions" section earlier in this chapter for information on how to change the ReplicateProject property via the Access UI.

You can use the adhSetJetObjectReplicable subroutine (from the basReplication-JRO module of the CH09.MDB database) to set the replicability of a table or query:

```
Public  Sub  adhSetJetObjectReplicable(strObj  As  String,  _
    Optional  fReplicable  As  Boolean)

    ' Set  the  replicability  of  Jet  object.
```

```
' Won't work on access objects.

Dim rpl As JRO.Replica

Set rpl = New JRO.Replica
Set rpl.ActiveConnection = CurrentProject.Connection

rpl.SetObjectReplicability strObj, "Tables", fReplicable

Set rpl = Nothing
End Sub
```

You use the GetObjectReplicability method of the Replica object to determine the replicability of an object. This method works for both Jet and Access objects. Its syntax is shown here:

```
return = replica.GetObjectReplicability(objectname, _
    objecttype)
```

where:

- *replica* is a Replica object variable.

- *objectname* is the name of the object.

- *objecttype* is the type of object; use "Tables" for tables or queries; *objecttype* can also be set the name of one of the Access containers: Forms, Reports, Scripts, Modules, or DataAccessPages.

- *return* is True if the object is replicable or False if it is not.

You can use the GetObjectReplicability method either before or after the database is replicated for both Jet and Access objects. For example, to check if the tblCustomer table is replicable, you could use the following:

```
fRep = rpl.GetObjectReplicability("tblCustomer", "Tables")
```

To check if the dapOrder data access page is replicable, you could use this code:

```
fRep = rpl.GetObjectReplicability("dapOrder", _
    "DataAccessPages")
```

You can use the adhGetObjectReplicable function (from the basReplicationJRO module of the CH09.MDB database) to get the replicability status of a database object:

```
Public Function adhGetObjectReplicable( _
  strObj As String, _
  strType As String) As Boolean
    ' Determines whether an object is replicable.
    ' Works on both Jet and Access objects.
    Dim rpl As JRO.Replica

    Set rpl = New JRO.Replica
    Set rpl.ActiveConnection = CurrentProject.Connection

    adhGetObjectReplicable = _
      rpl.GetObjectReplicability(strObj, strType)

    Set rpl = Nothing
End Function
```

# Partial Replication

As mentioned earlier in this chapter, a partial replica is a replica that contains a subset of the data contained in the full replicas of a replica set. You can create partial replicas using the Partial Replica Wizard, JRO, or DAO. Because its use is so straightforward, we won't discuss the Partial Replica Wizard other than to mention that you start it by selecting Replication ➢ Partial Replica Wizard. Instead, we'll focus on how to create a partial replica using JRO.

Creating partial replicas is a bit more involved than creating regular (full) replicas using JRO, but it's not that difficult. The process involves three basic steps that you must follow in order:

1. Create an empty partial replica.

2. Define filters for the partial replica.

3. Populate the partial replica.

Each of these steps is discussed in the following sections.

## Creating an Empty Partial Replica

To create a partial replica, you use the CreateReplica method of a full replica, setting the ReplicaType argument to jrRepTypePartial. For example, the following code creates a new empty partial replica based on a full replica:

```
rplFull.CreateReplica ReplicaName:="c:\docs\partial.mdb", _
    Description:="A partial replica", _
    ReplicaType:=jrRepTypePartial
```

When you create an empty partial replica, the new partial replica contains all the replicated tables and queries from the full replica, but the tables are empty.

**NOTE**  You can't create a partial replica from an existing partial replica; you must use a full replica.

## Defining Filters for a Partial Replica

You define the rows that a partial replica will contain by appending filters to the Filters collection of the partial replica. You can set two types of filters: *table filters* and *relationship filters*.

For most partial replicas, you'll have five different types of tables:

- You create a table filter for one or more main (driving) tables that you use to drive the partial replica. For example, for a traveling salesperson database, you might create partial replicas based on State of the tblCustomer table. (Alternately, you might choose to base a filter on the EmployeeID field of the tblEmployee table.) In many cases, you will only have one driving table.

- Jet automatically includes rows from the one side of any one-to-many relationships with the main tables. In the salesperson database example, there wouldn't be any tables on the one side of any one-to-many relationships with tblCustomer table.

- You create relationship filters for any rows you wish to be included in the partial replica because they appear on the many side of one-to-many relationships with the main tables. This might include a series of relationships. For the salesperson database example, two relationships would qualify: the relationship between tblCustomer and tblOrder, and the relationship between tblOrder and tblOrderDetail.

- You create a table filter with criteria of True for any tables that should contain all rows. This might include tables that are unrelated to the main tables. You might also decide that for some tables on the many side of one-to-many relationships with the main tables, you'd rather have all the rows rather than the relationship-filtered rows. In that case, you would create a table filter with criteria of True in lieu of creating a relationship filter.

- The partial replica won't contain any rows in tables for which you have not defined table or relationship filters. You can also create a table filter with the criteria of False for these tables, but this is unnecessary.

## Table Filters

You use the following syntax to define a table filter:

```
replica.Filters.Append  tablename,  jrFilterTypeTable,  _
    filtercriteria
```

where:

- *replica* is a Replica object variable pointing to the partial replica.

- *tablename* is the name of the table.

- *filtercriteria* is the SQL WHERE clause defining the filter (minus the WHERE keyword); use True to include all rows from the table or False to exclude all rows from the table.

For example, to define a filter on the tblCustomer table so that rows only in which the State was equal to "NY" were included in the partial replica, you would use:

```
rplPartial.Filters.Append  "tblCustomer",
    jrFilterTypeTable,  "State  =  'NY'"
```

To include all the rows from the tblProduct table in a partial replica, you would use the following:

```
rplPartial.Filters.Append  "tblProduct",  _
    jrFilterTypeTable,  True
```

---

**TIP**   For performance reasons, you should create indexes for fields on which you define filters.

---

## Relationship Filters

You use this syntax to define a relationship filter:

```
replica.Filters.Append tablename, _
    jrFilterTypeRelationship, filtercriteria
```

where:

- *replica* is a Replica object variable pointing to the partial replica.

- *tablename* is the name of the table on the foreign key side (many side) of the relationship.

- *filtercriteria* is the name of the relationship.

For example, to create a relationship filter for the relationship named "CustomerOrder" between tblCustomer and tblOrder, you might use the following:

```
rplPartial.Filters.Append "tblOrder", _
    jrFilterTypeRelationship, "CustomerOrder"
```

The hardest part of creating a relationship filter is determining the relationship name, because most of the time these names are created automatically for you. To get around this problem, we've created a function, adhGetRel, which you can find in the basReplicationJRO module of the CH09.MDB chapter database, that uses ADOX to determine a relationship name given the name of the two tables involved in the relationship. Here's the source code for adhGetRel:

```
Public Function adhGetRel(strCnn As String, _
    strOne As String, _
    strMany As String) As String
    ' Returns the relationship name for two
    ' one-to-many related tables.
    ' Assumes there is only one foreign key
    ' relationship between the two tables.
    Dim cat As ADOX.Catalog
    Dim fk As ADOX.Key
    Dim strRel As String

    Set cat = New ADOX.Catalog
    cat.ActiveConnection = strCnn

    strRel = ""
    For Each fk In cat.Tables(strMany).Keys
        If fk.RelatedTable = strOne _
```

```
        And  fk.Type  =  adKeyForeign  Then
            strRel  =  fk.Name
            Exit  For
        End  If
    Next  fk

    adhGetRel  =  strRel
    Set  fk  =  Nothing
    Set  cat  =  Nothing
End  Function
```

You pass adhGetRel a connection string, the name of the table on the one side of the relationship, and the name of the table on the many side of the relationship. It returns the relationship name as a string. If no relationship is found, it returns an empty string. adhGetRel assumes there is only one relationship defined between the two tables; if more than one relationship exists, it returns the first one it finds.

The adhGetRel function works by iterating through the Keys collection of the many-side table until it finds a foreign-key relationship with a RelatedTable property value that matches the name of the one-side table.

## Populating a Partial Replica

Once you've defined the filters for a partial replica, you use the PopulatePartial method to populate the partial replica with filtered rows from the full replica, using the following syntax:

```
replica.PopulatePartial  fullreplica
```

where:

- *replica* is a Replica object variable pointing to the partial replica.

- *fullreplica* is fully-qualified path to the full replica that will be used to populate the partial replica.

The partial replica must be opened exclusively. In addition, the executing code can't be running from the partial replica. For example, to populate a partial replica with records from C:\FULLREPLICA.MDB, you could use the following code:

```
rplPartial.PopulatePartial  "c:\fullreplica.mdb"
```

When you execute the PopulatePartial method, Jet performs the following steps in order:

1. Propagates any unpropagated changes to the full replica. (This step is skipped for empty partial replicas.)

2. Removes all existing records from the partial replica. (Again, this step is skipped for empty partial replicas.)

3. Populates the partial replica with records based on the currently defined filters.

You use the PopulatePartial method to both populate new replicas and repopulate existing replicas. When you execute this method on a replica with existing data, Jet clears out any orphaned records from the replica prior to the repopulation of records. A record can be orphaned when a user edits a record so that it no longer meets the currently defined filter.

**NOTE**      The PopulatePartial method is not equivalent to the Synchronize method and should be used only to repopulate data in an existing replica. Because Jet has to delete and recopy all records to the partial replica, the PopulatePartial method is much slower than the Synchronize method. Furthermore, you can't execute the PopulatePartial method using Internet or indirect synchronization.

## A Partial Replica Example

Say that you wished to create a partial replica based on a replicated version of the CH09.MDB database with the following parameters:

- Include rows from tblCustomer where State = "OR"

- Include all rows from the tblEmployee, tblPaymentMethod, tblProduct, and tblSiteOption tables

- Include related rows from the tblOrder and tblOrderDetail tables

The adhCreatePartialReplicaExample subroutine (from basReplicationJRO in the CH09.MDB) database creates a replica based on these parameters. The complete example is shown in Listing 9.1.

**⟳ Listing 9.1**

```
Public Sub adhCreatePartialReplicaExample( _
  strPartial As String)
    ' Creates a new partial replica from
    ' the current replica.
    ' Sets several filters in the process
    ' and populates the new partial replica.

    Dim rplPartial As JRO.Replica
    Dim rplFull As JRO.Replica
    Dim strConnect As String
    Dim strCustOrderRel As String
    Dim strOrderOrderDetailRel As String

    Set rplFull = New JRO.Replica
    Set rplPartial = New JRO.Replica

    ' Set the ActiveConnection to the full replica
    Set rplFull.ActiveConnection = CurrentProject.Connection

    ' Step 1: Create the empty partial replica
    rplFull.CreateReplica ReplicaName:=strPartial, _
      Description:="Partial replica", _
      ReplicaType:=jrRepTypePartial
    Set rplFull = Nothing
    Debug.Print "Partial replica created."

    strConnect = _
      "Provider=Microsoft.Jet.OLEDB.4.0;" & _
      "Data Source=" & strPartial & ";"

    ' Step 2: Set filters for the partial replica
    ' This example creates the following filters:
    ' a. Table filter for tblCustomer: "State = 'OR'"
    ' b. All records from tblEmployee, tblPaymentMethod,
    '    tblProduct, and tblSiteOption.
    ' c. Follow relationships between tblCustomer and
    '    tblOrder and between tblOrder and tblOrderDetail

    ' First, grab the names of the two relationships
```

```
strCustOrderRel = adhGetRel(strConnect, _
  "tblCustomer", "tblOrder")
strOrderOrderDetailRel = adhGetRel(strConnect, _
  "tblOrder", "tblOrderDetail")
' The PopulatePartial method requires an
' exclusive connection to the partial replica
rplPartial.ActiveConnection = strConnect & _
  "Mode=Share Exclusive"

' Create the filters
rplPartial.Filters.Append "tblCustomer", _
  jrFilterTypeTable, "State = 'OR'"

rplPartial.Filters.Append "tblEmployee", _
  jrFilterTypeTable, True
rplPartial.Filters.Append "tblPaymentMethod", _
  jrFilterTypeTable, True
rplPartial.Filters.Append "tblProduct", _
  jrFilterTypeTable, True
rplPartial.Filters.Append "tblSiteOption", _
  jrFilterTypeTable, True

rplPartial.Filters.Append "tblOrder", _
  jrFilterTypeRelationship, _
  strCustOrderRel

rplPartial.Filters.Append "tblOrderDetail", _
  jrFilterTypeRelationship, _
  strOrderOrderDetailRel
Debug.Print "Partial replica filters set."

' Step 3: Populate partial replica
rplPartial.PopulatePartial CurrentProject.FullName
Debug.Print "Partial replica populated."

    Set rplPartial = Nothing
End Sub
```

The subroutine begins by creating the empty partial replica using the CreateReplica method. It then determines the names of the two relationships it will need to create the relationship filters, storing the names in a couple of string variables. Next, the table and relationship filters are created. Finally, the partial replica is populated with data from the full replica.

# Preventing Replication

Only users with the Administer permission for a database can convert it to a replicated design master. However, any user who can open a replica has the necessary permissions to create additional replicas from an existing replica. This is unfortunate because each replica in a replica set takes some overhead to track. Of course, this may not be a problem if you do not give users the ability to create replicas in your application, but these users will still be able to create replicas if they can open the database outside the confines of your application using Access or Replication Manager.

# Reversing Replication

Once replicated, a database can't be un-replicated—at least not directly. You can take the following steps, however, to create a nonreplicated version of a replicated design master. (You can't un-replicate a non–design master replica because you can't modify the design of its objects.)

1. Open the design master and document the existing relationships—either manually or by using the Database Documentor.

2. Delete all relationships in the design master.

3. Select a table in the database window and choose View ➤ Properties (or the equivalent from a shortcut menu). Uncheck the Replicated property and click the OK button. Repeat for all other replicated tables.

4. Create a new empty database and import all objects from the design master to the new database.

5. Open the new database created in Step 4, which should now contain all the objects from the replicated database. Using the relationship documentation created in Step 1, re-create all relationships in the new database.

There's an unfortunate side effect of un-replicating a database using these steps. Any fields that were foreign keys in the replica will have their DefaultValue property set to "GenUniqueID( )." Although this shouldn't cause any problems, Access will display "#Name?" in these fields when you are adding new rows to the tables. To remedy this situation, open the tables containing the foreign keys in design mode and delete the Gen-UniqueID function from the DefaultValue property of these fields. (Note, though, that the GenUniqueID function will reappear if you copy the table or import it into another database. If this is an issue, you'll need to duplicate the design of each of the problem tables and use append queries to copy the data to the new tables.)

---

**TIP**    We've created an Access 2000 add-in, UNREPLICATE2000.MDA (which you'll find on the CD that accompanies this book), that you can use to reverse replication. In addition to removing the replication fields, the add-in optionally renumbers AutoNumber fields to a sequential sequence.

---

# Synchronizing Replicas

When you synchronize two replicas, Jet copies schema changes and data updates between the two replicas. The default exchange method is two-way, which means that updates move in both directions. If you are using JRO, DAO, or Replication Manager to perform the synchronization exchange, you can also opt for a one-way data exchange between two replicas, but regardless of whether you choose two-way or one-way exchanges, Jet always propagates schema changes.

Synchronizing two databases is simple—Jet does all the work. It's up to you, however, to decide when to synchronize, with whom, how, and whether to use two-way or one-way synchronization. You're also responsible for making sure the two replicas are connected when you wish to synchronize them. In addition, you must be aware of how your replication topology affects the propagation of updates through your replica set. (See the "Replication Topologies" section earlier in this chapter.) Finally, you must manage any conflicts that occur as a result of the synchronization exchange. This last item is discussed in the "Managing Conflicts" section later in this chapter.

## Synchronizing Using the Access Menus

To synchronize two replicas using the Access menu commands, select Tools ➤ Replication ➤ Synchronize Now. Access responds with the Synchronize Database dialog box, as shown in Figure 9.17. Access fills the Directly with Replica combo box with the list of all known replicas that it stores in the MSysReplicas system table. It also sets the default replica to the one you last synchronized with using Access.

**FIGURE 9.17**
The Synchronize Database
dialog box

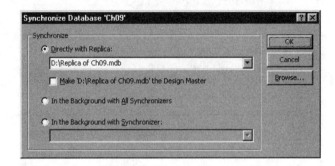

## Synchronizing Using Replication Manager

In addition to using the capabilities previously discussed in the area of replica management, you can use Replication Manager (and its companion Synchronizer program) to create synchronization schedules, perform the synchronizations, and view the results of synchronization exchanges. Although you can do all of this using JRO, you may ask yourself, "Why bother?" Replication Manager is Microsoft's preferred method for managing and automating synchronization exchanges, and for good reason: it makes the synchronization management process very easy.

You can synchronize a replica set using the Tools ➤ Synchronize Now command. When you execute this command, Replication Manager displays a dialog box similar to the one shown in Figure 9.18. At this time, you can choose to synchronize the selected replica with one of the following:

- All local members of the replica set managed by this synchronizer

- All members of the replica set at all locations

- The replicas at a specified remote site

**FIGURE 9.18**

Replication Manager's Synchronize Now dialog box

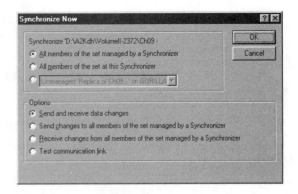

## Scheduled Synchronizations

While the ability to synchronize replicas on demand is certainly useful, Replication Manager's scheduling abilities are its real strong suit. You can set up a local synchronization schedule for all replica sets managed by the local synchronizer by right-clicking the local machine icon on the Replication Manager map and choosing Edit Locally Managed Replica Schedule from the shortcut menu. When you do this, Replication Manager displays the dialog box shown in Figure 9.19. You can schedule synchronizations on a weekly basis in 15-minute increments. This schedule applies to all local replicas managed by this synchronizer; there's no way to create individual schedules for different replica sets.

**FIGURE 9.19**

Use this dialog box to edit the synchronization schedule for locally managed replicas.

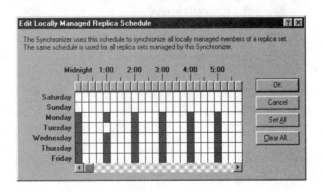

## Direct versus Indirect Synchronization

Replication Manager and Synchronizer support both direct and indirect synchronization modes. By default, when you initiate a synchronization exchange using Replication Manager/Synchronizer, your synchronizer performs the replication much as Access does. It opens both databases, determines which objects and records have changed, and proceeds to exchange data between the two replicas. This form of synchronization is called *direct synchronization* and works well when the replicas are located on two machines connected over a LAN.

Replication Manager and Synchronizer also support another form of synchronization called *indirect synchronization*. With indirect synchronization, your local synchronizer opens your local replica, establishes a link to a remote synchronizer, and exchanges packets of changes with the other synchronizer. This type of synchronization is safer and more efficient when using slower WAN and modem connections, because the remote replica is not opened over the connection.

If you use the direct synchronization method over a WAN or modem connection, the exchange will likely be slower. More important, you risk corrupting your database because a communications glitch could occur during a write to one of the replicas.

---

**TIP**    We strongly recommend you use the indirect synchronization method for WAN/modem synchronization exchanges.

---

## Configuring Replication Manager for Indirect Synchronizations

When configuring Replication Manager, you must indicate you will be performing indirect synchronizations before you do so. You can use the Configure Replication Manager Wizard (see Figure 9.20) to do this. Choose Tools ➢ Configure Microsoft Replication Manager to start the wizard.

**FIGURE 9.20**

The second screen of Replication Manager's configuration wizard asks if you want it to use indirect synchronization.

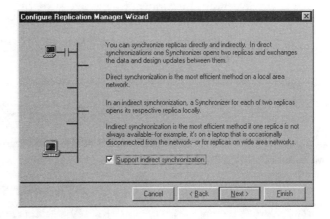

You will need to install and configure Replication Manager at each site that will be participating in indirect synchronizations.

## Synchronizing Replicas Indirectly

When you set up Replication Manager to manage a replica set, it assumes you will be performing only direct synchronizations. By default, any replicas you create using Replication Manager or Access at this site will support direct synchronization only. You'll need to perform the following steps to create a remote replica at a site with which you wish to indirectly synchronize:

1. Run Replication Manager on your local computer and create (or open) a managed replica set.

2. Make a regular DOS/Windows copy of the replica (*don't* create an additional replica) and move that copy of the replica to the remote site.

3. Run Replication Manager at the remote site and select File ➢ Open Replica Set. Replication Manager displays a dialog box informing you that "no synchronizer is currently managing the replica" and asks if "you want this synchronizer to manage this database?" Click Yes.

4. The two sites should now appear on the remote Replication Manager's map. Select the line connecting the two sites, right-click the mouse, and select Synchronize Now from the shortcut menu (see Figure 9.21). Replication Manager may take a while to complete the synchronization. Wait until the synchronization is complete.

**FIGURE 9.21**

Right-click the line connecting the two sites to bring up the indirect synchronization shortcut menu.

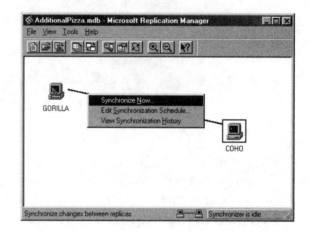

5. If you have Replication Manager open at the local site, select Tools ➤ Refresh Synchronization Window so that the remote site's icon appears on the local Replication Manager map.

After creating a remote replica following these steps, you synchronize, schedule synchronizations, or view the synchronization history between the two sites by selecting the line connecting the two sites, right-clicking the mouse, and selecting the appropriate shortcut menu (see Figure 9.21).

To edit the schedule for remote synchronization exchanges between two sites, right-click the line connecting the two sites and select Edit Synchronization Schedule. The Edit Schedule dialog box appears, as shown in Figure 9.22. The shading of each box indicates which synchronizer initiates the exchange; if the same time point is selected by both sites, both sites will attempt to initiate the exchange at the same time.

**FIGURE 9.22**
Use this dialog box to edit the synchronization schedule between the local and remote replicas.

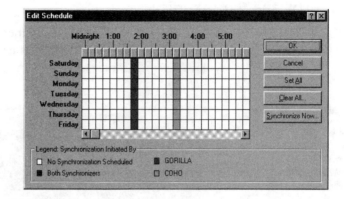

Once you have scheduled remote exchanges, it's up to you to ensure that the connection will be made prior to the synchronization exchange. If it's not, the synchronizer will log the changes to a temporary database located in the drop-box folder for that synchronizer. (This was the location specified when you first configured Replication Manager; you can change it using the Tools ➢ Configure Microsoft Replication Manager command.) The local synchronizer then continues to check every 15 minutes to see whether it can connect to the remote site. When it eventually connects to the remote synchronizer, it transfers the updates that have accumulated in the drop-box to the target synchronizer.

This feature allows you to easily configure laptop replicas to synchronize each time the laptop is connected to the network. Simply designate a dedicated drop-box folder for each laptop, which will receive all changes intended for that replica while the laptop is off the network. When the laptop returns, it will automatically be brought up-to-date.

**NOTE**      Although similar in concept to indirect synchronization, Internet synchronization is handled differently. See the "Internet/Intranet Synchronization" section later in this chapter for details on synchronizing over the Internet or across a corporate intranet.

## Controlling the Order of Synchronization Methods Used by the Synchronizer

When you configure Replication Manager using the Configure Replication Manager Wizard, one of the wizard screens displays the order of methods that the Synchronizer will use to synchronize replicas managed by the Synchronizer (see Figure 9.23).

**FIGURE 9.23**
On this screen of the Configure Replication Manager Wizard, you can adjust the order in which synchronization methods are attempted.

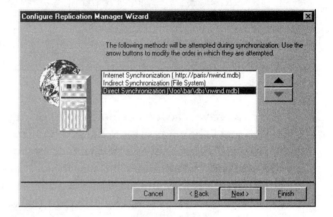

You can adjust the order in which the various synchronization methods are employed. If you haven't set up Replication Manager to use a particular method of synchronization—for example, Internet synchronization—that method will be skipped.

## Reviewing Synchronization History

Replication Manager includes the ability to view the log of synchronization activity. If you right-click the local machine icon and select View Local Synchronization History, you'll be able to view the history of all local synchronization exchanges. Similarly, if you right-click a remote computer icon (or the line connecting your local computer and the remote site) and select View Synchronization History, you'll be able to view the history of exchanges between the local and remote replicas. A sample of a remote synchronization history log, which is sorted in descending order by the time the exchange was initiated, is shown in Figure 9.24.

**FIGURE 9.24**
The Synchronization History
dialog box lists each
exchange in descending
date/time order.

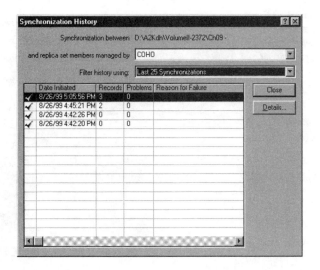

> **TIP**
> Regardless of whether you initially select to view the local or remote synchronization history, you can use the combo boxes that appear at the top of the dialog box to filter the list so it includes the history of local exchanges, all exchanges, exchanges with a particular synchronizer, the last 25 exchanges, only successful exchanges, only exchanges with conflicts, and so on.

If you select a record and click the Details button, a wealth of information regarding the selected exchange is revealed (see Figure 9.25), including:

- The direction of the exchange

- Whether the exchange was successful

- The number of data errors

- The number of conflicts

- The number and type of updates sent

- The number and type of updates received

- The number of design changes sent or received

**FIGURE 9.25**

The Synchronization Details dialog box reveals details regarding a particular exchange.

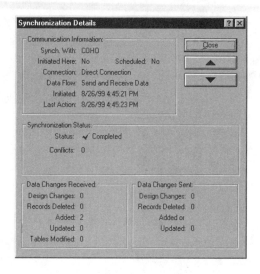

**TIP** When you browse the local or remote synchronization history logs using Replication Manager, you are actually viewing the history of all synchronization exchanges, not just those initiated by Replication Manager or the Synchronizer program. Thus, even if you use the Access menus, JRO, or DAO to synchronize replicas, you can still use Replication Manager to browse the exchange histories.

## Synchronizing Using JRO

You can programmatically initiate synchronization exchanges using the Synchronize method of the JRO Replica object. The syntax for this method is shown here:

```
replica.Synchronize target [, synctype] [, syncmode]
```

where:

- *replica* is a Replica object variable.

- *target* is a fully qualified path to the replica with which to synchronize.

- *synctype* is a constant specifying the type of synchronization to perform; can be jrSyncTypeExport (send changes only), jrSyncTypeImport (receive changes only), or jrSyncTypeImpExp (send and receive changes; the default)

- *syncmode* is a constant specifying the method of synchronization; can be jrSyncModeIndirect (use indirect synchronization), jrSyncModeDirect (use direct synchronization; the default), or jrSyncTypeModeInternet (use Internet synchronization)

Just as when using Replication Manager, you're responsible for ensuring that any remote connections are made prior to initiating a synchronization exchange using JRO.

To initiate an indirect, send-only exchange between the currently open database and c:\OtherReplica.Mdb, you could use the following code:

```
Set rpl = New JRO.Replica
Set rpl.ActiveConnection = CurrentProject.Connection
rpl.Synchronize "c:\OtherReplica.Mdb", jrSyncTypeExport, _
    jrSyncModeIndirect
```

The adhSyncReplicas subroutine synchronizes the current database replica with another replica. This routine is flexible—you can specify that the current database initiate the synchronization exchange or that the other replica initiate the exchange. In addition, you can pass it parameters to specify the type of exchange and the method used. You can find the adhSyncReplicas subroutine in the basReplication-JRO module of CH09.MDB. Its source is shown here:

```
Public Sub adhSyncReplicas(strTarget As String, _
    Optional fSyncFromThisReplica As Boolean = True, _
    Optional lngType As SyncTypeEnum = jrSyncTypeImpExp, _
    Optional lngMode As SyncModeEnum = jrSyncModeDirect)
    ' Synchronizes the current database
    ' with the specified target replica
    Dim rpl As JRO.Replica
    Dim strTo As String
    Dim cnn As ADODB.Connection

    Set cnn = CurrentProject.Connection
    Set rpl = New JRO.Replica

    ' If fSyncFromThisReplica is True, then
    ' the current replica drives replication.
    ' Otherwise, the other replica is the driver.
    If fSyncFromThisReplica Then
        Set rpl.ActiveConnection = cnn
        strTo = strTarget
```

```
    Else
        rpl.ActiveConnection = strTarget
        strTo = CurrentProject.FullName
    End If

    rpl.Synchronize Target:=strTo, _
      SyncType:=lngType, SyncMode:=lngMode

    Set rpl = Nothing
    Set cnn = Nothing
End Sub
```

> **NOTE**　If you execute synchronization code from a replica that has received design changes from a design master replica, you'll have to close and reopen the database for the changes to be incorporated into the schema of the open replica. Unfortunately, there's no way to close and reopen the currently open database from code that is running from the open database.

## Scheduling Synchronizations Using JRO

If you need to synchronize replicas on a regular basis and you've purchased Microsoft Office Developer, you may want to use Replication Manager instead of JRO to schedule synchronizations. It's easier to use, requires no programming, and maintains an excellent history of the exchanges. Creating your own synchronization schedule using JRO, however, does have its own advantages:

- It allows you to deliver an Access-only solution; you don't have to install and use Replication Manager and Synchronizer.

- You're not limited to a day-of-week schedule. For example, you could create a schedule based on the day of the month.

- You can synchronize at times other than at 15-minute intervals beginning on the hour.

- You can create a hybrid synchronization system that is based on both a regular timed schedule and update load. (See the next section.)

If you decide to implement a synchronization system using JRO, you'll need to decide how the process will be driven. Most likely, you'll employ a hidden form that's automatically loaded when the database is started with code attached to the form's Timer event. This form would probably follow a schedule that was stored in a table in the database. But where will this hidden form and table reside? Should it be part of the normal application database that runs on each desktop, or should it perhaps run only on selected desktops? One alternative might be to keep this form and table in a utility database that's kept separate from the rest of your application. This application could run off the file server or the database administrator's desktop.

## Synchronization Based on Number of Updates

You may wish to implement a synchronization system that is based on update load rather than (or in addition to) a regular schedule. You can ascertain the update load by counting the number of records in each replicated table in the database where the s_Generation field equals 0. This number represents the number of records that have been updated or added to the replica since the last synchronization exchange.

The sample form frmUpdateVolume in the CH09.MDB database contains code that does just that. If you open this form and click its command button, the code in Listing 9.2 executes. After a brief delay, the number of updated records in the replicated tables in the database is displayed in a text box on the form (see Figure 9.26).

**FIGURE 9.26**
frmUpdateVolume counts the number of updated records since the last synchronization exchange.

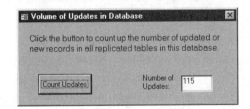

**Listing 9.2**

```
Private Sub cmdCount_Click()
    ' Count the number of updated/new
    ' records in any replicated tables
    ' in this database.
```

```
Dim lngCount As Long
Dim ctlCount As TextBox
Dim aob As AccessObject

DoCmd.Hourglass True

Set ctlCount = Me.txtCount
lngCount = 0

' Iterrate through all tables using
' CurrentData object's AllTables collection
For Each aob In CurrentData.AllTables
    'Only check replicated non-system tables
    If adhGetObjectReplicable(aob.Name, "Tables") And _
       Not IsSystemObject(aob) Then
        ' Count up number of records with
        ' s_Generation = 0
        lngCount = lngCount + DCount("*", aob.Name, _
           "[s_Generation]=0")
    End If
Next aob

ctlCount = lngCount
ctlCount.Enabled = True

Set ctlCount = Nothing
Set aob = Nothing
DoCmd.Hourglass False
End Sub
```

This routine works by iterating through the tables in the database using the CurrentData.AllTables collection. (See Chapter 6 in *Access 2000 Developer's Handbook, Volume 1: Desktop Edition* for more details on the CurrentData collections.) For each table, it checks to see if the table is replicated and not a system table, and if so, uses the DCount function to obtain a count of the table's records where the s_Generation field is 0.

Of course, this example doesn't do anything with the value, but once you've determined the number of updated or new records, you can easily decide whether it's time to synchronize. It's likely you'd call this code from a hidden form that is used to maintain a synchronization schedule for your application.

# Synchronizing Partial Replicas

You can synchronize partial replicas using the Access UI, JRO, DAO, or Replication Manager. A partial replica, however, can be synchronized only with a full replica.

If you change replica filters (see the "Defining Filters for a Partial Replica" section earlier in this chapter) and try to synchronize the replica prior to executing the PopulatePartial method, you will get a trappable error (3570—"The filters defining a partial replica have been changed. The partial replica must be repopulated."). You may wish to trap for this error in your code and execute the PopulatePartial method when this occurs.

# Internet/Intranet Synchronization

Access 2000 includes support for synchronization over the Internet or an intranet. In order to use Internet/intranet synchronization, your server must be running a Windows-based operating system. In addition, you must:

1. Install a copy of Access or an Access run-time application on the Web server.

2. Configure your Web server for Internet synchronization.

3. Install a copy of Replication Manager on the Web server.

4. Configure Replication Manager for Internet synchronization.

5. Set up your replica set for Internet synchronization.

> **NOTE**    Microsoft has published a white paper entitled "Internet Synchronization with Microsoft Jet 4.0." This paper, which is included on the CD that accompanies this book, describes in detail the steps you need to take to configure your server, configure Replication Manager, and set up your replica set for Internet synchronization.

## Synchronizing over the Internet Using Replication Manager

Once you've set up your network and enabled your replica set for Internet synchronization, select Tools ➢ Synchronize Now Across the Internet to synchronize a replica using a Web server. During the synchronization exchange, Replication Manager performs several steps. It indicates its progress with several status messages as it establishes the connection to the server, sends data to the server, and receives data from the server. Synchronization may take a while, especially if you have many changes or if you are using a slow dial-up line. If you are using a dial-up connection, you should establish the connection prior to synchronizing.

---

**NOTE**  While you can synchronize over the Internet/intranet at a single point in time, you can't schedule synchronization exchanges over the Internet/intranet using Replication Manager. If you need to schedule this type of exchange, use JRO instead. See the "Scheduling Synchronizations Using JRO" section earlier in this chapter for details.

---

## Synchronizing over the Internet Using Access

Once you've set up your network and enabled your replica set for Internet synchronization, you select Tools ➤ Replication ➤ Synchronize Now to perform an Internet/intranet synchronization. Access displays the Synchronize Database dialog box (see Figure 9.27). Select the Directly with Replica radio button and enter the `http:` address of the Web server. Click the OK button to begin the exchange.

---

**FIGURE 9.27**

Synchronizing over the Internet with Access

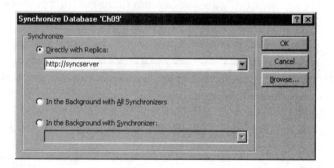

Unlike Replication Manager, Access does not display any messages during the exchange. This may lead you to prematurely believe that the session has hung, but be patient; the exchange will take several minutes even when involving only a small amount of data. If you are using a dial-up connection, you should establish the connection prior to initiating the synchronization exchange.

### Synchronizing over the Internet Using JRO

To perform a synchronization exchange over the Internet, you use the Synchronize method of the Replica object, setting the syncmode argument set to jrSyncTypeModeInternet. Here's the basic syntax:

```
replica.Synchronize domain/targetname synctype, _
    jrSyncTypeModeInternet
```

where:

- *replica* is a Replica object variable.

- *domain* is the domain name of the Web server for an Internet site or the machine name of the Web server for an intranet site.

- *targetname* is the name of the target replica on the Web Server without any path.

- *synctype* is a constant specifying the type of synchronization to perform; can be jrSyncTypeExport (send changes only), jrSyncTypeImport (receive changes only), or jrSyncTypeImpExp (send and receive changes; the default).

For example, to perform a two-way synchronization with a replica named SALES.MDB over the Internet via a server named Remote.com, you'd use this:

```
rpl.Synchronize "remote.com/Sales.Mdb", _
    jrSyncTypeImpExp, jrSyncTypeModeInternet
```

To perform a send-only synchronization with a replica named INVENT.MDB over a corporate intranet to a server named mis_dept, you'd use this:

```
rpl.Synchronize "mis_dept/Invent.Mdb", _
    jrSyncTypeExport, jrSyncTypeModeInternet
```

Once again, if you are using a dial-up connection, you should establish the connection prior to using the Synchronize method.

# Managing Conflicts

When you synchronize two replicas, Jet merges the updates from each of the replicas to create two replicas with the same data. Conflicts may arise anytime the same data is updated in both replicas.

## Row-Level versus Column-Level Tracking

In prior versions of Jet, conflicts would occur whenever the same row was modified in both replicas. Jet 4.0 supports two types of conflict tracking: row-level tracking and column-level tracking.

In *row-level tracking*, Jet flags a conflict every time the same row is updated by both replicas involved in the synchronization exchange. This was the only type of conflict tracking available in prior versions of the Jet engine.

In *column-level tracking*, Jet flags a conflict only when the same field (or column) is updated by both replicas. Column-level tracking produces fewer conflicts than row-level tracking.

### Customizing the Conflict Tracking Level

When you replicate a new Access 2000 database, Jet automatically enables column-level tracking by default. If you convert replicas created by prior versions of Access, row-level tracking is enabled.

You can change the type of conflict tracking employed by Jet prior to replicating a table. To use row-level tracking for a table, right-click on the table in the Access database container and select Properties from the popup menu. From the Properties dialog box, select the Row-Level Tracking checkbox to enable row-level tracking (see Figure 9.9 from earlier in the chapter).

---

**TIP**     Once an object is replicated, you can't directly change the conflict tracking level. You can work around this limitation by making the object local to the design master replica, changing its tracking level, and then re-replicating the object.

---

Using JRO, you can control the tracking level of a new replica set using the MakeReplica method of the Replica object. For example, to create a new replica set that uses row-level tracking as the default conflict tracking level, you could use the following code:

```
rpl.MakeReplicable  "c:\new.mdb",  ColumnTracking:=  False
```

JRO doesn't have any methods or properties to allow you to set the conflict tracking level of individual tables or replicas.

### Which Conflict Tracking Level Should You Use?

By enabling column-level tracking of conflicts, you may be able to drastically reduce the number of conflicts that occur in a replica set. However, column-level tracking has at least two disadvantages:

- It adds overhead to the tracking of updates and conflicts that may negatively impact performance.

- It allows users to inconsistently update records. For example, user A might change the address of a customer while user B changes the phone number, producing a merged customer record with inconsistent address and phone number information. This could be a problem in some applications where update consistency is critical.

You'll have to gauge your sensitivity to these disadvantages and weigh them against the obvious benefits afforded by using column-level tracking, before choosing which level of tracking to use. Remember that, if necessary, you can use column-level tracking for some tables and row-level tracking for others.

## Unified Treatment of Conflicts

In prior versions of the Jet engine, three types of synchronization problems could occur: *conflicts*, *data errors*, and *design errors*. This was an issue because data error and design errors were difficult to fix and almost always required a developer or database administrator to resolve.

Jet 4.0 simplifies the resolution of synchronization problems by treating all problems as conflicts. In addition, Jet now propagates the conflict information to both replicas. Previously, only the loser of a conflict was notified of the conflict.

## Replica Priority and Conflict Resolution

Jet 4.0 uses a new algorithm to initially resolve conflicts. Prior versions of Jet used an algorithm that chose a winner based on the total number of times the row was updated at each replica. This algorithm was simple for the Jet engine to execute but, in reality, wasn't much better than an algorithm that chose the winner randomly.

Jet 4.0 introduces a replica priority-based algorithm. Here's how it works:

- Each replica in the replica set is assigned a priority ranging from 0 to 100.

- The design master is assigned a priority of 90. Subsequent replicas are, by default, assigned a priority that is 90% of their parent replica. Anonymous and local replicas are assigned a fixed priority of 0.

- You can change the priority of a replica created using the Access menus or JRO. Once created, however, you cannot change a replica's priority.

- You must have database administer privilege to assign a priority to a replica that is greater than 90% of the parent replica's priority.

- When a conflict occurs, the replica with the highest priority value wins.

- If both replicas have the same priority, the replica with the lowest ReplicaID wins.

While not perfect, this conflict resolution scheme is better than the one used by prior versions of the Jet engine. Regardless, Jet doesn't have the final word on conflict resolution. You can use the Microsoft Replication Conflict Viewer or a custom conflict-resolution function to alter which replica wins the conflict battle. This is discussed later in the chapter. First, however, we need to discuss the different types of conflict that can occur.

## Types of Conflicts

Because Jet 4.0 treats all replication problems as conflicts, there are a number of different types of conflicts that can occur. The different types of conflicts that can occur and their resolution are summarized in Table 9.7

**TABLE 9.7:** Types of Conflicts

| Conflict | Occurs When | How Resolved |
|----------|-------------|--------------|
| Update/update | Two users update the same column of a row (when using column-level tracking) or the same row (when using row-level tracking). | Conflict is resolved by replica priority. |
| Update/delete | One user updates a row while a second user deletes the same row. | Deleted record wins. |
| Unique key violation | A record with the same primary key value or values is inserted in two or more replicas. | Conflict is resolved by replica priority. |

**TABLE 9.7:** Types of Conflicts *(continued)*

| Conflict | Occurs When | How Resolved |
|---|---|---|
| Validation rule | You change a table-level validation rule in one replica while at the same time, a user adds or updates records in another replica that fail to satisfy the new rule. | Conflict is resolved by replica priority. |
| Referential integrity | A user inserts a new record in one table that references a primary key value in another table. At the same time, a second user updates or deletes the referenced record in a second replica. | Conflict is resolved by replica priority. |
| Locked record | A record that needs to be updated during a synchronization exchange is locked by another user. | Synchronization fails. |

# The Microsoft Replication Conflict Viewer

When a synchronization exchange is complete, Jet checks if any conflicts have occurred. If Jet determines that one or more conflicts have occurred, it resolves the conflicts using the replica-priority algorithm previously discussed. It then creates a conflict table for each table containing synchronization conflicts, naming the conflict table *tablename*_Conflict, where *tablename* is the name of the table containing conflicts. Next, it places losing conflict records in the appropriate conflict table and replicates the conflict tables to both replicas.

**NOTE**   Unlike previous versions of the Jet engine, version 4.0 notifies both replicas of conflicts.

When you open a replica after a synchronization exchange that produced conflicts, Access informs you that the replica contains conflicts and asks you if you wish to resolve them now (as shown in Figure 9.28). If you answer Yes, Access launches the Microsoft Replication Conflict Viewer, a conflict viewer that is shared between Jet 4.0 and SQL Server 7.0. Initially, the conflict viewer displays a dialog box that summarizes the conflicts in the database (as shown in Figure 9.29).

**FIGURE 9.28**
Access has found conflicts in the current database.

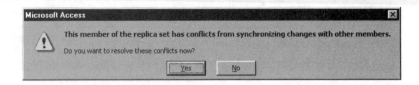

**FIGURE 9.29**
The Microsoft Replication Conflict Viewer lists the number of conflicts found in each table.

When you select a table and click the View button, the Microsoft Replication Conflict Viewer displays each of the conflicts for the table. The conflict viewer is shown in Figure 9.30 with an update/update conflict. In Figure 9.31, the conflict viewer is shown with a unique key violation. Figure 9.32 shows what the conflict viewer looks like when it encounters an update/delete conflict.

**FIGURE 9.30**

The Microsoft Replication Conflict Viewer displays a record containing an update/update conflict.

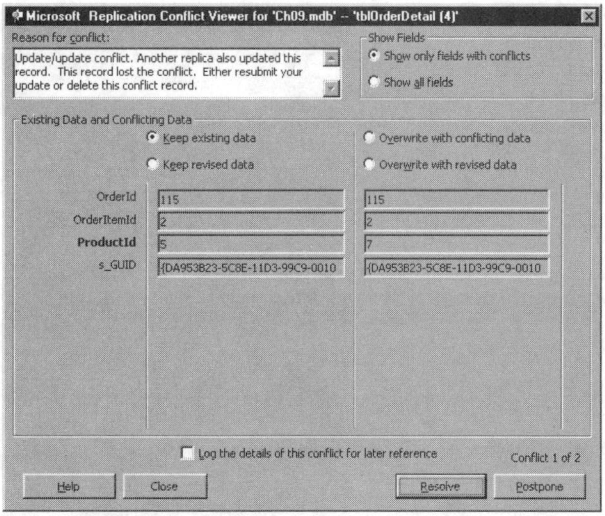

**FIGURE 9.31**

The Microsoft Replication Conflict Viewer displays a record containing a unique key violation.

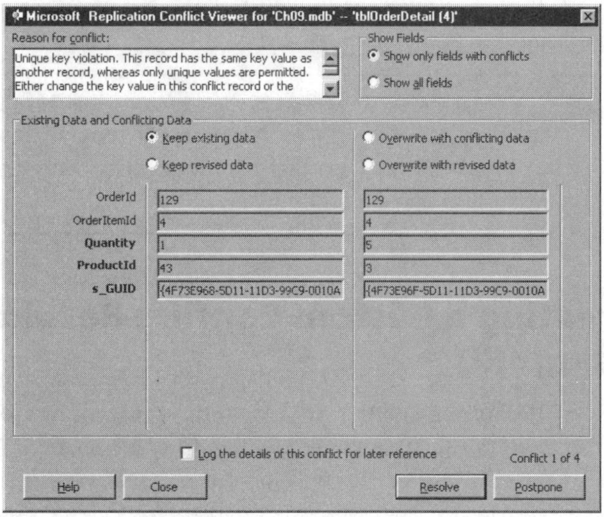

FIGURE 9.32

The Microsoft Replication
Conflict Viewer displays a
record containing an
update/delete conflict.

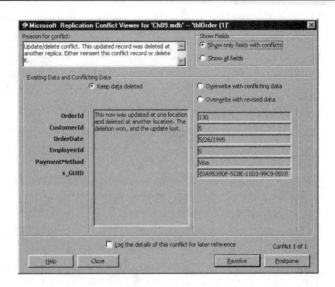

For each conflict record, you can opt to keep the original winner, keep the conflict record, or keep an edited version of either record.

> **TIP**  Each replica involved in the exchange will get to decide the status of conflicts. If
> you'd rather have only one user use the conflict viewer for a given set of conflicts,
> you should have that user synchronize with the other replica immediately after
> resolving the conflicts.

## Creating a Custom Conflict-Resolution Function Using JRO

If you're using the Access runtime system or a Visual Basic application, the Microsoft Replication Conflict Viewer won't be available. You will have to create your
own facility for reviewing and resolving conflicts. Even if you are using Access,
you may wish to resolve conflicts using a custom resolution algorithm rather than
depend on users to resolve conflicts.

## The ConflictFunction Property

You use the ConflictFunction property of the Replica object to get and set the name of a public Access VBA function that resolves conflicts for the replica set. For example, the following sets the ConflictFunction property to ConflictResolver:

```
rpl.ConflictFunction = "ConflictResolver()"
```

The parentheses are required.

To return to the default Microsoft Replication Conflict Viewer, set the Conflict-Function property to an empty string.

> **WARNING**    The Microsoft Jet replication documentation states that you can also set the Conflict-Function property to the GUID value of one of the replicas in the replica set. This tells Access to use the Microsoft Replication Conflict Viewer, but to report conflicts only to that replica. At the time of this writing, however, we were unable to get this feature to work.

## The ConflictTables Property

You can use the ConflictTables property to return a recordset that contains a record for each table containing conflicts. The returned recordset will contain two fields:

- *table_name*, which is the name of the table with conflicts

- *conflict_table_name*, which is the name of the conflict table for this table

For example, the following subroutine from basReplicationJRO prints the names of the tables with conflicts and their corresponding conflict tables to the debug window:

```
Public Sub adhDisplayConflictTables()
    Dim rpl As JRO.Replica
    Dim rstConflicts As ADODB.Recordset

    Set rpl = New JRO.Replica
    Set rpl.ActiveConnection = CurrentProject.Connection
    Set rstConflicts = rpl.ConflictTables

    Do While Not rstConflicts.EOF
        Debug.Print "Table: " & _
        rstConflicts("table_name");
```

```
            Debug.Print  ", Conflict Table: " & _
                rstConflicts("conflict_table_name")
            rstConflicts.MoveNext
        Loop

        rstConflicts.Close
        Set rstConflicts = Nothing
        Set rpl = Nothing
    End Sub
```

## An Example Conflict Resolution Function

The basReplicationJRO module contains a custom conflict function, adhSimple-Resolve, that you can use as a model for creating your own conflict resolution function. The adhSimpleResolve function iterates through all of the conflicts in a replica and deletes them without user intervention. That is, it accepts all of the winning records that were designated by the built-in replica priority algorithm. The adhSimpleResolve function is shown in Listing 9.3.

### ⟳ Listing 9.3

```
Function adhSimpleResolve() As Variant
    ' Iterates through conflict records
    ' and deletes them.
    On Error GoTo adhSimpleResolve_Err

    Dim cnn As ADODB.Connection
    Dim rpl As JRO.Replica
    Dim rstConTbls As ADODB.Recordset
    Dim rstConflict As ADODB.Recordset
    Dim strTable As String
    Dim strConflict As String
    Dim strMsg As String
    Dim lngCounter As Long

    DoCmd.Hourglass True

    Set cnn = CurrentProject.Connection
    Set rpl = New JRO.Replica
    Set rpl.ActiveConnection = cnn
```

```
' Get list of conflict tables.
Set rstConTbls = rpl.ConflictTables
Do While Not rstConTbls.EOF
    strTable = rstConTbls.Fields("table_name")
    strConflict = _
      rstConTbls.Fields("conflict_table_name")

    ' Create a recordset against the
    ' conflict table
    Set rstConflict = New ADODB.Recordset
    rstConflict.Open strConflict, cnn, adOpenKeyset, _
      adLockOptimistic, adCmdTable

    ' Count up conflicts and delete them
    Do While Not rstConflict.EOF
       lngCounter = lngCounter + 1
       rstConflict.Delete
       rstConflict.MoveNext
    Loop

    rstConflict.Close
    Set rstConflict = Nothing
    rstConTbls.MoveNext
Loop

strMsg = lngCounter & _
  " conflict records were processed!"
MsgBox strMsg, vbInformation + vbOKOnly, _
  adhSimpleResolve

adhSimpleResolve_Exit:
DoCmd.Hourglass False
If Not rpl Is Nothing Then
    Set rpl = Nothing
End If
If Not rstConflict Is Nothing Then
    Set rstConflict = Nothing
End If
If Not rstConTbls Is Nothing Then
    Set rstConTbls = Nothing
End If
Set cnn = Nothing
```

```
    Exit Function

adhSimpleResolve_Err:
    Select Case Err
    Case Else
        strMsg = "Error#" & Err.Number & "--" & _
          Err.Description
        MsgBox strMsg, vbCritical + vbOKOnly, _
          "Procedure adhSimpleResolve"
        Resume adhSimpleResolve_Exit
    End Select
End Function
```

You might wish to extend adhSimpleResolve with additional code, perhaps to log the conflict records to a central logging table or logging file.

To try out the adhSimpleResolve conflict resolution function, load a replicated version of CH09.MDB and enter the following into the debug window:

```
adhsetConflictFunction "adhSimpleResolve"
```

Now, whenever a replica contains conflicts, it will run adhSimpleResolve instead of loading the Microsoft Replication Conflict Viewer.

## Using the MSysConflicts Table

The sample adhSimpleResolve conflict resolution function simply deletes conflict records without investigating the nature of each conflict. A more intelligent conflict resolution function would gather information from the MSysConflicts table to help decide how the conflict should be resolved.

MSysConflicts contains metadata on all conflicts in the database. Table 9.8 describes the MSysConflicts fields.

You can use the information gathered from the MSysConflicts table to help create intelligent conflict-resolution functions. For example, say you wanted to create a query that:

- Listed all parent conflicts but no child conflicts

- Showed the losing and winning replicas

- Showed the count of conflicts and the count of child conflicts

- Showed the name of the conflict table and of the source table

**T A B L E  9 . 8 :**    The Fields of the MSysConflicts Table

| MSysConflicts Field | Description |
| --- | --- |
| BaseGuidSrc | A GUID that links to the GuidSrc field in MSysGenHistory. Used internally by Jet to handle the case where there are multiple conflicts on the same row from multiple sources, in order to determine the most recent conflict. You likely won't find this column useful. |
| BaseRowGuid | A GUID that links to the s_GUID field of the conflict table. It represents the "parent" conflict, so all child conflicts contain the same BaseRowGuid as the parent. When it's the same as the ConflictIdGuid, then this is the parent conflict. |
| BaseTableGuid | Links to the s_GUID field in MSysTableGuids and thus gives you the name of the source table for the conflict. |
| ConflictDescCode | Type of conflict (e.g., unique key, table validation, simultaneous update, foreign key, and so forth). |
| ConflictIdGuid | A GUID that links to the s_GUID field of the conflict table. When it's the same as the BaseRowGuid, then this is a parent conflict; otherwise, it is a child conflict. |
| InvolvedObjects | A text field which theoreticaly tells you info about where the conflict occurred like table and field. In practice, we have never seen it populated. |
| LosingReplicaId | Links to the s_GUID field in MSysReplicas and tells you which replica is the losing one. |
| Reason | Text that gives some context-sensitive info about the conflict, for display. |
| WinningGuidSrc | Links to the GuidSrc field in MSysGenHistory. Like BaseGuidSrc, this is used internally by Jet to handle the case where there are multiple conflicts on the same row from multiple sources, in order to determine the most recent conflict. Not normally useful. |
| WinningReplicaId | Links to the s_GUID field in MSysReplicas and tells you which replica is the winning replica. |
| WinningRowGuid | Links to the s_GUID field from the source table when there is still a source row that you might want to link to (such as in an update, update conflict, or in a duplicate primary key conflict). |
| s_GUID | Replication system field. Links to the ConflictRowGuid field in the conflict table. |
| s_Generation | Replication system field. Links to the s_Generation field in the conflict table. |
| s_Lineage | Replication system field. Links to the s_Lineage field in the conflict table. |

You could accomplish this by creating the following query (see qryConflict-Counts in the CH09.MDB database):

```
SELECT Max(tg.TableName) AS src_Table,
Max(st.SideTable) AS conflict_table,
Count(IIF(c_a.ConflictIdGuid <> c_a.s_Guid,Null, 1))
As CnfCount, Count(IIF(c_a.ConflictIdGuid =
c_a.s_Guid, Null, 1)) As CnfChildCount
FROM (((MSysTableGuids AS tg INNER JOIN
MSysSideTables AS st ON tg.s_GUID = st.TableGuid) INNER
JOIN MSysConflicts AS c ON st.TableGuid =
c.BaseTableGuid) INNER JOIN MSysReplicas AS r
ON c.WinningReplicaId = r.ReplicaId) INNER JOIN
MSysConflicts AS c_a ON c_a.ConflictIdGuid = c.s_Guid
WHERE c.ConflictIDGuid = c.s_Guid
GROUP BY tg.TableName;
```

This query produces a recordset containing all the source and conflict tables, as well as the count of conflicts and the associated child conflicts.

The following query returns the source and conflict fields from the tblOrder-Detail table in a single recordset (see qryOrderDetailConflicts in the CH09.MDB database):

```
SELECT tblOrderDetail.*, tblOrderDetail_Conflict.*
FROM (tblOrderDetail_Conflict INNER JOIN MSysConflicts ON
tblOrderDetail_Conflict.ConflictRowGuid =
MSysConflicts.s_GUID) LEFT JOIN tblOrderDetail ON
MSysConflicts.WinningRowGuid = tblOrderDetail.s_GUID
```

# Other Replication Issues

When developing database applications that will be replicated, you need to consider several additional issues, as described in the next few sections.

## Query Issues

Because of the extra fields that the replication process adds to tables, you may get strange results when using queries containing an asterisk (*) in the query grid (or the SELECT clause of a SQL statement). Append queries are especially a problem.

The solution is to avoid using the asterisk and instead explicitly add the desired fields to queries.

## Upgrading a Replica Set

Just like the upgrading of any production Access 97 application, you need to take care when upgrading a replicated application to Access 2000. You'll need to upgrade every replica of the replica set.

There are number of ways to approach the upgrade process. Here's one approach you may wish to take:

1. Create a backup copy of the design master of the replica set using Windows explorer.

2. Move this backup copy of the design master so that it's isolated from the other members of the replica set.

3. Upgrade the copy to Access 2000. Create additional replicas and test that everything is okay.

4. If everything checks out okay, delete the test replica set and upgrade each replica of the production replica set in turn. Synchronize all of the replicas.

## Removing a Replica from the Replica Set

To remove a replica from a replica set, first delete the replica and then attempt to synchronize with it using the Access menus. When Access realizes it has been deleted, it removes the replica from the replica set.

## Changing the Design Master

Normally, you won't need to change the design master status, but there may be times when you wish to designate another replica as the new design master. For example, say you are the database administrator for a replicated database and you will be going on vacation or transferring to another job. In cases like this you may wish to transfer design master status to your assistant, who normally uses a non–design master replica on the network.

Before you transfer design master status from one replica to another, compact the design master and synchronize all replicas with the current design master so they are at the same generation.

To transfer design master status from one replica to another using the Access menus, open the current design master and select Tools ➢ Replication ➢ Synchronize Now. In the Synchronize With combo box, choose the replica to which you wish to transfer design master status, and select the Make '*database*' the Design Master checkbox. (See Figure 9.17 earlier in this chapter.)

To transfer design master status using JRO code, follow these steps in your code:

1. Exclusively open both the current design master and the replica you wish to make the new design master.

2. Set the current design master's DesignMasterID property to the ReplicaID property of the new design master.

3. Synchronize the two replicas.

## Recovering the Design Master

In some cases, you may have to designate a new design master without the luxury of having the old design master around. This may be necessary, for example, if the design master becomes corrupted or is inadvertently deleted. In these cases, you must assign design master status to some other replica. You can do this by using the Tools ➢ Replication ➢ Recover Design Master command in Access.

You can recover the design master using JRO code by opening the new design master database exclusively and setting its DesignMasterID property to its ReplicaID property.

After changing the design master, synchronize all replicas with the new design master.

## Moving Replicas

You can use Replication Manager to move a replica from one location to another. Follow these steps:

1. Select File ➢ Move Replica.

2. Select the current location of the replica and click Open.

3. Select the destination folder and filename and click Save.

# Linked Tables

When you synchronize two replicas, Jet will exchange only the data in native Access tables, not in linked tables. You can, however, separately replicate and synchronize the database that contains the linked tables. If you're using a typical split database architecture (see Chapter 2), where users run an application from a local "application" database on their workstations linked to tables stored in a shared "data" database stored on the file server, you could choose to replicate just the application database, just the data database, or both.

---

**NOTE**    You can't replicate data stored in external non-Access tables.

---

## Design Considerations

If an application is to be used on a LAN only, you might keep a single nonreplicated data database on the file server with the application database replicated across the LAN, using a star topology with the file server as the hub node. As an alternative, you might wish to abandon the split database design and replicate the single database across the LAN using a star, ring, or fully connected topology.

If you wished to move a split application to a WAN or loosely connected network with—for example, multiple stars interconnected at their hub nodes—it may make sense to create two replica sets: one for the application databases that would be replicated to every desktop on the WAN, and a distinct replica set for the data databases that would remain on the file server hubs of each workgroup. Since application updates would be rare, you'd probably synchronize the application databases only when you needed to roll out a new version of the application. On the other hand, the data databases would be on a more regular synchronization schedule.

## Resolving Conflicts for "Data" Databases

Whenever you replicate a database that users will not normally open, you must have some automated system in place for detecting and resolving conflicts that might occur from synchronization exchanges between these replicas. This is necessary because the built-in Microsoft Replication Conflict Viewer or custom conflict resolution code will never be called, since the database won't normally be opened by a user. Thus, you'll have to create a VBA routine to automatically run after each synchronization exchange, logging and resolving conflicts and alerting the database administrator to any errors.

## Security Issues

Jet doesn't support replicating the workgroup file (SYSTEM.MDW) in a secured workgroup environment. Thus, on a LAN, you must either connect each replica to the workgroup file or copy the workgroup file to each workstation. For a WAN, you'll need to copy the workgroup file to each remote synchronization replica.

> **NOTE** You can't replicate a database that has a database password. You must remove the password before proceeding. Similarly, you can't create a database password for a replicated database.

In a secured system that's normally centrally controlled by a single database administrator, this shortcoming shouldn't affect you. However, in situations where you would normally distribute security responsibilities among users, you will have to address the following issues:

- Because permission changes are considered design changes, they can be made only at the design master.

- Unless you restrict user access to the account management features, users will be able to make changes to user and group accounts (including the changing of passwords) from any replica.

> **NOTE** Security information is stored in two places. Account information is stored in the workgroup file (SYSTEM.MDW), and permission information is stored along with the objects in each user database. Thus, only permission information will be replicated in a replicated database. See Chapter 8 for more details on Jet security.

Because you are restricted from making permission changes and these changes are kept in the user database, coordination of updates should not be a problem—they must be done at the design master and then propagated using the normal synchronization schedule. Changes to user accounts, however, present a problem: local account changes won't be replicated because they are stored in the workgroup file. The best approach may be to limit these types of security changes to one database administrator who can see that the multiple workgroup files are kept in sync.

**WARNING**   It's important that any permission changes that depend on changes to accounts be made only *after* updated workgroup files have been copied to each workstation. Otherwise you run the risk of the replicated databases being out of sync with the workgroup files.

## Compacting Replicas

When you make a number of schema changes at the design master, you should compact the database before synchronizing it with other replicas. This reduces the number of design changes that need to be transferred between replicas. In addition, it's a good idea to compact all replicas on a regular—perhaps daily or weekly—basis because replication will tend to bloat the databases.

The basReplicationJRO module of the CH09.MDB database contains a subroutine, adhCompactDatabase, that you can use to compact a database programmatically using the CompactDatabase method of the JRO JetEngine object.

**TIP**   When you compact replicated databases, you should compact each database *twice*. Jet performs the compact in two phases: first it performs the normal consolidation and recovery of deleted space, and *then* it goes through replicated objects and decides which ones to mark for deletion. However, because it has already finished reclaiming space from deleted objects, you need to compact a second time to finish the job. It won't hurt the replica to compact only once, but you will save additional space and make your replicas more efficient by compacting an extra time.

# SQL Server Replication

Whereas Jet uses a multi-master replication model, SQL Server replication is based on a "publish and subscribe" model. In SQL Server's replication world, you have publishers, distributors, and subscribers. While the underlying replication models are different, SQL Server replication can be configured to work in a manner similar to Jet replication.

A *publisher* is a server that makes data available to other servers. A *distributor*—which can be the same server as the publisher—is a server that helps distribute the published data. A *subscriber* is a server that receives replicated data from a publisher.

SQL Server publishes *publications*, which are groups of articles. *Articles* are tables or stored procedures you wish to publish. Subscriptions can either be *push subscriptions*—sent by the publisher to subscribers—or *pull subscriptions*—requested by the subscribers from the publishers.

## SQL Server Replication Modes

SQL Server can be configured to work in one of three different replication modes:

**Snapshot replication**   The publisher sends snapshots of publications to subscribers on a regular schedule that replace the contents of subscriber tables. Can be used with or without the immediate-updating subscriber option that allows subscribers to modify the data.

**Transactional replication**   The publisher replicates data within the context of a distributed transaction. While this type of replication guarantees tight consistency, it requires the subscribers to be connected to the publisher at all times. Like snapshot replication, transactional replication can be used with or without immediate-updating subscribers.

**Merge replication**   The publisher sends updates to subscribers on schedule. Subscribers can update data that is merged back into the publisher database. Works with the Microsoft Replication Conflict Viewer. This mode of replication is most like Jet replication.

You can configure snapshot or merge replication to work with non-SQL Server databases, including Jet 4.0 databases.

Configuring SQL Server for replication can be quite complex. There are a multitude of steps to be performed and decisions to be made. A complete discussion of SQL Server replication is beyond the scope of this chapter. We'll concentrate here on how to configure merge replication to a Jet subscriber.

**NOTE**  For more information on SQL Server replication, see the SQL Server documentation or *SQL Server 7 In Record Time* by Mike Gunderloy and Mary Chipman (Sybex, 1999).

# Configuring Merge Replication to a Jet Database

SQL Server merge replication is similar in many ways to Jet replication. So similar, in fact, that you can set up merge replication to work with both SQL Server and Jet subscribers. You can update records in both SQL Server and Jet replicas and use the Microsoft Replication Conflict Viewer to resolve any conflicts that might arise.

**NOTE**  MSDE can only act as a replication subscriber, not a publisher. Thus, you can't use it to perform merge replication to a Jet subscriber.

In order to replicate SQL Server data to a Jet database using merge replication, you must do the following in order:

1. Replicate the SQL Server database.

2. Create an Access subscriber.

3. Create a push subscription.

Each of these steps is discussed in the follow sections.

**TIP**  In order to use merge replication to a Jet subscriber with SQL Server 7.0, you must first apply the SQL Server 7.0 Service Pack 1 (or a later service pack if one is available).

## Replicating the SQL Server Database

To replicate the SQL Server database, start up SQL Server Enterprise Manager and follow these steps:

1. Highlight the name of the SQL Server in Enterprise Manager and select Tools ➤ Replication ➤ Create and Manage Publications.

2. From the Create and Manage Publications dialog box, select the database you want to replicate and click Create Publication.

3. SQL Server starts the Create Publication Wizard. Click the Next button on the first screen.

4. On the Choose Publication Type screen, select the Merge Publication option as shown in Figure 9.33.

**FIGURE 9.33**
Creating a merge publication using the SQL Server Create Publication Wizard

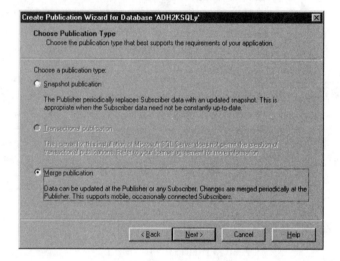

5. On the Specify Subscriber Types screen, select the Some Subscribers Will Be Microsoft Jet 4.0 Databases option.

6. On the Specify Articles screen, select the objects you wish to publish. You can elect to publish some or all of the tables listed, as shown in Figure 9.34.

7. On the Choose Publication Name and Description screen, name the publication.

8. On the Use Default Properties of the Publication screen, you can optionally elect to define filters or modify other properties of the publication.

9. On the last screen, click Finish to create the publication.

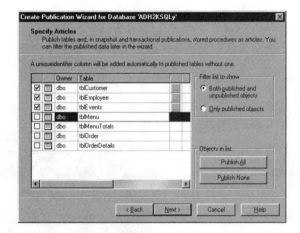

**FIGURE 9.34**
The Specify Articles screen of the SQL Server Create Publication Wizard

## Creating an Access Subscriber

Once the wizard is finished, you need to create an Access subscriber by following these steps:

1. Select Tools ➢ Replication ➢ Configure Publishing, Subscribers, and Distribution.

2. Click the Subscribers tab of the Publisher and Distributor Properties dialog box and click New Subscriber.

3. Select Microsoft Jet 4.0 Database and click OK, as shown in Figure 9.35.

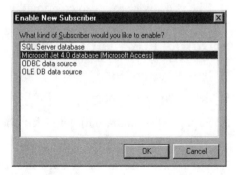

**FIGURE 9.35**
The Enable New Subscriber dialog box.

4. At the Enable Subscriber – Microsoft Jet 4.0 Database dialog box, click Add to add a new linked server.

5. At the Add Microsoft Jet Linked Server dialog box, fill in a name for the linked server and a path and filename for the Access database, as shown in Figure 9.36. The file won't exist yet; SQL Server will create it with the first synchronization.

**FIGURE 9.36**
Entering a linked server
name and database path
and name for the new Jet
merge subscriber

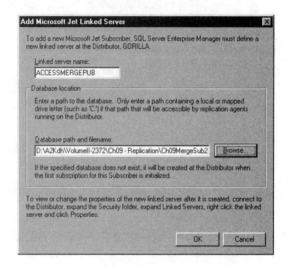

6. Back at the Enable Subscriber – Microsoft Jet 4.0 Database dialog box, enter a login name and password for the Jet database. If security is not enabled, enter **Admin** with a blank password.

7. Click OK twice to finish creating the new Jet subscriber.

## Creating a Push Subscription

The final step is to create a push subscription to the Jet subscriber:

1. Select Tools ➢ Replication ➢ Push Subscriptions to Others.

2. Expand the database folder, select the publication you want to push, and click Push New Subscription.

3. The Push Subscription Wizard starts. Click Next at the introductory screen.

4. At the Choose Subscribers screen, select the Jet subscriber you just created.

5. At the Set Merge Agent Schedule screen, configure any scheduling options you'd like.

6. At the Initialize Subscription screen, select the Yes, Initialize the Schema and Data at the Subscriber option and click Next.

7. At the Set Subscription Priority screen, set the desired subscription priority level as shown in Figure 9.37. SQL Server merge replication uses a priority-based conflict resolution algorithm much like Jet's.

8. At the Start the Required Services screen, select the SQLServerAgent service and click Next.

9. Click Finish to create the push subscription.

**FIGURE 9.37**

Entering a priority for the Jet subscriber

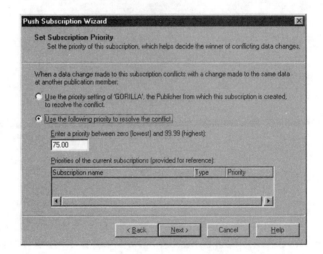

The wizard creates the subscription and informs you when the process is complete.

# Working with Merge Subscription Replicas

When you open a Jet merge subscription database in Access, as shown in Figure 9.38, it looks much like any regular Jet replication design master database. If you look a little more closely, however, you'll notice a few differences:

- It includes an extra user table: msmerge_delete_conflicts.

- All of the Tools ➤ Replication menu items except for Synchronize Now and Resolve Conflicts are disabled.

**FIGURE 9.38**

The database container of a Jet merge replica

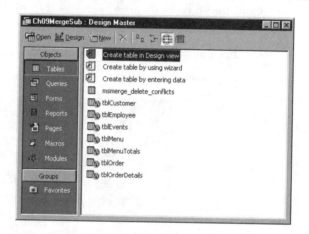

You make edits to the data in a SQL Server/Jet merge replica. You can also create forms, reports, and other Access objects. Only the tables will be replicated.

SQL Server/Jet merge replication uses a fixed hub and spoke star topology with the SQL Server publisher database as the hub. Jet replicas can synchronize only with the SQL Server publisher database.

---

**NOTE**    You can manage some of SQL Server replication features from the Tools ➤ Replication menus in an Access project file. However, not all of the features are available from the Access menus. In most cases, you're better off using SQL Server Enterprise Manager.

---

## Synchronizing Jet Merge Replicas

When you set up the push subscription, you created a schedule that SQL Server uses to synchronize between the master SQL Server database and the Jet replica. You can change the schedule and other properties of the subscription by following these steps:

1. From SQL Server Enterprise manager, select Tools ➢ Replication ➢ Create and Manage Publications.

2. Select the publication.

3. Click the Properties and Subscriptions button.

4. You can modify the schedule from the Status tab of the Subscription Properties dialog box.

You can initiate an ad hoc synchronization from Access by selecting Tools ➢ Replication ➢ Synchronize Now. Access displays a slightly modified version of the standard Synchronize Database dialog box, as shown in Figure 9.39.

**FIGURE 9.39**
Synchronizing a Jet merge
replica with SQL Server

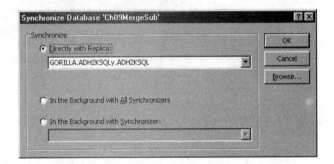

## Resolving Merge Replication Conflicts

Even though Access enables the Tools ➢ Replication ➢ Resolve Conflicts menu for Jet merge replicas, this menu doesn't do anything because Jet replicas are not notified of synchronization conflicts. You must use SQL Server Enterprise Manager to resolve conflicts.

To review any synchronization conflicts, right-click on the name of the SQL Server database in SQL Server Enterprise Manager and select All Tasks ➢ View

Replication Conflicts from the popup menu. SQL Server starts the Microsoft Replication Conflict Viewer.

Figure 9.40 shows a merge replication conflict as it appears in the Microsoft Replication Conflict Viewer. This is the same conflict viewer used by Jet replication.

**FIGURE 9.40**
This conflict was created by updating the same column in both the SQL Server master database and the Jet subscriber database.

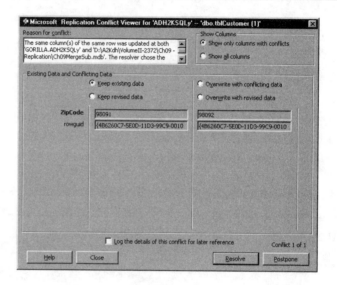

# Summary

Replication is an exciting technology. In this chapter we've explored replication in detail and covered the following topics:

- How replication works
- All the tools you can use to manage replication: Windows Briefcase, Access menus, Replication Manager, and JRO code
- When you should consider using replication
- Replication topologies
- The changes Jet makes to a replicated database
- Replicating a database

- Synchronizing replicas
- Resolving conflicts
- Creating a custom conflict resolution function
- Moving the design master
- Replicating databases with linked tables
- Replicating secured databases
- Compacting replicas
- Partial replication
- Internet-based synchronization
- Configuring SQL Server merge replication to a Jet subscriber

# Creating Data Access Pages

- Introducing data access pages

- Understanding how and why you might use data access pages

- Creating different types of data access pages

- Deploying data access pages

In creating Office 2000, Microsoft took on a huge challenge: it wanted each of the Office products to be able to present its native data in some format within a Web browser. This "browserability" needed to be transparent and simple to accomplish for the end user. In addition, Microsoft wanted each of the products to allow data editing from within the browser, if possible.

For products like Word and Excel, the products' data and its formatting are inextricably intertwined. That is, the only real way the teams could meet their goals was to provide round-trip data transformations from the native data store (.DOC or .XLS files) to the Web (in XML format) and back. For those products, this technique works well.

In Access, however, data and its presentation are not so tightly bound. You store data in one place and use a number of different possible techniques for displaying and editing that data. Therefore, the issues facing the Access team weren't as "cut and dry" as those facing the other teams. Although there may have been several possible alternatives, in the end the Access team produced a new technology, *data access pages*, which allows you to easily create Web-based pages that allow display and editing capabilities. In this chapter, we'll discuss the issues involved in creating and deploying data access pages (DAPs), taking a look at their various uses, the controls that Access provides for use on the pages, and several issues involved with deploying these pages for end-user applications.

This chapter focuses on design-time issues only. That is, you'll find information here on creating and designing DAPs, binding the DAPs to Jet or SQL Server data, and handling coding issues involving the location of DAPs. In Chapter 11, you'll find information about working with DAPs at runtime. Chapter 11 discusses scripting in general, and programming DAPs in specific. Once you've created a DAP and need to know how to make it do real work, you'll want to investigate the material in Chapter 11 as well.

Because data access pages store hard-coded links to their data source internally, and because Access stores hard-coded paths to the files containing the HTML for the data access page, the examples contained in this chapter will not operate correctly until you've reset these paths. To do that, open the basResetDAP module from CH10.MDB, place your cursor inside the first procedure (adhValidateDA-PLinks), and press the F5 key. (For more information on this procedure, see the "Deploying Data Access Pages" section at the end of this chapter.) Although you might want to run this procedure automatically in your applications, or provide a user interface for running this procedure, we opted not to do that, as every application needs to handle this situation differently.

The data access page control toolbox contains three controls provided by the Office Web Components: Office PivotTable, Office Chart, and Office Spreadsheet. We've put off coverage of these three useful components until Chapter 12, so that it follows the chapter on scripting. If you're interested in those particular components, check out Chapter 12.

# What Are Data Access Pages?

Data access pages allow you to display and (sometimes) edit data provided either by Jet or by SQL Server, in the context of a Web page. You use the data access page designer from within Access to create the pages (although you could just as easily use any other ActiveX-enabled designer, the Access designer makes this much easier), and you can display the pages either within Access—in Page view—or from Internet Explorer 5.0 or higher.

When you're working in Access, displaying a data access page in Page view is basically the same thing as displaying it in the browser. Access simply hosts a full instance of Internet Explorer in an Access window, so that you're seeing what users will see in a browser. The big difference is the location of the HTM files. Normally, if you want users to use a browser to view your pages, you'll want to place the pages (and the database, if you're reading data from an MDB file) on a Web server. If your application displays data access pages in Page view, the HTM files normally "live" in a local folder.

Basically, you can think of data access pages as a cross between forms and reports, available in a browser environment. In limited circumstances, users can edit data on a data access page (if you're showing data from only one data source, you've not grouped the data, and you have the appropriate rights). The most exciting part about data access pages, however, is the ability to interactively drill down into grouped data. This provides a report-like "feel," without needing to view all the data. Users can select just the subsets they want, based on the groupings you've created at design time. This chapter includes demonstrations you can walk through, creating various types of data access pages.

When you create a data access page within Access, you're actually creating two independent "pieces":

- The DataAccessPage object, within Access, which contains little more than the location of the associated HTM file

- The HTM file, which contains all the HTML and XML source code for your page

This separation causes its own share of deployment issues, some of which you'll find discussed at the end of this chapter. (In this chapter, we deal mostly with issues involved with deploying data access pages used within Access applications. For information on deploying data access pages in general, see Chapter 16.)

To link the HTM file with a data source, data access pages use a component from the Office Web Components (see Chapter 12 for more information on the Office Web Components) called the DataSourceControl control. This invisible control provides data linking for specific HTML and ActiveX controls that you place onto your data access pages, and makes it possible to group and sort data as well. Although you'll never see the DataSourceControl object, Access automatically creates an instance of this control (with a Name property value of "MSODSC") and adds it to your data access page when you first bind data to the page.

---

**WARNING**   Data access pages take advantage of ActiveX controls (the Office Web Components) that require an Office license. That is, anyone using Office Web Components must, legally, have an Office license (either an installed copy of an Office 2000 product, or a license purchased by a company as part of some licensing package). If for no other reason, this is reason enough not to use data access pages for public Web pages—unless Microsoft changes its licensing stance, you don't have the legal right to use these particular ActiveX controls in an environment where users don't necessarily have an Office 2000 license.

---

To sum up data access pages, think of an HTML file containing ActiveX controls that can be bound to Jet or SQL Server data. Microsoft Office provides ActiveX controls that manage the linking, sorting, and grouping, and the data access page designer makes it simple for you to create these bound Web pages.

---

**NOTE** At this time, because Access can only retrieve data using Jet or SQL Server, the limitation flows over to data access pages too. Data displayed on a data access page will either come from Jet (as data stored in an MDB file, or linked tables) or from SQL Server 6.5 or higher (as native SQL tables used in an Access Data Project [ADP file] , or linked server tables).

---

Data access pages provide a simple way to create Web pages for intranet reporting and data entry. If you're using them on a Web server, however, you may want to limit their use to SQL Server. With MDB files, all data processing must occur on the client. This means that Jet must be installed locally, and all data manipulation happens locally. Perhaps this isn't a problem, but it all works better using SQL Server data, where the processing occurs on some other machine.

# What Can You Do with Data Access Pages?

If you use data access pages within an application, you're likely to end up performing one of these three types of tasks:

- Analyzing data

- Reviewing data

- Entering or editing data

The following paragraphs describe how you can accomplish each of these goals, and each goal references a sample you'll find in the Northwind.MDB sample database that comes with Access.

## Analyzing Data

Users may want to be able to view and summarize data at will, collapse and expand various groups, and rearrange relationships to meet their needs. In order to allow users to analyze data, you'll most likely want to use the PivotTable control, available as part of the Office Web Components. You can bind this control to any standard data source, and users can work (read-only) with the control and its data interactively. You can also use one or more Office Chart controls to display the results of the analysis performed in the PivotTable control. See the Sales page in Northwind (see Figure 10.1) for an example of this type of page.

**FIGURE 10.1**
The Sales page in the Northwind sample database allows you to analyze data using the PivotTable and Office Chart controls.

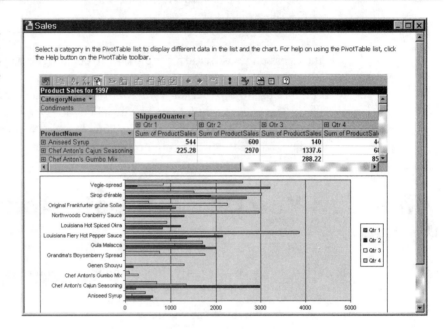

## Reviewing Data

Most commonly, you'll use data access pages to give users the ability to interact with groups of data, drilling down into the data as necessary. To create these types of pages (and this chapter includes a detailed walk-through to help you get started), you'll place bound controls on the page, grouping as necessary. Users can expand and contract levels until they find the data they need. To see an example showing this use of data access pages, see the Review Products page in the Northwind sample database (Figure 10.2).

**FIGURE 10.2**
The Review Products page in the Northwind sample database allows you to drill down into the various categories.

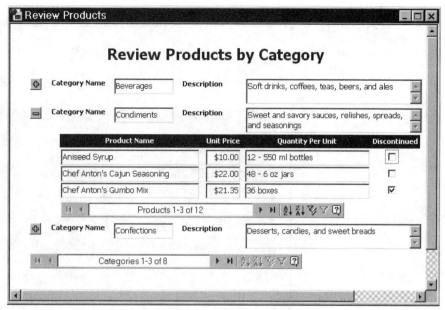

**FIGURE 10.2**
The Review Products page in the Northwind sample database allows you to drill down into the various categories.

## Entering or Editing Data

In limited circumstances, you can allow users to edit data on a data access page. In order for this option to be available, you must follow these rules:

- Your page can contain data from only a single source (one table or query, for example).

- You must use simple controls, like textboxes, combo boxes, and so on. You cannot use the bound PivotTable control.

- You can only display a single row at a time.

- You should customize the record navigation bar (setting properties of this ActiveX control) to manage your users' access to data. See the "The Record Navigation Control" section later in the chapter for more information. See the View Products page in Northwind for an example of a page that allows you to edit data (Figure 10.3).

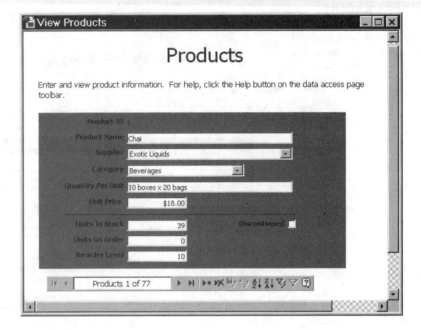

**FIGURE 10.3**
The View Products page in the Northwind sample database allows you to edit data.

## A Few Qualifying Words about Data Access Pages

There's no doubt about it: data access pages are a 1.0 technology, if that. The designer, to put as positive a spin on it as possible, needs a lot of work. There's no Undo capability, as amazing as that sounds! The whole concept requires Microsoft's Internet Explorer 5.0 (which every Office 2000 user has, of course, but what about the rest of the world?). We can't see any way that you'll want to use data access pages for anything but internal use, where you can control and verify browser support from all your users. You're limited to Jet and SQL Server data (not a terrible limitation, and Access suffers from the same exact limitation—all data must either go through Jet, as linked tables, or through SQL Server). Data access pages provide a simple way to get data into a browser, that's for sure. And Microsoft plans, as far as we know, to continue to improve the tools and the functionality in future versions. Right now? You'll have to decide for yourself. Work through the examples in this chapter, use the information here as a resource, and check out data access pages in limited tests. You may find that they solve a problem you need solved, and can do it right now.

# Creating Data Access Pages

Access provides several ways to get a data access page into your projects. This section introduces the techniques you can use for adding pages.

---

**NOTE**     You'll note one conspicuous absence, in terms of creating data access pages—Microsoft has provided no way to convert an existing form or report into a data access page. Although this is one common request, it's just not available as part of the package. Trigeminal Software has created a wizard to perform this task for you, however, and you'll find this tool on the book's accompanying CD.

---

## The Simplest Technique

Although you'll see a number of more flexible techniques in this chapter, the simplest way to add a data access page to your project is to follow these steps:

1. Select a table or query.

2. Choose Insert ➤ Page, or click the New Object toolbar icon and select Page from the menu.

3. From the New Data Access Page dialog box, select AutoPage: Columnar, then click OK.

4. Stand back, as Access creates a simple data access page for you.

---

**TIP**     Because this technique creates a page using simple controls, based on a single data source with no grouping, the data on the page should be editable (as long as the data source was editable).

---

## Using the Database Window Shortcuts

Unless you've turned off the display of the new object shortcuts (use the Tools ➤ Options ➤ General dialog box to turn this option on and off), you should see three built-in objects at the top of the list of available Page objects (see Figure 10.4). The following sections describe how to take advantage of each of these shortcuts.

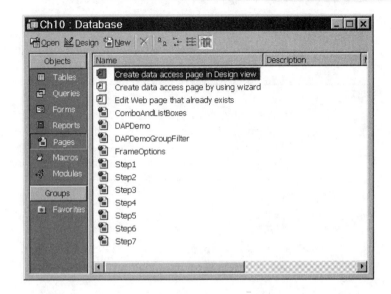

**FIGURE 10.4**
Unless you've hidden them,
the built-in new object
shortcuts make it easy to
get started with data
access pages.

## Create Data Access Page in Design View

If you select this shortcut, Access creates a new empty data access page and opens it in Design view. This is similar to opening a new form or report in Design view—what you do next is completely up to you. Most of this chapter focuses on creating new pages this way.

## Create Data Access Page by Using Wizard

Selecting this option brings up the Page Wizard, which walks you through the steps of creating a page. You can select fields, groupings, sorting, and a theme for your page. We won't insult your intelligence by walking you through the wizards here—it's definitely worth your time to stop and work through creating a few pages this way, however, if you've not already done so.

---

**TIP**    Using the wizard to create a page for you is a great way to see how to apply groupings and sorting to your pages.

---

Although we won't devote much time to styles and how you use them with data access pages, they do add an extra detail to worry about when deploying your pages. See the "Deploying Data Access Pages" section later in the chapter for more information.

### Edit Web Page That Already Exists

Selecting this option provides a useful solution to two problems you might encounter:

- How do you move a data access page from one database or project to another without changing the data source for the page to be the database/project you're in? (If you simply import the page, Access changes the data source for the page so that it attempts to retrieve its data from the current database or project.)

- How do you take an existing Web page and add data access page functionality to it?

When you add an existing Web page, Access opens the HTML document in Design view. If you decide to add it to your project, make sure you save it—at that point, Access actually creates the data access page shortcut in the Database window. If you decide not to save the page, Access won't add it at all.

---

**WARNING**    The way Access behaves when you add an existing page to your project can be confusing. Imagine that you've added an existing page, you make changes, and then close it. You decide, at this point, that you don't want to save your changes—you simply want to use it as it was originally, but you do want it available as a data access page in your project. If you select No when Access asks if you want to save your changes, the project ends up as if you'd never asked to add the existing page. Access doesn't add a shortcut to the existing page; to make that happen, you'll need to add the existing page and save it.

---

# Managing Data with Data Access Pages

Although you can create data access pages that aren't bound to any data source, one has to wonder why you'd bother. That is, there are much better HTML page designers out there. If you're working in Access, however, we're assuming you want to create bound pages, so that users can display (and in the rare instance, edit) data coming from your Access or SQL Server database.

## Creating a Moderately Complex Page on Your Own

Once you've run the wizards to see what data access pages can do and how much the wizards can do for you, you might like to create a reasonably complex page from start to finish. The steps presented in this section walk you through creating a complete (if somewhat ugly) data access page. If you want to apply a style to the pages, feel free, although the steps won't include that option.

TIP    Throughout these steps, the text will instruct you to take actions and create objects that we've not yet discussed. We suggest that you follow along, see what the page does, and fill in the details later as we work through various data access page topics in this chapter.

### Create an Editable Page

To get started, you'll create a data access page that allows you to edit data, pulled from qryCustomersWithFullName. This query takes all the fields from tblCustomer and adds a FullName calculated field. Follow these steps:

1.  From the Database window (using the sample database for this chapter), select Pages, click the New button, and select Design View from the New Data Access Page dialog box (or use whatever technique you like that ends up with an empty data access page).

2.  Click the "Click here and type title text" label on the page and enter **Customer Information**.

3.  Make sure the Field List window is visible, either using the appropriate toolbar icon or the View ➤ Field List menu item.

4.  In the Field List window, find the Queries node of the tree view and open it to select qryCustomersWithFullName. Open the query's field list by clicking the "+" sign next to its name.

5.  Drag each of the following fields to the grid on the page, arranging them so they look somewhat like Figure 10.5: CustomerID, FullName, and Phone.

Keep in mind that when you first create a page, the grid section is named Section: Unbound. After you place a bound control in that grid, the name changes to match the data source for the bound control.

Although it wasn't strictly necessary to place CustomerID on the page, the data wouldn't be editable if you didn't. This is, apparently, one of the limitations of using the data access page with a query as its data source: the data won't be read/write unless the primary key field is available on the page. Of course, CustomerID and FullName are read only, no matter what other restrictions apply, but with CustomerID on the page, Phone should be editable.

**FIGURE 10.5**
After placing fields on the page, arrange them like this.

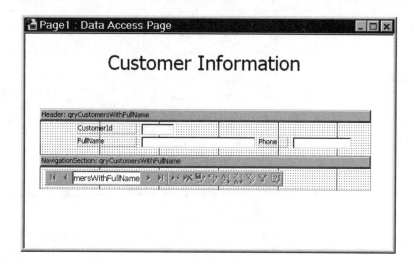

**NOTE**     There's nothing magical about the grid on a data access page. It allows you to place controls in a two-dimensional manner—that is, controlling the placement and size of the controls. If you place controls on the body of the page, they're still bound to the same data source, but you cannot manage their locations. This is the way most HTML documents work—controls appear in a linear (one-dimensional layout on the page).

6. Choose File ➤ Save to save the page. Assign it the name "Demo1" and save the HTM file in the same folder as the sample database. (If you closed the page, re-open it in Design view now.)

7. Choose View ➤ Page View and work with your simple, editable page. You should be able to edit the Phone field for any row of data. (You can use the navigation buttons on the Record Navigation control to move from one row to another.) Figure 10.6 shows how the page should look.

**FIGURE 10.6**

In Page view, you should be able to edit fields.

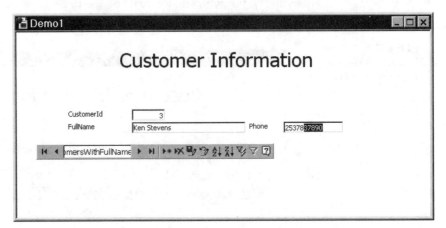

8. Try out the sorting and filtering buttons on the record navigation bar. These tools work just like the corresponding Access form tools. Select the FullName or Phone field and then select the A to Z sorting. You'll see that the data has been sorted at your request. When you're done, close the page.

9. Launch a copy of Internet Explorer 5.0 or higher and choose File ➤ Open to browse to the HTM file (named Demo1.HTM) you saved. Open the page, and it should look like Figure 10.7. Note that you can still edit phone numbers from the browser. Close the browser when you're done.

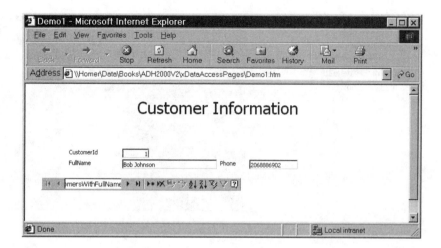

---

**NOTE**    If you have access to a Web server, you can set up a Web folder from any Office File Open or File Save dialog box and then save your page to the Web. Then use Internet Explorer to browse to your saved page, using an HTTP address (such as `http://www.yourserver.com/Demo1.htm`). If you have direct access to the Web server, you can simply copy the HTM file to the appropriate folder on the server (along with any subsidiary files).

---

10. Open the Demo1 page in Design view again, and open the Sorting and Grouping window. (You can either use the appropriate toolbar icon, or choose View ➢ Sorting and Grouping to display the window.) In this window, find the Data Page Size property, and change it from 1 to All. (See Figure 10.8.) Doing this will cause the page to display all the rows at once (like a continuous form in Access) when in Page view or in the browser, but will also make the data read-only. (Data access pages can only edit data shown one row at a time.)

11. Test the behavior in Page view to convince yourself that it works. You'll see all the rows at once, but you won't be able to modify the Phone field any more. Switch back to Design view once you're done.

**FIGURE 10.8**
Set the Data Page Size
value to All, in order to see
all rows without scrolling.
This makes the data
read-only, however.

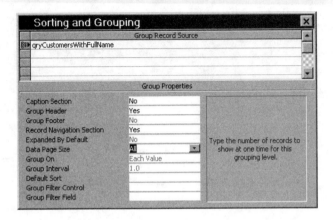

12. To finish off this section, spend some time working with the Record Navigation control. For example, modify the Show... properties (on the Other page of the Propeties window) to hide the buttons that aren't active with the page laid out as it is currently. Change the RecordsetLabel property to something like this (for more information on the RecordsetLabel property, see Table 10.5 later in the chapter) and then view the page in Page view again:

```
Customers |0 of |2;Customers |0-|1 of |2
```

13. When you're done, close and save the page.

**NOTE**  We've already saved a version of this page as Step1 in the chapter's database. You can use this as the starting point in the next exercise, if you don't wish to use your own page.

## Create a Group

In this section, you'll add a group to the page, showing information from both qryCustomersWithFullName and tblOrder. As with any page, once you add a grouping to the page, you can no longer edit the data, so this one will be for display purposes only.

**TIP**

In this, and all the rest of the pages you create, you can test the page either from within Access, or from Internet Explorer. The behavior should be the same either way. The step-by-step instructions won't prompt you to test both ways, but it can't hurt.

Follow these steps to create the sample grouped page:

1. Make sure your data access page is open in Design view. Delete all the existing controls from the page, one at a time.

2. With the page selected (you can click on the page's title bar to select it), find the DefaultControlType property on the Data page of the Properties window, and set it to be "Bound HTML" (as opposed to "Text Box"). These controls are more efficient than textboxes when displaying data.

**TIP**

Bound HTML controls display faster than Text Box controls, but they don't have attached labels. If you're creating a data access page that's to be used for displaying data, you should consider setting the DefaultControlType property to Bound HTML for the page.

3. From the Fields List window, select qryCustomersWithFullName and add the FullName and Phone fields to the page. Lay out the two controls horizontally across the top of the section, leaving some room at the left for the Expand control that Access will soon add to the page for you. After you've set this up, the page might look something like Figure 10.9.

**FIGURE 10.9**
The first step in creating a grouped page.

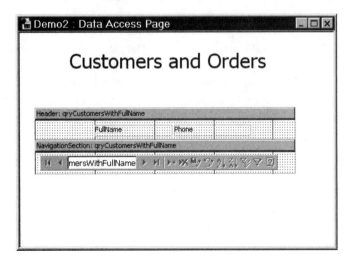

4. From the Fields List window, select tblOrder, and drag the OrderDate field over to the Header: qryCustomersWithFullName section. Don't drop the field yet, however! You want to create a new grouping section, and the easiest way to do so is to drop the field *below* the existing section. To do that, watch for the divider line between the sections, as shown in Figure 10.10. Once you see that divider, drop the field onto the divider itself.

**FIGURE 10.10**
Watch for the divider line with the arrows before dropping the grouped field(s).

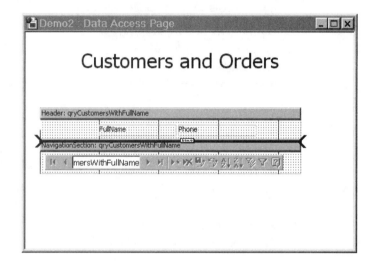

5. At this point, you've asked Access to join a query (qryCustomersWith-FullName) and a table (tblOrder). Because the data access page designer doesn't know how these two data sources are related, Access must ask you to supply the linking fields. Figure 10.11 shows the New Relationship dialog box, where you can select the field name(s). In this case, the dialog box "guesses" that CustomerID and Notes are related (they have the same names and data types). Remove Notes from each source by selecting the top-most, empty value in the combo box, and then click OK. Once you dismiss the dialog box, you'll see the grouped data access page, as shown in Figure 10.12. (Note that Access has added a new section for the tblOrder data and an Expand control to the original section.)

**FIGURE 10.11**
Choose fields from the lists to create the ad hoc join.

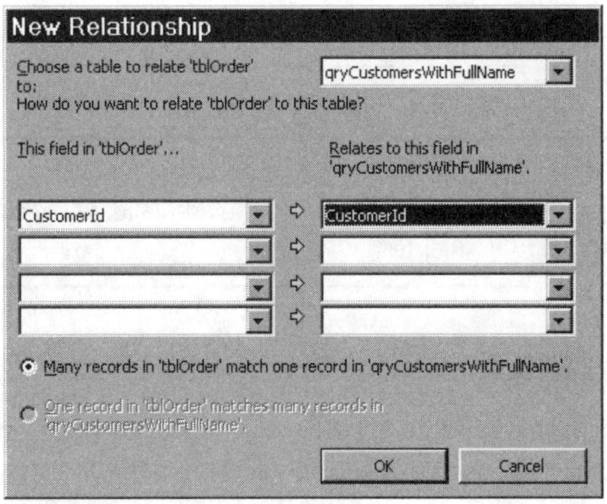

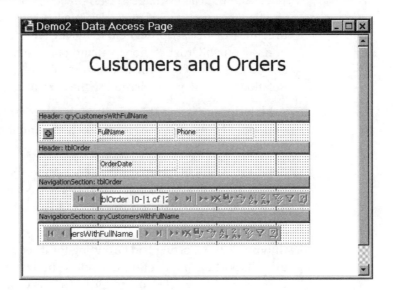

**FIGURE 10.12**
After you drop the grouped field, you'll have a new section for the group.

6. Choose View ➢ Page View to display the page as it would appear in a browser. Click on the "+" (Expand) control, to see that each customers' order dates appear as a grouping. Choose View ➢ Design View to revert to design view.

7. Save your page.

**NOTE**    This page has been saved for you in the sample database as Step2. You can use this as the starting point in the next exercise, if you don't wish to use your own page.

**TIP**    If you can't open Step2, or any other data access page in this sample database, make sure you've run the adhValidateDAPLinks, as discussed at the beginning of this chapter.

## Add Another Grouping Level

In this section, you'll add a third grouping, use the Sorting and Grouping dialog box to turn on a caption section, and change the number of rows displayed at once. Follow these steps to continue the demonstration:

1. With your data access page in Design view, select the Fields List window and find the query named qryOrderDetails. Open the query's list of fields, and drag the MenuDescription field to the area immediately above the NavigationSection: tblOrder section, watching for the double-arrowed divider (discussed in Step 4 of the previous section). Drop the field and dismiss the New Relationship dialog box, accepting the default suggestions.

2. Add the Quantity and Price fields to the Header: qryOrderDetails section. You should now see three Header sections, and three NavigationSection sections on your page.

   Because you might like to see the Description, Quantity, and Price fields displayed in a tabular format, it would be nice to have column headings for those fields. To do that, you'll need to add a caption section for your data, as shown in Step 3.

3. Choose View ➤ Sorting and Grouping (or its equivalent toolbar icon) to display the Sorting and Grouping window. In the top pane of the Sorting and Grouping window, click on qryOrderDetails to select that particular group, and then find the Caption Section property in the lower pane. Set the value of this property to Yes.

4. Rather than showing one row at a time, you might like to see all the rows at once. To do that, set the Data Page Size property to All.

5. If you're showing all the detail rows at once, there's no need to display the record navigation section, so set the Record Navigation Section property to No. Close the Sorting and Grouping window.

6. Add three Label controls to the Caption: qryOrderDetails section, and set their positions and text as shown in Figure 10.13. (We've set the Price and Quantity captions to be right-aligned, as the values in those fields will be right-aligned as well. We've also set the captions to be displayed bold, so they stand out on the page.)

**FIGURE 10.13**

Lay out the caption section like this.

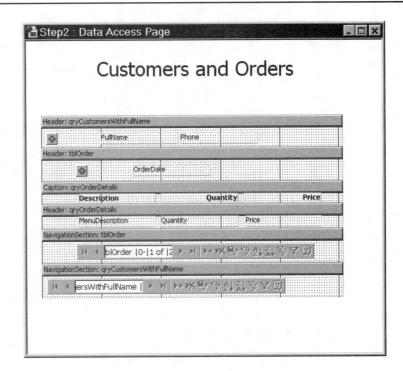

7. View the page either within Access or from Internet Explorer, and try opening the various sections. Note that the caption section only appears when the section above it is expanded, and that the page displays all the rows for the lowest-level detail section without navigation. Figure 10.14 shows how the page might look at this point.

**FIGURE 10.14**

After adding a third grouping with a caption section, your page should look like this.

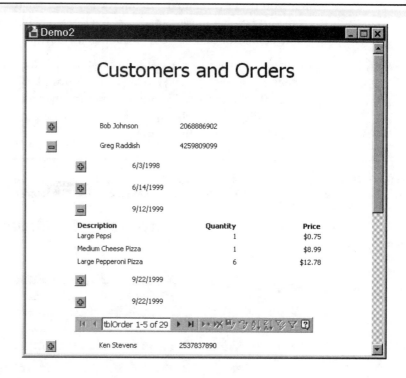

The chapter database includes a data access page named Step3, which includes all the steps taken up to this point.

## Create Summary Data

Once you've added a tabular grouping, you might like to add summary data—that is, sums for the Quantity and Price fields, to be displayed at the end of each order's data. Follow these steps to add summary data to your page:

1. Open your data access page in Design view once again and make sure the Sorting and Grouping window is visible.

2. Because you're adding a footer for the qryOrderDetails section, it makes sense to select that group in the Sorting and Grouping window. Unfortunately, you cannot. By design, the lowest-level group cannot have a footer section.

To work around this, you must add a footer section to the next higher grouping—tblOrder, in this example. Find the Group Footer property in the Sorting and Grouping window, and set it to Yes. This adds a Footer: tblOrder section to the page.

3. Select the Quantity textbox, in the Header: qryOrderDetails section, and press Ctrl+C to copy the control to the Windows Clipboard.

4. Select the Footer: tblOrder section, then press Ctrl+V to paste the copied control into this section. Access resets the ControlSource property for the control to GroupOfQuantity1: Quantity (indicating that this is a grouped field) and sets the TotalType property to Sum (which is exactly what you want). Move the new control so that it's right-aligned with, and immediately below, the original Quantity control.

5. Repeat the previous step for the Price control.

6. If you like, add a Label control to the Footer: tblOrder section, with the caption "Totals:". Once you're done, the page might look like the page shown in Figure 10.15.

**FIGURE 10.15**
After adding a group footer, your page might look like this.

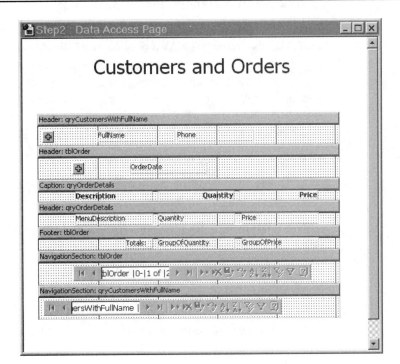

7. Run the page in Page view, then expand and contract the various sections to view the data. Note that you see summary information for the Quantity and Price fields. Go back to Design view when you're done.

You'll see, if you look carefully, that the summary information is visible as soon as you expand the tblOrder section—that is, the Header: tblOrder and Footer: tblOrder sections become visible at the same time. This can either be seem as an advantage, or an issue. That's the way this page works, however.

---

**WARNING**   You won't be able to add a footer section for the lowest grouping on your page. You'll need to work around this limitation. In the example page, you created a footer for the next-higher grouping level.

---

**NOTE**   The chapter database includes a data access page named Step4, which includes all the steps taken up to this point.

---

## Work with a Group Filter Control

As you saw when you worked with the page so far, all the customer rows appear individually on the page. You may want to allow your users to select a particular customer and show only the orders for that customer. The Access data access page designer makes this simple by allowing you to place a listbox or combo box in a section, and use that control to filter the rows. (Access calls this a *group filter control*). In the following steps, you'll work through adding such a control to the demonstration page you've been building. Follow these steps:

1. Open your page in Design view.

2. Delete all the existing controls from the Header: qryCustomersWithFullName section (including the Expand control that Access added for you).

3. Make sure the Toolbox window is visible and then click on the Dropdown List (Combo box) control.

4. In the Fields List window, right-click on the qryCustomersWith-FullName.FullName field, and drag it over to the Header: qryCustomersWithFullName section. Release the mouse.

5. From the context menu, select Group Filter Control.

**WARNING**    Unless you follow the steps carefully, Group Filter Control won't be available on the context menu. You must select the Dropdown List (or List Box) control first, then right-click/drag the correct field, and then select Group Filter Control from the context menu. Not an easy operation.

6. If you like, modify the caption for the new control (perhaps "Select a Customer") and make the combo box wider.

7. Because you won't need a RecordNavigationControl control for the customer data, open the Sorting and Grouping window again, select the qryCustomers-WithFullName section in the window and set its Record Navigation Section property to No.

8. Display the page in Page view (or open in a browser) and select a customer from the combo box. As you do, the page displays just the orders for that particular customer.

**NOTE**    The chapter database includes a data access page named Step5, which includes all the steps taken up to this point.

That's the end of the "guided tour" section. You've seen how to create a simple editable page, as well as a more complex, grouped page. The rest of the chapter focuses on explaining the details of what you've done and how else you might use the data access page designer.

## What Is the Designer Doing?

As you're laying out controls and data fields on the data access page designer, what you're actually creating under the covers is an HTML document. Because of this, you should be aware that everything you place onto this page becomes an HTML element. For example, the header section (including the text "Click here and type title text") is an HTML element defined with <H1></H1> tags. The area immediately below this section is a paragraph defined with <P></P> tags. The data access page designer creates the following HTML source—along with a bunch of other HTML elements—when you enter the text shown in the graphic below (choose View ➤ HTML Source to view this source):

```
<CENTER>
<H1 id=HeadingText style="FONT-WEIGHT: normal">
```

```
Title Section </H1></CENTER>
<P>This is where you might place a description of your
 page, or instructions to your users.</P>
<P>Each line of text becomes a &lt;P&gt;&lt;/P&gt; section
 in the HTML document.
Press enter to create a new paragraph or let the text wrap
 to fit the page size.</P>
```

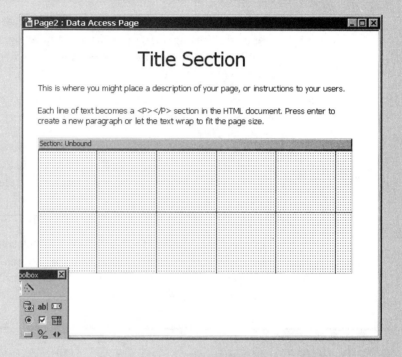

Other objects that you place on the page become different types of HTML elements: the sections become DIV elements, and controls become either intrinsic HTML controls or OBJECT tags. You may find it instructive to investigate the HTML created by the data access page designer (choose View ➤ HTML Source to display the Microsoft Development Environment with your page's source loaded).

## Working with Controls

If you're going to create data access pages yourself, or modify pages created by the wizards, you'll need to be able to create and manipulate controls on the data access page designer. This section introduces the skills and information you'll need in order to be able to work with this designer (which is very different from other Access tools).

Although the standard controls you can place on a data access page look and "feel" like Access controls, they are a different beast altogether. The data access page Label, Text Box, Frame, Option Button, Check Box, List Box, Dropdown List, and Command Button all look deceptively like their Access counterparts. These controls, however, expose radically different properties, methods, and events. This chapter deals only with design-time properties of these controls. For more information on working with methods and events of the data access page controls, see Chapter 11.

## Placing Controls on the Page

The steps required to place a control on the data access page are slightly different, depending on whether you're placing an unbound or bound control on the page.

### Working with Unbound Controls

If you want to place an unbound control onto a data access page, simply select the type of control you need in the control toolbox and then click and drag to place the control on the grid. This works, effectively, the same as placing Access controls on a form or report.

### Working with Bound Controls

If you need to place a bound control on a data access page, you have a number of options. First of all, note that when you first create a new data access page, the page is unbound. It's not until you add the first bound control to the page that Access sets up the necessary DataSourceControl object, linking the page to its data source.

The DataSourceControl is part of the Office Web Components set of ActiveX controls, provided by Office 2000. The data access page designer adds this invisible control to every bound data access page.

To place bound controls onto a data access page, first make sure that the Field List window is visible. If it's not, choose View ➤ Field List or click the Field List toolbar button. Choose one of these options to place controls on the page:

- Click a table name in the Field List window. Drag the table to the grid area of the page and let go. Access creates a bound PivotTable control (from the Office Web Components). The data in this control is read only.

- Right-click on a table in the Field List window. Drag the table to the grid area of the page and let go. Access provides a context menu with two available choices: Individual Controls and PivotTable List. If you choose Pivot-Table List, you end up with the same read-only grid discussed in the previous bullet point. If you choose Individual Controls, Access lays out the fields in the table in a two-dimensional columnar layout. Figure 10.16 shows how a page might look after right-clicking, dragging the tblEmployee table onto the page, and selecting Individual Controls.

**FIGURE 10.16**

This page was created by dragging the tblEmployee table to the page and selecting Individual Controls.

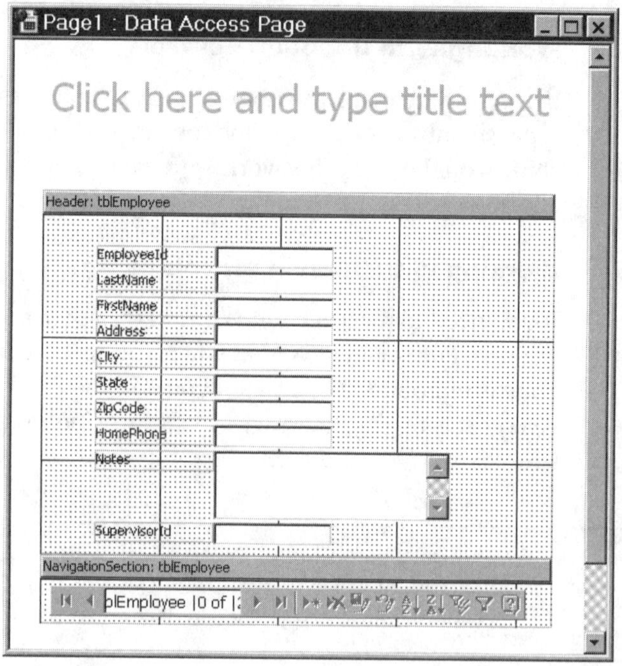

- Select any field in the Field List window. Click the Add To Page button at the bottom of the Field List window. Access adds the control in a columnar fashion, immediately below the previously added control.

- Right-click on any field in the Field List window. Choose Add To Page from the context menu. Access adds the control, just as if you'd clicked the Add To Page button.

- Double-click on any field in the Field List window. Access adds the control, just as if you'd clicked the Add To Page button.

- Click on any of the following controls in the control toolbox: Bound HTML, Text Box, Scrolling Text (Marquee), Frame, Option Button, Check Box, Dropdown List, List Box, Bound Hyperlink, and Image. Next, click and drag a field from the Field List to the grid area of the page. Access creates the selected control type, bound to the selected field.

- Select one of the control types listed in the previous bullet point, then select a field in the Field List window. Right-click and drag the field onto the grid area of the page. When you drop the field, you'll see the same context menu that was mentioned earlier in this section. Choose PivotTable List to create a pivot table containing the field and the primary key field(s) for the table.

- As a special case of the previous bullet point, select the Dropdown List control, then right-click/drag a field onto the page. When you release the field, the context menu will have enabled the third item on the list—Group Filter Control. This usage for the Dropdown List, discussed in detail later in the chapter (in the "Using the Group Filter Control" section), allows you to filter the displayed rows based on the value selected in this list.

---

**TIP**   While you're getting started with data access pages, you may find it useful to turn on the data access page control wizards. (Click the Control Wizards button at the top of the Control toolbox to turn them on.) The wizards will help you set properties for Dropdown List, List Box, and Command Button controls.

---

## Adding Fields from Multiple Tables

In the Field List window, you'll find a hierarchical listing of tables and queries, along with related tables. That is, if you've defined permanent relationships between a table listed in the Field List and other tables, Access can display the related tables in the hierarchical list. If you drag fields from multiple related tables to the same section on the page, Access perform a join between the tables for you and will allow you to edit data from the "most many" table. For example, if you were to drag the tblOrder:OrderDate field to the grid and then add the tblCustomer: LastName field, Access would display the joined tblCustomer/tblOrder data, and you would be able to edit the data from tblOrder. (The data from tblCustomer would be read only.)

---

**TIP**

If you drag fields from a single table onto the unbound section (the grid area), you'll see that Access creates a navigation section (including the record navigation control) at the same time. The section's title indicates the data source for the section. If you later place a field from a related source onto the same section, you may see the title of the navigation section change—it always displays the name of the "most many" data source.

---

If you attempt to drag fields from two tables that aren't related onto the same page, Access will request that you supply linking information. Figure 10.17 shows the dialog box you might see if you dragged fields from tblOrderDetails and tblCustomer to the same page. Because these tables aren't related, you won't be able to successfully supply linking information, but for tables that can be related (but for which there isn't a permanent relationship), this dialog box allows you to create ad hoc relationships.

**FIGURE 10.17**
Use this dialog box to create ad hoc relation-ships, as necessary.

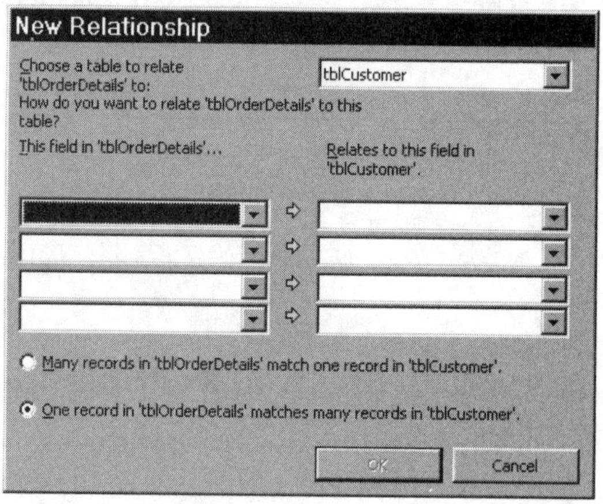

Generally, if you want fields from two tables, you'll want to create multiple group levels. It's easier to demonstrate this with an example, so you may want to follow along, using the tables provided in the chapter's database. (These steps mirror steps shown earlier in the chapter. For those who skipped the long walk-through, it's worth trying these few steps here.) Follow these steps to create a multi-section data access page:

1. Create a new data access page.

2. From the Field List, drag the tblCustomer:CustomerID field to the grid area of the data access page. Note that Access created a NavigationSection group for you.

3. From the Field List, drag the tblOrder:OrderDate field to the grid area, but drag it to the bottom of the Header:tblCustomer section. Don't let go yet! You should see the double-arrow divider, as shown in Figure 10.18.

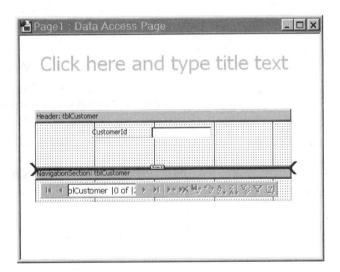

**FIGURE 10.18**
Drag fields from the related table to the area immediately below the existing section.

4. Drop the tblOrder:OrderDate field while you see the double-arrow divider line, and Access will create a new NavigationSection for you, as shown in Figure 10.19. If you look carefully at the original section, you'll see that Access has also added an Expand control (the square control with the "+" on it).

5. Add more fields, as you wish, to both Header sections.

**FIGURE 10.19**

When you drop a related field into a new section, Access creates the Header and NavigationSection for you.

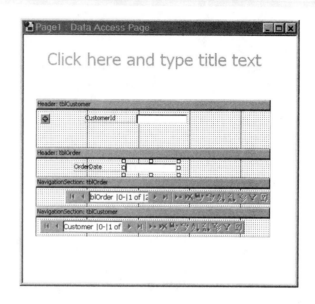

6. When you're ready, choose View ➤ Page View to display the page. You should see something like the page displayed in Figure 10.20. Because you placed the related data in its own group, you can expand and collapse the secondary group using the Expand control.

**FIGURE 10.20**

In Page view, you can expand or contract the detail section.

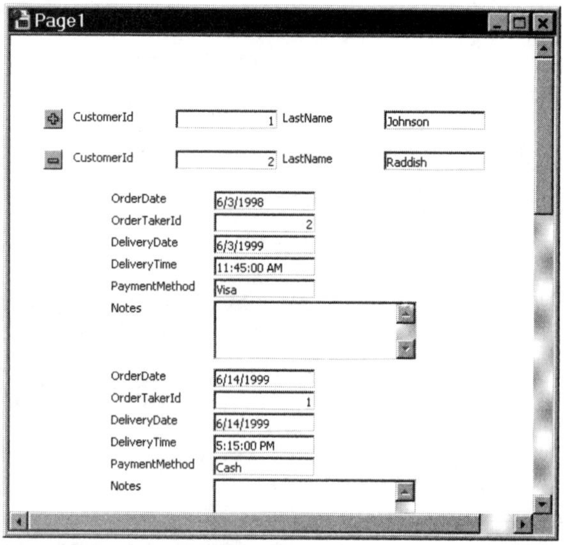

## Modifying the Layout

After designing your own page, or using the wizards to create a page for you, you'll inevitably need to modify the layout of the page. You'll immediately find that the data access page designer isn't nearly so friendly as the Access form designer. You can accomplish all the same sorts of tasks as you can when working with Access forms and reports, but it's all more difficult. This section works through some of the issues you'll encounter when modifying the layout of your data access pages. (We're assuming that you've mastered the basics of creating Access forms and reports and are interested here in the differences you'll find in the data access page designer.)

### Save Early and Often

We'll get this out of the way first: there's no Undo in the data access page designer. No, you weren't missing anything when you weren't able to find this functionality. It's simply not there. We've found it useful to save often, and to use the File ➤ Save As menu item, so that you assign your page a new name each time. This wastes disk space, but you can clean up all the extraneous pages once you're finished.

### Using the Grid

It appears that the snap-to-grid feature in the data access page designer only works half the time. That is, controls snap to the grid when you're moving them, but not when you're resizing. For this reason, you may find it easier to set the Width and Height properties of controls using the Properties window, rather than attempting to set their width and height correctly using a mouse.

### Moving Conjoined Controls

When you place a textbox onto a data access page, Access creates a textbox and an attached a label control. It's easy enough to resize either of the controls, and simple to move the label independently of its associated textbox. It's not possible, as far as we can tell, to move the textbox independently of its associated label, however. If you need to change the relative locations of the two controls, you'll need to drag the label, not the textbox. In addition, if you want to change the distance between the two controls, you'll need to move the label, not the textbox.

## Working with Groups of Controls

Fooled you! You can't. You can only work with individual controls (except for the child label with its parent, as mentioned in the previous paragraph). If you need to move a group of controls from one place to another on a page, you'll need to move each one individually. There's simply no way to select more than a single control (or parent/child label control pair).

You can, however, use the Alignment and Sizing toolbar, shown in Figure 10.21, to help overcome this missing functionality. Choose View ➤ Toolbars ➤ Alignment and Sizing to display the toolbar.

**FIGURE 10.21**
Use the Alignment and Sizing toolbar to manipulate groups of controls.

To try out this toolbar's functionality, follow these steps:

1. Create a new data access page.

2. Double-click on the LastName, FirstName, Address, City, State, and ZipCode fields from tblCustomer, so that Access places six textboxes on the page.

3. Stretch the LastName textbox, so that it's wider than the rest of the textboxes. Assume that you'd like the FirstName, and City textboxes to now be stretched to the same width as the LastName textbox.

4. Make sure the Alignment and Sizing toolbar is visible, as discussed previously.

5. Click on the LastName textbox to make sure it's selected.

6. Click the Size Width button (second from the right) on the toolbar.

7. Click on the control you'd like to have be the same width as the LastName textbox. Access will make it the same width. Notice that the focus moves back to the LastName textbox.

8. Repeat Steps 6 and 7 for each control you'd like to resize to match the LastName textbox.

As you can see, this is a somewhat arduous process. You must first select the "master" control, then click the toolbar button and select the "copycat" control for each control you want to modify.

The data access page designer provides a somewhat undiscoverable shortcut that makes formatting a bit simpler. If you double-click on the toolbar button for the action you want, it becomes "sticky." That is, rather than having to select a control, click a button, and then apply that to a second control, you can select a control, double-click a button, and then click once on each control to which you want to apply formatting without going back to the toolbar. When you're done applying the formatting, press the Escape key. You'll be amazed how much easier it is to format groups of controls this way, although it doesn't excuse the data access page designer for not allowing you to select multiple controls.

## Sets of Properties

The data access page controls share a large set of properties, and this section focuses on two of these sets: color properties and position properties. Because the properties apply to so many of the controls, it makes sense to "factor out" the discussion of these properties, and cover them in only one place.

### Setting Colors

Many properties involve colors. For example, the BackColor, BorderColor, and Color properties all require you to specify a valid HTML color value. HTML is flexible in this regard, and you have several options. You can specify any of the following (don't type the quotes into the Properties window):

- "Transparent," which causes the element to be painted with no color, inheriting the color of the element that's behind it.

- A hex value, in the format "#rrggbb" (where "rr" stands for the two-digit red component of the color, "gg" for green, and "bb" for blue). The DHTML help that comes with Office includes a Color Table page, a portion of which appears in Figure 10.22.

- A named color, selected from the colors available in the help file (a portion of which is shown in Figure 10.22).

- A named system color, selected from the system colors available in the help file (with names like "ActiveBorder," "ButtonFace," and so on).

- An expression using the rgb function, specifying the three components of the color as values between 0 and 255, such as "rgb(255, 0, 0)." (This example gives the same result as entering the values "red," or "#FF0000.")

---

**TIP**

If you need to convert from existing color values stored as long integers in VBA, we've provided the ColorToHex function in basHexColors. This simple function handles the brute force conversion from VBA's long integer "bbggrr" format for colors (once you convert color values into Hex) into HTML's "#rrggbb" format.

---

**FIGURE 10.22**

The DHTML help includes a Color Table page. Use it to help choose colors.

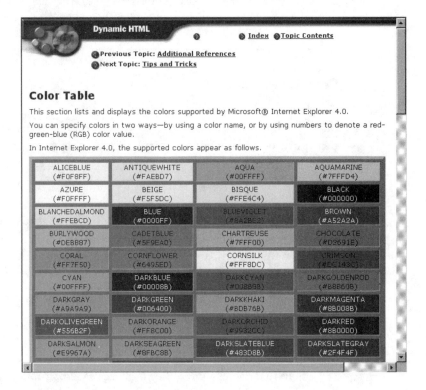

**Setting Positions**

Many properties require you to specify a location, such as the BackgroundX/Y, Left, Top, Width, and Height. In each case, you have a number of different ways you can supply the values. You can enter:

- A percentage of the parent size, using a value such as "50%."

- A measurement in one of several coordinate systems, using an abbreviation for the unit, such as "mm" for millimeters, "px" for pixels, "in" for inches.

- For some properties, such as BackgroundPositionX, you can provide specific location values, such as "Left," "Center," or "Right". See Table 10.5 later in this chapter for specifics.

## Working with the Tools

These next few sections discuss some of the controls you're likely to use as you design your data access pages. We'll describe uses of some of the simple controls and properties you'll want to set in order to use them.

## The Non-Helpful Data Page Properties Window

Unlike when you're working on an Access form or report, you cannot count on the Properties window for a data access page to help you much. Not only are many of the important properties confusing, poorly named, and inconsistent, but many properties that could supply a drop-down list of values don't. You're expected to simply know the possible values. In addition, some properties are available for controls for which they have no meaning, and often can't be changed (for example, the Type and Start properties for an option button). Focus on getting the control to do what you'd like, not on what each and every property does, or you'll waste inordinate amounts of time. (We know this, from personal experience.) We've supplied a large table, Table 10.5, which includes many of the properties you'll encounter as you design data access pages, along with possible values and descriptions of each. Having this table has helped us a great deal, and we hope it helps you too. By the way, online help on these topics generally doesn't. (Help, that is.)

## Label

The data access page Label control works similarly to the Access Label control. It cannot be bound to data, and simply displays static text. To set the caption of the label, you can click once on the label to select it, and then click again to enter Edit mode and edit in place. If you'd rather, you can go to the Properties window and edit the InnerText property there. (The Access F2 shortcut key does not work in the data access page designer.)

**WARNING**     Although the Label control has a DataFormatAs property (which can be set to either HTML or Text), we were unable to get a label control to display its InnerText property as anything besides text. (That is, we were unable to get it to render any HTML text correctly.)

## Bound HTML and Text Box Controls

The Bound HTML control displays HTML-rendered text and can be bound to a field in your data. This control provides the preferred method of displaying text on a data access page, because it incurs less overhead than does the Text Box control. Its contents are, however, read only. If you want to allow data editing on your page, you'll need to use the Text Box control. The Text Box control allows for editing as well as display, but displays slower and requires more resources.

You should consider these issues when working with these two controls:

- Bound HTML controls will almost always display more quickly. If you want your page to display as fast as possible, use Bound HTML controls.

- You can specify the default control type for the entire page. Select the page (choose Edit ➢ Select Page), and then change the DefaultControlType property in the Properties window for the page to be either Bound HTML or Text Box. From then on, any fields you drag onto the form will inherit the specified control type.

- Text Box controls have attached child label controls (see the ChildLabel property to find out which control is the child label). Bound HTML controls don't have a child label: if you want to display a label associated with the data displayed in the Bound HTML control, you'll need to place and maintain one yourself.

- If you want to display text including HTML tags, you must use the Bound HTML control. The Text Box control provides no mechanism for rendering HTML text. If you use the Bound HTML control, make sure you set the DataFormatAs property to HTML, if you want the control to render the HTML for you. (This means that you could place text into a table field like this—"This is BOLD text"—and the control would correctly interpret the tags and display the intended word in a bold font.) If you set the DataFormatAs property to be Text, then the control will display the text you send it without attempting to render it as HTML.

## Scrolling Text (Marquee)

The Scrolling Text (or Marquee) control allows you to display scrolling text. By setting properties of the control, you can specify the text, direction, number of loops, and speed of the scrolling. Table 10.1 lists and describes the properties of the Marquee control that affect its text display. (See Table 10.5 for more complete details on the properties of this control.)

**TABLE 10.1:**    Control Properties Pertinent to the Scrolling Text (Marquee) Control

| Property | Description |
| --- | --- |
| Behavior | Determines whether the text scrolls, slides, or alternates. |
| Direction | Allows you to specify the direction: left, right, up, or down. |
| InnerText | For an unbound Marquee control, determines the text that the control displays. For a bound control, determines the field name to be displayed. |
| Loop | Controls the number of times the text loops by (use –1 to loop indefinitely). |
| ScrollAmount | Number of pixels to scroll the text each time it moves. |
| ScrollDelay | Amount to delay between scrolls. |
| TrueSpeed | Determines whether the speed for a Marquee control's scrolling is based on the internal clock, with a minimum of 60ms, or based on the ScrollDelay and ScrollAmount properties. |

**WARNING**    Setting ScrollAmount too large and ScrollDelay too small can make testing your page within Access difficult. If your text is scrolling very quickly, Access can't catch mouse clicks as you attempt to switch from Page view to Design view. You'll still be able to close the page, however.

To create a bound Marquee control, first select the control in the toolbox, then click and drag a field from the field list window onto the page. Access will create the Marquee control and bind it to your selected field. As you move from row to row, the text in the scrolling region will change to reflect the selected row.

## Frame and Option Button

A Frame control allows you to choose a single option from a group of option buttons. Unlike an Access Option Group control, the data access page Frame control can contain only option buttons. Just like in Access, however, you should place the Frame control on the page first, and then place the option buttons within the frame.

To create a bound Frame control, first select the Frame control in the toolbox. Then drag the appropriate field from the Field List window to your page. When you "drop," Access creates a bound Frame control for you on the page. Then create as many Option Button controls as you need, inside the frame. Finally, set the Value property to match each of the possible values you'll want to display or enter using the frame. When you display the page, as you move from row to row in your data, the frame will select the appropriate option button, indicating the specific value for the selected field in the current row.

---

**TIP**     Unlike option buttons in Access, data access page option buttons use a text string as their value. This makes it possible to use a frame bound to the PaymentMethod field in tblOrder, and also to use option buttons to display the four values: "Cash," "Check," "Mastercard," and "Visa." In this environment, you won't have to write any code to convert from integer values to the appropriate text values.

---

**WARNING**     There's always a good side and a bad side. Although you can use text values to identify the option buttons within a frame, their comparisons to data are *case sensitive*. Unless you're sure that your data is pristine, using text values for your option buttons may not be a good idea. The sample page, FrameOptions, demonstrates this behavior. (When you move to a row and no option is selected, that indicates there's a case error.)

---

## List and Combo Boxes

In theory, list and combo boxes on data access pages work the same as bound list and combo boxes within Access. In actuality, many of the Access-specific features (value lists, list-filling callback functions, and so on) won't work here. Unless you care to delve into scripting, you'll need to bind the lists to some data source, so that they'll fill up from a column provided by a table or query.

Table 10.2 lists the properties you'll need to set if you want to display data from one data source and store it to another. (That's usually what you do with these controls: that is, you display a column of data from one data source and store the selection as a linking item into a second table—the table that's bound to the page as a whole.)

To make this clearer, we've provided a simple page, ComboAndListBoxes, shown in Figure 10.23. This page displays data from tblOrder and includes a combo box for selecting the customer and a list box for selecting the payment method. Table 10.2 includes a column indicating the fields used for each property, in this example.

**FIGURE 10.23**
Demonstration for combo and list boxes on a data access page.

**TABLE 10.2:** Properties Pertinent to Combo and List Boxes

| Property | Description | ComboBox | ListBox |
|---|---|---|---|
| ControlSource | Field, selected from the fields available in the page's data source, where selected value is to be stored/retrieved. | tblOrder.CustomerID | tblOrder.PaymentMethod |
| ListRowSource | Source of data for the list. Set this property before any of the other List... properties. | tblCustomer | qryPaymentMethod |

**T A B L E  1 0 . 2 :** Properties Pertinent to Combo and List Boxes *(continued)*

| Property | Description | ComboBox | ListBox |
|---|---|---|---|
| ListDisplayField | Field from the list's row source that's displayed in the control's list. | LastName | PaymentMethod |
| ListBoundField | Field from the list's row source that's stored and retrieved from the bound data source. | CustomerID | PaymentMethod |

**WARNING**    When you use a bound ComboBox control, beware that matches against underlying data are *case sensitive*. In this example, if a row contains "VISA" as a payment method, it won't match up against any item in the list box, which contains the text "Visa." You'll simply see nothing in the control for that row.

**TIP**    We were unable to find any way to have a combo box perform incremental searching as you type. If there's a property that controls this behavior, it is certainly well hidden.

Table 10.3 lists other properties associated with list and combo boxes that you may find useful

**T A B L E  1 0 . 3 :** Miscellaneous Combo and List Box Properties

| Property | Description |
|---|---|
| Length | Returns the number of items in the list. Appears in the Properties window, but you'll only use it in scripting code. |
| Multiple | If set to True, allows multiple selections. If you set this to True for a Combo Box, the control automatically becomes displayed as a List Box. Setting it back to False makes it appear again as a Combo Box. |
| SelectedIndex | Indicates the selected item in the list. For a bound control, setting this in the Properties window has no effect. |

Although you needn't create bound Combo or List Box controls, if they're unbound, you'll need to write some code to fill them with items. See Chapter 11 for more information on scripting data access pages.

## Hyperlink

The Hyperlink control allows you to insert a link that can navigate users to another page, to a bookmark within a page, or to send email. When you insert a Hyperlink control on a page, Access pops up the (rather dense) dialog box shown in Figure 10.24, allowing you to select the destination of the link.

**FIGURE 10.24**
Choose your hyperlink's destination from this dialog box.

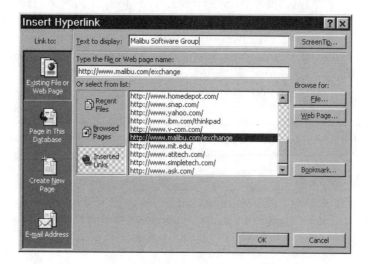

Although you can set properties individually for Hyperlink controls, we don't recommend it. If you need to modify the behavior of the hyperlink, simply right-click on the control and choose Hyperlink from the context menu. This brings up the dialog box shown in Figure 10.24 again, allowing you to modify any of the linking properties. If you want to set the properties manually (or if you intend to use scripting, as discussed in Chapter 11, to modify the behavior of the control at runtime), you may find the properties in Table 10.4 useful in adjusting the behavior of the Hyperlink control.

**TABLE 10.4:** Properties Pertinent to the Hyperlink Control

| Property | Description |
| --- | --- |
| Host | Specifies the location/port name, separated with a colon. You're better off setting the Href property instead. |
| Href | Specifies the location to which to navigate. |
| InnerText | Specifies the display text for the hyperlink. |
| Title | Specifies the tooltip text for the hyperlink. |

## Bound Hyperlink

Like the standard Hyperlink control, the Bound Hyperlink allows you to navigate to a new page or location. The difference here is that this control allows you to supply the hyperlink Href from a data source, possibly different for each row of data. In addition to the properties mentioned in Table 10.4, you'll also need to be concerned with the ControlSource property, which indicates the field supplying the hyperlink value.

**TIP**    We discovered some strange behavior for bound hyperlinks: when you first place a Bound Hyperlink control on a page, Access neglects to fill in the ControlSource property for you. (Rather, it fills in the ControlSource property on the Hyperlink property page, but that doesn't get carried over to the Data page, where it makes a difference.) It does set the InnerText and Href properties for you, however. If you manually go to the Data page and set the ControlSource property, the hyperlink will display correctly.

## Binding Hyperlinks to Hyperlink Fields

Although you might be tempted to bind the Hyperlink control to a Hyperlink field in an Access table, this won't work. You can only directly bind the Bound Hyperlink control to a text field. To do this, format the values in the text field as hyperlinks or email addresses.

If you want to bind a Hyperlink control to an Access field storing data in the *display-text#address#subaddress#screentip* format, you'll need to bind the control to individual portions of the hyperlink field. If you want to display a portion of a hyperlink field, you can bind a data access page control to that portion using the hyperlinkpart function provided by the Data Source Control on the page (MSODSC). For example, if you had a field named Link, you could create a bound Hyperlink control on a page and set the ControlSource property on the Data page of the Properties window to be:

```
=document.all.MSODSC.hyperlinkpart([Link], 0)
```

This sets the control's displayed value. You can also set the ControlSource property on the HyperLink page to be:

```
=document.all.MSODSC.hyperlinkpart([Link], 2)
```

This sets the control's address for linking.

## Image/HotSpot Image

The Image control and the HotSpot Image control are, effectively, the same control: they allow you to display images on your data access page. The big difference between the two is that the HotSpot Image control provides an active hyperlink, so that clicking on the image will navigate to a new location. The Image control can be bound; the HotSpot Image control cannot.

If you want to bind an Image control to data stored in a table, you must follow these steps:

1. Create a text field in a table containing paths of the images to be displayed. (The data access page will look for the images in the same folder as the page itself, unless you specify a full path for the images.)

2. When designing your page, select the Image control in the toolbox.

3. Drag the field containing the addresses onto the page. (This will create the Image control for you, and bind it to the field of addresses.)

You cannot bind a Jet OLE field containing actual images to an Image control—you must bind a text field (containing locations of images) instead.

To convert an Image control into a HotSpot Image control, simply add a hyperlink: right-click on the Image, select Hyperlink from the context menu, and set the linking properties of the control. (See the section on using the Hyperlink and Bound Hyperlink controls for more information.)

---

**WARNING**   Once we set the Hyperlink properties for an Image control (thereby turning it into a HotSpot Image control), we were unable to remove the linking properties. That is, we never found a way to convert it back into a normal Image control. Even deleting the associated properties in the Properties window didn't remove the link. You may need to delete and re-create the control, if that's your intent.

---

**NOTE**   What about the rest of the controls? Why no mention of the Office PivotTable, Chart, or Spreadsheet? Why nothing about the Movie control? Chapter 12 covers the Office Web Components. The Movie control is, well, just another ActiveX control. It's well documented, and doesn't have any direct equivalent from Access that requires "unlearning" of Access techniques. We can't cover every single ActiveX control here, and so we focused on the controls that are most likely to give you trouble.

---

## Hyperlinks to Data Access Pages

If you want to use links on one page to display data on another data access page, you're likely to want to limit the data on the second page to just information about the selected item on the first. That is, you'll often want to use hyperlinks as a drill-down mechanism. Access makes this easy: when you set up a hyperlink using the Insert Hyperlink dialog box, you can specify a filter in the Filter Criteria for the Data Access Page textbox on the dialog box. This filter (called a *server filter*, as its work is done by the database engine before the page is displayed) allows you to specify a SQL Where clause, limiting the rows that will appear on the new page. For more information on using this interesting feature and on other uses of hyperlinking with data access pages, see the white paper on the accompanying CD, "Connecting Data Access Pages Together" (Connecting DAPS.doc).

## Control Properties

As we worked on learning how to use the data access page designer, one thing became abundantly clear: this isn't the Access form designer! Not only is the design-time "feel" different, but most of the properties for familiar controls that you'll place onto data access pages are decidedly *unfamiliar*. As we attempted to create simple pages, we quickly became lost in the sea of new property names and values.

To make it easier for you, we've compiled a large table (Table 10.5) containing most of the properties associated with the simple elements (label, textbox, bound HTML, scrolling text, checkbox, option button, and so on) that you're likely to use on your pages. We've not documented here the controls that are clearly "foreign" (that is, controls from the Office Web Components, and the ActiveMovie control), but have focused on the simple controls you use every day.

Online help for these properties is decidedly unhelpful, so you may want to keep this table handy as you attempt to set properties associated with the elements you place on your data access pages. Note that not all properties listed in Table 10.5 apply to all controls—for example, the ListBoundField property applies only to list box and combo box controls, and the TrueSpeed property applies only to the Scrolling Text (Marquee) control.

---

**WARNING**    Microsoft did us a bit of a disservice when they created the Properties window for elements on data access pages. Note, for instance, that the TrueSpeed property appears just that way on the Properties window (that is, spelled with that particular combination of upper- and lower-case letters). Actually, the property is named "trueSpeed." Although VBA and VBScript don't care—they're not case-sensitive—JavaScript *does* care. If you're going to be scripting your pages, and you care to use JavaScript to do the scripting, you'll need to be aware of the exact spellings of the properties, which you can find in the DHTML help files.

---

## The Record Navigation Control

The record navigation bar that Access places onto each bound data access page is actually an ActiveX control supplied by the Office Web Components. This control works with the DataSource control to present data on a data access page. (See Chapter 12 for more information on Office Web Components.)

As with all other controls on data access pages, the RecordNavigationControl supplies many of the standard properties. In addition, the control provides some specific properties, listed in Table 10.6. You can set any of these properties in the Properties window, in VBA code at design time, or in scripting at runtime. (See Chapter 11 for more information on scripting.)

**T A B L E   1 0 . 5 :**   General Control and Page Properties

| PROPERTY NAME | DESCRIPTION | VALUES | COMMENTS |
|---|---|---|---|
| AccessKey | Specifies the accelerator key for the control or page | Any letter or number | This value allows you to press the Alt key, plus the specified letter or number, to set focus to the element. Although you can specify an AccessKey property for a page, it's not clear why you might. |
| Align | Specifies the alignment of the caption | "bottom", "center", "left", "right", "top", "textTop", "absMiddle", "baseline", "absBottom", "middle" | |
| AlinkColor | Specifies the color of a hyperlink as it's clicked | See BackgroundColor for options | Unlike most other color properties, this property converts its property settings into hex values when you enter them directly into the Properties window. That is, if you enter red, Access converts the value to #0000ff. |
| Alt | Specifies alternate text for graphic images, if the image can't be displayed | Any text string | |
| AlternateDataSource | ID property of an alternate data source (supposedly, if the original data source can't be found) | | |
| BackgroundColor | Specifies the background color for the control | "transparent", a color name, a hex color number (like #ffffff), a system color name (like "buttonface"), or a value created by calling the rgb function, and passing in three individual values (for example, "rgb(128,12, 256)") | Follow the help topics to the DHTML Color Table page for more information. |
| BackgroundImage | Specifies the background image for the control | "none", or the URL of an image to display | If you want, you can use the File:/// protocol to display a local file here. |

**T A B L E   1 0 . 5 :**   General Control and Page Properties *(continued)*

| PROPERTY NAME | DESCRIPTION | VALUES | COMMENTS |
|---|---|---|---|
| BackgroundPositionX | Specifies the offset from the left edge of the control | number of pixels ("10px"), percentage ("10%"), or "left", "center", "right" | If you repeat the image (see the BackgroundRepeat property), this coordinate indicates where the repetitions start, and fill from there. |
| BackgroundPositionY | Specifies the offset from the top edge of the control for the background image | number of pixels ("10px"), percentage ("10%"), or "top", "center", "bottom" | If you repeat the image (see the BackgroundRepeat property), this coordinate indicates where the repetitions start, and fill from there. |
| BackgroundRepeat | Specifies if and how the background image is repeated | "no-repeat" (don't repeat), "repeat-x" (repeat only in the x-direction), "repeat-y" (repeat only in the y-direction), "repeat" (repeat in both x- and y-directions | Repeats start at the offset specified in the BackgroundPositionX and BackgroundPositionY properties. |
| Behavior | Specifies the behavior of the Marquee control | "alternate" (alternate between sliding right and sliding left), "scroll" (scroll in the direction specified by the Direction property), or "slide" (slide text, once, in the direction specified by the Direction property) | Applies only to the Marquee control. See the Direction property as well. |
| BGProperties | Specifies behavior for the background image for a page | "fixed", "scroll" (default) | If set to "fixed", the background image doesn't move as you scroll the page. If "scroll" (or " "), the image scrolls with the page. |
| BorderColor | Specifies the border color | (See BackgroundColor) | Only has an effect if the BorderStyle and BorderWidth properties indicate that you want a border displayed. |
| BorderStyle | Specifies the border style | "none", "solid", "double", "groove", "ridge", "inset", "outset" | Use one of the specified words to get the effect you want. If BorderWidth is 0, you won't see any border. |

**T A B L E  1 0 . 5 :**  General Control and Page Properties *(continued)*

| PROPERTY NAME | DESCRIPTION | VALUES | COMMENTS |
| --- | --- | --- | --- |
| BorderWidth | Specifies the border width | "thin", "medium", "thick", or a numeric value (in pixels) | You can specify up to four different numeric values. These are interpreted as follows. One value: applies to all four sides. Two values: the first value is for top and bottom, second is for left and right sides. Three values: specifies top, right and left, and bottom widths. Four values: top, right, bottom, left, in that order. |
| BottomMargin | Specifies the bottom margin for a page and overrides the default margin | String representation of a decimal value, in pixels | If you attempt to leave this property empty, Access replaces the property with 15. You can specify 0 as a valid value, however. |
| Checked | Specifies whether a checkbox or option button has been selected | True or False | Applies only to checkbox and option button controls. |
| ChildLabel | Name of the control's child label (that is, the descriptive text associated with the control) | | You can specify the same label control for several other controls, allowing for some interesting design-time behaviors. Although you can specify any control you like here, only Label controls will "attach." |
| ClassName | Specifies the class of the given element | | Normally, you'll use this property to associate a particular style rule in a style sheet with a control. For label controls, for example, the class is "MSTheme-Label." |
| Color | Color to be used by the font or text rule | See BackgroundColor | Like other properties, this one is inherited from the parent. Setting the Color property of the SectionUnbound object allows you to specify color for all the controls you place on the section. |

**T A B L E  1 0 . 5 :**    General Control and Page Properties *(continued)*

| PROPERTY NAME | DESCRIPTION | VALUES | COMMENTS |
| --- | --- | --- | --- |
| ConsumesRecordset | Specifies whether data is supplied by the data source control | True or False | All bound controls have either their ControlSource property (if bound to a field) or ConsumesRecordset property (if bound to an entire recordset) property value set. |
| ControlSource | Name of the field within the page's data source to bind to this control | String | |
| Cookie | Unknown | | Undocumented, with unknown behavior. |
| DataEntry | Specifies whether a page is used only for data entry, or if the page's recordset should be populated with data from the data source | True or False (default) | If set to True, the page only allows you to add new rows. Once you've added a row, you can click the Save button on the record navigation toolbar to save it. |
| DataFormatAs | Specifies how the data should be rendered | "html", or "text" | Although this property exists for textbox controls, neither of the specified values is allowed. For the Bound HTML control, however, the values are accepted. Using "text" forces display of the exact text in the field. Using "html" causes the control to render the HTML (so that, for example, <b> and </b> tags format the text between them as bold). |
| DefaultCharacterSet | Unknown | | Undocumented, with unknown behavior. The default (in the U.S.) is "windows-1252", so it's relatively simple to guess that this specifies the character set and code page. |
| DefaultChecked | Determines whether a checkbox or option button is selected by default when the page is rendered | True or False | |

**TABLE 10.5:** General Control and Page Properties *(continued)*

| PROPERTY NAME | DESCRIPTION | VALUES | COMMENTS |
|---|---|---|---|
| DefaultControlType | Specifies the default control type to use for displaying text | ctlTypeTextBox (0) or ctlTypeBoundHTML (1) | Bound HTML controls allow your page to load faster, but are read only. |
| DefaultValue | Specifies the value to display in a control when you create a new row | String | In theory, the same concept as Access' DefaultValue property. Applies only to controls that have a Value property. |
| Dir | Specifies the direction of text, in language-specific environments | "ltr" (left-to-right) or "rtl" (right-to-left) | In English, the only effect of setting this property is to manage the alignment of the text: "rtl" forces right-aligned text, "ltr" forces left-aligned text |
| Direction | Specifies the direction the text scrolls in a Marquee control | "down", "left" (the default), "right", "up" | Applies only to the Marquee control. See also the Behavior property. |
| Disabled | Specifies whether the control is disabled | True or False | Similar to Access' Enabled property, except from the opposite point of view. The default for the Disabled property is False. |
| Display | Determines whether the element is rendered | "none", "block", "inline", "list-item", "table-header-group", "table-footer-group" | Specifying "none" causes the control to be removed from the page—that is, the page doesn't reserve any space for the control (as opposed to setting the Visible property to False, which simply hides the control). Specifying any other value renders the control, but doesn't affect its display. You can use the other values if you write code that manipulates different types of items. |
| Dynsrc | Specifies the address of a video clip or VRML world to be displayed in the window | | Why this property appears for the option button and checkbox controls is beyond us. |

**TABLE 10.5:**    General Control and Page Properties *(continued)*

| PROPERTY NAME | DESCRIPTION | VALUES | COMMENTS |
|---|---|---|---|
| ElementID | Enumerated value indicating the type of selected element | Long | Normally, passed as a parameter to an event procedure as an indication of the type of element that was selected. |
| FGColor | Specifies the foreground color for text on the page | Any color value (see BackGroundColor for specifics) | Unlike most other color properties, this property converts its property settings into hex values, when you enter them directly into the Properties window. That is, if you enter red, Access converts the value to #0000ff. |
| FontFamily | Specifies the font name to be used | Specify a comma-delimited list, containing either specific font names (such as "Tahoma") or generic font families (choose from "serif", "sans-serif", "cursive", "fantasy", "monospace") | Specify a list if you care to indicate what font to use if the font you want isn't available. If you use a generic font type (such as "serif"), the browser will select a font for you. If a font name contains spaces, make sure and place quotes around the font name. You can specify as many fonts as you like, separated with commas. |
| FontSize | Specifies the font size to be used | Absolute size, from this list: "xx-small", "x-small", "small", "medium", "large", "x-large", "xx-large"; or a relative size (based on the parent's font size), either "larger" or "smaller"; an absolute value for the size, such as "10pt"; or a percentage of the parent's font size, such as "80%" | Absolute font sizes scale to match the user's font preferences in the browser. |
| FontStyle | Specifies the font style | "normal", "italic", "oblique" | IE 4 (and 5) display italic and oblique text the same. |
| FontVariant | Selects the font variant | "normal", "small-caps" | IE 4 and 5 display small caps as all capitals, perhaps in a smaller font size. |

**TABLE 10.5:**  General Control and Page Properties *(continued)*

| PROPERTY NAME | DESCRIPTION | VALUES | COMMENTS |
|---|---|---|---|
| FontWeight | Specifies the weight of the font | "100", "200"..."900", "normal" (same as "400"), "bold" (same as "700"), "bolder", "lighter" | IE only supports normal (400) and bold (700). All other values are converted to one or the other of these values. |
| GridX, GridY | Specifies the number of dotted gridlines per inch | 1 through 24 | This is, obviously, a property you'll only change at design-time. |
| Height | Specifies the height of the control (for a page, the behavior is undocumented) | Specify a value ("40px", or "1.5in"), as a percentage of the parent ("40%"), or "auto" | For a page, the help link is broken, so it's unclear why this property is exposed for a page. Changing it doesn't appear to affect the behavior of the page. |
| Href | Specifies the location to which to navigate, for a Hyperlink control | Address of a page, or bookmark, or email address. See the special Insert Hyperlink dialog box for help in formatting this value. | |
| Hspace | Specifies the horizontal margin | Integer value, in pixels | Use this value to indicate an offset from the left edge of the page. |
| ID | Name of the element | | Just like the Access Name property for objects. |
| Indeterminate | Changes the state of a checkbox so that even if selected, the check appears greyed | True or False | Applies to both a checkbox and an option button control, but has no visual effect when set for an option button. |
| InnerText | Specifies the text to be displayed in a caption | | Similar to the Caption property of a label control on an Access form. Doesn't apply to a text box. For a Marquee control, specifies the scrolling text. |
| Lang | Specifies the language to use | | The specifier is an ISO standard language abbreviation. See the DHTML documentation for more information. |
| Left | Specifies the left coordinate of the control | Specify a value ("40px", or "1.5in", or "10mm"), as a percentage of the parent ("40%"), or "auto" | Added to the Hspace property (if that property is supplied for the element) to position the element. |

**T A B L E  1 0 . 5 :**   General Control and Page Properties  *(continued)*

| PROPERTY NAME | DESCRIPTION | VALUES | COMMENTS |
|---|---|---|---|
| LeftMargin | Specifies the left margin for the page | String representation of a decimal value, in pixels | This property sets the margin on the left side of the page, and effectively moves the 2D area of the page to the left or right, depending on the value. |
| Length | For list or combo boxes, returns the number of items in the control | | Surprisingly, you can set this property in the Properties window. If you set this for a list box, and you supply a value that would require scroll bars, the control displays scroll bars. You must actually add items to the control in order to populate it, however. |
| LinkColor | Specifies the color for the unvisited hyperlinks on a page | See BackgroundColor for options | Unlike most other color properties, this property converts its property settings into hex values when you enter them directly into the Properties window. If you enter red, Access converts the value to #0000ff. |
| ListBoundField | In a combo or list box, the field that's bound (as opposed to the field that's displayed) | | You must set the ListRowSource property before you set the ListBoundField property. The field name selected in this property must be available as a member of the ListRowSource recordset. |
| ListDisplayField | In a combo or list box, the field that's displayed (as opposed to the field that's bound) | | You must set the ListRowSource property before you set the ListDisplayField property. The field name selected in this property must be available as a member of the ListRowSource recordset. There can only be a single field in a combo box (as opposed to native combo box control in Access). |

**TABLE 10.5:** General Control and Page Properties *(continued)*

| PROPERTY NAME | DESCRIPTION | VALUES | COMMENTS |
|---|---|---|---|
| ListRowSource | In a combo or list box, specifies the source for the bound field and the display field | | You must set this property before setting the ListBoundField or ListDisplayField properties. |
| Loop | Specifies the number of times to repeat a marquee loop, or a sound or video loop | -1 (infinite), or a number greater than 0 | Documentation states that 0 is acceptable (and will loop once). Actually, the Property window rejects this value as invalid. |
| Lowsrc | Determines the lower-resolution image to be displayed in the element | | |
| MaxRecords | Specifies the maximum number of records that the connection will bring to the local computer | | The default value is 10,000. Making it smaller requires more trips to the server to retrieve data. Making it larger requires each data request to take more time. |
| Multiple | Determines whether you can select multiple items in a list or combo box. | True or False | If True, you can select multiple items. Unlike combo boxes in Access, you can set this property to True for combo boxes. Doing so effectively turns the control into a list box. |
| NoShade | If True, corresponding rule (line) control appears without the 3D shading | True or False | |
| NoWrap | Specifies whether the browser performs word wrap | True or False (default) | |
| Overflow | Specifies how to handle text that doesn't fit within the confines of the defined element area | "scroll", "hidden", "visible" (default), "auto" | "scroll" adds horizontal and vertical scrollbars, whether you need them or not. "hidden" simply hides overflow. "visible" shows overflow. "auto" decides whether you need horizontal or vertical scrollbars, and adds them as needed. |

**TABLE 10.5:**  General Control and Page Properties *(continued)*

| PROPERTY NAME | DESCRIPTION | VALUES | COMMENTS |
|---|---|---|---|
| Position | Specifies the type of positioning for an element | "static", "relative", "absolute", "fixed" | The default value is static, implying the control gets no special positioning and simply obeys the layout rules of HTML. See the DHTML help topic on Positioning for more information on using this property. |
| ReadOnly | Specifies whether the control's data is read only | True or False | Similar to the Locked property in Access. The default is False. |
| RecordsetType | Specifies the type of recordset to use for the data source control | dscSnapshot (1), or dscUpdatableSnapshot (2) | Setting this value to dscShapshot provides you with a read-only recordset. Use the default, dscUpdatableSnapshot to get a read/write recordset. |
| RecordSource | Specifies the recordset (or grouping definition) for the section | | This property is actually exposed as the RecordSource property of a GroupLevel object, provided by the DataSourceControl object |
| RightMargin | Specifies the right margin for the page | String representation of a decimal value, in pixels | |
| Scroll | Indicates whether a page displays scroll bars | yes (default), no, auto | It's unclear what effect this setting has—we could find no discernable differences. |
| ScrollAmount | Number of pixels to scroll the text each time it moves | Integer value indicating the number of pixels to scroll | Use a smaller value to force the text to scroll slower. See the ScrollDelay property for the interval between movements. (Marquee control only) |
| ScrollDelay | Amount to delay between scrolls | Integer value indicating number of milliseconds to wait (default is 85) | The larger this value, the slower the scroll. See the ScrollAmount property for the number of pixels to scroll each time the text moves. (Marquee control only) |
| SelectedIndex | 0-based index of the selected item within a combo box or list box | -1 (nothing is selected), 0 through the Length property - 1 | Although Access supplies this property on the Properties window, setting it at design time has no effect. |

**TABLE 10.5:** General Control and Page Properties *(continued)*

| PROPERTY NAME | DESCRIPTION | VALUES | COMMENTS |
|---|---|---|---|
| Src | Specifies the URL to be loaded by the object | Any value URL | |
| TabIndex | Specifies the order elements are visited when you use the Tab key to progress through controls | (Use any integer value) | Controls are visited in this order: All TabIndex values greater than 0, in ascending order (or source order, for duplicate TabIndex values); All TabIndex values equal to 0, in source order if there is more than one. Specify a TabIndex value of -1 to omit a control from the tab order. If you set a page's TabIndex property to anything other than -1, the page itself will get the focus at the appropriate time. |
| TagUrn | | | Undocumented usage. |
| TextAlign | Specifies the text alignment | "left", "right", "center", "justify" | Although "justify" was added for IE4, we were unable to see any difference between "left" and "justify". Perhaps you'll have better luck. |
| Title | Specifies advisory information for the control (For a Page, supplies the title bar caption) | | In IE, this property becomes the tool tip displayed as you hover your mouse over the control (similar to the ControlTipText property in Access). |
| Top | Specifies the top coordinate for the control | Specify a value ("40px", or "1.5in"), as a percentage of the parent ("40%"), or "auto" | |
| TopMargin | Specifies the right margin for the page | String representation of a decimal value, in pixels | |
| TotalType | The type of total to be displayed in the control | dscNone (0), dscSum (1), dscAvg (2), dscMin (3), dscMax (4), dscCount (5), dscAny (6), dscStdDev (7) | |

**TABLE 10.5:**  General Control and Page Properties *(continued)*

| PROPERTY NAME | DESCRIPTION | VALUES | COMMENTS |
|---|---|---|---|
| TrueSpeed | Determines whether the speed for a Marquee control's scrolling is based on the internal clock, with a minimum of 60ms, or based on the ScrollDelay and ScrollAmount properties | True or False | The default value of this property is False (for compatibility with IE3), which means that no matter how you set the ScrollSpeed property, text in a Marquee control will never move more often than every 60ms. If you set this property to True, then your ScrollSpeed property setting will take effect. |
| Type | Specifies a text string indicating the type of the control | Button, checkbox, file, hidden, image, password, radio, reset, submit, text, select-multiple, select-one, textarea | It's unclear whether there can be more possible options than the ones listed here. |
| UniqueTable | Name of the updateable table when a form is bound to a multi-table view or stored procedure | | |
| URL | Unknown | | This property is used by Access, but it's not documented, and its use isn't known. Leave this value alone. |
| UseRemoteProvider | Specifies whether the data source uses a remote provider | True or False | Use the default value (False) unless you're retrieving data using IIS from an HTTP/HTTPS address. Microsoft Remote Data Services provides an HTTP or HTTPS request to IIS, which retrieves the data using an OLE DB connection to the data. |
| Value | Sets or retrieves the value of the object | | Effectively allows you to specify text for an unbound control. For bound controls, the value of the field immediately replaces the Value property you've specified at design time. |

**TABLE 10.5:** General Control and Page Properties *(continued)*

| PROPERTY NAME | DESCRIPTION | VALUES | COMMENTS |
|---|---|---|---|
| Visibility | Specifies the visibility of the control | "visible", "hidden", "inherit" | If set to "inherit", the control gets this property from the parent element. Note that unlike the Display property, setting this property to "hidden" still reserves physical space for the control on the page. |
| VlinkColor | Specifies the color for the visited hyperlinks on a page | See BackgroundColor for options | Unlike most other color properties, this property converts its property settings into hex values, when you enter them directly into the Properties window. That is, if you enter red, Access converts the value to #0000ff. |
| Vrml | Specifies the URL of the VRML world to be displayed in the object | Any valid URL | Why does this apply to a checkbox control? Your guess is as good as ours. |
| Vspace | Specifies the vertical margin | Integer value, in pixels | Use this value to indicate an offset from the top edge of the section. |
| Width | Specifies the width of the element | Specify a value ("40px", or "1.5in"), as a percentage of the parent ("40%"), or "auto" | |
| ZIndex | Specifies the top-to-bottom order of the control on the page | An integer, or "auto" | "auto" (the default) specifies that the stacking order is bottom-to-top in the order that controls appear in the HTML source. Positive ZIndex values are positioned above negative (or lesser value). Two elements with the same ZIndex values are stacked according to source order. |

**TABLE 10.6:** Properties of the RecordNavigationControl control

| Property Name | Description | Comments |
| --- | --- | --- |
| DataSource | Specifies the ADO datasource object for the control. | |
| FontName | Specifies the name for the font used in the control's label. | |
| RecordsetLabel | Specify the label to display in the caption of the control. You can insert the following placeholders in the text: "I0" for the current row number, or the first row number if the control is displaying a range of rows; "I1" for the final row, if displaying a range of rows; and "I2" for the total number of rows. Provide two sets of text (one for single rows, one for groups of rows) separated with a semi-colon. | For example, you might use the text: "Customer I0 of I2;Customers I0 to I1 of I2". Invalid placeholders don't generate an error, but cause no value to be displayed. |
| RecordSource | Specifies the record source (the name of a recordset definition or grouping definition) It's possible that the Data Source Control supplies multiple recordset definitions, and this property specifies which one you'd like to use. | |
| ShowDelButton | Show the delete button? | |
| ShowFilterBySelectionButton | Show the filter-by-selection button? | |
| ShowFirstButton | Show the First button? | |
| ShowHelpButton | Show the Help button? | |
| ShowLabel | Show the label portion of the control? | |
| ShowLastButton | Show the Last button? | |
| ShowNewButton | Show the New button? | |
| ShowNextButton | Show the Next button? | |
| ShowPrevButton | Show the Previous button? | |
| ShowSaveButton | Show the Save button? | |
| ShowSortAscendingButton | Show the Sort Ascending button? | |
| ShowSortDescendingButton | Show the Sort Descending button? | |
| ShowToggleFilterButton | Show the Toggle Filter button? | |
| ShowUndoButton | Show the Undo button? | |
| IsButtonEnabled (method) | Determine whether a particular button is currently enabled. | Pass in one of the values supplied in the NavButtonEnum values (for example, navBtnUndo). |

# More Data Management Issues

Although you've seen, earlier in the chapter, how to create data access pages using various techniques, you may need to modify the behavior of the pages. Sooner or later, you'll need to modify the way the pages handle sorting, grouping, and filtering. This section discusses these issues, and elaborates on the various properties available to you.

## Grouping on any Field

Normally, your data access pages contain data grouped by the relationships between the data. That is, you might have a page that displays customer information, and, for each customer, information about the orders placed by the customer. Within in each order, you might display all the detail rows for that order.

What if you wanted to group all the orders for a given customer by the order date? That is, rather than seeing each individual order, you wanted to see the orders for each different date grouped together? To handle this situation, data access pages support grouping on any individual field within a group. This technique is tied to the concept of *promoting* and *demoting* controls on your page. Promoting a control creates a new section, grouping on that control's bound value. Demoting a control removes its section, and moves the control back to the normal header section for its group.

To see this technique in action, follow these steps:

1. Create a new data access page in the sample database for this chapter.

2. From the Field List window, drag the tblCustomer:CustomerID field to the Section: Unbound section of the new page.

3. Select the newly renamed Header: tblCustomer section and make it shorter (that is, drag the bottom of the section up so that the section takes up less vertical real estate).

4. From the Field List window, select the tblOrder: OrderDate field and drag it to its own section, underneath the Header: tblCustomer section (watch for the blue horizontal divider with the outward arrows on the ends).

5. Choose View ➢ Page View to view the page and expand a few customer rows to get the feel for how the page works. Go back to Design view when you're done.

6. Select the OrderDate textbox, right-click, and select Promote from the context menu. Access creates a new grouping section (named Header: tblOrderOrderDate) for you.

7. From the Field List window, drag the tblOrder: PaymentMethod field to the Header: tblOrder section.

8. View the page in Page view once again, expand a customer, and note that now the OrderDate field has an Expand button associated with it. Expand order dates, and you'll see that you've now grouped both on the CustomerID field and the OrderDate field.

You can use this same technique to group on the value of any bound control's field. If you promote a checkbox, for example, you'll end up with two groups (the rows for which the checkbox is checked, and the rows where it isn't). This technique works if your page contains only a single grouping, as well.

**TIP**   The Group On and Group Interval options on the Sorting and Grouping dialog box are only available for grouped fields. See the "Managing Sorting and Grouping" section later in this chapter for more information.

## Using Automatic Joins

Data access pages allow you to create joins "on the fly." That is, if you select fields from two related tables and place them onto the page, Access will do the work of creating the join for you. In addition, when you place fields from multiple tables within the same section, you can use the Group By Table toolbar icon to automatically separate out the two tables, grouping the page by the "one" side of the relationship.

**NOTE**   This is not the way forms and reports work—in those designers, if you want to base your form or report on the results of two joined tables, you'll need to either run a wizard to do the work for you or create a query that joins the tables for you. Data access pages allow you to do this as you're designing the page, in an ad hoc fashion.

To try out automatic joins and the Group By Table functionality, follow these steps:

1. Create a new data access page in Design view, in the sample database for this chapter.

2. From the Fields List window, drag the tblOrder.OrderDate field onto the unbound section.

3. From the Fields List window, drag the tblCustomer.LastName field onto the (now named) Header: tblOrder section.

   By following the steps so far, you've asked the DataSourceControl control that's providing the data for the page to create a join between tblOrder and tblCustomer. If you were doing this same sort of thing in an Access form or report, you'd need to stop and create a query to perform the join for you, and then create the form or report. Once the control has created the join for you, you can separate the two sources using the Group By Table functionality.

4. Add a few more fields from tblOrder onto the Header: tblOrder section.

5. Add a few more fields from tblCustomer onto the Header: tblOrder section.

6. Click on any field from tblCustomer. (This step is important!)

7. Click the Group by Table toolbar button (it's between the two arrow buttons, one pointing left, the other pointing right). At this point, Access takes all the fields from the selected table (tblCustomer) and promotes them to having a section of their own (Header: tblCustomer).

8. Run the page, either in Access or in Internet Explorer, and you'll see that the page is now grouped by all the fields from the tblCustomer table.

---

**TIP**  You can use the Group by Table button when you have selected any field from the "one" side of a relationship. If you select any control bound to a field from any other table, the Group by Table option won't be available.

---

## Using a Group Filter Control

Data access pages allow you to provide a drop-down list of values from which the users can select a value to use for filtering the data in a section. This control can be a list box or drop-down list (combo box) and creating it requires a few special steps:

1. In the control toolbox, select either the ListBox or the Dropdown List control.

2. In the Field List window, select the field on which you'd like to filter.

3. Right-click and drag the field to the section containing data for the selected table or query. When you release the mouse, choose Group Filter Control from the context menu.

4. Run the page. All the fields within the section will be empty, except the group filter control, which will contain a unique list of values from the selected field. Choose a value, and the rest of the controls will populate with the appropriate values for the first matching field. You can use the record navigation control to move to other rows that match the criteria.

It's easy to forget about using the right-click/drag technique to place the list box or drop-down list on the page: if you forget this step, your control will be a standard control and won't have any filtering effect.

For a demonstration of this technique, see DAPDemoGroupFilter in this chapter's sample database. This page uses a group filter control to draw information from qryCustomersWithFullName, filtering data from tblOrder. (This demo page also shows off some other data access page features, including using caption and footer sections.) Figure 10.25 shows the sample page in use.

**FIGURE 10.25**
Use a group filter control to filter data for just the particular row you need.

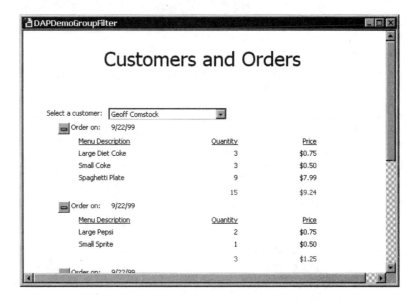

## Managing Sorting and Grouping

Each time you place fields from a different data source on your data access page, Access creates a new group for you. Just as on an Access report, each group has its own set of sorting and grouping properties, and you can use the Sorting and Grouping window to manage the properties for each section. (Choose View ➤ Sorting and Groupin,g or click the Sorting and Grouping toolbar icon to display the window, shown in Figure 10.26.)

**FIGURE 10.26**
Use the Sorting and Grouping window to modify the
group properties.

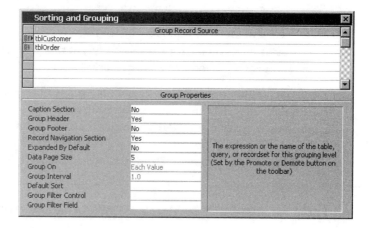

The Sorting and Grouping options, and how you might use each item, are described below:

**Caption Section**  Select Yes to add a caption section above the group header section. This section is useful if you want to display your data in a tabular format, and if you want to place field captions above the data. You'll only see this section when the next-higher group level is expanded, so that the detail rows are visible. You can't add bound controls to this section. If you change this value to No, and the Caption section already exists, Access will delete any existing controls within the section when it deletes the section.

**Group Header**  Select No to delete the header section (and all its controls) for the current grouping, or Yes to display the header section. The naming for this section is somewhat misleading: unlike a header section on an Access form or report (which corresponds to the Caption section here), the header section on a data access page is the section where you'll actually display the data for the grouping. (The help is displayed by pressing F1 in the Sorting and Grouping window is also misleading.)

**Group Footer**   Select Yes to display a footer section immediately above the record navigation section (if you're displaying that section) for the current group. This is a good place to put summary information and totals pertaining to the group. For reasons we can't guess, you cannot display the group footer for the lowest grouping level. Setting this value to No causes Access to remove the section and any controls it contains.

---

**WARNING**   Because you can't turn on the Group Footer section for the lowest-level grouping, you simply won't be able to display a footer for a page on which you're only displaying data in a single group. Of course, that's the only way your page will allow edits, so you can't have it both ways. If you want to display summary data about the grouping, you'll need to add multiple sections. Doing so makes the page read-only.

---

**Record Navigation Section**   Use this property to show or hide the record navigation control that manages the navigation from one row to the next. This section always goes below the group footer (if you've displayed that section), or below the group header. This section can't contain any bound controls. Setting this property to No removes the section and the record navigation control it controls; if you set it to No and you still want to display data in the group header section, you'll probably want to set the Data Page Size property to All, so that users don't require any navigation method to see all the rows. Of course, this means that your page must render all the rows in your record source.

---

**WARNING**   You should be careful about turning off the Record Navigation Section property and setting the Data Page Size property to All, unless you know that you won't have many rows of data. Asking the page to render all the rows in a large record-set before displaying anything to a user isn't a good idea. It's going to be slow.

---

**Expand by Default**   If set to Yes, the page will automatically expand the next-lower group level when the page is loaded. This means that the user won't have to expand the section (by clicking the Expand button). Of course, automatically expanding the section means that for each parent row, all the children rows will need to be retrieved before the page can display its data. This option isn't available unless there is a next lower section to expand.

---

**TIP**    Use this option judiciously. For each section you set to auto-expand, the page must do a great deal more work when loading. For fastest loading, make sure the top-level section has this property set to No.

---

**Data Page Size**    This option controls how many rows the page displays when the section appears. The window provides the values 1, 5, 10, and All, but you can type in any reasonable number you like. If you've set the Record Navigation Section property to No, you'll want to set this property to be All (or use a Group Filter Control to select the specific data to be displayed), so that users can see all the rows without navigation.

---

**TIP**    If you want to edit data on your data access page, you must set the Data Page Size property to 1, and you must have only a single grouping level. If either of these requirements isn't met, the page will be read only.

---

**Group On/Group Interval**    If the current section is a grouping section (that is, you've promoted a control and you're setting properties of its section), you can specify both the Group On and Group Interval properties. Group On allows you to specify the interval on which you want to group the data (for example, for date fields you can select Year, Qtr, Month, Week, and so on). Group Interval allows you to specify the number of units specified in the Group On property to group by. For example, if Group On is set to Weeks, and Group Interval is set to 2, then the output will be grouped into two week blocks. These properties aren't available except for grouped sections.

**Default Sort**    This property allows you to specify the sort order for the grouping. Specify field names, separated with commas. If you want to sort a field in descending order, add the text "DESC" after the field name. (You can use "ASC" after a field name to indicate that it's to be sorted ascending, but because that's the default, you needn't ever specify this text.)

For example, to sort a section on FirstName descending, and for matching first names on the LastName field, you can use a Default Sort value like this:

```
FirstName DESC, LastName
```

**Group Filter Control/Group Filter Field**   As mentioned in the previous section, you can use a list box or drop-down list (combo box) control to filter the rows showing within a section. These two properties specify the control to be used and the field on which to filter. You'll set these properties by creating the group filter control as defined in the previous section, and we've not found a need to alter these properties in this window.

# Managing Data Access Pages

As you work with your data access pages in various databases and projects, you'll need to decide where to place the pages. Sometimes you'll also need to move these from place to place or delete them. These seemingly simple actions have complex ramifications, because of the "under-the-covers" linkage between the Access data access page shortcuts and the actual HTM files.

## Placing Data Access Pages

It's tempting to place the HTM files associated with data access pages in the same folder as the database or project that's providing the page, but it's worth considering one important issue with this choice: data access pages are stored on disk as individual HTM files. That means, of course, that end users can touch them, study them, and (worst of all) modify them. Any end user, armed with Notepad, can ruin your page, and there's nothing you can do about it.

To avoid this issue, you might consider storing your HTM files on a Web server. If you have access to the Web server's file storage, you can simply place the HTM files there. If not, you'll need to first set up a Web folder within Office, and then you'll be able to store files on a Web server as easily as storing them in local file storage. By placing the files in a Web server, you make it much more difficult for the average user to find and modify the file. If you've managed the security on your Web server correctly, it should be impossible for anyone who isn't authorized to touch files to be able to modify your carefully crafted data access page.

Once you've placed the pages on a Web server, deploying your application is easy: you needn't distribute the pages—they're already deployed. If you're deploying data access pages using an MDB or ADP file as a container, you simply need to provide your end users with the appropriate file. If you're using data access pages with no associated database application, you tell your users the URL to navigate to, and you're all set.

---

**WARNING**    If you do place your pages on an Web site, you must be aware that some of the code provided in the "Deploying Data Access Pages" section will not work. That code relies on file system links to the HTM files, which isn't available once you've stored your pages on a Web server.

---

## Importing Data Access Pages

Just as with any other Access object, you can import a data access page from a different database or project file. When importing a data access page, however, you're not simply importing an Access object: you're also setting up a link to an external HTM file. After selecting the data access page to import from the external database or project, Access asks you to specify the name for the HTM file. That is, it makes a copy of the existing HTM file, and you must supply a new name for the file.

After you've supplied a name, Access checks the data source for the HTM and modifies the HTM file so that rather than retrieving its data from the original file, it now retrieves its data from the import destination file. If you don't want this behavior—that is, if you want the data access page to retrieve its data from its original source, rather than the current database or project—then you use a different technique. From the Database window, select Insert ➤ Page. From the New Data Access Page dialog box, shown in Figure 10.27, select Existing Web Page. Then, from the Locate Web Page dialog box, select your HTM file. Access will open the page in Design view. If you decide to add it to your project, close it and save your changes. If not, close it and cancel saving—Access will simply not add it to your project.

---

**TIP**    If you see the new object shortcuts in the Database window, you can select Edit Web Page That Already Exists from the list of available Page objects. This performs the same task as the steps outlined in the previous paragraph.

---

**FIGURE 10.27**
Use this dialog box to insert an existing Web page.

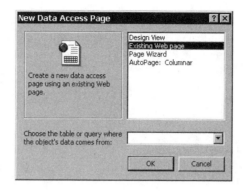

## Deleting Data Access Pages

When you attempt to delete a data access page from the Database window, you're not simply deleting an Access object: you're deleting an object that contains a shortcut to a file out in the file system, or on a Web server. Therefore, Access doesn't know, without asking, whether it should delete just the shortcut, or the shortcut and the external file.

Therefore, when you delete a data access page from within Access, you'll first see the Access dialog box confirming deletion of the shortcut (unless you've set the option within Access that allows it to delete objects without confirmation). Then you'll see the dialog box shown in Figure 10.28. This dialog box confirms that you want to delete the external file along with the Access shortcut. If you select Yes, Access will delete both the link and the HTM file. If you select No, it deletes the link, but leaves the HTM file intact.

**FIGURE 10.28**
Select whether to delete the external HTM file along with the Access shortcut.

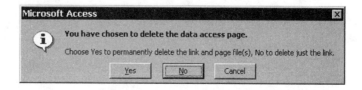

| TIP | Access does not make a special case for data access pages stored on a Web server. If you've set up a Web folder and have stored your page there, deleting the link and allowing Access to delete the HTM file will cause Access to go to the Web server and delete the file from the Web folder. Our point here is that although end users can't modify the HTM file on the Web server, you (and Access) can. |
|---|---|

# Deploying Data Access Pages

Although Chapter 16 focuses on the issues involved with deploying Access applications, data access pages present two specific issues that require careful planning and coding. We'll focus on those two issues in this section. Specifically, you must understand:

- How Access maintains links between your database (or project file) and the HTML files that make up the data access pages

- How the pages themselves link to the associated data source

What if you move the MDB (or ADP) file that contains links to the data access page files? What happens if you move the data source? You must be able to resolve both of these issues, at design-time, using code that fixes up path dependencies in your database. In this section, you'll find possible solutions to both of these important deployment issues.

## Creating Data Access Pages Programmatically

The code in this section uses the Access method, CreateDataAccessPage, to create new data access pages. This method allows you to create a new Page object within Access, either associated with a new HTM file or with an existing one. It does not, however, allow you to create controls on the page. What if you want to create a complete data access page from scratch, programmatically, just as you can with forms and reports, using the CreateControl and CreateReportControl functions? Access doesn't supply a CreatePageControl function, unfortunately.

To help us out, Trigeminal Software has provided a module for us, named basCreate, that contains a CreatePageControl function. This complex function allows you to create bound controls on a data access page programmatically. If you need to create your own data access page wizards or merely want to dig into the techniques involved in building data access pages programmatically, you can study the code in the basCreate module in the chapter database.

If you want to use this module, you'll need to use the Tools ➢ References menu to set a reference to Microsoft HTML Object Library. In addition, you'll need a reference to the Office Web Components type library. This one, however, may be tricky. Look for Microsoft Office Web Components 9.0 in the list of references. It may or may not appear, depending on your version of Office 2000. If it doesn't appear on the list of available references, you must use the Browse button on the References dialog box, find the folder that contains all the Office 2000 executables and DLLs, and locate MSOWC.DLL. This adds a reference named Microsoft Office Web Components 9.0.

## Linking Files and Data

Because working with data access pages will always involve managing files external to your MDB or ADP file, you'll need to be aware of the hard-coded linkage information stored in both the shortcut stored in the database, and in the HTML file that contains the data access page itself. If you break either of these links, you'll need to run code at your application's startup to fix up the broken links.

Although we think that most data access pages used in applications will take advantage of an intranet as the deployment scenario, you may find a need to deploy an MDB or ADP-based application that includes data access pages. In this case, the shortcut provided by Access (which refers to the actual HTML file), contains the full path to the file. If you break that link by moving the HTML file, you'll need to fix up the link to contain the actual address.

In addition, each data access page itself contains the connection information for its data connection. For Access databases, this information includes a full path and database name. If you've moved or changed the name of the data source, the data access page won't be able to display any data. If you're using SQL Server as the data source, it's possible that the server name may no longer be valid, or you may simply want to change the data source to be a different server. In either case, you'll need to fix the connection information so that your data access page can find its data. (Of course, if you're using an MDB to display your data access page, you're likely linking right back to the host database to find your data. Usually, however, this won't be the case. This is the least likely of all the deployment scenarios we've considered, but fixing up the links is still an important issue.)

In this chapter, we'll look only at the contingency that you're running a data access page from within an Access application, and that you can run VBA code in order to fix up these two issues.

## Fixing the Path from the Data Access Page to its Data Source

Imagine that you've created a database and added a number of data access pages to the application. You get the application working, and then you deploy it on a user's machine. Now, suddenly, all the data access pages won't work because they can no longer find the data.

What happened? If you investigate the contents of a data access page, you'll find, buried in the XML code making up the page, an ADO connection string. In order to link up to the appropriate data source, each data access page file contains a hard-coded path to its original data source. If you move the data source, you'll need to also fix that path before you can display the page and its data.

The DataSourceControl ActiveX control provides the link between the page and the data source. Listing 10.1 shows a portion of the HTML code from a sample data access page, with the data source printed in bold. In this fragment, you see properties of the DataSourceControl object; among the properties is the Data Source property provides the path to the data source.

### Listing 10.1

```
<OBJECT classid=CLSID:0002E530-0000-0000-C000-000000000046
codeBase=file:\\Tpwinnt\Z\msowc.cab#version=9,0,0,2710
 id=MSODSC><PARAM NAME="XMLData"
VALUE="<xml xmlns:a=&quot;urn:schemas-microsoft-
com:office:access&quot;>&#13;&#10; <a:DataSourceControl>
&#13;&#10;
<a:OWCVersion>9.0.0.2710</a:OWCVersion>&#13;&#10;
<a:ConnectionString>Provider=Microsoft.Jet.OLEDB.4.0;
User ID=Admin;Data Source=C:\MasterApplication\MyApp.mdb;
```

If you need to modify that data source, you'll need to provide some mechanism for opening the HTM file as a text file, finding that particular item within the text file, fixing it, and saving the entire mess back to disk. To make this process simpler, we've provided the adhResetDAPDataLink procedure in basResetDAP of the CH10.MDB database.

The adhResetDAPDataLink procedure does all the work for you. You send it three items:

- A reference to the data access page object within your application

- A string containing the path to the data source (or a server name, for SQL Server)

- A string containing the path to the HTM file that contains your data access page

Given these three bits of information, the procedure can open the HTM file, fix the data source, and save it back. The procedure has a few issues that we were not able to work around, however:

- The procedure must use the standard file system in order to open and modify the file. If you've stored your data access page on a Web server, this procedure won't be able to modify that file.

- The procedure reads the entire data access page into a single String variable. This type of variable is limited to storing around two billion characters. If your HTM file is larger than that, this procedure won't be able to help. (Of course, if your HTM file is larger than two billion characters, you've probably got lots of other problems!)

---

**TIP**    The procedures you'll find in this section use the AllDataAccessPages collection, a property of the CurrentProject object in Access. This collection contains all the saved data access pages, and each element of the collection is an AccessObject object.

---

The procedure can only change the location of the data source, not the type. That is, it won't be able to change the source from an Access database to SQL Server. Although this is feasible, it's a lot of work—you would need to replace the entire connection string, depending on the data source. Although it might be nice to be able to do this programmatically, we did not provide that functionality. Listing 10.2 contains the entire adhResetDAPDataLink procedure. Listings 10.3 and

10.4 contain the two subsidiary procedures required by adhResetDAPDataLink. FixPath (Listing 10.3) ensures that a file path ends with a trailing "\" (or "/", if the path is an HTTP path). GetFileName (Listing 10.4) takes in a full path and returns just the filename portion of the path.

---

**NOTE**    Although you can find code similar in purpose to adhResetDAPLink in the Northwind sample database that comes with Access 2000, you'll find that the code there is less "reusable", and is, perhaps, less efficient than the code we've provided. We think you'll find it easier to use our procedure than to attempt to extricate the functionality you need from the Northwind sample database.

---

**WARNING**    The use of data access pages, in general, will get very sticky if you include semicolons in your paths or data source names. Windows allows this, but data access pages do not. Although this isn't documented, to our knowledge, using a semicolon in a path or data source name will make it impossible for the data access page to link to its data source.

---

## Listing 10.2

```
Public Sub adhResetDAPDataLink( _
dap As AccessObject, _
strDataSource As String, _
strPathToHTM As String)

    ' Reset the link between a data access page
    ' and its data source.

    Dim strContent As String
    Dim strName As String
    Dim intFileNumber As Integer

    Dim lngPosStart As Long
    Dim lngPosEnd As Long
    Dim lngPosCnnStrStart As Long
    Dim lngPosCnnStrEnd As Long
```

```
Dim strExistingSource As String
Dim strOut As String
Dim strCnnStr As String
Dim strCompare As String

Const adhcSearch As String = "Data Source="
Const adhcConnectionStart As String = _
 "<a:ConnectionString>"
Const adhcConnectionEnd As String = _
 "</a:ConnectionString>"
Const adhcDash = "&amp;#45;"
Const adhcAmp = "&amp;amp;"
Const adhcQuot = "&amp;quot;"
Const QUOTE = """"

On Error GoTo HandleErrors

strName = FixPath(strPathToHTM) & _
 GetFileName(dap.FullName)
If Len(strName) > 0 Then
    intFileNumber = FreeFile
    Open strName For Input As #intFileNumber

    ' Look through the text file looking for
    ' the Connection String. Once found, change
    ' it to reflect the new database location and
    ' set it to an absolute path.

    strContent = Input(LOF(intFileNumber), _
     #intFileNumber)

    ' Look for the connection string part.
    lngPosCnnStrStart = InStr(1, _
     strContent, adhcConnectionStart)
    If lngPosCnnStrStart > 0 Then
        lngPosCnnStrStart = _
         lngPosCnnStrStart + _
         Len(adhcConnectionStart)
        lngPosCnnStrEnd = InStr(lngPosCnnStrStart, _
         strContent, adhcConnectionEnd)
        If lngPosCnnStrEnd > 0 Then
            strCnnStr = Mid$(strContent, _
```

```
            lngPosCnnStrStart, _
          lngPosCnnStrEnd - lngPosCnnStrStart)
    End If
End If

' Get rid of the nasty "&amp;xxx;" characters.
strCnnStr = Replace(strCnnStr, adhcDash, "-")
strCnnStr = Replace(strCnnStr, adhcAmp, "&")
strCnnStr = Replace(strCnnStr, adhcQuot, QUOTE)

' Search for the magic words, "Data Source=".
lngPosStart = InStr(1, strCnnStr, adhcSearch)
If lngPosStart > 0 Then
    ' If found, move past the magic words,
    ' and search for ";".
    lngPosStart = lngPosStart + Len(adhcSearch)
    lngPosEnd = InStr(lngPosStart, strCnnStr, ";")
    If lngPosEnd > 0 Then
        ' If you found a ";", then check to see
        ' if the data source matches the one passed
        ' in. If so, you're done, else replace it.
        strExistingSource = _
        Trim$(Mid$(strCnnStr, lngPosStart, _
        lngPosEnd - lngPosStart))

        ' If the DAP contains quotes around the
        ' data source, add quotes to the comparison
        ' text, as well.
        If Left$(strExistingSource, 1) = QUOTE Then
            strCompare = QUOTE & _
            strDataSource & QUOTE
          Else
            strCompare = strDataSource
        End If

        If StrComp(strExistingSource, _
        strCompare, vbTextCompare) <> 0 Then
            ' No match. Replace with the
            ' supplied data source.

            ' Put quotes around the database name.
            ' This can't hurt, and Access will
```

```
                                    ' remove them if they're unnecessary.
                                    strCnnStr = _
                                     Left$(strCnnStr, lngPosStart - 1) & _
                                     QUOTE & strDataSource & QUOTE & _
                                     Mid$(strCnnStr, lngPosEnd)

                                    ' Can't send back a string with bad
                                    ' characters in it. Put things back
                                    ' the way they were, being careful
                                    ' to replace "&" chars first.
                                    strCnnStr = Replace(strCnnStr, _
                                     "&", adhcAmp)
                                    strCnnStr = Replace(strCnnStr, _
                                     QUOTE, adhcQuot)
                                    strCnnStr = Replace(strCnnStr, _
                                     "-", adhcDash)

                                    ' Now need to build back the entire
                                    ' string, replacing the
                                    ' ConnectionString piece in there.
                                    strOut = Left$( _
                                     strContent, lngPosCnnStrStart - 1) & _
                                     strCnnStr & _
                                     Mid$(strContent, lngPosCnnStrEnd)

                                    ' Close the input file.
                                    Close #intFileNumber

                                    ' Get a new file number, open the file
                                    ' for output, and write the new HTML
                                    ' stream out.
                                    intFileNumber = FreeFile
                                    Open strName For Output _
                                     As #intFileNumber
                                    Print #intFileNumber, strOut
                            End If
                        End If
                    End If
                End If

        ExitHere:
            On Error Resume Next
```

```
        Close #intFileNumber
        Exit Sub

HandleErrors:
    Select Case Err.Number
        Case Else
            Err.Raise Err.Number, _
            Err.Source, Err.Description
    End Select
    Resume ExitHere
End Sub
```

◯ **Listing 10.3**

```
Private Function FixPath(strPath As String) As String

    ' Given a path (with no trailing file name), make
    ' sure the path ends with a trailing "\" or "/"
    ' (HTTP: requires "/", right?) That way, you can
    ' take the output of this function and tack on a
    ' file name without having to wonder if there's a
    ' separator or not.

    Dim strCh As String * 1

    On Error GoTo HandleErrors

    If StrComp(Left$(strPath, 4), _
      "HTTP", vbTextCompare) = 0 Then
        strCh = "/"
    Else
        strCh = "\"
    End If

    If Len(strPath) > 0 Then
        If Right$(strPath, 1) = strCh Then
            FixPath = strPath
        Else
            FixPath = strPath & strCh
        End If
```

```
        End If

ExitHere:
    Exit Function

HandleErrors:
    ' Not sure what errors could occur in here, besides
    ' catastrophic ones (out of memory, and so on), but
    ' it never hurts...
    Select Case Err.Number
        Case Else
            Err.Raise Err.Number, _
                Err.Source, Err.Description
    End Select
    ' This line doesn't do anything,
    ' given the current Select Case block.
    Resume ExitHere
End Function
```

### Listing 10.4

```
Private Function GetFileName(strFullPath As String) _
As String

    ' Given a full path, retrieve just the file name.
    ' (How many times have we written this code?)
    ' This version works with HTTP:// paths, as well,
    ' because you may store DAPs on a web server.

    Dim strFileName As String
    Dim lngPos As Long

    On Error GoTo HandleErrors

    ' First, convert any "/" to "\". Then, find
    ' the final "\" and pull off everything after that.

    strFileName = Replace$(strFullPath, "/", "\")
    lngPos = InStrRev(strFileName, "\")
    If lngPos > 0 Then
        strFileName = Mid$(strFileName, lngPos + 1)
    End If
```

```
        GetFileName = strFileName

ExitHere:
    Exit Function

HandleErrors:
    ' Not sure what errors could occur in here, besides
    ' catastrophic ones (out of memory, and so on), but
    ' it never hurts...
    Select Case Err.Number
        Case Else
            Err.Raise Err.Number, _
                Err.Source, Err.Description
    End Select
    ' This line doesn't do anything,
    ' given the current Select Case block.
    Resume ExitHere
End Function
```

The adhResetDAPDataLink procedure uses brute force to fix the broken linkage. Once the code has opened the file, it reads all the contents of the file into a local variable and searches for the text it needs to find: "Data Source=". If it finds that text, it extracts the current data source from the text and compares it to the data source you've specified in procedure's parameters. If the two items match, there's nothing more to be done. If they don't match, the procedure replaces the old data source with the new one and then writes the text back out. It's not elegant, but it works.

---

**NOTE**     To be honest, there's a bit more going on than the previous paragraph mentions. Because of the way data access pages store data source names internally, we found that ampersands (&), quotes, and double hyphens caused trouble. In each case, the data access page converted the character into a string like "&amp;amp;" for an ampersand, or "&amp;quot;" for a quote. Because adhResetDAPDataLink is looking for semicolons to delimit the data source name, you can imagine that this might cause some trouble. To work around it, the procedure replaces each offending combination with its original value, does all the work, and then replaces them back when it's done. There may be other characters and character combinations that we missed. If so, you'll need to modify the code (it should be obvious how to do it, given the examples we've provided). If you do find other "bad" characters, please let us know!

---

If, for example, your intent is to reset the data link within a data access page named "DAPDemo" so that it retrieves its data from the current project, you might write code like this (assuming that the HTM file is in the same path as the current project):

```
Call adhResetDAPDataLink( _
  CurrentProject.AllDataAccessPages("DAPDemo"), _
  CurrentProject.FullName, CurrentProject.Path)
```

You can use the AllDataAccessPages collection of the CurrentProject object (whether you're working in an MDB or an ADP file) to reference a particular data access page. CurrentProject.Name supplies the name of the current database, and CurrentProject.Path supplies just the path portion of the current database.

---

**WARNING**    If you attempt to run adhResetDAPDataLink when the data access page is in use, you'll get error 70 (Permission Denied) if the code tries to write to the HTM file.

---

## Handling the Path from the Database to the Data Access Page

If you create a database (or project) that contains data access pages and then move any of the corresponding HTM files to a new location, Access will no longer be able to locate those HTM files. (To try this out, change the name of the folder containing the sample database for this chapter. When you attempt to open a data access page in the new folder, Access will fail: it's looking for data access pages in the original folder, which no longer exists. You could also simply move the HTM files to a different folder and get the same results.) If you're deploying an Access application that includes data access pages, you'll want to make sure you include code that relinks the HTM files to the current database or project.

---

**NOTE**    Managing data access pages is really the same issue as managing linked tables, and you may want to create a user interface to manage this. In this chapter, we've provided no user interface—instead, we've supplied procedures you might call in order to relink the pages.

---

Given the location of the HTM file, you would think it should be easy to simply set some property of the DataAccessPage object within your database or project. And so did we—we looked in vain to find some way to simply change a property linking the shortcut stored within the database to the actual HTM file on the disk. If you hover your mouse over a data access page in a database (see Figure 10.29), the tooltip contains the path: clearly, Access knows where this thing is stored. But reading this visually from a tooltip doesn't do your code any good.

**FIGURE 10.29**

Hover your mouse over a data access page, and you'll find the path.

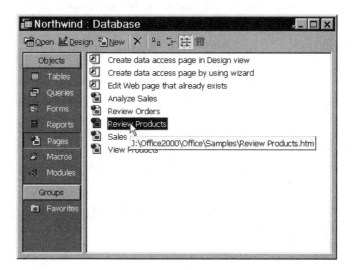

A little digging turned up the FullName property for all the AccessObject-type objects. That is, all of the All... collections contain AccessObject objects, and each of these has a FullName property. For most objects, this property contains an empty string. For data access pages, however, this property contains the full path to the associated HTM file. Unfortunately, this property is read only, and so we hit another brick wall.

The only known solution to this problem is (believe it or not) to delete the existing data access page from the database (not the associated HTM file from the hard drive, however), and then re-create a new one with the path you need. Yes, it's ugly, but it works. The code in adhResetDAPLink does this work for you. Given a reference to an existing data access page, and a path, the code resets the link to the HTM file. Of course, there are some issues to be considered:

- Because the adhResetDAPLink procedure does its work by deleting and then re-creating database objects, its use will lead to "database bloat." That is, as Access deletes and then creates objects, it doesn't necessarily reuse the space it has just freed up. This will, over time, cause your database to grow. Make sure you compact your database regularly if you use this code.

- The adhResetDAPLink procedure will cause some screen "flashing." Make sure you turn off screen updating somewhere upstream to the procedure (using DoCmd.Echo), so that you don't have to endure the unsightly screen flashing as the code creates and deletes objects from the database.

- If the data access page's data source can't be found, adhResetDAPLink will fail. Make sure you've verified the data source before you call this procedure to reset the links. In the next section, you'll see code that handles resetting both the data and the path—it must reset the data before it can work with the path information.

- In an MDE or ADE file, Access won't allow you to modify design-time properties of existing objects. If the code determines that it's been run from an MDE or ADE file, it gracefully fails and returns False. (See the ISMDE function in Listing 10.6.)

The adhResetDAPLink function, shown in Listing 10.5, follows these steps:

1. Tests to see if the current database/project is an MDE/ADE file. If so, the code sets the return value to be False and simply exits:

   ```
   If IsMDE() Then
       adhResetDAPLink = False
       GoTo ExitHere
   End If
   ```

2. Gets the filename portion of the data access page's FullName property and tacks that onto the end of the supplied path, creating the new full path for the HTM file:

   ```
   strFileName = GetFileName(dap.FullName)
   strFullPath = FixPath(strPath) & strFileName
   ```

3. Compares the new path to the data access page's FullName property—if they're the same, there's nothing to do, and the code sets the return value to be True and exits:

   ```
   If StrComp(dap.FullName, _
     strFullPath, vbTextCompare) = 0 Then
         ' There's nothing to do. The path already
         ' matches the path you're trying to set.
   ```

```
   ' Just get out now.
   adhResetDAPLink = True
   GoTo ExitHere
End If
```

4. Stores away the name of the current data access page, so that it can reset it once it has deleted and re-created the shortcut:

   ```
   strName = dap.Name
   ```

5. Deletes the original shortcut:

   ```
   DoCmd.DeleteObject acDataAccessPage, strName
   ```

6. Creates the new data access page, but doesn't create a new HTM file to go with it. This code simply creates a new object and sets its internal shortcut to the real HTM file:

   ```
   Call CreateDataAccessPage(strFullPath, _
     CreateNewFile:=False)
   ```

7. Closes the new data access page and saves it with the saved name:

   ```
   DoCmd.Close acDataAccessPage, strName, acSaveYes
   ```

### Listing 10.5

```
Public Function adhResetDAPLink( _
 dap As AccessObject, ByVal strPath As String) As Boolean

    ' Given the name for a DAP shortcut, and the
    ' full path of the actual HTM file, reset the DAP link.
    ' To do this, you must create a new DAP link (using
    ' the CreateDataAccessPage function), delete the
    ' original, and then rename the new one.

    Dim strName As String
    Dim strFileName As String
    Dim strFullPath As String
    Dim lngPos As Long

    Dim strOldName As String
```

```
' If this is an MDE, ain't no point in
' going on. In that case, simply return False
' and quit.
If IsMDE() Then
    adhResetDAPLink = False
    GoTo ExitHere
End If

On Error GoTo HandleErrors

' Get the new HTM file name:
strFileName = GetFileName(dap.FullName)
strFullPath = FixPath(strPath) & strFileName

If StrComp(dap.FullName, _
 strFullPath, vbTextCompare) = 0 Then
    ' There's nothing to do. The path already
    ' matches the path you're trying to set.
    ' Just get out now.
    adhResetDAPLink = True
    GoTo ExitHere
End If

' Store away the name of the DAP shortcut
' you want to end up with -- the same as the
' current DAP shortcut, which is about to
' get deleted.
strName = dap.Name

DoCmd.DeleteObject acDataAccessPage, strName
Call CreateDataAccessPage(strFullPath, _
 CreateNewFile:=False)
DoCmd.Close acDataAccessPage, strName, acSaveYes
adhResetDAPLink = True

ExitHere:
    Exit Function

HandleErrors:
    Select Case Err.Number
        Case Else
            Err.Raise Err.Number, _
```

```
                    Err.Source, Err.Description
        End Select
        ' This line doesn't do anything,
        ' given the current Select Case block.
        Resume ExitHere
End Function
```

The adhResetDAPLink procedure uses a few techniques you may not have seen before:

- To create a new DataAccessPage, the code calls the CreateDataAccessPage method of the Application object. This method can either open an existing HTML page as a data access page (as this example did), or it can create a new data access page and the associated HTM file.

- To determine if the current database/project is an MDE or ADE file, the code calls the IsMDE function, shown in Listing 10.6. This function attempts to retrieve the "MDE" property of the current database or project. If this property contains the value "T" (not the Boolean value True—the character "T"), the current file is an MDE/ADE file. In that case, the adhResetDAPLink procedure cannot relink the data access page, and so it must exit, returning False. (This code also relies on the ProjectType property of the Current-Project option. This allows the code to determine whether the code is running in a database or in a data project.)

**Listing 10.6**

```
Private Function IsMDE() As Boolean

    ' Is the current database/project an MDE/ADE file?

    Dim strValue As String
    On Error Resume Next

    ' The "MDE" property will contain "T" if this
    ' is an MDE or an ADE.
    If CurrentProject.ProjectType = acADP Then
        strValue = CurrentProject.Properties("MDE")
    Else
        strValue = CurrentDb.Properties("MDE")
```

```
      End If
      IsMDE = (strValue = "T") And (Err.Number = 0)
      Err.Clear
End Function
```

## Determining If a Link Is Broken

You may simply want to determine if a data access page's shortcut is broken or not, without attempting to create a new one. To make that possible, we've supplied the adhCheckLinkToDAP function, shown in Listing 10.7. This procedure simply attempts to use the Dir function to locate the file in the file system. If it succeeds, the file link is valid. If it fails and triggers a runtime error, either the link is invalid, or the file exists on a Web server. In that case, in the error handler, adhCheckLinkToDAP calls the adhCanOpenDAP function (shown in Listing 10.8), which attempts to physically open the data access page within Access. (This is a slow, ugly process, so you want to do anything possible to keep it from happening. If the HTM file is stored on a Web server, however, the Dir function can't find it and will trigger the runtime error that causes the code to load the page directly.) If the page opens successfully, adhCanOpenDAP returns True; otherwise, it returns False.

### Listing 10.7

```
Public Function adhCheckLinkToDAP( _
 dap As AccessObject) As Boolean

    ' Validate the file link for a specific DAP shortcut.

    On Error GoTo HandleErrors

    Dim strName As String
    strName = Dir(dap.FullName)

    ' Return success, if the file exists.
    adhCheckLinkToDAP = (Len(strName) > 0)

ExitHere:
    Exit Function
```

```
HandleErrors:
    adhCheckLinkToDAP = False
    Select Case Err.Number
        Case 52      ' Bad file name or number
            ' Perhaps the file name is http://?
            ' In that case, the simplest solution
            ' is to quietly try to open the thing,
            ' and see if that succeeds or not. This
            ' is MUCH slower than other techniques,
            ' so we reserve it for this case only.
            adhCheckLinkToDAP = adhCanOpenDAP(dap)
        Case Else
            ' What do we do? Return False?
    End Select
    Resume ExitHere
End Function
```

⟩ **Listing 10.8**

```
Public Function adhCanOpenDAP( _
 dap As AccessObject) As Boolean
    On Error Resume Next
    DoCmd.OpenDataAccessPage dap.Name
    adhCanOpenDAP = (Err.Number = 0)
    DoCmd.Close acDataAccessPage, dap.Name
    Err.Clear
End Function
```

# Fixing Both Issues in One Pass

If you need to create an application that uses data access pages deployed from an Access MDB or ADP file, you'll want to incorporate code that handles both of these issues. Providing a user interface to handle these issues is beyond the scope of this chapter, but we have provided a sample procedure, adhValidateDAPLinks (shown in Listing 10.9) that works through each of the data access pages in the application. This procedure first resets the data link and then, if the code can open the data access page, resets the file link to the HTM file as well.

**WARNING**    The adhValidateDAPLinks procedure assumes that the HTM files are in the same folder as the MDB or ADP file. If that's not the case in your application, you'll need to modify this sample procedure.

### Listing 10.9

```
Public Sub adhValidateDAPLinks()
    ' An example, showing how you might
    ' validate all DAP links.

    Dim lngDAPCount As Long
    Dim dap As AccessObject

    Dim i As Long

    On Error GoTo HandleErrors

    DoCmd.Echo False
    With CurrentProject.AllDataAccessPages
        lngDAPCount = .Count
        ' Must work backwards through the links,
        ' as adhResetDAPLink deletes and recreates
        ' DAPs. This messes Access' looping up
        ' seriously.
        For i = lngDAPCount - 1 To 0 Step -1
            Set dap = .Item(i)
            Call adhResetDAPDataLink(dap, _
             CurrentProject.FullName, CurrentProject.Path)
            If Not adhCheckLinkToDAP(dap) Then
                Call adhResetDAPLink(dap, _
                 CurrentProject.Path)
            End If
        Next i
    End With

ExitHere:
    Set dap = Nothing
    Exit Sub
```

```
HandleErrors:
    MsgBox "Error: " & Err.Description & _
      " (" & Err.Number & ")"
    Resume ExitHere
End Sub
```

> **NOTE**
>
> ValidateDAPLinks works its way backwards through the collection of available data access pages. It must do this: because the procedure may delete and re-create objects, Access assigns each new object a new ordinal position within its collection. If you used a For Each…Next loop to work through the collection, you would end up skipping over items. (Believe us, we tried it!) By working backwards through the items, the newly added items, at the end of the collection, don't conflict with the items that have yet to be touched. This is the same technique you might use any time you're modifying the contents of a collection within a loop—closing all open forms, for example.

## What about Themes?

If your data access page has a theme associated with it, you'll find one more issue that you'll need to grapple with. When you add a theme to a page, Access creates a subfolder of the folder containing your page, with the same name as your page plus "_files". In that folder, you'll find the theme's style sheet (CSS) files, the image files (GIF or JPG) used by the style, and an XML file describing the various parts of the theme.

When you move the HTM file that contains your data access page's layout to a new location, you must remember to move the subfolder as well, and to maintain the relative position of the folders.

# Summary

In this chapter, we've introduced the new data access page and its designer. There's no doubt that the designer needs work, but the pages you can create can be as complex and full-featured as you need. Deploying data access pages is simple: all you need is the data source, the HTM file (and perhaps some theme information) and Internet Explorer 5.0. Of course, because data access pages depend on technology that's part of Office, only Office users (or Office licensees) can legally use your pages.

This chapter focused on these particular issues:

- Introducing data access pages
- Why you might want to use data access pages
- Properties of the HTML controls used on data access pages
- Using the Sorting and Grouping properties
- Managing the two links used by data access pages—the link from the page to its data source and the link from the Access database or project to the page

Where do you go from here? If you're interested in scripting your pages (and you should be, if you intend to really use them in a production environment), you'll need to investigate Chapter 11, which deals with scripting in general, and working with data access pages in specific. If you want to use the Office Web Components, check out Chapter 12.

Take the time to work with data access pages. Don't be discouraged by the designer—save temporary copies of your pages, giving your page a new name as you save it each time, so you can back out any changes you make (the lack of Undo will, otherwise, drive you crazy). It will certainly improve in a later version. We think you'll find data access pages to be the simplest way to get Jet or SQL Server data up on the Web, and as long as you can limit your user base to Office 2000 users or licensees, data access page technology just might be an answer to your "I need to get this data onto the Web" needs.

# Scripting Data Access Pages

- Scripting data access pages

- Using the Microsoft Script Editor

- Debugging your scripts

- Understanding the events, properties, and methods of data access page objects

- Validating data

- Adding items to a drop-down list

In the last chapter you learned how to create data access pages and customize their design using the data access page designer. While you can do a lot with a basic data access page, sooner or later you're going to want to do something that requires scripting. This chapter takes a look at data access page scripting in detail.

---

**WARNING**   Because data access pages store hard-coded links to their data source internally, and because Access stores hard-coded paths to the files containing the HTML for the data access page, the examples contained in this chapter will not operate correctly until you've reset these paths. To do that, open the basResetDAP module, place your cursor inside the first procedure, adhValidateDAPLinks, and press the F5 key. (For more information on this procedure, see Chapter 10.) Although you might want to run this procedure automatically in your applications, or you might want to provide a user interface for running this procedure, we opted not to do that, as every application needs to handle this situation differently.

---

**NOTE**   We don't cover scripting the Office Web Components in this chapter. For information on scripting the Office Web Components, see Chapter 12.

---

# Good News/Bad News

Scripting data access pages is a good news/bad news proposition.

The *good news*: when creating data access pages you can use VBScript, a close relative of the familiar VBA programming language.

The *bad news*: in addition to learning VBScript, you'll need to learn the Microsoft Script Editor, the Internet Explorer Document Object Model (DOM), and the object models of the Data Source control and the Office Web Components. And if you thought the Access and ADO object models were complex, you'll be amazed to see how many events, properties, and methods are exposed by the DOM and the Data Source control.

In this chapter, we'll get you started putting together the pieces that are necessary to create effective data access pages that do what you want them to do.

# Microsoft Script Editor Orientation

The Microsoft Script Editor (MSE) is a color-coded HTML and script editor that you can use to add scripting code behind data access pages and other Microsoft Office documents. The MSE environment is depicted in Figure 11.1.

**FIGURE 11.1**
The Microsoft Script Editor

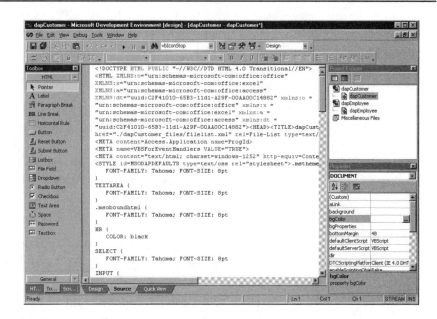

---

| **TIP** | MSE is actually a stripped-down version of the editor that comes with Microsoft Visual InterDev. |
| --- | --- |

---

| **NOTE** | In Chapter 14, we discuss how to use MSE to create Active Server Pages (ASPs). |
| --- | --- |

# Microsoft Script Editor Tour

The MSE environment includes a number of windows you can use to manage and edit your data access pages.

## Project Explorer

The Project Explorer window lists each of the pages you have opened for editing in MSE. It doesn't list all of the data access pages in the database, just those you have opened for editing with the MSE. The Project Explorer window is the window in the upper right-hand side of Figure 11.1.

## Properties Window

The Properties window lists the properties for the currently selected object. Depending on what you have selected, the Properties window might display the properties of the document (the page), a script, an HTML element, or another object. The Properties window is the window in the lower right-hand side of Figure 11.1.

## Page Editor

The MSE Page Editor supports three views that you can switch amongst using the tabs at the bottom of the window. You can see the Page Editor in the middle of Figure 11.1.

More than likely, you'll spend most of your time in Source view, which is a color-coded HTML and script editor you can use to edit the source of your data access pages. By default, each element on the page is color-coded according to a set of rules which you can customize using the Text Editor, Font And Colors section of the Options dialog box.

You can use Quick view to preview the Web page as it would look in Internet Explorer.

Design view is a WYSIWYG editor that lets you edit the elements of HTML and ASP pages visually. Unfortunately, when used with data access pages, Design view is unavailable. Microsoft would like you to use the data access page designer instead to visually edit your pages.

## Toolbox

You can use the MSE Toolbox to drag and drop HTML elements onto your pages. For data access pages, the Toolbox is of marginal utility because the elements on the Toolbox are light-weight HTML controls, not the data-bound controls supported by the data access page designer.

> **TIP** You can customize the Toolbox by dragging and dropping pieces of HTML and scripting code onto it. After dropping something on the Toolbox, MSE will give it the name "HTML Fragment." Right-click on the name and select Rename Item from the pop-up menu to change the name to something more descriptive.

## HTML Outline

The HTML Outline window (also known as the Document Outline window) displays a hierarchical view of the elements on the Web page opened in the Page Editor. You can use the HTML Outline window to navigate to page elements. To move to an element in the Page Editor, click on the element in the HTML Outline window. If the HTML Outline window is not displayed, select View ➤ Other Windows ➤ Document Outline.

In Figure 11.1 you can't see the HTML Outline window because it shares space with the Toolbox window. The HTML Outline window is displayed in Figure 11.2.

> **TIP** A nice feature of the MSE environment is that screen space is conserved by docking together related windows using a tabbed interface. By default, the HTML Outline window docks together with the Toolbox and Script Outline windows.

## Script Outline

The Script Outline window displays all the scriptable elements on the page in a hierarchical view. The Script Outline window, which is shown in Figure 11.3, has four nodes:

- Client Objects & Events
- Client Scripts
- Server Objects & Events
- Server Scripts

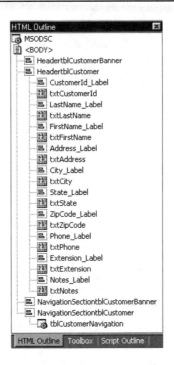

Only the first two nodes are useful when working with data access pages. You can use the Client Objects & Events node to create event handlers for the objects on the page and navigate to existing event handlers. The Client Scripts node displays all of the existing scripts on the page.

If the Script Outline window is not displayed, select View ➢ Other Windows ➢ Script Outline.

## Object Browser

The MSE environment, like the VBA environment, has an Object Browser you can use to browse the objects, collections, properties, methods, and events of the programmable objects on the page. To display the Object Browser, select View ➢ Other Windows ➢ Object Browser (or press the F2 key). The MSE Object Browser is shown in Figure 11.4.

**FIGURE 11.3**
The Script Outline window

**FIGURE 11.4**
The MSE Object Browser looks similar to the VBA Object Browser.

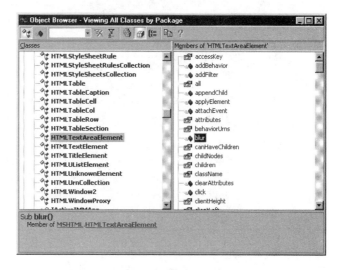

The MSE Object Browser looks similar to the VBA Object Browser but it works a little differently. By default, the MSE Object Browser doesn't display any object models. To browse an object model, you must first add the library to the Object Browser's list of packages and libraries.

To add a new library, click the Select Current Packages/Libraries toolbar button. MSE displays the Select Packages/Libraries dialog box as shown in Figure 11.5. Select the Other Packages and Libraries node and click the Add button to add a new library.

**FIGURE 11.5**
You use the Select Packages/ Libraries dialog box to add or remove type libraries from the Object Browser.

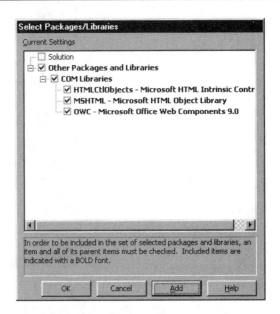

We've found the following type libraries to be most helpful when scripting data access pages:

**MSHTML (Microsoft HTML Object Library)**    This type library contains the complete IE 5 DOM object model.

**HTMLCtlObjects (Microsoft HTML Intrinsic Controls)**    This type library contains the HTML 3.2 form controls. (HTML 3.2 is an earlier browser-neutral version of the HTML specification.) While all the objects in this type library are also in MSHTML, we find it's often easier to work with this simplified version of the type library.

**OWC (Microsoft Office Web Components 9.0)**   This type library contains the objects in the Office Web Components object model.

These are the libraries we have found most useful, but you may find it helpful to add other type libraries to the object browser.

## Editing a Page in the Microsoft Script Editor

To open a data access page in MSE, you must first have the page open in Design view. Select Tools ➤ Macros ➤ Microsoft Script Editor, or right-click on the page and select Microsoft Script Editor from the pop-up menu.

When you first open a page in MSE you may be shocked to see a lot of unfamiliar tags. Here's the basic layout of a data access page:

```
<!DOCTYPE …>
<HTML …>
<HEAD><TITLE>…</TITLE>
meta tags
<STYLE>
 style attributes
</STYLE>
Data Source Control object
<META … XML …>
scripts
</HEAD>
<BODY>
controls
Navigation control object
</BODY>
</HTML>
```

You can ignore much of the data access page source code. Any scripts you add to the page using the Script Outline window will be added to the <HEAD> section of the page, between the last <META> tag and the </HEAD> tag. You can manually place scripts in other locations of the page—and they *may* work—but it's best to follow the lead of the Script Outline window and add your scripts in the same location.

Another area of the page that you may find of interest is the <BODY> section. Here's where you'll find all of the controls on the page. The mapping from data access page control to HTML tag might not always be obvious, so we've provided Table 11.1 to help you orient yourself.

**T A B L E  1 1 . 1:**    Control Mappings to HTML

| Data Access Page Control | HTML Tag |
| --- | --- |
| Bound HTML | <SPAN class=MSOBoundHTML> |
| Bound Hyperlink | <A> |
| Check Box | <INPUT type=checkbox> |
| Command Button | <BUTTON> |
| Data Source | <OBJECT> |
| Dropdown List | <SELECT> |
| Expand | <OBJECT> |
| Hotspot Image | <A> with embedded <IMG> |
| Hyperlink | <A> |
| Image | <IMG> |
| Label | <SPAN class=MSTheme-Label> |
| Line | <HR> |
| List Box | <SELECT> |
| Movie | <IMG> |
| Office Chart | <OBJECT> |
| Office Pivot Table | <OBJECT> |
| Office Spreadsheet | <OBJECT> |
| Option Button | <INPUT type=radio> |
| Option Group | <FIELDSET> |
| Record Navigation | <OBJECT> |
| Rectangle | <SPAN class=MicrosoftAccessRectangle> |
| Scrolling Text | <MARQUEE> |
| Section, bound | <DIV class=MSOShowDesignGrid> |

**TABLE 11.1:** Control Mappings to HTML *(continued)*

| Data Access Page Control | HTML Tag |
| --- | --- |
| Section, caption | <DIV class=MicrosoftAccessBanner> |
| Section, footer | <DIV class=MSOShowDesignGrid> |
| Section, header | <DIV class=MicrosoftAccessBanner> |
| Section, navigation | <DIV class=MSOShowDesignGrid> |
| Section, unbound | <DIV class=MSOShowDesignGrid> |
| Text Box | <TEXTAREA> |

**TIP**  The HTML written by the data access page designer is a bit difficult to read. You'll find many tags begin in the middle of a line of text and end several lines later. When you're trying to sort things out, you may find it helpful to insert line breaks to make the HTML more readable. Unfortunately, Access will reformat the HTML the next time you open the source of the page in the MSE environment. Still, it won't hurt anything to insert a few extra line breaks, even if they're only temporary.

# Adding Scripting Code to a Page

Once you've opened your page in MSE, you're ready to add some scripting code.

**TIP**  By default, any scripts you create use the VBScript language, but you can use JavaScript instead by clicking on any white space to select the Document object and using the Properties window to change the defaultClientScript property from VBScript to JavaScript. All the examples in this chapter use the VBScript language.

## Creating an Event Handler

To execute code in response to an event, select the object in the Script Outline window, click on the plus sign to the left of the object to expose its events, and double-click on the desired event. MSE responds by creating the shell of an event handler. All that's left is to write the code.

For example, double-clicking on the Data Source control's Current event produces the following event handler script:

```
<SCRIPT LANGUAGE=vbscript FOR=MSODSC EVENT=Current>
<!--

-->
</SCRIPT>
```

---

**WARNING**    When you use the Script Outline window to generate an event handler, it doesn't supply any arguments to the events. Some objects, however, require you to set up arguments to receive parameters from the event. If you don't include the necessary arguments, your event handler code will never be called. Thus, you will need to alter the event handler created by the Script Outline window for events that have arguments. See Table 11.2 and the "Supplying Event Handler Arguments" section later in this chapter for information on the arguments for many of the data access page object events.

---

## Creating a Global Script

Often, you'll want to create functions and subroutines that you can call from your event handlers. These procedures need to be placed in global scripts that aren't attached to a specific event. To create a global script, position the cursor where you wish to insert the script—the HEAD section of the page is usually the best place to add your global scripts, either before or after any event handlers—right-click on the page and select Script Block ➢ Client from the pop-up menu.

Here's what a global script block looks like:

```
<SCRIPT LANGUAGE=vbscript>
<!--

-->
</SCRIPT>
```

Of course, you could also enter the script block yourself.

---

**NOTE**    Any code you add to a global script outside of a procedure—called an *immediate script*—is executed as the page loads.

---

You can include scripts from script libraries by creating a special form of a global script using the following syntax:

```
<SCRIPT LANGUAGE=vbscript SRC="filename">
</SCRIPT>
```

Any scripting code you place in include script files is merged into the page as it loads.

---

**TIP**    The scripts that MSE writes always include HTML comment tags (<-- and -->) at the beginning and end of the scripts. These HTML tags are used so that older browsers that don't understand the <SCRIPT> tag will ignore the text, rather than displaying it in the browser. If you create your own client-side scripts, you should follow the lead of MSE and surround your scripts with HTML comment tags.

---

## Previewing a Page

To preview a page in Internet Explorer, right-click on the page and select View in Browser from the pop-up menu. MSE loads your page into IE. Alternately, you can switch back to Access, right-click on the page in the data access page designer, and select Page View from the pop-up menu to view the page in Access.

---

**WARNING**    When previewing pages from MSE, the editor copies your page—but not any include files—to a temp folder before loading the page in the browser. When previewed this way, code in include scripts will not execute.

---

## Debugging a Page

The MSE environment includes a debugger that you can use to debug your data access pages. To use the debugger, follow these steps:

1. Set one or more breakpoints in your code by clicking on the left-hand margin of the Page Editor. As in the VBE environment, MSE displays a red dot to indicate a breakpoint. You can't set breakpoints in HTML, only in your VBScript (or JavaScript) code.

2. Select Debug ➢ Start or press F5 to load the page into IE with debugging support.

3. Interact with the page. When any code hits a breakpoint, MSE suspends execution and displays the code in the debugger as shown in Figure 11.6.

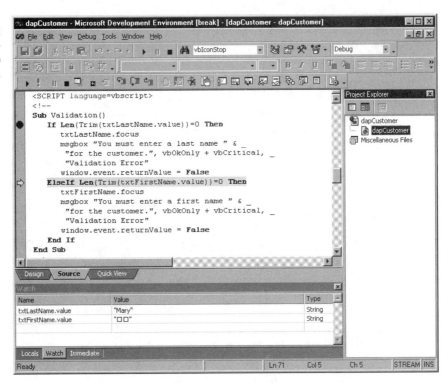

While debugging a page, you can step through your code using many of the same commands and windows supported by the VBA debugger. Here's a sampling of what you can do:

- To single-step through your code, select Debug ➢ Step Into or press F11.

- To procedure-step through your code, select Debug ➢ Step Over or press F10.

- To open the Immediate window, select View ➢ Debug Windows ➢ Immediate.

- To open the Locals window, select View ➢ Debug Windows ➢ Locals.

- To open the Watch window, select View ➢ Debug Windows ➢ Watch.

**NOTE** You can't use the MSE debugger to debug ASP server-side scripts because the MSE doesn't support server-side debugging. The Visual InterDev debugger, however, supports the debugging of both client and server-side (ASP) scripts.

# Client versus Server Scripting

Data access pages, along with any scripts you add to them, perform their magic using client-side scripting. That is, all (or most) processing, including data binding, is executed on the client machine. In contrast, when you create Active Server Pages (ASP), they perform all (or most) of their processing on the server. This has a number of ramifications, including:

- Data access pages will only work with Internet Explorer 5.0 or later (because of the data binding and controls they employ).

- Data access pages work with or without a Web server.

- Any scripting code you add to a data access page is executed on the client and thus must use the Document Object Model (DOM), not the ASP object model.

- Scripting code you add to the page can interact with the user and create dynamic effects without requiring a round-trip to the Web server. This means your client-side scripts will execute faster than the equivalent scripts in ASP pages.

**TIP** Creating data-driven Web pages using Active Server Pages is the subject of Chapter 14.

# VBScript versus VBA

When you add script to data access pages, you must use the VBScript scripting language. VBScript is a subset of VBA. (You can also use JavaScript, but we'll assume that most Access developers will want to code in VBScript because of its similarity to VBA.) One of the big differences between VBScript and VBA is that

VBScript doesn't support explicit datatypes. Instead, everything takes on the Variant datatype. The following code would be illegal in a VBScript script because VBScript doesn't support the As Datatype clause of the Dim statement:

```
' This is illegal in VBScript
Dim varString As Variant
```

Other major differences between VBA and VBScript:

- VBScript doesn't support custom collections.

- VBScript doesn't support early binding.

- VBScript lacks financial functions and file I/O statements.

- The only error handling VBScript supports is in the form of the On Error Resume Next statement.

- VBScript lacks any support for API calls or class modules (version 5.0 of VBScript—the version that ships with IE 5.0 and IIS 5.0—has added support for the Class statement which allows you to create your own objects; see the Microsoft scripting Web site at `http://msdn.microsoft.com/scripting/` for more details).

Many of the differences between VBScript and VBA are there to keep VBScript safer when executed on the client machine inside of a Web browser. For example, file I/O statements and API calls could be dangerous so they have been removed from the language. Other parts of VBA, such as support for custom collections and financial functions, are removed from VBScript to reduce the memory footprint of the language and make it faster.

---

**NOTE**    See Appendix B for a more complete list of the major differences between VBScript and VBA.

---

# Using Option Explicit

If you've been a VBA programmer for a while, you undoubtedly know the value of using the Option Explicit directive to require explicit variable declarations. You can add the Option Explicit directive to global scripts you create, but you can't use Option Explicit in the event handlers that the Script Outline window creates for you. That's because the event handler scripts the MSE editor creates are procedures and Option Explicit is not available from within an event procedure.

---

**TIP**  You can minimize the effect of not being able to use Option Explicit from event handlers by placing the majority of your code in procedures contained in global scripts (that contain the Option Explicit directive) and then calling these global procedures from your event handlers.

---

# Working with Data Access Page Objects

As mentioned at the beginning of this chapter, you will need to delve into both the IE Document Object Model (DOM) and the Office Web Components object model to script data access pages.

## The Document Object Model

A simplified view of the Internet Explorer Document Object Model (also known as the browser object model or the DHTML object model) is shown in Figure 11.7.

**FIGURE 11.7**
A simplified view of the Document Object Model

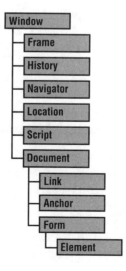

The major components of the DOM are explained below:

- The *Window* object is the top object in the DOM hierarchy. You can think of the Window object as representing the browser as a whole.

- The *Frame* object allows you to refer to other frames in a framed Web page.

- The *History* object allows you to manipulate the browser history. Essentially, it's a way to programmatically manipulate the browser's Back and Forward buttons.

- You use the *Navigator* object to query information about the browser implementation. You can use the Navigator object to determine, for example, the manufacturer of the browser (Microsoft or Netscape) or the major and minor version number of the browser.

- You can use the *Location* object to determine information about the URL of the current page. You can also use the Location object's HREF property to navigate to another page.

- The *Script* object provides programmatic access to scripts.

- The *Document* object represents the BODY of the Web page. Just about everything you place on a Web page will be a descendent of the Document object.

- The Link and Anchor objects provide a way to programmatically access the hyperlinks on the page. The *Link* object represents all hyperlinks with HREF attributes. The *Anchor* object represents all hyperlinks with NAME attributes.

- You use the *Form* object to reference any forms on the Web page.

- The *Element* objects represent the form controls on the page.

## The IE 5 Document Object Model

The view of the object model shown in Figure 11.7 and described in the previous section is compatible with HTML 3.2 and IE 3. With the releases of IE 4 and IE 5, the DOM has gotten quite a bit more complex, with every HTML tag now considered a scriptable object. Even though the version of the object model in Figure 11.7 is a simplified form of the objects in IE 5, it should prove helpful in understanding the hierarchies of objects. Most of the new objects added after IE 3 are direct descendents of the Document object. For example, the A, Span, and Div objects are all children of the Document object and represent programmatic versions of the A, SPAN, and DIV tags, respectively.

In addition to added objects, the IE 5 version of the DOM also defines a number of collections you can use to iterate through various groups of elements of the page. Chief among these collections is the Document.All collection, which you can use to iterate through all the elements on a page.

## The Data Source Control

The data binding functionality of data access pages revolves around the Data Source control (DSC). A simplified view of the DSC object model is depicted in Figure 11.8. This figure doesn't include several collections of the DataSourceControl object that you can use to iterate through items that the DataSourceControl object contains.

**FIGURE 11.8**
The Data Source control object model. Not displayed here are several collections of the DataSourceControl object.

---

**TIP**    A more complete object model diagram of the Data Source control and its objects, properties, methods, and collections can be found in the Microsoft Office Web Components Visual Basic help file. You can get to this help file by clicking on the Microsoft Office Web Components Visual Basic Reference node on the contents page of the main Access help file (or by separately loading the MSOWCVBA.CHM help file).

---

## Understanding Data Access Page Events

Understanding the events exposed by the objects on data access pages is the key to creating useful scripts. Table 11.2 summarizes the events of the major objects you'll find on a data access page.

In Table 11.2, we've included a complete list of the events of the DataSource-Control and many other Office Web Component objects. For other objects with a large number of events—the Document, HTML Element, Section, and Window objects—we've only included a subset of the available events. In these cases, we've tried to include the events that you are most likely to want to use.

**TABLE 11.2:** Selected Events of Data Access Page Objects

| Object | Event | Arguments | Description and Comments |
|--------|-------|-----------|--------------------------|
| DataSourceControl | beforecollapse | DSCEventInfo[1] | Before section is collapsed; cancel by setting DSCEventInfo.ReturnValue to False |
| | beforeexpand | DSCEventInfo | Before section is expanded; cancel by setting DSCEventInfo.ReturnValue to False |
| | beforefirstpage | DSCEventInfo | Before navigation to first page; cancel by setting DSCEventInfo.ReturnValue to False |
| | beforelastpage | DSCEventInfo | Before navigation to last page; cancel by setting DSCEventInfo.ReturnValue to False |
| | beforenextpage | DSCEventInfo | Before navigation to next page; cancel by setting DSCEventInfo.ReturnValue to False |
| | beforepreviouspage | DSCEventInfo | Before navigation to previous page; cancel by setting DSCEventInfo.ReturnValue to False |
| | current | DSCEventInfo | As section becomes current because of page opening, section expanding or collapsing, or user selection |
| | dataerror | DSCEventInfo | When data error occurs |

1   DSCEventInfo is an object with four properties: dataPage, section, returnValue, and error. Not all properties are appropriate for all events using the DSCEventInfo argument.

**T A B L E   1 1 . 2 :**   Selected Events of Data Access Page Objects *(continued)*

| Object | Event | Arguments | Description and Comments |
|---|---|---|---|
| | datapagecomplete | DSCEventInfo | When data binding for control is complete after a page open, navigation, or expansion |
| Document[2] | onafterupdate | | For bound pages, occurs after record is saved |
| | onbeforeupdate | | For bound pages, occurs before record is saved; a good place to add validation code; cancel by setting Window .Event.ReturnValue to False |
| | onclick | | User clicks mouse on page; cancel by setting Window .Event.ReturnValue to False |
| | oncontextmenu | | User right-clicks on page; set Window.Event.ReturnValue to False to cancel built-in context menu |
| | onhelp | | User presses F1 key; set Window.Event.ReturnValue to False to cancel built-in help |
| ChartSpace | click | ChartEventInfo[3] | When user clicks on chart |
| | datasetchange | | For bound charts, whenever underlying dataset changes |
| | dblclick | ChartEventInfo | When user double-clicks on chart |
| | keydown | ChartEventInfo | When user presses key; use ChartEventInfo.KeyChar to determine pressed key |
| | keypress | ChartEventInfo | When user presses and releases key; use ChartEventInfo.KeyChar to determine pressed key |
| | keyup | ChartEventInfo | When user releases key; use ChartEventInfo.KeyChar to determine pressed key |

2   The listed events for the Window, Document, Section, and HTML Element objects are a subset of the most-commonly used events. See on-line help for more complete list of events.

3   ChartEventInfo is an object with eight properties: altKey, button, ctrlKey, keyChar, keyCode, shiftKey, x, and y. Not all properties are appropriate for all events using the ChartEventInfo argument.

**TABLE 11.2:** Selected Events of Data Access Page Objects *(continued)*

| Object | Event | Arguments | Description and Comments |
|---|---|---|---|
| | mousedown | ChartEventInfo | When user clicks mouse button on chart |
| | mousemove | ChartEventInfo | When user moves mouse button over chart |
| | mouseup | ChartEventInfo | When user releases mouse button on chart |
| | selectionchange | | When user changes chart selection |
| DataPage | *none* | | See the events of the DataSourceControl and the Section objects |
| Expand Control | *none* | | See the events of the DataSourceControl object |
| HTML Element[1,4] | onafterupdate | | After data in a databound control is updated |
| | onbeforeupdate | | Before data in a databound control is updated; cancel by setting Window.Event .ReturnValue to False |
| | onblur | | As focus moves away from control |
| | onbounce | | When contents of marquee control reach a side; only occurs when the behavior is set to "alternate" |
| | onchange | | When contents of element are changed and committed by moving focus out of control; occurs before onblur event |
| | onclick | | When user clicks on the control; cancel by setting Window.Event.ReturnValue to False |

1   DSCEventInfo is an object with four properties: dataPage, section, returnValue, and error. Not all properties are appropriate for all events using the DSCEventInfo argument.
4   Not all listed events occur for all HTML elements.

**TABLE 11.2:** Selected Events of Data Access Page Objects *(continued)*

| Object | Event | Arguments | Description and Comments |
|---|---|---|---|
| | ondblclick | | When user double-clicks on the control; cancel by setting Window.Event.ReturnValue to False; occurs after onclick event |
| | onfinish | | When looping for marquee control is complete |
| | onfocus | | As control receives focus |
| | onkeydown | | When user presses key; can be cancelled; use Window.Event.KeyCode to determine keycode or pressed key |
| | onkeypress | | When user presses and releases key; can be cancelled; use Window.Event.KeyCode to determine Unicode value of pressed key |
| | onmouseout | | As user stops hovering over element with mouse pointer |
| | onmouseover | | As user hovers over element with mouse pointer |
| PivotTable | click | | When user clicks on pivot table |
| | dblclick | | When user double-clicks on pivot table |
| | pivottablechange | Reason[5] | Occurs whenever a PivotTable list field, field set, or total is added or deleted; check reason to determine what caused change |
| | query | Reason[6] | Occurs when pivot table list's query changes and needs to be re-executed |

5  Reason for pivottablechange event is an enumerated constant of type PivotTableReasonEnum. See Chapter 12 for information on how to use Office Web Component constants.

6  Reason for query event is an enumerated constant of type PivotQueryReasonEnum. See Chapter 12 for information on how to use Office Web Component constants.

**TABLE 11.2:** Selected Events of Data Access Page Objects *(continued)*

| Object | Event | Arguments | Description and Comments |
|---|---|---|---|
| | querycomplete | | When query completes |
| | selectionchange | | Whenever user changes pivot table selection |
| | viewchange | Reason[7] | Occurs whenever the user opens a different PivotTable list |
| Record Navigation Control | buttonclick | NavButton[8] | When user clicks on navigation bar button |
| Section1 | ondatasetcomplete | | As page is loaded, after data binding for page is complete |
| | ondatasetavailable | | After ondatasetcomplete but before page is rendered |
| | ondatasetchanged | | When record is updated or page is scrolled |
| | onfocus | | When section gets the focus |
| Spreadsheet | beforecommand | EventInfo[9] | Before user uses worksheet command; use EventInfo.command to determine command that triggered event; cancel command by setting EventInfo.returnValue to False |
| | calculate | EventInfo | When spreadsheet is recalculated |
| | canceledit | EventInfo | When user cancels edit mode |
| | change | EventInfo | When data in one or more cells change; occurs for both edits and copy/paste operations |

7   Reason for viewchange event is an enumerated constant of type PivotViewReasonEnum. See Chapter 12 for information on how to use Office Web Component constants.

8   NavButton is an enumerated constant of type NavButtonEnum. See Chapter 12 for information on how to use Office Web Component constants.

9   EventInfo is an object with 12 properties: altKey, button, command, ctrlKey, editData, keyChar, keyCode, range, returnValue, shiftKey, x, and y. Not all properties are appropriate for all events using the EventInfo argument.

**TABLE 11.2:** Selected Events of Data Access Page Objects *(continued)*

| Object | Event | Arguments | Description and Comments |
|---|---|---|---|
| | click | EventInfo | When user clicks on the spreadsheet |
| | command | EventInfo | After user uses worksheet command; use EventInfo.command to determine command that triggered event |
| | dblclick | EventInfo | When user double-clicks on the spreadsheet |
| | endedit | EventInfo | When user switches out of edit mode; cancel command by setting EventInfo.returnValue to False |
| | keydown | EventInfo | When user presses key; use EventInfo.KeyChar to determine pressed key |
| | keypress | EventInfo | When user presses and releases key; use EventInfo.KeyChar to determine pressed key |
| | keyup | EventInfo | When user releases key; use EventInfo.KeyChar to determine pressed key |
| | mousedown | EventInfo | When user clicks mouse button on spreadsheet |
| | mouseout | EventInfo | When user moves mouse out of a spreadsheet cell |
| | mouseover | EventInfo | When user moves mouse into a spreadsheet cell |
| | mouseup | EventInfo | When user releases mouse button on spreadsheet |
| | selectionchange | EventInfo | When user changes spreadsheet selection |
| | selectionchanging | EventInfo | When user drags mouse over selection |

**TABLE 11.2:** Selected Events of Data Access Page Objects *(continued)*

| Object | Event | Arguments | Description and Comments |
|---|---|---|---|
| | startedit | EventInfo | When user enters edit mode in a spreadsheet cell; cancel command by setting EventInfo.returnValue to False |
| | viewchange | EventInfo | When user changes the spreadsheet view |
| Window1 | onload | | As page is loaded |
| | onunload | | As page is unloaded |

## Supplying Event Handler Arguments

When you use the Script Outline window to generate an event handler, it doesn't supply any arguments to the events. Some objects, as illustrated in Table 11.2, require arguments. If you don't include the necessary arguments, your event handler code will never be called. Thus, you will need to alter the event handler created by the Script Outline window for events that have arguments.

For example, if you used the Script Outline window to create an event handler for the buttonclick event of the Record Navigation control that displayed a message "Button clicked!" when a button was clicked, the generated code along with your code would look like the following:

```
<SCRIPT event=ButtonClick FOR=tblCustomerNavigation
LANGUAGE=vbscript>
<!-
    ' This code will never execute!
    MsgBox "Button clicked!"
-->
</SCRIPT>
```

No matter how many times you click the button, however, your script will never execute until you modify the EVENT attribute to include the NavButton argument. This is true regardless of whether or not you plan on doing anything with the argument value.

Here's the modified version of the same script, this time, with the corrected EVENT attribute:

```
<SCRIPT event=ButtonClick(button) for=tblCustomerNavigation
language=vbscript>
<!--
    ' This code will execute!
    MsgBox "Button clicked!"
-->
</SCRIPT>
```

With this simple change, the script now executes.

## Scripting Properties and Methods

The objects on data access pages have a number of properties and methods. The complete set of properties and methods are too numerous to list here, but we've summarized the properties and methods you're most likely to want to script in Table 11.3.

**T A B L E   1 1 . 3 :**   Selected Properties and Methods of Data Access Page Objects

| Object | Method/ Property | Item | Description and Comments |
|---|---|---|---|
| DataSource-Control | Method | GetContainingSection | Retrieves a reference to the containing section of an HTML element; takes a single argument: the HTML element |
| | Property | Connection | Returns a reference to the ADO Connection object used to supply data to the page |
| | | Constants | Returns an object that allows you to use named constants |
| | | CurrentSection | Returns a reference to the current section (the section containing the focus) |
| DataPage | Method | DeleteRecord | Deletes the current record |
| | | MoveFirst, MoveLast, MoveNext, and MovePrevious | Moves the current record to the appropriate record |
| | | NewRecord | Moves the current record to the new record |

**TABLE 11.3:** Selected Properties and Methods of Data Access Page Objects *(continued)*

| Object | Method/Property | Item | Description and Comments |
|---|---|---|---|
| | | Requery | Reruns the query underlying the DataPage |
| | | Save | Saves the changes to the current record |
| | | Undo | Undoes the changes to the current record |
| | Property | Filter | Returns or sets the client-side filter for the DataPage's recordset |
| | | IsFilterOn | Returns or sets the filter status; set to True to filter the recordset |
| | | Recordset | Returns a reference to the ADO Recordset object behind the DataPage |
| Document | Method | write | Writes HTML to the page |
| | Property | referrer | The URL of the previous page |
| Expand Control | Property | Bitmap | Returns or sets the type of bitmap displayed by the ExpandControl object |
| HTML Element | Method | focus | Moves the focus to the element |
| | Property | className | Returns the name of the class the element is a member of, if any |
| | | disabled | True if the element if disabled; False if enabled |
| | | id | The unique identifier for the element |
| | | innerHTML | For elements that are not form controls, the displayed text, including any embedded HTML tags |

**TABLE 11.3:**   Selected Properties and Methods of Data Access Page Objects *(continued)*

| Object | Method/ Property | Item | Description and Comments |
|---|---|---|---|
| | | innerText | For elements that are not form controls, the displayed text, not including any embedded HTML tags |
| | | length | For select controls, the number of options |
| | | selectedIndex | For select controls, the index of the selected item; for multi-select controls, this returns the first selected item (use the selected property of the control's options collection to find all selected items) |
| | | style | A reference to an object you can use to modify the CSS style attributes of the element |
| | | tagName | The HTML tag name, in CAPS sans angle brackets; that is, the tagName for an input control is "INPUT" |
| | | title | The tooltip text |
| | | type | For form controls, the type of control |
| | | value | For form controls, the value of the control |
| Location | Method | reload | Reloads the current page; takes a single argument, bReloadSource, which if True reloads the page from the server; otherwise page is loaded from client cache |
| | Property | href | Returns or sets the URL of the current page; when set to a URL, the browser navigates to the specified page |

**TABLE 11.3:** Selected Properties and Methods of Data Access Page Objects *(continued)*

| Object | Method/ Property | Item | Description and Comments |
|---|---|---|---|
| Record Navigation Control | Method | IsButtonEnabled | Returns True if the button (passed as an argument) is enabled |
| Section | Method | Collapse | Collapses the section |
| | | Expand | Expands the section |
| | | MakeCurrent | Makes the section the current section |
| | Property | DataPage | Returns a reference to the DataPage object for the section |
| | | HTMLContainer | Returns a reference to the HTML DIV element that contains the section; you can use HTMLContainer.children to reference fields in a section containing multiple records |
| | | IsExpanded | Returns True if the section is expanded |
| | | ParentSelection | Returns a reference to the parent Section object of the section |
| Window | Method | alert | Displays a dialog box with a message and an OK button |
| | | clearInterval | Stops a function from repeatedly executing at some interval; use in combination with setInterval |
| | | confirm | Displays a dialog box with OK and Cancel buttons; returns True if OK was selected |
| | | prompt | Displays a dialog box that prompts for a value; similar to the VBScript InputBox function |

**T A B L E   1 1 . 3 :**   Selected Properties and Methods of Data Access Page Objects *(continued)*

| Object | Method/ Property | Item | Description and Comments |
|---|---|---|---|
| | | setInterval | Sets the name of a function to repeatedly execute at some interval; similar to an Access form timer event |
| | | showModalDialog | Displays a page in a modal view; the displayed page can return a value |
| | Property | event | Returns a reference to the event object which you can use to determine information about the event that triggered an event handler; useful when taking advantage of event bubbling; useful properties of the event object include srcElement, cancelBubble, and returnValue |

**NOTE**    Methods and properties of the Chart, Pivot Table, and Spreadsheet controls are not included in Table 11.3. Their properties, methods, and collections are discussed in detail in Chapter 12.

In the next few sections, we'll illustrate the use of data access page objects, collections, events, properties, and methods with a number of examples.

# Validating Data

Just like forms, data access pages respect any validation rules you have defined in tables that supply data to the pages. For example, the dapOrder data access page is based on the tblOrder table that has several validation rules defined. If you attempt to save a record with an order date greater than the current date, the validation rule will be triggered as shown in Figure 11.9.

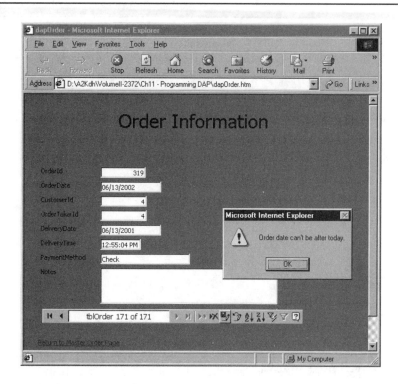

**FIGURE 11.9**
A validation rule on the
OrderDate field in tblOrder
is triggered from the
dapOrder data access page.

## Choosing an Event

You can also add your own custom validation rules to data access pages. There are several events you can hook your validation code up to, but probably the best event to use is the onbeforeupdate event of the document object. This event is fired right before the updates are committed to the database.

## The dapCustomer Page

The dapCustomer page in the CH11.MDB database incorporates some validation code that prevents users from leaving the FirstName or LastName fields blank. Figure 11.10 illustrates what happens when you leave the FirstName field blank. No validation rules exist in the tblCustomer table to enforce this rule; all of the code is behind the dapCustomer page.

**FIGURE 11.10**

This validation code is attached to the document object's onbeforeupdate event.

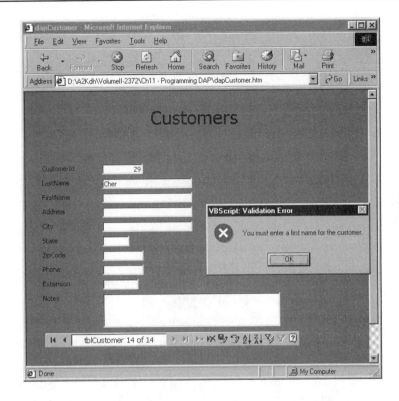

Here's the document object's onbeforeupdate event handler:

```
<SCRIPT event=onbeforeupdate for=document
language=vbscript>
<!--
    Call Validation()
-->
</SCRIPT>
```

The event handler calls the Validation subroutine that has been placed in a global script. Here's the source of the global script:

```
<SCRIPT language=vbscript>
<!--
Option Explicit
Sub Validation()
    If Len(Trim(txtLastName.value))=0 Then
```

```
            txtLastName.focus
            MsgBox "You must enter a last name " & _
              "for the customer.", vbOkOnly + vbCritical, _
              "Validation Error"
            window.event.returnValue = False
        ElseIf Len(Trim(txtFirstName.value))=0 Then
            txtFirstName.focus
            MsgBox "You must enter a first name " & _
              "for the customer.", vbOkOnly + vbCritical, _
              "Validation Error"
            window.event.returnValue = False
        End If
    End Sub
    -->
    </SCRIPT>
```

Unlike Access forms, HTML controls do not automatically strip out blanks entered into the control. This is why we have used the Trim function to first trim out blanks prior to checking for a zero-length string. (There's no need to check for Nulls because HTML controls can't store Nulls.)

The validation code uses the focus method to move the focus to the appropriate control prior to displaying the MsgBox dialog box. This way, the user will be at the correct control when he or she dismisses the dialog box.

The onbeforeupdate event is cancelled by using the returnValue property of the event object. By setting returnValue to False, we effectively cancel the event and thus abort the save:

```
window.event.returnValue = False
```

---

**TIP**    If at all possible, it's best to place validation rules at the table level. In the example shown here, we could have used the Required property of the underlying table fields to get the same effect, without any scripting code. While this example could have been solved using table-level rules, certain rules—for example, rules that involve multiple tables or complex processes—can't be placed at the table level.

---

# Employing Dynamic Styles and Event Bubbling

IE 5 supports the use of Cascading Style Sheet (CSS) styles. CSS styles work much like Word styles. Styles affect the look of the page and the elements on the page. Data access pages employ global CSS styles that are defined between the <STYLE> and </STYLE> tags in the HEAD section of the page. For example, here's a portion of the CSS styles defined in the dapSwitchboard page:

```
<STYLE id=MSODAPDEFAULTS
type=text/css rel="stylesheet">
.mstheme-label {
    FONT-FAMILY: Tahoma; FONT-SIZE: 8pt
}
TEXTAREA {
    FONT-FAMILY: Tahoma; FONT-SIZE: 8pt
}
.msoboundhtml {
    FONT-FAMILY: Tahoma; FONT-SIZE: 8pt
}
...
</STYLE>
```

## The Style Object

The style property of HTML elements provides a mechanism for retrieving a reference to the style object for the element. You can use the style object to programmatically manipulate the cascading style sheet (CSS) style attributes of an element, thus creating *dynamic styles*.

For example, you could use the following code to change the text of a control named ctlCity to 14 point blue text:

```
ctlCity.style.fontSize = 14
ctlCity.style.color = "blue"
```

You can find a complete list of the style attributes in the MSE help system, under "Dynamic HTML, DHTML References, CSS Attributes Reference, CSS Attributes."

**TIP**     When using the style object, you use properties that have the same name as the CSS style attributes, with one difference: the style properties don't have any hyphens. Thus the "font-size" *attribute* becomes the "fontSize" *property*.

## The Event Object and Event Bubbling

In the dapCustomer page, we took advantage of the event object to set the event object's returnValue property to False when we wished to cancel the event. In addition to the returnValue property, the event object provides several other properties, including srcElement.

The srcElement property returns a reference to the control that caused the event to occur. This allows you to create event handlers that respond to events triggered by child objects. By using the srcElement property you can create generic event handlers that handle events for child objects. This is referred to as *event bubbling*.

## The dapSwitchboard Page

The dapSwitchboard page uses dynamic styles and event bubbling to create a hovering effect for its four button controls. The dapSwitchboard page is shown in Figure 11.11.

**FIGURE 11.11**
This page takes advantage of dynamic styles and event bubbling to create a hovering effect for the buttons.

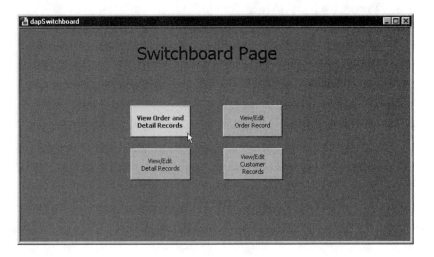

The onmouseover and onmouseout events provide the perfect hooks to create a hovering effect. The onmouseover event occurs when you hover the mouse over an element. The onmouseout event occurs when you stop hovering the mouse over an element.

The following event handlers from dapSwitchboard create the hovering effect shown in Figure 11.11:

```vbscript
<SCRIPT event=onmouseover for=SectionUnbound
language=vbscript>
<!--
    With window.event.srcElement
        If .tagName = "BUTTON" Then
            .style.color = "blue"
            .style.backgroundColor = "yellow"
            .style.fontWeight = "bold"
        End If
    End With
-->
</SCRIPT>

<SCRIPT event=onmouseout for=SectionUnbound
language=vbscript>
<!--
    With window.event.srcElement
        If .tagName = "BUTTON" Then
            .style.color = ""
            .style.backgroundColor = ""
            .style.fontWeight = ""
        End If
    End With
-->
</SCRIPT>
```

We've attached the "start hovering" code to the onmouseover event of the section that contains the button controls, SectionUnbound. This code executes whenever the mouse cursor is located over *any* element in the section, so we use the window .event.srcElement property to return a reference to the element that triggered the event and check its tagName property to determine if it's a button control. If the element is a button control, then we change the button's color, background-Color, and fontWeight properties to highlight the button.

The "stop hovering" code, which is attached to the onmouseout event of the section, reverses the actions of the "start hovering" code. While we could have changed the properties to specific values, we've chosen instead to set the properties to "" which restores the style properties to their original design-time values.

---

**TIP**   Although not shown in this example, you can set the cancelBubble property of the event object to True to cancel the bubbling of an event so that any parent objects don't see the event.

---

We've used button controls rather than hyperlinks on the dapSwitchboard page to make the page look more like an Access form. The code attached to the onclick event of each button control uses the href property of the location object to link to another page. Here's the script attached to the onlick event of the cmdCustomer button control:

```
<SCRIPT event=onclick for=cmdCustomer language=vbscript>
<!--
    window.location.href = "dapCustomer.htm"
-->
</SCRIPT>
```

---

**TIP**   Using button controls instead of hyperlink controls has an additional advantage: there's no way to specify a relative URL using a hyperlink control. This means that hyperlink properties may need to be changed if you move the pages to another folder or to a Web server. Using a button control and the window.location.href property, however, you can easily specify a relative URL—that is, a URL that's relative to the location of the current page and one therefore that doesn't need to be changed if the pages are moved to another folder—as we have in this example.

---

# Filtering Data

You can use the Filter and IsFilterOn properties of the DataPage object to filter the recordset behind a data access page section. Filtering is a two-step process:

1. Create the filter using syntax similar to the following:

```
MSODSC.Section("section").DataPage.Filter = filter
```

**2.** Turn the filter on using this syntax:

```
MSODSC.Section("section").DataPage.IsFilterOn = True
```

## The dapEmployee Page

The dapEmployee page, which is shown in Figure 11.12, uses a drop-down list to provide a navigational interface. When you select an item in the lstEmployeeFilter drop-down list, the following scripting code attached to the onchange event of the select control is executed:

```
<SCRIPT event=onchange for=lstEmployeeFilter
language=vbscript>
<!--
    Dim secData
    Set secData = MSODSC.GetContainingSection(EmployeeId)
    If Len(lstEmployeeFilter.value)> 0 Then
        ' Set the filter
        secData.DataPage.Filter = "EmployeeId=" & _
         lstEmployeeFilter.value
        ' Turn the filter on
        secData.DataPage.IsFilterOn = True
        ' Unselect the Employee
        lstEmployeeFilter.value = -1
        'Enable the Remove Filter button
        cmdRemoveFilter.disabled = False
    End If
-->
</SCRIPT>
```

In this example, the lstEmployeeFilter and the data-bound controls are located in different sections of the page. Thus, the script begins by using the GetContainingSection method of the DataSourceControl object to retrieve a reference to the section containing the recordset we wish to filter. You pass GetContainingSection a reference to an element in the section. We used "employeeid", but any element in the section would have sufficed.

**FIGURE 11.12**
The dapEmployee page

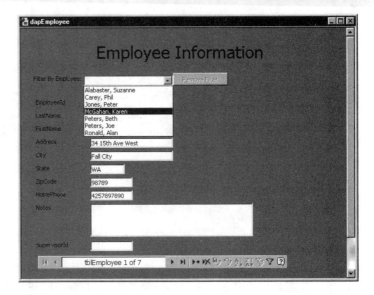

If the lstEmployeeFilter was located in the same section as the data-bound controls, we could have used the following code instead to get a reference to the section:

```
Set secData = MSODSC.CurrentSection
```

With a reference to the appropriate section in hand, the code sets the Filter property of the section's DataPage object using the following code:

```
secData.DataPage.Filter = "EmployeeId=" & _
  lstEmployeeFilter.value
```

The filter isn't executed, however, until the IsFilterOn property of the DataPage object is set to True as shown here:

```
secData.DataPage.IsFilterOn = True
```

The rest of the code in the event handler deselects the item in the drop-down list and enables the Remove Filter button.

## Removing the Filter

The following code, attached to the onclick event of the cmdRemoveFilter button control, removes the filter:

```
<SCRIPT event=onclick for=cmdRemoveFilter
language=vbscript>
```

```
<!--
    Dim secData
    Set secData = MSODSC.GetContainingSection(EmployeeId)
    ' Turn the filter off
    secData.DataPage.IsFilterOn = False
    ' Move the focus to the select control
    ' and disable the Remover Filter button
    lstEmployeeFilter.focus
    cmdRemoveFilter.disabled = True
-->
</SCRIPT>
```

The filter is removed by setting the DataPage object's IsFilterOn property to
False. The rest of the code in the script moves the focus back to the drop-down list
and disables the cmdRemoveFilter button.

# Drilling Down to Editable Data Using Server Filters

As you learned in Chapter 10, one of the problems with data access pages is that in
many cases the pages are read only. In fact, any time you use the Expand control,
multiple tables, or multiple sections, your page will be read only. That's a shame
because one of the best features of data access pages is their ability to create easy-
to-use drill-down interfaces.

One way to work around this dilemma is to create a main data access page that
you can use to drill down to the record you want to edit and then provide some
mechanism for opening another page with that record loaded. The dapOrderAnd-
Detail page accomplishes this by using a server filter.

## Client Filter versus Server Filter

Data access pages have two mechanisms for filtering records: client filters and
server filters. In an earlier example, we used the filter property to filter the records
on the dapEmployee page. When you use the filter property, the filter is applied on
the client-side to the DataPage object's recordset *after* the page is opened. In contrast, a server filter is applied on the server-side *before* the page is opened.

To apply a server filter, you must pass the page a filter in its URL query string. For example, you could use the following code to open the dapCustomer page with a particular customer record loaded:

```
window.location.href = _
   "dapCustomer.htm?serverfilter=""CustomerId=10"""
```

When you specify a server filter, you must enclose the filter in quotes. In this example, we've used pairs of quote characters to embed quotes within the href string. You must do this because the quote character is also used to delimit the entire string.

## The dapOrderAndDetail Page

The dapOrderAndDetail page is shown with a record expanded in Figure 11.13. Because this page contains data from multiple tables, it's read only. If you click the Edit Order button, the browser loads the dapOrder page, opened to the current order record (see Figure 11.14). Likewise, if you click the Edit Detail Record button, the browser loads the dapOrderDetail page, opened to the current order detail record (see Figure 11.15).

**FIGURE 11.13**

The dapOrderAndDetail page is read only, but pressing the Edit Order or Edit Detail Record button pulls up an editable version of the order or detail record.

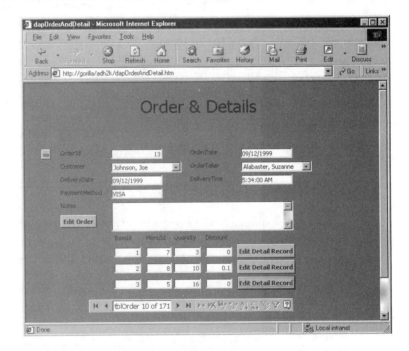

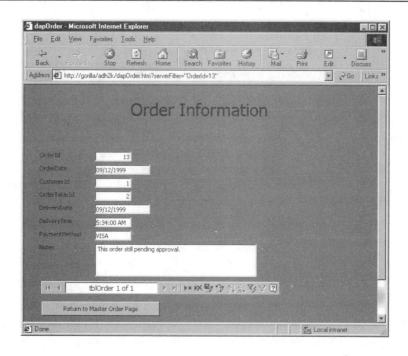

**FIGURE 11.14**
The dapOrder page is opened to the correct order record using a server filter.

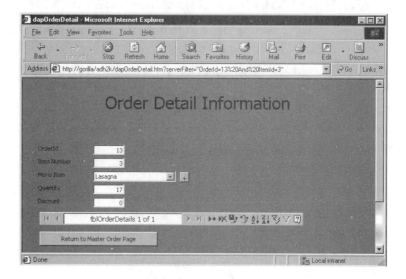

**FIGURE 11.15**
The dapOrderDetail page is opened to the correct order detail record using a server filter.

## Drilling Down to the dapOrder Page

Here's the code attached to the onclick event of the cmdOrderEdit button of the dapOrderAndDetail page:

```
<SCRIPT event=onclick for=cmdOrderEdit language=vbscript>
<!--
    Dim strFilter

    ' Navigate to the dapOrder page, passing
    ' along a server-filter for the page so
    ' that the current order record is displayed
    ' Notice that we've embedded quotes around the
    ' entire server filter.
    strFilter = """OrderId=" & OrderId.value & """"
    window.location.href = _
      "dapOrder.htm?serverFilter=" & strFilter
-->
</SCRIPT>
```

This code opens the dapOrder page, passing it a server filter that synchronizes the dapOrder page with the current record of the dapOrderAndDetail page. The server filter is built using the value property of the OrderID control.

## Drilling Down to the dapOrderDetail Page

Here's the code attached to the onclick event of the cmdDetailEdit button of the dapOrderAndDetail page:

```
<SCRIPT event=onclick for=cmdDetailEdit language=vbscript>
<!--
    Dim strFilter
    Dim sec

    Set sec = MSODSC.CurrentSection

    ' Navigate to the dapOrderDetail page, passing
    ' along a server-filter for the page so
    ' that the current detail record is displayed
    ' Notice that we've embedded quotes around the
    ' entire server filter.
    strFilter = """OrderId=" & _
     sec.HTMLContainer.children("OrderId1").value & _
     " And " & "ItemId=" & _
     sec.HTMLContainer.children("ItemId").value & """"
    window.location.href = _
```

```
        "dapOrderDetail.htm?serverFilter=" & strFilter
-->
</SCRIPT>
```

This code is a bit more involved than the cmdOrderEdit drill-down code. That's because the OrderDetail section displays multiple records. To retrieve the value of a field from a multiple-record section, you must use syntax like this:

```
MSODSC.CurrentSection.HTMLContainer.children("field").value
```

# Adding Items to a List

Many Access developers attach VBA code to the NotInList event of ComboBox controls to provide a mechanism for adding new items to a combo box list. Data access pages don't provide an equivalent of the NotInList event, but you can use a button control and some VBScript code to provide a similar feature that lets you add items to a drop-down or list box style select control.

## Using the Data Source Control's Connection

In order to add items to a bound select control's list, you have to open a connection to the database. Fortunately, the Data Source control already has an open ADO connection that you can share. You use the following syntax to reference the Data Source control's ADO Connection object:

```
MSODSC.Connection
```

Once you obtain a reference to the Data Source control's connection, you can execute commands and open recordsets against it.

## The dapOrderDetail Page

If you click the cmdAddToList button control (the button to the right of the Menu Item drop-down list control), you are prompted to enter the description of a new item to the list. The dapOrderDetail page is shown in Figure 11.16.

**FIGURE 11.16**
Adding a new item to the
Menu Item list

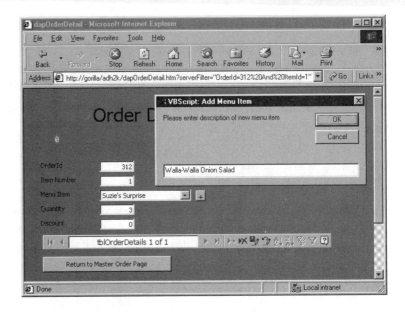

The script attached to the onclick event of the cmdAddToList button is shown here:

```
<SCRIPT event=onclick for=cmdAddToList language=vbscript>
<!--
    Dim varMenu
    Dim strInsert
    Dim varRecs

    varMenu = InputBox("Please enter description " & _
     "of new menu item", "Add Menu Item")
    If Len(varMenu)>0 Then
        ' Replace any apostrophes with two.
        varMenu = Replace(varMenu,"'","''")
        ' Construct an INSERT INTO statement and
        ' execute it using the MSODSC's Connection
        ' object.
        strInsert = "INSERT INTO tblMenu " & _
         "(MenuDescription) " & _
         "VALUES ('" & varMenu & "')"
        MSODSC.Connection.Execute strInsert, varRecs
```

```
        If varRecs = 0 Then
           MsgBox "Could not add new record.", _
             vbOKOnly + vbCritical, "Add Menu Item"
        Else
            ' Reload the page from the server
           window.location.reload(True)
        End If
    Else
          MsgBox "No new record was added.", _
             vbOKOnly + vbCritical, "Add Menu Item"
    End If
  -->
  </SCRIPT>
```

This script begins by requesting the description of the new menu item using the VBScript InputBox function. If the user enters a response, the script constructs an INSERT INTO statement and executes it against the CH11.MDB database using the Execute method of the MSODSC.Connection object.

If the INSERT INTO statement is successful, then script uses the reload method of the location object to force the browser to reload the page. By passing the reload method an argument of True, the page is reloaded from the server rather than the browser's cache. Once reloaded, the new menu item now appears in the drop-down list.

# Summary

In this chapter, you've looked at the scripting of data access pages in detail. You've learned:

- How to use the Microsoft Script Editor (MSE) to add scripts to data access pages
- How to use the Script Outline window to create event handlers
- How to debug scripts using the MSE's debugging features
- The differences between VBScript and VBA
- The layout of the IE 5 Document Object Model
- The object model of the Data Source control

- The significant events, properties, and methods of data access page objects

- How to validate data using scripting code

- How to employ dynamic styles and event bubbling to create a hovering effect

- How to filter data using both client-side and server-side filters

- How to create multiple-table data access pages that let you drill down to editable pages

- How to add items to a drop-down list

We've only scratched the surface of what you can script on a data access page. There are many additional objects, events, methods, properties, and collections that we didn't have the space to cover in this chapter. If you have a specific scripting need that we haven't shown here, you may want to consult Tables 11.2 and 11.3. You can also check out Chapter 12—which covers the scripting of the Office Web Components—or one of the following references:

- "Programming Data Access Pages" by Roy Leban. You'll find this Microsoft white paper on the CD that accompanies this book.

- "Connecting Data Access Pages Together" by Brett Tanzer. You'll also find this Microsoft white paper on the CD that accompanies this book.

- "Microsoft DHTML Help." This help file is part of the MSE help system.

- "Microsoft Office Web Components Visual Basic Help." This help file is part of the Access help.

---

**TIP**     For information on server-side scripting using Active Server Pages (ASP), see Chapter 14.

---

# Using the Office Web Components

- Introducing the Office Web Components

- Creating simple pages using the Office Web Components

- Using properties, methods, and events to script the Web Components

- Investigating the Spreadsheet, Chart, and PivotTable List Components

**E**ver since developers began creating applications hosted by Microsoft Office, those developers (including the authors of this book) have wanted a way to easily include functionality that wasn't a part of the application's "base" product. For example, Access developers have long wanted to insert attractive, easily programmed charts into their applications, yet the Microsoft Graph application was, and continues to be, a poorly documented memory hog. Developers have needed to include spreadsheet-like functionality in their applications, but loading a full copy of Excel just to get that functionality seemed like an onerous price to pay. The same goes for pivot table functionality that Excel provides: you can insert a pivot table into an Access form, but you're loading all of Excel just to work with that pivot table.

Finally, the Office 2000 development team has solved some of these issues for you. Microsoft has provided a set of controls/components that you can use in a data access page, on an Access form, on a standard Web page, or anywhere else COM components are supported. These components include an Excel-like spreadsheet, pivot table, and chart. In addition, the Web Components include the Data Source Control, which provides not only data for these components, but for Access data access pages, as well. (For more information on data access pages, see Chapter 10.)

This chapter introduces these components. Our intent is to discuss each component, and how you might use that component. The chapter database includes some instructive examples, both forms and data access pages, and includes code (VBA and VBScript) demonstrating how to manipulate these components. This chapter is not, however, a reference for developing with the Office Web Components. That would require an entire book on its own. We hope you'll find enough material here to get you started experimenting with the Office Web Components.

---

**TIP**　　　If you haven't done so already, we suggest you take the time to work through Chapter 10, covering data access pages, and Chapter 11, covering scripting, before using the material in this chapter. Here, the examples all assume that you're comfortable with both data access pages and scripting, using VBScript.

---

**TIP**　　Just as with the examples in Chapter 10, you'll need to reset the internal paths used for the data access pages in this chapter. Make sure you open the basResetDap module (copied in from the Chapter 10 sample database) and run the adhValidateDAPLinks procedure. This procedure resets both the links to data from the pages, and the links to the pages from within the Access database. You won't be able to load and run the pages until you do this.

## Getting Help

Microsoft's online help for programming the Office Web Components is, to be as polite as possible, really terrible. (On the other hand, the help topics on using the controls from the user interface are quite good.) Many programming topics include exactly one single sentence, often using the term being described in the help itself. You'll find very few "how's" and absolutely no "why's." If you're interested in going beyond the examples shown in this chapter, you will need to find a copy of the best and only book on this topic. Dave Stearns, program manager at Microsoft for the Office Web Components, has written a book specifically for developers incorporating Office Web Components into their applications. This book, *Programming Microsoft Office 2000 Web Components*, is from Microsoft Press, with ISBN number 0-7356-0794-X. Don't miss it if you want to take advantage of these components in your own applications. (For what it's worth, we believe that the uselessness of the online help and the availability of a detailed book from Microsoft Press are purely coincidental. You make up your own mind.)

# What Do You Get?

The Office Web Components include four distinct COM components. The following sections introduce each of the Office Web Components.

## Office Spreadsheet

This Excel-like spreadsheet control allows you to create grid-based data entry forms, with immediate recalculation. You can also bind data in cells to other controls on a Web page. This control looks and behaves like a single Excel worksheet, uses the same cell-referencing techniques, and allows you to use almost all the standard Excel spreadsheet functions. You can easily link Office Spreadsheet and Chart controls together, as shown in Figure 12.1.

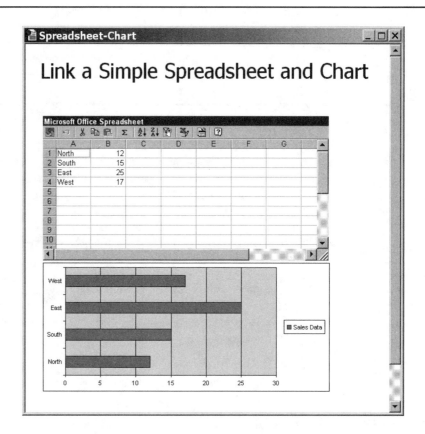

Because of the way this control (and the other Office Web Components) has been created, you needn't host it on a form in order for it to be useful. You can use the powerful Excel calculation engine in your applications without actually creating the Office Spreadsheet user interface anywhere at all. That is, you can invisibly instantiate and manipulate the Office Spreadsheet component with no host form or page. You'll see an example of this technique, later in the chapter.

**NOTE**    The concept of using COM components with no visual interface isn't unusual: as a matter of fact, that's how all communication between Access and ADO works. It is somewhat unusual for an ActiveX control to support both types of activation (that is, on a form, and from code). This additional functionality gives you more flexibility when using these controls.

## Office PivotTable

The Office PivotTable component allows you to analyze data, both from relational OLE DB data stores and from OLAP cubes. This powerful tool makes it simple for you to provide not only summary data (as you might in an Access crosstab query), but the control also allows users to interactively change the perspective on the data, viewing different field sets, sorting, grouping, and calculating values based on your data. Because the Office PivotTable control has a somewhat complex user interface, we've included a walk-through, demonstrating how you might interact with the control, later in the chapter. Figure 12.2 shows the results of that walk-through.

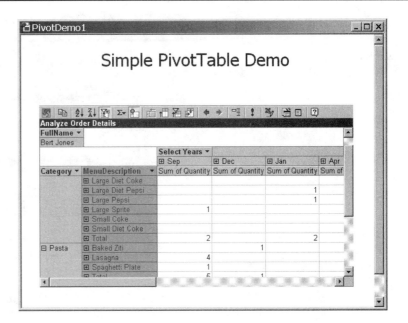

**FIGURE 12.2**
The Office PivotTable control makes it easy to create a summarized view of data that can be modified at run-time.

## Office Chart

The Office Chart control allows you to create almost all the standard two-dimensional (2D) Excel chart types, plus a Polar chart. (The Office Chart control doesn't support three-dimensional [3D] charts, in this version.) You can display multiple charts within the same charting space, allowing you to overlay different views of data on a single form or page. This control is far less resource-hungry than the standard Microsoft Chart component, and you can bind it to any of the other Office Web Components. That is, this control can retrieve its data from a spreadsheet, pivot table, or data source control. In addition, you can send it data using a standard ADO recordset, or even by passing in arrays containing the data points to be displayed. You'll find examples, later in the chapter, of binding the Office Chart control to different data sources.

The Office Chart component also includes a Chart Wizard (shown in Figure 12.3) that walks you through the process of creating a chart. This wizard isn't available in every host, but it does work in Access data access pages. Everything this wizard does, your own code can do as well, showing off the rich programming model of this component.

**FIGURE 12.3**
You can either use the Chart Wizard to create charts, or you can programmatically manipulate them at runtime.

## Data Source Control

The Data Source control is the least appreciated of the Office Web Components, mostly because it's invisible. You'll never see this control—it has no user interface—but it does all the data binding work behind the scenes. Whenever you use a data access page within Access, it's the Data Source control that provides the recordsets to be displayed on the page. This control acts as an intermediary between the database engine and the components that need the data, managing connections and providing recordsets as necessary. As you'll see, you can programmatically manipulate this control, adding to its collection of RecordsetDefs (objects that contain the information necessary to open a particular recordset), and working with its collections of groupings.

In this chapter, we won't focus on programming the Data Source control. You won't do it often, and when you do, you'll need more information than we have room for here. On the other hand, as an Access developer, you'll most likely find it easy to get started with the Data Source control, so we'll provide an example or two to get you going.

## Who Can Use These, and Where?

Basically, the Office Web Components are ActiveX controls, just like most other ActiveX controls. If you embed them on an Access (or any other) form, they need to be installed on users' machines before your forms will display correctly. If you use them on Web pages, they'll need to be downloaded to users' machines before the pages will display correctly. That is, they're no different from any other ActiveX control in how you deploy them as part of an application.

One difference, however, between these controls and other Active controls you might embed on a Web page is that many Office 2000 users will already have these installed on their machines. What if they don't? The DLL required by the Office Web Components (MSOWC.DLL) isn't small—it's over three megabytes—but that shouldn't affect any of your users. Office plays a neat trick here: when you embed one of these components onto a Web page, the CodeBase property of the control (that is, the location where the browser will look for the control if it's not already installed) is set to be the location from which you installed Office. Therefore, Web access to pages including these controls won't attempt to download the largish DLL from your site—instead, the browser will attempt to install them from the original installation location. You can override this behavior, but you needn't.

**NOTE**    It's important to note that the Office Web Components will only download using the file:// protocol. The controls cannot be downloaded using the standard Web http:// protocol. They'll have to be available as part of each user's file system, if they're not already installed locally. This means, of course, that you can't simply put the controls on a public Web site and expect that visitors without the controls can automatically download them from your site when they first visit your page.

Unlike most ActiveX controls, the Office Web Components don't allow unrestricted distribution. That is, when developers purchase most other ActiveX controls, they're purchasing an unlimited distribution license. You generally have the right to distribute applications written using those controls to anyone. The Office Web Components require each user to have an Office 2000 license. Does that mean that every user must have installed Office 2000? No, not at all. A company might purchase several hundred licenses, and roll out installations as necessary. Each user at the company has a valid Office 2000 license, but doesn't actually have Office 2000 installed. In this case, you can safely roll out an application using the Office Web Components to each employee at this company.

If every user must have a license, but doesn't necessarily need to have Office 2000 installed, what does that say for run-time license checking? In this version, there isn't any. Just as with most any other software component, the checking is based on the honor system. No part of the installation or use of the Office Web Components requires Office 2000 to be installed—it's just that the license agreement states that each user must have a license.

In addition, because users needn't have Office 2000 installed, you can use these controls in any host that supports ActiveX controls and COM components. You can use the controls in Office 97, or Visual Basic 6.0, or on a Web page where users won't have Office 2000 installed. Of course, in each of those scenarios, you'll need to consider how you're going to distribute the components to your users.

---

**TIP**

In all honesty, using the Office Web Components on an Access form requires some programming fortitude. Because there's no built-in support for data binding for these controls, as there is when you place them on a data access page in Access 2000, you'll end up writing a good deal of code. We attempted, when creating demos for this chapter, to create both an Access form and an Access data access page for most of the examples. It might appear that we were simply being generous, providing versions for two different sets of developers. Actually, it's just so much easier writing code in the VBA editor that we created forms first, and then converted the code to VBScript for the corresponding data access page. You might find this a useful technique as well, although the conversion does require some extra time. You won't find much coverage of using the Office Web Components on Access forms in this chapter, however, because they simply don't behave well there, in Design mode. (This isn't a fault of the Office Web Components—it's just a fact of the way Access handles ActiveX controls on its forms.)

---

What about browser support? Do these controls require Internet Explorer 5.0, as do data access pages? Although data access pages depend on functionality first available in IE5, the Office Web Components only require IE 4.01 or later. (IE 4.0 will fail to load the controls, as will IE 3.0.) If your intent is to create standard HTML pages using the Office Web Components, the only requirement is that their browsers support ActiveX controls fully.

What about Netscape users? We've not experimented with Netscape and ActiveX controls, and so cannot vouch for the plug-in that allows you to run ActiveX controls in that browser. One issue to consider is data binding. That is, once embedded within the plug-in that allows the page to download and display an ActiveX control, will the controls be able to communicate correctly, and provide data sources from one to the other? We don't know, and Microsoft is (unsurprisingly) quiet on the issue. We suggest limiting your use of Office Web Components (and any ActiveX control, for that matter) to situations in which you can control the browser that's used. What that boils down to is: just as with data access pages, you're best off using the Office Web Components only in local or intranet applications. Public Web sites using Office Web Components will be a problem until Microsoft achieves its goal of world domination in the browser arena.

## Server-Side Behavior

The Office Web Components all have an interesting, and potentially useful, ability. Each can be created programmatically, without a visible representation on any host form or page. That is, you can write code like this:

```
' In VBA code:
Dim owcSS as OWC.Spreadsheet
Set owcSS = New OWC.Spreadsheet

' or, in VBScript code:
Dim owcSS
Set owcSS = CreateObject("OWC.Spreadsheet")
```

Then, you can work with owcSS in your code as if referring to an Excel spreadsheet. You can do the same for pivot tables and charts, and they add an extra feature: in both cases, you can use the controls' ExportPicture method to save its image as a GIF file. This means that you can have an ASP page, on a Web server, providing static views of pivot tables and charts to Web clients that don't support ActiveX controls, or that don't have an Office 2000 license. You simply write code in the page to create the pivot table or chart, save the information as a GIF file, and then provide a page to the browser that includes the GIF file you've created. (For more information on using this technique, see Chapter 14.)

## Working with Scripting

As with most ActiveX components, the Office Web Components provide a large number of enumerated data values. That is, the components provide named groups of numeric values that are appropriate as values for specific properties and parameters. If you've worked with scripting at all, you know that these constants aren't generally available when writing script because you haven't associated the components' type library with the host's environment at design time. Normally, you need to either declare the constants you need or include a file containing all of the constants.

To make this easier for you, the Office Web Components development team politely provided a property of each component—the Constants property—which is itself an object with a Property Get procedure for each constant value. For example, in VBA, you might write code like this to set the data source for an Office Chart:

```
owcChart.DataSourceType = chDataSourceTypeSpreadsheet
```

Because the Office Web Components type library includes a value for chDataSourceTypeSpreadsheet (the value is 1), the VBA code knows what to do. If you write the same code in VBScript, however, one of two things will happen:

- If you've added "Option Explicit" to your code, you'll receive a run-time error when the interpreter hits that line.

- If you haven't added "Option Explicit" to your code, VBScript will see the expression, not know its value, and create it with a value of 0.

Both alternatives are unacceptable, although the first is less unacceptable than the second. To make use of the constants, your best bet is to declare a variable to refer to the Constants object, and then set the variable the actual object property. You'll find code like this in many of our examples:

```
Dim c
Set c = owcChart.Constants
' And then, later in the code...
owcChart.DataSourceType = c.chDataSourceTypeSpreadsheet
```

# Working with the Components at Design Time

If you're working within the data access page designer in Access (or within any other layout environment besides the Access form designer), the Office Web Components provide a Property Toolbox window, in which you can set properties appropriate to the current selection within the control. (When working on an Access form, you can set many of these properties from the normal Properties window, but not all.) This Property Toolbox, shown in Figure 12.4, allows you to select properties of the Spreadsheet control, including formatting, areas to show and hide, and protection.

**FIGURE 12.4**

Use the Property Toolbox to control the behavior of the Office Web Component at design time.

**TIP**
Because of the way Access forms host ActiveX controls, the Property Toolbox won't be available when working with any of the Office Web Components on Access forms. Within Access, you'll only see this window when working on data access pages.

To test out the Property Toolbox window, follow these steps:

1.  Create a new data access page.

2.  From the Toolbox window, select the Office Spreadsheet control, and place an instance of the control on the Unbound section of the page.

3.  Click on the control to select it. You may actually need to click twice: once to select the control, and again to make it active. (The border turns from a thin line to a thick, hashed border when the control's active.)

4.  Right-click on the control, and select Property Toolbox from the context menu.

Once you've displayed the toolbox, try changing properties of the control. This window works much like the standard Access Property window, except that it works in environments that don't support their own Property window—a browser window, for example.

Given this flexible tool, you'll need to note two important items:

- The Property Toolbox window is a cleverly concealed HTML page. That is, it's an instance of the Internet Explorer, hosted on a form, with some careful and tricky coding to make the various sections expand and collapse. The point here is that the toolbox uses the same programming interfaces as your own code, in order to modify the behavior of the controls. Anything that can be done using the Property Toolbox can be done from within your own code.

- You may not want users to be able to display the Property Toolbox at run time. To disable this feature, make sure you set the AllowPropertyToolbox property of the control to False. (You can also set this property on the Property Toolbox itself, in the Protection area of the toolbox.)

**NOTE**
Throughout this chapter, you won't see much coverage of working with the user interface for the three controls that have a user interface. Our concern here is demonstrating how you can get started programming these controls. If you're interested in UI features, start with the online help. If you're interested in digging into the programming features in more depth, see *Programming Microsoft Office 2000 Web Components*, by Dave Stearns, available from Microsoft Press.

## Using ActiveX Controls on Access Forms

In Volume I of this book, we suggested a specific technique for working with ActiveX controls on Access forms. In order to work with properties, methods, and events of an ActiveX control, you must always refer to the Object property of the control you see on the form. We've found it useful to create a private WithEvents variable in the form's module, and then, in the form's Load event procedure, set the variable to refer to the Object property of the ActiveX control, like this:

```
Private WithEvents owcSS As OWC.Spreadsheet


Private Sub Form_Load()
    Set owcSS = Me.ActiveXCtl0.Object
End Sub
```

If you don't need to react to events of the object, leave out the WithEvents keyword. Either way, from then on, in your form's module, use your variable when you need to refer to the control. This way, you can use early binding when referring to the control, and you can use the same object variable when writing event procedures. You'll find this technique used in all the Access form examples in this chapter.

## Working with VBA

When you use an external component from within VBA, you normally use the Tools ➤ References menu item to set a reference to the associated type library. That way, you get the benefits of early binding, IntelliSense, the Object Browser, and local help for the external objects. Search as you might from within Access, however, and you won't find the reference you need in the References dialog box.

Although it's not clear to us why, if you want to use the Office Web Components from within VBA, you'll need to set the reference manually. And you'll need to do it for each individual project.

**TIP**     If you insert one of the Office Web Component controls onto a form, you won't need to follow these steps. Adding one of these controls to a form loads the type library for you. The only time you'll need to follow these steps is when you're using the controls without placing one on a form. (See the "Server-Side Behavior" section earlier in this chapter for more information.)

To work with the Office Web Components from VBA, follow these steps:

1. Choose  Tools ➤ References to bring up the References dialog box.

2. Click the Browse button, and search for the folder where you installed Microsoft Office 2000. Within that folder, look for and select the Office folder.

3. Find and select the file named MSOWC.DLL—this file contains the type library you need.

4. Back in the References dialog box, look for the Microsoft Office Web Components 9.0 selection, as shown in Figure 12.5. If you don't see this item, you've selected the incorrect DLL.

**FIGURE 12.5**

After searching for MSOWC.DLL, you should see the associated item in the References dialog box.

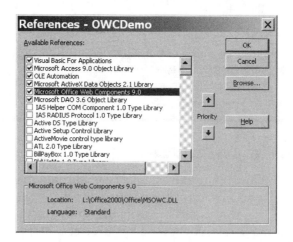

Now that you've got a basic idea of what the Office Web Components provide you, and when and how you can use these components, it's time to dig into the individual components. The rest of the chapter investigates each of the components in turn, showing how you can create Web pages using the controls individually and collectively.

---

If you're going to be programming these components, you'll need to make sure you've installed the help files for the Office Web Components. The most important help file is MSOWCVBA.CHM. Make sure this file is installed if you want help on the object models, properties, methods, and events of the Office Web Components.

---

# The Office Spreadsheet Component

If your form or page requires grid-based data entry or display, or requires the ability to modify values in a grid and see immediate recalculations elsewhere, the Office Spreadsheet component is made for you. As you'll see, not only can the control display data you've entered, you can also bind individual cells to formulas, or other controls on a page. The Office Spreadsheet control also provides an "invisible" server-side mode, where you can instantiate the control with no host of any sort, making it perfect for server-side calculations using the Excel spreadsheet calculation engine.

---

It's hard to count the number of times we've been asked for a way to provide a checkbook-like data entry system written in Access. This is a perfect situation for the Office Spreadsheet control. Although you can "fake it" with a datasheet, Access simply doesn't natively support the concept of a vertically calculated value within a datasheet.

---

## Using the Office Spreadsheet Control

Before you can use the Office Spreadsheet control, you normally place it onto a form, or a Web page. Getting an instance of the control onto a form is easy—you do it just like any other ActiveX control. That is, from your Access form, select the Insert ➤ ActiveX Control... menu item (see Figure 12.6), and choose Microsoft Office Spreadsheet 9.0 from the list of available controls. (One might wonder what happened to version 1 through 8, but as in all things Microsoft, version numbers aren't necessarily sequential.) Access will place an instance of the spreadsheet control on your form, filling the entire detail section.

> **TIP**
>
> In most host environments, Office Web Components can interact at design time. That is, you can enter data into a spreadsheet, or work with the grouping and filtering of a pivot table. This isn't true for Access forms, however. When using these controls on Access forms, you'll need to add data to the controls at run time instead, using VBA code.

If you're working in Access, and want to take an existing Excel spreadsheet and display it on a form or data access page using the Office Spreadsheet component, you have a number of choices:

- If you're creating a data access page, you can select the region you'd like to have appear on your page from within Excel, and copy it to the Windows Clipboard. Then, with the Unbound section selected in the data access page designer, paste the selection. Access will create a new Office Spreadsheet component for you, and will paste the region you've selected into the control. This isn't a perfect solution, however, as it loses some properties of the selected range, including protection. You'll need to manually enable protection for the new control, using its Property Toolbox.

> **TIP**
>
> Do not attempt the previous technique if you're creating an Access form—cutting and pasting an Excel region in a form creates an unbound object frame on the form, which causes all of Excel to be loaded when you run your form. If you're working with Access forms, you'll need to programmatically set up the spreadsheet, instead.

- From within Excel, select the range you'd like to display in the control, and then select File ➤ Save as Web Page.... Choose the Selection option (rather than saving the entire workbook), and make sure you check the Add Interactivity checkbox. (See Figure 12.7.) You can change the title if you like, and select the output filename. Click the Save button when you're ready. Back in Access, create a new data access page, and from the New Data Access Page dialog box, select Existing Web Page. Find the page you just created, and you'll see that you've got an Office Spreadsheet control on the page, ready to use.

**FIGURE 12.7**
Use the Save as Web Page... menu item in Excel to create a Web page containing an Office Spreadsheet.

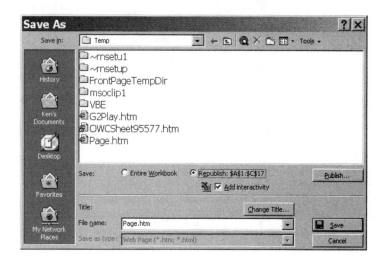

## Working with the SpreadSheet Control

Once you've placed an Office Spreadsheet control onto a data access page, you're ready to work with it as if you were working directly with an Excel spreadsheet. The sample data access page, SSControl (shown in Figure 12.8), allows you to enter page counts for book chapters, and, given the fact that all book chapters have an even number of pages, calculates the printed page count, and displays the total number of pages in an Unbound HTML control on the page. Take a moment and try out the page—note that you can't enter data into the spreadsheet except in the middle column, and that as you type, all the totals stay current.

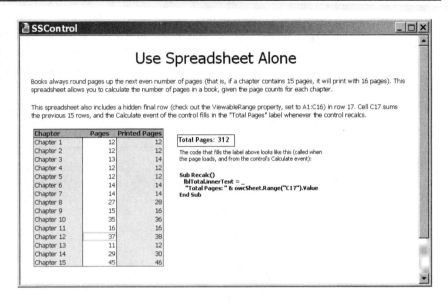

If you're unable to run the sample data access page, perhaps you neglected to run the adhValidateDAPLinks, in basResetDAP. Because data access pages store hard-coded paths internally, you must run this procedure to reset all the links between Access, the pages, and the associated data.

The following bullet points highlight issues we handled when designing this page:

- In this example, we've hidden all of the hints that this is a spreadsheet at all, including the toolbar, the titlebar, and the grid lines, using the Property Toolbox for the control.

- To set up the formulas in column C, we entered the following value in cell C2:

```
=B2+MOD(B2,2)
```

This expression takes the value in cell B2, and adds to it the remainder you get when you divide the value in B2 by 2. This calculation forces the number of pages to the next even number. Then, to copy it to the rest of column C, we copied cell C2 to the clipboard, selected cells C3:C15, and then pasted the formula. The spreadsheet fixes up the references so that each cell in column C refers to the corresponding cell in column B.

- To create the sum of all the pages, we entered the following formula into cell C17:

```
=SUM(C2:C16)
```

- The spreadsheet contains data in three columns and 17 rows. You only see 16 rows of data, because we set the ViewableRange property for the control to be A1:C16. (You can do this either in the Property Toolbox, or in the Properties window.) The 17th row contains the sum for the data in the other rows, but it's hidden, because the page displays the sum from cell C17 outside the spreadsheet.

- You can only type data into the middle column of the spreadsheet. To protect the other cells, you can display the Property Toolbox, select the Protection section, and enable protection. Then, you must select the range of cells where you do want to allow user input, and clear the Lock Cells checkbox on the Property Toolbox. Figure 12.9 shows the Property Toolbox and the Protection settings. Obviously, if you enable protection, you'll most likely want to disable use of the Property Toolbox at run time.

**FIGURE 12.9**
Use the Protection settings to control which cells the users can modify.

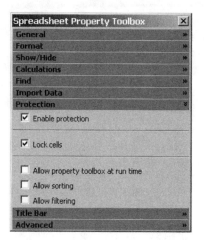

- Although the final row of the spreadsheet is hidden, you can see the total page count in an Unbound HTML control on the page. Code in the spreadsheet's Calculate event fills in the data. If you look at the script associated with the page, you'll find these procedures (for more information on the EventInfo object passed as a parameter to the Office Web Components events, see the "Working with Chart Events" section later in the chapter):

```
Sub owcSS_Calculate(EventInfo)
    Call Recalc
End Sub

Sub window_onLoad()
    Call Recalc
End Sub

Sub Recalc
    lblTotal.innerText =  "Total Pages: " & _
      owcSS.Range("C17").Value
End Sub
```

## Discovering Properties, Methods, and Events

Because the scripting editor doesn't provide an easy way to investigate members of the objects you're working with, you may want to mix development in both VBA and the script editor. We've found it easiest to set a reference to MSOWC.DLL from VBA, and then use the Object Browser and online help to figure out how all the objects interact, what their properties, methods, and events are, and prototype code in the VBA editor. Even when working with a data access page, you can begin your coding efforts in VBA, so you get the benefit of the tools VBA provides.

For example, if you want to refer to a control on a particular data access page, you can use an expression like this:

```
' In the Declarations area...
Private WithEvents owcSS As OWC.Spreadsheet

' In some procedure...
Set owcSS = DataAccessPages ("dapTest").document._
all("owcSSControl")
```

In this example, owcSSControl is the spreadsheet control on the data access page. From then on, in your VBA code, you could program against your VBA variable, referring to the control on the data access page. Of course, once you've got everything figured out, you can cut and paste the code over the script editor, removing syntax that VBScript won't allow. Although this technique isn't for everyone and every situation, it certainly made investigating these controls simpler for us.

Of course, the Microsoft Script Editor includes its own object browser, so you can get some of the benefits of the VBA Object Browser from within that environment as well. See Chapter 11 for more information on using that tool.

## Programming the Spreadsheet

The following example, intended to show off some of the features of the Spreadsheet control's object model, allows you to select the name of a table in the database, and then fill an Office Spreadsheet with all the data from the table. Because you cannot bind an Office Spreadsheet directly to a data source yet, you might want to display data in this grid format, or even allow users to calculate simple sums or work with the data offline.

This example works through many of the issues you need to solve in order to get data into an Office Spreadsheet control. We've provided this example both as an Access form (frmSSData) and as a data access page (SSData). In the text, we'll discuss the data access page example, only because its code is a bit less familiar to most readers. You might want to stop and experiment with either or both of these examples before reading on. (Figure 12.10 shows the data access page version of the example.)

If you were to solve this problem yourself, you'd need to answer several questions (many of these questions deal with ADO issues, not spreadsheet issues):

- How do you open a connection to the current database?

- How do you provide a combo box full of available tables and queries?

- Once you've selected a table or query, how do you retrieve all its data?

- Once you've got all the data, how to insert it into the spreadsheet control?

- How do you "freeze" the title row so it doesn't scroll?

The following sections provide solutions to each of these issues.

**FIGURE 12.10**
Once you've selected a
table or query name, script
in the page fills the spreadsheet with all the data.

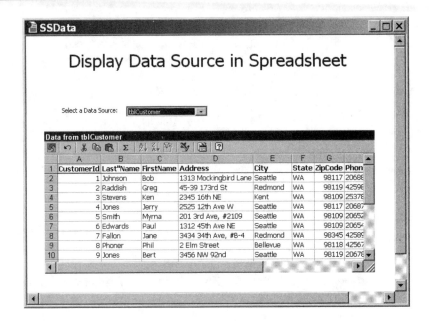

## Getting Data from a Recordset into a Spreadsheet

If your goal is to place data from an open recordset into a spreadsheet, your first thought might be to simply loop through all the columns, in all the rows, and place each value into the appropriate cell, programmatically. And, to be honest, that's exactly what you'll find in the Microsoft documentation, if you look.

Unfortunately, this technique is painfully slow. Even for moderately small recordsets, you'll be amazed at how long this takes. You could then try other techniques, such as creating tab-delimited lists, or arrays of values, but we found that using a combination of the ADO GetString function and the CSVData property of the Office Spreadsheet, you can fill a spreadsheet with data very quickly. The ADO GetString function retrieves all the data from a recordset, delimited as you specify in the function's parameters, and returns a string containing the data. (Normally, you'll use quotes and commas as delimiters.) The CSVData property of the Office Spreadsheet allows you to provide a string, containing quote-surrounded, comma-separated values; and the spreadsheet will parse out the data and display it. There may be a better way to do this, but we stopped looking once we saw how well this technique worked.

---

**NOTE**    The DAO and Excel teams worked together to provide the CopyFromRecordset method, in the previous version of Office. This made it simple to copy data from a recordset into a range in a spreadsheet. There doesn't appear to be a similar method for ADO recordsets.

---

**WARNING**    You won't want to use the code described here for large tables, or any data source that contains memo fields. Because this technique will retrieve all the data from all columns of your data source, it can be slow if there are too many rows, columns, or large text or binary values. If you want to modify the code so that it allows you to specify the fields to extract, or the number of rows, that might work better for you.

---

## Getting Started

To get started, the script portion of the data access page contains a few declarations:

```
Option Explicit
Dim cnn          ' ADODB.Connection
Dim c            ' OWC.Constants

Const QUOTE = """"

Const adClipString = 2
Const adSchemaTables = 20
```

The first constant is there only to make the code more readable. The second set of constants provides necessary ADO constants. (If only ADO provided a Constants object, as all the Office Web Components do, scripting ADO would be a lot easier!) The window_onload event procedure, shown in Listing 12.1, sets up important variables for the rest of the code.

---

### Listing 12.1

```
Sub window_onload()
    Set c = owcSS.Constants
    Set cnn = CreateObject("ADODB.Connection")

    ' Use the connection from the DataSourceControl.
    cnn.Open MSODSC.ConnectionString
```

```
        ' Load up the list of table/query names,
        ' and set up the empty spreadsheet.
        Call LoadSourceNames
        Call ResetSpreadSheet(owcSS)
    End Sub
```

Code in the window_onload event procedure sets up the page-wide variable c, containing a reference to the Constants property of the spreadsheet, and opens a persistent connection to the current database. Note that this code takes advantage of the fact that the Data Source control on the page (named MSODSC, by default) knows how to connect to the host database, and opens a connection based on the Data Source control's connection string. This way, there's only one place within the page containing information about the location of the database, and the code in basResetDAP can find and fix up that path. Finally, this code loads the combo box with a list of all the tables and queries in the database, and sets the spreadsheet up, ready to contain to data.

## Filling the List of Table and Query Names

Next, you'll need to fill the combo box with a list of table and query names. This problem really has two halves:

- How do you retrieve a list of table and query names?

- How do you fill a combo box with the names you find?

Both questions have been answered elsewhere in this book, in one volume or another, but it's worth reviewing the answers here. Listing 12.2 contains the entire LoadSourceNames procedure, which does all the work.

### Listing 12.2

```
    Sub LoadSourceNames()
        Dim opt
        Dim rst

        Set rst = cnn.OpenSchema(adSchemaTables)
        Do Until rst.EOF
            Select Case rst.Fields("TABLE_TYPE").Value
                Case "TABLE", "VIEW"
```

```
                    Set opt = document.createElement("OPTION")
                    opt.Text = rst.Fields("TABLE_NAME").Value
                    opt.Value = opt.Text
                    cboSource.add opt
                Case Else
                    ' Do nothing at all.
            End Select
            rst.MoveNext
        Loop
        rst.Close
        Set rst = Nothing
End Sub
```

LoadSourceNames begins by calling the OpenSchema method of the Connection object. This method retrieves a recordset containing information about the connection's schema—the actual information it retrieves depends on the constant you send it. (See Chapter 6 in *Access 2000 Developer's Handbook, Volume 1: Desktop Edition* for more information on using the OpenSchema method.) In this case, because the code sends the adSchemaTables constant, the recordset the method returns contains information about the tables (and queries) within the database. When you request information about tables, the recordset contains (among others) TABLE_NAME and TABLE_TYPE fields. In this example, you only want to include tables for which the TABLE_TYPE property contains either "TABLE" or "QUERY". Therefore, the Select Case in Listing 12.2 handles rows with those types, and disregards the rest. (The only reason we included this check here was to avoid displaying the system tables in the list.) The rest of the code takes care of retrieving the actual table name, creating a new Option element, and adding it to the combo box:

```
Set opt = document.createElement("OPTION")
opt.Text = rst.Fields("TABLE_NAME").Value
opt.Value = opt.Text
cboSource.add opt
```

In addition, this code fragment sets the Value property of each option, so that when you select a value from the list, the Value property of the combo box will contain the selected value. Finally, the code in Listing 12.2 closes the schema recordset.

## Selecting a Value

Once you've made a choice from the combo box, the control's Change event fires, and runs the code shown in Listing 12.3. This code checks to make sure you've selected a value containing the name of a table or query from the combo box (the first item in the list is empty, allowing you to clear the spreadsheet). If not, the code calls the ResetSpreadsheet procedure, clearing the spreadsheet and resetting the caption. If you did select a valid name, the code opens a recordset based on the selected table/query, and then calls FillSpreadsheet to display the data.

**Listing 12.3**

```
Sub cboSource_onChange()
    Dim rst

    If Len(cboSource.value) > 0 Then
        Set rst = CreateObject("ADODB.Recordset")
        rst.Open cboSource.Value, cnn
        Call FillSpreadsheet(rst, owcSS, _
          "Data from " & cboSource.Value)
        rst.Close
        Set rst = Nothing
    Else
        Call ResetSpreadsheet(owcSS)
    End If
End Sub
```

## Displaying the Data

The FillSpreadsheet procedure, shown in Listing 12.4, is the centerpiece of this example. This procedure sets up the spreadsheet, retrieves the data and inserts it into the spreadsheet, and then formats the spreadsheet correctly. The following paragraphs outline how this procedure does its work.

**Listing 12.4**

```
Sub FillSpreadsheet(rst, owcSS, strCaption)
    Dim owcSheet
    Dim strValues
```

```
Dim strFields

With owcSS
    .ScreenUpdating = False
    .TitleBar.Caption = strCaption
End With

Set owcSheet = owcSS.ActiveSheet
With owcSheet
    .Protection.Enabled = False
    .UsedRange.Clear
    .Cells.Font.Name = "Tahoma"
End With

strFields = GetFieldList(rst)

' If there's no rows, don't do this!
If Not (rst.BOF And rst.EOF) Then
    strValues = rst.GetString(adClipString,, _
     QUOTE & "," & QUOTE, _
     QUOTE & vbCr & QUOTE)

    ' Add quotes to the beginning and end.
    strValues = QUOTE & strValues & QUOTE

    ' The OWC Spreadsheet doesn't handle "" well when
    ' you use the CSVData property, so replace all
    ' empty strings with nothing at all.
    strValues = Replace(strValues, _
     QUOTE & QUOTE, vbNullString)
End If
' Fill the spreadsheet with the column headers and
' data (if there is any)
owcSS.CSVData = strFields & vbCr & strValues

With owcSheet
    .UsedRange.Locked = False

    With .Rows(1)
        .Font.Bold = True
        .Locked = True
    End With
```

```
            .UsedRange.AutoFitColumns
            .Protection.Enabled = True
            .Rows(2).FreezePanes c.ssFreezeTop
        End With

        owcSS.ScreenUpdating = True
    End Sub
```

### Handling Screen Updates

In order to make the screen display as clean as possible, the procedure turns off screen updating before doing any work, and then resets it when it's done, using the ScreenUpdating property of the Office Spreadsheet control:

```
With owcSS
    .ScreenUpdating = False
End With

' Do the work, and then...
owcSS.ScreenUpdating = True
```

### Working with the TitleBar

The Office Spreadsheet control has, as one of its properties, a TitleBar object. You can set the Visible property to control whether you see the title bar. You can format the interior of the title bar, using the Interior property, which is itself an object. Its only property at this time is Color, and you'll end up with expressions like this:

```
owcSS.TitleBar.Interior.Color = "red"
```

---

**TIP**     When specifying colors using the Office Web Components, you can use any of the normal HTML color values. That is, you can use named colors (like "red"), an RGB value (using the rgb function), or a hex value. See Chapter 10 for more information on using colors with data access pages.

---

In this example, the code sets the Caption property of the TitleBar object, so that it displays the strCaption parameter passed to the procedure:

```
With owcSS
    .TitleBar.Caption = strCaption
End With
```

### Setting Up the Active Sheet

Next, the procedure retrieves a reference to the ActiveSheet object (extraneous at the moment because there's only one sheet, but required so that when the control does support multiple sheets in a future version, existing code will continue to work). It then uses three properties of the Worksheet object—Protection, UsedRange (the entire range that's been used), and Cells (the entire set of cells in the sheet)—to disable protection, to clear out the used range of cells, and to set the font for the entire sheet:

```
Set owcSheet = owcSS.ActiveSheet
With owcSheet
    .Protection.Enabled = False
    .UsedRange.Clear
    .Cells.Font.Name = "Tahoma"
End With
```

### Retrieving the List of Fields

The next line from Listing 12.4 calls the GetFieldList procedure, which returns a string containing a comma-delimited list of all the fields in the recordset. The GetFieldList procedure, shown in Listing 12.5, builds up the list of available fields by looping through the Fields collection of the open recordset, surrounding each field name with quotes by calling the FixQuote procedure, also shown in Listing 12.5. (This code also replaces a quote within a name with two quotes, so that VBA can correctly parse the string.)

### Listing 12.5

```
Function FixQuote(varValue)
    ' Surround the field value with quotes, if it's
    ' not empty. If it is, simply return an empty string.
    If Len(varValue & "") > 0 Then
        FixQuote = QUOTE & _
          Replace(varValue, QUOTE, QUOTE & QUOTE) & QUOTE
    Else
        FixQuote = ""
    End If
End Function
```

```
Function GetFieldList(rst)
    ' Given a recordset, come up with a comma-delimited
    ' list of fields for the recordset.
    Dim fld
    Dim strFields

    For Each fld In rst.Fields
        strFields = strFields & "," & FixQuote(fld.Name)
    Next
    ' Remove the leading comma.
    GetFieldList = Mid(strFields, 2)
End Function
```

### Retrieving the Data

If there are any rows to retrieve (that is, if the recordset properties BOF and EOF aren't both True), it's time to do the work. This takes three distinct steps:

1. Retrieve the recordset as a string.

2. Surround the string with quotes.

3. Remove empty fields.

The goal here is to create a string containing quote-surrounded, comma-delimited values from the recordset.

---

**TIP**    The CSVValues property of the Office Spreadsheet doesn't handle empty strings correctly. That is, rather than displaying nothing, as you might expect, it displays "". Therefore, in this code, you'll find a step that replaces "" with vbNullString. That way, when the spreadsheet displays the text, empty columns won't contain extraneous characters.

---

The first step requires you to retrieve the data from the recordset, formatted as a comma-delimited string, with quotes around each field. To do that, call the Get-String method of the recordset, like this:

```
strValues = rst.GetString(adClipString,, _
    QUOTE & "," & QUOTE, _
    QUOTE & vbCr & QUOTE)
```

The first parameter to GetString (adClipString) indicates the type of string you want to create. At this point, adClipString is the only option, but the parameter is still required.

After this call, strValues will be a string containing data, like this (you can't see it here, but there's an extra vbCr at the end of this string, placed there by the Get-String method call):

```
Row1Field1","Row1Field2","Row1Field3","Row1Field4"
"Row2Field1","Row2Field2","Row2Field3","Row2Field4"
"
```

Of course, the current state of the string won't work—it requires quotes at both ends. The following line does this work, adding a quote at the start and at the end:

```
strValues = QUOTE & strValues & QUOTE
```

After running the code, the string of fields looks like this:

```
"Row1Field1","Row1Field2","Row1Field3","Row1Field4"
"Row2Field1","Row2Field2","Row2Field3","Row2Field4"
" "
```

Finally, because the Office Spreadsheet control doesn't handle "" the way you might expect, you need to remove the empty strings, using this code:

```
strValues = Replace(strValues, _
  QUOTE & QUOTE, vbNullString)
```

Once that's done, the output values look like they must, like this:

```
"Row1Field1","Row1Field2","Row1Field3","Row1Field4"
"Row2Field1","Row2Field2","Row2Field3","Row2Field4"
```

Now it's time to display the data in the spreadsheet.

### Displaying the Data

Finally, to display the data, the code sets the CSVData property of the Office Spreadsheet object. This parses out all the comma-separated values, and places them into the appropriate row and column. Of course, you want the field names to go into the first row, so you must combine the field titles with the field data, like this:

```
ssDemo.CSVData = strFields & vbCr & strValues
```

### Formatting the Sheet

The final step of this example formats the sheet correctly. Specifically, it seemed reasonable to "autofit" the used columns, make the field headers bold and locked (with the rest of the sheet unlocked), and to "freeze" the top row, so that as you scroll the data, the field names stay fixed.

To accomplish these goals, the FillSpreadsheet procedure in Listing 12.4 includes the following code:

```
With owcSheet
    .UsedRange.Locked = False

    With .Rows(1)
        .Font.Bold = True
        .Locked = True
    End With

    .UsedRange.AutoFitColumns
    .Protection.Enabled = True
    .Rows(2).FreezePanes c.ssFreezeTop
End With
```

Note that in order to lock the top row, but none of the rest, the code must first unlock all the data, then lock the first row, and finally set the Enabled property of the entire sheet's Protection object to True.

To freeze a section of the sheet, you call the FreezePanes method of a Range object (in this case, the range returned by owcSheet.Rows(2), the entire second row). You must specify which direction you want frozen—in this case, c.ssFreeze-Top indicates that you want to freeze the rows above the range.

---

**TIP**     As mentioned earlier, you may find it easier to work with the controls, and their somewhat complex object models, in VBA rather than in the script editor. Because the IntelliSense support in the VBA editor is more complete, you'll get more information as you're working. That's how we created this form and page pair—we created the example first on an Access form, and then later converted it to a data access page.

---

# Using the Spreadsheet Component without a Host

As part of your application, you may find that you need to take advantage of the calculation engine of an Excel-like spreadsheet. Or, perhaps you need to use one of the many built-in spreadsheet functions that aren't available in VBA. In either case, you don't need to display the user-interface for the spreadsheet. With most ActiveX controls, you would need to place a hidden instance of the control onto a form somewhere, and then use the features of the control programmatically.

You can accomplish these goals because the Office Spreadsheet component does not need to be hosted on a form, or on a page, in order to be instantiated and do its work. You can interact with the control, totally invisibly, with no user interface at all. This not only makes it possible to perform spreadsheet-like calculations from an ASP page on a Web server, without end users having a copy of the Office Web Components locally, but it also reduces the overhead required in using the control locally.

Imagine this scenario: you want to calculate the median number of items sold in an order, for all orders where more than one item is sold. Access queries can calculate the sum, count, max, min, and other aggregate values, but they cannot calculate the median of a list of numbers. Sure, you could write your own Median function (and it's not even very difficult) but if you need more than just this one simple calculation (use your imagination here), it makes sense to have the Office Spreadsheet do the work for you. This example, shown in Listing 12.6, opens a recordset, retrieves its data into a string (much like the previous example, but in a simpler case), creates an Office Spreadsheet component invisibly, inserts the data, sets up a cell to perform the calculation, and retrieves the data from the spreadsheet.

### Listing 12.6

```
Function TestOWCSS() As Long
    ' Return the median number of items
    ' sold on a single order, when the number
    ' of items sold is greater than 1.
    Dim ss As OWC.Spreadsheet
    Dim rst As ADODB.Recordset
    Dim strValues As String
    Dim lngRows As Long

    ' Normally, you'd add error handling to a procedure
```

```
' like this, but this is just attempting to prove
' a point.

Set rst = New ADODB.Recordset
rst.Open _
 "SELECT Quantity FROM tblOrderDetails " & _
 "WHERE Quantity > 1", CurrentProject.Connection

' Get the rows from the recordset as a string,
' using a CR/LF as the row delimiter.
strValues = rst.GetString(adClipString)
rst.Close
Set rst = Nothing

' Create the OWC Spreadsheet, in memory. Insert
' the values, using the CSVData property.
Set ss = New owc.Spreadsheet
ss.CSVData = strValues

' Calculate the number of rows in the recordset (you
' couldn't get this from ADO because you opened a
' forward-only recordset).
lngRows = ss.ActiveSheet.UsedRange.Rows.Count

' Set up the formula, in cell B1, and return the value.
With ss.Range("B1")
    .Formula = "=MEDIAN(A1:A" & lngRows & ")"
    TestOWCSS = .Value
End With

' Release the spreadsheet component.
Set ss = Nothing
End Function
```

In this example, the code starts by doing all the necessary work with the record-set. That is, it opens the appropriate recordset, calls the GetString method to retrieve all the data, and then closes the recordset. This time, GetString's work is much simpler than in the previous example—in this case, you know that the column of data you care about is numeric, so there's no reason to worry about quotes. It also doesn't handle field names, as there's no need here. GetString's default row delimiter is a carriage return, so there's no need to do any work there, either.

```
Set rst = New ADODB.Recordset
rst.Open _
 "SELECT Quantity FROM tblOrderDetails " & _
 "WHERE Quantity > 1", CurrentProject.Connection

' Get the rows from the recordset as a string,
' using a CR/LF as the row delimiter.
strValues = rst.GetString(adClipString)
rst.Close
Set rst = Nothing
```

Next, the code instantiates the Office Spreadsheet component, and inserts the data just read from the ADO recordset, using the CSVData property:

```
' Create the OWC Spreadsheet, in memory. Insert
' the values, using the CSVData property.
Set ss = New owc.Spreadsheet
ss.CSVData = strValues
```

The code next calculates the number of rows in the data, using the UsedRange property of the Spreadsheet component. The code uses this value later, when it calculates the Median of the correct range:

```
' Calculate the number of rows in the recordset (you
' couldn't get this from ADO because you opened a
' forward-only recordset).
lngRows = ss.ActiveSheet.UsedRange.Rows.Count
```

Finally, the code inserts a formula into cell B1 on the spreadsheet, requesting the median of the inserted data, and then releases the reference to the Spreadsheet component:

```
' Set up the formula, in cell B1, and return the value.
With ss.Range("B1")
    .Formula = "=MEDIAN(A1:A" & lngRows & ")"
    TestOWCSS = .Value
End With
Set ss = Nothing
```

Basically, anything you can do with the Office Spreadsheet component visibly, you can do with it invisibly as well. You can, if you like, think of the Office Spreadsheet component as a calculation engine, rather than as a grid. Certainly, you'll need to investigate how to interact with spreadsheets in general—a much different task than working with databases—before making best use of this tool, but the Office Spreadsheet component makes a useful grid for data entry, calculation, and display.

# The Office PivotTable Component

In Excel, a pivot table is a special, interactive table that summarizes large amounts of data. You can easily rotate the rows and columns to get a different perspective on your data, and you can filter the data by displaying different pages. After you create the basic pivot table, it can easily be "pivoted." Pivoting involves dragging and dropping fields to new positions within the table for a different view of the data. Because the pivot table acts as a view on the data, you can't change or alter the original data source by pivoting. This allows you to adjust the pivot table in a myriad of ways without concern for harming the original data source.

If you want to, you can easily create a pivot table in Excel, and save it as a Web page, with interactivity. (See the "Using the Office Spreadsheet Control" section earlier in the chapter to review how you can publish an existing Excel solution to the Web, using the Office Web Components.) The real question for Access developers, however, is why you might want to use a pivot table at all.

To clearly describe the usefulness of a pivot table, take a look at a real world example. You work for a pizza store, and your manager has asked you to create a summary report for some historical data on product sales. She wants to know the answers to questions like these:

- What were the annual sales totals for each customer, category of products, and product?

- How many units were sold for each product?

- Which customers had the highest orders across the span of three years?

- Are certain categories selling more than other?

You're good with Access, and so you can easily create a query that combines all the necessary tables together to get the raw data. (In the sample database, that query is qryOrderDetails, shown in Figure 12.11.) The list consists of rows of sales information for each product, including the product category, the employee that sold it, and the date on which it was sold. However, it will take some serious work to combine the information to answer the questions your manager is asking. At this point, you have two options: create several reports, each providing the answer to a specific question; or find a tool that allows you to quickly summarize the information interactively—the pivot table.

**FIGURE 12.11**
The qryOrderDetails query

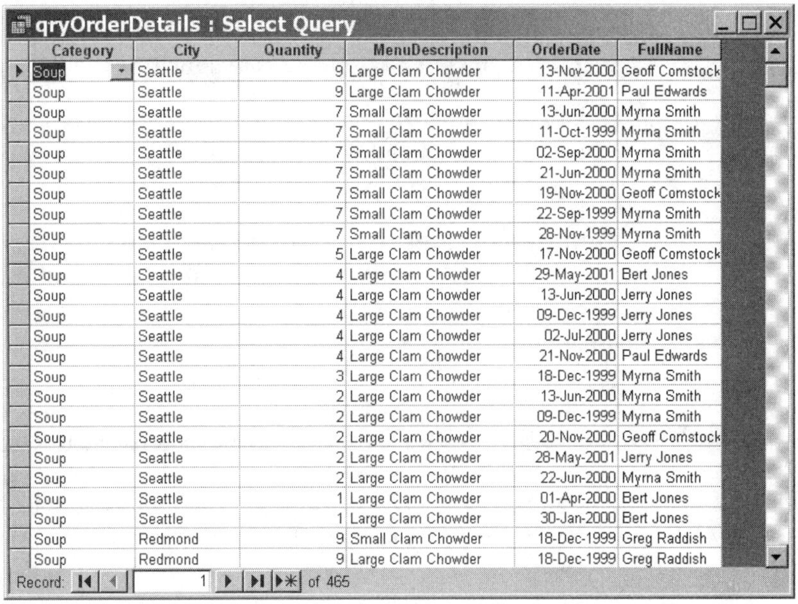
qryOrderDetails : Select Query

| Category | City | Quantity | MenuDescription | OrderDate | FullName |
|---|---|---|---|---|---|
| Soup | Seattle | 9 | Large Clam Chowder | 13-Nov-2000 | Geoff Comstock |
| Soup | Seattle | 9 | Large Clam Chowder | 11-Apr-2001 | Paul Edwards |
| Soup | Seattle | 7 | Small Clam Chowder | 13-Jun-2000 | Myrna Smith |
| Soup | Seattle | 7 | Small Clam Chowder | 11-Oct-1999 | Myrna Smith |
| Soup | Seattle | 7 | Small Clam Chowder | 02-Sep-2000 | Myrna Smith |
| Soup | Seattle | 7 | Small Clam Chowder | 21-Jun-2000 | Myrna Smith |
| Soup | Seattle | 7 | Small Clam Chowder | 19-Nov-2000 | Geoff Comstock |
| Soup | Seattle | 7 | Small Clam Chowder | 22-Sep-1999 | Myrna Smith |
| Soup | Seattle | 7 | Small Clam Chowder | 28-Nov-1999 | Myrna Smith |
| Soup | Seattle | 5 | Large Clam Chowder | 17-Nov-2000 | Geoff Comstock |
| Soup | Seattle | 4 | Large Clam Chowder | 29-May-2001 | Bert Jones |
| Soup | Seattle | 4 | Large Clam Chowder | 13-Jun-2000 | Jerry Jones |
| Soup | Seattle | 4 | Large Clam Chowder | 09-Dec-1999 | Jerry Jones |
| Soup | Seattle | 4 | Large Clam Chowder | 02-Jul-2000 | Jerry Jones |
| Soup | Seattle | 4 | Large Clam Chowder | 21-Nov-2000 | Paul Edwards |
| Soup | Seattle | 3 | Large Clam Chowder | 18-Dec-1999 | Myrna Smith |
| Soup | Seattle | 2 | Large Clam Chowder | 13-Jun-2000 | Myrna Smith |
| Soup | Seattle | 2 | Large Clam Chowder | 09-Dec-1999 | Myrna Smith |
| Soup | Seattle | 2 | Large Clam Chowder | 20-Nov-2000 | Geoff Comstock |
| Soup | Seattle | 2 | Large Clam Chowder | 28-May-2001 | Jerry Jones |
| Soup | Seattle | 2 | Large Clam Chowder | 22-Jun-2000 | Myrna Smith |
| Soup | Seattle | 1 | Large Clam Chowder | 01-Apr-2000 | Bert Jones |
| Soup | Seattle | 1 | Large Clam Chowder | 30-Jan-2000 | Bert Jones |
| Soup | Redmond | 9 | Small Clam Chowder | 18-Dec-1999 | Greg Raddish |
| Soup | Redmond | 9 | Large Clam Chowder | 18-Dec-1999 | Greg Raddish |

Record: 1 of 465

The most important feature of a pivot table is its ability to summarize large amounts of data into a clear and flexible format. By following the steps described in the next section, you can quickly create a summary report for the sales data like the one shown in Figure 12.12. You can easily adjust the new pivot table for various views and calculations based on the data. For instance, your manager can now easily:

- Filter the data displayed by the pivot table to see only sales information for Pizza products.
- Change the sales data to reflect averages instead of total sales.

- Add the Month or Year field to see data grouped by month or year.

- Hide specific products that don't need to be seen.

Your manager should be more than satisfied with the flexibility of the pivot table that you have created as well as with your resourcefulness. And there you have it: wealth and fame based on the capabilities of the Office PivotTable component!

Why use a pivot table? Pivot tables can be used in almost any environment to simplify data analysis. Rather than creating multiple static reports based on the same data source, you can opt to create a single pivot table that can be altered by the user to fit their specific needs. Some additional benefits to including pivot table reports in your analytical arsenal include the following:

**Data comparison**     Pivot tables allow you to easily compare field values across multiple categories. By limiting the amount of detail displayed, you can quickly compare subtotals for various groups.

**Summarizing large groups of data**     A large list of data is easier to understand when placed in a pivot table. Rather than hunting for the rows of information you need, a pivot table can quickly and easily group similar data together for analysis.

---

**NOTE**     This isn't the place to delve deeply into how pivot tables work in Excel, nor how to create them. If you're interested in digging deeper into this technology, you might start with *Mastering Excel 2000: Premium Edition*, by Mindy Martin, Steven Hansen, and Beth Klingher (Sybex, 1999), from which we've loosely borrowed a few sections describing pivot tables, with permission of the authors and publisher.

---

**TIP**     This whole section will make much more sense once you've done a little work with pivot tables. On the other hand, most of our examples look and feel like simple Access crosstabs, so if you have ever created a crosstab query, you should be all set for now. To fully take advantage of the Office PivotTable control, using either its user interface, or its object model, you'll need to understand more about pivot tables and their underlying technology than we can discuss here.

---

# Getting Started with the Office PivotTable Control

Although we tend to avoid step-by-step walkthroughs in this book, using pivot tables is so foreign to most Access developers that it seemed worthwhile working this exercise together. To get you comfortable with the Office PivotTable control, this section walks you through creating a data access page containing an instance of the control. By the end of these steps, you'll have created the pivot table shown in Figure 12.12. Your goal is to group the data in qryOrderDetails first by Category, and then by MenuDescription, calculate the amount sold of each item, grouped by months, and filter based on the customer.

**FIGURE 12.12**

After working through the steps in this section, you'll have a pivot table that looks something like this.

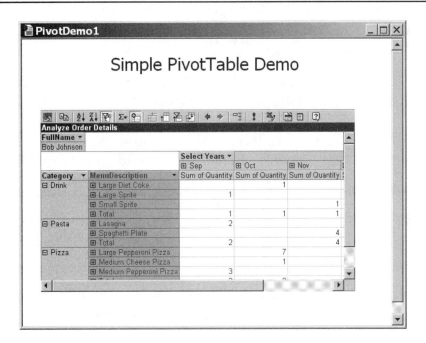

| TIP | If you haven't worked through Chapter 10 (introducing data access pages) this section may be difficult going. We suggest you take time now to read and try out the examples in that chapter before continuing with this chapter. |

To build your own data access page, including an Office PivotTable control, follow these steps:

1. In the sample database for this chapter, create a new data access page in Design view.

2. From the Field List window, find the qryOrderDetails query, and then click and drag it onto the Unbound section of the new data access page. This creates an Office PivotTable control for you. (This action does not place a NavigationBar control on the form, but it does bind the Office PivotTable to the invisible Data Source control (named MSODSC) on the page.)

3. To make things easier, expand the new PivotTable control to fill as much space as possible on the data access page. It doesn't need to fill your whole screen, but you should make it at least four times as large as the default size for the control.

4. Make sure the PivotTable control is selected. Click on a cell inside the control (watching to see that the border turns into a thick, hashed border). Right-click to bring up the context menu, and select Property Toolbox.

5. On the Property Toolbox, expand the Show/Hide section, and make sure all the items are selected. (You might want to select Field List last, because it often appears right on top of the Property Toolbox window.)

6. Click on the title bar for the control, and note how the available items on the Property Toolbox change. Expand each section in the Property Toolbox to see what properties are available. Try changing the caption and the background, to see how the Toolbox works.

7. You won't be needing the OrderDate field, so remove it. To do that, click and select the field title, then drag the field somewhere on the page outside the control. The cursor will change to indicate that you're removing a field (see Figure 12.13), and release the mouse. (There are other ways to remove a field, just as there are multiple ways to accomplish just about anything with this control. This is the method that's simplest to demonstrate, however.) Repeat for the City field, which you also don't need in this example.

**FIGURE 12.13**
Drag fields off of the
Office PivotTable control
to remove them from
the pivot table.

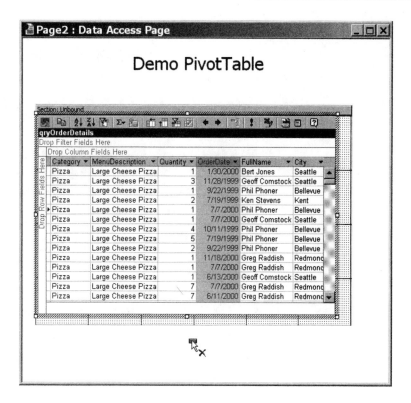

8. It's time to start grouping, so drag the MenuDescription field to the Drop
Row Fields Here section, creating a row header. Notice that you've now
grouped the data by MenuDescription, as shown in Figure 12.14.

**TIP**    As you drag the field, watch the blue border markers. These indicate where you'll
be dropping the field.

9. Drag the Category field to the left of the MenuDescription field, creating a
second row header.

**FIGURE 12.14**
Creating a new row header groups the data by that field.

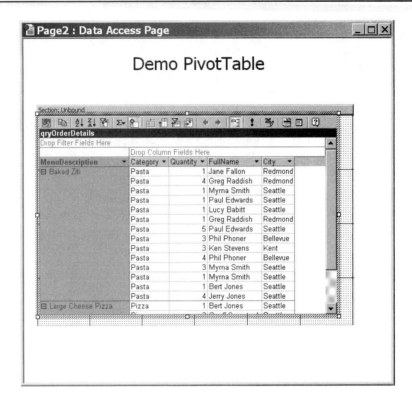

10. Drag the FullName field to the Drop Filter Fields Here section. This creates a filter field, allowing you to control exactly which rows of data appear in the pivot table.

11. Select the Quantity column, right-click, then choose AutoCalc ➤ Sum. (You can get the same effect clicking the Autocalc button on the toolbar.)

12. Stop here and try out Expand context menu item (or the Expand toolbar item) for the Category and MenuDescription fields. By expanding and contracting these fields, you can see how much of any item has been sold, both by category, and by item. Also, try clicking the drop-down arrow next to the FullName field. Select a single customer to filter the rows for just that particular customer. At this point, your page should look something like Figure 12.15.

**FIGURE 12.15**

After setting up row headers and filter fields, your page should look like this.

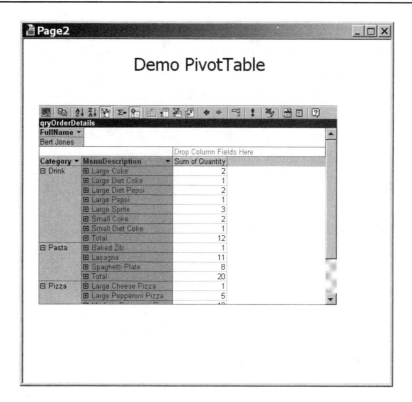

If you want to expand or contract and entire column, select the header for the column first, then use the Expand menu or toolbar item.

13. To group the sales information by month, you need to add a column header field. If the PivotTable Field List window isn't visible, use the Property Toolbox window to show it.

14. From the PivotTable Field List window, find the OrderDate by Months item and open the node (click on the "+") to select Months. Drag this to the Drop Column Fields Here section, to create a column header field. Now you see all the sums broken out by months. To see information for a particular year, select the Months drop-down list, and choose one or more years.

15. The caption for that drop-down list might be confusing to your end users, so use the Property Toolbox to change it. In the Office PivotTable control, select the Months drop-down, then in the Property Toolbox, open up the Captions section. Change the caption from Months to Select Years.

16. Switch to Page view, and try changing all the options. You can even move fields around at run time. For example, you can move the Months to be a filter field, and then choose years that filter the data.

These steps walked you through the bare minimum use of the Office PivotTable control. You've seen how to create the control and bind it to data, how to move columns around, and how to filter data. As you can see, you can make changes to the design of the control both at design time, and at run time.

---

**TIP**   Don't forget that everything you see in the Property Toolbox is written in DHTML, and therefore, uses the public interfaces provided by the control to manipulate its behavior. Anything you see available in the Property Toolbox (and more), you can control yourself, from VBA or scripting code.

---

## Where Is the Data Coming From?

Data for the PivotTable component can come from a number of different places:

**Relational data**   Using OLE DB: In this case, you're counting on the control to create its own summary data, and to group and filter fields as you request. That is, you request two-dimensional sets of data from some database engine, and the control does the work of creating third (and more) dimensions, based on summaries and groupings.

**OLAP data**   Normally from some OLAP server, such as SQL Server 7.0: In this case, all the work is done remotely, so the performance is significantly improved. In addition, OLAP servers generally allow you to create multi-dimensional representations of your data (normally called "cubes") that can be stored. Therefore, when you need to retrieve data from the cube, the server has already performed the necessary calculations and can quickly retrieve the information you request via the Office PivotTable component. You don't even need to be attached to a server. That is, you can save a cube file to disk, and retrieve data from that. Of course, in that case, the performance will be a little slower, as the control must load much of the cube file into memory on first use. When you use a server-side cube file, the dimension structures are most likely already in RAM, and can load faster.

**XML data**    Created using the Save method of an ADO recordset: ADO allows you to save an opened recordset in XML format. Using this data with an Office PivotTable requires a separate bit of OLE DB "plumbing," and won't be discussed here. (If you're interested in using XML data with the Office PivotTable component, you'll need to investigate the "mspersist" OLE DB provider. For more information, see *Programming Microsoft Office 2000 Web Components*, by Dave Stearns, available from Microsoft Press..)

# Programming the PivotTable Control

Before you can work with the PivotTable control programmatically, you'll need to know a few things about its object model. First of all, the control itself has two completely distinct object hierarchies:

**PivotView object**    Allows you to manipulate the view presented in the control. Using this object, you can add fieldsets (that is, one or more logically grouped sets of fields) to the various axes (row, column, data, or filter). You can also use this object to add totals, and modify the way any field or cell is displayed. Use the ActiveView property of the Office PivotTable control to retrieve a reference to this object.

**PivotData object**    Allows you to manipulate the data filling the PivotTable control. This object actually represents the data displayed in the control, and allows you to get at specific data items, and at the available fields. Use the ActiveData property of the Office PivotTable control to retrieve a reference to this object.

NOTE    Although it's not part of the PivotTable control explicitly, you can't forget about the Data Source control that's providing data for all the examples you'll see here. You can bind the PivotTable control to various data sources, but all the examples here use the Data Source control.

In this section, we'll work through two examples using the PivotTable control. In the first example, you'll see how to programmatically "pivot" the control, how to change the layout of the control, and how to react to events of the control. In the second example, you'll see how to persist the layout information, so that you can save and restore layout information from one session to another.

## Working with the PivotView Object

This example is based on the sample data access page, PivotTableObjects, shown in Figure 12.16. This page includes a pivot table, similar to the one you created in the "Getting Started with the Office PivotTable Control" section, as well as a series of checkboxes that allow you to control the behavior of the Office PivotTable control. The following sections explain what happens when you select each checkbox, how the checkboxes are initialized when the page first opens, and how the page keeps the checkboxes current, even if you make changes to the layout using the control's user interface directly.

---

**NOTE**    In the examples that follow, all code fragments will include the With...End With constructs, so you can tell which objects are being manipulated. The actual code may look slightly different, but we've attempted to make each fragment readable, on its own.

---

**FIGURE 12.16**
Work with this example to see how you can manipulate and react to changes to the PivotTable control's interface.

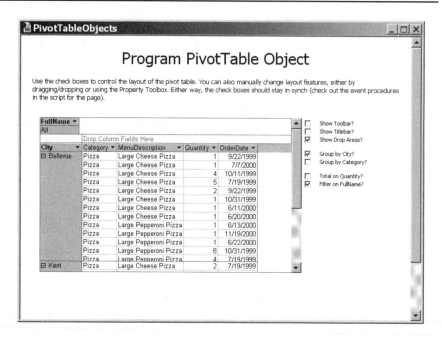

## Making Things Happen

As you can see in Figure 12.16, the page contains three checkboxes that control the "look" of the control (toolbar, titlebar, and drop areas); two checkboxes allowing you to group on City and Category; and two checkboxes allowing you to filter and total. Most of these checkboxes take an action that affects the ActiveView property of the PivotTable control, and the following paragraphs describe the actions of each one.

> **NOTE**     Throughout this example, code will refer directly to the PivotTable control on the sample page, which is named *pt*.

### Changing the Control Layout

The Show Toolbar? checkbox controls the display of the PivotTable control's toolbar. In the onClick event for the checkbox, the associated code sets the DisplayToolbar property of the PivotTable control to be the same as the checked property of the checkbox:

```
Sub chkShowToolbar_onClick()
    pt.DisplayToolbar = chkShowToolbar.checked
End Sub
```

> **NOTE**     DisplayToolbar is a property of the control itself, rather than of the ActiveView property of the control. This is the only property of the control itself that this example modifies.

The Show Titlebar? checkbox sets the Visible property of the ActiveView's Title-Bar property to be the same as the checked property of the checkbox. (The TitleBar property is itself a PivotLabel object, with other properties such as Caption, Font, BackColor, ForeColor, and HAlignment.) When you click this checkbox, the following code executes:

```
Sub chkShowTitlebar_onClick()
    pt.ActiveView.TitleBar.Visible = _
    chkShowTitleBar.checked
End Sub
```

The Show Drop Areas? checkbox controls the display of three different "areas" of the control: the filter area, the column header area, and the row header area.

Each of these areas corresponds to a different object property of the ActiveView object: the RowAxis, ColumnAxis, and FilterAxis properties. In each case, the code needs to set the Label property's Visible property to match the state of the checkbox:

```
Sub chkShowDropAreas_onClick()
    Dim blnShow
    blnShow = chkShowDropAreas.checked

    With pt.ActiveView
        .RowAxis.Label.Visible = blnShow
        .ColumnAxis.Label.Visible = blnShow
        .FilterAxis.Label.Visible = blnShow
    End With
End Sub
```

### Changing the Row Headings

The next two checkboxes (Group by City? and Group by Category?) work with row headers, adding or deleting the City or Category fields from the row header area. In each case, the code adds or deletes a FieldSet object from the RowAxis object's FieldSets collection. What's a FieldSet? Although, in this simple example, each field acts individually, in some pivot table scenarios you might have groups of related fields, such as OrderDate and DeliverDate for a particular order. Each FieldSet object in the pivot table can be added or removed from the axes' collection of fieldsets. In this case, because all the FieldSet objects contain only a single field, it's easy to refer to them by name—the unique identifier for each item in the collection is the name of the field itself.

Listing 12.7 shows the code that's run when you click the Group by City? checkbox (the code for the Group by Category? checkbox is the same, except for the field name). If you select the checkbox, then code runs that adds a FieldSet to the RowAxis object's FieldSets collection, like this (effectively):

```
With pt.ActiveView
    If chkGroupByCity.checked Then
        .RowAxis.InsertFieldSet .FieldSets("City")
    End If
End With
```

The full syntax for the InsertFieldSet method looks like this:

```
object.InsertFieldSet(FieldSet, [Before], [Remove])
```

where:

- *object* is an object that can insert a FieldSet, such as a RowAxis, DataAxis, FilterAxis, or ColumnAxis object.

- *FieldSet* specifies the field set to be inserted.

- *Before* specifies the index of the field set before which the inserted field set will be placed. Can be a numeric index, or a unique string value.

- *Remove* is reserved for future use.

The InsertFieldSet method guarantees that when it adds the FieldSet to a new axis, it removes it from its old location. In other words, this code removes the City FieldSet from the DataAxis collection of FieldSets, and adds it to the RowAxis FieldSets collection.

If you uncheck the checkbox, the code has to do a little more work. First of all, it must expand the column before removing it from the RowAxis FieldSets collection—it appears that, depending on the order in which you add and remove items, the data may simply disappear if you don't expand the column before removing it. (We learned this after noticing all the columns go away in the pivot table while working on this example. There may be other solutions, but this one works.) That code looks like this:

```
With pt.ActiveView
    .RowAxis.FieldSets("City"). _
    Fields(0).Expanded = True
End With
```

**NOTE**     You expand a full column by setting the Expanded property of the Field object, not the FieldSet object. (Remember, a FieldSet might contain multiple fields—these don't—and because there's only one field, you know it's field number 0.)

Next, the code removes the FieldSet from the RowAxis' collection of FieldSets:

```
With pt.ActiveView
    .RowAxis.RemoveFieldSet "City"
End With
```

The syntax for the RemoveFieldSet method looks like this:

```
object.RemoveFieldSet(FieldSetKey)
```

where:

- *object* is an object that has a FieldSets collection, such as a RowAxis, DataAxis, FilterAxis, or ColumnAxis object.

- *FieldSetKey* specifies the field set to be removed. Specify a numeric index, or a unique string key value.

In this case, however, simply removing it from the RowAxis FieldSets collections isn't enough: you must also add it back to the DataAxis FieldSets collection, like this:

```
With pt.ActiveView
    .DataAxis.InsertFieldSet .FieldSets("City")
End With
```

---

**TIP**    When you insert into a FieldSets collection, you must supply an entire FieldSet object. When you remove from the collection, you can simply supply an index, or a unique key value. Although you can pass a FieldSet object, you don't have to.

---

## Listing 12.7

```
Sub chkGroupByCity_onclick()
    With pt.ActiveView
        If chkGroupByCity.checked Then
            .RowAxis.InsertFieldSet .FieldSets("City")
        Else
            ' Make sure the field is expanded.
            ' Otherwise, it may get lost when you
            ' add it back to the data axis.
            .RowAxis.FieldSets("City"). _
            Fields(0).Expanded = True
            .RowAxis.RemoveFieldSet "City"
            .DataAxis.InsertFieldSet .FieldSets("City")
        End If
    End With
End Sub
```

### Adding a Filter

To add or remove a filter field, you'll need to work with the FieldSets collection of the FilterAxis object. The code required to do this is not much different than the code required to create a row header:

```
Sub chkFilterOnFullName_onclick()
    With pt.ActiveView
        If chkFilterOnFullName.checked Then
            .FilterAxis.InsertFieldSet _
            .FieldSets("FullName")
        Else
            .FilterAxis.RemoveFieldSet "FullName"
            .DataAxis.InsertFieldSet .FieldSets("FullName")
        End If
    End With
End Sub
```

This code is slightly simpler, however, because there's no need to expand the column before removing it. Other than that, the only difference between adding a row header and adding a filter is that for row headers, you work with the RowAxis object, and for filters, you work with the FilterAxis object.

### Adding a Total

To add a new total, you must take two steps. You must first add a new PivotTotal object to the PivotView's collection of totals, and then you must display the total on the axis where you want to see it. To create the PivotTotal object, you call the Add-Total method of the PivotView object. The syntax for this method looks like this:

```
object.AddTotal(Name, Field, Function)
```

where:

- *object* is the PivotTable control's PivotView object.

- *Name* specifies the name of the total. You needn't supply a name, and can use an empty string instead.

- *Field* specifies the field to be used to create the total. This must be a Pivot-Field object, normally a field within a FieldSet.

- *Function* specifies the function to be used to create the total. Can be plFunction-Sum (1), plFunctionCount (2), plFunctionMin (3), or plFunctionMax (4). (All these values are provided as properties of the Constants object of the Pivot-Table control.)

To insert the total into an axis, you call the InsertTotal method (which adds the PivotTotal object to the PivotTotals collection of the axis), with syntax like this:

```
object.InsertTotal(Total, [Before])
```

where:

- *object* is a PivotDataAxis object (in this example, the DataAxis property of the PivotView).

- *Total* specifies the PivotTotal object to be inserted.

- *Before* specifies the index of the total before which the inserted total will be placed. If you do not specify this argument, the total is inserted at the end of the collection.

Finally, to remove the total, you can either remove it from the view or from the axis. In this example, the code deletes from the view, using the DeleteTotal method. The syntax for the DeleteTotal method looks like this:

```
object.DeleteTotal(Total)
```

where:

- *object* is a PivotView object.

- *Total* specifies the name or number of the total to be removed.

Given those three methods, the Total on Quantity? checkbox executes the following code when you select it:

```
Sub chkTotalOnQuantity_onClick()
    With pt.ActiveView
        If chkTotalOnQuantity.checked Then
            ' Add a new total to the view. There's only
            ' one field in the Quantity fieldset, so use
            ' that for the total. Once you create the
            ' total, you need to show it on the "data"
            ' axis.
            .AddTotal "", _
            .FieldSets("Quantity").Fields(0), _
            c.plFunctionSum
            .DataAxis.InsertTotal .Totals(0)
```

```
            Else
                ' Simply delete the total from the view.
                ' That deletes it from the data axis, as well.
                .DeleteTotal .Totals(0)
            End if
        End With
    End Sub
```

## Handling Options at Startup

When you first open the page, the various checkboxes should correctly reflect the current settings of the options they're associated with. To make that happen, the page runs a series of procedures at startup, making sure that the correct checkboxes are checked. The window_onload event procedure runs two other procedures in the page, HandleViewChecks and HandleDataChecks. Each of those procedures calls several other procedures, which check the status of various properties, and set the associated checkboxes' values. Listing 12.8 shows HandleDataChecks and the procedures it calls. Listing 12.9 shows HandleViewChecks and the procedures it calls.

### Listing 12.8

```
Sub HandleDataChecks()
    HandleGroupBy
    HandleTotal
    HandleFilter
End Sub

Sub HandleGroupBy()
    ' Check to see if the "Group by..." checkboxes
    ' should be checked. In each case, look for the
    ' orientation of the fieldset object.
    With pt.ActiveView
        chkGroupByCity.checked = _
        (.FieldSets("City").Orientation = _
        c.plOrientationRowAxis)

        chkGroupByCategory.checked = _
        (.FieldSets("Category").Orientation = _
        c.plOrientationRowAxis)
```

```
        End With
    End Sub

    Sub HandleTotal()
        On Error Resume Next
        Dim strName
        With pt.ActiveView
            Err.Clear
            strName = .DataAxis.Totals("Sum of Quantity").Name
            chkTotalOnQuantity.checked = (Err.Number = 0)
        End With
        Err.Clear
    End Sub

    Sub HandleFilter()
        With pt.ActiveView
            chkFilterOnFullName.checked = _
              (.FieldSets("FullName").Orientation = _
                c.plOrientationFilterAxis)
        End With
    End Sub
```

**Listing 12.9**

```
    Sub HandleViewChecks()
        HandleLabel
        HandleTitleBar
    End Sub

    Sub HandleLabel()
        chkShowTitleBar.checked = _
          pt.ActiveView.TitleBar.Visible
        chkShowDropAreas.checked = _
          pt.ActiveView.RowAxis.Label.Visible
    End Sub

    Sub HandleTitleBar()
        chkShowToolbar.checked = pt.DisplayToolbar
    End Sub
```

In most of the procedures called by HandleDataChecks, the code works basically the same: it looks at the Orientation property of the appropriate FieldSet object. The procedure sets or clears checkboxes based on the value of the Orientation property.

The code must handle totals differently, as there's no associated Orientation property. In this case, the code turns off error handling, clears the error number, attempts to retrieve the Name property of the object in question, and checks Err. Number afterwards to tell if an error occurred. If so, the object doesn't exist, and the checkbox shouldn't be checked.

The procedures called by HandleViewChecks are simpler—they simply set the checked property of the appropriate checkbox to reflect the value of the associated PivotTable or PivotView property.

## Reacting to Events

Because the user of this page may change settings interactively, either by dragging fields around or by selecting options from the Property Toolbox, you want the checkboxes on the page to stay "in synch" with the PivotTable control. In order for that to happen, you must find an event that occurs whenever the user changes an option, and write code to update the checkbox accordingly.

The PivotTable control raises several events as you work with it interactively, but the two required by this example are the ViewChange and Query events. The ViewChange event occurs whenever the user changes any aspect of the PivotView object. When the control raises the event, it passes an enumerated value to your event procedure, indicating one of 45 or so reasons why the event might have occurred. Given the reason the event occurred, your code can react to the event appropriately. These reasons include things like changing the state of the title bar or the drop areas, changing the width of a column, changing colors, expanding or contracting a field, and so on. In this example, the only two reason values you need to watch for are plViewReasonLabelVisibleChange and plViewReasonDisplay-ToolbarChange (both available to you as properties of the Constants property of the PivotTable control). Listing 12.10 contains the code for the ViewChange event.

**NOTE**    Listings 12.10 and 12.11 include code to exit the procedure if the blnInitialized variable isn't True. This code ensures that these event procedures don't run when the page first loads. Because the control raises these events as it initializes, but before the window_onload event procedure runs, it doesn't make sense to run these unless the page has been completely loaded. Therefore, the blnInitialized variable is False until the end of the window_onload event procedure, which sets it to True.

### Listing 12.10

```
Sub pt_ViewChange(Reason)
    ' React to event that occurs when the
    ' pt's view changes.
    If Not blnInitialized Then
        Exit Sub
    End If
    Select Case Reason
        Case c.plViewReasonLabelVisibleChange
            Call HandleLabel
        Case c.plViewReasonDisplayToolbarChange
            Call HandleTitlebar
    End Select
End Sub
```

**NOTE**    Hopefully, as you study the two event procedures in this example, you'll see why we broke up the various procedures that handle the checkboxes on the page. Doing it the way we did makes it easier to call the same procedures at startup and later, when events occur.

The PivotTable control raises its Query event when you change some part of the query filling the control. When the Query event occurs, the PivotTable control also passes in an enumerated value (of about 20 possible values) indicating what changed, with respect to the query filling the control. In this case, the page needs to know if you add or remove a fieldset (this handles row, column, and filter axes), or add or remove a total. Listing 12.11 shows the sample's Query event procedure.

**Listing 12.11**

```
Sub pt_Query(Reason)
    ' React to event that occurs when the
    ' pt's query changes.
    If Not blnInitialized Then
        Exit Sub
    End If
    Select Case Reason
        Case c.plQueryReasonInsertFieldSet, _
          c.plQueryReasonRemoveFieldSet
            ' This happens whenever you  move
            ' a field from one axis to another,
            ' so you need to check for all the
            ' filtering/totalling/grouping options.
            HandleGroupBy
            HandleFilter
        Case c.plQueryReasonInsertTotal, _
          c.plQueryReasonRemoveTotal
            HandleTotal
    End Select
End Sub
```

In this example, you've seen how to manipulate the PivotTable control's Pivot-View object. You've seen how to add and delete row headers, filters, and totals, as well as how to modify the various aspects of the control's interface. There are many more objects, methods and properties that we couldn't cover here, but hopefully, this example has given you enough to get started. You should be able to use the Object Browser to dig deeper, if necessary.

---

**NOTE**    Why didn't we spend more time with the PivotData object? Unless you're interested in altering the workings of the PivotTable completely, or in creating a PivotTable control from scratch, you won't have much need to work with this object. The PivotView subtree of objects works with the view elements and the schema elements available as part of the view. The PivotData subtree (which we've not discussed at all in this chapter) represents the results of the most recent query that provided data for the pivot table. You might use the PivotData subtree (starting with the ActiveData object) if you need to gain access to the query result data, using the Cells, Members, and Aggregates collections.

---

# Persisting PivotTable Settings

If you allow a user to work with a PivotTable control, altering the groupings, filterings, totals, and so on, it might be nice to be able to save all the settings so that the user can retrieve them the next time the page is loaded. This turns out to be quite simple, as far as the control is concerned: the control politely provides the XMLData property that handles this issue. This read/write property allows you to both read (and store somewhere) and then write later when you want to restore the saved settings. In this section, we'll provide an example, both as an Access form (frmPTXMLData) and as a data access page (PTXMLData). Figure 12.17 shows the sample page, after it has restored a save layout.

**FIGURE 12.17**

The sample page allows you to save and restore pivot table layout settings.

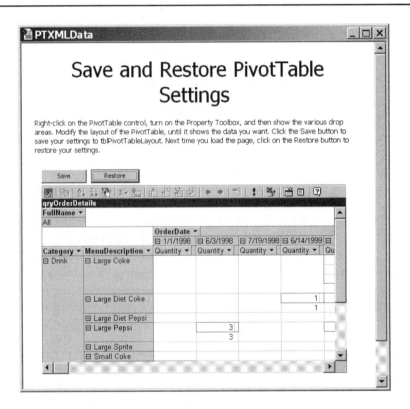

The PivotTable control's XMLData property saves (in XML format) information about the control that allows the control to render itself just the same way, in a later session. The problem isn't directly related to the PivotTable control, but rather, to the data storage. That is, where are you going to put that XML data so it's available the next time your page opens? You have a number of choices, including a cookie, a text file, a Session variable, or, as we've done in this example, in a database table. Because your data access page is reading data from a database, it makes sense that you might be able to store data back to the same database. This example saves and retrieves data from a table (tblPivotTableLayout) set up expressly for this purpose. This table contains two fields: FormName (the Primary Key, containing the name of the form or page containing the pivot table); and XMLData, containing the actual XML data that you want saved and restored.

Because the PivotTable control retrieves its display data from a Data Source control in this example, we decided to use the Data Source control as a data source for the XML save and restore operations as well. Although you could open a separate connection to the data source and use it to save and restore the layout data, there's no reason to do so. In addition, using this technique gives us a chance to provide a single, simple example that demonstrates how you can programmatically manipulate the Office Web Component's Data Source control.

> **NOTE**  In this example, the name of the PivotTable control is *pt*. You'll see this name scattered about the sample code—in each case, the name refers to the PivotTable control on the sample page.

## What You Need to Know About the Data Source Control

Among other things, the Data Source control acts as a "bucket" for recordset definitions, and provides a collection of RecordsetDef objects. Each of these objects defines a recordset, but doesn't actually return rows. You can assign each of these RecordsetDef objects a name, just as you can with any item you add to a collection. Later, when you need to open the recordset (either to return rows, or to execute some action), you use the Execute method of the Data Source control.

Because of the way the Data Source control was written, it can be used as a data source for the Office PivotTable, Office Chart, and many other ActiveX controls. In addition, using the ElementExtension object provided by the control, Access can bind native HTML controls to the Data Source control as well. This example, however, isn't concerned with the data binding capabilities of the control. Instead, here you simply need code that can set up a RecordsetDef object, and later execute it.

To create the RecordsetDef object, the window_onload event procedure calls the AddNew method of the RecordsetDefs collection of the Data Source control on the page (named MSODSC). The syntax for the Add method looks like this:

```
object.AddNew(Source, [RowsourceType], [Name])
```

where:

- *object* is the RecordsetDefs collection of the Data Source control.

- *Source* specifies the data source, just as the Source property might for an ADO recordset.

- *RowsourceType* optionally specifies the type of the new schema row source. Can be one of the dscRowsourceTypeEnum constants: dscTable (1), dscView (2), dscCommandText (3, the default value), dscProcedure (4), dscCommandFile (5).

- *Name* optionally specifies the name of the recordset definition. If you do not specify this argument, the method creates a name for you. We suggest you always specify your own, distinct name.

In the window_onload event procedure for the page, the code calls the AddNew method of MSODSC, creating a new RecordsetDef object named "LayoutInfo":

```
Sub window_onload()
    MSODSC.RecordsetDefs.AddNew _
      "SELECT * FROM tblPivotTableLayout " & _
      "WHERE FormName = '" & document.title & "'", _
      MSODSC.Constants.dscCommandText, "LayoutInfo"
End Sub
```

This RecordsetDef, when you later execute it, will return the one row from tblPivotTableLayout matching this particular page. (Because of the way we created this table, each page in your application must have a unique title. Feel free to use some other field as the primary key in tblPivotTableLayout, if this doesn't serve your needs.) For now, all the code has done is create the named RecordsetDef object, for later use. For all intents and purposes, this is similar to creating a saved QueryDef object in an Access database: it doesn't itself return rows, but when executed, can run an action or return the requested rows. In later procedures, when the page needs to read or write from tblPivotTableLayout, it will call the Execute method of this RecordsetDef to create the necessary recordset.

# Saving the XML Data

When you click the Save button on the sample page, the associated event procedure calls the adhSaveXMLData procedure, shown in Listing 12.12. This code calls the Execute method of the Data Source control, specifying the named RecordsetDef created in the window_onload event procedure. This code retrieves the row matching the title of the current page, if it exists. If there is no row (if rst.EOF is True) then the code adds a new row, and sets the Primary Key field (FormName) to be the title of the current document.

The "active ingredient" of the procedure is the line of code that takes the XMLData property of the PivotTable control, and places it into the XMLData field in the recordset. Once that's done, the code updates the recordset, and closes it.

**Listing 12.12**

```
Sub cmdSave_onClick()
    Call adhSaveXMLData(pt)
End Sub

Sub adhSaveXMLData(pt)
    ' Given a PivotTable control, save
    ' the XMLData information to tblPivotTableLayout.

    Dim rst
    Set rst = MSODSC.Execute("LayoutInfo")

    If rst.EOF Then
        rst.AddNew
        rst.Fields("FormName") = document.title
    End If

    ' Save the XMLData property.
    rst.Fields("XMLData") = pt.XMLData
    rst.Update

    rst.Close
    Set rst = Nothing
End Sub
```

## Retrieving the XML Data

Once you've saved a layout for the PivotTable control, you can retrieve it later. In this case, the example retrieves the layout information from the table where it was previously stored. To do that, the Restore button's onClick event procedure calls the adhRestoreXMLData procedure, shown in Listing 12.13.

This procedure is simpler than the adhSaveXMLData procedure, because this one only needs to retrieve the XML data if there's matching row in the recordset, and do nothing if there's not. The code calls the Execute method of the Data Source control again, specifying the RecordsetDef created in the window_onload event procedure. This recordset should contain either one row, or none. If the recordset contains a row, the code retrieves the XMLData field, and assigns it to the XMLData property of the PivotTable control. That's all there is to it!

**Listing 12.13**

```
Sub cmdRestore_onClick()
    Call adhRestoreXMLData(pt)
End Sub

Sub adhRestoreXMLData(pt)
    ' Given a PivotTable control, retrieve
    ' the XMLData information from tblPivotTableLayout.

    Dim rst

    Set rst = MSODSC.Execute("LayoutInfo")
    If Not rst.EOF Then
        pt.XMLData = rst.Fields("XMLData")
    End If

    rst.Close
    Set rst = Nothing
End Sub
```

## Try it Out!

To demonstrate the behavior discussed in this example, load the sample page, modify its layout by dragging fields to the various drop areas, and then click the

Save button. Close the page, and then reload it. Note that your changes have been lost, but not irretrievably! Click the Restore button, and after a moment of recalculation, your page should appear as you last saw it.

---

**NOTE**    If you're deploying pages on a Web server, you may not have write access to a convenient database in which to place your XML data. In that case, you might consider writing the data to a text file on the server, or to a cookie on the user's machine.

---

There's much more to the Office PivotTable component than we've been able to show you here. As you'll find, if you dig in deeper, you can control almost every aspect of this complex and useful view mechanism. We suggest that you spend time with this control—of all the Office Web Components, it's the one you're most likely to want to use, again and again.

# The Office Chart Component

The Office Chart component allows you to create customizable, programmable charts based on data from many different sources. Although this component looks as if it was based on the same charting engine as you'll find in Excel, it's actually a separate code base with similar functionality. The Office Chart component allows you to create all the 2-D charts from Excel, plus polar charts (but none of Excel's 3-D chart types). In addition, the Office Chart control allows you to create multiple charts in the same chart space, giving you the capability of overlaying charts of the same or differing types.

The Office Chart control can retrieve its data from any of these sources:

- Office Spreadsheet
- Office PivotTable
- Office Data Source control
- ADO recordsets
- Arrays containing literal values

In this section, you'll see examples binding charts to the Office Spreadsheet and PivotTable controls, as well as to an ADO recordset. In addition, one example will show how you can react to events raised by the Office Chart control as you move the mouse over the various elements of the chart.

## Creating a Simple Bound Chart

To get you started, this section will walk through the process of creating a simple chart that's bound to an Office Spreadsheet control. The goal is to end up with a page that looks like Figure 12.18. This data access page exists in the sample database as Spreadsheet-Chart.

**FIGURE 12.18**
Follow the steps to create a chart bound to an Office Spreadsheet control.

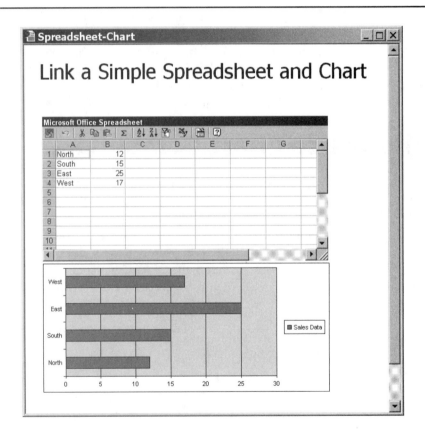

Follow these steps to create the sample page:

1. Create a new data access page, in Design view. Type in a title, if you like.

2. On the new page, insert an Office Spreadsheet control. In the spreadsheet, add values as shown in Figure 12.18.

3. Add a new Office Chart control to the page and place it underneath the existing Office Spreadsheet. When you drop the control, Access starts up the Microsoft Office Chart Wizard.

4. On the first page of the wizard, you can select the chart type and sub-type. Select Bar (the second option) and the default sub-type. Click Next to move to the next page.

5. On the second page, select the data source for the chart. In this case, your options are to choose from a Database table or query, or a Microsoft Office Spreadsheet. (You see that particular option because the other control on the page is a spreadsheet. Were you try this same experiment with a PivotTable control on the page, you'd see that option here instead.) Select the Microsoft Office Spreadsheet. The only option is to use the existing spreadsheet, so click Next to move to the next page.

6. On the third page, you tell the wizard what data you'd like to display in the chart. Note (for later use) that you must supply, basically, three sets of information: one or more *series*, each of which can contain 0 or more *values*, and a set of *categories*. Fill out the page so that it looks like Figure 12.19. When you're done, press Finish.

**FIGURE 12.19**
Set the categories, series, and values so they look like this.

7. Display the page in Page view (or, if you like, simply work with it in Design view—the controls are active either way) and change values in the spreadsheet. As you see, the controls are linked, and changes to the spreadsheet appear immediately in the chart.

## Charting Terminology

As you saw when you built a chart yourself, you must supply a number of bits of information before the chart can draw itself correctly. In Figure 12.20, we've created a simple example to demonstrate the various parts of a chart. The pivot table shows data from qryOrderDetails, with a Sum of Quantity totals field added so you can see total sales of each item, per customer. The pivot table has been filtered to only show a few customers.

> **NOTE**
>
> Figure 12.20 shows the sample page, GraphData. We'll discuss more about this example in the "Working with Chart Events" section later in the chapter. If you happen to move the mouse over the chart, you may notice some changes to the display of the chart. Don't worry: the "Working with Chart Events" section will explain what's going on.

In general, you must specify the following information in order to create a chart:

**Series**    A chart series represents a related group of data points. Each series can have a different chart type, so you can overlay series with different types. (Of course, some combinations can't work: you can't overlay a pie chart with a line chart, for example.) Generally, every data point in a series displays the same color. In Figure 12.20, each different food category represents a different series.

**Categories**    Generally, categories are groups of data points made up of one data point from each data series in the chart. Not all charts display a category axis: bar and column charts do, but x-y plots don't. In the case of an x-y plot, the data points are defined by the two coordinates, not by some single category. In Figure 12.20, each city represents a different chart category.

**Values**    Chart values are, basically, the intersection of a category and a series. In Figure 12.20, each bar represents a value. On a pie chart, each wedge generally represents both a value and a category (that is, the category provides a label for the wedge, whose value is the percentage of the whole). On an x-y plot, each point represents two values (the $x$ and $y$ values). On a high-low-close chart, each point represents three values.

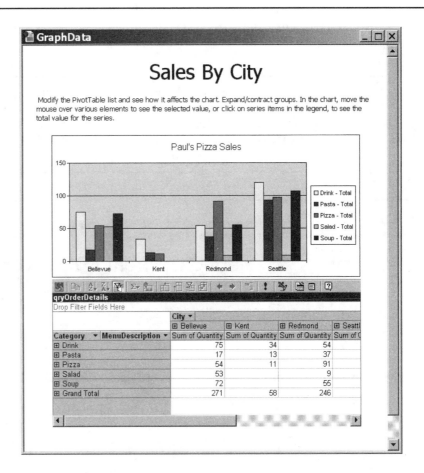

FIGURE 12.20
This simple chart, bound to a pivot table, demonstrates series, categories, and values.

**Axes**    As you might imagine, axes mean the same thing here as they did when you learned about charts in high school. In Figure 12.20, cities are on the *x* (or horizontal, or categories) axis, and values are on the *y* (or vertical, or values) axis.

## Creating and Manipulating a Chart Programmatically

To jump right in and demonstrate some of the scripting capabilities of the Office Chart control, the example in this section (the data access page named ChartFrom-Recordset) creates a pie chart based on data from a recordset. In addition, this example demonstrates how to modify layout properties of the chart: if you select the Animate the Chart checkbox, the chart will rotate, and the slices will move in and out from the center. Figure 12.21 shows the chart in mid-spin.

---

**TIP**    Throughout this example, we'll refer to the top-level chart object as the ChartSpace object. The object has this name, rather than the more obvious Chart, because the top-level object could contain multiple charts. The ChartSpace object contains a collection of WCChart objects. If you only have a single chart displayed, it's Charts(0) within the ChartSpace object's collection of charts.

---

**FIGURE 12.21**
You can create this chart programmatically, using data from a recordset.

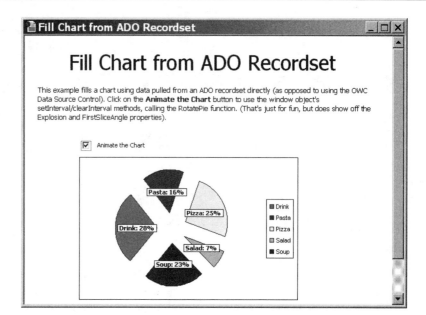

## Getting Started

The sample page creates its recordset in the window_onload event procedure, shown in Listing 12.14. In this procedure, the code first sets up a page-wide reference to the Constants property of the ChartSpace object:

```
Set c = owcChartSp.Constants
```

Then, it uses the Data Source control's ConnectionString property to open a new connection.

```
Set cnn = CreateObject("ADODB.Connection")
cnn.ConnectionString = MSODSC.ConnectionString
cnn.Open
```

Given that connection, the code can open a recordset based on the query qry-QuantityByCategory, which summarizes the quantity sold in each food category.

```
' Set up the recordset.
Set rst = CreateObject("ADODB.Recordset")
rst.Open "qryQuantityByCategory", cnn, adOpenStatic, _
 adLockReadOnly, adCmdView
```

Finally, the procedure calls the FillPieChartFromRecordset procedure (discussed in the next section) to set up and display the pie chart, passing in the control and the recordset to work with, along with the name of the field providing the categories and the field supplying the values. (In this example, owcChartSp is the name of the Office Chart control.)

```
' Fill in the pie chart.
Call FillPieChartFromRecordset( _
 owcChartSp, rst, "Category", "SumOfQuantity")
```

## Listing 12.14

```
Sub window_onload()
    Dim rst
    Dim cnn
    Dim strSQL

    Const adCmdTable = 2
    Const adOpenStatic = 3
    Const adLockReadOnly = 1

    Set c = owcChartSp.Constants

    Set cnn = CreateObject("ADODB.Connection")
    cnn.ConnectionString = MSODSC.ConnectionString
    cnn.Open
```

```
' Set up the recordset.
Set rst = CreateObject("ADODB.Recordset")
rst.Open "qryQuantityByCategory", cnn, adOpenStatic, _
  adLockReadOnly, adCmdView

' Fill in the pie chart.
Call FillPieChartFromRecordset( _
  owcChartSp, rst, "Category", "SumOfQuantity")
End Sub
```

## Creating the Chart from a Recordset

Listing 12.15 shows the procedure, FillPieChartFromRecordset, that does all the work in this example, and the following paragraphs work through all the details of this procedure. The code starts by clearing the current chartspace:

```
owcChartSp.Clear
```

Before you can display a bound chart (that is, a chart that's bound to some data source), you must set the DataSource property of the chart. You might use a Data Source control, a PivotTable control, a Spreadsheet control, or, as in this case, an ADO recordset. (In this example, owcChartSp is the name of the Office Chart control on the data access page.)

```
Set owcChartSp.DataSource = rst
```

Next, the code clears the chart space and creates a new chart within the chart space:

```
Set owcChart = owcChartSp.Charts.Add()
```

The code must tell the chart how to display its data (it's a pie chart), and, in this case, to display a legend:

```
With owcChart
    .Type = c.chChartTypePie
    .HasLegend = True
End With
```

Now comes the important code: telling the chart where to get its categories, values, and series from. In the case of a pie chart, you'll only need to specify categories and values, and if you're binding the chart to a recordset, you must supply the names of the fields to use for both these items. To do that, you call the SetData method of owcChart. The syntax for the SetData method looks like this:

```
object.SetData(Dimension, DataSourceIndex, [DataReference])
```

where:

- *object* is an expression that returns an object for which you might set data. In this case, it's a WCChart object.

- *Dimension* specifies the data dimension to be set. For a WCChart object, it can be one of twelve different values, such as chDimSeriesNames, chDimCategories, chDimValue. See online help for a complete list.

- *DataSourceIndex* specifies the index of the selected data source. In this example, the chart has only a single data source, numbered 0. If you were to fill the chart with literal data, you would use the chDataLiteral constant instead of an integer.

- *DataReference* optionally supplies a data reference as a field name, or a data reference in Excel format ("A1:C16", for example). If you're supplying data as literal values, (that is, when the DataSourceIndex property is set to chDataLiteral), you can set DataReference to a one-dimensional array or a tab-delimited string.

Given the syntax for the SetData method, you can see how the FillPieChartFromRecordset procedure uses the field names you've supplied in order to set up the chart:

```
With owcChart
    ' Hook up the two necessary data fields.
    .SetData c.chDimCategories, 0, strCategoriesField
    .SetData c.chDimValues, 0, strValuesField
End With
```

In this example, the code sets the Category field to be the "categories" field, and the SumOfQuantity field to be the "values" field. Once you've set those names, the chart can figure out how to display the data.

The remainder of the code works with properties of the data labels. To create data labels, you must first call the Add method of the DataLabelsCollection property of an item in the chart's SeriesCollection property.

**NOTE**
To be completely correct, the chart's SeriesCollection property contains a collection of WCSeries objects. Each WCSeries object has a DataLabelsCollection property. This collection contains WCDataLabels objects, each of which describes the data labels for the series. (Based on the fact that a series has a collection of WCDataLabels objects, it should be possible to create multiple data labels for a given series. We've not tried that.) The WCDataLabels object has a number of properties that the code in Listing 12.15 sets, to alter the display of the label for each pie slice.

The following code alters the data labels in these ways, setting the listed properties:

- Displays a percentage, and not the actual value of the slice (HasPercentage, HasValue)

- Displays the category name in the label (HasCategoryName).

- Sets the separator between the value and category name to be ": ", as opposed to the default "," (Separator)

- Sets the color for the interior to be white, and the border color to be black (Interior.Color, Border.Color)

- Sets the font of the label to Tahoma 8pt bold, in black (Font.Name, Font.Color, Font.Bold, Font.Size)

```
With owcChart
    ' Show a percentage, but not an absolute
    ' value. Also, show the category name.
    ' Use ":" as the separator between
    ' the category name and the percentage.
    With .SeriesCollection(0).DataLabelsCollection.Add
        .HasPercentage = True
        .HasValue = False
        .HasCategoryName = True
        .Separator = ": "

        ' Use 8pt black text on a white background,
        ' in Tahoma font.
        .Interior.Color = "white"
        .Border.Color = "black"
        With .Font
            .Name = "Tahoma"
```

```
                    .Color = "black"
                    .Bold = True
                    .Size = 8
            End With
        End With
End With
```

That's all it takes to create the chart shown in Figure 12.21.

---

⟩ **Listing 12.15**

```
Sub FillPieChartFromRecordset( _
 owcChartSp, rst, _
 strCategoriesField, _
 strValuesField)

    ' Given a chart control, pull data from the
    ' specified recordset.

    Dim owcChart

    owcChartSp.Clear

    Set owcChartSp.DataSource = rst
    Set owcChart = owcChartSp.Charts.Add()

    With owcChart
        .Type = c.chChartTypePie
        .HasLegend = True

        ' Hook up the two necessary data fields.
        .SetData c.chDimCategories, 0, strCategoriesField
        .SetData c.chDimValues, 0, strValuesField

        ' Show a percentage, but not an absolute
        ' value. Also, show the category name.
        ' Use ":" as the separator between
        ' the category name and the percentage.
        With .SeriesCollection(0).DataLabelsCollection.Add
            .HasPercentage = True
```

```
               .HasValue = False
               .HasCategoryName = True
               .Separator = ": "

               ' Use 8pt black text on a white background,
               ' in Tahoma font.
               .Interior.Color = "white"
               .Border.Color = "black"
               With .Font
                   .Name = "Tahoma"
                   .Color = "black"
                   .Bold = True
                   .Size = 8
               End With
           End With
       End With
   End Sub
```

**NOTE**   If you care to investigate, you'll find a similar example in the form frmChart-FromRecordset. The concepts are the same, but the code's written in VBA instead of in VBScript.

## Rotating the Chart

If you care to dig into it, you might find the RotatePie procedure, in the sample source code, interesting. This procedure, called every 200 milliseconds, modifies both the FirstSliceAngle property of the chart, and Explosion property of the first SeriesCollection object. The procedure uses a bit of tricky math to do its work. Each time it's called, the procedure increments the FirstSliceAngle by 20 degrees, but you can't keep incrementing this value—once it gets past 360, the chart raises an error. Therefore, the code uses the MOD operator to ensure that the value for the angle is between 0 and 359. (The MOD operator returns the remainder you get when you divide a the first operand by the second. For example, 340 MOD 360 is 340, but 360 MOD 360 is 0, and 380 MOD 360 is 20.) To handle the Explosion property (a value between 0 and 1000, indicating the percentage of the chart's radius where the tips of the slices are drawn), the code attempts to increase the property from 0 to 200, and then decrease back to 0 again, over and over. Although there are several ways to solve this problem, the code uses the Sin function, which provides values between −1 and 1, depending on its input. Given that value, the procedure multiplies the return value from the Sin function by 100, and adds the result to 100. This ends up with a value between 0 and 200, in a repeating pattern. If you're into high-school trig, have fun. Otherwise, just note that the RotatePie procedure does all the work of making those little sections move, and explode.

Another issue, in the data access page version of this example, is how you make something happen at regular intervals. (On the Access form example, we've simply added the code to the form's Timer event.) For a data access page, you can use the setInterval and clearInterval methods of the window object to specify a function to be called at regular intervals. See the window_onload event procedure in the sample page to see how it works.

## Working with Chart Events

Among the many other programmable features supplied by the Office Chart control, you're likely to find its capability for reacting to mouse events a measurable Benefit over the static nature of charts created with Microsoft Chart. As you'll see in this section, you can have a chart react to MouseOver and Click events, among others, so that your users can interact with the chart in ways that simply weren't possible in previous versions of Access.

**TIP**      Although this example uses a data access page to demonstrate the event functionality, you can react to the same events from an Access form.

Figure 12.22 shows the demonstration page, GraphData, discussed earlier in the chapter. Give it a try in Page view again, except this time, note that as you move your mouse over the bars of the chart, both the border of the "selected" bar and the title of the chart change to reflect the selection. In addition, if you click on one of the series displayed in the legend, the chart will select all the values in the series, and display the total for the food type in the chart title.

**FIGURE 12.22**

You can react to mouse movement and clicks on a chart, using event procedures.

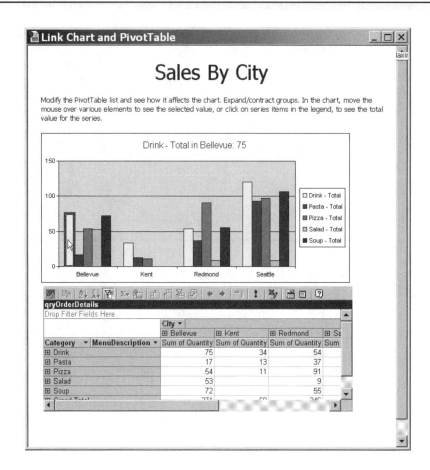

## Reacting to Events

In this example, the code for the page reacts to the MouseMove and Click events of the Office Chart object. That is, you'll find owcChart_MouseMove and owcChart_Click event procedures in the script associated with the GraphData data access page. Based on where the mouse is when the events occur, the code takes specific actions. Therefore, two questions might occur to you:

- How does the event procedure know where the mouse was when the event occurred? The code provides you with *x* and *y* coordinates of the location where the mouse was when the control raised the event. How does the control pass this information to your event procedure?

- How does the code convert coordinates into specific data points or chart elements on the screen? That is, how can you know what chart element you moved over, or clicked on, based on *x* and *y* coordinates?

The Office Chart control provides an elegant answer to the first question. If you think about how VBA handles event procedures, you'll remember that for different event procedures, VBA passes different parameters depending on the event. For example, the Form_Open and Form_Unload event procedures receive a single parameter named Cancel, the Form_KeyPress event procedure receives a single integer indicating the key that was pressed, and the Form_KeyDown event procedure receives two parameters (the keycode, and the shift state). This works fine in VBA, where the editor supplies the parameters and their types for you. When you're writing script, however, the editor can't supply this information: it's up to you to create the correct procedure signature when you write the code.

To make this simpler for you, any event procedure that requires information on input receives a single object as a parameter. This object (its data type is WCChartEventInfo, although the script code doesn't care) supplies a number of properties, only one or more apply to a given event procedure. The WCChartEventInfo object includes these properties:

- AltKey
- Button
- CtrlKey
- KeyChar
- KeyCode
- ShiftKey
- X
- Y

You would never use more than one or two of these in any given event procedure, and it's up to you to determine which one(s) are meaningful in the event you're reacting to. Using this technique makes it simple for you to write scripting code to react to the events, however. For example, both the MouseMove and Click events receive a WCChartEventInfo object as a parameter, and both make use of the X and Y properties, to indicate where the mouse was when the event occurred.

The next question is a bit tougher. That is, given an *x* and *y* coordinate within a chart, how can you tell what chart object, exactly, is underneath the mouse? To solve this problem, the Office Chart control provides the RangeFromPoint method: you supply *x* and *y* coordinates, and it returns the object underneath that coordinate.

This leads, unfortunately, to another question. The chart is made up of a number of different types of objects (values, legend entries, axes, blank space, and so on). How can you tell what type of object has been selected? To solve this, you can use the TypeName function, built into VBScript. This function returns the object type corresponding to the chart object that's under the mouse (that is, the return value from the RangeFromPoint method). In this example, the code looks for objects of type WCPoint (data points) or WCLegendEntry (legend entries). Once you know what type of object you're dealing with, your code can make intelligent choices about what to do.

---

**TIP**    For more information about the types of objects you might encounter inside a chart, use the VBA Object Browser. Search for all the objects that start with "WC". Not all of these objects can appear inside a chart, but you can be guaranteed that if an object appears inside a chart, its name starts with "WC".

---

As an example, take a look at the MouseMove event procedure for the chart, shown in Listing 12.16. This code declares an object (objSelection), and sets this object to refer to the return value from the RangeFromPoint method. As you can see, the code passes the EventInfo.x and EventInfo.y properties as parameters to RangeFromPoint, where EventInfo was the object passed as a parameter to the event procedure. If the TypeName function, passed objSelection, returns the text "WCPoint", the code knows that it's found a data point, and calls the SelectItem method (discussed in the next section) to highlight the item.

### Listing 12.16

```
Sub owcChart_MouseMove(EventInfo)
    Dim objSelection
    Set objSelection = owcChart. _
     RangeFromPoint(EventInfo.x, EventInfo.y)
    If TypeName(objSelection) = "WCPoint" Then
        Call SelectItem(objSelection)
    End if
    Set objSelection = Nothing
End Sub
```

The Click event procedure, shown in Listing 12.17, does much the same thing, but this procedure looks for legend entries: objects of type "WCLegendEntry". If that's what it finds, it sets objSelection to be the entire series collection associated with the legend entry (using the SeriesCollection property of the chart), and then calls the SelectItem method to select the entire series.

### Listing 12.17

```
Sub owcChart_Click(EventInfo)
    Dim objSelection

    Set objSelection = _
      owcChart.RangeFromPoint(eventInfo.x, eventInfo.y)
    If TypeName(objSelection) = "WCLegendEntry" Then
        Set objSelection = owcChart.Charts(0). _
          SeriesCollection(objSelection.Index)
        Call SelectItem(objSelection)
    End If
    Set objSelection = Nothing
End Sub
```

## Working with the Selection

When the code calls SelectItem (shown in its entirety in Listing 12.18), previous event procedures have either sent it a single point (with the type name "WCPoint") or an entire series (with the type name "WCSeries"). No matter which type of object SelectItem receives, its job is to reset the appearance of the last item selected so that is has a thin black border, and then make the currently selected object have a heavy red border. The code makes use of a page-level variable, ptLastSelection, which keeps track of the previously selected point (or series). The procedure starts out with this simple chunk of code:

```
If Not (ptLastSelection Is Nothing) Then
    With ptLastSelection.Border
        .Weight = 1
        .Color = "black"
    End With
End If
```

```
With objSelection.Border
    .Weight = 5
    .Color = "red"
End With
Set ptLastSelection = objSelection
```

As you may have noticed, the chart doesn't care if you're setting the border properties of a single point, or an entire series. Either way, you simply set the appropriate properties. The chart takes care of assigning the weight and color to the group of objects, if necessary.

Next comes the tricky part: as you move the mouse around, or click on the legend entry, the chart's title changes to indicate the value or series you've selected. To do this work, the code needs to be able to retrieve a value from a chart point (or add up all the values for an entire series). The chart control makes this possible, supplying the GetValue method of a WCPoint object. The syntax for GetValue looks like this:

```
object.GetValue(Dimension)
```

where:

- *object* is an expression that returns a WCPoint object.

- *Dimension* specifies the type of data to be returned for the specified point. Can be one of the enumerated values in the ChartDimensionsEnum type, such as chDimXValues, chDimYValues, chDimSeriesNames, chDimCategories. See the VBA Object Browser or online help for a complete list.

If you select a single point, the code builds up a string such as "Pizza – Total in Redmond: 91", using the series name ("Pizza"), the category name ("Redmond") and the value ("91"). If you select an entire series, the code adds up the values for all the points in the series, and creates a string such as "Soup – Total: 234". This time the code uses the series name ("Soup") and the total of the values ("234"). In each case, the procedure calls the GetValue method of the selected point (or points).

```
Select Case TypeName(objSelection)
    Case "WCPoint"
        strSeries = _
         objSelection.GetValue(c.chDimSeriesNames)
        strCategory = " in " & _
         objSelection.GetValue(c.chDimCategories)
```

```
        ' Get the single value.
        varValue = objSelection.GetValue(c.chDimValues)
    Case "WCSeries"
        strSeries = objSelection.Name
        strCategory = ""

        ' Add up all the values
        varValue = 0
        For Each pt in objSelection.Points
            varValue = varValue + _
              pt.GetValue(c.chDimValues)
        Next
    Case Else
        ' In case you add more click locations later.
End Select
```

The procedure ends by setting the Caption property of the chart's Title object to be the strings the code has created earlier in the procedure:

```
owcChart.Charts(0).Title.Caption = _
  strSeries & strCategory & ": " & CStr(varValue)
```

## Listing 12.18

```
Dim ptLastSelection

Sub SelectItem(objSelection)
    Dim varvalue
    Dim strCategory
    Dim strSeries
    Dim pt

    On Error Resume Next
    If Not (ptLastSelection Is Nothing) Then
        With ptLastSelection.Border
            .Weight = 1
            .Color = "black"
        End With
    End If
    With objSelection.Border
        .Weight = 5
        .Color = "red"
```

```
    End With
    Set ptLastSelection = objSelection

    Select Case TypeName(objSelection)
        Case "WCPoint"
            strSeries = _
             objSelection.GetValue(c.chDimSeriesNames)
            strCategory = " in " & _
             objSelection.GetValue(c.chDimCategories)

            ' Get the single value.
            varValue = objSelection.GetValue(c.chDimValues)
        Case "WCSeries"
            strSeries = objSelection.Name
            strCategory = ""

            ' Add up all the values
            varValue = 0
            For Each pt in objSelection.Points
                varValue = varValue + _
                 pt.GetValue(c.chDimValues)
            Next
        Case Else
            ' In case you add more click locations later.
    End Select
    owcChart.Charts(0).Title.Caption = _
     strSeries & strCategory & ": " & CStr(varValue)
    On Error Goto 0
End Sub
```

Take the time to dig into the mechanics demonstrated in this example. It's so easy to react to events of the Office Chart control, you'll be able to add useful interactivity to your charts, both on data access pages and on Access forms, with very little effort.

---

**TIP**    For information on creating and using the Office Chart control on a Web server, see Chapter 14.

---

# Summary

Hopefully, you've found enough information in this introduction to using and programming the Office Web Components to get you started. We've not made any attempt to be complete, nor comprehensive, in this coverage—there's simply not enough room for that. We've supplied a few examples, and shown you a good deal of code. If you want to dig deeper, you'll want to start by looking at the help files supplied with Office 2000. (Don't expect much in the way of programming help—those help files are skeletal, to be sure. But the help files covering the interactive nature of the components are more substantial.) Once you've worked through those, we suggest the book mentioned earlier in the chapter:

> *Programming Microsoft Office 2000 Web Components*
> Dave Stearns
> Microsoft Press
> ISBN: 0-7356-0794-X

This chapter's intent was to introduce you to the various Office Web Components: the Office Spreadsheet, Office PivotTable, and Office Chart controls, all derived from Excel functionality. In addition, both in this chapter and in Chapter 10, we used the Data Source control (also part of the Office Web Components) to provide data binding, and to act as a container for recordset definitions. Given the material here, and the examples provided, you have enough material to keep you busy for some time, and to get you started using these new additions to Microsoft Office.

Are the Office Web Components complete? Of course not—they're clearly a Version 1.0 product. But among all the 1.0 products we've seen come out of Microsoft, these are among the best. They work, they work quickly, they work well, and they're lightweight. If you're distributing standard Access applications, you can use them on Access forms. If you need to create server-side pages, using ASP, they work well created as COM components on the server. If you're creating Web applications where you can guarantee that your users both have Office 2000 licenses, and run Internet Explorer 5.0, the Office Web Components make a great addition to your programming arsenal.

# Using Access as a Web Client

- Understanding hyperlinks and HTML

- Using hyperlinks for intra-database navigation

- Creating a Web-search form

**A**s you've learned in the last three chapters, data access pages are a great way to analyze, review, and edit data from an Access 2000 database. Data access pages are one of the Web publishing features built into Access 2000. In the next chapter, you'll learn about additional ways to publish Access data. But publishing is not the only Web-enabled thing that Access can do—Access can also serve the Web in a *client* or *browsing* capacity. Access tables support a hyperlink datatype and forms—the regular old Access forms—also support hyperlinking. In addition, you can use the Microsoft Web Browser ActiveX control on your Access forms to add Web browsing capabilities to your Access application.

# What Are Hyperlinks?

To understand how Access stores and uses hyperlinks, you need to know a little about what they are and how they're formed. Hyperlinks allow you to navigate to other documents both on and off the Web using Universal Resource Locators (URLs). URLs support Web addresses (such as our own http://www.developershandbook .com), as well as file locations on your hard disk. Normally you activate, or *follow*, a hyperlink by pointing to and clicking on it with your mouse. When a browser application follows a link, it locates the document at the given URL and processes it. Web browsers such as Microsoft Internet Explorer and Netscape Navigator use HTML (HyperText Markup Language) to display formatted text and graphics. In addition, Office 2000 applications have special provisions for navigating to documents created by other Office apps, launching the appropriate program, and displaying the file.

## Anatomy of an Access Hyperlink

A hyperlink in Access consists of four basic parts:

**Address**   Specifies the path to an object, document, Web page, or other destination.

**Display text**   Optional text that Access displays to the user at the hyperlink location. If you don't supply display text, Access displays the address instead.

**Subaddress**   A particular location in a document specified by the address.

**Screentip**   A control tip to display when the mouse pointer hovers over the field.

Table 13.1 lists some of the types of hyperlink addresses and subaddresses Access supports. This table is not meant to be comprehensive. In addition to the protocols noted there, hyperlinks can contain references to gopher:, news:, nntp:, telnet:, and other addresses. Check the Access online help for the full details. Of course, a protocol won't work if it hasn't been properly installed on your machine. You can't send e-mail from Access, for example, if your installation doesn't already know how to send e-mail.

**TABLE 13.1:**    Types of Hyperlink Addresses and Subaddresses

| Hyperlink Type | Address | Subaddress |
| --- | --- | --- |
| Access | Path to an Access database | Name of an Access object |
| Excel | Path to an Excel workbook file | Sheet name and range |
| PowerPoint | Path to a PowerPoint presentation file | Slide number |
| Word | Path to a Word document | Name of a bookmark in the document |
| World Wide Web | URL to a Web page | An anchor on the HTML page |
| ftp file | URL to an ftp file | Not supported |
| mailto | A e-mail address to send a message | Not supported |
| Local file of registered type | Path to a file on a local machine or on a LAN | Not supported |

# Creating an Access Hyperlink, the Hard Way

Access stores hyperlinks as plain text, with each component separated from the others by pound symbols (#). The format is:

*displaytext#address#subaddress#screentip*

*displaytext* is optional, but you must specify either an *address* or a *subaddress*. If you don't include *displaytext*, Access displays the *address* (or the *subaddress*, if no address is specified). Each portion of the hyperlink can be up to 2,048 characters in length.

**TIP**  Once you enter a hyperlink into a field and tab out of the field, Access displays the displaytext portion of the hyperlink. If you attempt to select the hyperlink by clicking it with the mouse, Access follows the link. To view or edit the complete hyperlink text, tab to the control or datasheet cell containing the hyperlink with the keyboard. If you prefer to use the mouse, right-click the hyperlink with the mouse, and then click the hyperlink to dismiss the pop-up menu and view or edit the text.

Table 13.2 lists some hyperlink examples, including the text Access displays to the user.

**TABLE 13.2:** Hyperlink Examples

| Hyperlink | Description | Access Displays | Screen Tip |
|---|---|---|---|
| http:// www.microsoft.com | Link to the default HTML document at http:// www.microsoft.com | http:// www.microsoft.com | None |
| Welcome to DevelopersHandbook .com#http://www .developershandbook .com/##The Web Site for this Book! | Link to the default HTML document at http:// www.developershand-book.com | Welcome to DevelopersHandbook.com | The Web site for this Book! |
| Sales Figures#\\salesserver\dat a\sales.xls#B5 | Link to cell B5 on the Last Quarter Sales Figures worksheet in the sales.xls workbook on the salesserver server | Sales Figures | None |
| Main Menu#file://c:\My Documents\MyApp.mdb #Form frmMain* | Link to the frmMain form in C:\My Documents\MyApp.mdb | Main Menu | None |
| ##Form frmOrder#Enter Orders | Link to the frmMain form in the current database | Form frmOrder | Enter Orders |

*The file://protocol designator is optional.

# Creating an Access Hyperlink, the Easy Way

While you can enter a hyperlink manually as we've just shown, Access provides a dialog box you can use to create the hyperlink more visually. Right-click a hyperlink field and select Hyperlink ➢ Edit Hyperlink to display the Edit Hyperlink dialog box.

The Edit Hyperlink dialog box is loaded—perhaps even overloaded—with features that make it easy to create most kinds of hyperlinks (see Figure 13.1).

**FIGURE 13.1**
Entering a Web page using the Edit Hyperlink dialog box

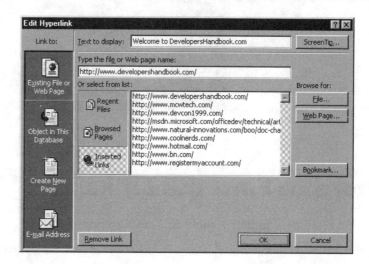

**TIP**
If you tried the Edit Hyperlink dialog box in Access 97 and thought it wasn't worth the effort, you may want to take another look at the Access 2000 Edit Hyperlink dialog box. It's much improved!

You can use the Edit Hyperlink dialog box to enter hyperlinks based on Web pages, local files, database objects, Office documents, or mail messages. You can use the icon bar along the left side of the dialog box to select the type of hyperlink you wish to create. When you select a different type of hyperlink, the dialog box changes to accommodate your choice. For example, if you select Objects in This

Database, the dialog box changes to show an inventory of the database's objects as shown in Figure 13.2.

**FIGURE 13.2**
Selecting a database object using the Edit Hyperlink dialog box

## Where to Find the Links

You'll find hyperlinks in Access in three places:

- Stored in tables in fields of the Hyperlink datatype
- Embedded in special properties of command button, label, and image controls of forms and printed reports
- In VBA code

### Field-Based Hyperlinks

You can use the Hyperlink datatype to store hyperlinks in a table just like normal text. The difference is that when Access displays the hyperlink—on a datasheet or in a bound control on a form—you can click it with your mouse to follow the link.

The tblHyperlinks1 table from the CH13.MDB sample database contains two fields: a text field, AddressType, and a hyperlink field, Hyperlink. As you tab to the Hyperlink field, you can view or edit the underlying hyperlink, as shown in Figure 13.3.

---

**TIP**    You must have the Behavior Entering Field option set to Go To Start of (or End of) Field in the Keyboard options tab to see the underlying hyperlink. If you have the Behavior Entering Field option set to Select Entire Field, you'll need to press the F2 key to see the underlying hyperlink.

---

**FIGURE 13.3**
When you tab to a hyperlink field, Access displays the full hyperlink text rather than the hyperlink's display text.

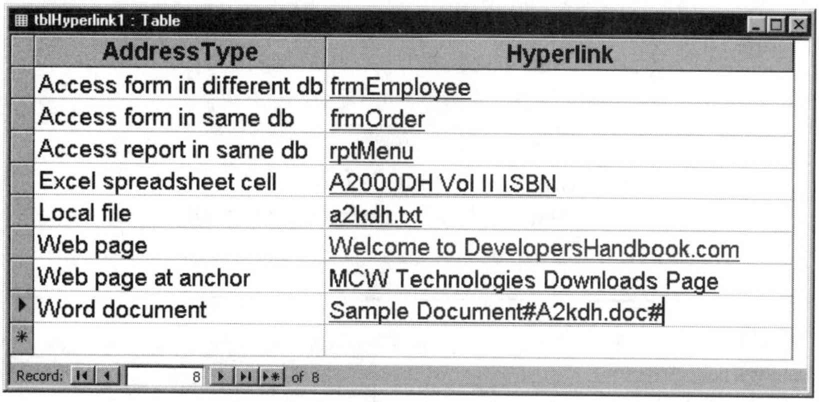

| AddressType | Hyperlink |
|---|---|
| Access form in different db | frmEmployee |
| Access form in same db | frmOrder |
| Access report in same db | rptMenu |
| Excel spreadsheet cell | A2000DH Vol II ISBN |
| Local file | a2kdh.txt |
| Web page | Welcome to DevelopersHandbook.com |
| Web page at anchor | MCW Technologies Downloads Page |
| Word document | Sample Document#A2kdh.doc# |

*tblHyperlink1 : Table*

*Record: 8 of 8*

You can enter a hyperlink into a table by entering it manually (using the syntax described earlier in this chapter) or by using the Edit Hyperlink dialog box shown in Figures 13.1 and 13.2.

---

**NOTE**    Underneath the covers, Jet stores hyperlink data internally as a memo field with a special bit mask on the field's Attributes property. Hyperlinks are really a function of how Access interprets these special memo fields. In fact, if you access the value of a hyperlink field from VBA, you get memo data with no special hyperlinking capabilities.

---

## Control-Based Hyperlinks

Access forms support hyperlinks for both bound and unbound controls.

## Using Bound Controls with Hyperlink Data

You can use text box, combo box and list box controls bound to fields with a Hyperlink datatype.

When you click a text box or combo box field containing a hyperlink, Access follows the hyperlink just like when you click a hyperlink in a datasheet. List boxes work a bit differently. When you click a hyperlink in a list box control, Access merely selects that item from the list box. To follow a hyperlink in a list box, you need to right-click the item in the list box and select Hyperlink ➤ Open from the pop-up menu.

---

**TIP**    If you've disabled the database's "Allow default shortcut menus" startup property, you won't get the pop-up menu.

---

The frmHyperlinkFields form in the CH13.MDB sample database demonstrates the use of a text box bound to the Hyperlink field of the tblHyperlink1 table (see Figure 13.4).

**FIGURE 13.4**
The second text box in frm-HyperlinkFields is bound to the Hyperlink field of tblHyperlink1, so it inherits the field's hyperlink behaviors.

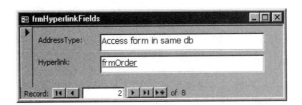

## Using Unbound Controls with Hyperlinks

You can associate hyperlinks with the following types of unbound controls:

- Labels
- Command buttons
- Image controls

For example, the frmHyperlinkControls form contains a label, a command button and an image control, all bound to the same hyperlink address (http://www.developershandbook.com). The frmHyperlinkControls form is shown in Figure 13.5.

**FIGURE 13.5**

You can associate command button, label, and image controls with hyperlinks.

You create control-based hyperlinks by entering each of the hyperlink parts into four different properties of the control:

| Hyperlink Part | Control Property |
| --- | --- |
| Address | HyperlinkAddress |
| Subaddress | HyperlinkSubAddress |
| DisplayText | Caption |
| ScreenTip | ControlTipText |

The image control doesn't have a Caption property.

As with field-based links in tables, you can use the Edit Hyperlink dialog box to help create the hyperlink. Click the Build button to the right of either the Hyperlink-Address or the HyperlinkSubAddress property on the control's property sheet to bring up this dialog box.

In addition to being able to associate hyperlinks to command buttons, labels, and image controls at design time, you can also set the HyperlinkAddress and HyperlinkSubAddress properties of labels, command buttons, and image controls at runtime to create dynamically linked controls.

The frmHyperlinkDynamic form (see Figure 13.6) demonstrates how you can create dynamically hyperlinked controls at runtime. When you choose a hyperlink from the combo box list, code attached to the combo box control's

AfterUpdate event sets the command button's HyperlinkAddress, HyperlinkSub-Address, and Caption properties:

```
Private Sub cboLinks_AfterUpdate()
    ' Dynamically set the Hyperlink properties
    ' of the cmdGo command button at runtime.
    ' Also display the address and subaddress
    ' parts of the hyperlink in textboxes.
    Dim ctlLinks As ComboBox
    Set ctlLinks = Me.cboLinks

    If Not IsNull(ctlLinks) Then
        Me.txtAddress = ctlLinks.Column(1)
        Me.cmdGo.HyperlinkAddress = ctlLinks.Column(1)

        Me.txtSubAddress = ctlLinks.Column(2)
        Me.cmdGo.HyperlinkSubAddress = ctlLinks.Column(2)

        Me.cmdGo.Caption = ctlLinks
    End If

    Set ctlLinks = Nothing
End Sub
```

**FIGURE 13.6**
The command button's hyperlink is created dynamically by code attached to the combo box's AfterUpdate event.

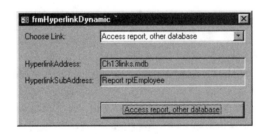

The row source for the cboLinks control is bound to the tblHyperlink2 table. The code also sets the value of the two text boxes for display purposes only.

## Hyperlinks on Reports

Hyperlinks operate differently on reports than they do on forms. Hyperlinks are operational only when the report is exported to an HTML document. You export a report using the File ➤ Export command. Hyperlinks are visible but do not function in Print Preview view.

In reports, you use unbound label or bound text box controls to store hyperlinks. When exported as HTML documents, the reports can be published on a Web server, or the files can be directly loaded into a Web browser. This latter option may be useful because it allows you to distribute HTML versions of your reports without a copy of Access on each user's desktop.

For example, Figure 13.7 shows the published rptMenu report as it looks in Internet Explorer. We've included a label in the report's header with the following HyperlinkAddress:

```
MailTo:plitwin@developershandbook.com
```

**FIGURE 13.7**
The HTML version of a simple Access report with a label containing a MailTo: hyperlink

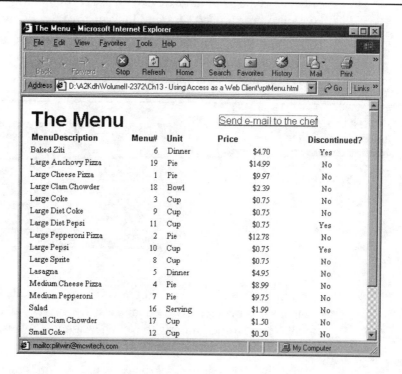

---

| **NOTE** | See Chapter 14 for more on publishing Access reports. |

# Using Hyperlinks for Intra-Database Navigation

While you might not need to link your workgroup's reporting system to the World Wide Web, you may wish to use hyperlinks to navigate within a database. Using just the subaddress portion of a hyperlink, you can jump from one database form or report to another.

By combining this technique with another a feature that was introduced back in Access 97—lightweight forms—you can create user interfaces without any code or macros. Lightweight forms are forms with no VBA class module associated with them. Since Access does not need to load VBA when opening the form, it theoretically opens the form more quickly than a form that has VBA code behind it. Hyperlinks don't need VBA and thus are great for use with lightweight forms.

The frmLWSwitchboard form, shown in Figure 13.8, is a switchboard form that lets you navigate among several forms and reports in the CH13.MDB database. This lightweight form was constructed using no VBA code or macros.

**FIGURE 13.8**
This lightweight switchboard form contains no code or macros but is fully functional.

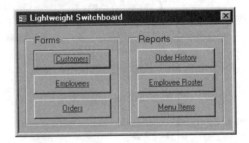

All Access forms start out as lightweight. Access adds a class module only if you try to insert VBA code. You can make a "heavyweight" form lightweight by setting its HasModule property to No in Design view. This, however, destroys any existing VBA code in the form's module.

While using hyperlinks for database navigation is nice, it does have several drawbacks. First, Access displays the text of the command button as it does other hyperlinks, using colored, underlined text. After you've followed a hyperlink, the text changes color.

You can control how Access formats hyperlinks by setting properties of the Options dialog box. You can find the hyperlink settings by clicking the Web Options button on the General tab. Unfortunately, because this is a global setting, it will affect all hyperlinks. A better solution is to change the formatting properties of the *control* (ForeColor and FontUnderline) after you've inserted the hyperlink address; these settings will override the settings that Access made when you added the hyperlink to the control. Access also changes the mouse cursor to the hyperlink hand when you move it over the control. You can't change this easily, but it's a small price to pay for simple, no-code navigation.

> **NOTE**    Lightweight forms are a nice idea in theory, but in practice it's doubtful you'd ever notice a significant improvement in performance over a similar form that used VBA code for navigation.

# Controlling Hyperlinks with VBA

As mentioned earlier in the chapter, you can set the HyperlinkAddress and HyperlinkSubAddress properties of a control using VBA code. In addition, you can manipulate hyperlinks as objects. Hyperlink-based controls—unbound label, command button, and image controls, *as well as* text box, combo box, and list box controls that have been bound to Hyperlink type fields—have an additional property, HyperLink, that doesn't appear on the controls' property sheet. You use this property to establish a reference to a Hyperlink object. The methods and properties of the Hyperlink object are summarized in Table 13.3.

**TABLE 13.3:**    Properties and Methods of the Hyperlink Object

| Type | Property/Method | Description |
| --- | --- | --- |
| Property | Address | Address portion of the hyperlink. |
| | EmailSubject | The subject for mailto hyperlinks; referring to this property for non-mailto hyperlinks causes a runtime error. |
| | ScreenTip | Screentip portion of the hyperlink. |
| | SubAddress | Subaddress portion of the hyperlink. |
| | TextToDisplay | Displaytext portion of the hyperlink. |

**TABLE 13.3:** Properties and Methods of the Hyperlink Object *(continued)*

| Type | Property/Method | Description |
|------|-----------------|-------------|
| Method | AddToFavorites | Adds the hyperlink to the favorites list. |
| | CreateNewDocument | Creates a new document associated with the hyperlink. |
| | Follow | Jumps to the hyperlink using the default browser. |

# The Hyperlink Object Properties

You can use the Hyperlink object properties at runtime to retrieve or set the various portions of a hyperlink.

The following code from frmHyperlinkObject displays the various parts of a hyperlink in a message box using the Hyperlink object properties:

```
Private Sub cmdAddress_Click()
    Dim hlk As Hyperlink
    Dim strMsg As String

    On Error Resume Next
    Set hlk = Me.txtLink.Hyperlink

    strMsg = "Address: " & hlk.Address & vbCrLf & _
      "SubAddress: " & hlk.SubAddress & vbCrLf & _
      "TextToDisplay: " & hlk.TextToDisplay & vbCrLf & _
      "ScreenTip: " & hlk.ScreenTip & vbCrLf
    strMsg = strMsg & "EMailSubject: " & hlk.EmailSubject

    MsgBox strMsg, vbInformation + vbOKOnly, _
      "Parsed Hyperlink"

    Set hlk = Nothing
End Sub
```

Be aware that the EmailSubject property won't exist unless the hyperlink is a mailto hyperlink. Thus, if you try to access this property for another type of hyperlink, you'll trigger a runtime error. This code deals with this potential issue by using an "On Error Resume Next" statement and attempting to grab the properties in two statements.

# The AddToFavorites Method

As you can probably guess from its name, the AddToFavorites method adds the hyperlink to your browser's list of favorite sites. Its syntax is quite simple because it has no parameters:

```
hyperlink.AddToFavorites
```

For example, to add the hyperlink stored in the txtLink text box control to your browser's favorites list, you might use the following code:

```
Me.txtLink.Hyperlink.AddToFavorites
```

# The Follow and FollowHyperlink Methods

The Follow method links directly to a specified hyperlink. It takes several arguments, as shown here:

```
hyperlink.Follow [newwindow] [, addhistory] [, extrainfo]_
[, method] [, headerInfo]
```

The arguments are described in Table 13.4.

**TABLE 13.4:**   Arguments of the Follow Method

| Argument | Description | Default Value |
| --- | --- | --- |
| newwindow | Boolean value that, when set to True, opens the document in a new window. | False |
| addhistory | Boolean value that, when set to True, adds the hyperlink to the History folder. | True |
| extrainfo | String or byte array that specifies additional information about the hyperlink. You can use this argument to specify a search parameter for a CGI, IDC, or ASP file. | Null |
| method | Integer that specifies the format of the extrainfo argument. Can be msoMethodGet, for a string argument that is appended to the URL (it appears at the end of the URL with a question mark separating the string from the rest of the URL), or msoMethodPost, for a string or byte array that is posted to the page. | Null if extrainfo is null; msoMethodGet for non-null extrainfo values |
| headerInfo | String that specifies additional http header text that is passed to the browser. | Zero-length string |

The FollowHyperlink method of the Application object is very similar to the Follow method of the Hyperlink object. With the FollowHyperlink method, however, you don't need to establish a reference to a Hyperlink object. Instead you can use FollowHyperlink to jump to any arbitrary address. Its syntax is shown here:

```
[Application.]FollowHyperlink address [, subaddress]_
[, newwindow] [, addhistory] [, extrainfo] [, method]_
[, headerInfo]
```

where *address* and *subaddress* are the address and subaddress parts of the hyperlink. The rest of the arguments are the same as for the Follow method.

## A Simple Example

The frmHyperlinkObject form in the chapter database demonstrates the use of the Follow method (and some of the other properties and methods) of the Hyperlink object. This form is shown in Figure 13.9. When a user clicks the Follow Hyperlink button on frmHyperlinkObject, the following code is executed:

```
Private Sub cmdFollow_Click()
    Me!txtLink.Hyperlink.Follow
End Sub
```

**FIGURE 13.9**
The frmHyperlinkObject
form demonstrates various
properties and methods of
the Hyperlink object.

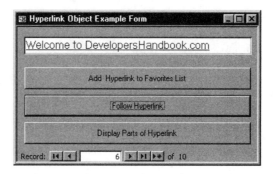

## Creating a Web Search Form Using the ExtraInfo and Method Parameters

The frmWebSearch form in the sample database illustrates how you can use the extrainfo and method parameters of the FollowHyperlink method of the Application object to pass search parameters to a Web page. This form lets you enter a string to search for on the Web using one of three popular search engine sites: Alta Vista, Yahoo, or Excite (see Figure 13.10). If you enter a search string like that shown in Figure 13.10, and then click the Perform Search button, the Follow-Hyperlink method opens your default browser and passes it the hyperlink address and extrainfo arguments, in this case displaying the results of the search, as shown in Figure 13.11.

**FIGURE 13.10**
Performing a search on the entered search string.

**FIGURE 13.11**
Result of the search specified in Figure 13.10.

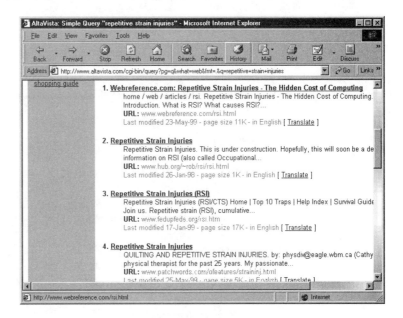

The code attached to the Click event of the cmdSearch button is shown in Listing 13.1. The subroutine begins by replacing spaces in the search string with a plus sign (+) using the VBA Replace function. The cmdSearch_Click subroutine then uses the FollowHyperlink method of the Application object, passing it the address of the selected Web search engine. The extrainfo parameter is formatted in the correct querystring syntax for the particular search engine. This varies from a simple "p=*searchstring*" for the Yahoo engine to more complex strings for the AltaVista and Excite sites. (We determined the correct querystrings by performing searches using our browser and observing the address passed to the search page.) In addition, the method argument is set to "msoMethodGet."

⤵ **Listing 13.1**

```
Private Sub cmdSearch_Click()

    ' Search for a string using one of
    ' three search web sites.

    Dim varSearch As Variant

    Const adhcSiteAltaVista = 1
    Const adhcSiteYahoo = 2
    Const adhcSiteExcite = 3

    varSearch = Replace(Me!txtSearch, " ", "+")

    Select Case Me.optSite
    Case adhcSiteAltaVista
        Application.FollowHyperlink _
         Address:="http://altavista.digital.com/" & _
          "cgi-bin/query", _
         ExtraInfo:="pg=q&what=Web&fmt=.&q=" & _
         varSearch, Method:=msoMethodGet, _
         AddHistory:=True
    Case adhcSiteYahoo
        Application.FollowHyperlink _
         Address:="http://search.yahoo.com/bin/search", _
         ExtraInfo:="p=" & varSearch, _
         Method:=msoMethodGet, _
         AddHistory:=True
    Case adhcSiteExcite
        Application.FollowHyperlink _
         Address:="http://excite.com/search.gw", _
```

```
            ExtraInfo:="search=" & varSearch & _
            "&collection=Web&searchButton.x=11&" & _
            "searchButton.y=8", _
            Method:=msoMethodGet, _
            AddHistory:=True
    End Select
End Sub
```

You can use the extrainfo argument, with the method argument set to mso-MethodGet, to pass information via the querystring portion of the URL to a CGI, IDC, or ASP page. You can also use the extrainfo argument, with the method argument set to msoMethodPut, to pass information via a posted form to a CGI, IDC, or ASP page.

# The CreateNewDocument Method

The Hyperlink object's CreateNewDocument method creates a new document from a hyperlink. Here's its syntax:

```
hyperlink.CreateNewDocument filename, editnow, overwrite
```

where:

- *filename* is the path and filename of the document you wish to create (can be .DOC, .HTM, .HTML, .ASP, .XLS, .RTF, .TXT, among others; defaults to HTML format)

- *editnow* is True if you wish to edit the document or False if you do not

- *overwrite* is True if it's okay to overwrite an existing file or False if it's not okay

The following code from frmCreateNewDoc form demonstrates the use of the CreateNewDocument method:

```
Private Sub cmdCreateNewDoc_Click()
    Me.txtLink.Hyperlink.CreateNewDocument _
        Me.txtLink.Value, Me.chkEdit.Value, True
    MsgBox Me.txtLink.Value & " created.", _
        vbOKOnly + vbInformation, Me.Name
End Sub
```

# The HyperlinkPart Method

The HyperlinkPart method of the Application object accepts a complete hyperlink and returns a specified part of it, such as the display text or subaddress. Its syntax is shown here:

```
strReturn = HyperlinkPart(hyperlink [, part])
```

*part* can be any of the following constants:

| | |
|---|---|
| acAddress | The address portion of hyperlink |
| acDisplayText | The displaytext portion of the hyperlink |
| acDisplayedValue | The value displayed by Access for the hyperlink; the default |
| acFullAddress | The address and subaddress portions of the hyperlink, delimited by "#" |
| acScreenTip | The screentip portion of the hyperlink |
| acSubAddress | The subaddress portion of the hyperlink |

For example, the LinkToSite subroutine shown in Listing 13.2 (from the basHyperlink module of CH13.MDB) searches for a Web site in a table of favorite sites and then links to the Web site.

**Listing 13.2**

```
Sub adhLinkToSite(strSite As String)
    ' Link to a web site

    Dim rst As ADODB.Recordset
    Dim strAddress As String
    Dim strSubAddress As String
    Dim varLink As Variant

    ' Find record in database
    Set rst = New ADODB.Recordset
    rst.Open _
     "SELECT Hyperlink FROM tblWebJumps WHERE " & _
     "SiteName = '" & strSite & "'", _
```

```
            CurrentProject.Connection, _
            adOpenForwardOnly, adLockReadOnly, adCmdText

        ' If record was found, link to site
        If Not rst.EOF Then
            varLink = rst("Hyperlink")
            strAddress = HyperlinkPart(varLink, acAddress)
            strSubAddress = HyperlinkPart(varLink, acSubAddress)

            Debug.Print "Site found...linking to " & _
             IIf(strSubAddress = "", "", _
             strSubAddress & " at ") & strAddress

            FollowHyperlink strAddress, strSubAddress
        Else
            Debug.Print "Site not found."
        End If

        rst.Close
        Set rst = Nothing
    End Sub
```

LinkToSite attempts to locate the record in the tblWebJumps table with a Site-Name equal to the passed-in strSite argument. If it finds a match, it uses Hyperlink-Part to parse the address and subaddress portions of the address stored in the Hyperlink field and then uses the FollowHyperlink method to jump to that hyperlink. For example, if you entered the following in the Debug window using the CH13.MDB sample database, the http://www.fmsinc.com page would appear in your browser:

```
    Call adhLinkToSite("FMS")
```

# Using the Microsoft Web Browser Control

When you click a Web-based hyperlink or execute code that employs the Follow or FollowHyperlink method, Access starts up your default Web browser and passes it the necessary information to display the desired Web page. This works well in many situations, but sometimes it would be nice if you could browse Web pages in place on a form. You can accomplish this by using the Microsoft Web

Browser Control (WebBrowser). The Microsoft control is automatically installed when you install Internet Explorer 3 (or later) on your machine.

Some of the more useful properties, methods, and events of the Web Browser control are summarized in Table 13.5.

**TABLE 13.5:** Selected Properties, Methods, and Events of the Microsoft Web Browser Control (the WebBrowser Object)

| Type | Property/Method | Description |
| --- | --- | --- |
| Property | Application | Object variable pointing to the application that contains the WebBrowser object |
| | Busy | Boolean value specifying whether the WebBrowser control is engaged in a navigation or downloading operation |
| | Container | Object variable pointing to the container of the WebBrowser control |
| | Document | Object variable pointing to the active document, if any |
| | Height | Returns or sets the height, in pixels, of the frame window that contains the control |
| | Left | Returns or sets the distance between the left edge of the control's container and the left edge of the control in the coordinate system of the container |
| | LocationName | Returns the name of the currently displayed resource—either the title of the Web page or, if the browser is displaying a folder or file, the UNC path |
| | LocationURL | Same as LocationName except that for Web pages, LocationURL returns the URL address of the page |
| | Parent | Object variable pointing to the form that contains the control |
| | Top | Returns or sets the distance between the top edge of the control's container and the top edge of the control in the coordinate system of the container |
| | TopLevelContainer | Boolean value indicating whether the browser object is a top-level container |
| | Type | String representing the type of the contained document object |
| | Width | Returns or sets the width, in pixels, of the frame window that contains the control |

**TABLE 13.5:** Selected Properties, Methods, and Events of the Microsoft Web Browser Control (the WebBrowser Object) *(continued)*

| Type | Property/Method | Description |
|------|-----------------|-------------|
| Method | GoBack | Navigates backward one item in the history list |
| | GoForward | Navigates forward one item in the history list |
| | GoHome | Navigates to the home page as specified in the Internet Explorer Options dialog box |
| | GoSearch | Navigates to the search page as specified in the Internet Explorer Options dialog box |
| | Navigate | Jumps to a new URL; takes one required parameter, URL, and four optional parameters: Flags, TargetFrameName, PostData, and Headers; Flags can be one or more of: navOpenInNewWindow (1), navNoHistory (2), navNoReadFromCache (4), and navNoWriteToCache (8) |
| | Refresh | Reloads the currently displayed page |
| | Refresh2 | Reloads the currently displayed page; takes one parameter, Level, which can be REFRESH_NORMAL (1), REFRESH_IFEXPIRED (2), or REFRESH_COMPLETELY (3) |
| | Stop | Stops any pending navigate or download operations |
| Events | BeforeNavigate2 | Triggered immediately prior to navigation to a new URL; passes several parameters to event procedure, including URL and Cancel |
| | NavigateComplete2 | Triggered when navigation is complete; passes several parameters to event procedure, including URL |
| | DownloadBegin | Triggered immediately prior to content being downloaded |
| | DownloadComplete | Triggered when the download operation is complete |
| | ProgressChange | Triggered repeatedly during download; you can use this event to update a progress meter during download of a document; passes the Progress and ProgressMax parameters to event procedure |

The CH13.MDB sample database contains an example of using the WebBrowser control in a form named frmWebBrowser (see Figure 13.12). This Access-based Web browser form, complete with search capabilities, was created with surprisingly little code. The code behind frmWebBrowser is shown in Listing 13.3.

**FIGURE 13.12**
You can use the Microsoft Web browser control to create a Web browser embedded in an Access form.

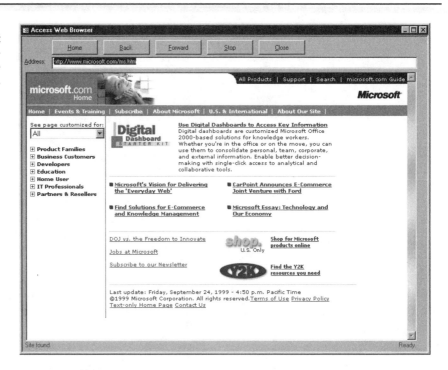

## Listing 13.3

```
Private Sub cmdBack_Click()
    On Error Resume Next
    Me.ocxWeb.GoBack
End Sub

Private Sub cmdClose_Click()
    DoCmd.Close
End Sub

Private Sub cmdForward_Click()
    On Error Resume Next
    Me.ocxWeb.GoForward
End Sub
```

```
Private Sub cmdHome_Click()
    On Error Resume Next
    Me.ocxWeb.GoHome
End Sub

Private Sub cmdStop_Click()
    Me.ocxWeb.Stop
    Me.lblStatusNav.Caption = ""
    Me.lblStatusDL.Caption = "Download aborted."
End Sub

Private Sub ocxWeb_BeforeNavigate2(ByVal pDisp As Object, _
 URL As Variant, Flags As Variant, _
 TargetFrameName As Variant, _
 PostData As Variant, Headers As Variant, Cancel As Boolean)
    Me.lblStatusNav.Caption = "Navigating to " & URL & "..."
    Me.txtSearch = URL
End Sub

Private Sub ocxWeb_DownloadBegin()
    Me.lblStatusDL.Caption = "Downloading data..."
End Sub

Private Sub ocxWeb_DownloadComplete()
    Me.lblStatusDL.Caption = "Ready."
End Sub

Private Sub ocxWeb_NavigateComplete2( _
 ByVal pDisp As Object, URL As Variant)
    Me.lblStatusNav.Caption = "Site found."
    Me.txtSearch = URL
End Sub

Private Sub txtSearch_AfterUpdate()
    ' Navigate to a URL
    Me.ocxWeb.Navigate Me.txtSearch
End Sub
```

| TIP | Looking for the Web Browser control help file? So are we. While Office 97 shipped with a help file for the IE 3 control, we haven't been able to locate the help file for the IE 5 control. If you have a copy of your Office 97 CD, you can find the Office 97 version of the Web Browser control help file at \Valupack\Access\Webhelp\Iexplore.hlp. |
|---|---|

# Summary

Access 2000 has a number of features that make it useful as a Web client. We've covered most of these, including:

- Understanding hyperlinks
- Creating hyperlink fields
- Creating hyperlink controls on forms
- Creating hyperlinks on reports
- Programmatically manipulating hyperlinks
- Creating lightweight forms
- Using hyperlinks for intra-database navigation
- Using the Web Browser control

# Publishing Access Data on the Web

- Using the Export dialog box to publish HTML and Active Server Pages (ASP) Web pages

- Building dynamic, data-driven ASP pages from scratch

- Using the Office Web Components on ASP pages to create charts on the fly

**A**s mentioned in Chapter 10, data access pages have a number of limitations that may make them unsuitable for data publishing. The limitations of data access pages include: licensing issues—users must own a copy of Microsoft Office; compatibility issues—users must be running Internet Explorer 5 or later; and flexibility issues—sometimes you want to publish data that doesn't look like a data access page.

It's not well known, but you *can* publish Access 2000 data without using data access pages. This chapter starts by exploring the built-in publishing capabilities of Access. But we don't stop there. We also look at how to hand craft Active Server Pages (ASP) using the VBScript language and ADO. Unlike data access pages, however, the pages you'll learn to build in this chapter work with virtually any browser because all of the scripting code runs on the Web server.

# Publishing Access Data Using the Export Dialog Box

Access 97 included a wizard, the Publish to the Web Wizard, that you could use to create Web documents from one or more Access objects. The Publish to the Web Wizard is noticeably absent from Access 2000, a casualty of the move to data access pages. While the wizard is gone, however, much of its underpinnings are still there in Access 2000.

## What's Wrong with Data Access Pages?

Data access pages aren't always the right tool for the job. They require—on the client machine—Internet Explorer 5, a license for Microsoft Office, and a copy of the Jet engine (unless you're accessing SQL Server data). That's a pretty hefty requirement for the client.

## Selecting a Publishing Format

The Export dialog box supports the publishing of tables, queries, reports, and the datasheets behind forms for both Access databases and projects. For Access projects, the Export dialog box additionally supports the publishing of SQL Server views and stored procedures. You can publish objects to one of three different formats: Hypertext Markup Language (HTML), Internet Database Connector (IDC), or Active Server Pages (ASP).

## HTML Format

When you publish an object to the HTML format, Access takes a snapshot of the data and creates an HTML page containing a table that looks similar to an Access datasheet. The data is saved as text to a file with the .HTML extension.

The HTML format is ubiquitous, supported by all Web browsers and servers on dozens of different platforms.

## IDC Format

When you publish an object to the IDC format (also referred to as the IDC/HTX format), Access generates a SQL statement to represent the data. When you use this format, you must supply an ODBC data source name (DSN) that is used at runtime to connect the Web page back to the database. Access saves the SQL statement and DSN to an IDC file. At the same time, Access generates an HTML Extension (HTX) file that contains a template of the formatted output. At runtime, the Web server runs the query and generates an HTML document from the IDC and HTX files that it sends back to the Web browser.

The IDC format is supported by Microsoft and compatible Web servers. Because all the processing is performed on the Web server, the generated pages work with any Web browser.

## ASP Format

Like the IDC format, when you publish an object to the ASP format, Access generates a SQL statement to represent the data. Also like the IDC format, you must supply an ODBC data source name (DSN) that is used at runtime to connect the Web page back to the database. Access saves both the SQL statement and formatting information to an ASP file using VBScript scripting code. The data access portion of the ASP code uses ADO to access the data. At runtime, the Web server runs the ASP code and generates an HTML document that it sends back to the Web browser.

The ASP format is supported by Microsoft and compatible Web servers. Because the ASP code is executed on the Web server, the generated pages work with any Web browser.

### Contrasting the Formats

These three Web publishing formats are contrasted in Table 14.1.

**TABLE 14.1:** The Web Publishing Formats Supported by the Export Dialog Box

| Format | Advantages | Disadvantages |
| --- | --- | --- |
| HTML | Simple, works with any Web server and any Web client. Can be used to retain a permanent record. | Produces static, unlinked files. You need to republish to update. |
| IDC | Dynamically linked to the database. Works with any Web browser. | Requires a Microsoft or compatible Web server. Limited in functionality; no scripting language support. |
| ASP | Dynamically linked to the database. Works with any Web browser. Employs the familiar VBScript language and ADO object model. Can be extended by editing the scripting code. | Requires a Microsoft or compatible Web server. |

**NOTE**   The functionality of the older IDC format has been supplanted by the newer and more powerful ASP format. Because of this, we recommend using the ASP format instead of the IDC format for the publication of dynamic pages. We won't discuss the IDC format any further in this chapter.

## Publishing an Object

To publish an object, select the object in the database container window and choose File ➢ Export. Access displays the Export dialog box as shown in Figure 14.1.

The Export dialog box allows you to export an object to a wide variety of formats, most of which are unrelated to Web publishing. To select one of the Web formats, use the Save as Type drop-down control and select HTML Documents

(*.html; *.htm) for HTML, Microsoft IIS 1-2 (*.htm; *.idc) for IDC, or Microsoft Active Server Pages (*.asp) for ASP format.

**FIGURE 14.1**
The Export dialog box

## Publishing HTML Pages

When publishing from an Access database, you can publish tables, queries, forms, and reports to the HTML format. From an Access project, you can publish tables, views, stored procedures, forms, and reports. When you publish forms, Access publishes the underlying datasheet associated with the form, not the formatted form. For reports, however, Access publishes a reasonable facsimile of the formatted report.

---

**TIP**    If you plan on publishing SQL Server data, you might also want to take a look at the SQL Server Web Assistant. This wizard that ships with SQL Server—but not MSDE—generates HTML pages from SQL Server tables, stored procedures, or SQL statements.

---

When you select the HTML format from the Export dialog box and uncheck the Save Formatted checkbox, Access creates an HTML page without any further questions. For example, if you publish the tblCustomer table from the CH14.MDB database, you'll end up with a fairly plain Web page that looks like the one shown in Figure 14.2. Notice the lack of any headings and the less-than-pleasing way that Nulls are displayed (see the last two columns).

**FIGURE 14.2**

Exporting tblCustomer without formatting produced this page.

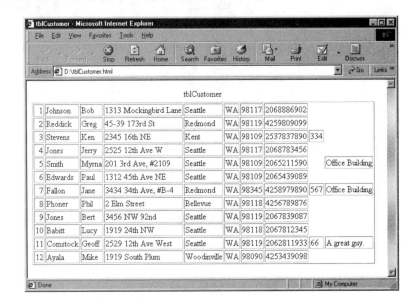

If you check the Save Formatted checkbox, Access prompts you for the name of an HTML template file. Templates are discussed later in the chapter in the "Using Templates" section. You don't have to use a template to produce a formatted page, however. Delete the name of a template file if one is displayed and click OK to produce a formatted page without using a template. If you publish the tblCustomer table from CH14.MDB, you should get a page that looks like the one shown in Figure 14.3. Contrast this page with the unformatted page shown earlier in Figure 14.2.

**TIP**   If you check the AutoStart checkbox, Access loads the formatted page into Internet Explorer as soon as it's finished creating it.

When publishing a table, Access attempts to mimic the colors and special formatting, if any, you've used when formatting the table's datasheet. Thus, if you've customized the properties of the datasheet to display blue text on a green background, Access uses the same colors when creating the HTML page.

Publishing a query, view, stored procedure, or form to the HTML format works the same way as publishing a table.

**FIGURE 14.3**
Exporting tblCustomer with formatting but without any template produced this page.

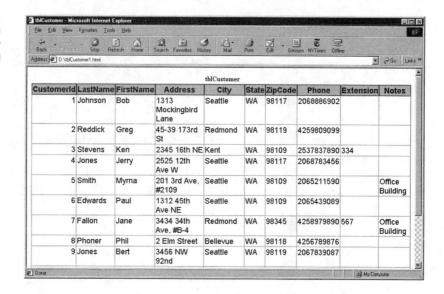

---

**NOTE**   When you publish a form to the HTML format, Access creates a Web page that looks like the datasheet associated with the form. The generated page will not look like the form in Form view.

---

## Publishing Reports

When you publish a report, Access attempts to create a Web page that looks similar to the printed report. As Access creates the published Web page, it positions textboxes and labels on the Web page to mimic the look of the report. In addition, Access attempts to format textboxes and labels with the same justification, alignment, font, font size, font color, and font style used on the report. Unfortunately, when publishing reports to HTML, Access is unable to publish the background colors of sections or controls, nor does it publish line, rectangle, image, object frame, graph, or custom controls. Thus, the resulting Web page may or may not suit your needs.

For example, the rptMenu report is shown as it looks in Preview view of Access in Figure 14.4. The same page is shown after exporting it to the HTML format in Figure 14.5.

**FIGURE 14.4**
The original Access rptMenu report

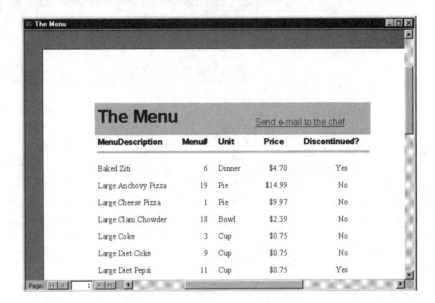

**FIGURE 14.5**
The HTML version of the rptMenu report

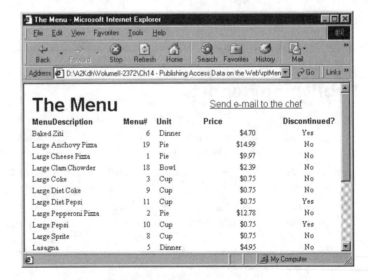

For reports that span multiple pages, Access generates an HTML page for each page of the report and links them altogether using hyperlinks at the bottom of each page.

---

**TIP**     You can use a use a template file to control the look of the published reports. Templates are discussed in the "Using Templates" section later in the chapter.

---

## Publishing ASP Pages

When you publish a table, query, view, or form to the ASP format, Access creates a formatted Web page that looks much like the formatted Web pages produced by the HTML format. The difference with the ASP format is that the generated Web page is dynamically linked back to the database, so that it reflects the state of the database at the time the page is *viewed*. This is in marked contrast to an object published to the HTML format that represents a static snapshot of the recordset at the time the page was *published*.

---

**WARNING**     At the time we went to press, the Access 2000 Export dialog box had trouble publishing parameter queries and stored procedures. When you publish a parameter query from an Access database, Access creates a SQL statement with a syntax error. Also, when you publish a stored procedure—with or without parameters—from an Access project, Access again creates a SQL statement that doesn't work. It's possible that Microsoft will fix these bugs in a future service pack release of Access.

---

When you specify Microsoft Active Server Pages (*.asp) in the Save as Type drop-down menu of the Export dialog box, Access displays the Microsoft Active Server Pages Output Options dialog box, as shown in Figure 14.6.

When publishing an ASP page, you'll need to supply an ODBC data source name (DSN) in the Data Source Information section of the Microsoft Active Server Pages Output Options dialog box. The DSN doesn't have to exist at this time, but you'll need to create it before using the published page. The DSN will be used at runtime to connect back to the database.

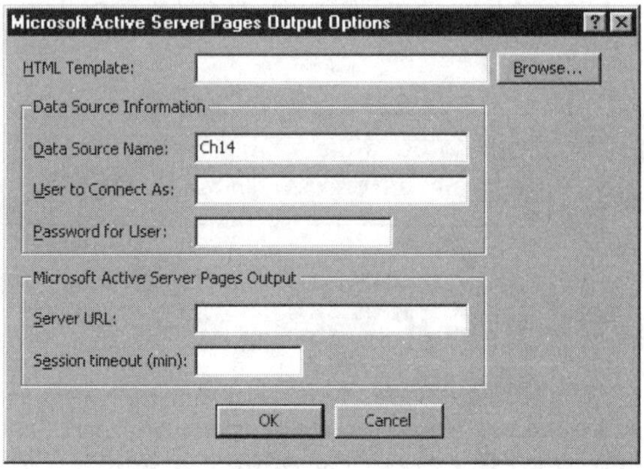

**FIGURE 14.6**
You use this dialog box to
link the published ASP page
back to the database.

**FIGURE 14.6**
You use this dialog box to
link the published ASP page
back to the database.

You can leave the User to Connect As and Password for User fields blank, unless the database is secured. If you're publishing SQL Server data, you need to enter the SQL Server username and password here.

The generated ASP page caches ADO objects using the ASP Session object. By default, these objects are maintained for 20 minutes, but you can shorten this time by entering a value into the Session Timeout field. See the discussion of the ASP Session object later in the chapter for more details. There's no need to enter any information into the Server URL field. (This field was sometimes necessary when publishing forms with embedded subforms in Access 97.)

**NOTE**    As when publishing to the HTML format, you can optionally include the name of a template file to be used in formatting the resulting Web page.

## What about Publishing Editable Forms?

The Access 97 Publish to the Web Wizard (and the Access 97 Save As dialog box) included the capability to publish editable forms to the ASP format. This capability has been removed from Access 2000, presumably because the functionality is replaced by data access pages and required the Web browser to host the obsolete HTML Layout ActiveX control.

## Configuring the Web Server for ASP

Unlike pure HTML pages and data access pages, ASP pages require Web server processing. Thus, you must configure a Web server before you can view an ASP page in your browser. If you've already set up your Web server to host ASP pages, you can just copy the published pages to an existing Web server folder. If not, you'll have to create and configure a Web server folder to host your pages.

To configure your Web server to host ASP pages, follow these steps:

1. Decide where you'd like to place the ASP pages. If you want to host your pages in the Web server's root folder, skip ahead to Step 2. Otherwise, create a new folder below the Web server's root publishing directory using Windows Explorer. For example, if you want to use a folder named AccessPages and your root Web folder path is C:\inetpub\wwwroot, you'd create a folder with the path C:\inetpub\wwwroot\AccessPages.

2. Start the Personal Web Manager program and click the Advanced icon (see Figure 14.7).

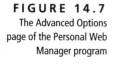

**FIGURE 14.7**
The Advanced Options page of the Personal Web Manager program

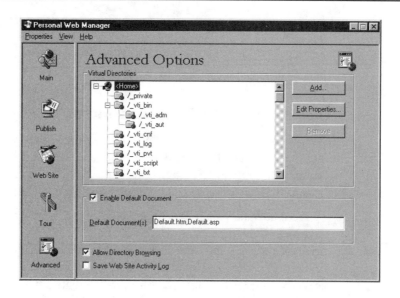

3. If you're using the root Web folder, select the <Home> folder and click Edit Properties to edit the properties of the home (root) directory. Make sure the

Scripts checkbox is checked. If you created a new folder in Step 1, then select the <Home> folder and click the Add button instead. Browse to the folder you created in Step 1, assign the folder an alias name (usually the same name as the folder without its path), and check both the Read and the Scripts checkboxes (see Figure 14.8). Click OK to dismiss the Add/Edit Directory dialog box and close the Personal Web Manager program window.

**NOTE**    These steps shown here assume you are using Microsoft Personal Web Server running on Windows 95/98 or Windows NT Workstation. The exact steps you follow will depend on the particular Web server you use.

**FIGURE 14.8**
Creating a new Web directory using Personal Web Manager

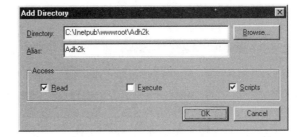

## Creating the ODBC Data Source

When you export an Access object to the ASP format, you must specify a data source name (DSN) of an ODBC data source. The Web server uses the DSN at runtime to link the ASP page back to the database that contains the data. This means that you need to create the DSN on the Web server machine.

To create a new DSN, start the control panel ODBC applet on the Web server machine. Click the System DSN tab of the ODBC Data Source Administrator dialog box and click the Add button, as shown in Figure 14.9, to create a new system data source. If the published data comes from an Access database, select Microsoft Access Driver and follow the prompts to create a new Access data source. If the published data comes from a SQL Server database, select the SQL Server driver instead and follow the prompts to create a new SQL Server data source.

**FIGURE 14.9**

The System DSN tab of the
ODBC Data Source Admin-
istrator dialog box

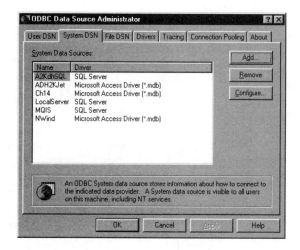

## Viewing ASP Pages

Once you've configured the Web server, set up the ODBC system DSN on the Web
server, and copied the ASP files to the Web server folder, you're ready to view
your ASP page using your Web browser. Start your browser and enter a URL into
the address box of the browser using the following syntax:

```
http:///server_name/folder_name/page_name
```

where:

- *server_name* is the name of the Web server machine or domain hosting your
  Web site.

- *folder_name* is the name of the virtual Web folder hosting your pages. You
  can omit "/folder_name" if the ASP pages are located in the root Web folder
  (wwwroot).

- *page_name* is the name of the ASP page, complete with extension.

For example, if you published tblMenu from the sample database to the tblMenu
.asp file in the A2kdh virtual Web folder of a Web server named gorilla, you'd
enter the following URL:

```
http://gorilla/Adh2k/tblMenu.asp
```

Figure 14.10 shows the ASP version of the published tblMenu table as seen in Internet Explorer 5.0.

**FIGURE 14.10**

The tblMenu.asp page

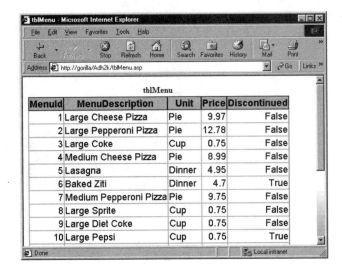

## Using Templates

You can use a template to help give your published Web pages a consistent look. A template file is nothing more than an HTML page with tokens that represent where you'd like Access to place various parts of the published page.

The *tokens* are HTML comments that Microsoft has defined to represent elements of the generated page. The Access template tokens are detailed in Table 14.2.

**TABLE 14.2:** Access Template Tokens

| Token | Access Replaces Token With |
| --- | --- |
| <!--AccessTemplate_Title--> | Name of the exported object |
| <!--AccessTemplate_Body--> | The details rows |
| <!--AccessTemplate_FirstPage--> | A hyperlink to the first page of output* |
| <!--AccessTemplate_PreviousPage--> | A hyperlink to the prior page of output* |
| <!--AccessTemplate_NextPage--> | A hyperlink to the next page of output* |

*Useful only for reports.

**TABLE 14.2:**   Access Template Tokens *(continued)*

| Token | Access Replaces Token With |
|---|---|
| <!- -AccessTemplate_LastPage- -> | A hyperlink to the last page of output* |
| <!- -AccessTemplate_PageNumber- -> | Current page number* |

*Useful only for reports.

The last five tokens in Table 14.2 make sense only when you've published a report that spans more than one page. Thus, you may wish to create two versions of your template: one version for reports that includes the pagination tokens and one version for all other pages that doesn't include these tokens.

Here's a sample template named A2KDHTempateNav.htm that demonstrates the use of the Access template tokens for publishing reports:

```
<HTML>
<HEAD>
<TITLE><!--AccessTemplate_Title--></TITLE>
</HEAD>
<BODY bgColor="#87ceeb">
<BR CLEAR="all">
<!--AccessTemplate_Body-->
<P>
<TABLE>
<TR>
<TD><A HREF="<!--AccessTemplate_FirstPage-->">First
   Page</A><TD>
<TD><A HREF="<!--AccessTemplate_PreviousPage-->">Prev
   Page</A><TD>
<TD><A HREF="<!--AccessTemplate_NextPage-->">Next
   Page</A><TD>
<TD><A HREF="<!--AccessTemplate_LastPage-->">Last
   Page</A><TD>
</TR>
</TABLE>
</BODY>
</HTML>
```

The Web page shown in Figure 14.11 was generated from the rptCustomer-Orders report and the A2KDHTempateNav.htm template.

**FIGURE 14.11**
The last page of the
multi-page rptCustomer-
Orders report

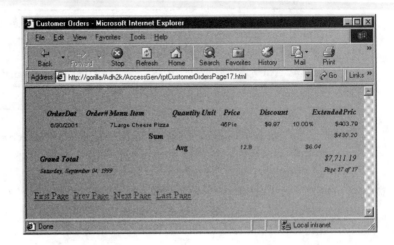

## Using the OutputTo Method

You can use the OutputTo method of the DoCmd object (or the OutputTo macro action) to programmatically generate Web pages in HTML, IDC, or ASP format. The syntax of the OutputTo method, which you can also use to export objects to other, non-Web formats, is shown here:

```
DoCmd.OutputTo objecttype [,objectname] [,outputformat]_
[,outputfile] [,autostart] [,templatefile]
```

The parameters of the OutputTo method are described in Table 14.3.

**T A B L E  1 4 . 3 :**   Parameters of the OutputTo Method

| Parameter | Description | Default Value |
|---|---|---|
| objecttype | One of the object type constants (acOutputDataAccessPage, acOutputForm, acOutputModule, acOuputQuery, acOutputReport, acOutputServerView, acOutputSoredProcedure, or acOutputTable) | *None*; required |
| objectname | Name of the object you wish to output | The active object |
| outputformat | One of the output format constants (acFormatASP, acFormatDAP, acFormatHTML, acFormatIIS, acFormatRTF, acFormatSNP, acFormatTXT, or acFormatXLS) | *None*; if left missing, Access prompts you for the value |

**TABLE 14.3:** Parameters of the OutputTo Method  *(continued)*

| Parameter | Description | Default Value |
| --- | --- | --- |
| outputfile | Name of the output file | *None*; if left missing, Access prompts you for the value |
| autostart | Boolean value; when True Access automatically starts the host application for that object after the output file is generated (this is ignored for the acFormatASP and acFormatIIS formats) | False |
| templatefile | Name of an optional template file | *None* |

For example, you might use the following subroutine (which can be found in the basPublish module of the CH14.MDB database) to publish objects using the OutputTo method, as shown in Listing 14.1.

### Listing 14.1

```
Sub adhPublishObject(strObject As String, _
 strOutputFile As String, _
 Optional intObjectType As _
 AcOutputObjectType = acOutputTable, _
 Optional intFormat As String = acFormatHTML, _
 Optional strTemplateFile As String = "")
     ' Publish an object using OutputTo

    On Error GoTo PublishObjectErr
    DoCmd.Hourglass True

    If strTemplateFile = "" Then
        DoCmd.OutputTo ObjectType:=intObjectType, _
          ObjectName:=strObject, _
          OutputFormat:=intFormat, _
          OutputFile:=strOutputFile, _
          AutoStart:=False
    Else
        DoCmd.OutputTo ObjectType:=intObjectType, _
          ObjectName:=strObject, _
          OutputFormat:=intFormat, _
```

```
            OutputFile:=strOutputFile, _
            AutoStart:=False, _
            TemplateFile:=strTemplateFile
    End If

    DoCmd.Hourglass False

    MsgBox strObject & _
      " was successfully published to the " & _
      strOutputFile & " file.", _
      vbInformation + vbOKOnly, "PublishObject Sub"

PublishObjectEnd:
    Exit Sub
PublishObjectErr:
    DoCmd.Hourglass False
    MsgBox "Error " & Err.Number & ": " & _
      Err.Description, _
      vbCritical + vbOKOnly, "adhPublishObject Error"
    Resume PublishObjectEnd
End Sub
```

---

**TIP**  When you use the OutputTo method with the ASP and IDC formats, Access determines the data source name, username, and password values from the last time you published ASP pages using the Export dialog box. These values are stored in Registry keys under the \HKEY_CURRENT_USER\ Software\Microsoft\Office\9.0\Access\Settings node.

---

# Hand-Coding Active Server Pages

If your needs are basic, the pages generated by the Export dialog box may serve you well. More than likely, however, you're going to want to create data-driven pages that go beyond the Export dialog box's capabilities. You certainly wouldn't build your Access database on forms and reports generated exclusively by the wizards, so why limit yourself to Web pages that only the Export dialog box is capable of generating?

Fortunately, if you're an Access developer then you should have no trouble learning ASP. The great thing about ASP is that it's based on the same technologies you're likely already familiar with: HTML, VBScript, and ADO.

# What Tool to Use

Before you can start creating ASP pages, you'll need to decide on an editor to use. There are a number of choices to choose from, including Notepad, the Microsoft Script Editor, and Visual InterDev.

## Using Notepad

Like HTML pages, ASP pages are just text. Thus, you can use a plain old text editor like Windows Notepad to edit your ASP pages.

What you get with Notepad is a lean and mean text editor that's there at a moments notice. What you don't get is color coding, IntelliSense support, and project management. On the other hand, you can't beat the price.

## Using Microsoft Script Editor

Office 2000 ships with the Microsoft Script Editor (MSE), a color-coded editor that you can use to add scripting behind data access pages and other Microsoft Office documents.

MSE is actually a stripped-down version of the editor that comes with Visual InterDev (see the next section). The MSE environment includes a color-coded editor, an HTML toolbox, HTML and script outline tools, and a property sheet window. MSE is shown in Figure 14.12 with an ASP page loaded.

---

**NOTE**     The MSE environment is described in detail in Chapter 11.

---

To launch MSE from inside of Access 2000, you need to load a data access page. Once loaded, however, there's nothing to prevent you from creating HTML or ASP pages that aren't part of the Access database project. Even better: you can launch MSE from outside of Access by simply creating a shortcut to the executable file, MSE.EXE. You should find this file in the following location on your machine:

```
C:\Program Files\Microsoft Visual Studio\Common\IDE\IDE98\MSE.EXE
```

**FIGURE 14.12**
The Microsoft Script Editor

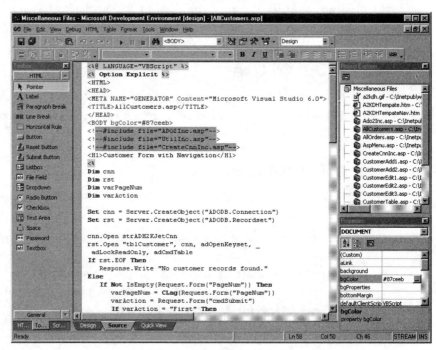

You can create new HTML and ASP pages from inside of MSE by selecting File ➤ New File and selecting HTML Page from the New tab of the New File dialog box. To change the HTML page to an ASP page, simply use the ASP extension when saving the file.

While MSE is based on Visual InterDev and has much of the same functionality as its older sibling, it does lack a few of Visual InterDev's more powerful features. MSE has no project or Web site management tools, no direct support for browsing ASP pages, and no server-side debugging capabilities. Still, if you own a copy of Access 2000 (or Office 2000)—and if you've gotten this far in the book, we think it's safe to assume that—you already own a copy of the Microsoft Script Editor.

### Using Visual InterDev

Visual InterDev, a component of Microsoft Visual Studio, is a wonderful development environment for creating data-driven Web sites. It uses the same basic editor as the Microsoft Script Editor, but adds additional features, including:

- The ability to create and manage Web sites and Web projects
- The ability to preview both HTML and ASP pages (with MSE, you must enter the URL of ASP pages into the browser manually)
- Extensive source-code control features, including integration with Visual SourceSafe
- Full client and server-side debugging capabilities
- Design-time controls for rapid application development
- The Microsoft Visual Data Tools

---

**TIP**    If you plan on doing any extensive ASP development, get yourself a copy of Visual InterDev—it's well worth the cost!

---

## Previewing Your Hand-Coded ASP Pages

If you're using Notepad or MSE to develop your ASP pages, you'll have to copy your ASP pages to a Web server folder before you can preview your pages in your browser. (This presumes you've already set up and configured your Web server—if not, see the "Configuring the Web Server for ASP" section earlier in this chapter.) Then, you'll need to open your Web browser and enter a URL that points to the page on your Web server using the HTTP protocol. For more information on how to do this, see the "Viewing ASP Pages" section earlier in this chapter.

If you're using Visual InterDev, you can preview your ASP pages by simply right-clicking on the page and choosing View in Browser from the pop-up menu. Visual InterDev automatically takes care of saving your page to the Web server folder and opening the page using the HTTP protocol.

# The Anatomy of an ASP Page

An ASP page is an HTML page that contains embedded scripts that the ASP engine executes on the Web server. You can write these scripts in VBScript, JavaScript, or some other scripting language.

In addition to HTML and embedded scripts, your ASP pages will need to interact with the ASP object model. The ASP object model allows you to pass data back and forth to the Web browser, create and use global variables, and instantiate ActiveX Server components. You'll use this last feature of the ASP object model to employ ADO objects and other external ActiveX Server components in your ASP pages.

The next few sections examine the various pieces that make up an ASP page.

# ASP Scripts

ASP pages consist of HTML and scripts. You embed scripts in an ASP page using the ASP script tags "<%" and "%>". For example, the following ASP page, First.asp, contains a line of HTML text followed by a line of text that is generated by a script:

```
<HTML>
<HEAD>
<TITLE>First.asp</TITLE>
</HEAD>
<BODY>
<H1>A Simple ASP Example</H1>
This text is pure HTML.
<P>
<%
Response.Write "This text created by an ASP Script."
%>
</BODY>
</HTML>
```

Notice how the ASP script is embedded directly in the ASP page. Everything between the opening ASP script tag (<%) and the closing ASP script tag (%>) is considered a script and is thus executed on the Web server by the ASP scripting engine. Everything on the page outside of the script tags is treated as plain HTML and thus it is just passed back to the browser untouched.

All of the ASP examples in the chapter contain an additional hyperlink at the bottom of each page that you can use to jump to a home page (AspMenu.asp) that lists all of the samples and provides an easy way to navigate from one sample to another. To simplify the listings we haven't included this hyperlink in the source code listings.

The First.asp page is shown as it looks in Internet Explorer 5.0 in Figure 14.13.

**FIGURE 14.13**
The First.asp page

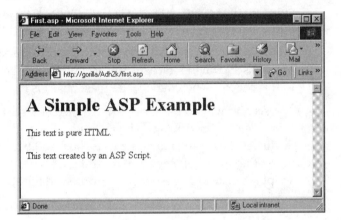

## What the Browser Sees

The Web browser never sees the ASP script. It only sees the results of executing the ASP script, which are shown here:

```
<HTML>
<HEAD>
<TITLE>First.asp</TITLE>
</HEAD>
<BODY>
<H1>A Simple ASP Example</H1>
This text is pure HTML.
<P>
This text created by an ASP Script.
</BODY>
</HTML>
```

Because all of the scripting code in an ASP page executes on the server, you can view ASP pages with just about any browser, even if that browser doesn't support VBScript or any scripting language. Contrast this to data access pages that require Internet Explorer 5.0 or later.

# Sending Information Back to the Browser

As mentioned in the last section, everything executed within an ASP script is executed on the server and is never seen by the Web browser. That is, unless you use one of two techniques to pass text back to the Web browser.

One way to pass text back to the browser is to use Write method of the Response object, as shown in First.asp. This technique will be discussed in more detail later in this chapter when the ASP Request object is more formally introduced.

A second way to pass text back to the browser is to use the special "<%= *expression* %>" script tag. When you use this ASP tag, the ASP scripting engine evaluates the expression and passes the result back to the browser. For example, here's the same ASP page, but this time we have used the "<%= *expression* %>" script tag instead of Response.Write to send the string back to the browser:

```
<HTML>
<HEAD>
<TITLE>Second.asp</TITLE>
</HEAD>
<BODY>
<H1>A Second ASP Example</H1>
This text is pure HTML.
<P>
<%= "This text created by an ASP Script."%>
</BODY>
</HTML>
```

Neither technique for returning text to the browser is better than the other. Sometimes it's more convenient to use the Reponse.Write method, which allows you to output the text in the middle of a script. At other times, it may be more convenient to use the "<%= *expression* %>" technique. The "<%= *expression* %>" technique differs from Response.Write in that it requires you to create a separate script every time you want to send output to the browser. At times, however, this is more convenient, especially when outputting text to cells of an HTML table.

# VBScript

As mentioned earlier, you have the choice of using VBScript, JavaScript, or another scripting language such as PERL to create ASP scripts. We think it's safe to say that the majority of Access developers will feel most at home using VBScript, a subset of the familiar VBA language, so we'll use VBScript as the scripting language for all of the examples in this chapter.

By default, Internet Information Server and Personal Web Server assume you are using VBScript as your scripting language. However, the Web server administrator can change the default language. Thus, it's important to designate the scripting language on each and every ASP page you create. That way, your pages will always work, no matter what the default scripting language is set to. To set the scripting language for the page, you use a special script tag that must appear on the first line of the page:

```
<%@ LANGUAGE="VBScript" %>
```

The following ASP page contains a script that displays a string and then uses the VBScript StrReverse function to display the string in reverse order:

```
<%@ LANGUAGE="VBScript" %>
<HTML>
<HEAD>
<TITLE>Third.asp</TITLE>
</HEAD>
<BODY>
<H1>This ASP Example uses a VBScript Function</H1>
<%
Dim varString

varString = "The quick brown fox jumped over the lazy dog."

Response.Write "The String: " & varString
Response.Write "<BR>"
Response.Write "The String Reversed: " & _
  StrReverse(varString)
%>
<P>
<I>Brought to you by the Access 2000 Developer's
Handbook, Volume II</I>
</BODY>
</HTML>
```

The Third.asp page is shown as it looks in Netscape Navigator in Figure 14.14.

**FIGURE 14.14**
The Third.asp page reverses
a string using the VBScript
StrReverse function.

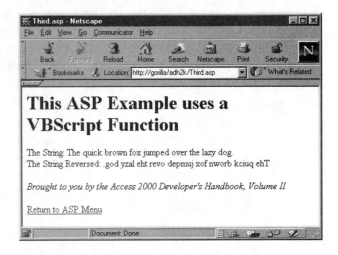

## Immediate Scripts versus Procedures

VBScript can live in one of two places: inside of a subroutine or function procedure or in an immediate script. An *immediate script* is any VBScript code on an ASP page that is not contained within a procedure.

All immediate scripts are executed immediately, as the page loads. If it helps, you can think of immediate script code as attached to an invisible page load event.

## Option Explicit

Every experienced Access developer knows the importance of using explicit variable declarations. You tell VBA to require you to declare every variable you use with the Option Explicit statement. VBScript also supports the Option Explicit statement, but in order for it to be interpreted correctly, you must place the Option Explicit statement at the top of the page, immediately underneath the <%@ LANGUAGE %> statement, in a script by itself.

For example, here's the top of a typical ASP page with the language set to VBScript and Option Explicit enabled:

```
<%@ LANGUAGE="VBScript" %>
<% Option Explicit %>
<HTML>
<HEAD>
```

## VBScript versus VBA

As stated previously, VBScript is a subset of VBA. One of the big differences between VBScript and VBA is that VBScript doesn't support explicit datatypes. Instead everything takes on the Variant datatype. The following code would be illegal in a VBScript script because VBScript doesn't support the As Datatype clause of the Dim statement:

```
' This is illegal in VBScript
Dim varString As Variant
```

---

**NOTE**    See Chapter 11 and Appendix B for a more complete discussion of the differences between VBScript and VBA.

---

# The ASP Object Model

ASP exposes five objects that you can manipulate from your ASP scripts. These objects are summarized in Table 14.4.

**TABLE 14.4:**   The ASP Objects

| Object | Purpose |
| --- | --- |
| Application | Used to persist global variables to all users of the Web application |
| Request | Used to retrieve information posted to the page by the prior Web page |
| Response | Used to send information back to the Web browser |

**TABLE 14.4:**  The ASP Objects *(continued)*

| Object | Purpose |
| --- | --- |
| Server | Used to instantiate ActiveX Server objects and perform several utility functions |
| Session | Used to persist global variables from one page to another of a single user session |

The next few sections examine each of the ASP objects in turn.

## Outputting Information with the Response Object

You use the Response object to send information to the Web browser. The Response object has a number of properties, methods, and collections that are summarized in Table 14.5.

**TABLE 14.5:**  The Collections, Properties, and Methods of the Response Object

| Type | Item | Purpose |
| --- | --- | --- |
| Collection | Cookies | Used to write collections of cookies to the user's machine. |
| Property | Buffer | Controls whether ASP buffers the page sent back to the browser. If True, then the page is only sent back to the browser when it has completely executed; if False, the page is sent back to the browser in chunks. |
| | ContentType | Determines how the browser should treat the content of the page; defaults to "text/HTML." |
| | Expires | The time, in minutes, that the browser should expire the page. If the user returns to the page before the page expires, the browser displays a locally cached version of the page; otherwise it requests a new page. You can turn off caching by setting Expires to -1. |
| | ExpiresAbsolute | The date and time that the browser should expire the page. |
| | Status | Sets the status line of the HTTP header. |
| Method | AddHeader | Adds information to the HTTP header of the page. |
| | AppendToLog | Writes information to the Web server's log. |
| | BinaryWrite | Writes binary information to the page without character conversion. |

**TABLE 14.5:**  The Collections, Properties, and Methods of the Response Object  *(continued)*

| Type | Item | Purpose |
|------|------|---------|
| | Clear | Erases information from a buffered page; only available when Buffer = True. |
| | End | Terminates processing of the current page and sends any buffered output to the browser. |
| | Flush | Sends any buffered output to the browser and continues processing; only available when Buffer = True. |
| | Redirect | Redirects the page to another URL; must be used before any content is written to the page. |
| | Write | Writes text to the browser page. |

The most commonly used method of the Response object is the Write method. The First.asp page from earlier in the chapter used Response.Write to write a string to the page:

```
<%
Response.Write "This text created by an ASP Script."
%>
```

When generating pages based on data that changes often, you may wish to tell the browser not to cache the page. You can accomplish this by using the Response .Expires property, as shown here:

```
<%
Response.Expires = -1
%>
```

At the beginning of a page you may wish to conditionally redirect a user to another page. The following ASP code checks to see if the user has logged in and redirects the user to the login page if they have not (the example makes use of a Session variable which we'll discuss in a later section):

```
<%
If Not Session("Login") Then
    Response.Redirect "login.asp"
End If
%>
```

You can persist information from one browser session to another by storing cookies on the user's system. The following code writes an array of two cookies to the user's machine:

```
<%
Response.Cookies("LoginInfo").Expires = "12/31/2002"
Response.Cookies("LoginInfo")("LoginDate") = Date()
Response.Cookies("LoginInfo")("LoginName") = "Mel"
%>
```

By default, any cookies you write are temporary unless you use set the Expires property to a date value. For privacy purposes, cookies are associated with the Web server's domain name, so a Web site can only read the cookies that it has written. On the user's system, cookies are read and written by the browser.

---

**NOTE**    Some older browsers don't support cookies. In addition, users can turn off cookies when using browsers that support them.

---

## Retrieving Information with the Request Object

You use the Request object to retrieve various pieces of information from form fields, the URL query string, and the HTTP header. The Request object contains five collections that are summarized in Table 14.6.

**TABLE 14.6:**   The Collections of the Request Object

| Collection | Purpose |
|---|---|
| ClientCertificates | Retrieves values from client certificates. |
| Cookies | Retrieves the values of cookies stored on the client machine. |
| Form | Retrieves the values of form controls posted to the page. |
| QueryString | Retrieves the values of any URL query string variables posted to the page. |
| ServerVariables | Retrieves values from the HTTP header. |

The most commonly used collections of the Request object are the Form and QueryString collections.

## Using the Form Collection

You use the Form collection to retrieve the values of form controls posted to the page using the Post method. The basic syntax is as follows:

```
variable = Request.Form("fieldname")
```

For example, let's say you constructed the following page (userinfor1.htm) to collect a visitor's name and e-mail address:

```
<HTML>
<HEAD><TITLE>userinfo1.htm</TITLE></HEAD>
<BODY>
<H1>Tell Us About Yourself</H1>

<FORM METHOD="POST" ACTION="userinfo2.asp">
First Name:<INPUT TYPE="text" SIZE="20"
NAME="txtFName">

<P>Last Name:<INPUT TYPE="text" SIZE="20"
NAME="txtLName">

<P>Email Address?
<INPUT TYPE="text" SIZE="40"
NAME="txtEMail">

<P><INPUT TYPE="submit" VALUE="Submit">
<INPUT TYPE="reset" VALUE="Reset">
</FORM>
</BODY>
</HTML>
```

In order to be able to retrieve form fields from a form using the Request object's Form collection, you must set the METHOD attribute of the <FORM> tag to "post" and set the ACTION attribute to the name of the ASP page that the form will post to.

The userinfo1.htm page is shown in Figure 14.15.

FIGURE 14.15
This form collects information from visitors to the
Web site and posts
the form to the
userinfo2.asp page.

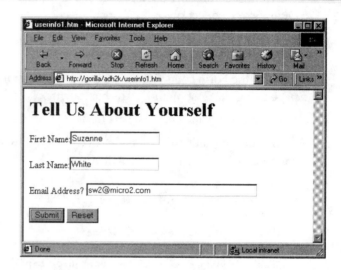

The userinfo2.asp page uses the Form collection to retrieve the values of the
form fields and display them on the page. Of course, this is a very basic example.
In reality, you'd probably save the values to a table in a database, but for now
we'll keep it simple. Here's the source for userinfo2.asp:

```
<%@ LANGUAGE="VBScript" %>
<% Option Explicit %>
<HTML>
<HEAD><TITLE>userinfo2.asp</TITLE></HEAD>
<BODY>
<H1>Your Current Personal Data</H1>
<FONT SIZE="4">
<P>First Name: <%=Request.Form("txtFName")%>
<P>Last Name: <%=Request.Form("txtLName")%>
<P>Email Address: <%=Request.Form("txtEmail")%>
</FONT>
</BODY>
</HTML>
```

The userinfo2.asp page is shown in Figure 14.16.

**FIGURE 14.16**

This page uses the Request.Form collection to retrieve the values of fields posted to the page.

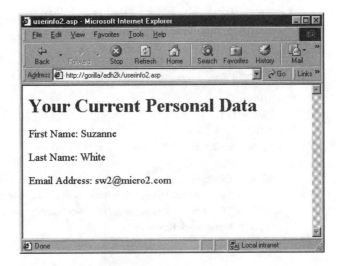

## Making Use of the QueryString Collection

The *query string* is that portion of the URL after the question mark. Often, the query string is used to pass information from one page to another, outside of a form. Also, any form with the METHOD attribute set to "get" sends its information to the next page via the query string.

You construct a query string using the following syntax:

```
url?item1=value1&item2=value2 …
```

You separate multiple items from each other using the ampersand character (&). Query strings have special encoding rules that you need to follow when you wish to pass certain characters. For example, you must replace spaces in the query string with the plus sign (+).

---

**TIP**  You can use the URLEncode method of the Server object (discussed later in the chapter) to encode any string you wish to pass in the query string so that it is not misinterpreted.

---

You use the QueryString collection of the Request object to retrieve items from the query string. The basic syntax is as follows:

```
variable = Request.QueryString("itemname")
```

For example, the productuse1.htm page contains three hyperlinks that all point to the same ASP page, productuse2.asp, but with a different query string:

```
<HTML>
<HEAD><TITLE>productuse1.htm</TITLE></HEAD>
<BODY>
<H1>Where Do You Use Our Product?</H1>

<P><A HREF="productuse2.asp?Use=home">At Home</A>
<P><A HREF="productuse2.asp?Use=work">At Work</A>
<P><A HREF="productuse2.asp?Use=workandhome">
At Both Work and Home</A>
</BODY>
</HTML>
```

The productuse1.asp page is shown in Figure 14.17. The productuse2.asp page displays the choice made by the user by retrieving the Use item from the Request object's QueryString collection:

```
<%@ LANGUAGE="VBScript" %>
<% Option Explicit %>
<HTML>
<HEAD><TITLE>productuse2.asp</TITLE></HEAD>
<BODY>
<H1>Where You Use Our Product</H1>
<FONT SIZE="4">
<%
Dim varUse

Response.Write "You use our product "
Response.Write "<FONT COLOR=""red"">"
Select Case Request.QueryString("Use")
Case "home"
   varUse = "at home"
Case "work"
   varUse = "at work"
Case "workandhome"
   varUse = "both at work and at home"
End Select
```

```
Response.Write varUse & ".</FONT>"
%>
</FONT>
</BODY>
</HTML>
```

**FIGURE 14.17**

The hyperlinks on this page each point to the same page, productuse2.asp, but with different query string values.

If you clicked the At Both Work and Home hyperlink of productuse1.htm, you should see a page that looks similar to the one shown in Figure 14.18. If you look closely at the figure you can see the following query string in the URL of the productuse2.asp page:

```
http://gorilla/adh2k/productuse2.asp?Use=workandhome
```

**FIGURE 14.18**

This Request.QueryString collection can be used to reveal where the product is used.

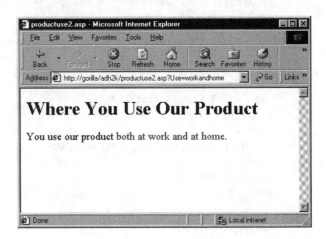

**TIP**    You can use a shortcut syntax to retrieve an item from one of the Request object's collections. For example, instead of using Request.Form("product") and Request.QueryString("color"), you can use Request("product") and Request("color"). When you use this shortcut syntax, ASP looks for the item in each of its collections. While this shortcut syntax may be convenient, it does come at a slight performance penalty.

## Sharing Data with the Application Object

The Application object lets you share global variables across all users of a Web site. Because multiple users may attempt to write to an Application variable at the same time, the Application object has a pair of methods, Lock and Unlock, that you need to use when writing values to Application variables. The Application methods are summarized in Table 14.7.

**T A B L E   1 4 . 7 :**    The Methods of the Application Object

| Method | Purpose |
| --- | --- |
| Lock | Locks the Application object for writing |
| Unlock | Releases the lock on the Application object placed by the Lock method |

The basic syntax for writing to an Application variable is as follows:

```
Application.Lock
    Application("variable") = value
Application.Unlock
```

For example, you could use the Application object to create a simple hit counter. Here's the source of hits.asp that implements a hit counter using the Application object:

```
<%@ LANGUAGE="VBScript" %>
<% Option Explicit %>
<HTML>
<HEAD><TITLE>hits.asp</TITLE></HEAD>
<BODY>
<FONT SIZE="5">
<%
' Track hits for this Web site.
Application.Lock
```

```
    Application("hits") = Application("hits") + 1
Application.UnLock

Response.Write "You are visitor #" & _
 Application("hits") & " to this Web site!"
%>
</FONT>
</BODY>
</HTML>
```

Hits.asp is shown in Figure 14.19.

**FIGURE 14.19**
The hits.asp page uses the
Application object to
implement a Web site
hit counter.

## Managing State with the Session Object

One of the difficulties in building Web applications is the management of state.
When you're programming an Access application against Jet or SQL Server, your
connection to Access persists between calls. You don't have to worry about managing state because a consistent connection to Access, VBA, and the database is
maintained between calls to your procedures. When working with Web pages,
you don't have this luxury. The HTTP protocol that the browser and Web server
use to communicate with each other is a *stateless* protocol, meaning that every
request for a page is considered a separate, independent request.

In order to maintain state, you must ensure that data is passed from page to
page. One way to accomplish this is to pass data along using HTML forms or the
URL query string. The ASP engine gives you another alternative: the Session
object. You can use the Session object to pass information amongst all the pages
of your Web project.

## What Defines a Session?

ASP defines a session as beginning the moment you connect to any page in the Web site. By default, this session is maintained for 20 minutes since the last request for a page. That is, the session doesn't end until a user has not requested another page for more than 20 minutes. When a session ends, the memory set aside to store variables associated with that session is released.

## How the Session Works

When you first connect to a page, the ASP engine looks in the HTTP header request for a SessionID cookie. If no SessionID cookie is present, then ASP assigns the request a new SessionID value that it writes back to the browser in the HTTP response. Thereafter, when you request another page on the Web site, the ASP engine compares the SessionID cookie of the requesting page with its list of active sessions and if a match is found, it passes all the variables associated with the session along to the new request. Any time a match is not found, either because no SessionID cookie is found or because the SessionID cookie has expired, a new SessionID is assigned.

The SessionID cookies that the ASP engine uses to maintain sessions are temporary cookies that are erased when the browser is closed.

## Using the Session Object

The Session object has two properties and a single method that are summarized in Table 14.8.

**TABLE 14.8:**   The Properties and Methods of the Session object.

| Type | Item | Purpose |
| --- | --- | --- |
| Property | SessionID | Returns the long integer that uniquely identifies the current session. |
| | Timeout | Length of time in minutes (since the last request) before a session is automatically abandoned; defaults to 20 minutes; you can also modify this globally for the Web server using the IIS management tool. |
| Method | Abandon | Destroys the current Session and erases its variables. |

To create or write to an existing session variable, you use the following syntax:

```
Session("session_variable")  = value
```

To read the value of a session variable, you use this syntax:

```
local_variable = Session("session_variable")
```

We've created a three-page example that demonstrates how to store a user's name and e-mail address in session variables. Here's part of the code from the second of three pages (sessionvar2.asp) that is used to store the information in session variables:

```
<%
' Save the form fields to session
' variables of the same name.
Session("txtFName") = Request.Form("txtFName")
Session("txtLName") = Request.Form("txtLName")
Session("txtEMail") = Request.Form("txtEmail")
%>
```

And here's the code on sessionvar3.asp that we use to retrieve the values of the three session variables:

```
<!--Grab the variables from the
Session object-->
<P>First Name: <%=Session("txtFName")%>
<P>Last Name: <%=Session("txtLName")%>
<P>Email Address: <%=Session("txtEmail")%>
```

Using the Session object makes it easy to persist information between various pages of the application, regardless of the particular path a user takes through your application. To accomplish the same effect using the URL query string or form fields requires a lot more work.

## Potential Problems with the Session Object

The simplicity of the Session object, unfortunately, comes at a price. The Web server must set aside memory for each session. While this may not sound like a lot of memory, all ASP processing occurs on the server and thus each session will eat up another chunk of memory for at least 20 minutes (unless the TimeOut property of the Session object is reduced). If you use the Session object, your ability to scale your Web application to support a large number of users will be impacted. On the other hand, this may not be a problem if your Web site will be hosted on an intranet and will have a small number of users.

You can make the memory used by the Session object even worse by storing object variables in the Session object. If you've dug into the ASP code generated by the Access Export dialog box, you'll see that this is exactly what pages generated by the Export dialog box do. This is an especially bad idea unless you can guarantee a small number of users requesting pages from the Web server.

**TIP**    If creating and destroying ADO objects on every page seems like a bad idea, think again. Internet Information Server and Personal Web Server automatically cache ADO connections to databases. This means that when you set a Connection object to Nothing, the Web server automatically keeps the connection around for several minutes and then passes the connection off to other page requests, significantly reducing the performance penalty associated with destroying ADO connections while maintaining scalability.

Another potential issue with using the Session object: the Session object uses cookies to do its work. Thus, the user's Web browser must support cookies and cookie support must be turned on. If cookies are not enabled, then each request for a page will be assigned a new SessionID and the session variables will not be passed along to the new page. The memory will be still tied up for each page until the session times out, but the data will be unavailable.

**TIP**    If you're using a Microsoft Web server running on Windows NT or Windows 2000, you can use the IIS Administrator program to disable the Session object.

So what can you do to persist session data if you decide not to use the Session object? You can pass information from page to page using hidden Form fields or the URL query string. You can also use cookies and database tables to store user information rather than pass it all from page to page.

## Extending the ASP World with the Server Object

The ASP Server object lets you call ActiveX Server components (also known as COM components) from your ASP pages. You can also use several utility methods of the Server object to encode strings. The methods and properties of the Server object are summarized in Table 14.9.

TABLE 14.9: The Properties and Methods of the Server Object

| Type | Item | Purpose |
|------|------|---------|
| Property | ScriptTimeout | The number of seconds to wait before terminating a script; default is 90 seconds |
| Method | CreateObject | Instantiates an ActiveX Server object |
| | HTMLEncode | Encodes text so that it can be passed to an HTML page without being interpreted as HTML |
| | MapPath | Maps a Web virtual folder path to the Windows file system; this is useful when you need to supply a component with the name of a file |
| | URLEncode | Encodes text so that it can be used as the query string portion of a URL |
| | URLPathEncode | Encodes text so that it can be used as the name of a page or other resource; you use this method to encode everything in the URL to the left of the query string |

By far the most important method of the Server object is the CreateObject method. You use CreateObject to instantiate (or create) external ActiveX Server objects.

For example, you could use the following ASP code to instantiate an ADO Connection object:

```
<%
Dim cnn
Set cnn = Server.CreateObject("ADODB.Connection")
' ...
%>
```

---

**NOTE**     We'll show complete examples that create and use ADO Connection, Recordset, and Command objects later in the chapter.

---

# Using Include Files

One of the difficulties in ASP development is that every page is an independent entity. One page can't normally call functions and subroutines in another page.

(ASP's support for remote scripting does let you call procedures in other page, but we've found it very difficult to get working.) You can, however, use the server-side include directive to work around this shortcoming. A server-side include directive tells the ASP engine to merge the contents of a file into a page before the page is processed.

You use the following syntax to merge the contents of another file into an ASP page:

```
<!--#include file="file_name"-->
```

The server-side include directive is actually a special form of an HTML comment that is interpreted by the ASP engine before it executes any scripts on the page. The include directive must appear outside any ASP scripts in the HTML portion of a page. Include files are merged into the page where the include directive occurs.

For example, the following excerpt from the customeradd2.asp page (which is discussed in more detail later in the chapter) merges the contents of three include files into the customeradd2.asp page:

```
<%@ LANGUAGE="VBScript" %>
<% Option Explicit %>
<HTML>
<HEAD>
<TITLE>CustomerAdd2.asp</TITLE>
</HEAD>
<BODY bgColor=#87ceeb>
<!--#include file="ADO2Inc.asp"-->
<!--#include file="UtilInc.asp"-->
<!--#include file="CnnInc.asp"-->
<H1>New Customer</H1>
<%
' This page adds a new Customer record
' using an Access insert query.


' ---------------------------------------------
' This page won't work with the SQL Server
' version of the database because the
' SQL Server database doesn't contain the query.
' ---------------------------------------------
Dim cnn
Dim cmd
Dim varRecords
Dim prm

'  ...
```

Include files can contain HTML or ASP scripts. You can use include files for a number of purposes, including:

- HTML that you wish to appear on every page, such as logos, navigation bars, and copyright information

- Constants and variables; the ADO2Inc.asp include file from the example contains a number of ADO constants

- Utility functions; the UtilInc.asp include file from the example contains several utility functions, including one that converts zero-length strings to Nulls

---

**TIP**    Unlike Access VBA code, the ADO constants are not automatically available from ASP pages. Thus, you might use an include file to define the ADO constants. Microsoft ships a VBScript version of the ADO constants that you can include in your pages, but the file (adovbs.inc) is 376 lines long and uses numerous constants that are rarely needed. We've created an include file named ADO2Inc.asp that contains a subset of the most commonly used ADO constants. This include file is only 75 lines long.

---

# Creating Data-Driven ASP Pages

If you've worked your way to this point in the chapter, you should now have all the pieces in place to start creating data-driven ASP pages. The only pieces we haven't covered specifically in this chapter are HTML and ADO. We'll have to assume you are comfortable with HTML. If not, you may want to pick up a copy of a good HTML book such as *Mastering HTML 4 Premium Edition*, by Deborah S. Ray and Eric J. Ray (Sybex, 1999).

We'll also assume at this point in the book you are comfortable with ADO. ADO shouldn't be a problem because earlier chapters of this book and its sibling volume (*Access 2000 Developer's Handbook, Volume I: Desktop Edition*) are chock full of ADO examples.

## The CustomerTable.asp Example

The CustomerTable.asp page, which is shown in Figure 14.20, displays all of the records from tblCustomer table in an HTML table.

FIGURE 14.20

The CustomerTable.asp
page displays customer
records.

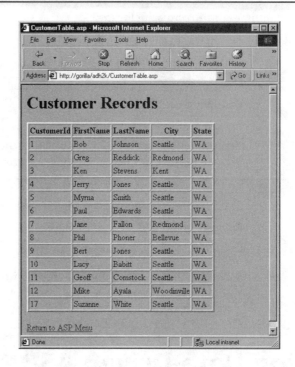

## Include Files and Connection Strings

Here's the first part of CustomerTable.asp source:

```
<%@ LANGUAGE="VBScript" %>
<% Option Explicit %>
<HTML>
<HEAD>
<TITLE>CustomerTable.asp</TITLE>
</HEAD>
<BODY bgColor=#87ceeb>
<!--#include file="ADO2Inc.asp"-->
<!--#include file="CnnInc.asp"-->
<H1>Customer Records</H1>
```

We use this portion of the source code to set VBScript as the default scripting
language for the page, require variable declarations, and create the HTML header
for the page. We also use two include directives to include the contents of ADO2Inc
.asp and CnnInc.asp. ADO2Inc.asp contains a subset of the complete ADO 2.1

constants. CnnInc.Asp creates a variable, strADH2KCnn, and sets it to a connection string that points to the sample database. Here's the source for CnnInc.asp:

```
<%
Dim strADH2KCnn

' Fix this path up to point to the Ch14 Access database.
strADH2KCnn = "Provider=Microsoft.Jet.OLEDB.4.0;" & _
 "Data Source=D:\A2kdh\VolumeII-2372\" & _
 "Ch14 - Publishing Access Data on the Web\Ch14.MDB;"

' Or comment the above out and uncomment this version to
' point to the SQL Server version of the sample database.
' Of course, you'll have to run the scripts to create the
' database first.
' --------------------------------------------------------
' Note: most, but not all examples in this chapter
' work against the SQL Server version of the database.
' --------------------------------------------------------
'strADH2KCnn = "Provider=SQLOLEDB;" & _
' "Data Source=Gorilla;Database=ADH2KSQL;" & _
' "User Id=sa;Password=;"
%>
```

By placing the connection string in an include file and using this include file in all the data-driven chapter examples, we make adjusting the connection string easy. You can adjust the connection string in this one file and automatically the connection string is modified for all the chapter examples.

---

**NOTE**
Most, but not all the data-driven ASP examples in this chapter will work with either the CH14.MDB Access database or the ADH2KSQL SQL Server database. A few examples won't work with the SQL Server database because they make use of saved Access queries that don't exist in the SQL Server version of the database. If you want the examples to use the Access version of the database, you will need to fix up the path to the database in the first assignment statement of CnnInc.asp so that it points to the location of the CH14.MDB database on your system. If you'd rather the examples use the SQL Server version of the database, then comment out the first assignment statement of CnnInc.asp and uncomment the second assignment statement after creating the ADH2KSQL database from the scripts we've included on the CD. (See the Introduction of this book for more details on creating the ADH2KSQL database.)

---

## Creating the Recordset

The next piece of code from CustomerTable.asp creates Connection and Recordset objects and checks if any records were found:

```
<%
Dim cnn
Dim rst

Set cnn = Server.CreateObject("ADODB.Connection")
Set rst = Server.CreateObject("ADODB.Recordset")

cnn.Open strADH2KCnn
rst.Open "tblCustomer", cnn, adOpenForwardOnly, _
  adLockReadOnly, adCmdTable

If rst.EOF Then
    Response.Write "No customer records found."
Else
%>
```

You use the CreateObject method of the Server object to instantiate ADO objects. Once created, the connection is opened using the strADH2kCnn connection string that was defined in the CnnInc.asp include file.

## Creating the HTML Header

The next portion of the page is pure HTML. This HTML code creates the table and sets up the header row:

```
<TABLE BORDER=2>
    <TR>
        <TH>CustomerId</TH>
        <TH>FirstName</TH>
        <TH>LastName</TH>
        <TH>City</TH>
        <TH>State</TH>
    </TR>
```

## Filling in the Detail Rows

The next portion of the page is a mixture of HTML and VBScript. This code creates the detail rows of the table within a Do...While loop and fills the cells with the values from the current record. At the bottom of the loop, the MoveNext method is used to move to the next record and the loop is exited when EOF is reached:

```
<%
    Do While Not rst.EOF
%>
    <TR>
        <TD><%=rst("CustomerId")%></TD>
        <TD><%=rst("FirstName")%></TD>
        <TD><%=rst("LastName")%></TD>
        <TD><%=rst("City")%></TD>
        <TD><%=rst("State")%></TD>
    </TR>
<%
        rst.MoveNext
    Loop
%>
```

## Cleaning Up

The last piece of the CustomerTable.asp page closes the table and releases the ADO objects. We also provide a link back to the switchboard page:

```
</TABLE>
<%
End If
Set rst = Nothing
Set cnn = Nothing
%>
<P>
<A HREF="AspMenu.asp">Return to ASP Menu</A>
</BODY>
</HTML>
```

# Inserting Records

The CustomerAdd1.asp and CustomerAdd2.asp pages provide a mechanism for adding a new record to the customer table.

This example won't work with the SQL Server version of the database because it makes use of an Access action query. You could easily modify it, however, to use a SQL Server stored procedure instead.

## The CustomerAdd1.asp Page

The CustomerAdd1.asp page collects the values of the fields using a standard HTML form. In fact, there is no ASP scripting on this page so we could have named it with the HTM or HTML extension. CustomerAdd1.asp is shown in Figure 14.21.

**FIGURE 14.21**
You can use this page to add a new customer record to the database.

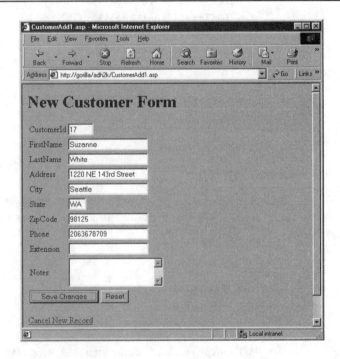

Here's the HTML behind the CustomerAdd1.asp page. Because we will be using the Request.Form collection to retrieve the posted data in CustomerAdd2.asp, we must set the Method attribute of the FORM tag to "Post":

```
<HTML>
<HEAD>
<TITLE>CustomerAdd1.asp</TITLE>
</HEAD>
```

```
<BODY bgColor=#87ceeb>
<H1>New Customer Form</H1>
<FORM METHOD="Post" ACTION="CustomerAdd2.ASP">
<TABLE>
   <TR>
      <TD>CustomerId</TD>
      <TD>    <INPUT Name="txtCustomerId" SIZE=5></TD>
   </TR>
   <TR>
      <TD>FirstName</TD>
      <TD><INPUT Name="txtFirstName" SIZE=20></TD>
   </TR>
   <TR>
      <TD>LastName</TD>
      <TD><INPUT Name="txtLastName" SIZE=20></TD>
   </TR>
   <TR>
      <TD>Address</TD>
      <TD><INPUT Name="txtAddress" SIZE=20></TD>
   </TR>
   <TR>
      <TD>City</TD>
      <TD><INPUT Name="txtCity" SIZE=20></TD>
   </TR>
   <TR>
      <TD>State</TD>
      <TD><INPUT Name="txtState" SIZE=3></TD>
   </TR>
   <TR>
      <TD>ZipCode</TD>
      <TD><INPUT Name="txtZipCode" SIZE=20></TD>
   </TR>
   <TR>
      <TD>Phone</TD>
      <TD><INPUT Name="txtPhone" SIZE=20></TD>
   </TR>
   <TR>
      <TD>Extension</TD>
      <TD><INPUT Name="txtExtension" SIZE=20></TD>
   </TR>
   <TR>
      <TD>Notes</TD>
```

```
        <TD>
        <TEXTAREA Name="tarNotes" ROWS=3 COLS=20></TEXTAREA>
        </TD>
     </TR>
  </TABLE>
  <TABLE>
     <TR>
        <TD><INPUT name="cmdSubmit" type=submit
        value="Save Changes"></TD>
        <TD><INPUT name="cmdSubmit" type=reset
        value="Reset"></TD>
     </TR>
  </TABLE>
  </FORM>
  <A HREF="CustomerEdit1.asp">Cancel New Record</A>
  <P>
  <A HREF="AspMenu.asp">Return to ASP Menu</A>
  </BODY>
  </HTML>
```

---

**TIP**　　Even though CustomerAdd1.asp is pure HTML, we have named it with an ASP extension. There's an advantage to making all of the pages in a Web site into ASP pages: you can then turn off Read rights to the folder to improve security. This works because HTML pages require Read rights while ASP pages require the Script Execute right. If you have a mixture of both pages, you need to assign both rights to the Web site folder. If you limit the pages to ASP pages—and name any static HTML page with the ASP extension—then you don't have to assign the Read right, making your Web a little more secure.

---

## The CustomerAdd2.asp Page

The CustomerAdd2.asp page is responsible for retrieving the field values from the Request.Form collection and inserting the new record into tblCustomer. Here's the beginning of the page:

```
<%@ LANGUAGE="VBScript" %>
<% Option Explicit %>
<HTML>
<HEAD>
<TITLE>CustomerAdd2.asp</TITLE>
```

```
</HEAD>
<BODY bgColor=#87ceeb>
<!--#include file="ADO2Inc.asp"-->
<!--#include file="UtilInc.asp"-->
<!--#include file="CnnInc.asp"-->
<H1>New Customer</H1>
```

This page includes a third include file, UtilInc.asp. The UtilInc.asp include file contains several utility functions, including Z2Null, a function used to convert zero-length strings to Nulls.

The next piece of the page creates a connection to the database and an ADO Command object:

```
<%
' This page adds a new Customer record
' using an Access insert query.

' -----------------------------------------------
' This page won't work with the SQL Server
' version of the database because the
' SQL Server database doesn't contain the query.
' -----------------------------------------------
Dim cnn
Dim cmd
Dim varRecords
Dim prm

Set cnn = Server.CreateObject("ADODB.Connection")
Set cmd = Server.CreateObject("ADODB.Command")

cnn.Open strADH2KCnn
Set cmd.ActiveConnection = cnn
cmd.CommandType = adCmdStoredProc
cmd.CommandText = "qryCustomerInsert"

Set prm = cmd.CreateParameter("CustomerId", adInteger, _
 adParamInput, ,Z2Null(Request.Form("txtCustomerId")))
cmd.Parameters.Append prm
Set prm = cmd.CreateParameter("FirstName", adVarWChar, _
 adParamInput, 255, Z2Null(Request.Form("txtFirstName")))
cmd.Parameters.Append prm
Set prm = cmd.CreateParameter("LastName", adVarWChar, _
```

```
adParamInput, 255, Z2Null(Request.Form("txtLastName")))
cmd.Parameters.Append prm
Set prm = cmd.CreateParameter("Address", adVarWChar, _
 adParamInput, 255, Z2Null(Request.Form("txtAddress")))
cmd.Parameters.Append prm
Set prm = cmd.CreateParameter("City", adVarWChar, _
 adParamInput, 255, Z2Null(Request.Form("txtCity")))
cmd.Parameters.Append prm
Set prm = cmd.CreateParameter("State", adVarWChar, _
 adParamInput, 255, Z2Null(Request.Form("txtState")))
cmd.Parameters.Append prm
Set prm = cmd.CreateParameter("ZipCode", adVarWChar, _
 adParamInput, 255, Z2Null(Request.Form("txtZipCode")))
cmd.Parameters.Append prm
Set prm = cmd.CreateParameter("Phone", adVarWChar, _
 adParamInput, 255, Z2Null(Request.Form("txtPhone")))
cmd.Parameters.Append prm
Set prm = cmd.CreateParameter("Extension", adVarWChar, _
 adParamInput, 255, Z2Null(Request.Form("txtExtension")))
cmd.Parameters.Append prm
Set prm = cmd.CreateParameter("Notes", adLongVarWChar, _
 adParamInput, 255, Z2Null(Trim(Request.Form("tarNotes"))))
cmd.Parameters.Append prm
```

The Command object is used to execute an insert query with a number of parameters. In Chapter 6, we discussed in detail how to use the Command object's Parameters collection to append parameters to a SQL Server stored procedure. The technique also works with Access parameter queries, as we have shown here.

HTML forms, like VB forms (but not Access forms) don't store Nulls. Instead, any blank strings are stored as zero-length strings. Thus, we use the Z2Null function from UtilInc.asp to convert zero-length strings from the HTML controls to Nulls.

The remaining code on the page executes the Command object, checks if it worked, and informs the user appropriately. The code also destroys the ADO objects:

```
cmd.Execute varRecords
If varRecords <> 0 Then
    Response.Write "New record added!"
```

```
Else
    Response.Write "Unable to add new record."
End If

Set prm = Nothing
Set cmd = Nothing
Set cnn = Nothing
%>
<P>
<A HREF="CustomerEdit1.asp">Return to Customer Menu</A>
</BODY>
</HTML>
```

The CustomerAdd2.asp page is shown in Figure 14.22, after a successful record addition.

**FIGURE 14.22**
A new customer record has been successfully added.

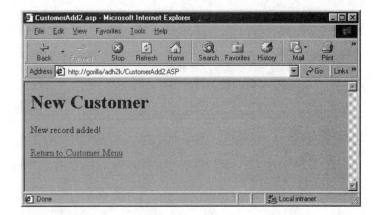

## Drilling Down

A common need in application development—on any platform—is the ability of the user to see a list of records and drill down into one of the records. The CustomerEdit1.asp, CustomerEdit2.asp, and CustomerEdit3.asp pages create a drill-down interface for viewing and editing customer records.

**NOTE**

This example won't work with the SQL Server version of the database because it makes use of Access action queries. You could easily modify it, however, to use SQL Server stored procedures instead.

## The CustomerEdit1.asp Page

The CusotmerEdit1.asp page presents a table of customer records similar to the CustomerTable.asp page shown earlier in the chapter. The table of customers in CustomerTable1.asp, however, includes hyperlinks that drill down to a given record for editing.

Here's the first portion of the page:

```
<%@ LANGUAGE="VBScript" %>
<% Option Explicit %>
<HTML>
<HEAD>
<TITLE>CustomerEdit1.asp</TITLE>
</HEAD>
<BODY bgColor=#87ceeb>
<!--#include file="ADO2Inc.asp"-->
<!--#include file="CnnInc.asp"-->
<H1>Select a Customer Record</H1>
<%
Dim cnn
Dim rst
Dim strSQL

Set cnn = Server.CreateObject("ADODB.Connection")
Set rst = Server.CreateObject("ADODB.Recordset")

cnn.Open strADH2KCnn

strSQL = "SELECT CustomerId, " & _
  "LastName + ', ' + FirstName As FullName, " & _
  "City, State FROM tblCustomer " & _
  "ORDER BY LastName, FirstName"
rst.Open strSQL, cnn, adOpenForwardOnly, _
```

```
    adLockReadOnly, adCmdText

If rst.EOF Then
    Response.Write "No customer records found."
Else
```

The code creates a recordset based on a SQL string that grabs CustomerID, City, and State from tblCustomer and creates a computed field, FullName, that concatenates the customer's last name and first name together.

Just like in CustomerTable.asp, the next portion of code creates an HTML table and fills it with the rows from the tblCustomer table. The difference is in the first column of the table. Rather than just displaying the full customer name, each displayed name is a hyperlink that displays the customer name, but is linked to CustomerEdit2.asp, passing the CustomerID number to the page via the query string:

```
%>
<TABLE BORDER=2>
    <TR>
        <TH>Customer Name</TH>
        <TH>City</TH>
        <TH>State</TH>
    </TR>
<%
    Do While Not rst.EOF
%>
    <TR>
        <TD><A HREF="CustomerEdit2.asp?CustomerId=
        <%=rst("CustomerId")%>"><%=rst("FullName")%></A></TD>
        <TD><%=rst("City")%></TD>
        <TD><%=rst("State")%></TD>
    </TR>
<%
        rst.MoveNext
    Loop
%>
</TABLE>
<%
End If
Set rst = Nothing
```

```
Set cnn = Nothing
%>
<P>
<A HREF="CustomerAdd1.asp">Add a New Customer</A>
<P>
<A HREF="AspMenu.asp">Return to ASP Menu</A>
</BODY>
</HTML>
```

The CustomerEdit1.asp page is shown in Figure 14.23.

**FIGURE 14.23**
The CustomerEdit1.asp
page displays a list of customer records with hyper-
links to each record.

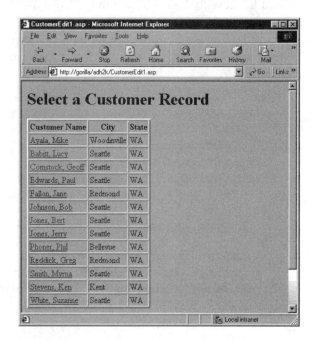

## The CustomerEdit2.asp Page

The CustomerEdit2.asp page is responsible for pulling the existing customer record into an HTML form for editing, as shown in Figure 14.24.

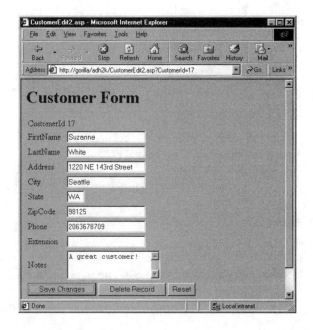

**FIGURE 14.24**
CustomerEdit2.asp displays a customer's record for editing.

Here's the start of the page:

```
<%@ LANGUAGE="VBScript" %>
<% Option Explicit %>
<HTML>
<HEAD>
<TITLE>CustomerEdit2.asp</TITLE>
</HEAD>
<BODY bgColor=#87ceeb>
<!--#include file="ADO2Inc.asp"-->
<!--#include file="CnnInc.asp"-->
<H1>Customer Form</H1>
<%
Dim cnn
Dim rst
Dim strSQL

Set cnn = Server.CreateObject("ADODB.Connection")
Set rst = Server.CreateObject("ADODB.Recordset")
```

```
If IsEmpty(Request.QueryString("CustomerId")) Then
    Response.Write "This page should be called from " & _
     "<A HREF=""CustomerEdit1.asp"">CustomerEdit1.asp</A>."
    Response.End
End If
strSQL = "SELECT * FROM tblCustomer " & _
 "WHERE CustomerId=" & Request.QueryString("CustomerId")

cnn.Open strADH2KCnn
rst.Open strSQL, cnn, adOpenKeyset, _
 adLockReadOnly, adCmdText
If rst.EOF Then
    Response.Write "No customer records found."
    Response.End
End If
%>
```

The SQL string for the recordset is constructed using the CustomerID passed in the query string to the page. The page includes a little error checking code that looks for an empty query string or empty recordset and executes a Response.End method after reporting the problem if either of these conditions are met.

The next part of the page creates the form with its ACTION attribute set to the CustomerEdit3.asp page:

```
<FORM METHOD="Post" ACTION="CustomerEdit3.ASP">
    <INPUT Name="txtCustomerId" Type=Hidden
    VALUE="<%=rst("CustomerId")%>" SIZE=5>
<TABLE>
    <TR>
        <TD>CustomerId</TD>
        <TD><%=rst("CustomerId")%></TD>
    </TR>
    <TR>
        <TD>FirstName</TD>
        <TD><INPUT Name="txtFirstName"
        VALUE="<%=rst("FirstName")%>" SIZE=20></TD>
    </TR>
    <TR>
        <TD>LastName</TD>
        <TD><INPUT Name="txtLastName"
        VALUE="<%=rst("LastName")%>" SIZE=20></TD>
    </TR>

... page continues ...
```

A table with no border is used to align the controls nicely within the form. This is a commonly used trick on Web pages.

We don't want users editing the CustomerID value, so we display it as uneditable text on the page. We also need to pass its value to the next page with the form, but plain HTML text doesn't get posted to the next page so we also include the CustomerID value in a hidden form input control.

The values of the fields are placed into the controls by setting each control's VALUE attribute equal to the value returned from the appropriate field in the recordset using this syntax:

```
VALUE="<%=rst("field_name")%>"
```

We've only shown here the source for the first few of the form controls. The rest of the controls are filled similarly.

After the textbox input controls, we've placed two submit input controls and one reset input control on the form:

```
<TD><INPUT name="cmdSubmit"
type=submit value="Save Changes"></TD>
<TD><INPUT name="cmdSubmit"
type=submit value="Delete Record"></TD>
<TD><INPUT name="cmdSubmit"
type=reset value="Reset"></TD>
```

We've given the submit buttons the same name but different values. Since we named the submit buttons, the value will be posted to the CustomerEdit3.asp page along with the values of the other controls. This way, we'll be able to tell on the next page if the user clicked the Save Changes button or the Delete Record button.

## The CustomerEdit3.asp Page

The final piece to this three-piece puzzle is the CustomerEdit3.asp page. Like the CustomerAdd2.asp page, this page uses parameterized action queries to update or delete the customer record. Here's the script from the page:

```
<%
' This page updates the Customer record
' using one of three Access action queries.


' -------------------------------------------------
' This page won't work with the SQL Server
' version of the database because the
' SQL Server database doesn't contain the queries.
' -------------------------------------------------
```

```
Dim cnn
Dim cmd
Dim varRecords
Dim prm

Set cnn = Server.CreateObject("ADODB.Connection")
Set cmd = Server.CreateObject("ADODB.Command")

cnn.Open strADH2KCnn
Set cmd.ActiveConnection = cnn
cmd.CommandType = adCmdStoredProc

Select Case Request.Form("cmdSubmit")
Case "Save Changes"
   cmd.CommandText = "qryCustomerUpdate"
   Set prm = cmd.CreateParameter("CustomerId", adInteger, _
    adParamInput, ,Z2Null(Request.Form("txtCustomerId")))
   cmd.Parameters.Append prm
   Set prm = cmd.CreateParameter("FirstName", adVarWChar, _
    adParamInput, 50, Z2Null(Request.Form("txtFirstName")))
   cmd.Parameters.Append prm
   Set prm = cmd.CreateParameter("LastName", adVarWChar, _
    adParamInput, 50, Z2Null(Request.Form("txtLastName")))
   cmd.Parameters.Append prm
   Set prm = cmd.CreateParameter("Address", adVarWChar, _
    adParamInput, 50, Z2Null(Request.Form("txtAddress")))
   cmd.Parameters.Append prm
   Set prm = cmd.CreateParameter("City", adVarWChar, _
    adParamInput, 50, Z2Null(Request.Form("txtCity")))
   cmd.Parameters.Append prm
   Set prm = cmd.CreateParameter("State", adVarWChar, _
    adParamInput, 2, Z2Null(Request.Form("txtState")))
   cmd.Parameters.Append prm
   Set prm = cmd.CreateParameter("ZipCode", adVarWChar, _
    adParamInput, 10, Z2Null(Request.Form("txtZipCode")))
   cmd.Parameters.Append prm
   Set prm = cmd.CreateParameter("Phone", adVarWChar, _
    adParamInput, 10, Z2Null(Request.Form("txtPhone")))
   cmd.Parameters.Append prm
   Set prm = cmd.CreateParameter("Extension", adVarWChar, _
    adParamInput, 5, Z2Null(Request.Form("txtExtension")))
   cmd.Parameters.Append prm
```

```
    Set prm = cmd.CreateParameter("Notes", adVarWChar, _
      adParamInput, 100, Z2Null(Trim(Request.Form("tarNotes"))))
    cmd.Parameters.Append prm

    cmd.Execute varRecords
    If varRecords <> 0 Then
       Response.Write "Record updated!"
    Else
       Response.Write "Unable to update record."
    End If
Case "Delete Record"
    cmd.CommandText = "qryCustomerDelete"
    Set prm = cmd.CreateParameter("CustomerId", adInteger, _
      adParamInput, ,Z2Null(Request.Form("txtCustomerId")))
    cmd.Parameters.Append prm
    cmd.Execute varRecords
    If varRecords <> 0 Then
       Response.Write "Record deleted!"
    Else
       Response.Write "Unable to delete record."
    End If
End Select

Set prm = Nothing
Set cmd = Nothing
Set cnn = Nothing
%>
```

The VBScript code branches based on the value of the cmdSubmit button obtained from the Request.Form collection. If cmdSubmit equals "Save Changes," then the qryCustomerUpdate query is used to update the customer record. Otherwise, if cmdSubmit equals "Delete Record," then the qryCustomerDelete query is used to delete the customer record. Both queries require parameters that are appended to the Command object's Parameters collection. The values of the parameters are grabbed from the prior page using the Request.Form collection.

## Providing Recordset Navigation

Access forms (as well as data access pages) normally have recordset navigation controls you can use to navigate from one record to another. While letting users freely navigate around a large recordset via an ASP page is usually not a good idea, there are times when, with a limited number of records, recordset navigation may prove useful.

While recordset navigation on Access forms comes for free, the same cannot be said for inherently stateless ASP pages. On first thought, you might attempt to solve the problem by storing the Recordset object in a Session variable. In fact, this is what forms generated by the Access 97 Publish to the Web Wizard did. This sort of scheme is a bad idea (see the "Potential Problems with the Session Object" section earlier in this chapter) because it eats up a potentially large amount of memory on your Web server, depends on cookies being enabled in user browsers, and ultimately reduces the scalability of your application.

## A Better Solution

A better solution is to use the AbsolutePosition property of the ADO Recordset object, a hidden form control, and a set of four submit buttons to create a page that looks like the one shown in Figure 14.25.

**FIGURE 14.25**

The AllCustomers.asp page, shown here in Netscape Navigator, displays customer records with record navigational controls.

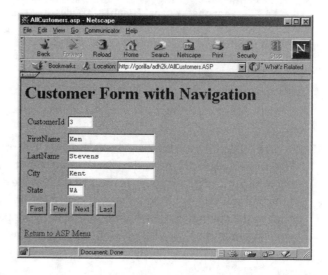

## The AbsolutePosition Property

The Recordset object has a property, AbsolutePosition, that you can use to read and update the position of the current record cursor within the recordset. To determine the position of the current record, you use syntax like this:

```
variable = recordset.AbsolutePosition
```

To move to a record with a different position in the recordset, you can use this syntax:

```
recordset.AbsolutePosition = position
```

The AbsolutePosition property is not supported by all types of recordsets. Some providers may not support it at all. Access and SQL Server server-side cursors only support the AbsolutePosition property when you create static or keyset recordsets.

## The AllCustomers.asp Page

The AllCustomers.asp page begins much like the other data-driven ASP examples in this chapter:

```
<%@ LANGUAGE="VBScript" %>
<% Option Explicit %>
<HTML>
<HEAD>
<TITLE>AllCustomers.asp</TITLE>
</HEAD>
<BODY bgColor=#87ceeb>
<!--#include file="ADO2Inc.asp"-->
<!--#include file="CnnInc.asp"-->
<H1>Customer Form with Navigation</H1>
<%
Dim cnn
Dim rst
Dim varPageNum
Dim varAction

Set cnn = Server.CreateObject("ADODB.Connection")
Set rst = Server.CreateObject("ADODB.Recordset")

cnn.Open strADH2KCnn
rst.Open "tblCustomer", cnn, adOpenStatic, _
```

```
   adLockReadOnly, adCmdTable
If rst.EOF Then
   Response.Write "No customer records found."
Else
```

When you click one of the recordset navigation controls shown in Figure 14.25, the form posts the form controls to itself. Yes, the ACTION attribute for the form is set to "AllCustomers.asp." Here's the code—shown slightly out of sequence—that creates the HTML form and navigational controls:

```
<FORM METHOD="Post" ACTION="AllCustomers.ASP">
   <INPUT TYPE="hidden" Name="PageNum"
   VALUE="<%=rst.AbsolutePosition%>">
<TABLE>
   <TR>
      <TD>CustomerId</TD>
      <TD><INPUT Name="txtCustomerId"
      VALUE="<%=rst("CustomerId")%>" SIZE=5></TD>
   </TR>
   <TR>
      <TD>FirstName</TD>
      <TD><INPUT Name="txtFirstName"
      VALUE="<%=rst("FirstName")%>" SIZE=20></TD>
   </TR>
   <TR>
      <TD>LastName</TD>
      <TD><INPUT Name="txtLastName"
      VALUE="<%=rst("LastName")%>" SIZE=20></TD>
   </TR>
   <TR>
      <TD>City</TD>
      <TD><INPUT Name="txtCity"
      VALUE="<%=rst("City")%>" SIZE=20></TD>
   </TR>
   <TR>
      <TD>State</TD>
      <TD><INPUT Name="txtState"
      VALUE="<%=rst("State")%>" SIZE=3></TD>
   </TR>
   </TR>
</TABLE>
<TABLE>
   <TR>
```

```
        <TD><INPUT name=cmdSubmit
        type=submit value="First"></TD>
        <TD><INPUT name=cmdSubmit
        type=submit value="Prev"></TD>
        <TD><INPUT name=cmdSubmit
        type=submit value="Next"></TD>
        <TD><INPUT name=cmdSubmit
        type=submit value="Last"></TD>
      </TR>
    </TABLE>
  </FORM>
```

The hidden PageNum control stores the current value of the AbsolutePosition property. This way, when one of the navigational controls is pressed, we'll know the prior position in the recordset.

The navigation buttons are submit controls with the same name. When the page is submitted to itself, we'll be able to tell which button was pressed by checking its value.

The following code—which actually comes before the form code—retrieves the value of the PageNum and cmdSubmit controls. These controls tell us where we were and where we need to go, respectively. Here's the code that retrieves the values from the Request.Form collection and saves the values to two variables, varPageNum and varAction:

```
    ' If not the first time visiting the form
    ' then handle record navigation.
    If Not IsEmpty(Request.Form("PageNum")) Then
        varPageNum = CLng(Request.Form("PageNum"))
        varAction = Request.Form("cmdSubmit")
```

When moving to the first or last record in the recordset, there's no need for AbsolutePosition. Instead, we use the MoveFirst or MoveLast methods of the Recordset object:

```
        ' First and Last are easy.
        If varAction = "First" Then
            rst.MoveFirst
        ElseIf varAction = "Last" Then
            rst.MoveLast
```

When someone clicks the Next or Prev buttons, we either increment or decrement the value of varPageNum. That's not enough, however, since we may have already been at the first or last record in the recordset. The beginning of the recordset is easy to tackle—if varPageNum is less that 1, just set it to 1.

The other end of the recordset could be handled similarly, but alas, we don't want to take the potentially expensive hit associated with moving to the end of the recordset just to determine the RecordCount of the recordset. So, we use a different tack. We attempt the MoveNext and then checks to see if we've overshot the recordset by checking if the AbsolutePosition property equals the special constant adPosEOF or –3. If this is the case, then we reposition ourselves one record prior to EOF, that is, the last record in the recordset.

Here's the Nex/Prev recordset navigation code:

```
Else
    ' Move a single page forward or back.
    If varAction = "Next" Then
        varPageNum = varPageNum + 1
    ElseIf varAction = "Prev" Then
        varPageNum = varPageNum - 1
    End If
    ' Check if overshot BOF.
    If varPageNum < 1 Then
        varPageNum = 1
    End If
    ' Attempt to position record.
    rst.AbsolutePosition = varPageNum
    ' Back up one record if at EOF.
    If rst.AbsolutePosition = adPosEOF Then
        ' Could have also used rst.MoveLast
        rst.AbsolutePosition = varPageNum - 1
    End If
    End If
End If
%>
```

NOTE    The AllCustomers.asp example doesn't provide any way to save an edited record, but it could easily be extended to support both editing and navigation.

# Paginating a Recordset

We've created another example, AllOrders.asp, that demonstrates a set of properties of the Recordset object you use can use to split your recordset into pages and navigate from one page to another. The previous example, AllCustomers.asp, used a related property, AbsolutePosition, to move one record at a time. The pagination properties, however, allow you to move in customizable chunks of records.

## The Pagination Properties and Methods

The pagination properties are summarized in Table 14.10.

**TABLE 14.10:**   The Recordset Pagination Properties

| Property | Purpose |
| --- | --- |
| PageSize | Size of a page; you set the PageSize property to divide the recordset into a set of equal-sized pages (the last page will be less than or equal to the page size). |
| PageCount | The number of total pages in the recordset; read only after you have set the PageSize property. |
| AbsolutePage | The number of the current page; can be between 1 and PageCount; read/write. |

You use the PageSize property to set the page size of a recordset. Once set, you can navigate to the beginning of a page using the AbsolutePage property. The read-only PageCount property tells you the total number of pages in the recordset.

## The AllOrders.asp Page

AllOrders.asp uses the recordset pagination properties to display records from the tblOrder table in 10-record pages. AllOrders.asp is shown in Figure 14.26.

**FIGURE 14.26**

The AllOrders.asp page displays 10 order records at a time, allowing you to easily navigate from one page to another.

The AllOrders.asp page begins by creating the connection and opening a static, read-only Recordset object. The script then sets the PageSize property to a page size of 10 and grabs the total number of pages from the PageCount property:

```
<%@ LANGUAGE="VBScript" %>
<% Option Explicit %>
<HTML>
<HEAD>
<TITLE>AllOrders.asp</TITLE>
</HEAD>
<BODY bgColor=#87ceeb>
<!--#include file="ADO2Inc.asp"-->
<!--#include file="CnnInc.asp"-->
<H1>Order Table with Pagination</H1>
<%
Dim cnn
Dim rst
Dim varPageNum
Dim varPageCnt
```

```
Dim varAction
Dim intRow

Set cnn = Server.CreateObject("ADODB.Connection")
Set rst = Server.CreateObject("ADODB.Recordset")

cnn.Open strADH2KCnn
rst.Open "tblOrder", cnn, adOpenStatic, _
 adLockReadOnly, adCmdTable
' Set page size to 10 and store away the
' total number of pages.
rst.PageSize = 10
varPageCnt = rst.PageCount

If rst.EOF Then
    Response.Write "No customer records found."
Else
```

## Page Navigation Code

The page navigation code in this example is a little more complex than the record-set navigation from AllCustomers.asp. It begins by determining the previous page number and the requested action from the Request.Form collection:

```
' If not first time visiting form, then
' need to handle page navigation.
If Not IsEmpty(Request.Form("PageNum")) Then
    varPageNum = CLng(Request.Form("PageNum"))
    varAction = Request.Form("cmdSubmit")
```

Like in the AllCustomers.asp example, the First and Last Page actions are easily handled:

```
' First and Last Page requests are easy.
If varAction = "First Page" Then
    rst.AbsolutePage = 1
ElseIf varAction = "Last Page" Then
    rst.AbsolutePage = varPageCnt
Else
```

The Prev and Next Page actions require a bit more work because you need to check for overshooting of the recordset boundaries. Here's the code to move backwards a page:

```
' Prev Page request.
If varAction = "Prev Page" Then
    If varPageNum = 1 Then
        ' If at first page, then
        ' stay there.
        varPageNum = 1
    ElseIf varPageNum = adPosEOF Then
        ' If at EOF, then varPageNum = -3,
        ' so need to special case.
        varPageNum = varPageCnt - 1
    Else
        ' Otherwise, back up 1 page.
        varPageNum = varPageNum - 1
    End If
```

When on the last page, ADO sets AbsolutePage to a value of –3 (adPosEOF), so the code needs to handle this occurrence specially. Also, you don't want to back up past the first page. Otherwise, the code just decrements the page number.

Here's the code to handle moving to the next page:

```
' Next page request.
ElseIf varAction = "Next Page" Then
    ' If at EOF or the last page,
    ' then stay at last page.
    If varPageNum = adPosEOF Or _
     varPageNum = varPageCnt Then
        varPageNum = varPageCnt
    Else
        ' Otherwise, move to next page.
        varPageNum = varPageNum + 1
    End If
End If
```

If the recordset is on the last page or EOF, then the code simply sets the page number to the last page. Otherwise, it just increments the page number.

With the page number calculated, it's time to move to the desired page. If this is the first time visiting the form, then the recordset will already be at the first page, but the code still needs to set varPageNum to 1:

```
            ' Now move to the calculated page.
            rst.AbsolutePage = varPageNum
        End If
    Else
        ' First time visiting form, so set
        ' varPageNum to 1 for future reference.
        varPageNum = 1
    End If
%>
```

## Displaying a Page Worth of Records

The next portion of code creates the table header. It's pure HTML:

```
<TABLE BORDER=2>
    <TR>
        <TH>OrderId</TH>
        <TH>OrderDate</TH>
        <TH>CustomerId</TH>
        <TH>OrderTakerId</TH>
        <TH>DeliveryDate</TH>
        <TH>PaymentMethod</TH>
    </TR>
```

This code outputs the page of records.

```
<%
    ' Now move through all the rows on
    ' the current page.
    For intRow = 1 to rst.PageSize
%>
    <TR>
        <TD><%=rst("OrderId")%></TD>
        <TD><%=rst("OrderDate")%></TD>
        <TD><%=rst("CustomerId")%></TD>
        <TD><%=rst("OrderTakerId")%></TD>
        <TD><%=rst("DeliveryDate")%></TD>
        <TD><%=rst("PaymentMethod")%></TD>
    </TR>
```

```
<%
        If intRow < rst.PageSize Then
           rst.MoveNext
           ' If hit EOF on last page,
           ' back up one record.
           If rst.EOF Then
              rst.MovePrevious
              Exit For
           End If
        End If
   Next

   ' Set varPageNum to actual page number.
   varPageNum = rst.AbsolutePage
%>
</TABLE>
```

The code executes a MoveNext unless it is at the last record of the page. Of course, it's entirely possible—in fact, probable—that the last page will have less than 10 records. So the code has to handle the possibility that it will run into EOF. If it does, then it backs off one record.

The navigation controls are implemented by placing submit controls on a form that posts to itself:

```
<FORM METHOD="Post" ACTION="AllOrders.ASP" Name="frmOrder">
   <INPUT Name="PageNum" TYPE="Hidden"
   VALUE="<%=varPageNum%>">
<TABLE>
   <TR>
      <TD><INPUT name=cmdSubmit type=submit
      value="First Page"></TD>
      <TD><INPUT name=cmdSubmit type=submit
      value="Prev Page"></TD>
      <TD><INPUT name=cmdSubmit type=submit
      value="Next Page"></TD>
      <TD><INPUT name=cmdSubmit type=submit
      value="Last Page"></TD>
      <TD>     </TD>
      <TD ALIGN="right">
      Page <%=varPageNum%> of <%=varPageCnt%> pages</TD>
   </TR>
</TABLE>
</FORM>
```

The code stores the current page number in a hidden input control named Page-Num and displays the current page number to the right of the navigation controls.

# Using the Office Web Components from ASP Pages

In Chapter 12 you learned about the Office Web Components. The Web Components provide sophisticated spreadsheet, pivot table, and charting capabilities as COM components. The examples in Chapter 12 showed how to use the Office Web Components from data access pages running in the user's Web browser.

You can also instantiate and use the Office Web Components from ASP pages. This usage of the Web Components has at least two advantages. Because the ASP code runs entirely on the server:

- You can use any Web browser

- You only need a license to use the components on the Web server machine

In these next sections, we look at examples of using the Office Spreadsheet and Chart controls on ASP pages. If you've already read Chapter 12, the examples should look familiar—they're modeled closely after examples in that chapter.

---

**NOTE**    We don't explain how to use the Office Web Components here, just how to use them on ASP pages. For more information on the Office Web Components, their object models, and how to program them, see Chapter 12.

---

## Using the Office Spreadsheet Component from an ASP Page

The Office Spreadsheet Component provides Excel's spreadsheet calculation engine in a small package. You can use the Spreadsheet Component to calculate statistics such as the median, perform linear regression analysis, and do just about anything you can do with Microsoft Excel.

## The SSComponent.asp Page

The SSComponent.asp page demonstrates how to call the component's spread-sheet calculation engine from an ASP page. SSComponent.asp uses the Spreadsheet Component to calculate the median value of a single-column recordset. Here's the portion of the page that creates the recordset and calls the CalculateMedian function:

```
Dim cnn
Dim rst
Dim varMedian

Set cnn = Server.CreateObject("ADODB.Connection")
Set rst = Server.CreateObject("ADODB.Recordset")

cnn.Open strADH2KCnn

rst.Open _
 "SELECT Quantity FROM tblOrderDetails " & _
 "WHERE Quantity > 1", cnn,adOpenStatic, _
 adLockReadOnly, adCmdText

' Call CalculateMedian which uses the
' Office Spreadsheet Component to calculate
' the median of a one-column recordset.
varMedian = CalculateMedian(rst)

rst.Close
Set rst = Nothing

%>
This example page uses the Office Spreadsheet Web Component
to calculate the median number of items
sold on a single order, when the number
of items sold is greater than 1.
<P>
The Spreadsheet component is instantiated on the server
from an ASP script. The data comes from the
tblOrderDetails table of the
CH14.MDB database. No processing was performed
on the client!
<P>
<FONT COLOR="red">And the Answer = <%=varMedian%>.</FONT>
```

This code creates a recordset that contains the Quantity field of the tblOrderDetails table for all records where Quantity is 2 or more and passes the recordset to the CalculateMedian function.

## Calculating the Median

The CalculateMedian function uses the Spreadsheet Component to calculate the median of Quantity for the recordset. Here's the CalculateMedian function:

```
Function CalculateMedian(rst)
    ' Return the median from a
    ' single-column recordset.
    Dim ss
    Dim strValues
    Dim lngRows

    Const adClipString = 2

    ' Get the rows from the recordset as a string,
    ' using a CR/LF as the row delimiter.
    strValues = rst.GetString(adClipString)

    ' Create the OWC Spreadsheet, in memory. Insert
    ' the values, using the CSVData property.
    Set ss = Server.CreateObject("owc.Spreadsheet")
    ss.CSVData = strValues

    ' Calculate the number of rows in the recordset (you
    ' couldn't get this from ADO because you opened a
    ' forward-only recordset).
    lngRows = ss.ActiveSheet.UsedRange.Rows.Count

    ' Set up the formula, in cell B1, and return the value.
    ss.Range("B1").Formula = "=MEDIAN(A1:A" & lngRows & ")"

    CalculateMedian = ss.Range("B1").Value

    ' Release the spreadsheet component.
    Set ss = Nothing
End Function
```

CalculateMedian uses the GetString method of the passed Recordset object to create a delimited string out of the Quantity field. The returned string is then fed to the spreadsheet using the Spreadsheet object's CSVData property.

Once the data is in the Spreadsheet control's spreadsheet, it's only a matter of using the component's Median function to calculate the median of the range of data and return the median in the return value of CalculateMedian.

The result of this less than exciting page is shown in Figure 14.27.

**FIGURE 14.27**

The value on this ASP page was calculated using the Office Spreadsheet component running on the server in an ASP page.

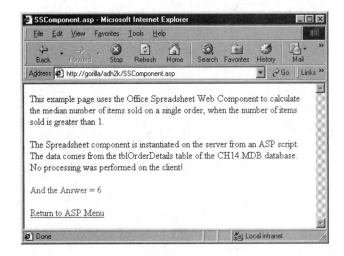

# Using the Office Chart Component from an ASP Page

They say a picture is worth a thousand words. With the Office Chart Component you can save thousands of words by generating dynamic, data-driven charts on the Web server from your ASP pages.

### The ChartComponent.asp Page

The ChartComponent.asp page demonstrates how to use the Chart Component to generate a pie chart from a query. This example is based on the ChartFromRecordset.htm data access page from Chapter 12.

The ChartComponent.asp page creates a recordset based on a GROUP BY query that returns the quantity of items sold by category. The code then passes the recordset to the FillPieChartFromRecordset subroutine that creates a new chart, sets its DataSource property to the recordset, and formats the chart as a pie chart. The created chart is returned to the immediate script where a random filename is generated and the ExportPicture method of the Chart Component is used to save the chart to a GIF file. The generated GIF image is then used to display the chart on the ASP page. As in the last example, all the processing occurs on the server so the Chart Component only needs to exist on the Web server machine. Figure 14.28 shows the chart created by the ChartComponent.asp page.

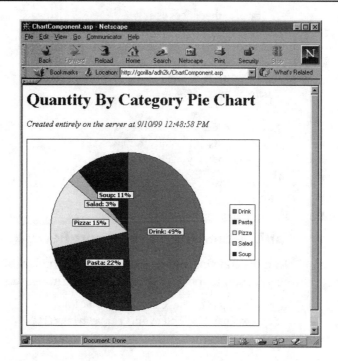

Here's the beginning of the ChartComponent.asp page:

```
<%@ LANGUAGE="VBScript" %>
<% Option Explicit %>
<!--#include file="ADO2Inc.asp"-->
<!--#include file="CnnInc.asp"-->
<%
Dim rst
Dim cnn
```

```
Dim strSQL
Dim owcChartSp
Dim strWebGIF
Dim strFileGIF
Dim c

Set cnn = Server.CreateObject("ADODB.Connection")
cnn.ConnectionString = strADH2KCnn
cnn.Open strADH2KCnn

' Set up the recordset.
strSQL = "SELECT Category, " & _
  "Sum(Quantity) AS SumOfQuantity " & _
  "FROM tblMenu INNER JOIN tblOrderDetails " & _
  "ON tblMenu.MenuId = tblOrderDetails.MenuId " & _
  "GROUP BY Category"

Set rst = Server.CreateObject("ADODB.Recordset")
rst.Open strSQL, cnn, adOpenStatic, _
  adLockReadOnly, adCmdText
```

The recordset is based on a GROUP BY SQL statement that returns the sum of Quantity by Category.

## Calling the FillPieChartFromRecordset Subroutine

Next, the code instantiates the Chart Component and passes the chart and the recordset off to the FillPieChartFromRecordset subroutine:

```
' Instantiate the Chart Component.
Set owcChartSp = Server.CreateObject("OWC.Chart")
Set c = owcChartSp.Constants

' Fill in the pie chart.
Call FillPieChartFromRecordset( _
  owcChartSp, rst, "Category", "SumOfQuantity")
```

The FillPieChartFromRecordset subroutine takes the recordset and creates a pie chart from it:

```
Sub FillPieChartFromRecordset( _
  owcChartSp, rst, _
  strCategoriesField, _
  strValuesField)
```

```
' Given a chart control, pull data from the
' specified recordset.

Dim owcChart

owcChartSp.Clear

Set owcChartSp.DataSource = rst
Set owcChart = owcChartSp.Charts.Add()

With owcChart
    .Type = c.chChartTypePie
    .HasLegend = True

    ' Hook up the two necessary data fields.
    .SetData c.chDimCategories, 0, strCategoriesField
    .SetData c.chDimValues, 0, strValuesField

    ' Show a percentage, but not an absolute
    ' value. Also, show the category name.
    ' Use ":" as the separator between
    ' the category name and the percentage.
    With .SeriesCollection(0).DataLabelsCollection.Add
        .HasPercentage = True
        .HasValue = False
        .HasCategoryName = True
        .Separator = ": "

        ' Use 8pt black text on a white background,
        ' in Tahoma font.
        .Interior.Color = "white"
        .Border.Color = "black"
        With .Font
            .Name = "Tahoma"
            .Color = "black"
            .Bold = True
            .Size = 8
        End With
    End With
End With
End Sub
```

See Chapter 12 for more detailed information on how the FillPieChartFrom-Recordset subroutine works.

## Living in Two Worlds

After the FillPieChartFromRecordset subroutine has performed its magic, the following code uses the Chart Component's ExportPicture method to create a GIF file from the chart:

```
' Create a unique file name using Rnd. This
' version of the file name will be used when
' accessing the file via ASP Objects.
Randomize
strWebGIF = "Temp" & Int(10000*Rnd()) & ".gif"
' Convert the relative name to name of file
' in current Windows folder using MapPath.
' This version of name is needed by Web components
' which work with Windows file system.
strFileGIF = Server.MapPath(strWebGIF)

' Export the chart previously created to a
' GIF file using the file system name.
owcChartSp.ExportPicture strFileGIF, _
  "gif", 450, 350

' Clean up
Set rst = Nothing
Set cnn = Nothing
Set owcChartSp = Nothing
```

This example requires that you work in two file system worlds: the virtual file system of the Web site, and the Windows file system. When placing image files onto a Web page, you need to work in the Web site's virtual file system. But the Office Web Components don't know anything about the Web site's world. They need real, hard-coded paths to a file. The bridge between these two systems is the Server.MapPath method. MapPath takes a Web site filename and converts into the Windows file system. That way, both the ASP page and the Office Web Component can both work with the same file, but from their own little worlds.

The code generates a random filename, which will be located in the same folder as the ASP page. Server.MapPath takes this virtual file system name and converts it to a path and name that can be handed off to the Chart Component.

**NOTE**   You can also use the Scripting.FileSystemObject object to generate a random filename. The Scripting component ships with IIS and Personal Web Server.

The only thing left to do is to create the HTML to host the newly created GIF file. The code that does this is shown here:

```
%>
<HTML>
<HEAD><TITLE>ChartComponent.asp</TITLE></HEAD>
<BODY>
<H1>Quantity By Category Pie Chart</H1>
<I>Created entirely on the server at <%=Now()%></I>
<P><IMG SRC="<%= strWebGIF%>"
ALT="A dynamically-created pie chart">
<P>
<A HREF="AspMenu.asp">Return to ASP Menu</A>
</BODY>
</HTML>
```

**WARNING**   In this example, we haven't provided a mechanism for deleting the temporary GIF file. This could become a problem if this was used on an active Web site. We've provided a page, DelTempFiles.asp, that uses the Scripting.FileSystemObject object to delete the temp files. You could incorporate the script from DelTemp-Files.asp into your home page, or run it on some regular basis to clear out the temp files.

## What the Browser Sees

To prove that the Web browser is doing no processing, you might want to take a look at the Web page's source when viewing the page in your favorite browser. If you do, you should see source that looks like the following:

```
<HTML>
<HEAD><TITLE>ChartComponent.asp</TITLE></HEAD>
<BODY>
<H1>Quantity By Category Pie Chart</H1>
<I>Created entirely on the server at 9/10/99 12:48:58
PM</I>
<P><IMG SRC="Temp3131.gif"
```

```
ALT="A dynamically-created pie chart">
<P>
<A HREF="AspMenu.asp">Return to ASP Menu</A>
</BODY>
</HTML>
```

---

**NOTE**    The Office Web Component examples presented in this chapter will work with either the CH14.MDB Access database or the ADH2KSQL SQL Server database. See the "Creating Data-Driven ASP Pages" section earlier in this chapter for information on how to change the connection string to point to the SQL Server version of the sample database.

---

# Summary

While data access pages are a great way to make Access data available on an intranet site, they have several shortcomings that prevent their widespread use. In this chapter we looked at a couple of alternatives to data access pages: static HTML and ASP pages.

We looked at how to generate static HTML and dynamic ASP pages using the Access Export dialog box. We also looked in detail at how to create data-driven ASP pages from scratch using VBScript and ADO and examined why these hand-coded pages are more flexible, powerful, and efficient than the Access-generated pages. We looked at several different ASP examples, including examples that edited, inserted, and deleted database records; examples that demonstrated how to display paginated recordsets; and examples that showed how to employ the Office Web Components on the Web server.

# Using Source Code Control

- Understanding source code control

- Exploring source code control integration in Access 2000

- Using Microsoft Visual SourceSafe with Access

- Controlling Visual SourceSafe with VBA

As the popularity of Microsoft Access grew over time among both commercial and corporate developers, it began to show a weakness when multiple developers used it to contribute to a single database development project. Not only was it difficult for two or more developers to work simultaneously on a single database (for instance, changes to modules required other developers to close and reopen the database), but it was impractical, if not impossible, to track changes to individual database objects. "Pure" language developers (those working in C, C++, Visual Basic, and so on) created a solution to this problem long ago in the form of *source code control* applications. These applications use a network directory to store copies of a program's source files and regulate access to them. Until recently Access has been incompatible with source code control programs because, instead of having separate source files that are combined to create a single executable program, Access applications are stored in a single, binary file format. Microsoft remedied the situation and built source code control compatibility into Access 97. This capability remains, relatively unchanged, in Access 2000. In this chapter we look at how source code control is supported, as well as how to use it with Microsoft's control program, Visual SourceSafe.

# What Is Source Code Control?

The driving principle behind source code control (abbreviated SCC in this chapter) is simple. Any programmer involved in a development project is allowed to use source files to compile, or *build*, a version of the application. Only one developer, however, is given the privilege to modify a source file at any given time. This eliminates the chance that two developers will overwrite each other's changes by working on the same source file at the same time. If the development tool has properly integrated source code control, the mechanics of making this work are transparent to the developer. The following sections explain the concepts encompassed in source code control, all of which apply generally to development tools that support SCC. Later sections cover how Access 2000 supports and uses these concepts.

## Source Code Control Provider

At the heart of source code control is the actual software that manages access to source files, called the SCC *provider*. Microsoft offers a provider called Visual SourceSafe that you can use with its Visual Basic, VBA, Visual FoxPro, Visual

InterDev, and Visual C++ languages, as well as with Access. Other third party software is also available. A provider can follow either the file-server or client-server deployment model, with provider software running on each developer's computer or on a centralized server. In each case, a centralized database or directory structure stores source code files.

SCC provider software usually supports distinct user accounts, just as the database server or network software does. Each developer wishing to use any managed source code files must have an account with the provider. This ensures that only authorized users can access the valuable files and provides a convenient way to track changes to them.

## Projects and Source Files

Before you can begin using source code control with your programming language, you must set up a *project* on the server. Most providers let you do this as a separate step or by importing an existing development project. At a minimum, the SCC project defines the source code files to be managed. Depending on the provider, you may also be able to set other project options.

Most providers let you share source files among several projects. This is extremely useful for managing "utility" functions that are used in many different applications.

## Check In and Check Out

When you want to work on a particular source file, you must "check out" the file from the project on the server. After making sure no other developer already has the file checked out, the provider copies the latest version of the file to your computer so you can modify it. When you have made your changes and want others to be able to use them in their copies of the application, you check the file back in. In this sense source code control is like a library with the SCC provider acting as librarian.

## Multiple Check Out and Merge

Some source code control providers offer the ability to have multiple developers check out the same source file. While this can potentially lead to problems, it is sometimes necessary, especially with source files for generic or "utility" functions.

During the check in process, the SCC provider compares the version being checked in with the current version. If it detects conflicts it cannot resolve, you must manually merge the two files. Many provider programs automatically resolve some conflicts (for example, if the file being checked in is a complete superset of the current version), but you will have to cope with many conflicts yourself.

## Get

If you don't want to modify a particular file but want only to include it in your copy of the application, you perform what's known as a *get* or *sync*. This copies the most recent copy from the server to your computer, overwriting the existing version stored there. Developers typically perform gets periodically during the day to bring in changes to source code files made by other developers.

## Diff and Restore

Most SCC providers support *versioning*. When a developer checks in a source file, rather than simply overwriting the copy on the server, the provider archives it, logging the date and time it was checked in and by whom. This allows you to compare versions, called performing a *diff* (for difference). The provider software usually displays the versions side by side with any changes highlighted. Should you wish, you can *restore* an older version of the source file, making it the current one.

# Support for Source Code Control in Access 2000

As mentioned earlier in this chapter, the main reason earlier versions of Access were incompatible with source code control programs was their single, binary file structure. Not only did this make check in and check out useless, but given the changing structure of the binary file contents, performing a diff on two functionally equivalent databases would always show changes. It took an act of Access Program Management to add specific support for SCC programs to the base product. In this section, we explain how Microsoft chose to support source code control in Access 2000.

**NOTE**    Other than bug fixes, there were no changes to the level of support for source code control between Access 97 and Access 2000.

## Source Code Control Add-In

Before you can use source code control features of Access, you must purchase a copy of Microsoft Office 2000 Developer (MOD). (This used to be called Office Developer Edition and is a replacement to the venerable Access Developer's Toolkit.) It includes the add-in and DLLs that implement the link between Access and a source code control provider. Once you've installed the add-in from the MOD and a source code control provider, Access invokes the add-in at key points in the development process (when you open a database or create a new object, for example). The add-in then communicates with the SCC provider using a standard set of functions to perform actions such as check in, check out, and get.

**NOTE**    Unlike ODE, Office 2000 Developer also includes a copy of Visual SourceSafe in the box, meaning you have everything you need to use source code control in Access 2000.

**TIP**    The full Microsoft Office 2000 Developer product includes all the applications in Office 2000 Premium (Access, Excel, etc.). If you've already purchased a copy of Office 2000, Microsoft offers a version of MOD that includes just the incremental tools and add-ins, including the Access SCC add-in.

## What about the VBA Source Code Control Add-in?

With Office 2000 Developer, Microsoft has created a new add-in that takes advantage of the extensibility architecture in VBA 6 to provide source code control features to any VBA 6 application. Any application *except* Access, that is. The VBA source code control add-in only works with the contents of a VBA project (standard and class modules) and ignores any other document or application data. In this sense it's much less functional than the Access-specific add-in, which manages forms, reports, queries and data as well. It is for this reason that the VBA add-in specifically disables itself when it detects it's running under VBA in Access.

> Nevertheless, now that source code control is available in other VBA-enabled products, it is easier than ever to share source code with any application that uses VBA. You can maintain a single source code control database that includes projects written in Access, Excel, Word, or any or dozens of third party VBA-enabled products. For more information on sharing source files between projects, see the "Sharing and Branching" section later in this chapter.

## The Process

In the "Working with VSS from Access 2000" section later in this chapter, we explain the exact steps to manage a database project using a source code control provider. Here, however, we discuss the process in general.

After installing the appropriate software (a provider and the SCC add-in), you (as a single developer who has the most up-to-date copy of the MDB or ADP file) begin the process by creating a source code control project from an existing Access database or project. Creating a project from an existing database produces the appropriate source files on the source code control server and makes them available to other developers.

Once the project exists on the server, you want to allow other developers to begin using it. You start by creating a new Access database or project on each developer's workstation and, in effect, importing all the objects from the project on the server. These developers work on their own copies of the database. You create each database using the SCC add-in menu commands, however, not by creating a database and importing objects yourself. Other developers can then work with the objects in their own copies of the database, checking objects in and out as necessary.

Eventually you'll want to remove a database from source code control so you can distribute it to your users. To do this you simply compact the database. Access asks, each time you compact a database, whether you want to remove it from source code control. If you answer Yes, Access breaks the link from the SCC project, and you will no longer be able to use SCC commands.

---

**WARNING**   Once you've removed a database from source code control, there is no way to re-establish the link with the SCC project. The only solution is to start from scratch.

---

## Object Exchanges

An Access database combines two things that are normally separate in other development environments: data and application objects (queries, forms, reports, macros, and modules). Access 2000 treats these separately when it comes to source code control. When Access exchanges application objects with an SCC provider, it exports each object as a separate text file. These files define the properties of each object and, where applicable, any VBA code the object contains, using a format similar to the one Microsoft Visual Basic has used for years. Everything else an Access database can contain (tables, relationships, command bars, custom properties, and import/export specifications) remains in a single, binary file that the SCC add-in treats as a separate component.

Figure 15.1 illustrates how Access treats objects under source code control. When you retrieve them from the SCC provider, Access reassembles them into a single MDB or ADP file. For details on the file structure, see the "Object Text File Formats" section later in this chapter.

**FIGURE 15.1**

How Access treats database objects under source code control

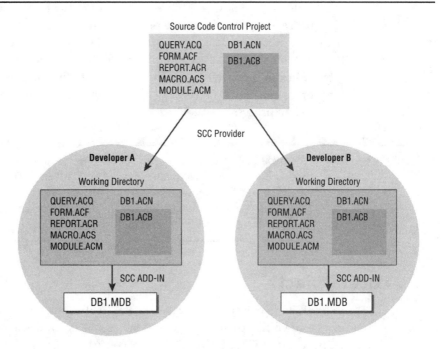

**NOTE**    The binary file containing a database's tables, relationships, and other objects is, itself, an Access database that contains these objects and nothing more. Even though Access Data Projects contain no data, Access still creates a binary component containing toolbar settings, etc.

While the exchange of objects is accomplished with text files, it is important to remember that developers themselves still work with an Access database or project. The conversion to text files and back is completely transparent. Developers working with a database under source code control each maintain a separate MDB or ADP file on their own hard disk. When you check out or get objects from the SCC project, the SCC add-in copies them, as text, to your hard drive and then integrates them into your local MDB or ADP file. When you check them back into the project, the process is reversed. The add-in instructs Access to export the objects to your local hard drive and then copies them back to the project on the server.

## Check In and Check Out Rules

To modify database objects and save them back to the project, you must check them out from the SCC project. You can check out application objects individually, just as with other language products such as Visual Basic and C++. If you want to modify any data objects (tables and so on), however, you must check out the entire binary database component. While you have objects checked out, no other user can check them out. The exception to this rule is modules. Multiple developers can check out a single module and then merge their changes during the check in process.

**NOTE**   When you have a database under source code control, Access prompts you to check out objects whenever you attempt to open them in Design view. This goes for all the traditional application objects, as well as such things as relationships and VBA project information. You can bypass these dialog boxes by using the SetWarnings action to turn them off.

## Local Objects

In addition to objects that are part of an SCC project, you can maintain local objects in your copy of the Access database. This applies to everything except tables. (You can't create local tables, because all tables are stored as a single binary object.) Local objects exist only in your database and are useful for testing and experimentation. After creating a local object, you can add it to the SCC project.

# Local Source File Storage

Because Access breaks up a database into separate source files while working with an SCC provider, it must have a place to store these files. In SCC nomenclature, this location is sometimes called the *working directory*. It is the place on a developer's hard drive where files are stored when they are checked out, as well as before they are checked back in to the project.

Access implements a working directory by creating a subdirectory beneath the directory where the local MDB or ADP file is stored. This subdirectory has the same name as the database and an extension of .SCC. For example, if the database was called CH15.MDB, the working directory would be called CH15.SCC. Within this directory the SCC add-in would place all the source files for the database as necessary during exchanges with the SCC provider.

---

**NOTE**    Access and the SCC add-in create this directory when you open the database and delete it when you close it. While it exists, any files it contains that are not checked out will be marked as read only to prevent inadvertent changes. Unlike other development tools, however, these files are *not* used to build a compiled program directly. You should not, therefore, edit these files; if you do, your changes will be lost during the next get, check out, or check in action.

---

# Source Code Control Options

Access lets you customize how it interacts with your source code control provider via the Source Code Control Options dialog box shown in Figure 15.2. Open the dialog box by selecting Tools ➢ SourceSafe ➢ Options. The options for each of the four questions shown in Figure 15.2 are Yes, No, and Ask. Select Ask if you want Access to prompt you. Select one of the other options if you want actions to happen automatically.

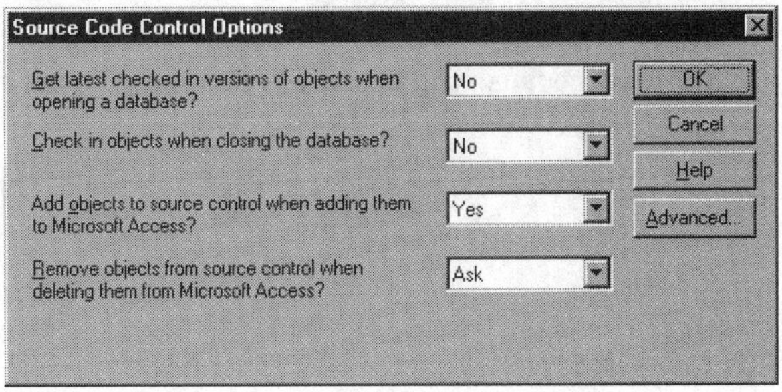

**FIGURE 15.2**
Options dialog box that controls how Access works with your SCC provider

| Source Code Control Options | |
| --- | --- |
| Get latest checked in versions of objects when opening a database? | No |
| Check in objects when closing the database? | No |
| Add objects to source control when adding them to Microsoft Access? | Yes |
| Remove objects from source control when deleting them from Microsoft Access? | Ask |

OK / Cancel / Help / Advanced...

## Changes to Objects under Source Code Control

Placing a database and its objects under source code control produces changes to those objects and the way you use them. First of all, Access adds a number of properties to the database and its objects. Table 15.1 lists the properties that are added to the Database object. The one of most interest is SccStatus, which indicates the status of an object with regard to source code control.

**TABLE 15.1:**    Properties Added to a Database under Source Code Control

| Property | Description |
| --- | --- |
| SccStatus | Bit mask indicating the current status of an object. See code examples for bit mask values. |
| SccDatabasePath | Local path of the database under source code control. |
| SccPath | Path to the source code control project containing the database. |
| SccAuxPath | Additional directory information used by a source code control provider. |
| SccUserName | Source code control username of the developer who created this copy of the database. |

**WARNING**    The information in this section is based on our own experimentation. The SCC properties are not documented or officially supported by Microsoft. As with any undocumented feature, these properties may change in future versions. Use this information at your own risk.

In addition, the SccStatus property is added to each object in the database under source code control. Local objects do not have an SccStatus property. The bit mask values are the same as those for a database.

You can use the SccStatus property to determine the status of any object in a database. For example, the adhSccStatus function shown in Listing 15.1 accepts an object variable and returns a status message. Note the error handling. This is required because the SccStatus property won't exist for objects that aren't under source code control.

## Listing 15.1

```
Private Const conUnderSCC = &H1
Private Const conCheckedOutByMe = &H2
Private Const conCheckedOutByOther = &H4
Private Const conCheckedOutByMe2 = &H1000
Private Const conPropNotFound = 3270
Private Const conInvalidProp = 2455

Function adhSccStatus(objAny As Object) As String
    Dim lngStatus As Long
    Dim strTemp As String

    On Error GoTo HandleError

    ' Get status value--this will cause an error if the
    ' object isn't under source code control
    lngStatus = objAny.Properties("SccStatus")

    ' Build base string
    strTemp = "Object is under source code control and "

    ' Compare status against constants
    If (lngStatus And conCheckedOutByMe) Then
        strTemp = strTemp & "checked out by you."
    ElseIf (lngStatus And conCheckedOutByOther) Then
        strTemp = strTemp & "checked out by someone else."
    Else
        strTemp = strTemp & "not checked out."
    End If

    adhSccStatus = strTemp

ExitHere:
    Exit Function
HandleError:
    Select Case Err.Number
        Case conPropNotFound, conInvalidProp
            adhSccStatus = _
            "Object is not under source code control."
```

```
            Case Else
                MsgBox Err.Description, vbExclamation, _
                    "Error " & Err.Number
        End Select
        Resume ExitHere
    End Function
```

Access also provides visual feedback for objects that are under source code control. Special icons in the database window designate these objects. You can see them in Figure 15.3. They include:

- The lock, indicating an object in the SCC database

- The checkmark, indicating that you have the object checked out

- The small person, indicating that another user has the object checked out

Local objects won't have any icons at all.

**FIGURE 15.3**
Access uses icons to indicate the status of objects in a database under source code control.

In addition to the new properties, you should be aware that changes to an object might affect the source file in the server project. For example, renaming an object in your copy of the database renames it in the project as well. The next time another developer's copy of the database changes, that developer's local object will be renamed. Given the potential complications involved in renaming objects (hard-coded references in code being one), you should use care when renaming objects. You must check out the binary data object in order to rename tables, command bars, or relationships. Renaming an object will fail if another user has the object checked out.

Deleting an object also has an effect on the project. When you delete an object from your database, the SCC add-in asks whether you want to delete it from the project as well. If you choose to do this, other developers will not be able to check out or use the object.

## Source Code Control Restrictions

While source code control offers many benefits, there are several restrictions regarding which Access features are allowed in databases under source code control. Specifically, there are three classes of databases that you cannot place under source code control:

- Secured databases

- Replicated databases

- Enabled databases

If you want to secure or replicate a database, develop it under source code control first, and then apply security or replication to the finalized database.

Another restriction concerns relationships involving queries. Any relationship involving a query is ignored when you place a database under source code control. This is necessary for Access to treat queries as separate objects and not part of the binary data object.

Finally, beware of changes made to a database programmatically using ADO. For example, it is possible to create a new table using VBA. Since ADO knows nothing about the presence of a source code control add-in, it will not create the property values necessary to add the database to an SCC project. The next time the binary data object is updated, your changes will be overwritten.

# Using Microsoft Visual SourceSafe

If you don't currently have a source code control provider, you can use a copy of Microsoft's SCC product, Visual SourceSafe (VSS), which ships with Office 2000 Developer. VSS also ships as a separate product and is bundled with the Enterprise Editions of Visual Studio, Visual C++, and Visual Basic.

# Setting Up Source Code Control

Installing Visual SourceSafe is a two-step process. First, you install the server components on a networked computer. This creates a database that VSS will use to store project files. Then VSS copies setup files that developers can use to install the client software on their computers. You must install the client files on each computer where you want to use source code control.

---

**TIP**  You can install both the server and client files on a single computer. This allows you to use source code control features such as versioning and histories (see the "Working with Histories and Differences" section later in this chapter) even if you're the only developer working on a project.

---

## Installing SourceSafe Server Files

To install the VSS server files, run SETUP.EXE from the VSS CD-ROM. You have the option of installing server files, client files, or a stand-alone installation (see Figure 15.4). Be sure to choose the last option if you intend to use the computer as both a VSS server and a client.

**FIGURE 15.4**
The VSS Setup dialog box lets you specify the installation type.

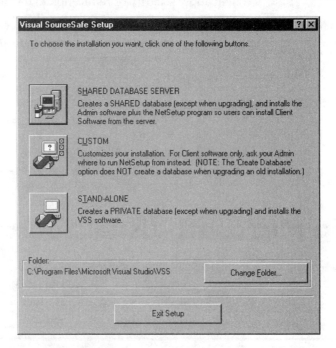

### Installing SourceSafe Client Files

Once the server files have been installed, you can install client files on each workstation that needs access to project files. The simplest way to do this is to run the NETSETUP.EXE file from the directory on the server where you installed VSS. To do this, connect to the VSS share and run NETSETUP.EXE. The setup program copies the VSS program files and automatically creates a reference to the VSS database.

## Creating SourceSafe User Accounts

Visual SourceSafe includes an integrated security component to ensure that only authorized developers have access to project files. Before using VSS with Access, you should use the VSS Administrator application to add user accounts. When you install the server files, the setup program creates an icon for the Administrator program. Figure 15.5 shows the program's main window. It lists the existing user accounts and which ones, if any, are logged into VSS.

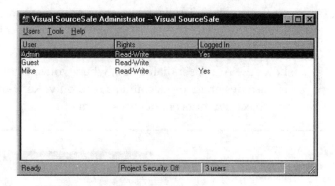

**FIGURE 15.5**
VSS Administrator program showing user accounts

VSS creates two accounts for you: Admin and Guest. Admin is the administrator account you must use to create user accounts. When you launch VSS or the Administrator program, you are prompted to log in. Figure 15.6 shows the Login dialog box. You'll also need to log in the first time you use a VSS function from Access.

**FIGURE 15.6**
Visual SourceSafe Login
dialog box

You can have VSS use a user's network name and password as that user's login information. This eliminates the need for developers to manually log in to VSS. To enable this feature, use the Options dialog box in the VSS Administrator application.

Admin is created with a blank password, so leave that field blank when you log in for the first time. We recommend, however, that you change the password as soon as possible. To change an account's password, select the account from the Administrator program's main window and select Users ➤ Change Password.

To create new accounts for your developers, select Users ➤ Add User. Figure 15.7 shows the Add User dialog box, where you specify a name and password. You can also designate the account as read only. Read-only accounts can perform gets on project files but cannot check them out.

**FIGURE 15.7**
Adding a new VSS user
using the Add User
dialog box

User-level authentication is the default security scheme VSS uses. This allows any user with a valid VSS account complete access to any and all projects and files. Using the VSS Administrator application, you can enable project-level security, which restricts access to projects and files on a user-by-user basis.

# Running Visual SourceSafe

While you'll normally interact with VSS through the Access user interface, you can also run VSS interactively as a separate application. Figure 15.8 shows the VSS Explorer window. It operates just like the Windows Explorer. The left-hand pane shows all the projects that VSS is currently managing. The right-hand pane shows the source files that make up the project.

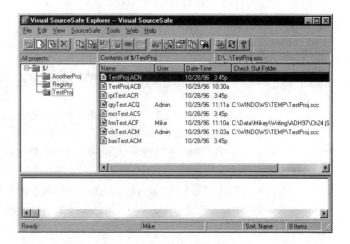

VSS uses a hierarchical structure to manage projects. Every project can have subprojects, which themselves can have subprojects, and so on. All projects descend from a root project represented by the symbols "$/" in the left-hand pane. You can create projects that are part of other projects and operate on them independently or as a component of their parent (called *recursively* by VSS documentation). For example, you can perform diffs on entire projects in VSS, including any subprojects.

When you select a project from the left-hand pane, VSS displays all the files that make it up in the right-hand pane. VSS displays the filename (note that those in Figure 15.8 are Access components), the date and time it was last modified, and check out information if applicable. If a file has been checked out, VSS shows you who checked it out and the directory on the workstation to which that user copied it.

Using VSS Explorer, you can create new projects, add and remove files from projects, view file histories, perform diffs and restores, and print a number of reports. We'll leave exploring all its functionality up to you and concentrate on the Access VSS interface in the remainder of this chapter.

---

**TIP**     The Visual SourceSafe Explorer is most useful to project managers and lead developers. It shows who has what checked out, and you can use it to troubleshoot errors by performing diffs and restores.

---

# Working with VSS from Access 2000

This section explains the basics of using VSS from within Access 2000. It is not meant to replace the Access or VSS documentation, so not every aspect of using VSS is covered. This section should, however, provide you with a fundamental understanding of how Access and VSS interact.

To use VSS from Access, you need to install both the VSS client files and the Access source code control option that comes on the Microsoft Office 2000 Developer CD-ROM. Once you've accomplished that, you'll be able to access the source code control commands on the Tools menu. If you install the SCC support files but do *not* install VSS, you'll receive an error message when you open a database or project (see Figure 15.9). Click No to dispense with the dialog box and prevent it from appearing again.

---

**FIGURE 15.9**
Error message you receive if you install SCC support but no SCC provider

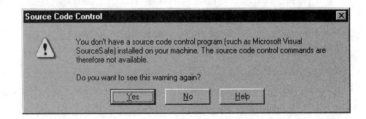

**TIP**
Some people inadvertently perform a complete install of the MOD without realizing that it includes the source code control integration features. If you see the warning dialog box and want to remove the source code control add-in, you can rerun the setup program and choose the Add/Remove option.

# Placing a Database under Source Code Control

The first step in using an Access database with source code control is to add it to a VSS project. To place a database under VSS source code control, open it in Access and select Tools ➢ SourceSafe ➢ Add Database to SourceSafe. Access warns you that it must first close the database before it can add it to SourceSafe. If you have any open, changed objects, you can click No and save them and then select the menu command again. Otherwise you will be prompted with a dialog box for each object.

**WARNING**
Do not use the Add Files command in VSS Explorer to add a database to a project. VSS by itself cannot cope with an MDB file's binary structure. It will add the entire file to the project instead of exporting and adding individual object files.

## Selecting a VSS Project

After you give Access permission to add the database to SourceSafe, it closes and reopens the database. You will then have to log in to VSS using the Login dialog box (unless you're using network logons as VSS user accounts) shown earlier in Figure 15.6. Access then prompts you with a dialog box like the one shown in Figure 15.10, listing all the VSS projects and subprojects. You can either enter the name of a new project in the text box or select an existing project from the tree view window. If you want to create a new project, you can either enter a complete path in the text box (for example, "$/Sales/Inventory"), or select an existing project and enter just the name of the new subproject. In the latter case, VSS creates a new subproject beneath the selected project. Click the Create button to create a new project immediately and display it in the tree view window. If you don't click the Create button, VSS automatically creates the new project when you click OK.

FIGURE 15.10

**FIGURE 15.10**
Use this dialog box to select or create a VSS project for your database.

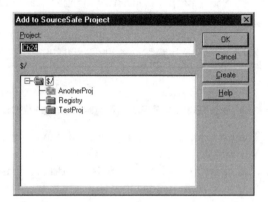

WARNING

**WARNING**   Make sure you leave the text box blank if you want to place the database into an existing project. Otherwise VSS will create a new subproject beneath the selected project and place your database there.

**NOTE**   Access will not let you add a database to a VSS project that already contains a database under source code control.

## Adding Objects to the Project

After choosing a VSS project name, you are presented with another dialog box. This one, shown in Figure 15.11, gives you the opportunity to add database objects (including the binary data object) to the VSS project. You don't have to add any objects at this time. This dialog box is accessible whenever you're working in a database under source code control just by selecting the Add Objects command from the SourceSafe menu. If you decide not to add any objects, Access will create only the ACN file (the one that defines the database name) in the VSS project.

You can select as many or as few objects as you like from the Objects To Be Added list. If you have a lot of objects in your database, you can view only those of a given type by selecting it from the Object Type combo box. Note the high-lighted entry in Figure 15.11 (Other: Data and Misc. Objects). This is the entry for the binary data component.

**FIGURE 15.11**
Use this dialog box to add objects to the VSS project.

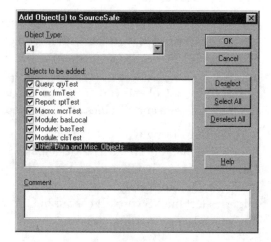

After making your selections, click OK to add them to the VSS project. You'll see a VSS dialog box that logs the status of each object as it is added to the project. Normally this dialog box, shown in Figure 15.12, disappears automatically after all the objects have been added successfully. If any errors or warnings occur, it remains open so you can examine them.

**FIGURE 15.12**
The Visual SourceSafe dialog box shows status and error messages during processing.

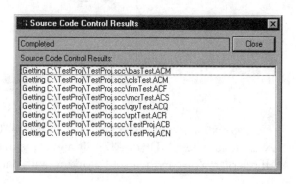

## Creating a Database from a VSS Project

Once one developer has created a VSS project from an Access database, other developers can begin working with it. You cannot, however, simply copy the MDB or ADP file to other workstations, because it contains custom properties that apply to the original VSS user. If you attempt to open a database placed under source code control and you aren't the VSS user who created it, Access issues a warning message and disables all source code control functions.

To begin working with a database under source code control, you must use the SourceSafe menu to create a new database. Select Tools ➢ SourceSafe ➢ Create Database from SourceSafe Project. You'll be prompted with the dialog box shown in Figure 15.13 to specify a local working directory and to select a VSS project folder. Select the VSS project containing the database you created using the previously listed steps.

**FIGURE 15.13**
Creating a new database from a Visual SourceSafe project

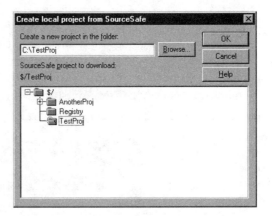

After making your selections, click the OK button. Access and Visual SourceSafe will create a new MDB or ADP file and copy all the objects from the VSS project on the server. You can then start working with database objects under source code control.

# Working with Objects in a VSS Project

Adding objects to a VSS project is only the first step in using source code control features with Access. If you want to make changes to objects, you'll need to check them out, as described in the next section.

---

**NOTE**    If you decided not to add all the objects in the database when you added it to SourceSafe, or if you have created new local objects, you can add objects to a VSS project by selecting the Add Objects command from the SourceSafe menu.

---

## Checking Out Objects

As mentioned earlier in this chapter, Access prompts you to check out objects whenever you attempt to open them in design mode. You can also check out objects interactively using a VSS-supplied dialog box. To open this dialog box, shown in Figure 15.14, select Tools ≻ SourceSafe ≻ Check Out.

---

**FIGURE 15.14**
Visual SourceSafe dialog box for checking out objects

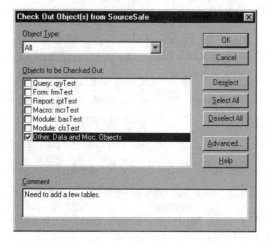

---

**TIP**    Access also features a Source Code Control command bar with buttons for the most frequently used SCC commands. To display this command bar, choose View ≻ Toolbars or right-click and select it from the command bar menu.

---

The dialog box lets you select one or more objects to check out at the same time. Use the Object Type drop-down list to view objects of a given type or all objects in the project. Place a checkmark next to those you wish to check out in the Objects to be Checked Out list. Use the Comment text box to enter a comment regarding why you are checking out these objects. Comments are stored in the VSS database and can be read and/or printed by the project administrator.

Click the Advanced button to open the dialog box shown in Figure 15.15. The options shown on the dialog box control what happens during the check out process.

**FIGURE 15.15**
Visual SourceSafe
advanced check out options

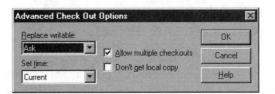

The Advanced Check Out Options are described below:

**Replace Writable**   Determines how VSS reacts when it finds a file in the working directory that is not read only. It can prompt you (Ask), replace the file with the one being checked out (Replace), skip the file (Skip), or merge the two files (Merge).

**Set Time**   Determines what date and time information VSS sets on the checked out file. Your choices are:

- Current, for the current date and time

- Modification, for the last time the file was modified

- Check In, for the date and time the file was last checked in

**Allow Multiple Checkouts**   If checked, VSS allows multiple check outs on the file.

**Don't Get Local Copy**   If checked, VSS marks the file as checked out but does not copy the latest version to your working directory.

## Undoing a Check Out

Occasionally you may want to reverse or "undo" a check out. For example, suppose that after checking out an object and making numerous changes, you discover you've approached a problem from a completely wrong direction—that you've reached a programming dead end. Rather than trying to remember all the changes you've made to the object and repealing each one individually, you can use VSS to undo the check out, thus reverting to the current VSS project version.

To do this, select Tools ≻ SourceSafe≻ Undo Check Out or right-click on an object in the database window. SourceSafe warns you that undoing a check out will overwrite any changes to the object.

## Checking In Objects

Once you have made changes to an object that you want to share with others, you must check the object back in to the VSS project. Select the Check In menu command to open the dialog box shown in Figure 15.16. Like the Check Out dialog box, you can view only those objects of a particular type or all objects. You can also supply a comment indicating what changes were made that will be saved along with the objects.

**FIGURE 15.16**
Visual SourceSafe dialog box for checking objects back in to VSS

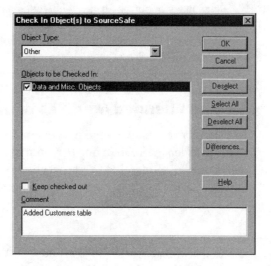

If you want to continue working on the objects, select the Keep Checked Out checkbox. This instructs VSS to check the objects into the project on the server so other developers can retrieve them, along with your changes, but leaves the objects checked out to you so you can continue editing them.

Before checking in the objects, you can view the differences between them and those currently in the VSS project on the server by clicking the Differences button. For application objects, this displays the VSS Differences dialog box. (See the "Working with Histories and Differences" section later in this chapter for more information on using this dialog box). For the binary data object, VSS informs you if there is a difference but does not display the information in the Differences dialog box.

## Retrieving Checked In Objects

If you are working with several developers on the same database project, you will occasionally want to merge changes made by other developers into your copy of the database. To do this, select an object in the database window and choose Get Latest Version from the SourceSafe or right-click menu. This replaces the current version of the object with the one stored in the VSS database.

**WARNING**   Be cautious about doing this with code-bearing objects such as forms, reports, and modules. Other developers may have checked in their changes with references to other procedures that you may not have declared in your copy of the database. This will prevent your application from compiling.

## Merging Changed Modules with Multiple Check Outs

Visual SourceSafe allows several users to check out any text file from a VSS project. This lets more than one person make changes to an object at the same time. While it is preferable to restrict checkouts to a single developer, sometimes multiple checkouts are necessary due to the size and complexity of a source file. Access supports multiple checkouts for code modules only.

**NOTE**   To enable multiple checkouts, you must run the VSS Administrator application and select the Allow Multiple Checkouts option from the that application's Options dialog box.

When checking in source files that have been checked out by multiple developers, VSS must merge the file being checked in with the one in the VSS database. Merging involves integrating changes made to the local copy with the current version in the VSS project. VSS uses a rather sophisticated pattern-matching algorithm to process the merge and to spot conflicts. Therefore, VSS can often perform the merge automatically if there are no direct conflicts between files. For example, if only new procedures are added to a code module, VSS adds the new procedures to the VSS database copy of the file. Changes to the same line of code, or any other change that short-circuits the pattern-matching algorithm, will cause conflicts that VSS cannot resolve on its own.

When conflicts are detected, VSS displays its Merge dialog box, shown in Figure 15.17. This dialog box contains three panes. The upper-left and -right panes show the current VSS project version of the file alongside the local version. The lower pane shows the results of the merge. It is up to you to sort out the differences and, where there are conflicts, to pick a "winner."

**FIGURE 15.17**
The Merge dialog box lets you resolve conflicting changes to a file.

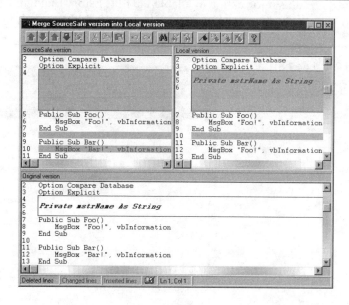

To make the process easier, VSS color-codes each conflict to indicate which lines have been added, changed, or removed. You can use the toolbar to move quickly from one conflict to the next. For each conflict, you have the option of discarding your changes and reverting to the VSS database version, discarding the version in the VSS database, or accepting both sets of changes (where applicable). For example, if two new, different procedures exist in the two versions, you could decide to accept both. On the other hand, in the case of conflicts within a single line of code, you must pick one winner. To select a winner, simply click on it in the appropriate upper pane. You can also right-click on a conflict and select from menu commands that accept the change, discard it, or apply both.

When you are done merging the two files, close the Merge dialog box. VSS prompts you to confirm that the merge was successful. If you were able to resolve all the conflicts, click Yes to check in the file. If not, perhaps because you needed to check with another developer, Click No to keep the object checked out.

## Working with Histories and Differences

As you begin to save numerous versions of an object, you may want to look back at previous incarnations. This is called viewing the *history* of an object. VSS makes this information available via the History dialog box, shown in Figure 15.18, which you can open by selecting Tools ≻ SourceSafe ≻ Show History.

**FIGURE 15.18**
Viewing the history of checkins made for a source file

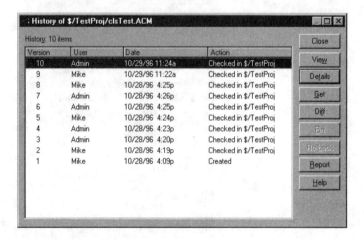

The History dialog box lists the version number, the username of the developer who checked in that version, the date and time of the checkin, and the action that initiated the new version. You can view a version's details, such as any comments or labels associated with it, by clicking the Details button. This opens a secondary dialog box.

Using the History dialog box, you can retrieve any version of the file into your copy of the database by clicking the Get button. You can also view the differences between your local copy and any other version by selecting that version and clicking the Diff button. If there are differences between the two versions, VSS displays the Differences dialog box shown in Figure 15.19.

**FIGURE 15.19**

Viewing differences between two versions of a source file

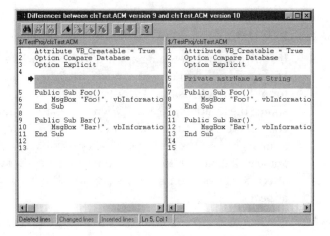

VSS uses the same highlighting here as in the Merge dialog box. You can use the toolbar to move from difference to difference, but you cannot make changes using this dialog box. You'll have to manually note the differences and change them in your local copy.

In addition to viewing differences between your local copy of an object and a version in the history list, you can view the differences between any two versions in the VSS database. Just select the first version you want to examine, hold down the Ctrl key, and click on another version. Then click the Diff button.

**TIP**    You can also compare your local copy of an object with the version in the VSS database by selecting Tools ➤ SourceSafe ➤ Show Differences.

If you discover a critical error in your local version of an object and correcting it manually would be impractical, you can use the History dialog box to restore a prior version. Simply select the version you want to restore (click the View button to examine it if you're unsure) and click the Rollback button. Restoring a version of an object deletes all subsequent versions permanently, so use care when doing this. VSS does not, however, merge the restored version into your local copy of the database. Your database will still contain the newer, yet flawed, version. We recommend, therefore, that after performing a rollback, you immediately perform a get on the latest version.

## Sharing and Branching

If you've been developing applications for a while, you probably have modules of source code that you share between projects. This is an especially useful technique for utility functions that are not application dependent. VSS supports sharing of source files among projects. When you share a source file using VSS, only one copy of the file actually exists in the VSS database; however, you can include it in as many projects as you like. Whenever you make changes to the file in one project and check it back in to the VSS database, all other projects that use the file are affected. The next time a get is performed in those projects, your changes will appear.

When using source code control integration in Access, you can select source files from any other project for inclusion in the current database. You do this using the Share With dialog box, shown in Figure 15.20, which you can open by selecting Tools ➢ SourceSafe ➢ Share Objects.

**FIGURE 15.20**
Use this dialog box to share source files from other projects.

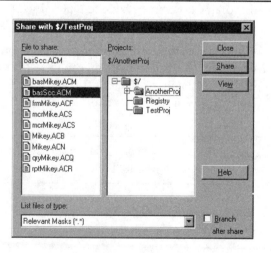

Use the Projects list to view source files in a particular project. You can select any project except the current one. If you select the current project, no files are displayed in the Files to Share list. Choose one or more files to share from this list. After making your selections, click the Share button. This marks the files as shared in the VSS database, adds them to the current project, and copies the latest version of each to your local database. You can then work with them as you would any other source file.

The opposite of sharing is branching. *Branching* is performed on a shared file and breaks the link between projects using the file. It creates a new, native copy of the file in the project where the branch is created. From that point forward, changes in the new copy do not affect other projects that use the file.

You cannot perform branching directly through Access. You must run Visual SourceSafe itself. To do this, select Tools ➢ SourceSafe ➢ Run SourceSafe. From the VSS Explorer window, select the project where you want to create the branch and select the shared file. Select Branch from the SourceSafe menu or click the Branch Files toolbar button.

# Controlling SourceSafe with VBA

Visual SourceSafe versions 5 and 6 support an Automation interface that allows you to execute SourceSafe procedures using any Automation client, including Microsoft Access. Using this interface plus a few undocumented Access methods, you could write your own VSS integration tool. In this section we briefly explain the Automation interface and show you how to use it. This section is not meant to replace the VSS documentation or tools such as the Object Browser. We do not, therefore, include complete descriptions of every object class, property, and method. Instead, we highlight a select few using simple examples. For a complete reference to the VSS Automation interface, consult the VSS Web page at `http://msdn.microsoft.com/ssafe`.

---

**NOTE**    It is not clear to the authors *why* you would want to reinvent the wheel by using the VSS Automation interface in this manner. Understanding how VSS and Access work together, however, may help you in using the products effectively. You might also choose to integrate the functionality into other VBA host products.

---

To demonstrate some of these techniques, we've developed a small application called the VSS Project Explorer (see Figure 15.21). To use this application, just open the frmVSSExplorer form in CH15.MDB. You are prompted to log in to a VSS database, and then the form displays a list of all the projects in that database. Double-click on a project name to view any subprojects. Use the Files tab to see a list of the files associated with a project.

**FIGURE 15.21**
Our VSS Project Explorer
demonstrates the VSS
Automation interface.

You can use the VSS Explorer to view source files in a separate window or print version and to check out information to the Debug window. Most of the source code included in this section is contained in the Explorer form's module.

## Visual SourceSafe Object Model

Visual SourceSafe features a fairly simple and straightforward object module. In fact, it consists of only four object classes: VSSDatabase, VSSItem, VSSVersion, and VSSCheckout. All of these except VSSDatabase also have associated collections. Figure 15.22 illustrates the object model. Note that the VSSItem object below VSSDatabase represents the results of calling the database's VSSItem method. Once you have a pointer to this object, you can access collections of all the other objects it contains.

**FIGURE 15.22**

Visual SourceSafe Automa-
tion object model

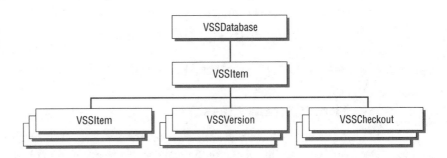

Before attempting to write any Automation code, be sure to add a reference to
the Visual SourceSafe 6.0 Object Library to your VBA project. If the type library is
not added to the reference list when you install VSS, you can find it in the \win32
subdirectory of your VSS install directory. The type library filename is SSAPI.DLL.

## The VSSDatabase Class

SourceSafe's VSSDatabase class represents an entire VSS database, including all
the projects and subprojects defined therein. All Automation sessions begin by
declaring a new instance of this class and calling its Open method. Open accepts
three arguments: a path to a VSS INI file containing the database to use, a VSS user
name, and a password. The following code snippet illustrates this:

```
Dim vdb As New VSSDatabase

' Make sure the path to srcsafe.ini is accurate!
vdb.Open "C:\VSS\SRCSAFE.INI", "Admin", ""
```

Once you've opened the database, you can start manipulating items in the database. To obtain a pointer to an item (represented by the VSSItem class, explained
in the next section), use the VSSDatabase's VSSItem method. VSSItem accepts an
item specification (similar in concept to a file path and name) as an argument.
Depending on the specification, you can get a pointer to any project or item in the
database. For example, to get a pointer to the root project, you could use the code
shown here:

```
Dim vit As VSSItem

' Get a reference to the root project
Set vit = vdb.VSSItem("$/")
```

Alternately, the following code fragment obtains a reference to a file called basSccFunctions.acm in the Chapter15 project:

```
Dim vit As VSSItem

Set vit = vbd.VSSItem("$/Chapter15/basSccFunctions.acm")
```

## The VSSItem Class

As you may have deduced by now, the VSSItem class can refer to either a project or a source file. Once you have a pointer to a VSSItem object, you can check its Type property to determine exactly what it is. Type returns 0 (VSSITEM_PROJECT) for a project and 1 (VSSITEM_FILE) for a file.

While we can't include all the details here, suffice it to say that the VSSItem class implements obvious properties such as Name, IsCheckedOut, IsDifferent, Local-Spec, Parent, and VersionNumber, among others. For methods, you can use Add, CheckIn, CheckOut, Get, and UndoCheckout.

The VSS Project Explorer uses some of these properties and methods to copy a version of a source file to a temporary directory where it can be viewed using the frmVSSFileViewer form (see Figure 15.23). Listing 15.2 contains the ViewFile procedure that accomplishes this.

**FIGURE 15.23**

Viewing a source file from a VSS project

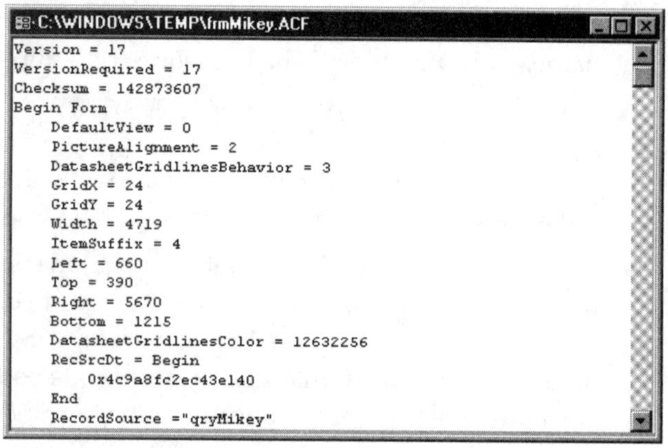

```
C:\WINDOWS\TEMP\frmMikey.ACF
Version = 17
VersionRequired = 17
Checksum = 142873607
Begin Form
    DefaultView = 0
    PictureAlignment = 2
    DatasheetGridlinesBehavior = 3
    GridX = 24
    GridY = 24
    Width = 4719
    ItemSuffix = 4
    Left = 660
    Top = 390
    Right = 5670
    Bottom = 1215
    DatasheetGridlinesColor = 12632256
    RecSrcDt = Begin
        0x4c9a8fc2ec43e140
    End
    RecordSource ="qryMikey"
```

### Listing 15.2

```
Private Sub ViewFile(vitFile As VSSItem)
    Dim strTempFile As String
    Dim frmViewer As New Form_frmVSSFileViewer
    Dim frmAny As Form
    Dim cb As Long

    ' Make sure it's a file
    If vitFile.Type = VSSITEM_PROJECT Then
        MsgBox "Cannot view projects.", _
          vbExclamation, Me.Caption
    ' Make sure it's text
    ElseIf vitFile.Binary Then
        MsgBox "File is binary and cannot be viewed.", _
          vbExclamation, Me.Caption
    Else

        ' Create a temp file name
        strTempFile = Space(255)
        cb = adh_apiGetTempPath(255, strTempFile)
        If cb > 0 Then
            strTempFile = Left(strTempFile, cb)
            strTempFile = strTempFile & mvitCurrFile.Name

            ' See if we already have it open
            For Each frmAny In mcolViewers
                If frmAny.File = strTempFile Then
                    frmAny.SetFocus
                    Exit Sub
                End If
            Next

            ' Perform a "get" to grab the file
            vitFile.Get strTempFile

            ' Set the viewer form's File property (this
            ' reads the file's contents)
            frmViewer.File = strTempFile

            ' Make the form visible and add it to our
```

```
               ' collection to keep it around
               frmViewer.Visible = True
               mcolViewers.Add frmViewer

               ' Getting the file makes it read-only.
               ' Remove this attribute
               SetAttr strTempFile, vbNormal

               ' Delete the temp file
               Kill strTempFile
           End If
       End If
   End Sub
```

You'll notice that the procedure first verifies that the VSSItem being passed in is, in fact, a file and not a project by examining its Type property. It then checks the Binary property to ensure that it's a text file. After constructing a filename from the system temp directory and the VSSItem's Name property, the procedure calls the object's Get method. This instructs VSS to copy the file from the VSS database to the location specified by the method's argument. After this happens, a new instance of frmVSSFileViewer is opened, and it reads the file into a text box. The ViewFile procedure can then delete the file by calling the Kill function (after removing the read-only attribute VSS placed on the file during the Get operation).

## The VSSVersion Class

Since one of the reasons for using a source code control program is to maintain past versions of files, the VSS Automation interface implements a class that allows you programmatic access to these. The VSSVersion class has properties specific to a particular version of a source file, such as Comment, Date, Username, and VersionNumber. Additionally, the VSSVersion class implements a VSSItem property, which returns a pointer to a VSSItem object representing the actual source file. Using the VSSItem property, you can manipulate all the versions of a file, including the current one.

You access versions using properties of a VSSItem. Use the Versions (plural) property to iterate through all versions using a For...Each loop, or the Version (singular) property to reference an individual version. (VSSItem objects do not have a true Versions collection.) For example, the following procedure iterates all the versions of a given file, printing information to the Debug window:

```
Private Sub PrintVersionInfo(vit As VSSItem)
    Dim ver As VSSVersion

    Debug.Print "Version info for " & vit.Name
    Debug.Print "===================================="
    For Each ver In vit.Versions
        With ver
            Debug.Print "Version " & .VersionNumber, _
                .UserName, .Date, .Action, .Comment
        End With
    Next
End Sub
```

To reference a particular version of a file, however, you would use code like the following, which prints the file name of the original version:

```
Debug.Print vit.Version(1).Name
```

## The IVSSCheckout Class

Finally, the IVSSCheckout interface implements properties pertaining to the status of an object when it is checked out. You can use the Checkouts collection of a VSSItem object to view this information. If an object is not checked out, there will be no members of this collection. Checkouts will contain a single IVSSCheckout object under normal situations when a user has the object checked out. If you allow multiple developers to check out an object, the collection could potentially contain several IVSSCheckout objects.

The IVSSCheckout interface implements properties such as UserName, Machine, LocalPath, Date, and Comments that inform you of who has the object checked out, where it is, and when that user checked it out. The following procedure lists information for a given VSSItem object:

```
Private Sub PrintCheckoutInfo(vit As VSSItem)
    Dim vck As IVSSCheckout
    Dim c As Integer

    Debug.Print "Check out info for " & vit.Name
    Debug.Print "===================================="
    For Each vck In vit.Checkouts
```

```
        c = c + 1
    With vck
        Debug.Print "Check out " & c, _
            .UserName, .Machine, .LocalSpec, .Date, _
            .Comment
    End With
Next
End Sub
```

# Access Source Code Control Methods

To support source code control integration, Access implements two methods: SaveAsText and LoadFromText. Normally these are called only by the SCC integration add-in that comes with the Microsoft Office Developer. You can, however, write VBA code that calls these methods.

---

**TIP**    SaveAsText and LoadFromText are "hidden" methods and do not show up in the VBA Object Browser by default. To view these methods, open the Object Browser, right-click on the window, and select Show Hidden Members from the pop-up menu.

---

## The SaveAsText Method

SaveAsText does just that—it saves an Access object to a text file so it can be loaded into VSS or some other source code control application. SaveAsText takes three arguments: an object type (use the Access constants acQuery, acForm, and so on), an object name, and a filename. Access will create a text definition of the object at the specified location. As an example, the following code creates a text file called C:\QUERY1.ACQ containing the definition of a query, Query1:

```
Application.SaveAsText acQuery, "Query1", "C:\QUERY1.ACQ"
```

## The LoadFromText Method

The counterpart to SaveAsText is LoadFromText. LoadFromText takes the same three arguments and uses the definition information in the text file to create or re-create an object in the current database. The code snippet shown here creates a new version of Query1 from the text file:

```
Application.LoadFromText acQuery, "Query1", "C:\QUERY1.ACQ"
```

If an object of the same name and type already exists, LoadFromText overwrites it. Because LoadFromText is a hidden method intended to be used only by the source code control integration add-in, Access does not warn you when this happens. Use LoadFromText with care.

While LoadFromText will create the object in the database, it does not mark it as being under source code control. To do that, you must add the SccStatus property to the object yourself.

# Object Text File Formats

We could fill most of a chapter discussing just the text file formats Access uses for exchanging objects. Obviously we can't do that, but we do want say a few words about it. Because you can use the SaveAsText and LoadFromText methods apart from source code control, the text file format does open up some interesting possibilities.

## File Usage and Naming

We've already mentioned that Access exports individual text files for each of the application objects in a database, plus one binary file for the data objects. Access names these files using the object or database name and a file extension that denotes the object type. You can see this in Figure 15.8, shown earlier in the chapter. Access uses the file extensions .ACQ, .ACF, .ACR, .ACS, and .ACM to denote queries, forms, reports, macros (scripts), and modules, respectively. The extension .ACB denotes the binary data object for Jet databases, while .ACP is used for ADP files. Finally, Access creates a zero-byte file with the file extension .ACN to denote the name of the database or project. It's important that you do not delete this file from the project. If you do, other developers will not be able to create new databases based on the project.

## Object Definitions

Access uses a format that is similar to that used by Visual Basic. It uses a nested, hierarchical structure to describe objects. Components of an object are represented by blocks of text that specify property values. Listing 15.3 shows the definition of a simple query that selects all the fields from a sample table with a criterion on the ID field.

**Listing 15.3**

```
Operation = 1
Option = 0
Where ="(((tblTest.ID)=5))"
Begin InputTables
    Name ="tblTest"
End
Begin OutputColumns
    Expression ="tblTest.*"
End
dbBoolean "ReturnsRecords" ="-1"
dbInteger "ODBCTimeout" ="60"
dbByte "RecordsetType" ="0"
dbBoolean "OrderByOn" ="0"
Begin
End
Begin
    State = 0
    Left = 40
    Top = 22
    Right = 778
    Bottom = 323
    Left = -1
    Top = -1
    Right = 731
    Bottom = 154
    Left = 0
    Top = 0
    ColumnsShown = 539
    Begin
        Left = 38
        Top = 6
        Right = 134
        Bottom = 83
        Top = 0
        Name ="tblTest"
    End
End
```

You can see evidence of properties in the listing. Some, such as ODBCTimeout and RecordsetType, are DAO properties. Others are used by Access to build the QBE display. Listing 15.4 shows a simple macro with two actions. The first action opens a form and the second displays an informational dialog box.

### Listing 15.4

```
Version = 131074
ColumnsShown = 0
Begin
    Action ="OpenForm"
    Argument ="frmTest"
    Argument ="0"
    Argument =" "
    Argument =" "
    Argument ="-1"
    Argument ="0"
End
Begin
    Action ="MsgBox"
    Argument ="The form has been opened!"
    Argument ="-1"
    Argument ="4"
    Argument ="Test Macro"
End
```

Again, notice the properties and their values. In the case of macros, each Begin…End block marks a single macro action. Begin and End statements denote complex properties and, in the case of forms and reports, are nested to indicate object containment.

While it will take you some time to fully explore and map the structure of these files, it does open the door for additional approaches to object creation.

# Summary

In this chapter we've explained the basic concepts behind source code control. We showed you how Access fits into the source code control universe by decomposing its databases into separate components. We explained how to use Access with one particular source code control provider, Microsoft Visual SourceSafe. Finally, we explored using SourceSafe's Automation interface to manage source code control projects using VBA. The chapter covered these key concepts:

- What source code control projects are
- How you work with source files in a controlled environment
- How Access supports source code control integration
- How to install and use Microsoft Visual SourceSafe
- How to manage a database project using source code control
- How to control VSS using Automation from VBA

With this knowledge in hand (and Access 2000's source code control integration features), managing large development projects involving numerous programmers should be easier than ever.

# Setup and Deployment

- Understanding the Access Runtime

- Understanding the Windows Installer

- The Windows Installer Automation Interface

- Using the Package and Deployment Wizard

- Editing Installer files

- Deploying data access pages

**A**fter many weeks of effort, you've finally got your Access solution working perfectly. Now what? The end of development does not represent the end of your responsibilities as a professional application developer. What remains is to deploy your solution to the computers of your application's end users. In this chapter, you'll learn about the Microsoft Office 2000 Developer tools that help you with this deployment. We'll also dig into the new Microsoft Installer and the tools that currently exist to help you create and maintain Windows-compliant setup programs.

# Understanding the Access Runtime

When you purchase Microsoft Office 2000 Developer, part of what you're buying is a redistribution license for the Microsoft Access Runtime. The Runtime is a variation of Access that allows end users to run, but not modify, Access applications. There are some major differences between the Access Runtime and the full Access product. The following conditions apply when your application is running within the Access Runtime:

- The Database window is permanently hidden.

- The Visual Basic Editor is permanently hidden.

- All Design views are permanently hidden and cannot be used. Note in particular that the Filter by Form and Server Filter by Form windows are considered Design views, so you can't use these modes in a Runtime application.

- The built-in toolbars are unavailable, but you can still display custom toolbars.

- Many commands (all those related to designing objects) are dropped from the menus and shortcut menus.

- Any untrapped error is fatal and causes your application to exit without warning. This applies to any macro error and any error in VBA code that's not handled by your own error handler.

---

**TIP**      Because the database window is permanently hidden when executing under the Runtime version, it's important to have either a startup form or an AutoExec macro specified. Otherwise, your application's users will be left staring at an empty screen, with no way to open any objects.

---

# Runtime Architecture

To ensure that the Runtime version of Access functions identically to the full retail version (except in areas where the functionality is deliberately removed), Microsoft employs an interesting strategy. The Runtime executable is the exact same program as the retail executable. Whether you get retail or Runtime functionality is controlled by the presence of license keys (which are actually GUIDs) in a certain part of the Windows Registry. There's one license key for the Runtime and a different license key for retail Access.

You can force retail Access into Runtime mode by using the /runtime switch on the command line. For example, creating a shortcut with this command line will launch Access, load the ADH2KSQL.ADP project, and open Access in Runtime mode:

```
C:\Program Files\Microsoft Office\Office\msaccess.exe C:\ADH2KSQL.adp /
runtime
```

Table 16.1 shows the possible modes of launching Access, both retail and Runtime.

**TABLE 16.1:** Access Launch Parameters

| Retail key present? | Runtime key present? | /runtime Used? | Result |
| --- | --- | --- | --- |
| No | No | No | Will not launch |
| No | No | Yes | Will not launch |
| No | Yes | No | Launches as Runtime |
| No | Yes | Yes | Launches as Runtime |
| Yes | No | No | Launches as retail |
| Yes | No | Yes | Launches as Runtime |
| Yes | Yes | No | Launches as retail |
| Yes | Yes | Yes | Launches as Runtime |

As you can see, the retail key overrides the Runtime key, but the /runtime switch overrides the retail key. This allows you to easily test the functionality of your Access application in the Runtime without actually installing the Runtime on your computer.

**WARNING**     Of course, there's another consequence of this architecture. Suppose you deploy an application using the Access Runtime to a customer's computer and that customer then installs the retail version of Access on the same computer. Your application can now be opened within retail Access. This means that using security to protect any parts of your application that are proprietary is a necessity, even if you plan to distribute it with the Runtime.

# Understanding the Windows Installer

Microsoft Office 2000 is the first application that uses the new Windows Installer technology (formerly code-named "Darwin"). Several years in development, the Windows Installer is designed to help control severe problems associated with previous installation technologies:

- Setup programs that take forever because they install everything locally.

- Lack of administrative control over end-user installations.

- Software that needs administrative rights to install properly.

- Setup programs must use different APIs for different platforms (Windows 95, Windows 98, Windows NT, Windows 2000).

- Software can't be uninstalled completely or without breaking other software.

- Setup programs are unable to repair broken software without a complete reinstall.

The Windows Installer acts as a single point of contact for all software that needs to be installed on your computer. Instead of each application using its own calls directly to the operating system to copy files, write Registry keys, and perform other setup tasks, applications call services from the Windows Installer. This allows the Windows Installer to perform several critical functions:

- Features can be "advertised" so that they appear to be installed without taking the time to actually install them.

- Administrators can control exactly what gets installed on computers in an enterprise.

- Software can be installed even when the user can't modify the desktop or Registry directly.

- Setup programs use one uniform API on all platforms.

- All changes during setup can be "rolled back" for a clean uninstall.

- Software can be repaired or reinstalled by calling the Windows Installer.

The Windows Installer delivers all of these benefits, but at the moment it's version 1.0 technology. The Windows Installer service is a native part of Windows 2000, and it's installed on other versions of Windows by its own bootstrap installation program. Microsoft has clearly indicated that this is the way they expect all future software to be installed on Windows. In particular, to obtain the Windows 2000 compatible logo, your application must use the Windows Installer for its setup program.

In addition, the Windows Installer installs the Microsoft Access Runtime, so it's a natural fit to add your own application to that installation if you're distributing the Runtime with your application.

> **NOTE**    The Windows Installer keeps all the information it needs to perform a setup in a database with the file extension .MSI. Unfortunately these databases are not in Jet or SQL Server format, so they can't be managed directly with Access. You'll learn about tools for editing Installer databases later in this chapter.

## The Windows Installer SDK

If you're going to do any serious work with the Windows Installer, you absolutely need a copy of the Windows Installer Software Development Kit (SDK). There are two ways to get a copy of this SDK:

- It's included in the Windows Platform SDK, a part of the Microsoft Developer Network, under Management Services\Setup\Windows Installer.

- It can be downloaded from the Windows Installer SDK page on Microsoft's Web site at `http://msdn.microsoft.com/developer/sdk/wininst.asp`.

Even if you have a copy of the Platform SDK, you'll probably want to download a copy of the SDK from the Web site. The downloadable version includes numerous tools that are not included in the Platform SDK version.

Table 16.2 lists the components of the Windows Installer SDK.

**TABLE 16.2:** Windows Installer SDK Components

| Component | Description |
| --- | --- |
| INSTMSI.EXE | This is the installer for the Installer service itself. There's one version for Windows 95 or 98, and another for Windows NT 4.0. You generally won't have to worry about this file if you're using the Access Runtime, because it's already included in the Runtime setup. |
| MSI.CHM | Hypertext help for the Windows Installer. This is essential reading if you're planning to customize an installation. |
| MSITOOL.HLP | Help for the various tools included in the Windows Installer SDK. |
| C++ Source, Header and Library files | These are examples for developers who wish to use the Windows Installer APIs directly. You won't need them if you're working solely with Office applications. |
| INSTLR1.ADM | This is a Group Policy Editor file for Windows NT 4.0 and Windows 2000 administrators who wish to customize the behavior of the Windows Installer service. |
| ORCA.MSI | Installation package for the "Orca" Installer database editor. Orca is a very simple database editor that comes with the SDK. |
| MSIVAL2.MSI | Installation package for the Installer database validation tool. |
| MSIDB.EXE | Command-line tool to import and export text files from Installer databases. |
| MSIINFO.EXE | Command-line tool to set or inspect summary information from Installer databases. |
| MSIMERG.EXE | Command-line tool to merge two Installer databases. |
| MSITRAN.EXE | Command-line tool to apply transform files to Installer databases. A *transform file* is a separate Installer database that's designed to preselect options in an existing Installer database, or to add new components to the existing database. |
| MSIZAP.EXE | Command-line tool to remove selected Windows Installer information from a computer. Normally you should use the Windows Installer Cleanup Tool, discussed later in this chapter, instead. |
| MSISPY.MSI | Installation package used for examples in the Installer SDK. MsiSpy itself is a program for listing the components that are being managed by the Windows Installer on your computer. |

**TABLE 16.2:** Windows Installer SDK Components *(continued)*

| Component | Description |
|---|---|
| Patching files | Documentation and examples for building Installer patches, which are designed to adjust the functionality of existing products. This is an advanced topic that we won't discuss further. |
| SCHEMA.MSI | Blank Installer database. |
| UISAMPLE.MSI | Installer database demonstrating the creation of a user interface for a setup program. |

In the remainder of this section we'll describe the major concepts you need to understand to make use of Windows Installer technology:

- Installation packages
- Features and components
- Installation phases
- Advertisement and installation-on-demand
- Versioning rules

## Installation Packages

The Windows Installer is designed to use *installation packages*. These are structured storage files that contain a database of actions for the Installer to perform, a summary information stream, and possibly other streams. An installation package can even contain binary components in the form of embedded .CAB files, making it possible to deliver an entire installation as a single (although probably large) file. Installation packages have the .MSI extension by default.

The Windows Installer makes a distinction between a product and a package. A *product* is a particular piece of software identified by a product code, which is a GUID. A *package* is an installer package designed to install a product. Packages are identified by package codes, which are also GUIDs. If you make a minor change to your application and repackage it, you can keep the same product code, but you must change the package code if there's been any change at all to the installer package.

**WARNING**   All GUIDs used by the Windows Installer (including product codes, package codes, and component codes) can use only upper case letters. If you're using the GUID-GEN utility to generate these codes, you'll need to manually convert lower case letters to upper case letters.

## Features and Components

The Windows Installer divides applications into features and components. It's important to understand the distinction between the two; otherwise, you'll be confused by much of the Windows Installer documentation, as well as the structure of the Installer database.

A *feature* is a part of an application that a user understands as an independent entity. For example, if your application includes a separate help file you might choose to make "online help" a feature of the application. Features can be organized hierarchically. In the Windows Installer world, if you install a child feature, you automatically install the parent feature. So if you have a "multi-language reporting" feature that's a child of a "multi-language editing" feature, choosing to install multi-language reporting automatically forces the installation of multi-language editing.

A *component*, by contrast, is a part of an application that makes sense to a developer. A component could be a group of files that all get installed to the same folder, a COM component together with the Registry entries needed to make it work, or a single file with a Windows shortcut to be placed on the desktop.

While features are part of a single application, components can actually be shared by many applications. For example, both the Access Runtime installation package and the Office Premier installation package include a component named Global_Graph_Core, which contains all of the files and Registry settings required for the language-independent portion of Microsoft Graph. When the Windows Installer is installing a component, it checks to see whether that particular component is already installed on the computer. If so, it just increments a counter rather than performing the same setup steps all over again. Components are uniquely identified by GUIDs called component codes.

The Windows Installer decides whether a particular component is installed by checking for the presence of a key file on the computer where the installation is being performed. If that file is found, the Windows Installer assumes that the entire component is installed and functioning properly.

The relationship between features and components is many-to-many. That is, a single feature may call for many components, and many features may install a single component.

## Installation Phases

The Windows Installer performs an installation in at least two, and possibly three, phases:

- Acquisition
- Execution
- Rollback

During the acquisition phase, the Windows Installer inspects the features that the user has chosen as well as any other choices made in the setup user interface and develops an internal installation script. This script lists all of the individual actions (for example, copying a file or writing a Registry key) that the Windows Installer must perform.

During the execution phase, the Windows Installer reads the script and performs the actions. This phase is carried out by a system service that runs at an elevated privilege. Thus it can perform actions such as writing Registry keys even if the current user of the computer cannot perform these actions. During this phase, the Windows Installer creates a rollback script that tells it how to undo each action it has performed. It also saves hidden copies of any files that it deletes or overwrites.

If anything goes wrong during the execution phase, the Windows Installer enters the rollback phase. During this phase it reads the rollback script and reverses every action that was performed during the execution phase.

**WARNING**  Any error in setup is 100% fatal to the installation process. For example, if you include a COM server that can't be registered on a particular computer, the Installer will automatically enter the rollback phase and none of your setup will be executed on that computer.

## Advertisement and Installation-on-Demand

The Windows Installer supports advertised applications. An *advertised application* is one that appears to be present without actually being installed. In this case, Start menu entries will be present, the application's files will be correctly associated with the application, the application's icon will be displayed, and the Registry entries for the application will be written to the computer. However, files and folders associated with an advertised application are generally not created.

Advertisement works together with installation-on-demand. When the user actually tries to run an advertised application, it calls back to the Windows Installer, which then performs the installation.

Installation-on-demand works at the feature level as well as at the application level. Your application can be installed with all features, yet use advertising for most of them. Only features actually activated by the user will be installed. If you've ever seen a Windows Installer dialog box when choosing something from the menus within an Office 2000 program, you've watched installation-on-demand in action.

---

**TIP**　　　On Windows 2000 *only*, installation-on-demand extends to COM components. So if your application advertises a server for MyProgram.MyObject, calling CreateObject("MyProgram.MyObject") from within a Visual Basic program will automatically install the server. Be careful, though, because this type of advertising is not supported on other versions of Windows.

---

## Versioning Rules

When you're running an installation, the Windows Installer may find that a particular file already exists in the target location. In this case, it follows a set of rules to determine whether to install a new copy of the file:

1. All other things being equal, the file with the highest version wins, whether this is the file in the installation package or the one already on the computer.

2. A file with version information always wins over a file with no version information.

3. If the file being installed has a different language than the file on the computer, the new file wins.

4. If the file supports multiple languages, install the new file if it supports any languages that are not supported by the file on the computer.

5. If the file supports multiple languages, and the file on the computer supports all of the languages supported by the new file, keep whichever file supports more languages.

6. If the modified date for the file on the computer is later than the creation date for that file, assume it's been customized by the user and do not install a new file.

## Developing Components

As you prepare your own application to be installed by the Windows Installer, you'll need to break it up into features and components. While the choice of features is more or less arbitrary (you get to decide how it makes sense to split functionality from a user's point of view) there are a number of rules that have to be followed when creating components.

- A component is the same in all applications that require it.

- All files in a component must be installed in a single directory.

- A single key file must identify every component. The version of the component is determined by the version of this file. If a newer version of this file is on the target computer, the component will not be installed.

- If the component includes a COM server, this server must be the key file for the component. A component can include at most one COM server.

- A component can include at most one file that is a target for a desktop or Start menu shortcut.

- No file can ever be included in more than one component. This rule applies across everything: versions and applications, even across multiple companies. So, for example, if the Access Runtime installation package includes a redistributable file in a particular component, the only way you can install that file is to install that exact component.

- No Registry entry, shortcut or other resource can be included in more than one component.

- If a component is not 100% backwards compatible with a previous version of the same component, then it's a new component and must be assigned a new component code. This rule applies any time you don't know for certain that the new component can replace the old component everywhere without causing any problems. Note that when you change the component code, you're creating a new component, and thus must change every filename, shortcut name, Registry key, and other resource in the component.

The Windows Installer SDK suggests a step-by-step procedure for breaking your application into components:

1. List all of the files, folders, shortcuts and Registry keys required by your application.

2. Identify any of these resources that are already in other Windows Installer packages and pick up the components from those packages. In some cases, you'll be able to do this by using Windows Installer merge modules. A *merge module* is an installer database, provided by a component vendor, that's designed to be merged into other installation packages rather than to be installed by itself.

3. Define a new component for each .EXE, .DLL and .OCX file in your application. Make these files the key files of their components.

4. Define a new component for each .CHM or .HLP file. Make these files the key files of their components. Add the associated .CHI or .CNT files to these components.

5. If there are any files left that are the targets of shortcuts, define a new component for each of these files.

6. For any leftover files, define a component for each folder containing files. If there's any possibility of a group of these files being broken up in the future, break them into multiple folders and components now.

7. Add Registry keys to the components they're most closely associated with. If necessary, define an additional component for general Registry settings that are not associated with a particular component.

## Using the FeatureInstall property

Access 2000 provides some programmatic control over installation-on-demand with the Application.FeatureInstall property. The possible values for this property are shown in Table 16.3.

**TABLE 16.3:**   Values for the FeatureInstall Property

| Value | Description |
| --- | --- |
| msoFeatureInstallNone | Specifies that installation-on-demand should not take place (the default). |
| msoFeatureInstallOnDemand | Specifies that the user should be prompted to install new features that are referenced from your code. Figure 16.1 shows the prompt dialog box in the case of the Office Assistant feature. If the user answers Yes, the feature is installed and the progress meter displayed during installation. |
| msoFeatureInstallOnDemandWithUI | Specifies that the feature should be automatically installed, and that the progress meter should be displayed during installation. |

**TIP**   To use constants with the Application.FeatureInstall property, you must set a reference to the Microsoft Office 9.0 Object Library.

**FIGURE 16.1**
Office Install-on-Demand
prompt

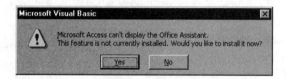

Install-on-demand, of course, works only with features that have been advertised. In the Office 2000 setup, advertised features are those for which the user chooses Installed on First Use when installing Office. If the user chooses Not Available for a feature, it will never be installed on demand, no matter how you set the FeatureInstall property.

To see the FeatureInstall property in action, you can use the frmShowAssistant form in the CH16.MDB sample database. This form allows you to choose one of the possible values for the FeatureInstall property and then try to show the Assistant. The Assistant is a separate feature of Office 2000 that can be set to install on first use. If you've already installed Office, you can set your Assistant to install on first use (that is, the next time you try to use it) by following these steps:

1. From Control Panel, run the Add/Remove Programs applet.

2. Choose Microsoft Office 2000.

3. Choose Add or Remove Features.

4. Expand the Office Tools node of the available features tree.

5. Click on the node for Office Assistant and select Installed on First Use.

Once you've done this, any use of a property of the Assistant object in your code will tell Access to attempt to install the Assistant feature on your computer. For example, Listing 16.1 shows the code from frmShowAssistant.

> **Listing 16.1**

```
Private Sub cmdShowAssistant_Click()
    ' Attempt to show the Assistant,
    ' with various settings of the
    ' Application.FeatureInstall property

    On Error GoTo HandleErr

    Select Case grpAssistant.Value
        Case 1  ' optFeatureInstallNone
            Application.FeatureInstall = _
            msoFeatureInstallNone
        Case 2  ' optFeatureInstallOnDemand
            Application.FeatureInstall = _
            msoFeatureInstallOnDemand
        Case 3  ' optFeatureInstallOnDemandWithUI
            Application.FeatureInstall = _
            msoFeatureInstallOnDemandWithUI
    End Select

    Assistant.On = True
    Assistant.Visible = True

ExitHere:
    Exit Sub

HandleErr:
    MsgBox "Error " & Err.Number & ": " & _
    Err.Description
    Resume ExitHere
End Sub
```

If you experiment with this form, you'll discover that you get Error –2147467259, "Method 'On' of object 'Assistant' Failed," under any of these circumstances:

- The FeatureInstall property is set to msoFeatureInstallNone.

- The FeatureInstall property is set to msoFeatureInstallOnDemand and the user chooses not to install the feature.

- The FeatureInstall property is set to msoFeatureInstallOnDemand or msoFeatureInstallOnDemandWithUI and the user clicks the Cancel button in the progress dialog box.

You can also receive the same error if the user cancels an installation-on-demand and you attempt to install another feature before the Windows Installer service has reset. You can see this problem by choosing msoFeatureInstallOn-DemandWithUI, clicking "Show Assistant", canceling the dialog box, and immediately clicking Show Assistant a second time. There's no way to tell this from any of the other causes of the error.

> **NOTE**
> You can't control the wording of the alert that is presented when Application .FeatureInstall is set to msoFeatureInstallOnDemand and the user attempts to use a demand-installed feature. You may wish to use msoFeatureInstallOnDemand-WithUI and present your own MessageBox to the user instead.

## Repair & Reinstall

When you run Microsoft Office Setup in maintenance mode (that is, by choosing Microsoft Office from the Add/Remove Programs Control Panel applet after you've completed your Office installation) one of your choices is to reinstall or repair your Office installation. Actually, there are three possible choices on this dialog box, shown in Figure 16.2. These choices correspond to different command lines passed to the Windows Installer software:

**Reinstall Office**    Invokes the installer with the command-line switch /fecums

**Repair Errors in My Office Installation**    Invokes the installer with the command line switch /focum

**Repair Errors in My Office Installation *and* Restore My Shortcuts**    Invokes the installer with the command line switch /focums. This is also the way the installer is invoked when you choose Detect and Repair from the Help menu within Access.

FIGURE 16.2
Repair and reinstall choices

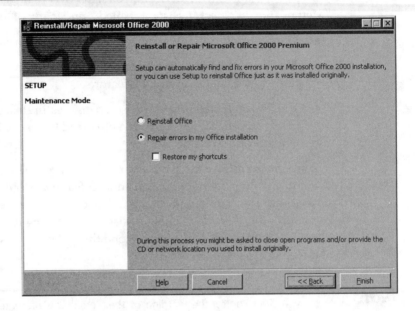

Table 16.4 lists the various available modifiers to the /f switch for the Windows Installer. You're not limited to just the combinations supported by the setup user interface, nor do you have to go through the Add/Remove Programs applet to use this switch. You can invoke the Installer in repair mode directly from a command window with a command line such as

```
<path>\setup.exe /f<modifiers> data1.msi
```

Here <path> is the path to the Office CD-ROM or network installation point and <modifiers> is any combination of modifiers from Table 16.4.

**TABLE 16.4:**   Windows Installer Repair Modifiers

| Modifier | Description |
| --- | --- |
| a | Reinstall all files, regardless of checksum or version. |
| c | Reinstall if a file is missing or corrupt. This switch only operates on files with a checksum stored in the installation databases's File table. |
| d | Reinstall if a file is missing, or a different version is installed. |
| e | Reinstall if a file is missing, or an earlier or equal version is installed. |

**TABLE 16.4:**   Windows Installer Repair Modifiers *(continued)*

| Modifier | Description |
| --- | --- |
| m | Re-create all Registry keys that to to the HKEY_LOCAL_MACHINE or HKEY_CLASSES_ROOT Registry keys. Also rewrite all information from the Class, Verb, PublishComponent, ProgID, MIME, Icon, Extension, and AppID tables. Reinstall all localized components. |
| o | Reinstall if a file is missing, or an earlier version is installed. |
| p | Reinstall if a file is missing, or verify it against the source if it is present. |
| s | Reinstall all shortcuts and icons, replacing any that are present or cached. |
| u | Re-create all Registry keys that go to the HKEY_CURRENT_USER or HKEY_USERS Registry keys. |
| v | Forces use of the package on the source media rather than any locally cached copy. |

# The Windows Install Clean Up Utility

The Windows Installer caches quite a bit of information on your computer when you perform an installation. Some of this information is cached in the Registry and some in disk files. It's possible for this information to get corrupted, in which case the Installer may not be able to repair or reinstall a particular product, or properly service install-on-demand requests. You may also not be able to uninstall a product if the Installer database has become corrupted.

Corruption can result from:

- Registry or disk crashes

- User edits to the Registry

- A crash during the installation of a program

- Multiple instances of the Installer running at one time

Microsoft has released the Windows Install Clean Up utility to help recover from these problems. Figure 16.3 shows this utility in action. It lists all of the products that are known to the Windows Installer on your system and lets you remove any or all of these products along with the cached installation information.

FIGURE 16.3
Windows Install Clean Up
utility

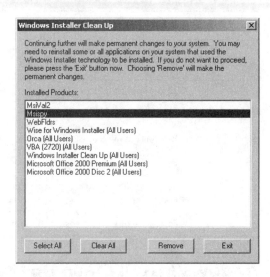

The Windows Install Clean Up utility maintains a log file of its actions in Windows\Temp\MSICU.LOG. You can use this file to determine what actions the utility has taken. Of course, you'll need to reinstall from the original source media any application that you uninstall with this utility.

To obtain a copy of the Windows Install Clean Up utility, refer to article Q238413 in the Microsoft KnowledgeBase. You can access this article online at `http://support.microsoft.com/support/kb/articles/q238/4/13.ASP`. You can also receive a copy of this article by e-mail by sending a message to `mshelp@microsoft.com` with the subject "Q238413". The article contains the latest information on where to download the utility, which comes in separate versions for Windows $9x$ and Windows NT.

Using the Windows Install Clean Up utility should be treated as a last resort for fixing setup problems. But sometimes you'll need to use that last resort.

# The Windows Installer Automation Interface

The Windows Installer SDK documents the complete API for the Windows Installer. It also documents the automation interface for the Windows Installer, which is automatically installed on your computer the first time you use the Windows Installer to set up an application. Figure 16.4 shows a sample of the information that's available through the automation interface. This form, frmInstallerAutomation in CH16.MDB, displays information on installed packages as well as the components and features in the selected package.

**FIGURE 16.4**

Retrieving information from the Windows Installer automation interface

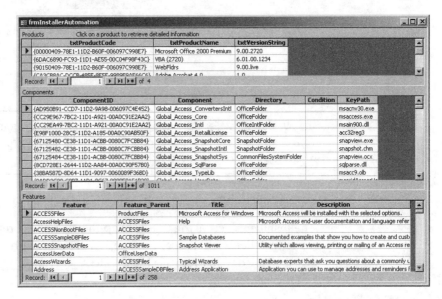

Because the automation interface can be used to retrieve information from any of the tables in an installer package, it's a good choice any time your application needs to know something about software that was installed by the Windows Installer.

You could edit installer packages through the Installer automation interface, but there's no need. As you'll see later in this chapter, there are several applications designed to edit installer packages directly.

## Installer Objects

Figure 16.5 shows the Windows Installer objects that we'll be using in this chapter. For the complete Windows Installer object model, refer to the Windows Installer SDK.

**FIGURE 16.5**
Windows Installer objects

---

**TIP**

The Windows Installer SDK help will not properly launch from the Visual Basic object browser. You should launch the help file directly from the Help folder where you installed the SDK instead.

---

The objects in the Windows Installer are described below:

- The Installer object is the top-level application object representing the Windows Installer itself. It does not support creation with the VBA New keyword. Instead, you must use the CreateObject function to obtain an instance of the Installer object.

- The Products object is a collection of all the products known to the Windows Installer on this computer. It's stored as an array of strings.

- The Session object represents a single installation session. This might be a session to actually install a product, or just one to connect to the database inside an installer package.

- The Database object represents the database within a particular installation package.

- The View object represents information retrieved from one or more tables within an installation database as specified by a SQL statement.

- The Record object represents a single record within a View object.

# Retrieving Product Information

The GetProductInfo procedure in basInstaller demonstrates the use of the Installer API to retrieve information about known products. Listing 16.2 shows the code that this procedure uses to move this information to a table in the Access database.

---

**NOTE**    To use this code in your applications you'll need to set a VBA reference to "Microsoft Windows Installer Object Library."

---

⤵ **Listing 16.2**

```
Sub GetProductInfo()
    ' Use the Installer Automation API to
    ' retrieve information about products
    ' installed on this computer
    Dim objInstaller As WindowsInstaller.Installer
    Dim varGUID As Variant

    Dim rstProducts As New ADODB.Recordset

    On Error GoTo HandleErr

    DoCmd.Hourglass True

    Set objInstaller = CreateObject( _
     "WindowsInstaller.Installer")

    CurrentProject.Connection.Execute _
     "DELETE * FROM tblProducts"
    rstProducts.Open "tblProducts", _
     CurrentProject.Connection, _
     adOpenKeyset, adLockOptimistic

    ' Stock a table with all of the products that the
    ' Windows Installer knows about on this computer
    For Each varGUID In objInstaller.Products
        With rstProducts
            .AddNew
            .Fields("ProductCode") = varGUID
```

```
                .Fields("ProductName") = _
                 objInstaller.ProductInfo(varGUID, "ProductName")
                .Fields("VersionString") = _
                 objInstaller.ProductInfo(varGUID, _
                 "VersionString")
                .Update
            End With
        Next varGUID
        rstProducts.Close

    ExitHere:
        DoCmd.Hourglass False
        Exit Sub

    HandleErr:
        MsgBox "Error " & Err.Number & ": " & _
         Err.Description
        Resume ExitHere
        Resume
    End Sub
```

After creating an instance of the Installer object, this procedure uses that object's Products property to retrieve the list of products. The Products property is an example of what the Installer SDK calls a StringList object. This property returns an array of strings, one for each known product (because of the limitations of COM in VBA, this array can only be retrieved into a variant using the For...Each syntax).

These strings are the product codes (GUIDs) of the known products. Those product codes in turn can be used with the objInstaller.ProductInfo property to retrieve information about the particular product. The ProductInfo property takes two arguments. The first is a product code, and the second is the name of a property to retrieve. Table 16.5 lists the available properties. Note that some of these properties are available for either advertised or installed products, while others are available only for installed products.

**TABLE 16.5:** ProductInfo Property Names

| Name | Description | Available for Installed Products only? |
| --- | --- | --- |
| AssignmentType | Information on advertising status | No |
| HelpLink | URL for technical support | Yes |
| HelpTelephone | Phone number for technical support | Yes |
| InstallDate | Date product was first installed | Yes |
| InstallLocation | Root folder of the installed product | Yes |
| InstallSource | Root folder that setup was performed from | Yes |
| InstalledProductName | Name of the installed product | Yes |
| Language | Product language | No |
| LocalPackage | Filename for the locally cached version of the package | Yes |
| PackageCode | GUID identifying the installer package | No |
| ProductID | Product ID entered by the user during licensing | Yes |
| ProductName | Product Name | No |
| Publisher | Publisher of the package | Yes |
| RegCompany | Company of registered owner of the software | Yes |
| RegOwner | Registered owner of the software | Yes |
| Transforms | List of customizations for the product | No |
| URLInfoAbout | URL for information about the product | Yes |
| URLUpdateInfo | URL for information regarding updating the product | Yes |
| Version | Product Version | No |
| VersionMajor | Major version number | Yes |
| VersionMinor | Minor version number | Yes |
| VersionString | Human-readable version | Yes |

## Retrieving Information from the Installer Database

The GetDetailInfo procedure in basInstaller demonstrates the use of the Installer automation model to retrieve information from the installer database within a particular installer package. You'll find the database schema documented in the Installer SDK. This schema includes quite a number of tables, and we won't review it in detail here. The process for retrieving the data is the same for any of these tables.

You call GetDetailInfo by passing the GUID representing the product code you want information for. GetDetailInfo starts its work by retrieving the particular installer database of interest:

```
Dim objInstaller As WindowsInstaller.Installer
Dim objSession As WindowsInstaller.Session
Dim objDatabase As WindowsInstaller.Database
Dim objView As WindowsInstaller.View
Dim objRecord As WindowsInstaller.Record

Dim rstComponents As New ADODB.Recordset
Dim rstFeatures As New ADODB.Recordset

On Error GoTo HandleErr

DoCmd.Hourglass True

' Open a session with the specified product
' and retrieve the installer database
Set objInstaller = CreateObject( _
 "WindowsInstaller.Installer")
Set objSession = _
 objInstaller.OpenProduct(strProductCode)
Set objDatabase = objSession.Database
```

Retrieving an installer database is a three-step process:

1. Create the Installer object.

2. Use the product code to open an Installer Session object using a particular installer package.

3. Use the Session object's Database property to retrieve a reference to the installer database.

Once it's connected to the installer database, GetDetailInfo uses SQL queries to retrieve information. Here, for example, is the code that retrieves component information from the database:

```
' Open an Installer view on the Components
' table in the Installer package
Set objView = objDatabase.OpenView( _
 "SELECT ComponentId, Component, Directory_, " & _
 "Condition, KeyPath FROM Component")
objView.Execute
Set objRecord = objView.Fetch
Do Until objRecord Is Nothing
    With rstComponents
        .AddNew
        .Fields("ComponentID") = _
         objRecord.StringData(1)
        .Fields("Component") = _
         objRecord.StringData(2)
        .Fields("Directory_") = _
         objRecord.StringData(3)
        .Fields("Condition") = _
         objRecord.StringData(4)
        .Fields("KeyPath") = _
         objRecord.StringData(5)
        .Update
    End With
    Set objRecord = objView.Fetch
Loop
```

You'll see that retrieving information from an installer database differs substantially from retrieving information from an Access database. To retrieve information from an installer database, you need to take these steps:

1. Obtain a valid Database object.

2. Use the Database object's OpenView method to create a View object. The OpenView method takes as its single argument a SQL statement specifying information to retrieve from the database.

3. Use the View object's Execute method to retrieve the data specified by the SQL statement.

**4.** Use the View object's Fetch method to create a Record object containing the next record in the view. You can only move forward through a view, and only one record at a time. When the records are exhausted, the Fetch method will return nothing.

**5.** Use ordinal numbers with the View object's StringData property to retrieve the information in the current record. You can't use field names here.

We'll use this knowledge of the Windows Installer technology when we look at tools for creating Windows Installer setup packages later in the chapter. First, though, let's look at the one setup tool that actually ships with Microsoft Office 2000 Developer: the Package and Deployment Wizard.

# The Package and Deployment Wizard

In addition to the Access Runtime and its redistribution license, Microsoft Office 2000 Developer contains an Office 2000 version of the Package and Deployment Wizard. Originally developed as a part of Visual Basic, this wizard takes a set of files and creates a setup program to install them on end users' computers. The Package and Deployment Wizard has some special knowledge of the Access Runtime, but as you'll see, this knowledge is not well integrated with the rest of the product.

> **WARNING** The Package and Deployment Wizard does not create Windows Installer packages. Instead, it creates stand-alone setups using a setup program authored in Visual Basic. Later in this chapter we'll discuss tools for creating true Windows Installer packages.

The Package and Deployment Wizard is shipped as a VBA add-in. After installing Microsoft Office 2000 Developer, follow these steps to finish installing the wizard:

**1.** Launch Access (or any other VBA host).

**2.** Open the Visual Basic Editor.

**3.** Choose Add-Ins ➢ Add-In Manager.

**4.** Choose VBA Package and Deployment Wizard from the list of add-ins.

5. Select the Loaded and Load on Startup checkboxes.

6. Click OK.

The Add-Ins menu should now contain an entry for the Package and Deployment Wizard.

## Using the Package and Deployment Wizard

To use the Package and Deployment Wizard to distribute your Access application, you must complete two steps. First, you need to create a package (a compressed file or set of compressed files containing the components of your application, as well as a setup program to install those components). Second, you need to deploy the package, making it available on distribution media or a Web site to end users who will install your application. In this section we'll show you the basic steps involved in using the Package and Deployment Wizard for these activities.

To start, open your application in Access and switch to the Visual Basic Editor. If you're used to the version of the Package and Deployment Wizard shipped with Visual Basic, you might be looking for a stand-alone program, but the version shipped with Microsoft Office 2000 Developer works as an add-in only. Choose Add-Ins ➤ Package and Deployment Wizard to start the wizard.

> **NOTE**     You must open your Access application in shared mode before you launch the Package and Deployment Wizard.

Click the Package button on the first screen of the wizard to start the packaging process. The wizard will analyze your Access application, looking for components that need to be distributed. Next, you must choose a type of package to create. Generally speaking, you should choose the Standard Setup Package. The other choice is to create a Dependency File, which is used to capture information about the components in an application without actually creating a setup program.

You next need to supply a location for the package. This should not be the same folder that your copy of the application resides in. The wizard will automatically propose creating a Package subfolder to hold the package.

If there are any components in the application that the wizard does not contain dependency information about, it will flag these for you now. As Figure 16.6 illustrates, the wizard doesn't know about dependency information for the ADO type library, which is used by all new Access applications. Because the Access Runtime automatically installs the necessary files for ADO to function, you can check the box for this type library so you're not prompted about it again in the future.

**FIGURE 16.6**

Missing Dependency Information warning from the Package and Deployment Wizard

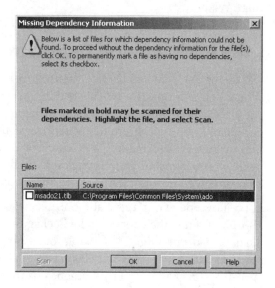

The wizard will next present you with a list of files to be included in the setup. Figure 16.7 shows a typical list of files. The wizard will automatically find a number of files for you:

- The Access project or database that's loaded when you launch the wizard

- Any data access pages from the current database or project

- Any type libraries listed under Tools ≻ References

- Any linked file-server data sources

- The files used by the setup program itself (ODESTKIT.DLL, ODEUNST .EXE, SETUP.EXE, SETUP1.EXE)

**TIP**

If you're going to redistribute the Access Runtime with your application, you should select the Include Access Runtime checkbox on this wizard panel and uncheck the reference to the ADO type library.

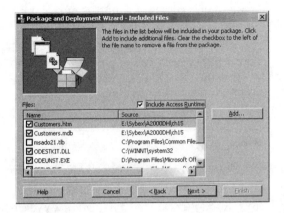

**FIGURE 16.7**
Choosing files to package

The first time you choose to include the Access Runtime, you'll have to tell the Package and Deployment Wizard where to find the Access Runtime files. These files are *not* automatically installed to your hard drive by the Microsoft 2000 Office Developer setup program. You can either leave them on the Microsoft Office Developer CD-ROM, and ensure that this CD-ROM is always available when you run the Package and Deployment Wizard, or you can copy the entire \ACCESSRT folder from the CD-ROM to your hard drive.

**TIP**    The Package and Deployment Wizard will complete its work much more quickly if you copy the Access Runtime files to your hard drive.

The next panel of the wizard allows you to choose the title displayed by the setup program and to specify a command to run when the setup program has completed its work. One use of this option is to allow you to automatically set up the MSDE at the end of your application's installation routine. We'll discuss this process later in this chapter.

The next panel of the wizard allows you to create Start menu groups and short-cuts. By default, the wizard creates a single group and a single shortcut, both with the name of your application. The shortcut will be pointing directly to the Access (MDB or ADP) file, and depends on the Windows file association to launch Access.

The next panel of the wizard allows you to verify the installation locations for the files you've included in the setup. For non-operating system files, the default location is coded with the $(AppPath) macro, which tells the wizard to install these files in the folder chosen by the user when they run the setup program. You can use either hard-coded paths or macros to specify installation locations. Table 16.6 lists the available macros you can use here.

**TABLE 16.6:** Package and Deployment Wizard Installation Path Macros

| Macro | Location |
| --- | --- |
| $(WinSysPath) | \Windows\System on Windows 95 or 98, or \Winnt\System32 on Windows NT or Windows 2000 |
| $(WinSysPathSysFile) | \Windows\System on Windows 95 or 98, or \Winnt\System32 on Windows NT or Windows 2000. In addition, the file is marked as a system file and not uninstalled if the user uninstalls your application. |
| $(WinPath) | \Windows on Windows 95 or 98, or \Winnt on Windows NT or Windows 2000 |
| $(AppPath) | The application folder chosen by the user when they run the setup program. |
| $(AppPath)\SubFolder | A subfolder created under the application folder chosen by the user when they run the setup program. |
| $(ProgramFiles) | The user's program files folder. |
| $(CommonFiles) | The user's common files folder. |
| $(MSDAOPath) | The location stored in the Registry for Data Access Objects. |

Next the wizard will allow you to specify whether any of the files you're using are shared files. Shared files are reference counted in the Registry. Each time an application installs one of these files a counter is incremented, and each time an application using a shared file is uninstalled, the counter is decremented. Only when the counter reaches zero is the file actually removed (that is, when the last application sharing the file is uninstalled). Generally, you won't want to mark your application's files as shared.

Finally, the wizard will let you supply a script name and click Finish. A Package and Deployment Wizard script contains a record of all the choices you made as your proceeded through the wizard. This makes it much easier to reload a project and make modifications in the future.

---

**WARNING**    If you're including the Access Runtime files, make sure the location where you're storing the package has at least 160 MB of free space to store a copy of the Runtime, as well as enough extra space for your application's files.

---

When the Package part of the wizard finishes its work, all of the necessary files to set up your application will have been created and stored on your hard drive. Then it's time to deploy the setup program. To do this, launch the Package and Deployment Wizard again (note that it will still be displayed if you've just finished building the package) and click the Deploy button.

The first panel of the wizard lets you select the package to deploy. The wizard keeps track of all the packages you've created. Next, you must choose whether to deploy to a folder or a Web server. If you want to create diskettes (not a practical idea if you're including the Access Runtime), a CD-ROM, or a network setup, select the folder option. If you want to make your setup package available on a Web server, select the Web publishing option. For most applications, you'll want to select the folder option.

Next, you must select a location for the package's deployment. This can either be a removable device or a network folder. Select a location and click Finish to deploy the setup package.

## Testing the Setup

Once you've completed the deployment step, you're ready to test your setup program. To do this, you'll want a computer that doesn't have your application or Access installed. You should check that your application functions correctly after the install and that you fully understand the setup process so that you can answer any questions your users may have.

Here's what will happen when the user runs the SETUP.EXE program that the Package and Deployment Wizard creates:

1.  Necessary files for the setup program to run will be copied to the user's hard drive.

2. If the user has an old version of the core COM files, they'll have to reboot their computer at this point. After the reboot, they'll need to run the setup program a second time.

3. If your setup contains the Access Runtime, setup checks the user's hard drive to see if Microsoft Access 2000 is installed. If it is present, setup skips installing the Runtime entirely (remember, the Runtime files are the same as the regular Access files, and the Runtime behaves just like regular Access if the retail licensing key is present in the Registry). If Access is not present, the user will see the dialog box shown in Figure 16.8.

<table>
<tr>
<td>

**FIGURE 16.8**

Prompt to install the Access Runtime

</td>
<td>

</td>
</tr>
</table>

4. After the user clicks OK, the Access Runtime setup will check for the presence of the Windows Installer core files on the system. If these files are not present, they will be installed. The Windows Installer then launches the Access Runtime setup from the Access Runtime installer package included as a part of your application's setup files.

5. The user can choose Install Now to automatically place the Runtime files in their default location, or Customize to choose a different location for the Runtime files. You can't prevent the user from choosing Customize, nor can you track the folder they've chosen to install the files to, so you better not depend on the program files in a specific location.

6. When the user selects a location, the Windows Installer will complete the Access Runtime installation. While this installation is going on, a progress meter will be displayed that prominently tells the user that the Access Runtime is being installed. You can't suppress this dialog box. The Runtime installation isn't especially fast, and may appear to hang. However, there's no Cancel button on the progress dialog box, so unless the user reboots this should not be a problem.

7. At the end of the Access Runtime setup, the user will need to reboot their computer again.

8. After the reboot, the user will see the Windows Update dialog box as Internet Explorer 5 setup completes (unless they already had Internet Explorer 5 installed on their computer). The Access Runtime setup installs Internet Explorer 5 without warning because some of the functionality of data access pages depends on this version of Internet Explorer.

9. After the Internet Explorer setup is complete, the Windows Installer takes over with another progress dialog box while it finishes registering the Access Runtime components.

10. After the Access Runtime setup is complete, the setup program for your application will finally launch. The user gets a chance to close applications and they can then pick a folder to use for the software installation (this is the folder that will be used to resolve the $(AppPath) macro if you used that macro during the Package phase of the Package and Deployment Wizard).

11. If you told the Package and Deployment Wizard to create any Start menu groups, the setup program will confirm the name of the group with the user.

12. Your application's files will be copied to the user's computer. When this is complete, setup will exit.

## Tips and Workarounds

Developers who remember the Access Setup Wizard from Microsoft Office 97 Developer Edition may feel a bit lost with the new Package and Deployment Wizard. The new technology can do almost anything the old Setup Wizard could do, but you may have to learn some new tricks.

The old Setup Wizard could automatically include a Workgroup file with your setup, and used the name of this file when building shortcuts. The new wizard requires you to perform this work manually. If you need a Workgroup file, you'll have to remember to add it to the file list yourself. You'll also need to modify the command line used for the shortcuts created by the setup program. You'll probably want to use a command line similar to this one:

```
$(AppPath)\Customers.mdb /runtime/wrkgrp$(AppPath)\Corporate.mdw
```

**TIP**  You should also add the runtime switch as shown above to force the application to launch with runtime functionality even if the user has retail Access installed on their computer.

While you're editing Start menu items, you might also want to add one to compact and repair your database. This is another nicety that the old wizard offered that isn't built into the new wizard. Compacting and repairing a database is accomplished using the /compact and/or /repair command line switches.

The old wizard had a panel devoted to creating Registry keys. The new one does not. However, the new wizard automatically runs any .REG file that you include in your file list at the end of the setup process. So, to create Registry keys on the user's computer, just export the required keys to a Registry file by using REGEDIT.EXE on your computer, and include that Registry file in your file list.

---

**WARNING**     There is no way to get the new wizard to resolve macros in Registry keys at installation time. This means you can't use it to register an Access wizard.

---

## Installing Access Projects

The Package and Deployment Wizard functions exactly the same within Access projects as it does within Access databases. However, if you need to distribute the back-end SQL database as well as the front-end Access project, you'll need to take some additional steps.

The Microsoft Office 2000 Developer CD contains a redistributable version of the MSDE database engine. This is not precisely the same as the version contained on the Microsoft Office 2000 Premium CD (which you are not allowed to redistribute). The core data engine is identical, but the redistributable version lacks the user interface tools for editing server-side objects.

---

**NOTE**     For more information on installing and configuring MSDE, see http://msdn.microsoft.com/vstudio/msde/.

---

The Microsoft Office 2000 Developer CD also contains a batch file for installing the redistributable version of MSDE. This batch file, located in the MSDE folder on the CD, can be invoked as a command-line program to run at the end of the setup created by the Package and Deployment Wizard.

In addition, if you want to automatically install a particular back-end database, you'll need to include the appropriate MDF and LDF (data and log, respectively) files in your setup disks. The Microsoft Office 2000 Developer CD includes a white paper showing how you can write code to load the database files into MSDE after MSDE is installed on the user's system. You could either insert this code into your Access project or into the setup program itself (see the next section for information on modifying the setup program).

---

**NOTE**　You should also consider what to do about SQL Server service packs, which also apply to MSDE. You might want to include the latest service pack in your installation and run it from the same batch file. Alternately, you might just want to tell users where to download the service pack.

---

# Customizing Setup

The setup program created by the Package and Deployment Wizard comes in two distinct parts. SETUP.EXE, the program that end users actually run, is a bootstrap program whose job it is to copy necessary infrastructure files to the user's hard drive. A separate program, SETUP1.EXE, does the real work of installing files, writing Registry keys, and so on.

You can customize the setup created by the Package and Deployment Wizard by customizing SETUP1.EXE. This is possible because SETUP1.EXE is written in Visual Basic 6, and the original source code is provided on the Microsoft Office 2000 Developer CD (in the ODETOOLS\V9\SAMPLES\UNSUPPRT\SETUP1 folder). To create a customized version of setup, you make changes to this source code, recompile, and replace the SETUP1.EXE that the Package and Deployment Wizard uses with your new version.

---

**NOTE**　You'll need Visual Basic 6 to modify SETUP1.EXE; it can't be opened in a VBA host such as Access.

---

The Visual Basic source code in SETUP1.VBP is actually pretty well commented. You'll find that most of the setup logic is contained in the Form_Load event of the frmSetup1 form. One useful trick demonstrated in this code is a method for customizing setup to make some components optional.

# Installer Switches

Another reason you might want to customize SETUP1.EXE would be to change the options that the Windows Installer uses when installing the Access Runtime. The Windows Installer is launched from the Exit_Setup procedure in the basSetup1 module in SETUP1.VBP. By default, the Installer is launched without any command-line switches. However, quite a number of switches are available, as shown in Table 16.7. These switches can be used with any Windows Installer application, not just the Access Runtime.

**TABLE 16.7:** Windows Installer Command-line Switches

| Switch | Description |
| --- | --- |
| /a <msifile> | Create an administrative install point from the specified installer package. |
| /i <msifile> | Specifies the name of the installer package to use. |
| /qn | Don't display any user interface. |
| /qb | Display only progress and error messages. |
| /qr | Display a "reduced" user interface, without collecting user information. |
| /qf | Display the full setup user interface. |
| /qn+ | Display only a modal dialog box at the end of the setup. |
| /qb+ | Display progress and error messages, and a modal dialog box at the end of the setup |
| /wait | Waits for the installation to complete before terminating the Installer program. |
| /f<options> | Repairs rather than installs the program. See Table 16.4 for valid repair options. |
| /x <msifile> | Uninstall the specified installer package. |
| /l<actions> <logfile> | Logs the specified actions to the specified log file. Actions are specified by choosing one or more of these characters: a (startup of actions), c (initial parameters), e (all error messages), I (all status messages), m (any out of memory error), r (messages from custom actions), p (termination properties), u (user requests), v (verbose output), w (all warnings) and + (append to existing file rather than overwrite). |

| TIP | You can also turn on logging by editing the SETUP.INI file in the root of the Access Runtime source folder. This file contains a Logging section where you can list the types of information that you'd like to log during the setup process. |
|-----|---|

# Editing Installer Files

Given the drawbacks of using the setups generated by the Package and Deployment Wizard, is there any other alternative for installing your application and the Access Runtime? There is, but it's not for the faint of heart. The Windows Installer SDK contains all of the necessary information to allow you to create or modify your own installer package. In particular, you can modify the installer package that Microsoft Office 2000 Developer contains, inserting the necessary entries to install your own application along with the Access Runtime.

The advantage to this strategy is obvious. Instead of multiple reboots and multiple setup programs, you can present the user with a single setup program followed by a single reboot. You can also modify the user interface displayed by the Installer during the Access Runtime setup so that it only contains the name of your product.

However, before you start, you should be aware that the Installer SDK documentation, while complete, is rather confusing. The existing tools for modifying installer packages also leave something to be desired. Nevertheless, we think the effort of taking this path, instead of using the Package and Deployment Wizard, justifies the results.

In this section, we'll discuss the most common changes that you might want to make to the Access Runtime installer package. Then we'll take a look at the process of making those changes with three different tools:

- Orca, the Microsoft editor for installer packages

- InstallShield for Windows Installer

- Wise for Windows Installer

You can download Orca for free. The other two editors are commercial applications that offer substantially more functionality than Orca provides.

TIP As this book went to press, Microsoft had just released another setup creation tool called the Visual Studio Installer. This tool, which integrates directly into the Visual Studio development environment, offers based MSI creation and editing functionality and is available free to registered Visual Studio 6 users (this includes users of any of the Visual Studio products, including Visual Basic). For more information see `http://msdn.microsoft.com/vstudio/downloads/vsi/default.asp`.

## Installer Database Tables

The Windows Installer is completely database-driven. That is, the actions it takes when installing a package are completely dictated by rows stored in database tables within the package. A package contains 75 or more tables (the number isn't fixed, because individual package designers can add custom tables to a package) that define the files to be installed, the user interface to show during setup, the Registry entries to be made, and so on.

Much of the Installer SDK is devoted to explaining these tables and their interactions in detail. Learning exactly what goes on within the installer is beyond the scope of this book. In order to customize the Access Runtime installer package, we'll concentrate on the following changes:

- Customizing the user interface

- Adding new files

- Adding new shortcuts

- Adding new Registry keys

Table 16.8 shows the installer package tables that need to be modified to perform these tasks.

**T A B L E  1 6 . 8 :**  Selected Installer Package Tables

| Table | Use |
|-------|-----|
| ActionText | Messages displayed during installation |
| Binary | Stores binary information such as graphics and custom installer DLLs |
| Component | Available components |
| Control | User interface controls |

**TABLE 16.8:** Selected Installer Package Tables *(continued)*

| Table | Use |
|---|---|
| CreateFolder | Folders to be created for particular components |
| Dialog | User interface dialog boxes |
| Directory | Folder layout for the product |
| Feature | Features in the product |
| FeatureComponents | Association between components and features |
| File | Files to be installed |
| Media | List of source media |
| Property | Advertised properties and a list of tokens that can be substituted in other tables |
| Registry | List of Registry keys to create |
| Shortcut | List of shortcuts to create |

# Common Editing Tasks

Before we get to specific editing tools, let's take a look at the individual tasks you might want to perform. Each of these tasks requires modifying one or more tables in the installer database.

## Altering Summary Information

When you're creating your own installer package, you should clearly mark it as your own package. You cannot simply keep the package and product codes supplied with the Access Runtime. In the world of the Windows Installer, it's not acceptable for two packages to have the same codes, no matter how minor the differences between the packages.

Some of the information you'll need to customize is stored in the Summary Information Stream. The Summary Information Stream is a structured storage stream within the installer package, rather than one of the database tables. The various package editing tools all provide some way to edit the Summary Information Stream. This stream provides overall information on the installer package, some of which is visible in Windows Explorer, as shown in Figure 16.9.

**FIGURE 16.9**
Part of the Summary
Information Stream
displayed in Windows
Explorer

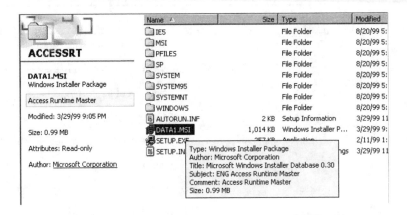

There are also some entries in the Property database table that you should customize. The Property table contains global variables for the Windows Installer.

Table 16.9 lists the summary information and properties that you should customize for any Windows Installer package.

**TABLE 16.9:** Installer Package Summary Information

| Name | Location | Description |
|------|----------|-------------|
| Author | Summary Information Stream | Author of the package. This is normally the company name, not an individual name. |
| Comments | Summary Information Stream | Comments on the installer package. Microsoft says that this string should be set to "This installer database contains the logic and data required to install <product name>," although that's not what it contains for the Access Runtime. |
| DiskPrompt | Property | Name used by the Installer when creating a dialog box to prompt for a disk. |
| Manufacturer | Property | Author of the package. Normally the same as Author, above. |

**TABLE 16.9:** Installer Package Summary Information *(continued)*

| Name | Location | Description |
| --- | --- | --- |
| ProductCode | Property | GUID that identifies the product installed by this package. |
| ProductName | Property | Name of the product installed by this package. |
| PRODUCTNAMEARM | Property | Name of the product installed by this package (used in the setup user interface). |
| ProductVersion | Property | Version of the product installed by this package. |
| Revision Number | Summary Information Stream | Despite its name, this property contains the GUID that is the package code for this package. |
| Subject | Summary Information Stream | Name of the product installed by this installer package. |
| Template | Summary Information Stream | Indicates the platforms where the Installer will allow this package to be run. The format is \<platform>,\<platform>;\<language>, \<language>. For example, "Intel,Alpha;1033" would indicate that this package only runs on US English (1033 codepage) but on either the Intel or Alpha platform. If you omit the platform, it tells the installer that it's OK to run this package on any platform. If you set the language to 0 it tells the installer that it's OK to run this package on any language. So for a general-purpose install, you'll want to set this property to ";0" (without the quotes). |

Of these properties, it is absolutely imperative that you set the ProductCode property and the Revision Number in the Summary Information Stream to unique GUIDs. If you don't do this, your application won't install on any computer that's already had the Access Runtime installed.

You can use the GUIDGEN.EXE tool to generate GUIDs. This tool is shipped with Microsoft Visual Studio. You can also generate GUIDs by creating a table in Access 2000 with an AutoNumber field set to be a ReplicationID. As you add records to this table, Access will generate GUIDs for the AutoNumber field. These GUIDs are generated with letters entirely in upper case, so they're immediately suitable for use in an installer package.

## Customizing the User Interface

The Windows Installer dynamically constructs the user interface displayed during setup based on information stored in the Dialog table, the Control table, and some related tables. In addition, the InstallUISequence table and related tables control the order in which the user interface is displayed.

The Access Runtime installer package contains an extremely simple user interface. We recommend that for your first forays into using this installer package as the basis for your own package, you limit yourself to modifying this interface's appearance but not its functionality. That is, you should limit your modifications to changing captions and pictures, and not attempt to insert additional controls or dialog boxes until you've gained some experience working with installer packages.

The Dialog table in the Access Runtime installer package contains information on 28 separate dialog boxes. Some of these dialog boxes will never actually be displayed. For example, although the Dialog table contains the user interface for choosing an Internet Explorer installation level, this portion of the interface is not used in the current Access Runtime installation. Table 16.10 lists the dialog boxes contained in the Dialog table that you might want to modify.

**TABLE 16.10:** Important Dialog Boxes in the Access Runtime Installer Package

| Dialog Box Name | Purpose |
|---|---|
| BrowseDialogARM | Shown when the user chooses to browse for an installation location. |
| Cancel | Confirmation dialog box when the user clicks Cancel in any other dialog box. |
| ConfirmUninstall | Confirmation dialog box when the user chooses to uninstall the product from Control Panel. |
| ErrorDialog | Used to show any errors during the installation process. |

**TABLE 16.10:**    Important Dialog Boxes in the Access Runtime Installer Package *(continued)*

| Dialog Box Name | Purpose |
| --- | --- |
| ExitDialog | Shown when the setup is completed successfully. |
| FatalError | Used to show any fatal errors during the installation process. |
| FilesInUse | Lists running applications that should be closed before installation proceeds. |
| InstallLocationARM | Shows the chosen install location when the user chooses a custom installation. |
| InstallingShortARM | Progress dialog box during installation. |
| MModeARM | Initial dialog box shown when the user chooses the application from the Add/Remove Programs Control Panel applet. |
| OutOfDisk | Shown when the installer runs out of disk space during the installation. |
| PreActionDialogARM | Shown when the Installer is initializing. |
| ReadyToInstallARM | Dialog box that allows the user to select Install Now or Customize. |
| Reboot | Warning from the Installer that a reboot is needed to complete the installation. |
| Reinstalling | Dialog box shown during maintenance mode setup. |
| ReinstallRepairARM | Dialog box that allows the user to choose whether to repair or reinstall during maintenance mode setup. |

The simplest way to understand the information stored in the Dialog table is to take a look at entries for one particular dialog box. Here's what the table contains for the ReadyToInstallARM dialog box, which is the one where the user chooses whether to do a default or customized installation:

- The Dialog field contains the name of the dialog box. This is the primary key of the table.

- The HCentering and VCentering fields control the initial positioning of the dialog box. These fields are calibrated in percent of screen size, regardless of the user's screen settings. In the case of ReadyToInstallARM, both fields have the value 50, which tells the Installer to center this dialog box.

- The Width and Height fields control the size of the dialog box. ReadyTo-InstallARM has a width of 450 and a height of 307. These are in pixel units.

- The Attributes field is a set of bit flags that control the style of the dialog box. Table 16.11 shows the flags that can be set in this field. For the ReadyToInstall-ARM dialog box, this field is set to 39, which specifies that the dialog box keeps track of the disk space required for the installation, that the dialog box can be minimized, and that the dialog box is modal and visible.

- The Title field contains the caption of the dialog box. For the ReadyToInstall-ARM dialog box, this is set to "[PRODUCTNAMEARM]: Ready To Install". The square brackets indicate that PRODUCTNAMEARM is the name of a property stored in the Property Table. Thus, to change the name of the product everywhere, you just have to edit the corresponding row in the Property table.

- The ControlFirst field specifies the name of the Control that will be selected when the dialog box is first displayed. For ReadyToInstallARM, this is the InstallNow control.

- The ControlDefault and ControlCancel fields specify the names of the default and cancel controls on the dialog box. In the case of ReadyToInstallARM, these are, respectively, the InstallNow and Cancel controls.

**TABLE 16.11:** Dialog Attribute Flags

| Flag | Value | Meaning |
| --- | --- | --- |
| Visible | 1 | The dialog box is visible. |
| Modal | 2 | The dialog box is modal. |
| Minimize | 4 | The dialog box may be minimized. |
| SysModal | 8 | The dialog box is system modal. |
| KeepModeless | 16 | If set, other Installer dialog boxes are not destroyed when this dialog box is created. |
| TrackDiskSpace | 32 | The dialog box makes periodic calls to the Installer to determine whether there's enough disk space for the installation. |
| UseCustomPalette | 64 | If set, the dialog box uses the palette from the first control in the dialog box. If not set, the dialog box uses the default palette. |

**TABLE 16.11:**    Dialog Attribute Flags *(continued)*

| Flag | Value | Meaning |
|------|-------|---------|
| RTLRO | 128 | The dialog box is displayed for right-to-left languages. |
| RightAligned | 256 | All text is right-aligned in controls. |
| LeftScroll | 512 | The scrollbar is located on the left side of the dialog box. |
| Error | 65536 | This is the dialog box that the Installer should use for error messages. |

In addition to the Dialog table, each dialog box has entries in the Control table. As you might guess, this table has one row for every control on every dialog box for this installer package. These rows provide the information that the Windows Installer uses to place controls on dialog boxes when they are displayed. As an example, we'll examine the fields for the InstallNow control on the ReadyToInstall-ARM dialog box:

- The Dialog_ and Control fields form a two-part primary key for this table. The Dialog_ field holds the name of the dialog box that this control will appear on, and is a foreign key back to the Dialog field of the Dialog table. (In general, foreign key fields in the installer database are named with a trailing underscore.) The Control field is the name of the control itself. So, for this control, the Dialog_ field holds the value ReadyToInstallARM and the Control field holds the value InstallNow.

- The Type field specifies the type of control, in this case PushButton. The Windows Installer natively supports the 22 types of controls listed in Table 16.12. There's also provision in the Installer SDK for using custom controls.

- The X, Y, Width and Height fields specify the size and location of the control. These values are all given in pixels. The X and Y fields specify the top and left of the control relative to the top left corner of the dialog box. Negative values are not allowed, so you can't hide a control by moving it outside of the dialog box.

- The Attributes field is a bit-mapped list of flags for the control. Table 16.13 lists the possible values that you can set in this field.

- The Property field lists the name of a property that gets the value from a list box, combo box, or radio button. This field should be blank for all other types of controls.

- The Text field gives the caption of the control. In the case of graphical controls, such as the InstallNow control we're looking at, this field will match the Name property from a row in the Binary table. The Data property in the corresponding row of the Binary table will be the graphic to display on the control. In the case of controls displaying text, this can be a formatted property. For example, the Text property of the InstallNowText control on the same dialog box is set to "{\TahomaBold8}[TYPICALINSTALLTEXT]". Here, the {\TahomaBold8} portion is a foreign key into the TextStyle table, which controls the formatting of the text. The [TYPICALINSTALLTEXT] portion is a foreign key into the Property table, which holds the actual text.

- The Control_Next field holds the name of the next control in the tab order for this dialog box.

- The Help field can hold two parts, separated by a pipe ( | ) character. The first part is the tooltip to use for the control. The second part is reserved for context-sensitive help, which is not yet implemented in the Installer. You need to include the pipe even if you're just specifying a tooltip.

**TABLE 16.12:** Windows Installer Native Control Types

| Type | Description |
| --- | --- |
| Billboard | Graphic from the Billboard table |
| Bitmap | Static bitmap |
| Checkbox | Checkbox |
| ComboBox | Combo box |
| DirectoryCombo | Directory selection control |
| DirectoryList | Treeview displaying a path |
| Edit | Textbox |
| GroupBox | Rectangle that groups other controls |
| Icon | Static icon |
| Line | Horizontal line |
| ListBox | Listbox |
| ListView | ListView |
| MaskedEdit | Textbox with an editing mask |

**TABLE 16.12:**   Windows Installer Native Control Types *(continued)*

| Type | Description |
|------|-------------|
| PathEdit | Textbox designed for editing paths |
| ProgressBar_Control | Bar graph that responds to progress messages from the Installer |
| PushButton | Command button |
| RadioButtonGroup | Group of option buttons |
| ScrollableText | Textbox with scrollbar |
| SelectionTree | TreeView based on information in the Feature table |
| Text | Static text (label) |
| VolumeCostList | Summary of disk space taken on each drive when installing |
| VolumeSelectCombo | Combo box for selecting a drive |

**TABLE 16.13:**   Control Attribute Flags

| Flag | Value | Meaning |
|------|-------|---------|
| Visible | 1 | Control is visible. |
| Enabled | 2 | Control is enabled. |
| Sunken | 4 | Control is displayed three-dimensionally. |
| Indirect | 8 | If this bit is set, the value in the Property field is the name of the name of a property. If it's not set, the value in the Property field is the name of a property. |
| IntegerControl | 16 | Control accepts integers only. |
| RTLRO | 32 | Control uses right-to-left reading order. |
| RightAligned | 64 | Text is right-aligned in the control. |
| LeftScroll | 128 | Any scrollbar appears to the left of the control. |
| MultiLine | 65536 | Allows multiple lines of text (edit control only). |
| Transparent | 65536 | Background of the control is transparent (text controls only). |
| Progress95 | 65536 | If set, the progress bar is displayed as a series of small rectangles. If not set, the progress bar is displayed as a continuous rectangle (progress bar control only). |

**TABLE 16.13:** Control Attribute Flags *(continued)*

| Flag | Value | Meaning |
|---|---|---|
| RemovableVolume | 65536 | Display all removable volumes (volume controls only). |
| SortedControl | 65536 | Entries are sorted (combo and list box controls only). |
| ComboListControl | 131072 | If set, combo box controls are limited to values appearing in the list (combo box controls only). |
| FixedVolume | 131072 | Display all fixed volumes (volume controls only). |
| NoPrefix | 131072 | Ampersands in the control's text are not interpreted as hot keys. |
| PushLikeControl | 131072 | Forces checkboxes and option buttons to be drawn as pushbuttons, but does not change their logic. |
| Bitmap | 262144 | Control displays a bitmap (Pushbutton control only). |
| NoWrap | 262144 | Do not wordwrap text in the control. |
| RemoteVolume | 262144 | Display all networked volumes (volume controls only). |
| CDRomVolume | 524288 | Display all CD-ROM volumes (volume controls only). |
| FormatSize | 524288 | Values in the control are converted to KB, MB or GB as appropriate. |
| Icon | 524288 | Control displays an icon (Pushbutton control only). |
| FixedSize | 1048576 | Control displays pictures in their native size. If not set, control stretches pictures to fit (Pushbutton control only). |
| RAMDiskVolume | 1048576 | Display all RAM disk volumes (volume controls only). |
| UsersLanguage | 1048576 | Control uses fonts from the user's default code page. If not set, the control uses fonts from the database's default code page. |
| FloppyVolume | 2097162 | Display all floppy drive volumes (volume controls only). |
| IconSize16 | 2097162 | Use the 16x16 icon (Pushbutton control only). |
| ControlShowRollbackCost | 4194304 | Include backup files in displaying disk space required (VolumeCostList control only). |
| IconSize32 | 4194304 | Use the 32x32 icon (Pushbutton control only). |
| IconSize48 | 6291456 | Use the 48x48 icon (Pushbutton control only). |

## Adding a File

One of the major reasons you might want to modify the Access Runtime installer package is to add your own database to the list of files that it installs. You might also want to add a help file, or an HTML file that links back to your corporate server, or to other files. The process of modifying an installer package to include more files starts, not surprisingly, with the File table.

The File table lists every single file that the installer package contains (by default, the Access Runtime setup installs an amazing 457 files). This table has the following fields:

- The File field is the primary key of the table, and should be the filename. In cases where the filename might be localized (for example, README.TXT) this should be the un-localized name. Because this is the primary key of the File table, you can't have two different files of the same name in the same installer package, even if they're installed to different target folders on the end user's computer.

- The Component_ field is the name of the component that contains this file (remember, components represent the division of your application into units that make sense to you). This field is a foreign key into the Component table, which we'll discuss below. You should create a component to contain your own files. For example, if you're modifying the Access Runtime installer package to install a database named CUSTOMERS.MDB and an associated help file CUSTOMERS.HLP, and you don't plan to localize these files, you might wish to assign both of them to a component named Global_Customers.

- The FileName field contains the actual name of the file in the installation. This might be a localized name. This name is assumed to be in short file-name (8.3) syntax; you must provide a short filename for each file because the target volume might not support long file names. If you wish, you can also provide a long filename, separated from the short filename by a pipe character. For example, the FileName field might be set to "CUST.MDB | Customers.mdb," which would install the file using the long name if possible and the short name otherwise.

- The Version field can contain a version string, in which case it's the version number of the file. It can also be blank, for a file that does not contain internal version information. It can also be the File field from another record in the File table. In this case, the installation of this file is controlled not by its own version information but by the version information of the listed file, which is termed a Companion Parent file.

- The Language field contains one or more language IDs, separated by commas. It can also contain 0 for language-neutral files.

- The Attributes field is a bit-mapped field of flags. Table 16.14 lists the available flag values for this field.

- The Sequence field controls the order of installation to the source media for compressed files. Since the Access Runtime uses uncompressed source files, you can simply leave this set to 1 for all files.

**T A B L E   1 6 . 1 4 :**   File Attribute Flags

| Flag | Value | Meaning |
|------|-------|---------|
| ReadOnly | 1 | Install the file as read only. |
| Hidden | 2 | Install the file as a hidden file. |
| System | 4 | Install the file as a system file. |
| Vital | 512 | If this file can't be installed for any reason, the installation of the entire component containing the file fails. |
| Checksum | 1024 | The file contains a checksum to check for corruption. Generally, databases and text files don't contain checksum information. |
| NonCompressed | 8192 | The file is not compressed on the source media. You'll want to set this bit for all the files you add to the installer package. |
| Compressed | 16384 | The file is compressed on the source media. |

Once you've added your files to the File table, you need to add a corresponding component to the Component table. The Component table has these fields:

- Component is the primary key of the table. This is the unique name of the component. This name only has to be unique across all components in the current installer package.

- The ComponentID field contains a unique GUID identifying this version of the component in the specified language. Any time you make any change to a component, or add anything to it, you'll need to create a new ComponentID for it. This field can also be set to null if you don't want installer to track this component. However, for files you add, you should almost certainly generate a ComponentID.

- The Directory_ field is a foreign key referring to the Directory table, which we'll discuss in a moment.

- The Attributes field is, once again, a bitmapped set of flags. Table 16.15 lists the flags that you can use for Attributes in the Component table.

- The Condition field allows you to create logic governing whether or not a component is installed. You'll probably want to leave this blank so that your additional components are always installed.

- The KeyPath field indicates the file that the Installer looks for to determine whether this component is already installed on a computer. This field is either a foreign key to the File table, a foreign key to the Registry table, or a foreign key to the ODBCDataSource table. If you're modifying the Access Runtime setup to include your own database, then that database should be the KeyPath.

**TABLE 16.15:** Component Attribute Flags

| Flag | Value | Meaning |
| --- | --- | --- |
| LocalOnly | 0 | Component can only be run from the installed location. |
| SourceOnly | 1 | Component can only be run from the source location. |
| Optional | 2 | Component can run locally or from the source. |
| RegistryKeyPath | 4 | The KeyPath lists the name of a Registry key. This is probably the setting you want if the component is inserting entries into the HKEY_CURRENT_USER hive of the registry. |
| SharedDllRefCount | 8 | The Installer increments the refcount for the component, and creates the refcount Registry key if it doesn't already exist. |
| Permanent | 16 | This component is not removed if the product is uninstalled. |
| ODBCDataSource | 32 | The KeyPath lists the name of an ODBC data source. |
| Transitive | 64 | The Installer re-evaluates any conditions if the product is reinstalled. |
| NeverOverwrite | 128 | The component never overwrites files already on the machine regardless of version information. |

Along with the entry in the Component table, you'll probably want to make an entry in the Directory table. This table has only a few fields:

- The Directory field is the primary key, and a unique logical identifier for this directory.

- The Directory_Parent field is a foreign key back into the Directory table, listing the parent (if any) of the directory.

- The DefaultDir property is the name of the directory under its parent directory.

**TIP**   If you want your application to be installed to the location the user browses to in the Customize dialog box (the same folder that's the root of the Access runtime install), just set the Directory field in the Component table to the special value TARGETDIR.

After creating the entries in the File, Component and Directory tables, you still have to make the files available for the user to install. You do this by making an entry in the FeatureComponents table. Remember, features break the product up into logical units that make sense to the user.

In a full-featured install, you might create multiple features. However, in the Access Runtime installer package, everything is part of a single huge feature. Because there's no user interface to allow the users to choose particular features, you need to just add your own component to this master feature. To do so, add a row to the FeatureComponents table with the Feature_ field set to "AccessRuntimeMaster" and the Component_ field set to the name of your component.

## Adding a Shortcut

Adding a shortcut to an installer package is much simpler than adding a file to a package. That's because all the shortcut information is stored in the Shortcut table, which has these fields:

- The Shortcut field is a logical identifier for the shortcut, and the primary key of the table.

- The Directory_ field is a foreign key to the Directory table. It specifies the folder where this shortcut will be created.

- The Name field is the filename (without the .LNK suffix) to be used to the shortcut. You can use the ShortName | LongName syntax here if you like.

- The Component_ field is a foreign key to the Component table. It specifies the component that installs this shortcut.

- The Target field specifies the target of this shortcut. You use the syntax [#*filename*] for this field, where *filename* is the name of a file that's part of the same component as the shortcut.

- The Arguments field holds any command-line arguments for the shortcut.

- The Description field holds the description for the shortcut.

- The Hotkey field can contain a hotkey for the shortcut. The Installer documentation recommends that you leave this field blank to avoid any possible conflict with hot keys the user has assigned to other shortcuts.

- The Icon field is a foreign key pointing to the Icon table. If you leave this field blank, the shortcut uses the icon from the Target file.

- The IconIndex field holds the index of the icon in the target. By default, this is zero, the default icon.

- The ShowCmd field specifies how the program should be launched when the shortcut is executed: 0 for normal, 3 for maximized, 7 for minimized and inactive (no other values are valid here).

- The WkDir field is a foreign key to the Directory table. It holds the working directory that should be used for the shortcut's target.

## Adding a Registry Key

Adding a Registry key also involves modifying only a single table, the Registry table. Here are the fields in the Registry table:

- The Registry field is a logical name that uniquely identifies this registry key. It's the primary key in the table.

- The Root field specifies the registry hive that will hold this key. It can be 0 for HKEY_CLASSES_ROOT, 1 for HKEY_CURRENT_USER, 2 for HKEY_LOCAL_MACHINE or 3 for HKEY_USERS. It can also be set to –1 to specify HKEY_CURRENT_USER for per-user installation and HKEY_LOCAL_MACHINE for per-machine installation. The Access Runtime installer package isn't designed for per-machine installation so you should avoid this value.

- The Key field holds the path to the Registry key under the specified root. This value should appear without a leading slash.

- The Name field holds the Registry value name. If this is null, the value is written to the default Registry key.

- The Value field holds the data to be written. Hexadecimal values should be prefixed with #x, integer values with #, and string values do not require a prefix. The Installer SDK contains instructions on using multiple-string values here as well.

- The Component_ field is a foreign key to the Component table. It specifies the component that this key is a part of.

---

**TIP**    The Value field may include names in square brackets that are resolved by reference to the Property table.

---

## Editing Tools

Knowing what changes you want to make to the installer package is most of the job of modifying the Access Runtime installation. However, there's still the problem of actually making the changes. As of this writing, we know of three tools that you can use to make these changes:

- Microsoft Orca

- InstallShield for Windows Installer

- Wise for Windows Installer

In this section, we'll take a brief look at each of these tools to help you make a choice between them for your own installation needs.

### Microsoft Orca

Microsoft Orca (shown in Figure 16.10) is the only one of these tools that's available for free. When you download the Windows Installer SDK, one of the files it contains is ORCA.MSI. This is an installer package for Microsoft Orca, which is a simple editor for installer databases.

**FIGURE 16.10**
Microsoft Orca

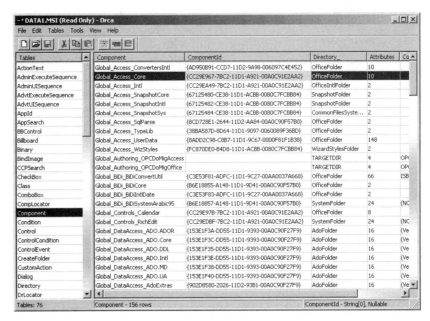

The basic interface of Orca is very simple. It lists all of the tables in the database down the left-hand side of its main window, and all of the rows in the selected table on the right-hand side of the main window. You can edit data by clicking in it, and add a new row by selecting Add Row from the context menu in the right-hand pane. The rows in the current table can be sorted by clicking on column headers, and the columns can be resized with the mouse.

You can edit the Summary Information Stream with Orca by choosing View ➤ Summary Information. This opens the dialog box shown in Figure 16.11. This dialog box doesn't allow you to edit all of the summary information, but it does include the most important fields. When you create a new installer package with Orca, it automatically generates new Product and Package IDs for the package.

Orca also contains a dialog preview mode, accessible from Tools ➤ Dialog Preview. This mode, shown in Figure 16.12, lets you choose any dialog box to view on screen. Orca calls into the actual Installer APIs to give you a true picture of the dialog box. The Dialog Preview window also shows the buttons on the various dialog boxes and the other dialog boxes that they link to. And when a dialog box is open in preview mode, buttons that link to other dialog boxes are also active.

**FIGURE 16.11**

Editing summary informa-
tion with Orca

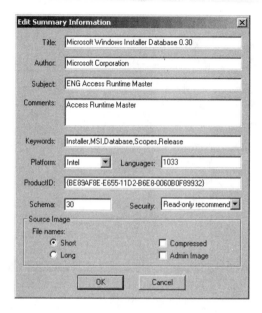

**FIGURE 16.12**

Orca dialog preview mode

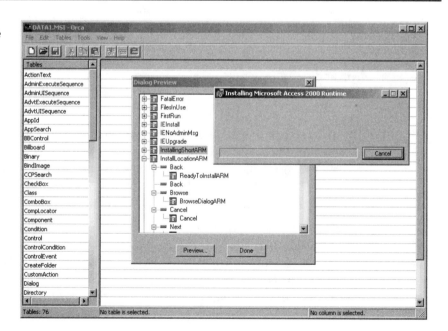

Unfortunately, the Dialog Preview window does not function as a dialog designer. If you want a visual design tool for dialog boxes, you'll need to look elsewhere. Orca only lets you design dialog boxes by making entries to the Dialog and Control tables.

Orca also has hooks in it for validating installer packages. However, that functionality is not active in the current version. You'll have to check your installer package for validity the old-fashioned way, by testing it.

## InstallShield for Windows Installer

InstallShield for Windows Installer comes from InstallShield Software Corporation (http://www.installshield.com) at a list price of $795. Rather than presenting the data in the installer package as raw tables, the InstallShield product (shown in Figure 16.13) uses the tables as the source for a large number of custom views, each with their own design tools.

**FIGURE 16.13**
InstallShield for Windows Installer

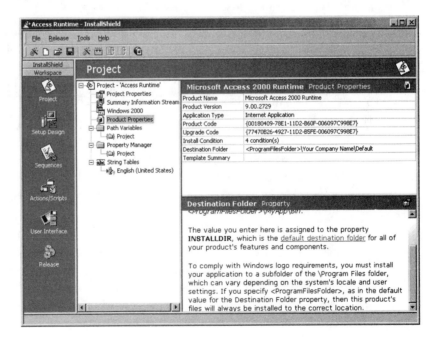

Although InstallShield stores projects in its own proprietary format, it's able to open standard .MSI installer packages and import their contents to an InstallShield project. InstallShield uses an edit-and-build metaphor, so after making changes to your project, you need to rebuild the final setup. Among other advantages, this functionality lets you build multiple setups (for example, to support different languages) from a single project.

---

**TIP**

InstallShield for Windows Installer will initially refuse to open the Access Runtime MSI file, because it's marked as being a pre-release schema. You can fix this by opening the MSI file in Microsoft Orca and, on the Summary Properties dialog box, changing the Schema property from 30 to 100.

---

InstallShield presents everything in DHTML pages, so a lot of the online help is integrated directly with the editing tools. This help tells you not just how the product works, but also what you need to do in order to build a logo-compatible setup program.

Editing summary information stream properties is done from the Project view shown in Figure 16.13. You might have to hunt around a bit to find some of the properties, but they're all there, and integrated with the Property table rows that describe the project. Any time that a property is meant to be a GUID, InstallShield presents a button to automatically generate a new GUID, which is a nice touch.

Figure 16.14 shows the InstallShield Dialog Editor. As you can see, this is a true visual editor for dialog boxes, very similar to the Access form design view. Modifying dialog boxes by working with this editor is much simpler than trying to do so by directly editing the raw Control and Dialog tables. InstallShield also supports a "test run" mode that allows you to run your project's user interface without actually installing any software.

InstallShield's Setup Design view, shown in Figure 16.15, allows you to create and associate new features and components. The parts of a component (files, Registry keys, shortcuts and so on) are logically grouped with the components, so you don't need to go chasing them all over multiple database tables. Each of these has its own dedicated editor, and they all work well.

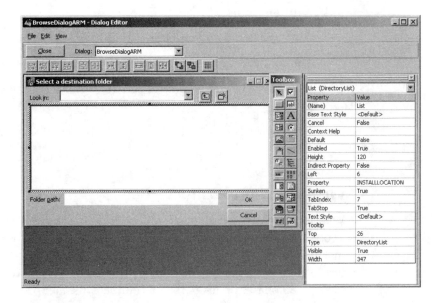

**FIGURE 16.14**
The InstallShield Dialog Editor

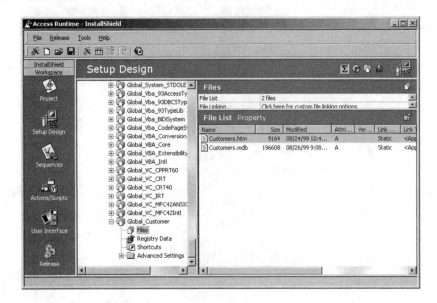

**FIGURE 16.15**
InstallShield Setup Design view

InstallShield also offers a lot of extras and nice touches. Additional features of this product include:

- A wizard that validates your project for internal consistency

- The ability to start off a new project by importing a Visual Basic project file

- A Project Wizard that guides you through the process of starting a new project

- Internal checks for "Best Practices" recommended by Microsoft

- A Power Editor mode that lets you edit database tables directly

## Wise for Windows Installer

Wise for Windows Installer, from Wise Solutions (`http://www.wisesolutions.com`) is another full-featured editor. This $795 package works directly with installer packages, and allows you to customize all aspects of the installation. Figure 16.16 shows this package in its Installation Expert mode, which walks you through all phases of developing a complete installer package.

**FIGURE 16.16**
Wise for Windows Installer

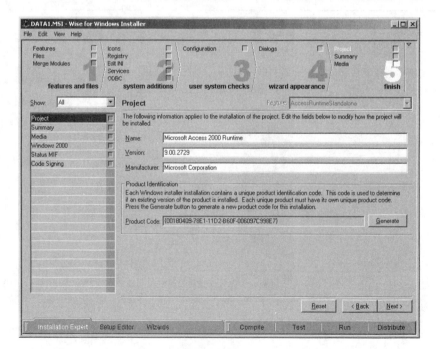

For making small changes to an existing installer package you'll probably want to run Wise for Windows Installer in Setup Editor mode. This mode, shown in Figure 16.17, allows you to make changes to all the information stored in the Installer package. The panel shown in the figure is displaying some of the Summary Information Stream properties. As you can see, the same view will let you view the contents of the Properties table.

**FIGURE 16.17**
Editing Summary
Information with Wise
for Windows Installer

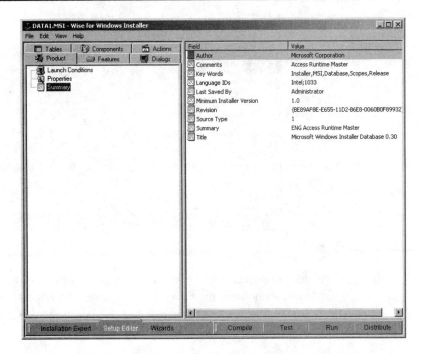

Like InstallShield, Wise includes a dialog editor, shown in Figure 16.18. This editor uses property sheets and context menus to allow you to edit dialogs and controls. The editing is less visual than that provided by InstallShield's editor, but the rendering of the dialog box as it's being edited is closer to that actually displayed by the Windows Installer.

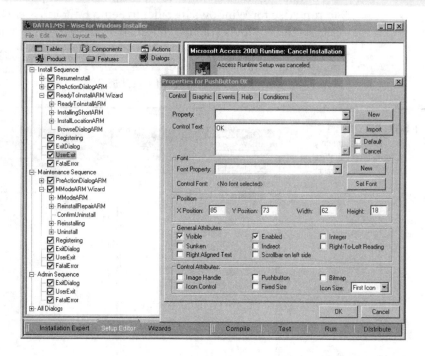

Wise uses separate tree views to manage Components and Features. Editing the Components node in the Features tree makes the association between the two. As with InstallShield, everything relating to a component is grouped in one place for easy editing.

Wise offers a number of other useful tools to make your setup process simpler. These include:

- A Verification Wizard that checks your installer package for common mistakes and violations of the Windows 2000 specification

- The ability to import existing setups or SMS packages, as well as Visual Basic applications

- A wizard that monitors changes made to your system while you set up or run a program and uses these changes as the basis for a new package

- Easy code signing of installer packages

- Automatic checking for upgrades to the Wise package via their web site

# Deploying Data Access Pages

If your application includes data access pages, there are several extra issues that you need to consider when deploying the application:

- Required files
- Required software and licenses
- Link fix up

Data access pages are stored as external HTML files, not as part of your Access database or project. What this means is that you need to include those external files if you want the data access pages to be available when you deploy your application. If you're using the Package and Deployment Wizard, it will automatically add the HTML files to your setup files. If you're modifying the Access Runtime installer package on your own, you need to remember to include the HTML file for each and every data page that you want to display on the end user's computer.

In an installer package you should put data access pages into the same component as the database to which they refer, because they're not much good without that database.

Another issue to consider is the browser on the target computer. For any data access page containing any data at all, the end user must be using Internet Explorer 5.0 or higher in order to view the data on the page. Previous versions of Internet Explorer won't work. Neither will any version of another browser such as Netscape Navigator or Opera. If you can't ensure that end users will be using Internet Explorer 5.0, you shouldn't be using data access pages for any critical information.

The Access Runtime setup automatically installs Internet Explorer 5.0, so if you're distributing your application with the Access Runtime you're covered.

End users must also have Office 2000, or the Office Web Components, installed on their computer to view data access pages. Again, these components are installed by the Access Runtime installer package. If you're not using the Access Runtime, users must have a valid Office 2000 license to view data access pages.

Finally, you need to be aware that the path to the target database is hard-coded within the HTML that makes up a data access page. If there's any chance that users will place your application and the associated data access pages in a folder that is different from the one where the pages were created, you'll need to provide a way to fix up these hard-coded paths. You'll find code to do this in the "Deploying Data Access Pages" section of Chapter 10.

# Summary

This chapter has reviewed deployment and installation issues for Microsoft Access applications. We covered both the supported Microsoft process of using the Package and Deployment Wizard to deploy your application, and the unsupported (but we think superior) process of modifying the Access Runtime installer package to create a unified setup for the Runtime and your application.

This chapter has covered these major topics:

- The Access Runtime architecture
- The Windows Installer
- The Windows Installer SDK
- Windows Installer concepts
- The Application.FeatureInstall property
- Repairing and reinstalling Office
- The Windows Install Cleanup utility
- The Windows Installer automation interface
- The Package and Deployment Wizard
- Installing Access projects
- Editing installer databases
- Tools for editing installer databases
- Deploying data access pages

# The Reddick VBA Naming Conventions, Version 6

The purpose of the Reddick VBA (RVBA) Naming Conventions is to provide a guideline for naming objects in the Visual Basic for Applications (VBA) language. Having conventions is valuable in any programming project. When you use them, the name of the object conveys information about the meaning of the object. These conventions attempt to provide a way of standardizing that meaning across the body of VBA programmers.

VBA is implemented to interact with a host application—for example, Microsoft Access, Microsoft Visual Basic, AutoCAD, and Visio. The RVBA conventions cover all implementations of the VBA language, regardless of the host application. Some of the tags described in this appendix may not necessarily have an implementation within some of the particular host programs for VBA. The word *object*, in the context of this appendix, refers to simple variables and VBA objects, as well as to objects made available by the VBA host program.

While I am the editor of these conventions, they are the work of many people, including Charles Simonyi, who invented the Hungarian conventions on which these are based, and Stan Leszynski, who co-authored several versions of the conventions. Many others, too numerous to mention, have also contributed to the development and distribution of these conventions.

These conventions are intended as a guideline. If you disagree with a particular part of the conventions, simply replace that part with what you think works better. However, keep in mind that future generations of programmers may need to understand those changes, and place a comment in the header of a module indicating what changes have been made. The conventions are presented without rationalizations for how they were derived, although each of the ideas presented has a considerable history to it.

## Changes to the Conventions

Some of the tags in the version of the conventions presented here have changed from previous versions. Consider all previous tags to be grandfathered into the conventions—you don't need to go back and make changes. For new development work, I leave it up to you to decide whether to use the older tags or the ones suggested here. In a few places in this appendix, older tags are shown in {braces}. As updates to this appendix are made, the current version can be found at http://www.xoc.net.

# An Introduction to Hungarian

The RVBA conventions are based on the Hungarian conventions for constructing object names (they were named for the native country of the inventor, Charles Simonyi). The objective of Hungarian is to convey information about the object concisely and efficiently. Hungarian takes some getting used to, but once adopted, it quickly becomes second nature. The format of a Hungarian object name is

```
[prefixes]tag[BaseName[Suffixes]]
```

The square brackets indicate optional parts of the object name. These components have the following meanings:

| Component | Description |
|-----------|-------------|
| Prefixes | Modify the tag to indicate additional information. Prefixes are all lowercase. They are usually picked from a standardized list of prefixes, given later in this appendix. |
| Tag | Short set of characters, usually mnemonic, that indicates the type of the object. The tag is all lowercase. It is usually selected from a standardized list of tags, given later in this appendix. |
| BaseName | One or more words that indicate what the object represents. The first letter of each word in the BaseName is capitalized. |
| Suffixes | Additional information about the meaning of the BaseName. The first letter of each word in the Suffix is capitalized. They are usually picked from a standardized list of suffixes, given later in this appendix. |

Notice that the only required part of the object name is the tag. This may seem counterintuitive; you may feel that the BaseName is the most important part of the object name. However, consider a generic procedure that operates on any form. The fact that the routine operates on a form is the important thing, not what that form represents. Because the routine may operate on forms of many different types, you do not necessarily need a BaseName. However, if you have more than one object of a type referenced in the routine, you must have a BaseName on all but one of the object names to differentiate them. Also, unless the routine is generic, the BaseName conveys information about the variable. In most cases, a variable should include a BaseName.

# Tags

You use tags to indicate the data type of an object, and you construct them using the techniques described in the following sections.

## Variable Tags

Use the tags listed in Table A.1 for VBA data types. You can also use a specific tag instead of obj for any data type defined by the host application or one of its objects. (See the "Host Application and Component Extensions to the Conventions" section later in this appendix.

**TABLE A.1:**   Tables for VBA Variables

| Tag | Object Type |
| --- | --- |
| bool {f, bln} | Boolean |
| byte {byt} | Byte |
| cur | Currency |
| date {dtm} | Date |
| dec | Decimal |
| dbl | Double |
| int | Integer |
| lng | Long |
| obj | Object |
| sng | Single |
| str | String |
| stf | String (fixed length) |
| var | Variant |

Here are several examples:

```
lngCount
intValue
strInput
```

You should explicitly declare all variables, each on a line by itself. Do not use the old-type declaration characters, such as %, &, and $. They are extraneous if you use the naming conventions, and there is no character for some of the data types, such as Boolean. You should always explicitly declare all variables of type Variant using the As Variant clause, even though it is the default in VBA. For example:

```
Dim intTotal As Integer
Dim varField As Variant
Dim strName As String
```

## Constructing Properties Names

Properties of a class present a particular problem: Should they include the naming convention to indicate the type? To be consistent with the rest of these naming conventions, they should. However, it is permitted to have property names without the tags, especially if the class is to be made available to customers who may not be familiar with these naming conventions.

## Collection Tags

You treat a collection object with a special tag. You construct the tag using the data type of the collection followed by the letter s. For example, if you had a collection of Longs, the tag would be lngs. If it were a collection of forms, the collection would be frms. Although, in theory, a collection can hold objects of different data types, in practice, each of the data types in the collection is the same. If you do want to use different data types in a collection, use the tag objs. For example:

```
intsEntries
frmsCustomerData
objsMisc
```

## Constants

Constants always have a data type in VBA. Because VBA will choose this data type for you if you don't specify it, you should always specify the data type for a constant. Constants declared in the General Declarations section of a module should always have a scope keyword of Private or Public and be prefixed by the scope prefixes m or g, respectively. A constant is indicated by appending the letter c to the end of the data type for the constant. For example:

```
Const intcGray As Integer = 3
Private Const mdblcPi As Double = 3.14159265358979
```

Although this technique is the recommended method of naming constants, if you are more concerned about specifying that you are dealing with constants rather than their data type, you can alternatively use the generic tag con instead. For example:

```
Const conPi As Double = 3.14159265358979
```

## Menu Items

The names of menu items should reflect their position in the menu hierarchy. All menu items should use the tag mnu, but the BaseName should indicate where in the hierarchy the menu item falls. Use Sep in the BaseName to indicate a menu separator bar, followed by an ordinal. For example:

```
mnuFile (on menu bar)
mnuFileNew (on File popup menu)
mnuFileNewForm (on File New flyout menu)
mnuFileNewReport (on File New flyout menu)
mnuFileSep1 (first separator bar on file popup menu)
mnuFileSaveAs (on File popup menu)
mnuFileSep2 (second separator bar on file popup menu)
mnuFileExit (on File popup menu)
mnuEdit (on menu bar)
```

# Creating Data Types

VBA gives you three ways to create new data types: *enumerated* types, *classes*, and *user-defined* types. In each case, you will need to invent a new tag that represents the data type that you create.

## Enumerated Types

Groups of constants of the Long data type should be made an enumerated type. Invent a tag for the type, append the letter *c*, then define the enumerated constants using that tag. Because the name used in the Enum line is seen in the object browser, you can add a BaseName to the tag to spell out the abbreviation indicated by the tag. For example:

```
Public Enum ervcErrorValue
    ervcInvalidType = 205
    ervcValueOutOfBounds
End Enum
```

The BaseName should be singular, so that the enumerated type should be ervcErrorValue, not ervcErrorValues. The tag that you invent for enumerated types can then be used for variables that can contain values of that type. For example:

```
Dim erv As ervcErrorValue
Private Sub Example(ByVal ervCur As ervcErrorValue)
```

While VBA only provides enumerated types of groups of the Long type, you can still create groups of constants of other types. Just create a set of constant definitions using an invented tag. For example:

```
Public Const estcError205 As String = "Invalid type"
Public Const estcError206 As String = "Value out of bounds"
```

Unfortunately, because this technique doesn't actually create a new type, you don't get the benefit of the VBA compiler performing type checking for you. You create variables that will hold constants using a similar syntax to variables meant to hold instances of enumerated types. For example:

```
Dim estError As String
```

## Tags for Classes and User-Defined Types

A class defines a user-defined object. Because these invent a new data type, you will need to invent a new tag for the object. You can add a BaseName to the tag to spell out the abbreviation indicated by the tag. User-defined types are considered a simple class with only properties, but in all other ways are used the same as class modules. For example:

```
gphGlyph
edtEdit
Public Type grbGrabber
```

You then define variables to refer to instances of the class using the same tag. For example:

```
Dim gphNext As New gphGlyph
Dim edtCurrent as edtEdit
Dim grbHandle as grbGrabber
```

## Polymorphism

In VBA, you use the Implements statement to derive classes from a base class. The tag for the derived class should use the same tag as the base class. The derived classes, though, should use a different BaseName from the base class. For example:

```
anmAnimal (base class)
anmZebra (derived class of anmAnimal)
anmElephant (derived class of anmAnimal)
```

This logic of naming derived classes is used with forms, which are all derived from the predefined Form base class and use the frm tag. If a variable is defined to be of the type of the base class, then use the tag, as usual. For example:

```
Dim anmArbitrary As anmAnimal
Dim frmNew As Form
```

On the other hand, if you define a variable as an instance of a derived class, include the complete derived class name in the variable name. For example:

```
Dim anmZebraInstance As anmZebra
Dim anmElephantExample As anmElephant
Dim frmCustomerData As frmCustomer
```

# Constructing Procedures

VBA procedures require you to name various items: procedure names, parameters, and labels. These objects are described in the following sections.

## Constructing Procedure Names

VBA names event procedures and you cannot change them. You should use the capitalization defined by the system. For user-defined procedure names, capitalize the first letter of each word in the name. For example:

```
cmdOK_Click
GetTitleBarString
PerformInitialization
```

Procedures should always have a scope keyword, Public or Private, when they are declared. For example:

```
Public Function GetTitleBarString() As String
Private Sub PerformInitialization
```

## Naming Parameters

You should prefix all parameters in a procedure definition with ByVal or ByRef, even though ByRef is optional and redundant. Procedure parameters are named the same as simple variables of the same type, except that arguments passed by reference use the prefix r. For example:

```
Public Sub TestValue(ByVal intInput As Integer, ByRef_
rlngOutput As Long) Private Function GetReturnValue(ByVal_
 strKey As String, ByRef rgph As Glyph) As Boolean
```

## Naming Labels

Labels are named using upper- and lowercase, capitalizing the first letter of each word. For example:

```
ErrorHandler:
ExitProcedure:
```

# Prefixes

Prefixes modify an object tag to indicate more information about an object.

## Arrays of Objects Prefix

Arrays of an object type use the prefix a. For example:

```
aintFontSizes
astrNames
```

## Index Prefix

You indicate an index into an array by the prefix i, and, for consistency, the data type should always be a Long. You may also use the index prefix to index into other enumerated objects, such as a collection of user-defined classes. For example:

```
iaintFontSizes
iastrNames
igphsGlyphCollection
```

## Prefixes for Scope and Lifetime

Three levels of scope exist for each variable in VBA: Public, Private, and Local. A variable also has a lifetime of the current procedure or the lifetime of the object in which it is defined. Use the prefixes in Table A.2 to indicate scope and lifetime.

**TABLE A.2:** Scope Prefixes

| Prefix | Object Type |
| --- | --- |
| (none) | Local variable, procedure-level lifetime, declared with Dim |
| s | Local variable, object lifetime, declared with Static |
| m | Private (module) variable, object lifetime, declared with Private |
| g | Public (global) variable, object lifetime, declared with Public |

You also use the m and g constants with other objects, such as constants, to indicate their scope. For example:

```
intLocalVariable
mintPrivateVariable
gintPublicVariable
mdblcPi
```

VBA allows several type declaration words for backward compatibility. The older keyword Global should always be replaced by Public, and the Dim keyword in the General Declarations section should be replaced by Private.

## Other Prefixes

Table A.3 lists and describes some other prefixes.

**TABLE A.3:** Other Commonly Used Prefixes

| Prefix | Object Type |
| --- | --- |
| c | Count of some object type |
| h | Handle to a Windows object |
| r | Parameter passed by reference |

Here are some examples:

```
castrArray
hWndForm
```

## Suffixes

Suffixes modify the BaseName of an object, indicating additional information about a variable. You'll likely create your own suffixes that are specific to your development work. Table A.4 lists some generic VBA suffixes.

**TABLE A.4:**  Commonly Used Suffixes

| Suffix | Object Type |
| --- | --- |
| Min | The absolute first element in an array or other kind of list. |
| First | The first element to be used in an array or list during the current operation. |
| Last | The last element to be used in an array or list during the current operation. |
| Lim | The upper limit of elements to be used in an array or list. Lim is not a valid index. Generally, Lim equals Last + 1. |
| Max | The absolutely last element in an array or other kind of list. |
| Cnt | Used with database elements to indicate that the item is a Counter. Counter fields are incremented by the system and are numbers of either type Long or type Replication Id. |

Here are some examples:

```
iastrNamesMin
iastrNamesMax
iaintFontSizesFirst
igphsGlyphCollectionLast
lngCustomerIdCnt
varOrderIdCnt
```

## File Names

When naming items stored on the disk, no tag is needed because the extension already gives the object type. For example:

```
Test.Frm (frmTest form)
Globals.Bas (globals module)
Glyph.Cls (gphGlyph class module)
```

# Host Application and Component Extensions to the Conventions

Each host application for VBA, as well as each component that can be installed, has a set of objects it can use. This section defines tags for the objects in the various host applications and components.

## Access 2000, Version 9 Objects

Table A.5 lists Access object variable tags. Besides being used in code to refer to these object types, these same tags are used to name these kinds of objects in the form and report designers.

**TABLE A.5:** Access Object Variable Tags

| Tag | Object Type |
| --- | --- |
| Aob | AccessObject |
| Aop | AccessObjectProperty |
| Aops | AccessObjectProperties |
| App | Application |
| Bfr | BoundObjectFrame |
| Chk | CheckBox |
| Cbo | ComboBox |
| Cmd | CommandButton |
| Ctl | Control |
| Ctls | Controls |
| Ocx | CustomControl |
| Dap | DataAccessPage |
| Dcm | DoCmd |
| Frm | Form |
| Frms | Forms |
| Fcd | FormatCondition |

**TABLE A.5:**   Access Object Variable Tags  *(continued)*

| Tag | Object Type |
| --- | --- |
| Fcds | FormatConditions |
| Grl | GroupLevel |
| Hyp | Hyperlink |
| Img | Image |
| Lbl | Label |
| Lin | Line |
| Lst | ListBox |
| Bas | Module |
| Ole | ObjectFrame |
| Opt | OptionButton |
| Fra | OptionGroup (frame) |
| Brk | PageBreak |
| Pal | PaletteButton |
| Prps | Properties |
| Shp | Rectangle |
| Ref | Reference |
| Refs | References |
| Rpt | Report |
| Rpts | Reports |
| Scr | Screen |
| Sec | Section |
| Sfr | SubForm |
| Srp | SubReport |
| Tab | TabControl |
| Txt | TextBox |
| Tgl | ToggleButton |

Some examples:

```
txtName
lblInput
```

For ActiveX custom controls, you can use the tag ocx as specified in Table A.5 or more specific object tags that are listed later in this appendix in Tables A.14 and A.15. For an ActiveX control that doesn't appear in the Tables A.14 or A.15, you can either use ocx or invent a new tag.

## DAO 3.6 Objects

DAO is the programmatic interface to the Jet database engine shared by Access, Visual Basic, and Visual C++. The tags for DAO 3.6 objects are shown in Table A.6.

**TABLE A.6:**  DAO Object Tags

| Tag | Object Type |
| --- | --- |
| cnt | Container |
| cnts | Containers |
| db | Database |
| dbs | Databases |
| dbe | DBEngine |
| doc | Document |
| docs | Documents |
| err | Error |
| errs | Errors |
| fld | Field |
| flds | Fields |
| grp | Group |
| grps | Groups |
| idx | Index |
| idxs | Indexes |
| prm | Parameter |

**TABLE A.6:** DAO Object Tags *(continued)*

| Tag | Object Type |
|---|---|
| prms | Parameters |
| pdbe | PrivDBEngine |
| prp | Property |
| prps | Properties |
| qry | QueryDef |
| qrys | QueryDefs |
| rst | Recordset |
| rsts | Recordsets |
| rel | Relation |
| rels | Relations |
| tbl | TableDef |
| tbls | TableDefs |
| usr | User |
| usrs | Users |
| wrk | Workspace |
| wrks | Workspaces |

Here are some examples:

```
rstCustomers
idxPrimaryKey
```

Table A.7 lists the tags used to identify types of objects in a database.

**TABLE A.7:** Access Database Explorer Object Tags

| Tag | Object Type |
|---|---|
| tbl | Table |
| qry | Query |

**TABLE A.7:** Access Database Explorer Object Tags *(continued)*

| Tag | Object Type |
| --- | --- |
| frm | Form |
| rpt | Report |
| mcr | Macro |
| bas | Module |
| dap | DataAccessPage |

If you wish, you can use more exact tags or suffixes to identify the purpose and type of a database object. If you use the suffix, use the tag given from Table A.7 to indicate the type. Use either the tag or the suffix found along with the more general tag, but not both. The tags and suffixes are shown in Table A.8.

**TABLE A.8:** Specific Object Tags and Suffixes for Access Database Explorer Objects

| Tag | Suffix | Object Type |
| --- | --- | --- |
| tlkp | Lookup | Table (lookup) |
| qsel | (none) | Query (select) |
| qapp | Append | Query (append) |
| qxtb | XTab | Query (crosstab) |
| qddl | DDL | Query (DDL) |
| qdel | Delete | Query (delete) |
| qflt | Filter | Query (filter) |
| qlkp | Lookup | Query (lookup) |
| qmak | MakeTable | Query (make table) |
| qspt | PassThru | Query (SQL pass-through) |
| qtot | Totals | Query (totals) |
| quni | Union | Query (union) |
| qupd | Update | Query (update) |

**TABLE A.8:** Specific Object Tags and Suffixes for Access Database Explorer Objects *(continued)*

| Tag | Suffix | Object Type |
|-----|--------|-------------|
| fdlg | Dlg | Form (dialog) |
| fmnu | Mnu | Form (menu) |
| fmsg | Msg | Form (message) |
| fsfr | SubForm | Form (subform) |
| rsrp | SubReport | Form (subreport) |
| mmnu | Mnu | Macro (menu) |

Here are some examples:

```
tblValidNamesLookup
tlkpValidNames
fmsgError
mmnuFileMnu
```

When naming objects in a database, do not use spaces. Instead, capitalize the first letter of each word. For example, instead of Quarterly Sales Values Table, use tblQuarterlySalesValues.

There is strong debate over whether fields in a table should have tags. Whether you use them is up to you. However, if you do use them, use the tags from Table A.9.

**TABLE A.9:** Field Tags (If You Decide to Use Them)

| Tag | Object Type |
|-----|-------------|
| lng | Autoincrementing (either sequential or random) Long (used with the suffix Cnt) |
| bin | Binary |
| byte | Byte |
| cur | Currency |
| date | Date/time |
| dbl | Double |
| guid | Globally unique identified (GUID) used for replication AutoIncrement fields |

**TABLE A.9:** Field Tags (If You Decide to Use Them) *(continued)*

| Tag | Object Type |
| --- | --- |
| int | Integer |
| lng | Long |
| mem | Memo |
| ole | OLE |
| sng | Single |
| str | Text |
| bool | Yes/No |

## Visual Basic 6 Objects

Table A.10 shows the tags for Visual Basic 6 objects.

**TABLE A.10:** Visual Basic 6 Object Tags

| Tag | Object Type |
| --- | --- |
| app | App |
| chk | CheckBox |
| clp | Clipboard |
| cbo | ComboBox |
| cmd | CommandButton |
| ctl | Control |
| dat | Data |
| dir | DirListBox |
| drv | DriveListBox |
| fil | FileListBox |
| frm | Form |
| fra | Frame |
| glb | Global |

**TABLE A.10:**   Visual Basic 6 Object Tags *(continued)*

| Tag | Object Type |
| --- | --- |
| hsb | HScrollBar |
| img | Image |
| lbl | Label |
| lics | Licenses |
| lin | Line |
| lst | ListBox |
| mdi | MDIForm |
| mnu | Menu |
| ole | OLE |
| opt | OptionButton |
| pic | PictureBox |
| prt | Printer |
| prp | PropertyPage |
| scr | Screen |
| shp | Shape |
| txt | TextBox |
| tmr | Timer |
| uctl | UserControl |
| udoc | UserDocument |
| vsb | VscrollBar |

## Microsoft ActiveX Data Objects 2.1 Tags

Office 2000 provides version 2.1 of the ActiveX Data Objects library. Table A.11 lists the recommended tags for this version of ADO.

**TABLE A.11:**  ADO 2.1 Object Tags

| Tag | Object Type |
| --- | --- |
| cmn {cmd} | Command |
| cnn {cnx} | Connection |
| err | Error |
| errs | Errors |
| fld | Field |
| flds | Fields |
| prm | Parameter |
| prms | Parameters |
| prp | Property |
| prps | Properties |
| rst | Recordset |

# Avoiding Object Confusion

Many of the ADO, ADOX, and JRO tags overlap with existing DAO tags. Make sure you include the object library name in all references in your code, so there's never any possibility of confusion. For example, use

```
Dim rst As ADODB.Recordset
```

or

```
Dim cat As ADOX.Catalog
```

rather than using the object types without the library name. This will not only make your code more explicit and avoid confusion about the source of the object, but will also make your code run a bit faster.

## Microsoft ADO Ext. 2.1 for DDL and Security (ADOX) Tags

In order to support DDL and security objects within Jet database, Microsoft provides ADOX, an additional ADO library of objects. Table A.12 lists tags for the ADOX objects.

**TABLE A.12:** ADOX Object Tags

| Tag | Object Type |
|-----|-------------|
| cat | Catalog |
| clms | Column |
| clm | Columns |
| cmd | Command |
| grp | Group |
| grps | Groups |
| idx | Index |
| idxs | Indexes |
| key | Key |
| keys | Keys |
| prc | Procedure |
| prcs | Procedures |
| prp | Property |
| prps | Properties |
| tbl | Table |
| tbls | Tables |
| usr | User |
| usrs | Users |
| vw | View |
| vws | Views |

## Microsoft Jet and Replication Objects 2.1

In order to support Jet's replication features, ADO provides another library, JRO. Table A.13 lists suggested tags for the JRO objects.

**TABLE A.13:** JRO Object Tags

| Tag | Object Type |
| --- | --- |
| flt | Filter |
| flts | Filters |
| jet | JetEngine |
| rpl | Replica |

## Microsoft SQL Server and Microsoft Data Engine (MSDE) Objects

Table A.14 lists tags for Microsoft SQL Server and the Microsoft Data Engine (a limited-connection version of SQL Server 7) objects.

**TABLE A.14:** SQL Server/MSDE Object Tags

| Tag | Object Type |
| --- | --- |
| tbl | table |
| proc | stored procedure |
| trg | trigger |
| qry | view |
| dgm | database diagram |
| pk | primary key |
| fk | foreign key |
| idx | other (nonkey) index |
| rul | check constraint |
| def | default |

## Microsoft Common Control Objects

Windows 95 and Windows NT have a set of common controls that are accessible from VBA. Table A.15 lists the tags for objects created using these controls.

**T A B L E  A . 1 5 :**  Microsoft Common Control Object Tags

| Tag | Object Type |
| --- | --- |
| ani | Animation |
| btn | Button (Toolbar) |
| bmn | ButtonMenu (Toolbar) |
| bmns | ButtonMenus (Toolbar) |
| bnd | Band (CoolBar) |
| bnds | Bands (CoolBar) |
| bnp | BandsPage (CoolBar) |
| btns | Buttons (Toolbar) |
| cbr | CoolBar |
| cbp | CoolBarPage (CoolBar) |
| hdr | ColumnHeader (ListView) |
| hdrs | ColumnHeaders (ListView) |
| cbi | ComboItem (ImageCombo) |
| cbis | ComboItems (ImageCombo) |
| ctls | Controls |
| dto | DataObject |
| dtf | DataObjectFiles |
| dtp | DTPicker |
| fsb | FlatScrollBar |
| imc | ImageCombo |
| iml | ImageList |
| lim | ListImage |
| lims | ListImages |
| lit | ListItem (ListView) |
| lits | ListItems (ListView) |
| lsi | ListSubItem (ListView) |

**TABLE A.15:** Microsoft Common Control Object Tags *(continued)*

| Tag | Object Type |
| --- | --- |
| lsis | ListSubItems (ListView) |
| lvw | ListView |
| mvw | MonthView |
| nod | Node (TreeView) |
| nods | Nodes (TreeView) |
| pnl | Panel (Status Bar) |
| pnls | Panels (Status Bar) |
| prb | ProgressBar |
| sld | Slider |
| sbr | StatusBar |
| tab | Tab (Tab Strip) |
| tabs | Tabs (Tab Strip) |
| tbs | TabStrip |
| tbr | Toolbar |
| tvw | TreeView |
| udn | UpDown |

## Other Custom Controls and Objects

Finally, Table A.16 lists the tags for other commonly used custom controls and objects.

**TABLE A.16:** Tags for Commonly Used Custom Controls

| Tag | Object Type |
| --- | --- |
| cdl | CommonDialog (Common Dialog) |
| dbc | DBCombo (Data Bound Combo Box) |
| dbg | DBGrid (Data Bound Grid) |

**TABLE A.16:**  Tags for Commonly Used Custom Controls  *(continued)*

| Tag | Object Type |
| --- | --- |
| dls | DBList (Data Bound List Box) |
| gau | Gauge (Gauge) |
| gph | Graph (Graph) |
| grd | Grid (Grid) |
| msg | MAPIMessages (Messaging API Message Control) |
| ses | MAPISession (Messaging API Session Control) |
| msk | MaskEdBox (Masked Edit Textbox) |
| key | MhState (Key State) |
| mmc | MMControl (Multimedia Control) |
| com | MSComm (Communication Port) |
| out | Outline (Outline Control) |
| pcl | PictureClip (Picture Clip Control) |
| rtf | RichTextBox (Rich Textbox) |
| spn | SpinButton (Spin Button) |

# Summary

Using a naming convention requires a considerable initial effort on your part. The payoff comes when either you or another programmer has to revisit your code at a later time. Using the conventions given here will make your code more readable and maintainable.

*Greg Reddick is the President of Xoc Software, a software development company developing programs in Visual Basic, Microsoft Access, and C/C++. He leads training seminars in Visual Basic for Application Developers Training Company and is a co-author of* **Microsoft Access 95 Developer's Handbook,** *published by Sybex. He worked for four years on the Access development team at Microsoft. Greg can be reached at* grr@xoc.net *or at the Xoc Software Web site at* http://www.xoc.net.

# VBA versus VBScript

**V**BScript is a scripting language based on a subset of the VBA language. Unlike VBA, VBScript code is always interpreted at runtime; there's no way to compile your scripts.

VBScript contains much of the functionality of the VBA language, but there are number of features that are not supported or are only partially supported in the language. The differences between the VBA and VBScript languages are summarized in Table B.1.

**TABLE B.1:**   The Differences between VBA and VBScript

| VBA Feature | VBScript Support for Feature |
| --- | --- |
| Arrays | Option Base is not supported, nor can you specify the lower bound for an array; all array dimensions start at 0. |
| Collections | Custom collections not supported. In addition, you can't refer to elements in built-in collections with bang (!). |
| Conditional Compilation | Not supported. |
| DoEvents | Not supported. |
| GoTo, GoSub, On GoSub | Not supported. |
| On Error GoTo, Resume, Resume Next, Resume label, Erl, and Error | Can't set or use error handlers. Only error handling supported is in-line using On Error Resume Next. The Err object is supported. |
| Line numbers, line labels | Not supported. |
| CVar, CVDate, Str, Val | Not supported. |
| Variable declarations | VBScript supports only variant variables. You can use Dim, Public, and Private statements; however, you can't specify datatypes. You can't use the Optional, ParamArray, and Static keywords. |
| For…Next loops | Fully supported, except that VBScript doesn't like when you specify the index variable in the Next statement. For example, "Next" is okay, but "Next intl" is not. |
| User defined types | Not supported. |
| With…End With | Supported in version 5.0 but not earlier versions. |
| Date and Time statements | Not supported, but the Date and Time functions are supported. |
| Timer | Not supported. |

**TABLE B.1:**  The Differences between VBA and VBScript  *(continued)*

| VBA Feature | VBScript Support for Feature |
| --- | --- |
| DDE statements and functions. | Not supported. |
| Declare statement | API calls not supported for safety reasons. |
| Class modules, Property procedures | Not supported prior to version 5.0. Property procedures and a new keyword, Class, are supported in version 5.0. |
| Debug object | Not supported. |
| End and Stop | Not supported. |
| File I/O statements and functions | Not supported for safety reasons. From ASP pages, however, you can use the Scripting objects to read and write files. |
| Financial functions | Not supported. |
| Operators | Like operator not supported. |
| Option Statements | Option Compare, Option Private Module, Deftype not supported. |
| Select Case | Use of operators in Case clauses not supported. |
| String manipulation | Mid statement, LSet, RSet, StrConv not supported. |

**TIP**    Version 5.0 of VBScript is included with Internet Explorer 5.0 and Internet Information Server 5.0.

# INDEX

**Note to the Reader:** Throughout this index **boldfaced** page numbers indicate primary discussions of a topic. *Italicized* page numbers indicate illustrations.

# G

# H

# Q

# T

# What's on the CD?

This CD is a valuable companion to the book. It provides a wealth of information in a readily usable format to aid in your Access development efforts. We've included every significant example presented in the text—and not just the VBA code. We've also included all the tables (with sample data), queries, forms, reports, stored procedures, views, and so on—everything you need to get you up and running instantly. The CD also contains a number of Microsoft-authored white papers on replication and data access pages, several free and shareware utility programs, and demonstrations of commercial products.

Here's just a sampling of what you'll find on the CD:

- An Access add-in that reverses database replication

- Several free add-ins from Trigeminal Software for managing Access 2000 replication, security, and data access pages

- A class module that you can employ to easily add a record lock timeout feature to your forms

- Lots of sample code that demonstrates how to create lean and mean stored procedure interfaces, how to control concurrency in client-server applications, how to programmatically manipulate security and replication, how to script the Office Web components, how to create dynamic ASP pages, and more

- Demos of all the award-winning Access add-ins from FMS, Inc

- A free utility program from Database Creations, as well as demo versions of their accounting and other Access 2000 add-on software

- WinZip, the premier Windows shareware programming for zipping and unzipping files

- Demo versions of WebWhacker and *Click*Book (a printing utility that makes it easy to print code listings or anything else, in a compact, easy-to-carry format), all from BlueSquirrel Software

For more information about the CD, including installation instructions, see the "About the CD" section in the Introduction of this book and the README.TXT file in the root folder of the CD.

---

**NOTE**    If you use Windows Explorer to copy the sample database files directly from the CD to your hard disk, the files will be marked as read only. Either run the supplied Chapter.exe self-extracting zip file, or, after you've copied files manually, use Windows Explorer to clear the Read Only attribute of the file.

---

# X

# Y

# Z